15e

# Contemporary Business Mathematics

## for Colleges

15e

# Contemporary Business Mathematics

## for Colleges

**James E. Deitz, Ed.D.**
*Past President of Heald Colleges*

**James L. Southam, Ph.D.**
*San Francisco State University*

SOUTH-WESTERN
CENGAGE Learning™

Australia • Brazil • Japan • Korea • Mexico • Singapore • Spain • United Kingdom • United States

SOUTH-WESTERN
CENGAGE Learning™

**Contemporary Business Mathematics for Colleges, 15e**
**James E. Deitz, Ed.D., and James L. Southam, Ph.D.**

Vice President of Editorial, Business: Jack W. Calhoun

Vice President/Editor-in-Chief: Alex von Rosenberg

Senior Acquisitions Editor: Charles McCormick, Jr.

Associate Developmental Editor: Julie Klooster

Editorial Assistant: Bryn Lathrop

Marketing Manager: Bryant T. Chrzan

Marketing Coordinator: Suellen Ruttkay

Marketing Communications Manager: Elizabeth Shipp

Senior Content Project Manager: Kim Kusnerak

Rights Account Manager—Text: Scott Bragg

Managing Media Editor: Matt McKinney

Media Editor: Chris Valentine

Frontlist Buyer, Manufacturing: Beverly Breslin

Production Service: International Typesetting and Composition

Copyeditor: Alan Biondi

Compositor: International Typesetting and Composition

Art Director: Stacy Jenkins Shirley

Internal Designer: Grannan Graphic Design, Ltd.

Cover Designer: cmiller design

Cover Images: © Getty Images

Photography Manager: John Hill

Photo Researcher: Rose Alcorn



Library of Congress Control Number: 2008936672

Student Edition ISBN 13: 978-0-324-66315-0

Student Edition ISBN 10: 0-324-66315-3

Student Edition with CD ISBN 13: 978-0-324-66316-7

Student Edition with CD ISBN 10: 0-324-66316-1

**South-Western Cengage Learning**
5191 Natorp Boulevard
Mason, OH 45040
USA

Cengage Learning products are represented in Canada by Nelson Education, Ltd.



Printed in the United States of America
2 3 4 5 12 11 10

# To the Student

*Contemporary Business Mathematics for Colleges* presents an arithmetic-based, basic approach to business mathematics. It emphasizes a practical, skill-building approach to prepare students for future careers in business through step-by-step development of concepts, numerous practice exercises, and a focus on real-world application of techniques. The text progresses from the most basic to more complex business mathematics topics.

During its previous editions, *Contemporary Business Mathematics for Colleges* sold more copies than any other business mathematics textbook. As always, the goal of this new fifteenth edition is to make a successful book even better. This edition continues to maintain its coverage of practical, real-world, business math problems, and offers step-by-step solutions to help you solve these problems. The content of the new edition continues to be focused entirely on business mathematics with its emphasis on both the needs of contemporary business students and the requirements of shorter regular and online courses. *Contemporary Business Mathematics for Colleges* presents the basic principles of mathematics and immediately applies them in a series of practical business problems. This new edition continues to provide a balance among conceptual understanding, skill development, and business applications.

In the modern business environment, managers, employees, and consumers all need knowledge of and skill in business mathematics. Although computers and calculators are used to do many of the calculations, it is important to understand the concepts behind mechanical computations. The purpose of this business mathematics textbook is to increase your mathematics knowledge and to develop your skills at applying this knowledge. This will make you a more valuable employee and a wiser consumer.

## KEY FEATURES

*Contemporary Business Mathematics for Colleges* uses special features to aid you in reading, learning, and practicing for your exams.

**Integrated Learning Objectives:** These icons identify the sections of each chapter where each specific Learning Objective is addressed. The Learning Objectives are there to remind you of the organization of the chapter.

**Concept Checks:** At the end of the section for each Learning Objective is a Concept Check to reinforce your understanding of that particular Learning Objective.

**Step-by-Step Problem-Solving Approach:** Short, concise text sections are followed by examples with step-by-step solutions. You will learn mathematical concepts by immediately applying practical solutions to common business problems, and you will gain confidence in your own problem-solving skills by studying the way example problems are worked out.

**Business Examples and Problems:** Abundant practical business problems and examples from a variety of businesses will help you better relate to the material as you see how it is applied to modern life.

**Bottom Line:** This end-of-chapter feature ties each Learning Objective to self-test problems (with answers). You have the opportunity to check whether you have mastered the chapter's key skills before moving on to the assignments.

**Self-Check Review Problems:** Located at the end of each chapter, self-check review problems provide yet another opportunity for you to test yourself before completing the end-of-chapter assignments. Answers are provided at the end of the text.

**Video Icons:** Video icons are placed where appropriate throughout the text to direct you to video clips. The clips cover 12 major mathematical concepts and apply them to a series of practical business problems. A digital version of the video segments is included on the Student CD-ROM for easier access.

**Microsoft® Excel Templates:** Spreadsheet templates give you practice with both mathematics and spreadsheet software where relevant. The Excel templates were prepared by Adele Stock, faculty, Minnesota State Colleges and Universities, and are available on the Student CD-ROM.

**Student Resource CD-ROM:** The Student CD-ROM is packaged with every new text. It includes the Excel templates, digitized Topic Review Videos, and the Math in Employment Tests. These tests are supplementary material for use in class or for review by the individual student.

**Product Website:** The text Website at www.cengage.com/bmath/deitz provides financial calculator material from Chapter 23, online quizzes, Internet links for the text, and more. The online quizzes may be used as practice before assignments or exams. Your instructor may also use them as additional assignments for you.

## SUGGESTIONS TO IMPROVE YOUR STUDY

The special features in *Contemporary Business Mathematics for Colleges* are meant to help you focus your study. Keeping up with the coursework and making consistent use of the features will improve your performance on homework assignments and exams.

1. Read the text and study the step-by-step illustrations and examples carefully.
2. Work the Concept Check and the Bottom Line problems. These features will give you a comprehensive review of the problems in each chapter, before you get to the assignments.
3. Read the instructions carefully for each assignment before solving the problems.
4. Your instructor may tell you whether you are to work in groups or by yourself. However, you will not have learned until you can do the calculations yourself. Ask your instructor for help if you have difficulty understanding what you are asked to do, or how to do it.
5. Before working a problem, try to estimate your answer. The early chapters present methods for doing this.
6. Use shortcuts in your calculations to increase your confidence. Shortcuts are presented in several chapters.
7. Write numbers neatly and clearly, and align them in columns to help avoid errors.
8. Space is provided on the assignment sheets to compute most problems. Show each step in the solution so that if you make an error, your instructor can help you locate the cause.
9. Record your scores for each assignment on the Progress Report at the end of the book.

# Acknowledgments

We would like to acknowledge the work of reviewers and verifiers who provided suggestions about this edition's reorganization and comments about other ways to continually improve the accuracy in our text.

Barbara Bidwell Gray Coombs, Academy of Court Reporting, Columbus, OH
Paul H. Martin, Aims Community College
Veronica Liebold Cook, Austin Community College
Melissa Kemp, Bauder College
Diane F. Hendrickson, Becker College
Karen May, Blinn College
Ellen Sawyer, College of DuPage
Yvonne Block, College of Lake County
Pamela N. McGlasson, College of San Mateo
Rhonda Coleman-Posey, Copiah-Lincoln Community College
Pam Perry, Hinds Community College
Allan L. Sheets, International Business College, Indianapolis
Carol A. Perry, Marshall Community & Technical College
Susan Bell, Mendocino College
Steve Hixenbaugh, Mendocino College
Deborah H. White, Mendocino College
Dr. Jamie L. Summerville, Mid-Continent University
Lana K. LaBruyere, Mineral Area College
Susan J. Peterson, Minnesota State Community and Technical College—Moorhead
Amanda Hardin, Mississippi Delta Community College
Dr. Patrick J. Nedry, Monroe County Community College
Julia L. Angel, North Arkansas College
Dawn W. Stevens, Northwest Mississippi Community College—Desoto Center
Diane Andrews Hagan, Ohio Business College
Joyce Coleman, Palo Verde College
Sharon J. Brown, Randolph Community College
Nicholas Providence, Valencia Community College
Marilyn K. St. Clair, Weatherford College
Kathy H. Scott, Western Piedmont Community College

We also thank the staff at South-Western who worked to make this new edition the best business mathematics text possible: Sr. Content Project Manager, Kim Kusnerak; Sr. Acquisitions Editor, Charles McCormick, Jr.; Marketing Manager, Bryant Chrzan; and Associate Developmental Editor, Julie Klooster.

James E. Deitz
James L. Southam

# About the Authors

## JAMES E. DEITZ

### *PAST PRESIDENT OF HEALD COLLEGES*

Author ***James E. Deitz*** brings both a thorough understanding of effective education today and a practical business knowledge to the latest edition of this leading text. Dr. Deitz earned his bachelor's degree in accounting from Memphis State University and doctorate of education from UCLA. Dr. Deitz has been an educator for more than 35 years, including professorships with UCLA and Los Angeles State College and a long-standing position as President of Heald Colleges. An active member of the business community, Dr. Deitz is a recognized international speaker and has served on regional educational accrediting commissions. Dr. Deitz serves currently on the Executive Committee and Board of Trustees of Dominican University of California and as a member of the Board of Directors of Bank of Marin. He has authored several texts in addition to this best-selling ***Contemporary Business Mathematics for Colleges.***

## JAMES L. SOUTHAM

### *SAN FRANCISCO STATE UNIVERSITY*

Author ***James L. Southam*** has a diverse background of professional, educational, and teaching experience in business and mathematics. Dr. Southam holds bachelor's and master's degrees in mathematics education from Southern Oregon College, a Ph.D. in mathematics from Oregon State University, an MBA in finance from University of California, Berkeley, and a law degree from University of California, Hastings. Dr. Southam's 40 years of teaching experience include San Francisco State University College of Business, California State University, Stanislaus, Southern Oregon College, Oregon State University, and the University of International Business and Economics in Beijing. Both domestically and internationally, Dr. Southam has participated in business ventures, has been a business consultant, and is a successful author. He is a member of the San Francisco State University Athletics Hall of Fame.

# BRIEF CONTENTS

# CONTENTS

# CONTENTS

# CONTENTS

15e

# Contemporary Business Mathematics

## for Colleges

# Part 1

# Fundamental Review

# 1

# Fundamental Processes

## Learning Objectives

By studying this chapter and completing all assignments, you will be able to:

Learning Objective 1 Use shortcuts to add rapidly and accurately.

Learning Objective 2 Use shortcuts to subtract rapidly and accurately.

Learning Objective 3 Use shortcuts to multiply rapidly and accurately.

Learning Objective 4 Use shortcuts to divide rapidly and accurately.

Learning Objective 5 Estimate answers before doing calculations.

# Addition

**Learning Objective 1**

Use shortcuts to add rapidly and accurately.

About half of all computations used in business involve addition. The more skilled you become in adding, the more rapidly you will get accurate answers. Addition is the process of finding the **sum** (total) of two or more **addends** (any of a set of numbers to be added).

## NUMBER COMBINATIONS

Certain aids can help you add more accurately and rapidly. One of the most helpful is to combine any two numbers that total 10. The following combinations total 10. Practice the combinations until you can identify them instantly.

| | | | | | | | | |
|---|---|---|---|---|---|---|---|---|
| 1 | 2 | 3 | 4 | 5 | 9 | 8 | 7 | 6 |
| 9 | 8 | 7 | 6 | 5 | 1 | 2 | 3 | 4 |

When these combinations are found sequentially in any column of numbers, you should add them as 10. In example A, by using the combinations of 10, you can simply add down the column by saying "9 plus 10 is 19, plus 10 is 29, plus 8 is 37" (or "9, 19, 29, 37").

The number 3 is carried over to the top of the next column and written in a small figure above the number 7. The combinations of 10 are used in adding the center column by simply saying "10, 20, 30."

In adding the tens and hundreds, you carry over the number 3 from the tens and hundreds total. You can simply say "8, 18, 28, 32."

**EXAMPLE A**

| | | | |
|---|---|---|---|
| | 3 | 3 | |
| | 5 | 7 | 9 |
| | 4 | 2 | 4 |
| | 6 | 8 | 6 |
| | 9 | 0 | 3 |
| | 1 | 5 | 7 |
| | 4 | 5 | 8 |
| 3, | 2 | 0 | 7 |

Also, you should learn to recognize the combinations of three numbers that total 10.

| | | | | | | | |
|---|---|---|---|---|---|---|---|
| 1 | 1 | 1 | 1 | 2 | 2 | 2 | 3 |
| 1 | 2 | 3 | 4 | 2 | 3 | 4 | 3 |
| 8 | 7 | 6 | 5 | 6 | 5 | 4 | 4 |

When three numbers totaling 10 appear in sequence in a column, you should combine them and add them as 10. In example B, you might add the numbers in the ones column as you add down the column, "10, 18, 28, 38, 41." Write the number 4, which is carried over as a small figure above the 1 in the tens column. Then use the combinations of 10 in adding the tens column by saying "5, 15, 25, 35, 43."

**EXAMPLE B**

| | | | | |
|---|---|---|---|---|
| | | 4 | | |
| (5) | | 1 | 7 | |
| | | 6 | 2 | |
| (15) | | 4 | 1 | (10) |
| | | 2 | 8 | (18) |
| | | 2 | 5 | |
| (25) | | 6 | 5 | (28) |
| | | 5 | 4 | |
| | | 2 | 4 | |
| (35) | | 3 | 2 | (38) |
| (43) | | 8 | 3 | (41) |
| | 4 | 3 | 1 | |

## REPEATED DIGITS

When you're adding a column in which many of the digits are the same, it is often quicker to count the number of repeated digits and then multiply the digit by that number. In example C, the ones column totals 33: $10 + 10 + 7 + 6$. The tens column shows five 4s, equaling 20: $5 \times 4 = 20$. The 3 that was carried over and the 5 are then added to the 20 for a total of 28 in the tens column. The total for the problem is 283.

**EXAMPLE C**

| | | | | |
|---|---|---|---|---|
| | | 3 | | |
| | | 4 | 1 | |
| | | 4 | 9 | (10) |
| (5 × 4) | | 4 | 8 | |
| | | 4 | 2 | (10) |
| | | 4 | 7 | |
| | | 5 | 6 | (13) |
| | 2 | 8 | 3 | (33) |

## ADDING FROM LEFT TO RIGHT (COLUMNS OF TWO-DIGIT NUMBERS)

When adding columns of two-digit numbers, you can easily count by tens and add the ones column to your total.

**EXAMPLE D**

Count:

| | |
|---|---|
| 12 | 12 |
| 24 | 22, 32 + 4 = 36 |
| 51 | 46, 56, 66, 76, 86 +1 = 87 |
| 43 | 97, 107, 117, 127 + 3 = 130 |
| 32 | 140, 150, 160 + 2 = 162 |
| 162 | |

With practice, you can learn to count the tens by their number:

| | |
|---|---|
| 12 | 12 |
| 24 | 32 + 4 = 36 |
| 51 | 86 + 1 = 87 |
| 43 | 127 + 3 = 130 |
| 32 | 160 + 2 = 162 |
| 162 | |

## CHECKING ADDITION

You should always check the accuracy of your addition. To do so, add the columns again in the opposite direction—that is, if you added down, add up for the check.

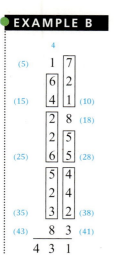

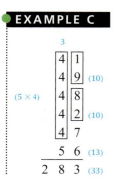

## HORIZONTAL ADDITION

When using business records, you may need to add numbers horizontally. You may check several horizontal additions by adding the columns vertically and then adding these totals horizontally. This method is called **cross-checking.** The sums obtained by adding the totals horizontally and vertically should be the same.

**EXAMPLE E**

| | | | | | | | | | | |
|---|---|---|---|---|---|---|---|---|---|---|
| 282 | + | 346 | + | 723 | + | 409 | + | 716 | = | 2,476 |
| 113 | + | 806 | + | 629 | + | 916 | + | 620 | = | 3,084 |
| 240 | + | 318 | + | 718 | + | 312 | + | 309 | = | 1,897 |
| 716 | + | 501 | + | 423 | + | 716 | + | 114 | = | 2,470 |
| 872 | + | 417 | + | 909 | + | 704 | + | 472 | = | 3,374 |
| 2,223 | + | 2,388 | + | 3,402 | + | 3,057 | + | 2,231 | = | 13,301 |

### CONCEPT CHECK 1.1

Add horizontally and vertically; compare horizontal and vertical totals to verify accuracy. Use combinations to simplify addition.

| | | | | | | | | |
|---|---|---|---|---|---|---|---|---|
| 1 | | 1 | | 1 | | | | |
| 24 | + | 76 | + | 63 | = | 163 | (4 + 6) | |
| 36 | + | 24 | + | 25 | = | 85 | (6 + 4) | (Note horizontal combinations) |
| 27 | + | 43 | + | 12 | = | 82 | (7 + 3) | |
| 87 | + | 143 | + | 100 | = | 330 | | |

COMPLETE ASSIGNMENT 1.1.

# Subtraction

Subtraction is the process of finding the difference between the **minuend** (number from which subtraction is being made) and the **subtrahend** (number being subtracted); the result is the **difference.** When the subtrahend is greater than the minuend, the result is a negative difference. In business, a negative difference may be called a **credit balance.** A credit balance is frequently shown in parentheses.

Learning Objective **2**

Use shortcuts to subtract rapidly and accurately.

**EXAMPLE F**

| Positive Difference | | Negative Difference (Credit Balance) |
|---|---|---|
| $18.88 | Minuend | $12.00 |
| −3.63 | −Subtrahend | −13.50 |
| $15.25 | Difference | ($ 1.50) |

## CHECKING SUBTRACTION

To check subtraction, use addition. If 209 is subtracted from 317, the difference is 108. You can check this result by adding the difference (108) to the subtrahend (209). The sum is 317. You can use the same procedure to check subtraction with a negative difference (credit balance).

**EXAMPLE G**

| Subtract: | Check: |
|---|---|
| 317 | 108 |
| −209 | +209 |
| 108 | 317 |

**EXAMPLE H**

| Subtract: | Check: |
|---|---|
| $21.10 | ($ 3.40) |
| −24.50 | +24.50 |
| ($ 3.40) | $ 21.10 |

## HORIZONTAL SUBTRACTION

When using some business forms, you may have to subtract numbers horizontally. You can check a number of horizontal subtractions by adding the columns vertically and then subtracting these totals horizontally. This answer should equal the total of the differences in the column at the right.

**EXAMPLE I**

| Minuend | | Subtrahend | | Difference |
|---|---|---|---|---|
| $ 120 | − | $ 20 | = | $100 |
| 283 | − | 10 | = | 273 |
| 440 | − | 110 | = | 330 |
| $ 269 | − | $149 | = | $120 |
| $1,112 | − | $289 | = | $823 |

## ✔ CONCEPT CHECK 1.2

| Subtract: | Check: | Subtract horizontally: Check by comparing totals |
|---|---|---|
| 276 | 142 | 27 − 13 = 14 |
| −134 | +134 | 24 − 11 = 13 |
| | | 36 − 10 = 26 |
| 142 | 276 | 87 − 34 = 53 |

COMPLETE ASSIGNMENT 1.2.

# Multiplication

**Learning Objective 3**

Use shortcuts to multiply rapidly and accurately.

Multiplication, stated simply, is repeated addition. When two numbers (called **factors**) are multiplied, one number is repeated as many times as there are units in the other. The factor that is multiplied is called the **multiplicand.** The factor that indicates how many times to multiply is the **multiplier.** The result is the **product.**

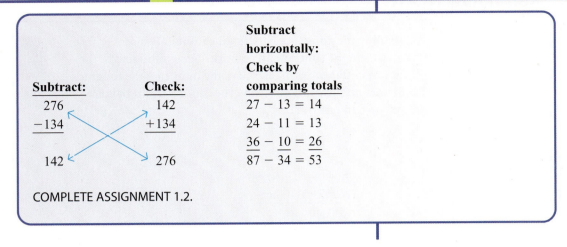

### STEPS to Multiply Two Numbers

1. Make the smaller factor the multiplier.
2. Multiply from right to left.
3. Add the products to get the final product.

### EXAMPLE J

| | | | In other words: |
|---|---|---|---|
| | 456 | (multiplicand) | |
| STEP 1 | ×237 | (multiplier) | 7 × 456 = 3,192 |
| STEP 2 | 3 192 | (product) | 30 × 456 = 13,680 |
| STEP 2 | 13 680 | (product) | 200 × 456 = 91,200 |
| STEP 2 | 91 200 | (product) | 237 × 456 = 108,072 |
| STEP 3 | 108,072 | (final product) | |

## CHECKING MULTIPLICATION

The best method of checking multiplication is to divide the product by the multiplier to obtain the multiplicand. Example K shows the relationship between multiplication and division.

**EXAMPLE K**

| | | | |
|---|---|---|---|
| Multiplicand | 22 | → | 22 |
| Multiplier | ×6 | → | 6)132 |
| Product | 132 | → | ↑ (132) |

## MULTIPLYING NUMBERS ENDING IN ZERO

To multiply a number by 10, simply add a zero to the end of the number. To multiply a number by 100, add two zeros to the end: 10 × 46 = 460; 7,689 × 100 = 768,900.

**STEPS to Multiply Numbers with Zeros**

1. Make the multiplier the factor with the smaller number of digits after ignoring zeros at the right-hand side of the number.
2. Ignore the right-hand zeros and multiply the remaining numbers.
3. Insert the zeros ignored in Step 2 to the right-hand side of the product.

**EXAMPLE L**

| | | |
|---|---|---|
| STEP 1 | 370 × 200: | Make 2 the multiplier. |
| | | Ignored: |
| | 37 | (1 zero) |
| | ×2 | (2 zeros) |
| STEP 2 | 74 | (3 zeros) |
| STEP 3 | 74 000 = | 74,000 |

**EXAMPLE M**

| | | |
|---|---|---|
| STEP 1 | 1,200 × 160,800: | Make 12 the multiplier. |
| | | Ignored: |
| | 1,608 | (2 zeros) |
| | ×12 | (2 zeros) |
| | 3 216 | |
| | 16 08 | |
| STEP 2 | 19,296 | (4 zeros) |
| STEP 3 | 19,296 0000 = | 192,960,000 |

## MULTIPLYING WHEN THE MULTIPLIER CONTAINS ZERO NOT ON THE END

Often a zero appears in the center of the multiplier rather than at the end. To multiply 42,674 by 401, first multiply the multiplicand by 1 and write down the product. Then multiply by 4 (which is really 400) and write the result two places, instead of one, to the left. In other words, one extra place is left for each zero in the multiplier.

**EXAMPLE N**

| | |
|---|---|
| 42,674 | |
| × 401 | |
| 42 674 | |
| 17 069 6 | (2 places) |
| 17,112,274 | |

Whenever more than one zero appears in the multiplier, the multiplication process is similar. To multiply 33,222 by 2,004, as in example O, first multiply 33,222 by 4. Then multiply 33,222 by 2, writing the answer three places to the left. Remember, extra places must be left for the two zeros (1 place + 2 extra places = 3 places).

**EXAMPLE O**

```
   33,222
  × 2,004
  132 888
66 444        (3 places)
66,576,888
```

## MULTIPLYING THE PRODUCT OF TWO FACTORS

Sometimes in business you will need to multiply two factors and then multiply the product of those factors by a third factor. As shown in example P, you begin by multiplying the first two factors and then multiplying that product by the third factor.

**EXAMPLE P**

$21 \times 30 \times 15 = 9{,}450$

```
 21        630
×30       ×15
630  →    3150
          630
          9,450
```

## MULTIPLYING BY 25

A shortcut for multiplying by 25 is to multiply by 100 (increase by two zeros) and divide by 4.

**EXAMPLE Q**

$321 \times 25$

$32{,}100 \div 4 = 8{,}025$

**EXAMPLE R**

$828 \times 25$

$82{,}800 \div 4 = 20{,}700$

## MULTIPLYING BY 50

A shortcut for multiplying by 50 is to multiply by 100 (increase by two zeros) and divide by 2.

**EXAMPLE S**

$732 \times 50$

$73{,}200 \div 2 = 36{,}600$

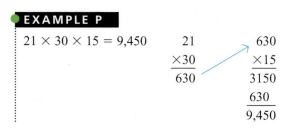

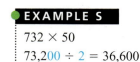

## CONCEPT CHECK 1.3

To multiply by 10, add one zero to the end of the number:
$36 \times 10 = 360$
To multiply by 100, add two zeros to the end of the number:
$36 \times 100 = 3{,}600$

COMPLETE ASSIGNMENT 1.3.

**Multiply:**

```
   214  → multiplicand
 ×102   → multiplier
   428
 21 4     (two places)
21,828  → product
```

**Check:**

```
       214
102)21,828
```

# Division

Division is the process of finding how many times one number (the **divisor**) is contained in another (the **dividend**). The result is called the **quotient.** If anything remains after the division is completed, it is called the **remainder.** In example T, $47 \div 2 = 23$ with a remainder of 1, 47 is the dividend, 2 is the divisor, 1 is the remainder, and 23 with a remainder of (1) is the quotient.

Learning Objective 4

Use shortcuts to divide rapidly and accurately.

**EXAMPLE T**

```
  23 (1)
2)47
  4
  7
  6
  1
```

**STEPS in Long Division**

1. Write the divisor in front of and the dividend inside of a division bracket ( $\overline{)\quad}$ ).
2. Use only as many digits at the left of the dividend as you need as the first partial dividend in order to have a number that is equal to or larger than the divisor.
3. Write the number of times the divisor will go into the partial dividend selected in Step 2.
4. Multiply the divisor by this answer, write the product under the partial dividend, and subtract.
5. Next to the remainder thus obtained, bring down the next digit of the dividend to form the second partial dividend.
6. Divide as before and repeat the process until all the digits of the dividend have been used.

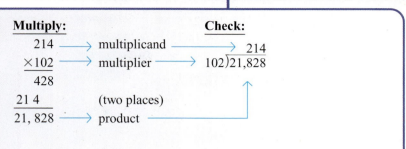

**EXAMPLE U**

| | |
|---|---|
| 174 | STEP 3 |
| 164)28,536 | STEPS 1 & 2 |
| 16 4 | STEP 4 |
| 12 13 | STEP 5 |
| 11 48 | STEP 6 |
| 656 | |
| 656 | |
| 0 | |

When the partial dividend is smaller than the divisor, a zero must be placed in the quotient above that digit. This process is continued until the partial dividend is at least as large as the divisor. Then continue the long division steps, as shown in example V.

**EXAMPLE V**

20,402 (17)
34)693,685
68
13 6
13 6
085
68
17

## CHECKING DIVISION

To check division, simply multiply the quotient by the divisor and add any remainder to the product. The result will equal the original dividend. (Examples W and X provide checks for examples U and V.)

**EXAMPLE W**

174
×164
696
10 44
17 4
28,536

**EXAMPLE X**

| | | |
|---|---|---|
| quotient | = | 20,402 |
| divisor | = | × 34 |
| | | 81 608 |
| | | 612 06 |
| | | 693,668 |
| remainder | = | + 17 |
| dividend | = | 693,685 |

*Note:* Division is the reverse process of multiplication.

## DIVIDING BY 10

To divide by 10, drop the digit at the extreme right of the dividend; the dropped digit will be the remainder.

**EXAMPLE Y**

790 ÷ 10 = 79 (0 remainder)

**EXAMPLE Z**

3,652 ÷ 10 = 365 (2 remainder)

## DIVIDING BY 100

To divide by 100, drop the two right-hand digits of the dividend—they will be the remainder.

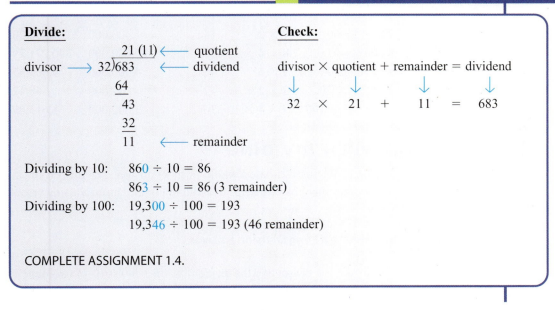

**EXAMPLE AA**

81,400 ÷ 100 = 814 (0 remainder)

**EXAMPLE BB**

257,948 ÷ 100 = 2,579 (48 remainder)

## DIVIDING WHEN THE DIVISOR AND DIVIDEND END WITH ZEROS

When a divisor and dividend both end with zeros, a division shortcut is to delete the ending zeros common to both and then divide.

**EXAMPLE CC**

| Both Divisor and Dividend End with Zeros | Zeros Common to Divisor and Dividend Have Been Dropped | Answer |
|---|---|---|
| 8,400 ÷ 200 | 84 ÷ 2 | 42 |
| 46,000 ÷ 2,300 | 460 ÷ 23 | 20 |
| 42,000 ÷ 100 | 420 ÷ 1 | 420 |
| 20,000,000 ÷ 4,000 | 20,000 ÷ 4 | 5,000 |
| 2,760 ÷ 270 | 276 ÷ 27 | 10 (6 remainder) |
| 3,200 ÷ 1,000 | 32 ÷ 10 | 3 (2 remainder) |

### CONCEPT CHECK 1.4

**Divide:**

```
                21 (11) ⟵ quotient
divisor ⟶ 32)683      ⟵ dividend
             64
              43
              32
              11      ⟵ remainder
```

**Check:**

divisor × quotient + remainder = dividend

32 × 21 + 11 = 683

Dividing by 10: 860 ÷ 10 = 86

863 ÷ 10 = 86 (3 remainder)

Dividing by 100: 19,300 ÷ 100 = 193

19,346 ÷ 100 = 193 (46 remainder)

COMPLETE ASSIGNMENT 1.4.

# Estimating

Learning Objective 5

Estimate answers before doing calculations.

## ESTIMATING WHEN MULTIPLYING

Is estimating important? *Yes*, it is! In using a calculator to make computations, you may possibly omit keystrokes, accidentally repeat keystrokes, or incorrectly shift or omit decimal points. There is a great deal of difference between 3 times $14.87 and 3 times $1,487. When working with calculations in any manner—such as entering items into a spreadsheet, a cash register, or a calculator—you should *always* have a mental estimate of the final product.

Mentally estimating an answer provides a good method for checking whether your product is a reasonable answer.

Video: Estimating Answers

**STEPS to Estimate a Multiplication Answer**

1. Round both the multiplicand and multiplier to the nearest 10 for two-digit numbers, the nearest 100 for three-digit numbers, the nearest 1,000 for four-digit numbers, etc.
2. Drop the zeros to the right of the nonzero numbers.
3. Mentally multiply the nonzero numbers to determine the base product.
4. Reinsert *all* zeros dropped in Step 2.

**EXAMPLE DD**

| | | | Reinsert Zeros | | |
|---|---|---|---|---|---|
| **Problem** | **Round to** | **Drop Zeros** | **Base Product** | **Estimated Answer** | **Real Answer** |
| 68 × 21 | 70 × 20 | 7 × 2 | 14 | 1,400 | 1,428 |
| 693 × 1,957 | 700 × 2,000 | 7 × 2 | 14 | 1,400,000 | 1,356,201 |
| 7,869 × 43,242 | 8,000 × 40,000 | 8 × 4 | 32 | 320,000,000 | 340,271,298 |
| 9 × 511,739 | 9 × 500,000 | 9 × 5 | 45 | 4,500,000 | 4,605,651 |
| 31 × 22 × 71 | 30 × 20 × 70 | 3 × 2 × 7 | 42 | 42,000 | 48,422 |
| 891 × 39 × 104 | 900 × 40 × 100 | 9 × 4 × 1 | 36 | 3,600,000 | 3,613,896 |

## ESTIMATING WHEN DIVIDING

Before doing long division problems, estimate a whole-number answer. The process of mentally estimating whole-number answers helps to avoid major and embarrassing errors.

**STEPS to Estimate a Long Division Answer**

1. Round both the divisor and the dividend to the nearest 10 for two-digit numbers, the nearest 100 for three-digit numbers, the nearest 1,000 for four-digit numbers, etc.
2. Drop the number of zeros common to both.
3. Mentally divide the remaining divisor into the remaining dividend.

**EXAMPLE EE**

| Problem | Round to | Drop Zeros | Estimated Answer | Real Answer |
|---|---|---|---|---|
| 77 ÷ 39 | 80 ÷ 40 | 8 ÷ 4 | 2 | 1.97 |
| 196 ÷ 63 | 200 ÷ 60 | 20 ÷ 6 | 3* | 3.11* |
| 2,891 ÷ 114 | 3,000 ÷ 100 | 30 ÷ 1 | 30 | 25.36 |
| 592 ÷ 29 | 600 ÷ 30 | 60 ÷ 3 | 20 | 20.41 |
| 18,476 ÷ 384 | 20,000 ÷ 400 | 200 ÷ 4 | 50 | 48.11 |
| 917 ÷ 186 | 900 ÷ 200 | 9 ÷ 2 | 4* | 4.93* |
| 21,716,412 ÷ 40,796 | 20,000,000 ÷ 40,000 | 2,000 ÷ 4 | 500 | 532.32 |
| 99,624 ÷ 476 | 100,000 ÷ 500 | 1,000 ÷ 5 | 200 | 209.29 |
| 29,200 ÷ 316 | 30,000 ÷ 300 | 300 ÷ 3 | 100 | 92.41 |

*Because 20 ÷ 6 and 9 ÷ 2 would result in remainders, we can reasonably assume that the real number will be *larger*.

## CONCEPT CHECK 1.5

ESTIMATING MULTIPLICATION ANSWERS

| Problem | Round to | Drop Zeros | Base Product | Reinsert Zeros Estimated Answer | Real Answer |
|---|---|---|---|---|---|
| 47 × 31 | 50 × 30 | 5 × 3 | 15 | 1,500 | 1,457 |
| 498 × 221 | 500 × 200 | 5 × 2 | 10 | 100,000 | 110,058 |

ESTIMATING DIVISION ANSWERS

| Problem | Round to | Drop Zeros | Estimated Answer | Real Answer |
|---|---|---|---|---|
| 88 ÷ 29 | 90 ÷ 30 | 9 ÷ 3 | 3 | 3.03 |
| 9,811 ÷ 394 | 10,000 ÷ 400 | 100 ÷ 4 | 25 | 24.90 |

COMPLETE ASSIGNMENT 1.5.

## Chapter Terms for Review

| | | | |
|---|---|---|---|
| addend | dividend | multiplicand | remainder |
| credit balance | divisor | multiplier | subtrahend |
| cross-checking | factors | product | sum |
| difference | minuend | quotient | |

## Try Microsoft® Excel

Try working the problems using the Microsoft Excel templates found on your student CD. Solutions for the problems are also shown on the CD.

# THE BOTTOM LINE

*Summary of chapter learning objectives:*

| Learning Objective | Example |
|---|---|

### 1.1

Use shortcuts to add rapidly and accurately.

Add the following, using the technique indicated.

| **Number combinations** | | **Repeated digits** | **Counting by tens** |
|---|---|---|---|
| 1. 8 | 2. 18 | 3. 52 | 4. 23 |
| 2 | 62 | 58 | 41 |
| 3 | 43 | 57 | 37 |
| 2 | 27 | 52 | 56 |
| + 5 | + 80 | + 51 | + 42 |

Add and then check by adding both vertically and horizontally.

5. 22 + 54 + 63 + 37 = _____
   27 + 82 + 44 + 19 = _____
   83 + 39 + 72 + 12 = _____
   91 + 71 + 21 + 84 = _____
   __ + __ + __ + __ = _____

### 1.2

Use shortcuts to subtract rapidly and accurately.

Subtract the following and then check by addition.

6. 228 − 134 = ____  ____ + 134 = ____

7. 335 − 217 = ____  ____ + 217 = ____

8. 53 − 18 = ____  ____ + 18 = ____

Subtract horizontally and check.

9. 245 − 130 = _____
   432 − 212 = _____
   381 − 270 = _____
   183 − 111 = _____
   ___ − ___ = _____

### 1.3

Use shortcuts to multiply rapidly and accurately.

Multiply.

10. 227 × 143

**Multiplying by numbers ending in zero**

11. 437 × 100

12. 879 × 10

**Multiplying by 25**

13. 354 × 25

**Multiplying by 50**

14. 846 × 50

Answers: 1. 20 2. 230 3. 270 4. 199 5. 821 6. 94 7. 118 8. 35 9. 518 10. 32,461 11. 43,700 12. 8,790 13. 8,850 14. 42,300

# THE BOTTOM LINE

*Summary of chapter learning objectives:*

| Learning Objective | Example |
|---|---|
| **1.4** Use shortcuts to divide rapidly and accurately. | Divide and check the answer by multiplication. 15. 27)1,512   27 × ____ ____ <br> **Dividing by numbers ending in 0** <br> 16. 8,430 ÷ 10 = ____ <br> 17. 127,400 ÷ 100 = ____ <br> **Dividing when both divisor and dividend end with zeros** <br> 18. 7,400 ÷ 200 = ____ <br> 19. 53,200 ÷ 400 = ____ <br> 20. 140,000 ÷ 2,000 = ____ |
| **1.5** Estimate answers before doing calculations. | Estimate these multiplication answers. Show your rounding, dropping of zeros with base product, estimated answer, and real answer. |

| Problem | Round to | Dropped Zeros and Base Product | Estimated Answer | Real Answer |
|---|---|---|---|---|
| 21. 47 × 31 | ____ | ____ | ____ | ____ |
| 22. 498 × 221 | ____ | ____ | ____ | ____ |

Estimate these division answers. Show your rounding, dropping of zeros, estimated answer, and real answer.

| Problem | Round to | Drop Zeros | Estimated Answer | Real Answer |
|---|---|---|---|---|
| 23. 88 ÷ 29 | ____ | ____ | ____ | ____ |
| 24. 9,811 ÷ 394 | ____ | ____ | ____ | ____ |

Answers: 15. 56 16. 843 17. 1,274 18. 37 19. 133 20. 70 21. 50 × 30; 5 × 3 = 15; 1,500; 1,457
22. 500 × 200; 5 × 2 = 10; 100,000; 110,058 23. 90 ÷ 30; 9 ÷ 3; 3; 3.03
24. 10,000 ÷ 400; 100 ÷ 4; 25; 24.90

SELF-CHECK

# Review Problems for Chapter 1

1. $8 + 9 + 3 + 12 + 6 =$ ________
2. $32 + 47 + 36 + 12 =$ ________
   $17 + 22 + 17 + 11 =$ ________
   $14 + 98 + 47 + 81 =$ ________
   $77 + 62 + 21 + 44 =$ ________
   ___ ___ ___ ___ = ________
3. $\begin{array}{r} 9{,}078 \\ -6{,}382 \\ \hline \end{array}$
4. $717 \div 14 =$ ________
5. $98 \times 13 =$ ________
6. $789 \div 36 =$ ________
7. $842 \div 200 =$ ________
8. $974 \div 12 =$ ________
9. $27\overline{)876} =$ ________
10. $2{,}006 \times 304 =$ ________
11. $395 \div 79 =$ ________
12. $800 \div 25 =$ ________
13. $4{,}000{,}000 \div 400 =$ ________
14. $\$370 - \$148 =$ ________
    $\$422 - \$109 =$ ________
    $\$982 - \$777 =$ ________
    $___ − $___ = ________
15. $\begin{array}{r} 1{,}472 \\ \times 28 \\ \hline \\ \hline \end{array}$
16. $704 \times 1{,}002 =$ ________
17. $704 \div 25 =$ ________
18. $16{,}000 \div 25 =$ ________
19. $6{,}000{,}006 \div 300 =$ ________
20. $77{,}777 \div 707 =$ ________

**Estimate answers for each of the following.**

21. $78 \times 29 =$ ________
22. $103 \times 19 =$ ________
23. $397 \times 200 =$ ________
24. $3{,}982 \times 99 =$ ________
25. $1{,}503 \times 600 =$ ________
26. $396 \div 79 =$ ________
27. $892 \div 29 =$ ________
28. $9{,}891 \div 480 =$ ________
29. $3{,}111 \div 59 =$ ________
30. $6{,}219 \div 3{,}114 =$ ________

**Answers to the Self-Check can be found in Appendix B at the back of the text.**

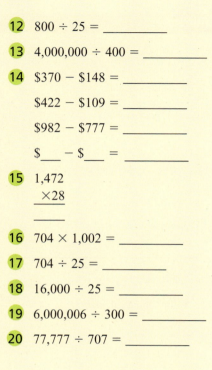

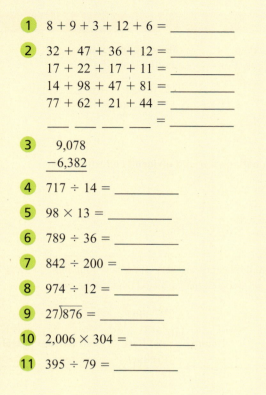

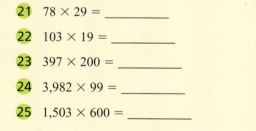

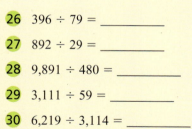

# Assignment 1.1: Addition

Name

Date Score

Learning Objective 1

**A (10 points) Add the following. Where possible, use combinations of 10. (1 point for each correct answer)**

| 1. | 2. | 3. | 4. | 5. | 6. | 7. | 8. | 9. | 10. |
|---|---|---|---|---|---|---|---|---|---|
| 17 | 41 | 19 | 34 | 97 | 50 | 72 | 82 | 38 | 63 |
| 43 | 29 | 54 | 33 | 44 | 54 | 99 | 43 | 39 | 37 |
| 35 | 17 | 14 | 43 | 33 | 54 | 99 | 47 | 22 | 44 |
| 42 | 36 | 81 | 37 | 76 | 47 | 89 | 93 | 45 | 36 |
| 43 | 44 | 28 | 36 | 32 | 59 | 47 | 58 | 47 | 24 |
| 37 | 15 | 11 | 34 | 72 | 54 | 63 | 34 | 25 | 21 |
| 23 | 56 | 43 | 32 | 34 | 55 | 40 | 22 | 13 | 19 |
| 58 | 62 | 51 | 38 | 76 | 55 | 62 | 46 | 29 | 25 |
| 12 | 66 | 76 | 32 | 27 | 35 | 68 | 73 | 79 | 75 |

Score for A (10)

**B (10 points) Add the following. (1 point for each correct answer)**

| 11. | 12. | 13. | 14. | 15. | 16. | 17. | 18. | 19. | 20. |
|---|---|---|---|---|---|---|---|---|---|
| 209 | 782 | 127 | 920 | 347 | 852 | 251 | 885 | 275 | 773 |
| 301 | 280 | 145 | 751 | 399 | 428 | 271 | 115 | 342 | 417 |
| 116 | 438 | 665 | 359 | 354 | 112 | 244 | 316 | 342 | 200 |
| 214 | 473 | 818 | 822 | 334 | 238 | 234 | 584 | 898 | 416 |
| 375 | 655 | 682 | 807 | 192 | 959 | 589 | 736 | 505 | 204 |

Score for B (10)

**C (10 points) Add the following. (1 point for each correct answer)**

| 21. | 22. | 23. | 24. | 25. |
|---|---|---|---|---|
| 248.28 | 201.22 | 234.81 | 238.69 | 326.52 |
| 820.14 | 513.14 | 371.60 | 982.30 | 217.38 |
| 306.80 | 250.54 | 271.37 | 376.48 | 267.34 |
| 521.98 | 2,647.55 | 408.55 | 728.90 | 118.66 |

| 26. | 27. | 28. | 29. | 30. |
|---|---|---|---|---|
| 703.91 | 126.92 | 442.71 | 535.13 | 233.48 |
| 422.38 | 32.15 | 71.93 | 44.78 | 607.22 |
| 721.05 | 873.19 | 416.90 | 208.17 | 211.25 |
| 446.21 | 872.52 | 236.19 | 6,481.29 | 211.25 |

Score for C (10)

**D** **(10 points) Add the following. Use the count-by-10s-and-add-the-1s method. (1 point for each correct answer)**

| **31.** | **32.** | **33.** | **34.** | **35.** | **36.** | **37.** | **38.** | **39.** | **40.** |
|---|---|---|---|---|---|---|---|---|---|
| 10.76 | 20.43 | 33.79 | 45.86 | 33.27 | 11.43 | 88.71 | 94.32 | 55.93 | 22.79 |
| 31.43 | 82.76 | 42.56 | 22.18 | 98.21 | 27.43 | 56.32 | 74.23 | 10.70 | 43.28 |
| 88.33 | 30.42 | 12.70 | 33.81 | 90.01 | 11.51 | 83.70 | 21.44 | 30.46 | 12.48 |
| 33.08 | 64.22 | 21.20 | 10.04 | 11.33 | 21.48 | 44.12 | 63.01 | 47.05 | 53.20 |
| 12.33 | 56.03 | 22.19 | 80.31 | 33.04 | 11.80 | 23.51 | 34.20 | 80.11 | 30.22 |

Score for D (10)

**E** **(30 points) Business Application. The following is the first part of a weekly sales summary—the Weekly Sales Report for the computer department. Complete the totals, both horizontal and vertical, and verify your addition by comparing the vertical and horizontal grand totals. (2 points for each column/row; 4 points for grand total)**

**DEPARTMENT SALES REPORT**

**Week of December 11–17, 20XX**

**Department: COMPUTERS**

| SALESPERSON | SUN | MON | TUE | WED | THU | FRI | SAT | TOTAL |
|---|---|---|---|---|---|---|---|---|
| Whalen | $3,443 | — | — | $8,643 | $3,176 | $7,885 | $9,378 | |
| Tsao | — | $8,772 | — | $9,483 | $7,339 | $8,113 | $9,771 | |
| Culver | $8,722 | $2,443 | $3,114 | $5,729 | $6,193 | — | — | |
| Hernandez | $6,117 | $8,783 | — | — | $5,685 | $9,473 | $11,492 | |
| Ingake | — | $3,114 | $8,492 | $7,652 | $3,994 | $14,119 | $12,378 | |
| Greenberg | — | — | $5,141 | $2,739 | $8,941 | $2,836 | $10,242 | |
| Total | | | | | | | | |

Score for E (30)

**F** **(30 points) Business Application. The following is the second part of the weekly sales summary—the Consolidated Sales Report for the entire store. Fill in the figures from the Department Sales Report and complete the totals, both horizontal and vertical. Verify your addition by comparing the horizontal and vertical grand totals. (2 points for each column/row; 2 points for grand total)**

**STORE SALES REPORT**

**Week of December 11–17, 20XX**

| DEPARTMENT | SUN | MON | TUE | WED | THU | FRI | SAT | TOTAL |
|---|---|---|---|---|---|---|---|---|
| Home Audio | 3,465 | 1,147 | 1,523 | 2,403 | 1,773 | 2,873 | 3,432 | |
| Auto Audio | 1,278 | 1,785 | 1,713 | 2,117 | 2,563 | 3,499 | 9,971 | |
| Video/TV | 15,230 | 12,377 | 10,429 | 9,384 | 8,773 | 11,245 | 13,486 | |
| Computers | 18,282 | 23,112 | 16,747 | 34,246 | 35,328 | 42,426 | 53,261 | |
| Telecomm | 849 | 722 | 531 | 733 | 1,012 | 1,239 | 1,375 | |
| Games | 882 | 248 | 379 | 287 | 415 | 978 | 1,015 | |
| Repairs | 732 | 892 | 384 | 658 | 981 | 1,043 | 1,774 | |
| Total | | | | | | | | |

Score for F (30)

# Assignment 1.2: Subtraction

Name ______________________

Date ______________ Score ______________

Learning Objective 2

**A (18 points) Subtract the following. (1 point for each correct answer)**

| | | | | | | | | |
|---|---|---|---|---|---|---|---|---|
| **1.** 77 − 16 | **2.** 90 − 17 | **3.** 72 − 25 | **4.** 63 − 29 | **5.** 84 − 48 | **6.** 38 − 49 | **7.** 92 − 16 | **8.** 83 − 65 | **9.** 30 − 14 |
| **10.** 39 − 36 | **11.** 20 − 13 | **12.** 13 − 26 | **13.** 73 − 14 | **14.** 63 − 19 | **15.** 68 − 39 | **16.** 99 − 27 | **17.** 57 − 43 | **18.** 27 − 39 |

Score for A (18)

**B (12 points) Subtract the following. Then check your subtraction by adding the subtrahend and the difference and comparing your total to the minuend. (2 points for each correct answer)**

| | | | | | |
|---|---|---|---|---|---|
| **19.** 584 − 173 | **20.** 963 − 874 | **21.** 103 − 310 | **22.** 714 − 30 | **23.** 616 − 333 | **24.** 9,999 − 3,264 |

Score for B (12)

**C (6 points) Subtract the following. (1 point for each correct answer)**

| | | | | | |
|---|---|---|---|---|---|
| **25.** $97.17 − 23.19 | **26.** $0.79 − 0.88 | **27.** $71.69 − 10.87 | **28.** $43.21 − 47.18 | **29.** $80.41 − 41.80 | **30.** $99.32 − 18.66 |

Score for C (6)

**D (9 points) Subtract the following. ($1\frac{1}{2}$ points for each correct answer)**

| | | | | | |
|---|---|---|---|---|---|
| **31.** $2,011.11 − 3,400.07 | **32.** $964.38 − 201.83 | **33.** $9,011.09 − 795.08 | **34.** $7,430.29 − 2,597.73 | **35.** $3,385.03 − 233.42 | **36.** $1,029.27 − 89.27 |

Score for D (9)

**E (15 points) Subtract the following. Sometimes a double subtraction is necessary. The following problems are of this type. (3 points for each correct final answer)**

| | | | | |
|---|---|---|---|---|
| **37.** $477.09 − 564.27 − 124.13 | **38.** $11,739.93 − 3,142.18 − 1,694.25 | **39.** $734.12 − 672.18 − 13.14 | **40.** $745.89 − 250.15 − 224.13 | **41.** $1,837,042.03 − 6,218.18 − 39,917.16 |

Score for E (15)

**F** **(20 points) Business Application. In many cases, multiple subtractions are required to complete a business transaction. (1 point for each intermediate answer; 2 points for each final answer)**

WINTER CATALOG CLEARANCE SALE ON SOFTWARE AND GAMES
10% REDUCTIONS ON CATALOG ORDERS
10% PREFERRED CUSTOMER DISCOUNTS
MAIL-IN REBATE OFFERS

| Item | Sierra Half-Life | The Sims 2 | Grand Theft Auto | Street Legal | Zoo Tycoon |
|---|---|---|---|---|---|
| List price | $43.95 | $45.70 | $42.25 | $49.95 | $53.75 |
| Less 10% catalog rate | −4.40 | −4.57 | −4.23 | −5.00 | −5.38 |
| | | | | | |
| Less 10% preferred customer rate | −3.96 | −4.11 | −3.80 | −4.50 | −4.84 |
| | | | | | |
| Mail−in rebate | −7.50 | −6.25 | −7.50 | −6.75 | −5.75 |
| Your price | | | | | |

Score for F (20)

**G** **(20 points) Business Application. Maintaining a budget involves both addition and subtraction. Keeping a budget sometimes involves a continuous record of cash income and expenses. Study the example and then complete the balances. (2 points for each balance)**

| Date 2/1/98 | To | Subtract Expenses | Add Income | Balance |
|---|---|---|---|---|
| | | | | $1,475.38 |
| 2/2/98 | Salary income | | $700.00 | 2,175.38 |
| 2/3/98 | Hinson Real Estate | $550.00 | | 1,625.38 |
| 2/5/98 | PG&E | 23.22 | | |
| 2/6/98 | Pacific Bell | 18.76 | | |
| 2/6/98 | Macy's | 43.22 | | |
| 2/10/98 | Chevron | 15.75 | | |
| 2/16/98 | Salary income | | $700.00 | |
| 2/17/98 | Fitness USA | 25.00 | | |
| 2/18/98 | John Simms, D.D.S. | 30.00 | | |
| 2/23/98 | Prudential Insurance | 17.73 | | |
| 2/25/98 | Visa | 85.42 | | |
| 2/27/98 | General Motors Finance | 257.87 | | |

Score for G (20)

# Assignment 1.3: Multiplication

Name ______________________________

Date ______________ Score ______________

Learning Objective 3

**A** **(12 points) Multiply the following. ($\frac{1}{2}$ point for each correct answer)**

| | | | |
|---|---|---|---|
| **1.** $2 \times 13 =$ ____ | **2.** $7 \times 17 =$ ____ | **3.** $14 \times 52 =$ ____ | **4.** $22 \times 22 =$ ____ |
| **5.** $9 \times 10 =$ ____ | **6.** $5 \times 15 =$ ____ | **7.** $15 \times 16 =$ ____ | **8.** $60 \times 7 =$ ____ |
| **9.** $8 \times 9 =$ ____ | **10.** $6 \times 12 =$ ____ | **11.** $12 \times 12 =$ ____ | **12.** $55 \times 9 =$ ____ |
| **13.** $6 \times 8 =$ ____ | **14.** $8 \times 12 =$ ____ | **15.** $4 \times 20 =$ ____ | **16.** $62 \times 70 =$ ____ |
| **17.** $6 \times 6 =$ ____ | **18.** $7 \times 22 =$ ____ | **19.** $8 \times 11 =$ ____ | **20.** $14 \times 700 =$ ____ |
| **21.** $2 \times 14 =$ ____ | **22.** $9 \times 22 =$ ____ | **23.** $8 \times 17 =$ ____ | **24.** $70 \times 70 =$ ____ |

Score for A (12) ____

**B** **(24 points) Find the products. (2 points for each correct answer)**

| | | | | | |
|---|---|---|---|---|---|
| **25.** 1,728 × 42 | **26.** 3,026 × 372 | **27.** 38,246 × 8,297 | **28.** 5,017 × 201 | **29.** 3,600 × 300 | **30.** 8,179 × 81 |
| **31.** 8,222 × 509 | **32.** 67,406 × 3,006 | **33.** 1,236 × 444 | **34.** 27,000 × 420 | **35.** 8,125 × 279 | **36.** 4,007 × 308 |

Score for B (24) ____

**C** **(10 points) Multiply by using shortcuts. (2 points for each correct answer)**

| | | | | |
|---|---|---|---|---|
| **37.** 3,684 × 50 | **38.** 4,999 × 50 | **39.** 6,642 × 25 | **40.** 3,212 × 50 | **41.** 1,500 × 25 |

Score for C (10) ____

**D** **(18 points) Multiply the three factors. (2 points for each final product)**

| | | |
|---|---|---|
| **42.** $33 \times 32 \times 31 =$ ____ | **43.** $51 \times 9 \times 60 =$ ____ | **44.** $45 \times 45 \times 45 =$ ____ |
| **45.** $14 \times 100 \times 7 =$ ____ | **46.** $915 \times 40 \times 20 =$ ____ | **47.** $10 \times 10 \times 10 =$ ____ |
| **48.** $30 \times 30 \times 30 =$ ____ | **49.** $17 \times 34 \times 1{,}013 =$ ____ | **50.** $1{,}500 \times 9 \times 3 =$ ____ |

Score for D (18) ____

**E** **(12 points) Complete each group of five multiplication problems and then add the five products. (1 point for each correct answer)**

**51.** 12 × 12.00 = ________

**52.** 27 × 8.16 = ________

**53.** 104 × 3.52 = ________

**54.** 6 × 92.92 = ________

**55.** 55 × 32.50 = ________

**56.** Total = ________

**57.** 21 × 7 × 16 = ________

**58.** 13 × 101 × 22 = ________

**59.** 33 × 14 × 7 = ________

**60.** 99 × 11 × 100 = ________

**61.** 3 × 88 × 100 = ________

**62.** Total = ________

________
Score for E (12)

**F** **(24 points) Business Application. Complete the merchandise inventory TOTAL column. (1 point for each correct total; 8 points for correct grand total)**

**MERCHANDISE INVENTORY**
**JUNE 30, 20xx**

| Stock Number | Description | Price | # in Stock | Total |
|---|---|---|---|---|
| G473-2 | Linspire 4.5 | $39.99 | 58 | |
| G763-4 | Spysweeper | $39.99 | 172 | |
| G865-A | Encarta | $49.95 | 98 | |
| G2238-1 | Turbo Tax | $34.99 | 225 | |
| G873-2 | Ever Quest 2 | $42.75 | 88 | |
| S876-3 | Microsoft Word | $98.77 | 178 | |
| S4433 | Uninstaller 4 | $32.59 | 85 | |
| S887-32 | Doom 3 | $45.79 | 110 | |
| S4536 | Netscape Navigator | $38.79 | 100 | |
| S1322 | Norton Utilities 7.0 | $67.85 | 68 | |
| S458-2 | Quicken | $27.75 | 205 | |
| S5382 | City of Heros | $95.69 | 80 | |
| E5673-E | Typing Tutor | $26.59 | 108 | |
| E82-18 | Atari Atar | $52.49 | 25 | |
| E2442 | Adobe 6 | $45.29 | 307 | |
| E3578-1 | Perfect Spanish | $44.79 | 80 | |
| | | | TOTAL | |

________
Score for F (24)

# Assignment 1.4: Division

Name

Date Score

Learning Objective 4

**A (10 points) Divide the following problems mentally. ($\frac{1}{2}$ point for each correct quotient)**

| | | |
|---|---|---|
| **1.** 72 ÷ 6 = ______ | **2.** 75 ÷ 5 = ______ | **3.** 66 ÷ 22 = ______ |
| **4.** 110 ÷ 5 = ______ | **5.** 126 ÷ 3 = ______ | **6.** 189 ÷ 21 = ______ |
| **7.** 88 ÷ 22 = ______ | **8.** 144 ÷ 12 = ______ | **9.** 360 ÷ 20 = ______ |
| **10.** 135 ÷ 9 = ______ | **11.** 990 ÷ 33 = ______ | **12.** 361 ÷ 19 = ______ |
| **13.** 156 ÷ 12 = ______ | **14.** 900 ÷ 15 = ______ | **15.** 1,782 ÷ 18 = ______ |
| **16.** 84 ÷ 12 = ______ | **17.** 104 ÷ 2 = ______ | **18.** 357 ÷ 17 = ______ |
| **19.** 126 ÷ 7 = ______ | **20.** 315 ÷ 15 = ______ | |

Score for A (10)

**B (10 points) Divide by shortcut methods. Express remainders in parentheses. (1 point for each correct answer)**

| | | |
|---|---|---|
| **21.** 1,818 ÷ 333 = ______ | **22.** 107,300 ÷ 100 = ______ | **23.** 97,600 ÷ 100 = ______ |
| **24.** 2,200 ÷ 100 = ______ | **25.** 7,800 ÷ 20 = ______ | **26.** 6,450 ÷ 320 = ______ |
| **27.** 9,005 ÷ 100 = ______ | **28.** 387 ÷ 10 = ______ | **29.** 7,600 ÷ 1,000 = ______ |
| **30.** 3,250,000 ÷ 10,000 = ______ | | |

Score for B (10)

**C (50 points) Divide. Show the remainder in parentheses after the whole number in the quotient. (2 points for each correct answer)**

| | | | |
|---|---|---|---|
| **31.** 21)478 | **32.** 13)2,795 | **33.** 23)14,076 | **34.** 7)4,919 |
| **35.** 36)6,436 | **36.** 23)478 | **37.** 271)50,001 | **38.** 33)97,382 |
| **39.** 926)926,007 | **40.** 77)12,770 | **41.** 506)10,238 | **42.** 9)818,173 |
| **43.** 700)362,497 | **44.** 111)34,173 | **45.** 88)97,817 | **46.** 13)$67,209 |
| **47.** 6)$13.20 | **48.** 54)78,540 | **49.** 51)100 | **50.** 26)111,013 |
| **51.** 66)73,428 | **52.** 1,014)20,016 | **53.** 66)17,209 | **54.** 65)372,000 |
| **55.** 29)58,004,316 | | | |

Score for C (50)

**D** **(10 points) Divide and check the following problems. (2 points for each correct answer)**

**56.** 22)1,364 **57.** 31)1,395 **58.** 92)7,284 **59.** 21)2,214 **60.** 42)711

**Check:**

× ____ × ____ × ____ × ____ × ____

\+ ____ + ____ + ____

= ____ = ____ = ____ = ____ = ____

Score for D (10)

**E** **(20 points) Business Application. As an estimator for a printing company, you must estimate the paper costs for printing jobs. Paper is priced by the ream, which is 500 pages. Compute the paper costs of the jobs. (1 point for each correct computation)**

| No. of Booklets | No. of Pages | Total Pages | Reams of Paper | Cost per Ream | Total Paper Cost |
|---|---|---|---|---|---|
| 250 | 66 | | | $2.00 | |
| 120 | 150 | | | $4.25 | |
| 75 | 220 | | | $4.83 | |
| 110 | 250 | | | $3.75 | |
| 25 | 280 | | | $3.15 | |
| 30 | 250 | | | $4.10 | |
| | | Total reams | | Total paper cost | |

Score for E (20)

# Assignment 1.5: Estimating

Name ______________________

Date ______________ Score ______________

Learning Objective 5

**A** **(60 points) Estimate an answer for each of the following problems. Show your rounding, dropping of zeros with base product, and final estimate. (1 point for each correct answer)**

| Problem | Round to | Dropped Zeros and Base Product | Estimated Answer |
|---|---|---|---|
| **1.** 1,095 × 427 | | | |
| **2.** 78,221 × 6,099 | | | |
| **3.** 34,007 × 80 | | | |
| **4.** 56 × 1,528 | | | |
| **5.** 18 × 2,855 × 93 | | | |
| **6.** 20 × 17 × 19 | | | |
| **7.** 2,997 × 13 | | | |
| **8.** 41 × 19 × 3 | | | |
| **9.** 212 × 101 × 99 | | | |
| **10.** 23 × 10,322 | | | |
| **11.** 777 × 777 | | | |
| **12.** 29,301 × 21 | | | |
| **13.** 72,111 × 108 | | | |
| **14.** 13 × 100 × 6 | | | |
| **15.** 99 × 99 × 99 | | | |
| **16.** 28 × 42 | | | |
| **17.** 111 × 39 | | | |
| **18.** 7 × 99 | | | |
| **19.** 204 × 17 | | | |
| **20.** 11 × 12 × 13 | | | |

______________
Score for A (60)

**B** **(20 points) Estimate an answer for each of the following problems. Show your rounding, dropping of zeros with base product, estimated answer, and real answer. (1 point for each correct answer)**

| Problem | Round to | Dropped Zeros and Base Product | Estimated Answer | Real Answer |
|---|---|---|---|---|
| **21.** 883 × 294 | | | | |
| **22.** 42,100 × 412 | | | | |
| **23.** 19,965 × 492 | | | | |
| **24.** 89 × 33 | | | | |
| **25.** 689 × 203 | | | | |

Score for B (20)

**C** **(20 points) Estimate an answer for each of the following division problems. Show your rounding, dropping of zeros, estimated answer, and real answer. (1 point for each correct answer)**

| Problem | Round to | Drop Zeros | Estimated Answer | Real Answer |
|---|---|---|---|---|
| **26.** 123 ÷ 41 | | | | |
| **27.** 612 ÷ 12 | | | | |
| **28.** 4,836 ÷ 78 | | | | |
| **29.** 19,760 ÷ 95 | | | | |
| **30.** 21,390 ÷ 690 | | | | |

Score for C (20)

# Fractions

2

## Learning Objectives

By studying this chapter and completing all assignments, you will be able to:

Learning Objective 1 Change improper fractions and mixed numbers.

Learning Objective 2 Change fractions to lower and higher terms.

Learning Objective 3 Add fractions and mixed numbers.

Learning Objective 4 Subtract fractions and mixed numbers.

Learning Objective 5 Multiply fractions, mixed numbers, and whole numbers.

Learning Objective 6 Divide fractions, mixed numbers, and whole numbers.

**Fractions** are a natural part of cultures around the world. Very young children who cannot yet read learn simple fractions such as one half and one third when their parents teach them about sharing a candy bar or a pizza. Before the development of inexpensive handheld calculators, fractions were more important than they are today because they permitted shortcuts in arithmetic. However, fractions are still important in some industries. Moreover, the rules of fractions will always remain very important in algebra and higher mathematics.

# Notation and Vocabulary of Fractions

A restaurant cuts its medium-sized pizzas into six pieces. Each piece is "*one sixth*" of the pizza. If you take two pieces of pizza, you have "*two sixths*" of the pizza. Using numbers, two sixths can be written as $\frac{2}{6}$. If you buy two medium-sized pizzas and cut each pizza into six pieces, you will have twelve pieces, or *twelve sixths,* written as $\frac{12}{6}$. If you eat one of the twelve slices of pizza, eleven pieces remain, or *eleven sixths,* written as $\frac{11}{6}$.

In the three fractions $\frac{2}{6}$, $\frac{12}{6}$, and $\frac{11}{6}$, the bottom number (6) is called the **denominator.** The top numbers (2, 12, and 11) are called **numerators.** $\frac{2}{6}$ is called a **proper fraction** because the numerator (2) is *smaller than* the denominator (6). $\frac{12}{6}$ and $\frac{11}{6}$ are called **improper fractions** because the numerators are *greater than, or equal to,* the denominators. Notice that $\frac{11}{6}$ represents one whole pizza plus $\frac{5}{6}$ of the second pizza. $\frac{11}{6}$ can be written as $1\frac{5}{6}$ which is called a **mixed number** because there is a whole number part (1) and a proper fraction $(\frac{5}{6})$.

Figure 2-1 illustrates these concepts. Diagram b represents a proper fraction. Diagrams a, c, and d all represent improper fractions. Diagram d also represents a mixed number.

**Figure 2-1**

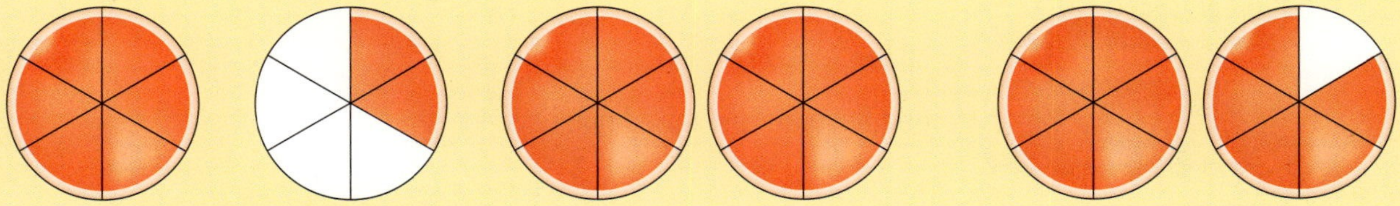


# Changing Improper Fractions and Mixed Numbers

**Learning Objective 1**

Change improper fractions and mixed numbers.

Using simple arithmetic, we can change improper fractions to mixed numbers and mixed numbers to improper fractions.

## STEPS to Change an Improper Fraction to a Mixed Number

1. Divide the numerator by the denominator.
2. The quotient is the whole-number part of the mixed number.
3. The remainder is the numerator of the fraction part.
4. The original denominator is the denominator of the fraction part.

### EXAMPLE A

Change $\frac{11}{8}$ to a mixed number.

STEP 1

$$\frac{11}{8} = 8\overline{)11} \quad \begin{array}{r} 1\ R3 \\ 8 \\ \hline 3 \end{array}$$

STEPS 2, 3, & 4

$$\text{Thus, } \frac{11}{8} = 1\frac{3}{8}$$

*Note:* Refer to Point A in Figure 2-2 to see where these numbers appear on a ruler.

**Figure 2-2**

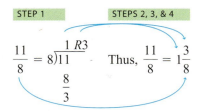

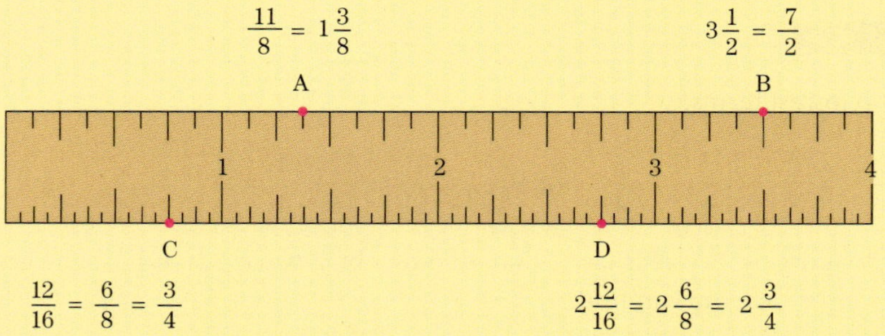


## STEPS to Change a Mixed Number to an Improper Fraction

1. Multiply the denominator of the fraction part by the whole number.
2. Add the numerator of the fraction part to the product of Step 1. The sum is the numerator of the improper fraction.
3. The denominator of the fraction of the mixed number is the denominator of the improper fraction.

### EXAMPLE B

Change $3\frac{1}{2}$ to an improper fraction.

STEP 1

$$2 \times 3 = 6$$

STEPS 2, 3

$$\text{Thus, } 3\frac{1}{2} = \frac{6 + 1}{2} = \frac{7}{2}$$

*Note:* Refer to Point B in Figure 2-2 to see where these numbers appear on a ruler.

# Changing Fractions to Lower and Higher Terms

**Learning Objective 2**

Change fractions to lower and higher terms.

Read Point C on the ruler shown in Figure 2-2. Point C marks the distance $\frac{12}{16}$ of an inch, but it could also be read as $\frac{6}{8}$ or $\frac{3}{4}$ of an inch. Thus $\frac{12}{16}$, $\frac{6}{8}$, and $\frac{3}{4}$ are three ways to write the same value. We say that $\frac{6}{8}$ is in **lower terms** and $\frac{12}{16}$ is in **higher terms** because 8 is a smaller denominator than 16. We also say that $\frac{3}{4}$ is in **lowest terms** because it cannot be changed to any lower terms. When we change a fraction to lower terms, we say that we are *reducing* the fraction to lower terms. If we change a mixed number such as $2\frac{12}{16}$ to $2\frac{3}{4}$, we say that we have reduced the mixed number to its lowest terms. When we change fractions to higher terms, we say that we are raising them to higher terms.

### STEPS to Reduce a Fraction to Lowest Terms

1. Divide both the numerator and the denominator by a common divisor greater than 1 to arrive at a reduced fraction.
2. If necessary, repeat Step 1 until the fraction cannot be reduced any further.

*Note:* If a fraction's numerator and denominator have no common divisor greater than 1, the fraction is already in lowest terms.

**EXAMPLE C**

Reduce $\frac{12}{16}$ to lowest terms.

$$\frac{12}{16} = \frac{12 \div 2}{16 \div 2} = \frac{6}{8} = \frac{6 \div 2}{8 \div 2} = \frac{3}{4} \quad \text{or else} \quad \frac{12}{16} = \frac{12 \div 4}{16 \div 4} = \frac{3}{4}$$

Note that dividing by 4 once is faster than dividing by 2 twice. Always use the greatest common divisor that you can find.

### STEPS to Raise a Fraction to Higher Terms

1. Divide the new denominator by the old denominator. The quotient is the *common multiplier.*
2. Multiply the old numerator by the common multiplier.
3. Multiply the old denominator by the common multiplier.

**Video**

Reducing and Raising Fractions

**EXAMPLE D**

Raise $\frac{3}{4}$ to twenty-fourths.

STEP 1

$$\frac{3}{4} = \frac{?}{24} \qquad 24 \div 4 = 6$$

STEPS 2 & 3

$$\text{So, } \frac{3}{4} = \frac{3 \times 6}{4 \times 6} = \frac{18}{24}$$

# Adding Fractions and Mixed Numbers

**Learning Objective 3**

Add fractions and mixed numbers.

Fractions and mixed numbers are all numbers, so they can be added and subtracted just like whole numbers. However, when you add fractions and/or mixed numbers, you must first find a **common denominator.** This is a denominator shared by all of the fractions and it also will be the denominator of the fraction part of the answer.

The smallest common denominator possible is called the **least common denominator.** If the least common denominator is not easily apparent, it may be quicker to use the first common denominator that you can discover and then reduce the answer to lowest terms. The product of all of the denominators always will be a common denominator, but very often there will be a smaller common denominator.

**Video**

Adding and Subtracting Fractions and Mixed Numbers

**STEPS to Add Two or More Fractions and/or Mixed Numbers**

1. If necessary, change the fraction parts to fractions with common denominators. The common denominator is the denominator in the fraction part of the answer.
2. Add the numerators to make the numerator of the fraction part of the answer. If there are any whole-number parts, add them to make the whole-number part of the answer.
3. If necessary, change an improper fraction to a mixed number and mentally add any whole number parts.
4. Reduce the fraction part of the answer to lowest terms.

**EXAMPLE E**

Add $2\frac{7}{8}$ and $4\frac{3}{8}$.
The fractions already have a common denominator of 8.

$$
\begin{array}{r}
2\frac{7}{8} \\
+4\frac{3}{8} \\
\hline
6\frac{10}{8} = 6 + 1\frac{2}{8} = 7\frac{1}{4}
\end{array}
$$

STEP 2 STEP 3 STEP 4

**EXAMPLE F**

Add $\frac{5}{6}$ and $\frac{3}{4}$.
A common denominator is $6 \times 4 = 24$.

$$
\begin{array}{r}
\frac{5}{6} = \frac{5 \times 4}{6 \times 4} = \frac{20}{24} \\
+\frac{3}{4} = \frac{3 \times 6}{4 \times 6} = \frac{18}{24} \\
\hline
\frac{38}{24} = 1\frac{14}{24} = 1\frac{7}{12}
\end{array}
$$

STEP 1

STEPS 2, 3, & 4

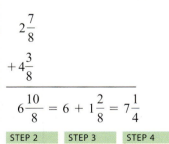

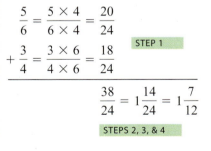

**EXAMPLE G**

Add $3\frac{5}{8}$ and $7\frac{5}{6}$.
The least common denominator is 24.

STEP 1

$$3\frac{5}{8} = 3\frac{15}{24}$$

$$+7\frac{5}{6} = +7\frac{20}{24}$$

$$10\frac{35}{24} = 10 + 1\frac{11}{24} = 11\frac{11}{24}$$

STEP 2 STEP 3

**CONCEPT CHECK 2.1**

a. Add $\frac{4}{5}$, $\frac{2}{3}$, and $\frac{5}{9}$.
The least common denominator is 45.

$$\frac{4}{5} = \frac{4 \times 9}{5 \times 9} = \frac{36}{45}$$

$$\frac{2}{3} = \frac{2 \times 15}{3 \times 15} = \frac{30}{45}$$

$$+\frac{5}{9} = \frac{5 \times 5}{9 \times 5} = +\frac{25}{45}$$

$$\frac{91}{45} = 2\frac{1}{45}$$

b. Add $1\frac{5}{6}$ and $2\frac{5}{9}$.
A common denominator is $6 \times 9 = 54$.

$$1\frac{5}{6} = 1\frac{45}{54}$$

$$+2\frac{5}{9} = +2\frac{30}{54}$$

$$3\frac{75}{54} = 4\frac{21}{54} = 4\frac{7}{18}$$

# Subtracting Fractions and Mixed Numbers

**Learning Objective 4**

Subtract fractions and mixed numbers.

The procedure for subtracting one fraction from another is almost the same as the procedure for adding one fraction to another. When you calculate $3\frac{1}{4} - \frac{3}{4}$, $3\frac{1}{4}$ is called the *minuend* and $\frac{3}{4}$ is called the *subtrahend*, as in the subtraction of whole numbers.

## BORROWING 1

Sometimes, as with $3\frac{1}{4} - \frac{3}{4}$, the fraction part of the minuend is smaller than the fraction part of the subtrahend. To make the fraction part of the minuend larger than the fraction part of the subtrahend, you have to "borrow 1" from the whole-number part of the minuend. Actually, you're just rewriting the minuend. Remember that $3\frac{1}{4}$ means $3 + \frac{1}{4}$, or the same as $2 + 1 + \frac{1}{4}$, $2 + \frac{4}{4} + \frac{1}{4}$, or $2\frac{5}{4}$. These are simply four different ways to express the same quantity. Figure 2-3 is useful in understanding borrowing.

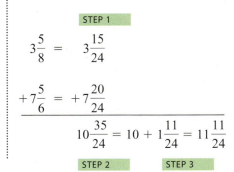

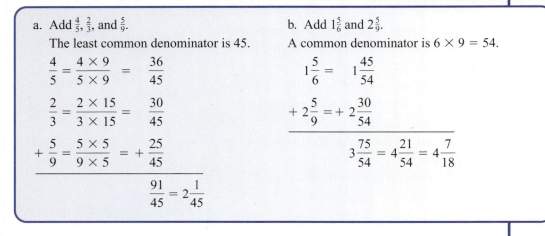

**Figure 2-3**

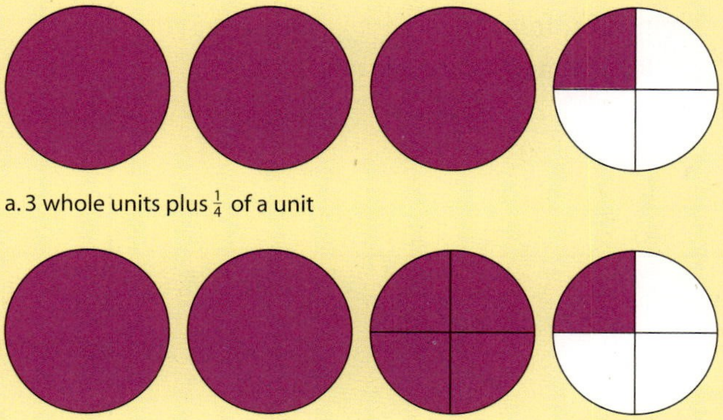

a. 3 whole units plus $\frac{1}{4}$ of a unit

b. 2 "whole units" plus $\frac{5}{4}$ of a unit

**Video**

Adding and Subtracting Fractions and Mixed Numbers

## STEPS to Subtract One Fraction or Mixed Number from Another

1. If necessary, change the fractions so that all fractions have a common denominator. The common denominator is the denominator in the fraction part of the answer.
2. If necessary, "borrow 1" from the whole-number part of the minuend so that the fraction part of the minuend is at least as large as the fraction part of the subtrahend.
3. Subtract the numerators in the fractions to make the numerator in the fraction part of the answer.
4. If there are any whole-number parts, subtract them to make the whole-number part of the answer.
5. Reduce the fraction part of the answer to lowest terms.

**EXAMPLE H**

STEP 3 STEP 5

$$\frac{7}{8} - \frac{3}{8} = \frac{7-3}{8} = \frac{4}{8} = \frac{1}{2}$$

**EXAMPLE I**

STEP 1 STEP 3

$$\frac{3}{4} - \frac{1}{5} = \frac{3 \times 5}{4 \times 5} - \frac{1 \times 4}{5 \times 4} = \frac{15}{20} - \frac{4}{20} = \frac{11}{20}$$

**EXAMPLE J**

STEP 1

$$5\frac{3}{4} = 5\frac{9}{12}$$

$$-2\frac{1}{3} = -2\frac{4}{12}$$

STEPS 3 & 4

$$3\frac{5}{12}$$

**EXAMPLE K**

STEP 1 STEP 2

$$4\frac{4}{9} = 4\frac{8}{18} = 3\frac{18}{18} + \frac{8}{18} = 3\frac{26}{18}$$

$$-1\frac{5}{6} = -1\frac{15}{18} = -1\frac{15}{18} = -1\frac{15}{18}$$

STEPS 3 & 4

$$2\frac{11}{18}$$

## CONCEPT CHECK 2.2

a. Subtract $\frac{5}{6}$ from $\frac{7}{8}$.

The least common denominator is 24.

$$\begin{array}{rcr} \dfrac{7}{8} & = & \dfrac{21}{24} \\ -\dfrac{5}{6} & = & -\dfrac{20}{24} \\ \hline & & \dfrac{1}{24} \end{array}$$

b. Subtract $2\frac{9}{10}$ from $6\frac{5}{6}$.

The least common denominator is 30.

$$\begin{array}{rcrcr} 6\dfrac{5}{6} & = & 6\dfrac{25}{30} & = & 5\dfrac{55}{30} \\ -2\dfrac{9}{10} & = & -2\dfrac{27}{30} & = & -2\dfrac{27}{30} \\ \hline & & & & 3\dfrac{28}{30} = 3\dfrac{14}{15} \end{array}$$

COMPLETE ASSIGNMENT 2.1.

# Multiplying Fractions, Mixed Numbers, and Whole Numbers

**Learning Objective 5**

Multiply fractions, mixed numbers, and whole numbers.

In fractions, multiplication and division do not require common denominators. This means that multiplication and division are simpler than addition and subtraction. Recall that any mixed number can be changed to an improper fraction. Also, a whole number can be written as an improper fraction by writing the whole number in the numerator with a denominator of 1. For example, the whole number 5 can be written as the improper fraction $\frac{5}{1}$.

**Video**

Multiplication and Division of Mixed Numbers

**STEPS to Multiply Fractions, Mixed Numbers, and Whole Numbers**

1. If necessary, change any mixed or whole numbers to improper fractions.
2. Multiply all the numerators to get the numerator of the product.
3. Multiply all the denominators to get the denominator of the product.
4. Change the product to a proper fraction or mixed number in lowest terms.

**EXAMPLE L**

STEP 1 | STEPS 2 & 3 | STEP 4

$$1\frac{2}{3} \times \frac{4}{5} = \frac{5}{3} \times \frac{4}{5} = \frac{5 \times 4}{3 \times 5} = \frac{20}{15} = 1\frac{5}{15} = 1\frac{1}{3}$$

**EXAMPLE M**

STEPS 2 & 3 | STEP 4

$$\frac{2}{3} \times \frac{4}{5} \times \frac{5}{6} = \frac{2 \times 4 \times 5}{3 \times 5 \times 6} = \frac{40}{90} = \frac{4}{9}$$

*Note:* The word *of* often means *multiply* when it is used with fractions. For example, you know that "$\frac{1}{2}$ *of* 6 bottles" is 3 bottles. And $\frac{1}{2}$ *of* $6 = \frac{1}{2} \times \frac{6}{1} = \frac{6}{2} = 3$. For this reason, multiplication may even be the most important arithmetic operation with fractions. In verbal communication, we will often be saying expressions like "$\frac{1}{2}$ of 6."

# Canceling Common Factors in Numerators and Denominators

As the last step in example M, we reduced the fraction $\frac{40}{90}$ to its lowest terms, $\frac{4}{9}$. Recall that reducing this fraction means that we divide both the numerator and the denominator by 10. As an option, we can do that division in advance, before doing any multiplication. Examining the three numerators and three denominators, we discover that they have common factors of 2 and 5. Divide out, or **cancel,** both the 2 and the 5 in both the numerators and denominators as shown in example N. This division of the common factors is often called **cancellation.** Canceling common factors is an option; it is not required to calculate the correct product.

**EXAMPLE N**

Multiply the three fractions, using cancellation.

STEP 1 | STEPS 2 & 3 | STEP 4

$$\frac{2}{3} \times \frac{4}{5} \times \frac{5}{6} = \frac{2}{3} \times \frac{4}{\underset{1}{\cancel{5}}} \times \frac{\overset{1}{\cancel{5}}}{6} = \frac{2}{3} \times \frac{\overset{2}{\cancel{4}}}{\underset{1}{\cancel{5}}} \times \frac{\overset{1}{\cancel{5}}}{\underset{3}{\cancel{6}}} = \frac{2 \times 2 \times 1}{3 \times 1 \times 3} = \frac{4}{9}$$

**EXAMPLE O**

Multiply the fraction and the whole number, using cancellation.

STEP 1 | STEPS 2 & 3 | STEP 4

$$\frac{3}{4} \text{ of } 12 = \frac{3}{4} \times 12 = \frac{3}{4} \times \frac{12}{1} = \frac{3}{\underset{1}{\cancel{4}}} \times \frac{\overset{3}{\cancel{12}}}{1} = \frac{3 \times 3}{1 \times 1} = \frac{9}{1} = 9$$

**EXAMPLE P**

Multiply the fraction and the mixed number, using cancellation.

STEP 1 | STEPS 2 & 3 | STEP 4

$$\frac{2}{5} \text{ of } 2\frac{3}{4} = \frac{2}{5} \times 2\frac{3}{4} = \frac{2}{5} \times \frac{11}{4} = \frac{\overset{1}{\cancel{2}}}{5} \times \frac{11}{\underset{2}{\cancel{4}}} = \frac{1 \times 11}{5 \times 2} = \frac{11}{10} = 1\frac{1}{10}$$

**CONCEPT CHECK 2.3**

Multiply the fraction, whole number, and mixed number, using cancellation.

$$\frac{1}{8} \times 4 \times 2\frac{1}{3} = \frac{1}{8} \times \frac{4}{1} \times \frac{7}{3} = \frac{1}{\underset{2}{\cancel{8}}} \times \frac{\overset{1}{\cancel{4}}}{1} \times \frac{7}{3} = \frac{1 \times 1 \times 7}{2 \times 1 \times 3} = \frac{7}{6} = 1\frac{1}{6}$$

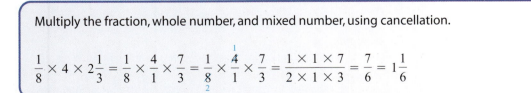

# Dividing Fractions, Mixed Numbers, and Whole Numbers

**Learning Objective 6**

Divide fractions, mixed numbers, and whole numbers.

Recall that with whole numbers, division is the *inverse* of multiplication. You can check a multiplication problem with division. With fractions, you actually perform a division problem by doing multiplication. That is, you *invert the divisor and multiply*.

**STEPS to Divide Fractions, Mixed Numbers, and Whole Numbers**

1. If necessary, change the dividend and/or the divisor from mixed or whole numbers to improper fractions.
2. Invert the divisor (that is, exchange the numerator and denominator).
3. Change the division symbol to a multiplication symbol.
4. Multiply the two factors (canceling where possible, if desired).
5. Write the result as a proper fraction or mixed number in lowest terms.

**VIDEO**

Multiplication and Division of Mixed Numbers

**EXAMPLE Q**

STEPS 2 & 3 | STEP 4

$$\frac{3}{10} \div \frac{2}{5} = \frac{3}{10} \times \frac{5}{2} = \frac{3}{\cancel{10}_{2}} \times \frac{\cancel{5}^{1}}{2} = \frac{3 \times 1}{2 \times 2} = \frac{3}{4}$$

**EXAMPLE R**

STEP 1 | STEPS 2 & 3 | STEP 4 | STEP 5

$$6 \div 1\frac{3}{5} = \frac{6}{1} \div \frac{8}{5} = \frac{6}{1} \times \frac{5}{8} = \frac{\cancel{6}^{3}}{1} \times \frac{5}{\cancel{8}_{4}} = \frac{3 \times 5}{1 \times 4} = \frac{15}{4} = 3\frac{3}{4}$$

## CONCEPT CHECK 2.4

Divide $3\frac{3}{4}$ *by* $1\frac{1}{2}$.

Change both mixed numbers to improper fractions: $\frac{15}{4} \div \frac{3}{2}$.

Invert the divisor $\frac{3}{2}$ to $\frac{2}{3}$ and multiply:

$$\frac{15}{4} \times \frac{2}{3} = \frac{\cancel{15}^{5}}{\cancel{4}_{2}} \times \frac{\cancel{2}^{1}}{\cancel{3}_{1}} = \frac{5 \times 1}{2 \times 1} = \frac{5}{2} = 2\frac{1}{2}$$

COMPLETE ASSIGNMENT 2.2.

## Chapter Terms for Review

cancel
cancellation
common denominator
denominator
fractions
higher terms
improper fraction
least common denominator
lower terms
lowest terms
mixed number
numerator
proper fraction

# THE BOTTOM LINE

*Summary of chapter learning objectives:*

| Learning Objective | Example |
|---|---|
| **2.1** Change improper fractions and mixed numbers. | 1(a). Change $\frac{18}{5}$ to a mixed number.<br>1(b). Change $2\frac{5}{6}$ to an improper fraction. |
| **2.2** Change fractions to lower and higher terms. | 2(a). Reduce $\frac{12}{30}$ to lowest terms.<br>2(b). Raise $\frac{7}{12}$ to sixtieths; that is, $\frac{7}{12} = \frac{?}{60}$. |
| **2.3** Add fractions and mixed numbers. | 3. Add $\frac{7}{8}$, $\frac{5}{6}$, and $2\frac{3}{4}$. |
| **2.4** Subtract fractions and mixed numbers. | 4. Subtract $1\frac{3}{4}$ from $4\frac{2}{5}$. |
| **2.5** Multiply fractions, mixed numbers, and whole numbers. | 5. Multiply: $\frac{2}{9} \times \frac{6}{7}$. |
| **2.6** Divide fractions, mixed numbers, and whole numbers. | 6. Divide: $1\frac{4}{5} \div \frac{3}{4}$. |

Answers: 1(a). $3\frac{3}{5}$ 1(b). $\frac{17}{6}$ 2(a). $\frac{2}{5}$ 2(b). $\frac{35}{60}$ 3. $4\frac{11}{24}$ 4. $2\frac{13}{20}$ 5. $\frac{4}{21}$ 6. $2\frac{2}{5}$

SELF-CHECK

# Review Problems for Chapter 2

**Write all answers as proper fractions or mixed numbers in lowest terms.**

1. Change $2\frac{5}{6}$ to an improper fraction _______
2. Change $\frac{90}{12}$ to a mixed number _______
3. Reduce $\frac{54}{63}$ to lowest terms _______
4. Raise $\frac{10}{14}$ to 56ths _______
5. Add $\frac{2}{3}$, $\frac{3}{5}$, and $\frac{3}{10}$ _______
6. Add $\frac{5}{8}$ and $1\frac{1}{6}$ _______
7. Add $\frac{3}{4}$, $2\frac{4}{5}$, and 4 _______
8. Subtract $\frac{1}{3}$ from $\frac{4}{5}$ _______
9. Subtract $\frac{8}{9}$ from $2\frac{5}{6}$ _______
10. Subtract $2\frac{4}{9}$ from $4\frac{1}{5}$ _______
11. Multiply $\frac{5}{6}$ by $\frac{12}{35}$ _______
12. Multiply $\frac{9}{16}$ by $1\frac{13}{15}$ _______
13. Multiply $2\frac{1}{10}$, $\frac{8}{15}$, and $2\frac{1}{12}$ _______
14. Divide $\frac{15}{16}$ by $\frac{5}{12}$ _______
15. Divide $1\frac{11}{25}$ by $\frac{24}{35}$ _______
16. Divide $1\frac{2}{7}$ by $1\frac{1}{14}$ _______
17. JoAnn Brandt decided to use an expensive, but effective, herbicide to kill weeds and brush on a client's land. For one part of the land, she needed $3\frac{2}{3}$ quarts of herbicide; for a second part, she needed $2\frac{3}{4}$ quarts; and for the third part, she needed $1\frac{5}{6}$ quarts. In total, how many quarts of herbicide did JoAnn need for this client? _________
18. An electrician had a piece of electrical conduit that was $12\frac{1}{2}$ feet long. She cut off two pieces that were $4\frac{3}{4}$ feet and $5\frac{2}{3}$ feet long, respectively. How many feet of conduit did she have left over? _________
19. The Central Hotel just hired a new chef. This chef makes a hot sauce that uses $1\frac{3}{4}$ tablespoons of chili powder, but he needs to increase the recipe by $3\frac{1}{2}$ times. How many tablespoons of chili powder should he use? _________
20. How many whole pieces of copper $2\frac{5}{8}$ inches long can be cut out of one piece that is $24\frac{1}{2}$ inches long? _________ How long is the shorter piece that is left over? _________

**Answers to the Self-Check can be found in Appendix B at the back of the text.**

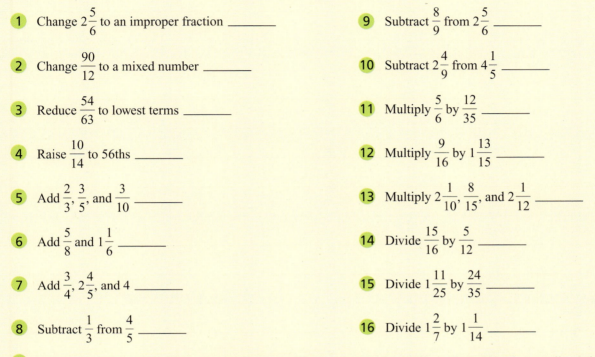

## Notes

# Assignment 2.1: Addition and Subtraction of Fractions

Name ______________________

Date ______________ Score ______________

Learning Objectives 1 2 3 4

**A (12 points) Change the improper fractions to whole numbers or to mixed numbers. Change the mixed numbers to improper fractions. (1 point for each correct answer)**

**1.** $\frac{13}{6}$ ______ **2.** $\frac{32}{10}$ ______ **3.** $\frac{18}{6}$ ______ **4.** $\frac{25}{15}$ ______

**5.** $\frac{23}{13}$ ______ **6.** $\frac{25}{8}$ ______ **7.** $3\frac{7}{10}$ ______ **8.** $2\frac{11}{12}$ ______

**9.** $2\frac{5}{8}$ ______ **10.** $3\frac{3}{4}$ ______ **11.** $6\frac{3}{5}$ ______ **12.** $4\frac{5}{6}$ ______

______ Score for A (12)

**B (15 points) In problems 13–20, reduce each fraction to lowest terms. In problems 21–27, raise each fraction to higher terms, as indicated. (1 point for each correct answer)**

**13.** $\frac{10}{25}$ ______ **14.** $\frac{9}{24}$ ______ **15.** $\frac{18}{30}$ ______ **16.** $\frac{12}{16}$ ______

**17.** $\frac{32}{48}$ ______ **18.** $\frac{24}{42}$ ______ **19.** $\frac{42}{60}$ ______ **20.** $\frac{16}{32}$ ______

**21.** $\frac{5}{6} = \frac{\quad}{18}$ **22.** $\frac{3}{4} = \frac{\quad}{20}$ **23.** $\frac{5}{8} = \frac{\quad}{24}$ **24.** $\frac{7}{12} = \frac{\quad}{36}$

**25.** $\frac{3}{7} = \frac{\quad}{35}$ **26.** $\frac{2}{3} = \frac{\quad}{15}$ **27.** $\frac{4}{5} = \frac{\quad}{45}$

______ Score for B (15)

**C (24 points) Add the following fractions and mixed numbers. Write the answers as fractions or mixed numbers, with fractions in lowest terms. (3 points for each correct answer)**

**28.** $\frac{1}{8} + \frac{3}{8}$ ______

**29.** $\frac{7}{10} + \frac{3}{10}$ ______

**30.** $\frac{9}{16} + 2\frac{11}{16}$ ______

**31.** $1\frac{2}{3} =$ ; $+ 2\frac{3}{4} =$ ______

**32.** $1\frac{1}{4} =$ ; $\frac{5}{8} =$ ; $+ 4\frac{11}{12} =$ ______

**33.** $4\frac{1}{2} =$ ; $3\frac{2}{3} =$ ; $+ \frac{5}{6} =$ ______

**34.** $\frac{4}{5} =$ ; $3\frac{5}{6} =$ ; $+ 5\frac{1}{3} =$ ______

**35.** $2\frac{5}{9} =$ ; $3\frac{8}{15} =$ ; $+ 1\frac{1}{5} =$ ______

______ Score for C (24)

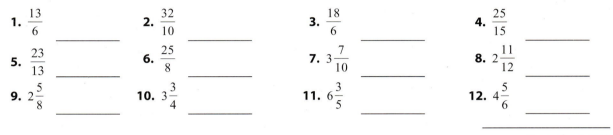

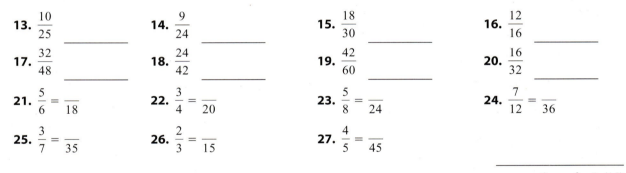

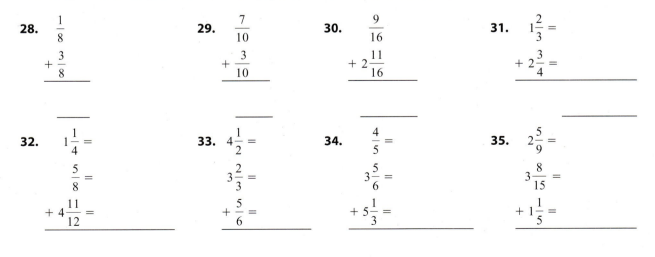

**D** **(24 points) Subtract the following fractions and mixed numbers. Write the answers as proper fractions or mixed numbers, with fractions in lowest terms. (3 points for each correct answer)**

**36.** $\frac{5}{8} - \frac{3}{8}$ = ______

**37.** $2\frac{7}{12} - 1\frac{5}{12}$ = ______

**38.** $\frac{3}{4} = \underline{\quad}$ ; $-\frac{5}{16} = \underline{\quad}$ ; ______

**39.** $2\frac{3}{4} = \underline{\quad}$ ; $-1\frac{1}{12} = \underline{\quad}$ ; ______

**40.** $3\frac{2}{3} = \underline{\quad} = \underline{\quad}$ ; $-2\frac{5}{6} = \underline{\quad} = \underline{\quad}$ ; ______

**41.** $3\frac{3}{5} = \underline{\quad} = \underline{\quad}$ ; $-1\frac{3}{4} = \underline{\quad} = \underline{\quad}$ ; ______

**42.** $6\frac{7}{8} = \underline{\quad}$ ; $-2\frac{2}{3} = \underline{\quad}$ ; ______

**43.** $4\frac{2}{5} = \underline{\quad} = \underline{\quad}$ ; $-1\frac{5}{6} = \underline{\quad} = \underline{\quad}$ ; ______

Score for D (24) ______

**E** **(25 points) Business Applications and Critical Thinking. Solve the following. Write your answers as fractions or mixed numbers in lowest terms. (5 points for each correct answer)**

**44.** A restaurant sells three different hamburgers, based on the amount of meat used: "The Mini" ($\frac{1}{5}$ lb); "The Regular" ($\frac{1}{3}$ lb); and "The Maxi" ($\frac{1}{2}$ lb). Students bought one of each to compare them. What was the total amount of meat used in the three hamburgers? ______

**45.** Jared Sines specializes in custom faux painting, but for the first coat he could combine leftover paints when the colors were relatively the same. He has three containers of different shades of white: $2\frac{2}{3}$ quarts, $2\frac{3}{4}$ quarts, and $2\frac{1}{2}$ quarts. If Jared combines the contents of all the containers, how many quarts of paint will he have? ______

**46.** Contractor Don Fleming has a top board that is $\frac{13}{16}$ inch thick. Don wants to use wood screws to attach it to a bottom board. If a wood screw is $1\frac{1}{2}$ inches long, how much of the screw will be left over to go into the bottom board? ______

**47.** Robert Landles is planning to attach a plywood panel to a wall using nails that are $1\frac{3}{4}$ inches long. The panel is $\frac{3}{8}$ inch thick. Beneath the panel is a layer of sheetrock that is $\frac{1}{2}$ inch thick. How many inches of the nail should go into the wood frame that is underneath the sheetrock? ______

**48.** Paris Fabric Center sold four pieces of wool fabric to a tailor. The pieces measured $3\frac{1}{4}$ yards, $2\frac{1}{3}$ yards, $1\frac{3}{4}$ yards, and $4\frac{1}{2}$ yards in length. How many yards of fabric did the tailor purchase? ______

Score for E (25) ______

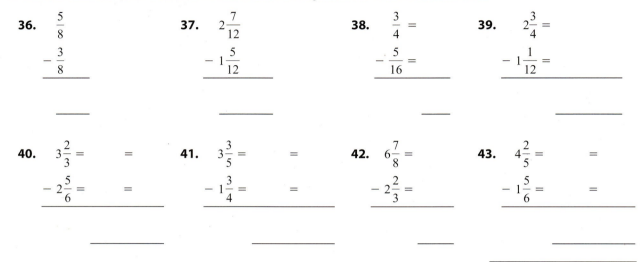

# Assignment 2.2: Multiplication and Division of Fractions

Name

Date Score

Learning Objectives 1 2 5 6

**A** **(32 points) Change whole or mixed numbers to improper fractions and multiply. Cancel if possible. Where the word *of* appears, replace it with the multiplication symbol. Write the answers as mixed numbers or proper fractions in lowest terms. (4 points for each correct answer)**

**1.** $\frac{4}{15} \times \frac{5}{8} =$ ________

**2.** $\frac{3}{10} \times \frac{6}{7} \times \frac{5}{6} =$ ________

**3.** $\frac{3}{4}$ of $\frac{5}{6} =$ ________

**4.** $\frac{5}{18} \times \frac{4}{9} \times \frac{3}{10} =$ ________

**5.** $4\frac{1}{2} \times 1\frac{5}{9} =$ ________

**6.** $\frac{3}{8}$ of $12 =$ ________

**7.** $1\frac{7}{8} \times 12 \times \frac{3}{10} =$ ________

**8.** $1\frac{1}{3} \times 1\frac{7}{8} \times 1\frac{1}{5} =$ ________

________
Score for A (32)

**B** **(32 points) Change the mixed numbers to improper fractions and divide. Cancel where possible. Write the quotients as mixed numbers or proper fractions in lowest terms. (4 points for each correct answer)**

**9.** $\frac{7}{8} \div \frac{3}{4} =$ ________

**10.** $\frac{4}{15} \div \frac{7}{10} =$ ________

**11.** $\frac{5}{6} \div \frac{4}{9} =$ ________

**12.** $\frac{7}{10} \div 2\frac{4}{5} =$ ________

**13.** $6\frac{1}{4} \div 4\frac{3}{8} =$ ________

**14.** $3\frac{5}{6} \div 1\frac{7}{12} =$ ________

**15.** $3\frac{1}{3} \div \frac{4}{5} =$ ________

**16.** $2\frac{1}{3} \div 1\frac{3}{4} =$ ________

________
Score for B (32)

**C** **(36 points) Business Applications and Critical Thinking. Use fractions and mixed numbers to solve each of the following. State the answers as whole numbers, proper fractions, or mixed numbers in lowest terms. (6 points for each correct answer)**

**17.** Last week, East Shore Concrete Co. built a small driveway that required $5\frac{1}{3}$ cubic yards of concrete. This week, the company must build another driveway that is $2\frac{1}{2}$ times larger. How many yards of concrete will be required? ________

**18.** Athena Nguyen bought eight pieces of copper tubing that were each $6\frac{3}{4}$ inches long. What was the total length of tubing that Athena bought? (Give the answer in inches.) ________

**19.** Linda Johanssen had $2\frac{1}{4}$ quarts of liquid fertilizer in a container. Her supervisor asked her to mix $\frac{2}{3}$ of the fertilizer with water and save the remainder. How many quarts of fertilizer did Linda mix with water? ________

**20.** Landscaper Roger Hillman needs several pieces of PVC irrigation pipe, each 3 feet 4 inches long. PVC pipe comes in 20-foot lengths. How many pieces can Roger cut out of one length of pipe? (*Hint:* 4 inches equal $\frac{1}{3}$ foot.) ________

**21.** Robert Burke has a diesel-powered generator on his ranch. The generator has a tank that holds $3\frac{3}{4}$ gallons of diesel fuel. He stores the diesel fuel in 55-gallon drums (barrels). How many times can Robert refill his generator from one drum of fuel? ________

**22.** Home builders Bill and John Walter are planning a narrow stairway to an attic. The stairs will each be 2 feet 8 inches long. They will cut the stairs from boards that are 8 feet long. How many whole stairs can they cut from one 8-foot board? (*Hint:* 8 inches is $\frac{2}{3}$ foot.) ________

________
Score for C (36)

# 3 Decimals

## Learning Objectives

By studying this chapter and completing all assignments, you will be able to:

- **Learning Objective 1** Read decimal numbers.
- **Learning Objective 2** Round decimal numbers.
- **Learning Objective 3** Add two or more decimal numbers.
- **Learning Objective 4** Subtract one decimal number from another.
- **Learning Objective 5** Multiply two decimal numbers.
- **Learning Objective 6** Divide one decimal number by another decimal number.
- **Learning Objective 7** Multiply and divide by decimal numbers that end with zeros.
- **Learning Objective 8** Approximate products and quotients.

# Fractions Versus Decimal Numbers

© DOUG KOONTZ/THE (FREDERICK) NEWS-POST/ASSOCIATED PRESS

McDonald's restaurant sells a hamburger sandwich called the Quarter Pounder. The sandwich is named for the amount of meat: one-quarter pound of ground beef. McDonald's—or anyone—can describe the same amount of meat in four different ways: 4 ounces, $\frac{1}{4}$ pound, 0.25 pound, or 25% of a pound. To express less than 1 pound, McDonald's could use smaller units, fractions, decimals, or percents.

All four expressions are useful, but which one is best? It may depend on what you're doing: whether you're buying or selling, whether you're speaking or writing, whether you're just estimating or making accurate financial records, or whether you're working with large volumes of something cheap or small quantities of something very expensive. For McDonald's, a Four Ouncer might not sell as well as a Quarter Pounder, but Bloomingdale's sells perfume by the (fluid) ounce rather than by the gallon, quart, pint, or even cup.

Verbal expressions such as "half of a candy bar" or "a third of the pizza" are so common that children learn them before they can even read. We reviewed fractions in Chapter 2. Because of calculators, most calculations are now performed using decimal numbers. We review decimals here in Chapter 3. Percents are a combination of decimal numbers and a few common fractions. Percents are as easy to use as decimals and also allow simple verbal expressions. We review percents in Chapter 5.

Chapter 3 has three main concepts: vocabulary, calculating, and estimating. Calculating with decimals is the same as with whole numbers except that there is a decimal point. Thus, calculating with decimals is actually "managing the decimal point," which your calculator does automatically. Estimating, which is important in checking your calculations, still requires that you "manage the decimal point."

# Decimal Numbers and Electronic Displays

A customer in a delicatessen might ask for "a quarter of a pound of salami, please" or perhaps "four ounces of salami." However, the food scale in the delicatessen probably has an electronic display and is calibrated only in pounds. It will likely display "0.25" or "0.250." As a fraction, a quarter of a pound is written as $\frac{1}{4}$ pound; three quarters of a pound is $\frac{3}{4}$ pound. In the U.S. monetary system, a quarter is the name of the coin whose value is twenty-five cents. And three quarters are worth seventy-five cents. When we write these monetary amounts, we write either whole numbers or decimals: 25¢ and 75¢, or \$0.25 and \$0.75. It is highly unlikely that anyone would ever write $\$\frac{1}{4}$ or $\$\frac{3}{4}$.

Almost all business transactions and record keeping are best done using decimals rather than fractions. The calculations are usually more straightforward and more accurate. Today, specialized calculators, computers, and measurement instruments have electronic displays that are calibrated in decimals, not fractions.

Modern gasoline pumps used in the United States are calibrated in gallons and typically measure the volume of gasoline sold accurate to three decimal places. Suppose that an automobile owner buys gasoline and the display shows 12.762 gallons. 12.762 is a number; it is called a **mixed decimal.** The 12 is the whole number part of the number; the 762 is the **pure decimal** part. The period (or dot) that separates the 12 from the 762 is the **decimal point.** We say that the number 12.762 has three **decimal places** because there are three digits to the right of the decimal point.

Many calculators and all computer spreadsheets permit you to change the number of decimal places that are displayed. A new calculator may be preset to display exactly two decimal places because that is how the monetary system is designed. Divide 1 by 3 with your calculator. The correct answer is 0.333333333 . . . repeating number that never stops. Count the number of 3s that appear in the calculator. That is the number of decimal places your calculator is set to display. Read the instruction manual. Perhaps you can change the display to show more or fewer decimal places. *Note:* Your calculator also displays a zero (0) to the left of the decimal point. We follow that same convention in this book. Every pure decimal number is preceded by a zero (0).

## Reading Decimal Numbers

**Learning Objective 1**

Read decimal numbers.

Reading decimal numbers, both mixed and pure, is like reading whole numbers: Each "place," or column, represents a different value. Starting at the decimal point and reading to the *left,* the places represent ones, tens, hundreds, thousands, and so on. Starting at the decimal point and reading to the *right,* the vocabulary is different: The places represent *tenths, hundredths, thousandths,* and so on.

Recall words such as *tenths, hundredths,* and *thousandths* from your review of fractions in Chapter 2. As money, the decimal \$0.10 represents 10¢, but also \$$\frac{10}{100}$. $\frac{10}{100}$ is pronounced as "ten *hundredths.*" But $\frac{10}{100}$ can be reduced to $\frac{1}{10}$ which is "one *tenth.*" Like fractions, the decimal 0.10 is read as "ten *hundredths*"; the decimal 0.1 is "one *tenth.*" At the gasoline pump, the display showed 12.762. As a fraction, it is written $12\frac{762}{1000}$. Both numbers are pronounced "twelve *and* seven hundred sixty-two *thousandths.* The decimal point is read as the word "*and.*"

Figure 3-1 illustrates the place values of the number system on both sides of the decimal point for the number 607,194.35824. The pure decimal part of the number in Figure 3-1 is 0.35824, which is pronounced "thirty-five thousand eight hundred twenty-four *hundred-thousandths.*"

**Figure 3-1** Number System on Both Sides of the Decimal Point

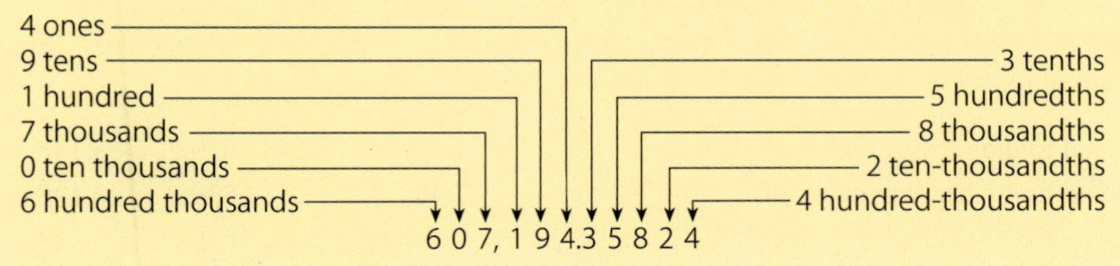


### READING LONG DECIMAL NUMBERS

The entire number in Figure 3-1—607,194.35824—is read as "six hundred seven thousand, one hundred ninety-four and thirty-five thousand eight hundred twenty-four hundred-thousandths." For a long number, reciting it orally is inefficient and can be confusing to the listener. For such a number, it may be better simply to read the digits and commas, from left to right. The word *point* is used for the decimal point.

**EXAMPLE A**

Recite orally the number 607,194.35824.

| Number | Oral Recitation |
|---|---|
| 607,194.35824 | "six zero seven comma one nine four point three five eight two four" |

**CONCEPT CHECK 3.1**

a. Write 37.045 using words: Thirty-seven and forty-five thousandths
b. Write fifteen and seven hundredths using digits: 15.07

# Rounding Decimal Numbers

**Learning Objective 2**

Round decimal numbers.

In the preceding section, you reviewed how to read and write decimal numbers such as 148.65392. However, in many business situations, if the whole number part is as large as 148, the digits on the extreme right may not be very important. Maybe only the digit in the tenths or hundredths column is significant. **Rounding off** such a number to make it simpler is common. You rounded off whole numbers in Chapter 1. The procedure is the same with decimal numbers.

**STEPS to Round Decimal Numbers**

1. Find the last place, or digit, to be retained.
2. Examine the digit to the right of the last digit to be retained.
3. **a.** If it is equal to or greater than 5, increase the digit to be retained by 1. Drop all digits to the right of the ones retained.
   **b.** If it is less than 5, leave the digit to be retained unchanged. Drop all digits to the right of the ones retained.

**EXAMPLE B**

Round 7.3951 and 148.65392 to one decimal place, to two decimal places, and to three decimal places.

| | | |
|---|---|---|
| Round to the nearest tenth | 7.3951 ⟶ 7.4 | 148.65392 ⟶ 148.7 |
| Round to the nearest hundredth | 7.3951 ⟶ 7.40 | 148.65392 ⟶ 148.65 |
| Round to the nearest thousandth | 7.3951 ⟶ 7.395 | 148.65392 ⟶ 148.654 |

## ROUNDING UP

Retail businesses, such as grocery stores, often use a different method of rounding to a whole number of cents. Suppose that a grocery store has lemons priced at 3 for $1.00. Usually the store will charge $0.34 for one lemon, even though $1.00 divided by 3 is $0.3333 (to four places). The store has rounded up to the next larger whole cent. To round up monetary amounts, always increase any partial cent to the next whole cent. For example, $27.842 would round up to $27.85.

## CONCEPT CHECK 3.2

a. Round 3.4681 to the nearest hundredth (that is, to two decimal places).

| | | |
|---|---|---|
| Find the hundredths digit. | 3.4681 | (The 6) |
| Examine the digit to the right of the 6. | 3.4681 | (It is greater than 5.) |
| Increase the 6 to a 7 and drop the digits 81 at the right. | 3.47 | (The answer) |

b. Round up 8.5014 to the *next* tenth (that is, to one decimal place).

| | | |
|---|---|---|
| Find the tenths digit. | 8.5014 | (The 5) |
| Increase the 5 to a 6 and drop the digits 014 at the right. | 8.6 | (The answer) |

# Whole Numbers, Decimal Numbers, and Arithmetic

In Chapter 1, we reviewed arithmetic with whole numbers. There were also some problems involving money in which the numbers contained decimal points. A whole number is simply a mixed decimal where the pure decimal part is zero. For simplicity, the zeros and the decimal point are omitted. In the examples that follow, when you see a whole number, you may need to place a decimal point at the right end and maybe even write one or more zeros after it. As you calculate, "manage the decimal point" as described in the following sections.

# Adding Decimal Numbers

To add two or more decimal numbers, follow these steps.

**Learning Objective 3**

Add two or more decimal numbers.

**STEPS to Add Decimal Numbers**

1. Arrange the numbers in columns, with the decimal points in a vertical line.
2. Add each column, from right to left, as with whole numbers. Insert the decimal point.

*Option:* You may want to write zeros in some of the right-hand columns of decimal numbers so that each number has the same number of decimal places.

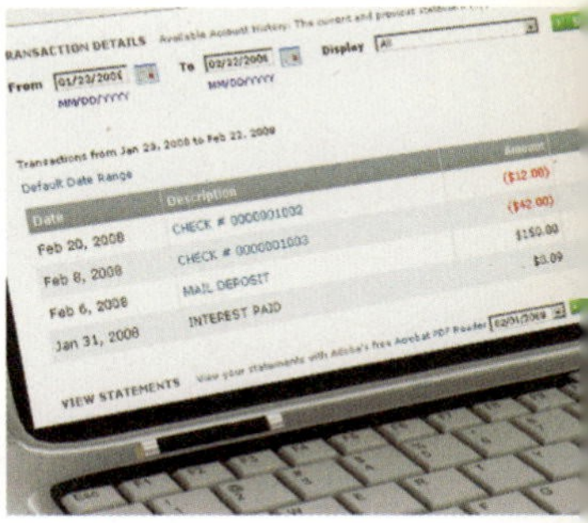

© R. ALCORN/CENGAGE LEARNING

**EXAMPLE C**

Add 4.326, 218.6004, 7.09, 15, and 0.87782.

| STEP 1 | STEP 2 | | STEP 2 WITH OPTION |
|---|---|---|---|
| 4.326 | 4.326 | | 4.32600 |
| 218.6004 | 218.6004 | | 218.60040 |
| 7.09 | 7.09 | or | 7.09000 |
| 15. | 15. | | 15.00000 |
| 0.87782 | + 0.87782 | | + 0.87782 |
| | 245.89422 | | 245.89422 |

**CONCEPT CHECK 3.3**

Add these decimal numbers: 8.95, 13.791, and 0.6.

| First align: | Then add: | Or, write zeros and add: |
|---|---|---|
| 8.95 | 8.95 | 8.950 |
| 13.791 | 13.791 | 13.791 |
| 0.6 | + 0.6 | + 0.600 |
| | 23.341 | 23.341 |

# Subtracting Decimal Numbers

**Learning Objective 4**

Subtract one decimal number from another.

Subtracting one decimal number from another is similar to subtracting whole numbers. When you aren't using a calculator, it may be helpful to write enough zeros so that both numbers have the same number of places. To subtract one decimal number from another, follow these steps.

**STEPS to Subtract Decimal Numbers**

1. Arrange the numbers in columns, with the decimal points in a vertical line.
2. If necessary, write enough extra zeros so that both numbers have the same number of decimal places.
3. Subtract each column, from right to left, as with whole numbers. Insert the decimal point.

**EXAMPLE D**

Subtract 4.935 from 12.8.

| STEP 1 | STEPS 2 & 3 |
|---|---|
| 12.8 | 12.800 |
| − 4.935 | − 4.935 |
| | 7.865 |

**EXAMPLE E**

Subtract 9.4 from 82.113.

| STEP 1 | STEPS 2 & 3 |
|---|---|
| 82.113 | 82.113 |
| − 9.4 | − 9.400 |
| | 72.713 |

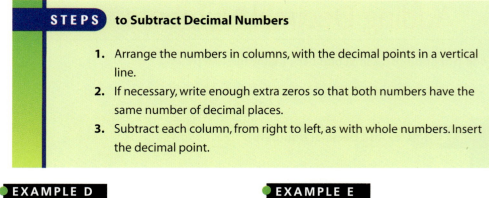

## CONCEPT CHECK 3.4

Subtract 53.784 from 207.6.

| Align: | Write zeros and subtract: |
| --- | --- |
| 207.6 | 207.600 |
| 53.784 | − 53.784 |
| | 153.816 |

COMPLETE ASSIGNMENT 3.1.

# Multiplying Decimal Numbers

To multiply one decimal number by another, follow these steps.

Learning Objective 5

Multiply two decimal numbers.

**STEPS to Multiply Decimal Numbers**

1. Multiply the two numbers as if they were whole numbers.
2. Count the *total* number of decimal places in the two original numbers.
3. **a.** In the product, place the decimal point so that the number of decimal places is the same as the number in Step 2. (Count from right to left.)

   **b.** If necessary, insert zeros in front of the left-hand digit to provide enough decimal places. (See example G.)

**EXAMPLE F**

3.764 × 2.1

| | | |
| --- | --- | --- |
| | 3.764 | (3 places) |
| | × 2.1 | (1 place) |
| STEP 1 | 3764 | |
| | +7528 | STEP 2 |
| STEP 3 | 7.9044 | (3 + 1 = 4 places) |

**EXAMPLE G**

3.764 × 0.0021

| | | |
| --- | --- | --- |
| | 3.764 | (3 places) |
| | × 0.0021 | (4 places) |
| STEP 1 | 3764 | |
| | +7528 | STEP 2 |
| STEP 3 | 0.0079044 | (3 + 4 = 7 places; insert 2 zeros) |

In business applications, zeros that come at the right end of the decimal part of the product are often omitted (example H). Do not omit zeros that come at the end of the whole-number part (example I). When the product is written in dollars and cents, exactly two decimal places are written, including zeros at the right end (example J). Please be aware that some calculators may not display any zeros at the right end of a decimal.

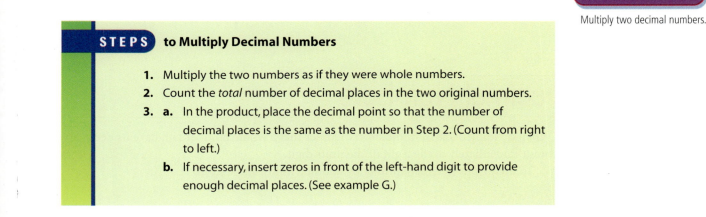

**EXAMPLE H**

$0.76 \times 0.5 = 0.380$ (3 places)
May be written as 0.38

**EXAMPLE I**

$12.5 \times 1.6 = 20.00$ (2 places)
May be written as 20

**EXAMPLE J**

$\$8.40 \times 6.5 = \$54.600$ (3 places)
Should be written as \$54.60

**CONCEPT CHECK 3.5**

a. Multiply $2.36 \times 3.4$

$$\begin{array}{rl} 2.36 & \text{(2 places)} \\ \times\ 3.4 & \text{(1 place)} \\ \hline 944 & \\ +7\,08 & \\ \hline 8.024 & \text{(3 places)} \end{array}$$

b. Multiply $0.236 \times 0.34$

$$\begin{array}{rl} 0.236 & \text{(3 places)} \\ \times\ 0.34 & \text{(2 places)} \\ \hline 9\,44 & \\ +70\,8 & \\ \hline 0.08024 & \text{(5 places; insert 1 zero)} \end{array}$$

## Dividing Decimal Numbers

**Learning Objective 6**

Divide one decimal number by another decimal number.

When dividing decimal numbers, remember that a whole number will have its decimal point immediately to the right of the units digit.

To divide one decimal number by another, follow these steps.

**STEPS to Divide one Decimal Number by Another**

1. Arrange the divisor, dividend, and division bracket ($\overline{)\quad}$) as in whole-number long division.
2. Move the decimal point in the divisor to the right until the divisor is a whole number. (You won't have to move it if the divisor is already a whole number.)
3. Move the decimal point in the dividend to the right exactly the same number of decimal places as you did in Step 2. If necessary, attach more zeros to the right end of the dividend. (See example K.)
4. Write the decimal point in the quotient directly above the new decimal point in the dividend (in Step 3).
5. Write zeros, if necessary, in the quotient between the decimal point and the first nonzero digit. (See example L.)
6. Divide as you would for whole numbers.

## EXAMPLE K

STEP 1 | STEP 2 | STEP 3 | STEP 4 | STEP 6

$$2.7 \div 0.15 \quad \textit{is} \quad 0.15\overline{)2.7} \quad = \quad 0.15.\overline{)2.70.} \quad = \quad 15.\overline{)270.} \quad = \quad \begin{array}{r} 18. \\ 15.\overline{)270.} \\ \underline{-15} \\ 120 \\ \underline{-120} \\ 0 \end{array}$$

## EXAMPLE L

STEP 1 | STEP 4 | STEPS 5 & 6

$$0.096 \div 4 \quad \textit{is} \quad 4\overline{)0.096} \quad = \quad 4.\overline{)0.096} \quad = \quad \begin{array}{r} 0.024 \\ 4.\overline{)0.096} \\ \underline{-8} \\ 16 \\ \underline{-16} \\ 0 \end{array}$$

Recall from Chapter 1 that, in long division with two whole numbers, you write a *remainder* when the division doesn't come out evenly, for example, 17 ÷ 8 = 2 with a remainder of 1. In division with decimals, you do not write remainders. You simply keep dividing until you have some required number of decimal places. To get the required number of decimal places, you may have to keep attaching zeros to the right end of the dividend. (See example M.)

## EXAMPLE M

Calculate 17 ÷ 8 to three decimal places.

STEP 1 | STEP 4 | STEP 6

$$17 \div 8 \quad \textit{is} \quad 8\overline{)17} \quad = \quad 8.\overline{)17.} \quad = \quad \begin{array}{r} 2. \\ 8.\overline{)17.} \end{array} \quad = \quad \begin{array}{r} 2.125 \\ 8.\overline{)17.000} \\ \underline{-16} \\ 10 \\ \underline{-\ 8} \\ 20 \\ \underline{-16} \\ 40 \\ \underline{-40} \\ 0 \end{array}$$

## CONCEPT CHECK 3.6

a. Divide 1.026 by 15.

$$15\overline{)1.026} = 15\overline{)1.0260}$$

```
   0.0684
15)1.0260
  -90
   126
  -120
     60
    -60
      0
```

b. Divide 0.009 by 0.4.

$$0.4.\overline{)0.0.09} = 4\overline{)0.0900}$$

```
   0.0225
 4)0.0900
   - 8
     10
   - 8
     20
    -20
      0
```

In example M, $17 \div 8 = 2.125$. But recall that $17 \div 8$ can also be written as the fraction $\frac{17}{8}$. 2.125 is called the **decimal equivalent** of $\frac{17}{8}$. Decimal equivalents can be useful when you are working with fractions and have a calculator available. Even with simple fractions, and no calculator, it is often simpler to use decimal equivalents because you don't need a common denominator.

### EXAMPLE N

Compute $\frac{1}{2} + \frac{3}{4} - \frac{2}{5}$. This requires that all fractions have a common denominator of 20. But $\frac{1}{2} = 0.5$, $\frac{3}{4} = 0.75$, and $\frac{2}{5} = 0.4$. Therefore, we have $\frac{1}{2} + \frac{3}{4} - \frac{2}{5} = 0.5 + 0.75 - 0.4 = 0.85$.

For difficult fractions, use a calculator to convert the fractions to their decimal equivalents. Then use the calculator to perform the required operation. (If possible, you should use the memory of your calculator to store the intermediate answers.)

### EXAMPLE O

Compute $\frac{8}{15} + \frac{7}{12} + \frac{3}{7}$.

| | |
|---|---|
| [8] [÷] [15] [=] gives | 0.53333333 |
| [7] [÷] [12] [=] gives | 0.58333333 |
| [3] [÷] [7] [=] gives | + 0.42857143 |
| | **1.54523809** |

The preceeding example assumes that your calculator is displaying eight decimal places. Also, if you use the memory to store the intermediate answers, your calculator may round off the intermediate answers and give you a final answer of 1.54523810 or 1.5452381. A few calculators make it easier to compute fractions with an "algebraic operating system" that automatically does multiplication and division before addition and subtraction. For those calculators, you might use keystrokes like these:

[8] [÷] [15] [+] [7] [÷] [12] [+] [3] [÷] [7] [=] **1.5452380,** or possibly **1.5452381**

Other calculators that do not have an "algebraic operating system" may have parentheses, permitting this type of calculation:

[(] [8] [÷] [15] [)] [+] [(] [7] [÷] [12] [)] [+] [(] [3] [÷] [7] [)] [=] **1.5452380,** or possibly **1.5452381**

## Using Multipliers and Divisors that End with Zeros

**Learning Objective 7**

Multiply and divide by decimal numbers that end with zeros.

In Chapter 1, we showed simple multiplication and division shortcuts when the multiplier or the divisor is a whole number ending in zeros (e.g., 30, 200, or 1,000). The same shortcuts may be used with decimal numbers. We just "manage the decimal point."

If the multiplier is 10, 100, 1,000, etc., there is just one step.

**Step 1** Move the decimal point in the multiplicand to the *right* the same number of places as the number of zeros in the multiplier. (See example P.) If necessary, attach zeros to the *right* end of the multiplicand before multiplying. (See example Q.)

**EXAMPLE P**

0.56 × 10 = 0.5.6 = 5.6

(1 place)

**EXAMPLE Q**

4.73 × 1,000 = 4.730 = 4,730

(3 places)

If the multiplier ends in zeros but has a first digit that is not 1 (for example, 300 or 2,000), there are two steps.

**Step 1** Multiply the multiplicand by the nonzero part of the multiplier.

**Step 2** Move the decimal point in the product from Step 1 to the *right* the same number of places as the number of zeros in the multiplier.

**EXAMPLE R**

Multiply 3.431 by 2,000

Multiply by 2: 3.431 × 2 = 6.862

Move the decimal point three places to the right: 6.862. ⟶ 6,862.

If the divisor is 10, 100, 1,000, etc., there is just one step.

**Step 1** Move the decimal point in the dividend to the *left* the same number of places as the number of zeros in the divisor. (See example S.) If necessary, attach zeros to the *left* end of the dividend. (See example T.)

**EXAMPLE S**

735.1 ÷ 100

735.1 ÷ 100 = 7.35.1 = 7.351

(2 places)

**EXAMPLE T**

9.64 ÷ 1,000

9.64 ÷ 1,000 = .009.64 = 0.00964

(3 places)

If the divisor ends in zeros but has a first digit that is not 1 (for example, 300 or 2,000), there are two steps.

**Step 1** Divide the dividend by the nonzero part of the divisor.

**Step 2** Move the decimal point in the quotient from Step 1 to the *left* the same number of places as the number of zeros in the divisor.

**EXAMPLE U**

Divide 615.24 by 300

Divide by 3: $615.24 \div 3 = 205.08$

Move the decimal point two places to the left: 2.05.08 ⟶ 2.0508

**CONCEPT CHECK 3.7**

a. Multiply 0.413 by 300

$0.413 \times 3 = 1.239$

Move the decimal point two places to the right:

1.23.9 ⟶ 123.9

b. Divide 4.375 by 10

Move the decimal point one place to the left:

$4.375 \div 10 =$ .4.375 ⟶ 0.4375

# Approximating Products and Quotients

**Learning Objective 8**

Approximate products and quotients.

Business people today almost always use calculators or computers to do important computations. But calculators are perfect only if every single key is pressed correctly. Often, you can discover a calculator error by doing some simple mental approximations. The objective is to determine whether the answer is approximately the right size—that is, whether the decimal point is in the correct position. To do so, we round each decimal number to only one nonzero digit and all the rest to zeros. Follow these steps.

**STEPS to Approximate a Multiplication Problem**

1. Round the first nonzero digit from the left end in each factor. (How does the digit to its right compare to 5?)
2. Change all the digits to the right of the first nonzero digit to zero.
3. Multiply the two new factors.
4. Place the decimal point in the product.

**EXAMPLE V**

Approximate $3.764 \times 7.4$

| | STEP 1 | STEPS 2 & 3 |
|---|---|---|
| 3.764 → | 4.000 | 4 |
| × 7.4 → | × 7.0 | × 7 |
| | | 28 |

**EXAMPLE W**

Approximate $0.089 \times 61.18$

| | STEP 1 | STEPS 2 & 3 |
|---|---|---|
| 0.089 → | 0.090 | 0.09 |
| × 61.18 → | × 60.00 | × 60 |
| | | 5.40 |

The actual answers are 27.8536 and 5.44502.

In division, the mental approximation will be easier if you change the decimal numbers so that the division will end evenly after one step. To do this, first round the divisor to one nonzero digit and then round the dividend to two nonzero digits, evenly divisible by the new divisor.

## STEPS to Approximate a Division Problem

1. Round the divisor to a *single nonzero digit* at the left, followed by all zeros.
2. Round the dividend to a *two-digit number* at the left, followed by all zeros. Select the two-digit number so that it is evenly divisible by the new divisor.
3. Divide the new dividend by the new divisor.
4. Place the decimal point correctly in the quotient.

**EXAMPLE X**

Approximate $4.764 \div 8.1$

STEP 1: $8.1\overline{)4.764} \longrightarrow 8.0\overline{)4.764}$

STEP 2: $\longrightarrow 8.\overline{)4.800}$

STEPS 3 & 4: $\longrightarrow 8.\overline{)4.8}$ = 0.6

$$\begin{array}{r} 0.6 \\ 8.\overline{)4.8} \\ -4.8 \\ \hline 0 \end{array}$$

**EXAMPLE Y**

Approximate $61.18 \div 0.089$

STEP 1: $0.089\overline{)61.18} \longrightarrow 0.090\overline{)61.18}$

STEP 2: $\longrightarrow 0.09\overline{)63.00}$

STEPS 3 & 4: $\longrightarrow 9.\overline{)6300.}$

$$\begin{array}{r} 700. \\ 9.\overline{)6300.} \\ -63\phantom{00.} \\ \hline 0\phantom{00.} \end{array}$$

The actual answers are 0.5881 and 687.4157 (to four decimal places).

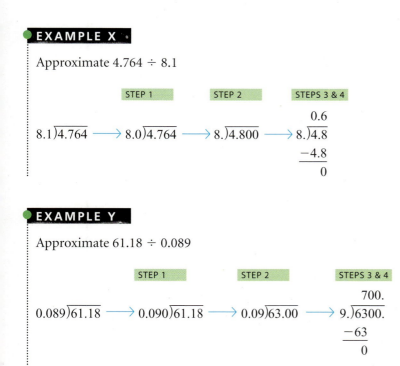

## CONCEPT CHECK 3.8

a. Approximate 6.891 × 0.614

6.891 → 7.000
0.614 → 0.600

| | |
|---|---|
| 0.6 | (1 place) |
| × 7 | (0 places) |
| 4.2 | (1 place) |

Compare with 6.891 × 0.614 = 4.231074

COMPLETE ASSIGNMENTS 3.2 and 3.3

b. Approximate 0.0738 ÷ 92.65

Remember to round off the divisor first.

92.65 → 90.00
0.0738 → 0.0720

$90\overline{)0.072} \longrightarrow 90\overline{)0.0720}$, quotient .0008

720
0

Compare with 0.0738 ÷ 92.65 = 0.000796546

## Chapter Terms for Review

decimal equivalent
decimal places
decimal point
mixed decimal
pure decimal
rounding off

## Try Microsoft® Excel

Try working the problems using the Microsoft Excel templates found on your student CD. Solutions for the problems are also shown on the CD.

1. Set up and complete the following tables using the appropriate Excel formulas.

| Date | Auto Sales | Part Sales | Total Sales |
|---|---|---|---|
| 6/4/10 | $ 36,628.14 | $ 1,782.28 | |
| 6/5/10 | $ 42,789.40 | $ 2,047.33 | |
| 6/6/10 | $ 58,334.98 | $ 1,132.48 | |
| 6/7/10 | $ 96,782.04 | $ 3,006.04 | |
| 6/8/10 | $ 29,765.55 | $ 2,333.33 | |
| Total | | | |

| Date | Total Receipts | Total Cash | Cash Short |
|---|---|---|---|
| 7/15/10 | $ 974.58 | $ 969.30 | |
| 7/16/10 | $ 888.07 | $ 888.02 | |
| 7/17/10 | $ 1,384.17 | $ 1,350.23 | |
| Total | | | |

| Date | Units Sold | Price Per Unit | Total Sales |
|---|---|---|---|
| 5/24/10 | 47 | $ 107.16 | |
| 5/25/10 | 63 | $ 107.16 | |
| 5/26/10 | 72 | $ 107.16 | |
| 5/27/10 | 39 | $ 107.16 | |
| Total | | | |

| Date | Total Sale | Price Per Unit | Units Sold |
|---|---|---|---|
| 5/24/10 | $ 5,036.52 | $ 107.16 | |
| 5/25/10 | $ 6,751.08 | $ 107.16 | |
| 5/26/10 | $ 7,715.52 | $ 107.16 | |
| 5/27/10 | $ 4,179.24 | $ 107.16 | |
| Total | | | |

# THE BOTTOM LINE

*Summary of chapter learning objectives:*

| Learning Objective | Example |
|---|---|
| **3.1** Read decimal numbers. | 1. Write 8.427 using words.<br>2. Write forty-one and eleven ten-thousandths using digits. |
| **3.2** Round decimal numbers. | 3. Round 0.506489 to the nearest thousandth (that is, to three decimal places).<br>4. Round up 13.26012 to the *next* hundredth (that is, to two decimal places). |
| **3.3** Add two or more decimal numbers. | 5. Add 82.9, 14.872, and 2.09. |
| **3.4** Subtract one decimal number from another. | 6. Subtract 14.5977 from 19.34. |
| **3.5** Multiply two decimal numbers. | 7. Multiply: $4.68 \times 3.5$ _____ |
| **3.6** Divide one decimal number by another decimal number. | 8. Divide: $0.084 \div 4$ _____<br>9. Divide: $0.064 \div 2.5$ _____ |
| **3.7** Multiply and divide by decimals that end with zeros. | 10. Multiply: $0.069782 \times 1000$ _____<br>11. Divide: 9.462 by 100 _____<br>12. Multiply: $0.0623 \times 20$ _____<br>13. Divide: 84.6 by 300 _____ |
| **3.8** Approximate products and quotients. | 14. Approximate $48.79 \times 0.47$ _____<br>15. Approximate $0.2688 \div 0.713$ _____ |

Answers: 1. eight and four hundred twenty-seven thousandths 2. 41.0011 3. 0.506 4. 13.27 5. 99.862 6. 4.7423 7. 16.38 8. 0.021 9. 0.0256 10. 69.782 11. 0.09462 12. 1.246 13. 0.282 14. 25 15. 0.4

SELF-CHECK

## Review Problems for Chapter 3

1 Write "one hundred sixteen and fourteen ten-thousandths" as a number __________

2 Write 6,431.719, using words __________

3 Round 3.475 feet to the nearest tenth __________

4 Round $12.667 to the nearest cent __________

5 Add 3.79475 and 739.85 __________

6 Add 12.42, 0.087, and 8.3 __________

7 Subtract 8.693 from 11.41 __________

8 Subtract 287.963 from 410.4511 __________

9 Multiply 3.722 by 0.483 (do not round off) __________

10 Multiply $19.75 by 22.45 (round off to the nearest cent) __________

**In problems 11 and 12, divide to three places and round to the nearest hundredth.**

11 Divide 45.88 by 14.2 __________

12 Divide $6.25 by 8.41 __________

**In problems 13 and 14, use shortcuts to solve each problem and round to the nearest hundredth.**

13 Multiply 86.493 by 100 __________

14 Divide $2,762.35 by 1,000 __________

**In problems 15 and 16, pick the best approximate answers from the possible answers.**

15 Multiply 48.98 by 11.2 __________ **(a)** 0.5 **(b)** 5 **(c)** 50 **(d)** 500 **(e)** 5,000

16 Divide $6.65 by 8.21 __________ **(a)** $0.008 **(b)** $0.08 **(c)** $0.80 **(d)** $8.00 **(e)** $80.0

17 DeLois McBryde owns a chain of very large, upscale bookstores. She decides to start selling coffee drinks such as espresso and cappuccino at one of her stores. During the first day, the store has total sales of $4,188.25. Of the total, $362.50 was from coffee drinks. How much of the total was from books and other items? __________

18 Gary Gehlert operates tennis and golf shops at a desert resort. Last year, he started selling on the Internet as well. He had the following profits last year: Tennis (shop), $52,418.12; Golf (shop), $168,078.51; Tennis (Internet), $28,570.12; and Golf (Internet), $32,904.82. What were the total profits from these sources? __________

19 Dean Treggas, a landscape contractor, needed to plant 226 one-gallon plants and 164 five-gallon plants. Dean uses about 0.8 cubic foot of planting soil for each one-gallon plant and 2.5 cubic feet of planting soil for each five-gallon plant. How many cubic feet of planting soil will Dean need for all these plants? __________

20 Planting soil is sold by the cubic yard. To two decimals, how many cubic yards of planting soil will Dean Treggas need to do his planting in question 19? (Hint: 1 cubic yard equals 27 cubic feet.) __________

**Answers to the Self-Check can be found in Appendix B at the back of the text.**

# Assignment 3.1: Addition and Subtraction of Decimal Numbers

Name ______________________

Date ______________ Score ______________

Learning Objectives 1 2 3 4

**A** **(13 points) Use digits to write each number that is expressed in words. Use words to write each number that is expressed in digits. (1 point for each correct answer)**

**1.** Six hundred thirteen ten-thousandths ______________________

**2.** Nineteen thousandths ______________________

**3.** Sixty-four hundredths ______________________

**4.** Seventy-six and seventy-one ten-thousandths ______________________

**5.** Eight hundred sixty and ninety-eight hundred-thousandths ______________________

**6.** Eighteen and six thousandths ______________________

**7.** 308.97 ______________________

**8.** 0.0004 ______________________

**9.** 492.3 ______________________

**10.** 0.081 ______________________

**11.** 42.0481 ______________________

**12.** 6.018 ______________________

**13.** 1,007.4 ______________________

______________
Score for A (13)

**B** **(24 points) Round as indicated. (1 point for each correct answer)**

**Nearest Tenth**

**14.** 6.3517 qt ________

**15.** 48.97 mi ________

**16.** 3.824 gal ________

**17.** 374.29 lb ________

**18.** 7.35 ft ________

**19.** 6.375 oz ________

**Nearest Cent**

**20.** $17.375 ________

**21.** $0.098 ________

**22.** $942.3449 ________

**23.** $8.1047 ________

**24.** $0.0449 ________

**25.** $52.996 ________

**Nearest Thousandth**

**26.** 5.37575 pt ________

**27.** 0.00549 gal ________

**28.** 14.6445 oz ________

**29.** 8.1855 in. ________

**30.** 8.9989 mi ________

**31.** 0.200499 lb ________

**UP to the *Next* Cent**

**32.** $9.681 ________

**33.** $0.159 ________

**34.** $72.535 ________

**35.** $2.0917 ________

**36.** $11.4405 ________

**37.** $0.6545 ________

______________
Score for B (24)

**C** **(27 points) Write the following numbers in columns, and then add. (3 points for each correct answer)**

**38.** 3.84, 42.81, 747.114

**39.** 0.7323, 4.084, 17.42

**40.** 15.4, 32.574, 9.51, 74.0822

**41.** 24.78, 71.402, 8.3176

**42.** 7.911, 64.3075, 288.69

**43.** 6.4, 3.211, 12.6, 7.07

**44.** 337.51, 6.1761, 16.078

**45.** 36.7, 208.51, 3.992

**46.** 0.592, 1.82, 0.774, 6.5

Score for C (27)

**D** **(36 points) Subtract the following. (3 points for each correct answer)**

**47.** $\begin{array}{r} 0.734 \\ -0.37 \\ \hline \end{array}$

**48.** $\begin{array}{r} 0.04264 \\ -0.00497 \\ \hline \end{array}$

**49.** $\begin{array}{r} 26.04 \\ -\ 8.625 \\ \hline \end{array}$

**50.** $\begin{array}{r} 0.7212 \\ -0.034 \\ \hline \end{array}$

**51.** $\begin{array}{r} 6.1 \\ -2.418 \\ \hline \end{array}$

**52.** $\begin{array}{r} 804.07 \\ -167.1 \\ \hline \end{array}$

**53.** $\begin{array}{r} 3.2525 \\ -2.843 \\ \hline \end{array}$

**54.** $\begin{array}{r} 708.932 \\ -419.058 \\ \hline \end{array}$

**55.** $\begin{array}{r} 0.365 \\ -0.189 \\ \hline \end{array}$

**56.** $\begin{array}{r} 4.37 \\ -1.9055 \\ \hline \end{array}$

**57.** $\begin{array}{r} 7.624 \\ -5.947 \\ \hline \end{array}$

**58.** $\begin{array}{r} 5.6976 \\ -4.6913 \\ \hline \end{array}$

Score for D (36)

# Assignment 3.2: Multiplication and Division of Decimal Numbers

Name ______________________

Date ______________ Score ______________

Learning Objectives 5 6 7 8

**A (32 points) Multiply the following. Round monetary products to the nearest cent. Do not round nonmonetary products. (4 points for each correct answer)**

**1.** $15.67 × 83.7 ______

**2.** $24.60 × 4.5 ______

**3.** $420.00 × 0.806 ______

**4.** $57.80 × 0.35 ______

**5.** 107.21 × 0.74 ______

**6.** 52.93 × 0.45 ______

**7.** 285.70326 × 0.28 ______

**8.** 816.04 × 0.403 ______

______ Score for A (32)

**B (24 points) Divide the following. Round monetary quotients to the nearest cent. Round nonmonetary quotients to two decimal places. (4 points for each correct answer)**

**9.** 7)$12.95 ______

**10.** 0.36 )$6.75 ______

**11.** 1.2)$54.30 ______

**12.** $1.5\overline{)2.59}$ ________

**13.** $0.11\overline{)0.6735}$ ________

**14.** $0.09\overline{)0.7888}$ ________

________
Score for B (24)

**C** **(12 points) Multiply and/or divide by just moving the decimal point or by doing some simple multiplication/division and moving the decimal point. Round monetary answers to the nearest cent. Do not round nonmonetary answers. (1 point for each correct answer)**

**15.** 0.0625 × 1,000 = ________

**16.** 50.708 × 100 = ________

**17.** 0.047 × 10,000 = ________

**18.** 763 ÷ 100 = ________

**19.** 6.32 ÷ 10 = ________

**20.** 27.469 ÷ 1,000 = ________

**21.** $72.41 × 300 = ________

**22.** $32.25 × 20 = ________

**23.** $0.12 × 6,000 = ________

**24.** $2.50 × 40 = ________

**25.** $86.50 ÷ 200 = ________

**26.** $9,612 ÷ 40 = ________

________
Score for C (12)

**D** **(32 points) For each of the following problems, underline the estimate that is most nearly correct. (2 points for each correct answer)**

| | | | | | |
|---|---|---|---|---|---|
| **27.** | 0.077 × 0.52 | **(a)** 4.0 | **(b)** 0.4 | **(c)** 0.04 | **(d)** 0.004 |
| **28.** | 76.7 × 0.8477 | **(a)** 0.064 | **(b)** 0.64 | **(c)** 6.4 | **(d)** 64 |
| **29.** | 0.38 × 71.918 | **(a)** 0.28 | **(b)** 2.8 | **(c)** 28 | **(d)** 280 |
| **30.** | 0.00907 × 6.12 | **(a)** 0.054 | **(b)** 0.54 | **(c)** 5.4 | **(d)** 54 |
| **31.** | 0.0782 × 0.5503 | **(a)** 0.0048 | **(b)** 0.048 | **(c)** 0.48 | **(d)** 4.8 |
| **32.** | 0.0417 × 0.0957 | **(a)** 0.04 | **(b)** 0.004 | **(c)** 0.0004 | **(d)** 0.00004 |
| **33.** | 268.25 × 0.9175 | **(a)** 27,000 | **(b)** 2,700 | **(c)** 270 | **(d)** 27 |
| **34.** | 0.0487 × 0.0059 | **(a)** 0.000003 | **(b)** 0.00003 | **(c)** 0.0003 | **(d)** 0.003 |
| **35.** | 19.1 × 6104 | **(a)** 120 | **(b)** 1,200 | **(c)** 12,000 | **(d)** 120,000 |
| **36.** | 7.958 ÷ 0.514 | **(a)** 16 | **(b)** 160 | **(c)** 1,600 | **(d)** 16,000 |
| **37.** | 3.575 ÷ 893.12 | **(a)** 0.004 | **(b)** 0.04 | **(c)** 0.4 | **(d)** 4 |
| **38.** | 0.0614 ÷ 0.00398 | **(a)** 0.15 | **(b)** 1.5 | **(c)** 15 | **(d)** 150 |
| **39.** | 8.397 ÷ 7.12 | **(a)** 0.12 | **(b)** 1.2 | **(c)** 12 | **(d)** 120 |
| **40.** | 0.5379 ÷ 0.591 | **(a)** 900 | **(b)** 90 | **(c)** 9 | **(d)** 0.9 |
| **41.** | 5.112 ÷ 0.0692 | **(a)** 70 | **(b)** 7 | **(c)** 0.7 | **(d)** 0.07 |
| **42.** | 2.671 ÷ 0.0926 | **(a)** 300 | **(b)** 30 | **(c)** 3 | **(d)** 0.3 |

________
Score for D (32)

# Assignment 3.3: Decimal Numbers in Business

Name ______________________

Date ______________________ Score ______

Learning Objectives 3 4 5 6

**A (36 points) Business Applications and Critical Thinking. Solve the following. Do not round your final answers. (6 points for each correct answer)**

**1.** Bob Jones had 24.75 feet of rope. He cut off a piece 16.5 feet long. How much did he have left?

__________

**2.** Cho Jewelers had only 12.7 ounces of gold on hand, so Mr. Cho bought 22.5 ounces more to make Christmas items. He used 18.7 ounces for gold rings. How much gold did he have left?

__________

**3.** Judy Taylor reads meters for the gas and electric company. She walked 3.6 miles on Monday; 3.7 miles on Tuesday, 2.9 miles on Wednesday, 3.25 miles on Thursday, and 3.4 miles on Friday. What was her total distance for the week?

__________

**4.** Four messenger service drivers need gasoline for their cars. Individually, they buy 12.4, 8.9, 11.7, and 13.9 gallons. How much do they purchase all together?

__________

**5.** A retail customer owes a total of $226.54 on her department store account. She visits the store to return an item that cost $47.79. While there, she buys two items that cost $55.88 and $67.50. What is her new account balance at the store?

__________

**6.** Parker Paving Co. delivered 6.2 tons of asphalt. It used 4.7 tons for a driveway and 1.2 tons for a walkway. How much asphalt was left?

__________

__________
Score for A (36)

**B** **(64 points) Business Applications and Critical Thinking. Solve the following business problems. Use shortcuts where possible. If necessary, round answers to two decimal places. (8 points for each correct answer)**

**7.** Bill Wells Hardware sells a large-diameter plastic pipe for $0.17 per foot and copper pipe for $1.32 per foot. How much will Katy Cruz save by using plastic pipe if she needs 400 feet of pipe? ________

**8.** Benoit Landscaping sent three truckloads of topsoil to a job. The soil cost $28.50 per cubic yard. Two trucks carried 7.25 cubic yards each; the third carried 6.75 cubic yards. What was the total cost of all the topsoil? ________

**9.** Wholesale, 1,000 2-ounce plastic bottles cost 3.5 cents each, and 2,000 4-ounce bottles cost 4.5 cents each. What is the total cost of all 3,000 bottles? ________

**10.** Evelyn Haynes often used her motorcycle as a delivery vehicle. One Monday, when regular gasoline was priced at $4.499 per gallon, Evelyn bought 2.62 gallons. The following Thursday, regular gasoline prices rose to $4.799 per gallon and she bought 2.87 gallons. What was the total amount that Evelyn spent for gasoline those two days? ________

**11.** Electrician Tom Stewart paid $95.50 for 500 feet of multistrand electrical wire. What was the cost per foot for this particular wire?

________

**12.** A pizza chef has 24 pounds of flour on hand. He needs 3.75 pounds of flour for one large recipe of pizza dough. How many recipes can he make with the flour on hand? (Round to the nearest tenth.) ________

**13.** Paint thinner costs $1.49 per gallon. How many gallons can a painting contractor buy for $100? (Round to the nearest tenth.) ________

**14.** Jackie Barner earns $22.60 per hour. How many hours did she work during a partial day for which her pay was $152.55? ________

________

Score for B (64)

# 4

# Word Problems and Equations

## Learning Objectives

By studying this chapter and completing all assignments, you will be able to:

Learning Objective **1** Use a systematic approach to solve word problems.

Learning Objective **2** Apply formulas to solve rate, time, and distance problems.

Learning Objective **3** Solve simple numerical equations.

Learning Objective **4** Recognize numerical relationships in a series.

Learning Objective **5** Do quick mental calculations through a process of rounding numbers.

# Solving Word Problems

Learning Objective 1

Use a systematic approach to solve word problems.

Word problems in business are solved by using a three-step approach and applying simple addition, subtraction, multiplication, and division.

**EXAMPLE A**

A company orders carpeting for three offices measuring 15 square yards, 15 square yards, and 10 square yards, respectively. A carpet dealer sells the carpet for $10 a square yard and gives a $50 discount when the sale is for three or more offices. How much would the company pay to have the three offices carpeted?

15 sq yd + 15 sq yd + 10 sq yd = 40 sq yd
40 sq yd × $10 = $400 gross price
$400 − $50 discount = $350 net price

VIDEO

Word Problems

**STEPS to Solve Word Problems**

1. Read the problem carefully.
2. Determine what is requested.
3. Determine the processes to use.

We use these steps to solve the word problem in example A.

**STEP 1** Read the problem carefully.

**STEP 2** Determine what is requested: How much money would the company pay?

**STEP 3** Determine the processes to use.
*Add* square yards in the three offices: 15 + 15 + 10 = 40.
*Multiply* the total square yards by the $10 per square yard cost: 40 × $10 = $400.
*Subtract* the $50 discount: $400 − $50 = $350.

Some word problems involve all four fundamental processes: addition, subtraction, multiplication, and division.

**EXAMPLE B**

Phoebe Elias owns half of a small bakery. Last week she baked 6 cakes on Monday, 9 on Tuesday, 11 on Wednesday, 8 on Thursday, and 6 on Friday. She sold all cakes for $9 each. It cost Phoebe $5 to make each cake; the rest was her profit on each cake. Phoebe split her profit evenly with her partner. How much did her partner receive from last week's cakes?

**STEP 1** Read the problem carefully.

**STEP 2** Determine what is requested: How much money did Phoebe's partner receive?

**STEP3** Determine the processes to use.
*Add* the cakes baked: 6 + 9 + 11 + 8 + 6 = 40.
*Subtract* the cost from the sales price: $9 − $5 = $4 profit per cake.
*Multiply* the number of cakes sold by the $4 profit per cake: 40 × $4 = $160.
*Divide* the total profit by 2: $160 ÷ 2 = $80 received by the partner.

## ✓ CONCEPT CHECK 4.1

Summary of steps for solving word problems:

1. Read the problem carefully.
2. Determine what is requested.
3. Determine the processes to use.

Problem: Maria wants to upholster three chairs. Two chairs will require 4 yards of material each; the third will require 3 yards. One material costs \$32 per yard; the other costs \$15 per yard. What is the difference between the costs of the two materials for upholstering the chairs?

Read the problem carefully.

Determine what is requested: Difference in cost between the two materials.

Determine the processes to use.
*Add* amount of material needed: 4 yd + 4 yd + 3 yd = 11 yd.
*Multiply* amount of material needed by cost per yard—first material: 11 yd × \$32 per yd = \$352.
*Multiply* amount of material needed by cost per yard—second material: 11 yd × \$15 per yd = \$165.
*Subtract* cost between the two materials: \$352 − \$165 = \$187 difference in cost.

# Solving Rate, Time, and Distance Problems

Learning Objective 2

Apply formulas to solve rate, time, and distance problems.

In some business word problems, you must compute how much is done in a given amount of time at a specific speed. These rate, time, and distance problems are solved with a simple formula: Rate (speed) × Time = Distance (amount done). If you are given any two factors, it is easy, by formula, to find the third.

Rate × Time = Distance
Distance ÷ Time = Rate
Distance ÷ Rate = Time

**EXAMPLE C**

Jan traveled at 35 miles per hour for 5 hours. How far did Jan travel?
35 mph × 5 hr = 175 mi
(Rate × Time = Distance)

**EXAMPLE D**

Jan traveled 175 miles in 5 hours. How fast was Jan traveling?
175 mi ÷ 5 hr = 35 mph
(Distance ÷ Time = Rate)

**EXAMPLE E**

At 35 miles per hour, how long would it take Jan to travel a total of 175 miles?
175 mi ÷ 35 mph = 5 hr
(Distance ÷ Rate = Time)

© JAMES BOULETTE/ISTOCK-PHOTO INTERNATIONAL

### EXAMPLE F

Jan and Ahmed start traveling toward each other from 300 miles apart. Jan is traveling at 35 miles per hour; Ahmed is traveling at 40 miles per hour. How much time will elapse before they meet?

Distance = 300 mi

Total rate = 35 mph (Jan) + 40 mph (Ahmed) = 75 mph

300 mi ÷ 75 mph = 4 hr

(Distance ÷ Rate = Time)

### EXAMPLE G

Jan and Ahmed start traveling toward each other from 300 miles apart. Jan is traveling at 35 miles per hour; Ahmed is traveling at 40 miles per hour. How much distance will Jan travel before they meet?

Total rate = 35 mph (Jan) + 40 mph (Ahmed) = 75 mph

Time = 300 mi ÷ 75 mph = 4 hr

Jan's distance = 35 mph (Jan's Rate) × 4 hr (Time) = 140 mi

### EXAMPLE H

Mary needs to type a term paper that will be 30 pages long. Each page contains about 200 words. If Mary can type 40 words per minute, how many minutes will it take her to complete the paper?

Choose a formula: We know distance (amount done) and speed (rate). Therefore, we choose the formula for time.

Distance (amount done) ÷ Rate (speed) = Time

30 pages × 200 words = 6,000 words ÷ 40 wpm = 150 min

### EXAMPLE I

Flora also had a paper to type, but hers was 9,000 words in length. She was able to type it in 150 minutes. How fast did she type?

Choose a formula: We know distance (amount done) and time. Therefore, we choose the formula for rate.

Distance (amount done) ÷ Time = Rate (speed)

9,000 words ÷ 150 min = 60 wpm

### EXAMPLE J

It is approximately 400 miles from San Francisco to Los Angeles. Roy's friends tell him that he can make the trip in 6 hours if he averages 60 miles per hour. Is this true?

Choose a formula: We know the rate and the time, so we choose the formula for distance.

Rate (speed) × Time = Distance (amount done)

60 mph × 6 hr = 360 mi

Can he get there in 6 hours? *No.*

## CONCEPT CHECK 4.2

The basic formulas:

a. Rate (speed) × Time = Distance (amount done)
   If you know any *two* factors, you can find the *third.*

b. Distance (amount done) ÷ Time = Rate (speed)

c. Distance (amount done) ÷ Rate (speed) = Time

Apply the appropriate formula to answer the following question: A machine that produces tortillas at the Baja Restaurant can produce 200 tortillas per hour, or 1,600 tortillas in an 8-hour day. A new machine can produce 3,000 tortillas in 6 hours. How many more tortillas per hour can the new machine produce than the old one?

Distance (amount done) ÷ Time = Rate

1,600 tortillas ÷ 8 hr = 200 per hr

3,000 tortillas ÷ 6 hr = 500 per hr

Difference: 500 − 200 = 300 more tortillas per hr

# Solving Simple Numerical Equations

Learning Objective 3

Solve simple numerical equations.

A **numerical sentence** in which both sides of an equal sign contain calculations is called an **equation.** For example, five plus five equals twelve minus two ($5 + 5 = 12 - 2$) is an equation, as is seven minus one equals thirty divided by five ($7 - 1 = 30 \div 5$).

For an equation to be true, the numbers on the left of the equal sign must always compute to the same answer as the numbers on the right of the equal sign. Moving a number from one side of the equation to the other changes its sign. A plus sign will change to minus; a minus sign will change to plus. A multiplication sign will change to division; a division sign will change to multiplication.

**EXAMPLE K** **Addition—Subtraction**

$6 + 4 + 5 = 17 - 2$

Change the − 2:

$6 + 4 + 5 + 2 = 17$

Now change the + 5:

$6 + 4 + 2 = 17 - 5$

**EXAMPLE L** **Multiplication—Division**

$3 \times 8 = 48 \div 2$

Change the ÷ 2:

$3 \times 8 \times 2 = 48$

Now change the × 8:

$3 \times 2 = 48 \div 8$

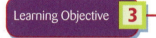

A numerical equation may have one value that is *unknown,* but still provide enough information to complete the sentence. To solve for the unknown value, you can *move* any or all of the known values to the other side of the equation by *reversing* their signs.

**EXAMPLE M**

$6 + 2 = 5 + ?$
Change a number
$6 + 2 - 5 = ?$
Therefore, $? = 3$

**EXAMPLE N**

$15 - 3 = 2 + ?$
Change a number
$15 - 3 - 2 = ?$
Therefore, $? = 10$

**EXAMPLE O**

$7 + 3 + 6 = 4 + 4 + ?$
Change a number
$7 + 3 + 6 - 4 - 4 = ?$
Therefore, $? = 8$

**EXAMPLE P**

$20 \div 5 = 2 \times ?$
Change a number
$20 \div 5 \div 2 = ?$
Therefore, $? = 2$

In business, numerical sentences with equations compare items. Note the following example.

**EXAMPLE Q**

Last year a company had sales of \$25,000 in Dept. A and \$20,000 in Dept. B. If sales this year were \$30,000 in Dept. A, what is the amount needed for Dept. B to equal last year's sales?

Last year: Dept. A \$25,000 + Dept. B \$20,000 = \$45,000
This year: Dept. A \$30,000 + Dept. B ? = \$45,000
Dept. B = \$45,000 − Dept. A \$30,000
Therefore, ? = \$15,000

## CONCEPT CHECK 4.3

Both sides of a true equation are equal. Each side may contain calculations.
$7 + 5 = 14 - 2$
$2 \times 9 = 36 \div 2$
A number may be moved from one side of an equation to the other by reversing its sign.

| | | | |
|---|---|---|---|
| $8 = 6 + 2$ | $8 - 2 = 6$ | $7 + 3 = 10$ | $7 = 10 - 3$ |
| $12 = 4 \times 3$ | $12 \div 3 = 4$ | $24 \div 12 = 2$ | $24 = 2 \times 12$ |

# Numerical Relationships in a Series

**Learning Objective 4**

Recognize numerical relationships in a series.

Relationships in a series of numbers may be found by comparing the first three or four terms in a series and then extrapolating the numbers that would most logically come next. For example, examining the series 320, 160, 80, 40 indicates that each term is found by dividing the preceding number by 2. The next two numbers in the series would logically be 20 and 10—that is, $40 \div 2 = 20$ and $20 \div 2 = 10$.

Examining the series 7, 14, 21, 28 suggests the addition of 7 to each preceding number. The next two numbers in this series would logically be 35 and 42 ($28 + 7 = 35$ and $35 + 7 = 42$).

In the series 5, 15, 35, 75, 155, seeing a relationship is difficult; however, a relationship does exist. Each number results from multiplying the preceding number by 2 and then adding 5. In this series, the next number would logically be 315 ($155 \times 2 + 5 = 315$).

Recognizing numerical and series relationships can be important in analyzing, communicating, and computing numbers. These relationship series are also used frequently in initial employment tests.

## CONCEPT CHECK 4.4

In studying relationships in a numerical series, look for patterns. Patterns most commonly fall into categories:

| | | |
|---|---|---|
| Addition | 2, 7, 12, 17, 22, 27 | (+5, or 32) |
| Alternating addition/subtraction | 12, 24, 18, 30, 24, 36, 30 | (+12, −6, or 42, 36) |
| Subtraction | 39, 32, 25, 18, 11, 4 | (−7, or −3) |
| Alternating subtraction/addition | 64, 59, 61, 56, 58, 53, 55 | (−5, +2, or 50, 52) |
| Multiplication | 4, 12, 36, 108, 324, 972 | (×3, or 2,916) |
| Division | 384, 192, 96, 48, 24 | (÷2, or 12) |

You can also devise patterns such as multiplication with addition or subtraction, division with addition or subtraction, and many other combinations.

# Making Quick Calculations by Rounding Numbers

**Learning Objective 5**

Do quick mental calculations through a process of rounding numbers.

Quick calculations are beneficial when working in business situations. *Rounding* odd and difficult-to-compute amounts to even whole numbers that are easier to compute is a technique often used in business. By rounding, you will be able to get quick and accurate answers without having to write out the computations.

**EXAMPLE R**

How much would 5 items at $2.99 each cost?

To make this computation easily, think "$2.99 is $0.01 less than $3.00." Then think "5 times $3 equals $15." Finally, think "$15.00 less $0.05 (5 × $0.01) is $14.95," which is the correct answer.

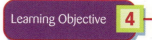

**EXAMPLE S**

The total cost of three equally priced dresses is \$119.85. How much does each dress cost?

To figure out this problem easily, think "\$119.85 is \$0.15 less than \$120.00." Then think "\$120 divided by 3 = \$40, and \$40.00 less \$0.05 (\$0.15 ÷ 3) is \$39.95," the correct answer.

**EXAMPLE T**

At 19 miles per gallon, how many miles would a car go on 9 gallons of gas?

To figure out this problem easily, think "19 is just 1 mile less than 20." Then think "9 times 20 = 180, and 180 minus 9 (9 × 1) is 171," the correct answer.

## CONCEPT CHECK 4.5

You may have noticed that making quick calculations is quite similar to making estimations, which you did in Chapter 1. In fact, quick calculation is only an additional step. After estimating an answer, you determine the degree to which the estimated, or rounded, answer differs from the actual answer by mentally correcting for the amount of the estimation or rounding.

COMPLETE ASSIGNMENTS 4.1 AND 4.2

## Chapter Terms for Review

equation

numerical sentence

## Notes

# THE BOTTOM LINE

*Summary of chapter learning objectives:*

| Learning Objective | Example |
|---|---|
| **4.1**<br><br>Use a systematic approach to solve word problems involving basic math processes. | Use the two-step process to solve the word problem.<br><br>1. Martha is preparing to make two dresses. One will require 3 yards of material; the other will require 4 yards of material. The material for the first dress costs \$12.00 per yard; the material for the second costs \$15.00 per yard. Buttons and trimming will cost \$8.00 for each dress. What will be the total cost?<br>Determine what is being requested.<br>Determine the processes to be used to solve the problem.<br>Answer: _____ |
| **4.2**<br><br>Apply formulas to solve rate, time, and distance problems. | 2. At an average rate of 50 miles per hour, how long would it take to drive 650 miles? _____<br>3. At an average rate of 60 miles per hour, how far could you drive in 6 hours? _____<br>4. If you drove 70 miles per hour and covered 280 miles, how much time did it take? _____ |
| **4.3**<br><br>Solve simple numerical equations. | 5. $5 \times 12 = 120 \div 2$ — Move the 2 to the opposite side of the equation.<br>6. $7 + 8 - 3 = 5 + 2 + ?$ — Solve for ? amount. |

Answers: 1. \$112 2. 13 hr 3. 360 mi 4. 4 hr 5. $5 \times 12 \times 2 = 120$ 6. 5

# THE BOTTOM LINE

*Summary of chapter learning objectives:*

| Learning Objective | Example |
|---|---|
| **4.4**<br>Recognize numeric relationships in a series. | Insert the next two numbers.<br>7. 4, 7, 6, 9, 8, 11, ______, ______ Pattern: ______<br>8. 12, 48, 24, 96, 48, ______, ______ Pattern: ______ |
| **4.5**<br>Do quick mental calculations through a process of rounding numbers. | 9. What is the cost of eight items at $3.99 each?<br>10. At 59 miles per hour, how far would a car go in 20 hours? |

Answers: 7. (+ 3, − 1) 10, 13 8. (× 4, ÷ 2) 192, 96 9. (8 × $4.00) = $32.00 − 0.08 = $31.92
10. (60 × 20) = 1200 − 20 = 1180 mi

SELF-CHECK

# Review Problems for Chapter 4

1 6 items at $5.99 each = __________

2 3 items at $2.48 each = __________

3 24 items at $1.99 each = __________

4 40 items at $2.02 each = __________

5 In the first four months of the year, a corporation had monthly earnings of $12,493, $6,007, $3,028, and $9,728. What were its total earnings in the four months? __________

6 If the corporation in question 5 had earnings of $74,500 at the end of the year, how much did it earn in the last eight months of the year? __________

7 If a tour bus gets 7 miles per gallon of gas and used 61 gallons in a week, how many miles did it travel in the week? __________

8 An employer earned $4,000. Half the earnings went into an employee bonus pool. The pool was split among five employees. How much did each employee receive? __________

9 A delivery firm bought 21 gallons of gas on Monday, 15 on Tuesday, 24 on Wednesday, 34 on Thursday, and 11 on Friday. If gas cost $2.15 per gallon, how much did the delivery firm pay for the week's gas?

__________

10 A store owner planned to give away $1,200 at Christmas. The owner gave $150 to each of five full-time employees and $50 to each of four part-time employees. The remainder was given to a local charity. How much did the charity receive? __________

11 How long would it take to travel 1,265 miles at 55 miles per hour? __________

12 Bob and Mary start traveling toward each other from 1,330 miles apart. Bob is traveling at 30 miles per hour, Mary at 40 miles per hour. How many hours elapse before they meet? __________

13 Bob and Mary start traveling toward each other from 960 miles apart. Bob is traveling at 25 miles per hour, Mary at 55 miles per hour. How far did Bob travel? __________

14 $41 - 6 = 27 +$ __________

15 $72 + 72 = 300 -$ __________

16 $10 \times 3 = 90 \div$ __________

17 Four items at $9 each = __________ items at $12 each

18 What is the next number in the series 3, 7, 8, 12, ? __________

19 What is the next number in the series 5, 20, 10, 40, ? __________

20 To find the price of seven items at $1.99 you would think: 7 times $__________ less 7 times $__________ = $13.93

**Answers to the Self-Check can be found in Appendix B at the back of the text.**

# Assignment 4.1: Word Problems, Equations, and Series

Name ______________________________

Date ______________ Score ______________

Learning Objectives 1 2 4

**A** **(20 points) Use the three-step process to solve the following word problems. (5 points for each correct answer)**

**1.** Mayberry Auto, Inc., conducted a direct-mail program. The manager determined that $30,000 in new business came from the program. If the profit was 40% of sales, how much profit did the program produce? ________

**2.** Martha's Beauty Salon charges $40 for a haircut, $48 for a facial, and $28 for hair coloring. If it had 20 haircut, 22 facial, and 18 coloring customers, what were its total sales? ________

**3.** Juan Lopez sold 11 life insurance policies with premiums totaling $24,200. He sold 14 auto policies with premiums totaling $31,920. Which type of policy had the greater premium per sale? ________

**4.** The Tulsa Taxi Service had four taxi vehicles. Two got 25 miles per gallon of gas; two got 20 miles per gallon of gas. The vehicles were each driven 8,000 miles per month. The gas cost $3.80 per gallon. What was the amount of the gas bill for the month? ________

Score for A (20) ________

**B** **(10 points) Do these problems without using scratch paper or an electronic calculator. (2 points for each correct answer)**

**5.** How much would you pay for 8 gallons of gasoline selling at $3.95 per gallon? ________

**6.** How many items would you have if you had 98 books, 98 cards, and 98 pencils? ________

**7.** What is the price of 15 items at $2.99 each? ________

**8.** How much would you have if you received $3.99 from one person, $7.99 from a second, $11.99 from a third, and $1.99 from a fourth? ________

**9.** If 27 people were divided into three equal groups and each group added 2 additional members, how many members would be in each group? ________

Score for B (10) ________

**C** **(10 points) Do the steps in the order in which they occur. Do these problems without using scratch paper or an electronic calculator. (1 point for each correct answer)**

**10.** 12 items at $3 each plus $2 tax = ________

**11.** 15 watches at $30 each less a $50 discount = ________

**12.** 3 lamps at $22 each plus 7 bulbs at $2 each = ________

**13.** 100 belts at $4 each less discounts of $60 and $30 = ________

**14.** 3 dozen scissors at $11.20 per dozen plus a $4 shipping charge = ________

**15.** 8 pounds of pears at $3 per pound plus 50¢ per pound for packaging = ________

16. \$38 sale price plus \$3 tax less an \$11 discount plus a \$5 delivery charge = ________

17. 6 bath towels at \$8 each and 4 hand towels at \$3 each plus \$2.50 tax = ________

18. 4 dozen brushes at \$25 per dozen plus \$5 tax plus \$7 shipping charge = ________

19. 2 shirts at \$30 each, 4 ties at \$10 each, and 7 pairs of socks at \$2 each = ________

Score for C (10)

**D (40 points) Complete the following equations by supplying the missing items. (4 points for each correct answer)**

20. $27 + 3 =$ ________ $+ 8$

21. $13 +$ ________ $= 7 + 28$

22. ________ $+ 4 = 4 + 16$

23. $400 = 17 - 2 +$ ________

24. $9 + 17 - 3 = 4 \times$ ________ $- 5$

25. $160 \div 4 + 2 = 7 \times 7 -$ ________

26. $13 - 11 \times$ ________ $= 8 \times 8 + 16$

27. ________ $\times 3 \times 3 = 9 \div 3 \times 9$

28. $64 \div 32 = 900 \div$ ________

29. $15 - 9 - 2 = 25 -$ ________

Score for D (40)

**E (20 points) In each of the following problems, a definite relationship exists among the numbers in each series. Extend each series two items by following the correct process. (1 point for each correct line)**

30. Extend each series below through addition.
   - a. 4, 8, 12, 16, ________
   - b. 1, 4, 5, 8, ________
   - c. 2, 4, 7, 11, 13, ________

31. Extend each series below through subtraction.
   - a. 50, 45, 40, 35, ________
   - b. 50, 45, 43, 38, ________
   - c. 100, 90, 81, 73, ________

32. Extend each series below through multiplication.
   - a. 4, 8, 16, 32, ________
   - b. 5, 25, 125, ________
   - c. 2, 4, 20, 40, ________

33. Extend each series below through division.
   - a. 15,625, 3,125, 625, 125, ________
   - b. 729, 243, 81, 27, ________
   - c. 10,000, 2,000, 1,000, 200, ________

34. Extend each series below through combinations of the four processes above.
   - a. 72, 75, 69, 72, ________
   - b. 200, 100, 300, 150, ________
   - c. 6, 9, 18, 21, 42, ________
   - d. 240, 120, 600, 300, 1,500, ________
   - e. 7, 4, 8, 5, 9, ________
   - f. 30, 10, 60, 20, ________
   - g. 10, 40, 20, 80, ________
   - h. 100, 50, 40, 20, ________

Score for E (20)

# Assignment 4.2: Word Problems, Formulas, and Equations

Name ______________________

Date ______________ Score ______________

Learning Objectives 1 2 3 4 5

**A (40 points) Solve the following word problems. (5 points for each correct answer)**

**1.** A store regularly sold 2 cans of soup for $1.28. It advertised a special sale of 6 cans for $3.12. A customer bought 12 cans at the sale. How much did the customer save over the regular price? ________

**2.** A sales representative's car gets 18 miles to a gallon of gas. It was driven 120 miles each day for 30 days. Gas cost an average of $2.27 per gallon. What was the sales representative's total 30-day cost for gas? ________

**3.** A store clerk sold a customer a ruler for $1.67, three pencils for $0.29 each, notebook paper for $0.99, and an eraser for $0.35 and was given $10.00 in payment. How much change did the clerk give the customer from the $10.00? (All prices include tax.) ________

**4.** A college student worked at a local store for $9.00 per hour, as his class schedule permitted. The student worked 3 hours each Monday, Tuesday, Wednesday, and Thursday. He also worked 2 hours each Friday and 8 hours each Saturday. How many weeks did the student have to work to earn $792 for a new bicycle?

________

**5.** A box, a crate, and a trunk weigh a total of 370 pounds. The crate weighs 160 pounds. The trunk weighs 4 pounds more than the box. What does the box weigh? ________

**6.** A hotel has 12 floors. Each floor has 30 *single-person* rooms and 40 *two-person* rooms. What is the total *guest* capacity of the hotel? ________

**7.** A department store offers its customers socks for $1.50 per pair or $15.00 per dozen. If two customers buy 1 dozen together and each pays half the cost, how much will each customer save by paying the quantity price? ________

**8.** Supply Clerk A ordered five staplers at $9 each and two large boxes of staples for $3 each. Supply Clerk B ordered a box of computer disks for $8.50 and a box of computer paper for $39.95. How much less did Clerk B spend than Clerk A? (All prices include tax.) ________

________________

Score for A (40)

**B** **(10 points) Solve the following time, rate, distance problems. (5 points for each correct answer)**

**9.** Wendy leaves St. Paul to travel the 2,000 miles to Los Angeles, driving at a speed of 55 miles per hour. Mark leaves Los Angeles to travel the same 2,000-mile route to St. Paul, driving at a speed of 45 miles per hour. How many miles will Mark have traveled when they meet? ________

**10.** Car A traveled to a destination 840 miles away at 60 miles per hour. Car B traveled to a destination 660 miles away at 55 miles per hour. How much longer did Car A travel than Car B? ________

________

Score for B (10)

**C** **(40 points) Solve each of the problems without writing any computations on paper and without using a calculator or a computer. (2 points for each correct answer)**

**11.** 5 items at \$1.99 = ________

**12.** 2 items at \$7.98 = ________

**13.** 4 items at \$19.98 = ________

**14.** 2 items at \$49.96 = ________

**15.** 15 items at \$0.99 = ________

**16.** 10 items at \$9.99 = ________

**17.** 6 items at \$3.95 = ________

**18.** 5 items at \$1.02 = ________

**19.** 19 items at \$40 = ________

**20.** 3 items at \$19.99 = ________

**21.** 20 items at \$40.05 = ________

**22.** 30 items at \$1.99 = ________

**23.** 20 items at \$39.98 = ________

**24.** 2 items at \$5.99 = ________

**25.** 48 items at \$5 = ________

**26.** 5 items at \$1.97 = ________

**27.** 7 items at \$7.97 = ________

**28.** 2 items at \$99.98 = ________

**29.** 30 items at \$2.98 = ________

**30.** 99 items at \$1.90 = ________

________

Score for C (40)

**D** **(10 points) In each of the following equations, rewrite the equation by moving the last number on each side of the equal sign to the other side and making appropriate sign changes so that the equation is still true. (Example: Given 13 + 7 + 2 = 10 + 12; Answer 13 + 7 − 12 = 10 − 2) (1 point for each correct equation)**

**31.** $6 + 4 + 5 = 17 - 2$

**32.** $6 \times 2 \div 3 = 8 \div 4 \times 2$

**33.** $9 - 3 - 3 = 2 + 1$

**34.** $8 \div 2 \times 4 = 24 \div 3 \times 2$

**35.** $20 + 1 - 7 = 16 - 2$

**36.** $3 \times 3 \times 3 = 18 \div 2 \times 3$

**37.** $12 + 3 - 5 = 7 + 3$

**38.** $7 \times 4 \div 2 = 28 \times 2 \div 4$

**39.** $64 - 32 - 16 = 8 + 8$

**40.** $63 \div 7 \times 2 = 3 \times 2 \times 3$

________

Score for D (10)

## Notes

Part 2

# Percentage Applications

# Percents

# 5

## Learning Objectives

By studying this chapter and completing all assignments, you will be able to:

Learning Objective 1 Change percents to decimals.

Learning Objective 2 Change fractions and decimals to percents.

Learning Objective 3 Find Base, Rate, and Percentage.

Learning Objective 4 Use percents to measure increase and decrease.

Learning Objective 5 Use percents to allocate overhead expenses.

Percents and percentages are used extensively in various business and nonbusiness applications. Airlines are required to publish the "on-time percentage" for each of their flights. Every bank publishes its loan rates as percents. The Food and Drug Administration (FDA) says that packaged foods must contain labels with nutritional information, much of which is written in percents. Colleges and universities often describe the ethnic diversity of their student bodies and faculty using percents.

## Changing Percents to Decimals

**Learning Objective 1**

Change percents to decimals.

We use percents because the word **percent** makes verbal and written communication easier. Suppose that we have a 5% sales tax. Which of these phrases sounds better: (a) "five percent," (b) "five-hundredths," (c) "one-twentieth," or even (d) "point zero five"? Imagine how complicated the latter three phrases would be if the sales tax rate were 5.25%. But by using the word *percent,* we can just say "five point two five percent."

Percents themselves are actually not used in arithmetic. Before you can do any calculation with a percent, you must change the percent to a decimal. If you use a calculator with a percent key [%], the calculator will first convert the percent to a decimal. Take a calculator with a percent key and observe the display closely. Enter **75%**; that is, press these three keys: [7] [5] [%]. After pressing the [%] key, the display shows **0.75.** There is no percent symbol and the decimal point has moved two places to the *left.* The calculator will use 0.75 in all of its calculations that involve 75%.

Sometimes a percent has a fractional part. For example, we might have a tax rate that is stated as $5\frac{1}{2}$%. Even using a calculator, first we must write the fraction as a decimal to get 5.5%. Using the calculator, press these keys: [5] [.] [5] [%]. After pressing [%], the display shows **0.055.** Notice that to move two places to the left, the calculator had to insert an extra zero.

**STEPS to Change a Percent to a Decimal**

1. If the percent has a fractional part, convert the fraction to its decimal equivalent.
2. Remove the percent symbol.
3. Move the decimal point two places to the *left* (insert zeros if needed).

**EXAMPLE A**

45% —STEP 2→ 45 —STEP 3→ .45. = 0.45

**EXAMPLE B**

175% —STEP 2→ 175 —STEP 3→ 1.75. = 1.75

**EXAMPLE C**

4.5% —STEP 2→ 4.5 —STEP 3→ .04.5 = 0.045

**EXAMPLE D**

$1\frac{3}{4}$% = 1.75% (STEP 1) —STEP 2→ 1.75 —STEP 3→ .01.75 = 0.0175

(*Note:* Check the answers to these examples with the percent key on your calculator.)

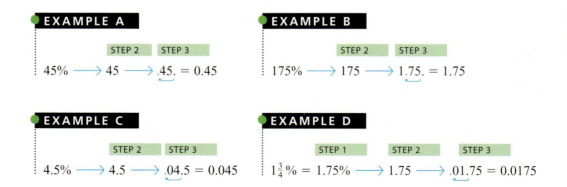

## CONCEPT CHECK 5.1

a. Change 250% to a decimal.

250% ⟶ 250 ⟶ 2.50. = 2.50 or 2.5

b. Change $\frac{1}{4}$% to a decimal.

$\frac{1}{4}$% = 0.25% ⟶ 0.25 ⟶ .00.25 = 0.0025

# Changing Decimals and Fractions to Percents

Learning Objective 2

Change fractions and decimals to percents.

Changing a decimal to a percent is exactly the opposite from changing a percent to a decimal: Move the decimal point two places to the *right*, and then write a percent symbol. If you have a fraction or a mixed number, first change it to a decimal as you did in Chapter 3. Then change the decimal to a percent. (A decimal point at the extreme right end of the percent is omitted—examples E, G, and J below.)

**STEPS to Change a Fraction or a Decimal to a Percent**

1. If the number is a fraction, or a mixed number, convert it to its decimal equivalent.
2. Move the decimal point two places to the *right* (insert zeros if needed).
3. Write a percent symbol at the *right* end of the new number.

**EXAMPLE E**

STEP 1 / STEP 2 / STEP 3

$\frac{4}{5}$ = 0.8 ⟶ 0.80. ⟶ 80%

**EXAMPLE F**

STEP 1 / STEP 2 / STEP 3

$1\frac{3}{8}$ = 1.375 ⟶ 1.37.5 ⟶ 137.5%

**EXAMPLE G**

STEP 2 / STEP 3

0.4 ⟶ 0.40. ⟶ 40%

**EXAMPLE H**

STEP 2 / STEP 3

1.1875 ⟶ 1.18.75 ⟶ 118.75%

**EXAMPLE I**

STEP 2 / STEP 3

2.5 ⟶ 2.50. ⟶ 250%

**EXAMPLE J**

STEP 2 / STEP 3

1 = 1. ⟶ 1.00. ⟶ 100%

(*Note:* To check these examples with your calculator, you can multiply the decimal number by 100 and write the percent symbol at the right end of the answer.)

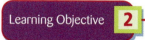

## CONCEPT CHECK 5.2

a. Change $2\frac{7}{10}$ to a percent.

$2\frac{7}{10} = 2.7 \longrightarrow 2.70. \longrightarrow 270\%$

b. Change 0.075 to a percent.

$0.075 \longrightarrow 0.07.5 \longrightarrow 7.5\%$

# Finding Base, Rate, and Percentage

**Learning Objective 3**

Find Base, Rate, and Percentage.

Suppose that you have \$5 and spend \$4 for breakfast. Example E showed that the fraction $\frac{4}{5}$ equals 80%. You can say that "you spent 80% of your money (\$5) for your breakfast (\$4)." Without the context of your breakfast, you have simply "80% of \$5 = \$4." In this book we call 80% the **Rate *(R)*,** \$5 the **Base *(B)*** amount, and \$4 the **Percentage *(P)*** amount. The Base and the Percentage amounts will always have the same units (e.g., dollars, feet, or pounds). The Rate is the percent. (The word *rate* comes from the word *ratio*—in this case, $\frac{4}{5}$.) It may make sense for you to think of the Base amount as the denominator in the rate (that is, ratio = $\frac{4}{5}$) because the denominator is the "base" (i.e., bottom) of the fraction.

*Note*: In practice, the terms *percent* and *percentage* are often used interchangeably. Sometimes, you will see the word *percentage* used to mean a rate and the word *percent* used to mean an amount. You will even see the two words *percentage rate* to mean the rate. In this book, however, we use only one meaning for each word.

**EXAMPLE K**

80% of \$5 = \$4
80% is the Rate
\$5 is the Base
\$4 is the Percentage

**EXAMPLE L**

25% of 20 ft = 5 ft
25% is the Rate
20 ft is the Base
5 ft is the Percentage

**EXAMPLE M**

50% of 60 gal = 30 gal
50% is the Rate
60 gal is the Base
30 gal is the Percentage

**Figure 5-1**

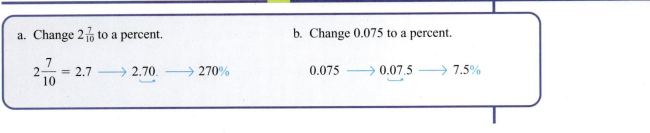

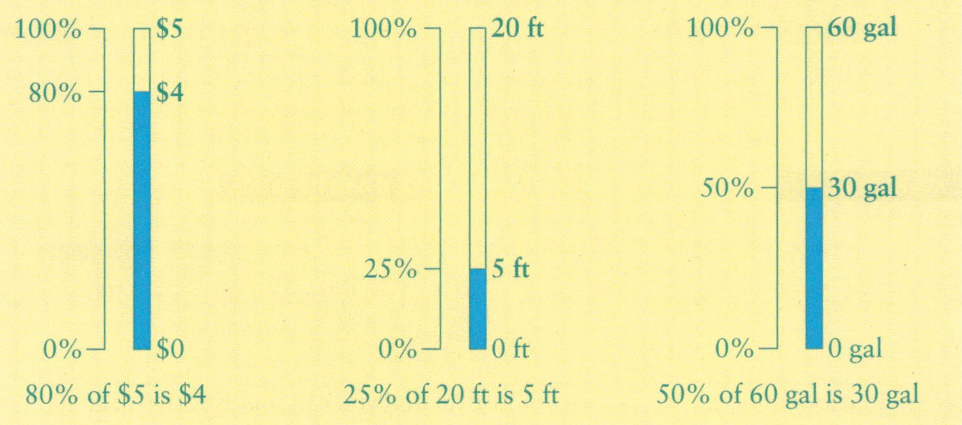

Figure 5-1 shows three diagrams, one each for examples K, L, and M. In each diagram, the Rate (or percent) is shown in the left-hand column. Each Percentage is represented by the shaded portion of the right-hand column. Each Base is represented by the entire height of the right-hand column.

The word *of* often appears in problems that involve percents. Recall from Chapter 2 that with fractions, *of* means *multiply*. We just showed that 80% $= \frac{\$4}{\$5}$. Also recall that you can "check" a division problem by multiplication. We would get 80% × \$5 = \$4. In words, we say that "80% *of* \$5 is \$4."

*Rule:* The number that follows the word *of* is the Base (and is the denominator in the fraction); the number that follows the word *is* is the Percentage amount.

The preceding examples illustrate the basic relationship among the Rate, Base, and Percentage: Rate × Base = Percentage. As a formula, it is written as $R \times B = P$ or as $P = R \times B$.

When you know any two of these three numbers, you can calculate the third by changing the formula:

If you want to find $B$, the formula becomes $B = P \div R$ or $P \div R = B$.
If you want to find $R$, the formula becomes $R = P \div B$ or $P \div B = R$.

**EXAMPLE N**

Find $P$ when
$R$ = 50% and $B$ = 300 yd

**EXAMPLE O**

Find $R$ when
$B$ = 30 lb and $P$ = 6 lb

**EXAMPLE P**

Find $B$ when
$P$ = \$45 and $R$ = 75%

**Figure 5-2**

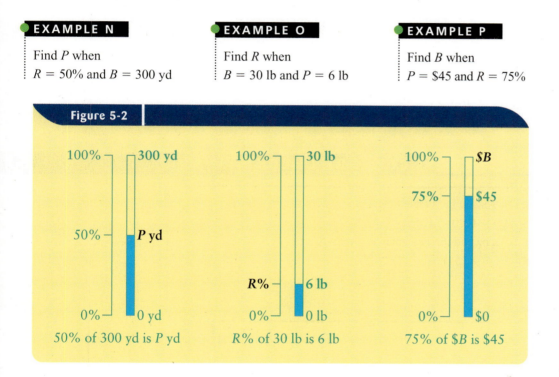

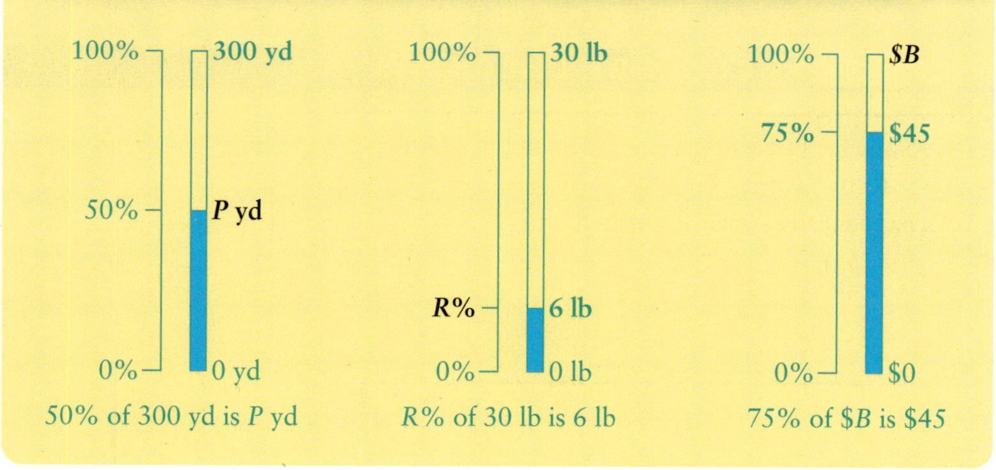


Figure 5-2 illustrates these relationships, which are calculated as follows:

$P = R \times B$
$P = 50\% \times 300$ yd
$P = 0.50 \times 300$ yd
$P = 150$ yd
[5] [0] [%] [×] [3] [0] [0] [=]

$R = P \div B$
$R = 6$ lb $\div$ 30 lb
$R = 0.20$
$R = 20\%$
[6] [÷] [3] [0] [=]

$B = P \div R$
$B = \$45 \div 75\%$
$B = \$45 \div 0.75$
$B = \$60$
[4] [5] [÷] [7] [5] [%] [=]

Note that in example O, the calculator cannot automatically "move" the decimal point two places to the right. If you want the calculator to do it, you "multiply by 100." It is faster to just move the decimal point places without a calculator.

## USING PERCENTS IN BUSINESS

Percent problems occur frequently in business. Examples Q and R are typical fundamental applications, in which we solve for the Base $(B)$ amount and the Rate $(R)$, respectively.

© STOCKBYTE/GETTY IMAGES

**EXAMPLE Q**

Lena Hoover is a financial analyst. In December, she received a \$600 bonus, which equaled 15% of her monthly salary. What was her monthly salary?

$P$ = amount of bonus = \$600
$R$ = rate of bonus = 15%
$B$ = monthly salary = ?
As $P \div R = B$,
$P \div R$ = \$600 ÷ 15% = \$600 ÷ 0.15 = \$4,000 monthly salary

**EXAMPLE R**

Last year Bayside Coffee Shop had total expenses of \$300,000. Of that total, \$210,000 was the expense for employee salaries. Last year at Bayside, the employee salary expense was what percent of total expenses?

$P$ = employee salaries = \$210,000
$R$ = ?
$B$ = total expenses = \$300,000
Since $P \div B = R$,
$P \div B$ = \$210,000 ÷ \$300,000 = 0.70 = 70%

**CONCEPT CHECK 5.3**

a. Find the Base when the Rate is 40% and the Percentage amount is 50 ft.
$B = P \div R$ = 50ft ÷ 40% = 50ft ÷ 0.40 = 125 ft
b. Find the Rate when the Base is 12 oz and the Percentage amount is 3 oz.
$R = P \div B$ = 3 oz ÷ 12 oz = 0.25 = 25%

COMPLETE ASSIGNMENT 5.1.

# Using Percents to Measure Increase and Decrease

**Learning Objective 4**

Use percents to measure increase and decrease.

In business, percents are used to measure change from one year to the next or from one month to the next. Real estate firms compare the number of homes sold this year with the number of homes sold last year. Read and carefully compare the following four statements about home sales last year and this year:

Joslin Realty sold 40% more homes this year than it did last year, when it sold 135 homes.

Rossi & Shanley Real Estate sold 25 more homes this year than last year, which represents 20% more homes sold this year than last year.

Real estate agent Nancy Lo sold 5 fewer homes this year than she did last year, when she sold 40 homes.

Charles Peterson, a real estate broker, sold 30 homes last year; this year he sold 36 homes.

The number of homes sold last year is the Base *(B)* amount (last year is called the *base year*). The change in homes sold can be reported as a number, which would be the Percentage amount *(P)*, or as a percent, which would be the Rate *(R)*. If any two of the three values are given, the third can be determined using one of the three formulas in this chapter.

**EXAMPLE S**

Find the number of additional homes *(P)* that Joslin Realty sold this year.

$B = 135$ and $R = 40\%$. Since $P = R \times B$,

$P = 40\% \times 135 = 0.40 \times 135 = 54$ more homes this year

**EXAMPLE T**

Find the number of homes that Rossi & Shanley Real Estate sold last year *(B)*.

$P = 25$ and $R = 20\%$. Since $B = P \div R$,

$B = 25 \div 20\% = 25 \div 0.20 = 125$ homes sold last year

**EXAMPLE U**

Find Nancy Lo's rate of decrease *(R)* from last year's sales.

$P = 5$ and $B = 40$. Since $R = P \div B$,

$R = 5 \div 40 = 0.125 = 12.5\%$ decrease

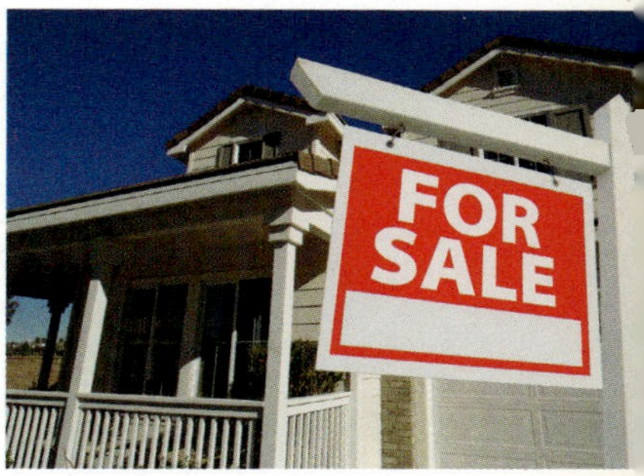



To find the percent change when the only numbers reported are the amounts *(B)* for last year and this year, the first step is to find the **amount of increase** or the **amount of decrease.** *P* is the difference between the amounts for the two years. Then use $R = P \div B$ to find the **rate of increase** or the **rate of decrease.**

**EXAMPLE V**

Find Charles Peterson's rate of change *(R)*.

Charles sold 30 homes last year *(B)* and 36 this year. The amount of change is

$P = 36 - 30 = 6$ more homes this year

The rate of change is

$R = P \div B = 6 \div 30 = 0.20 = 20\%$ increase

## COMPUTING AMOUNTS OF INCREASE AND DECREASE WITH A CALCULATOR

Review example S. Now consider a variation of example S that says, "Find the total number of homes that Joslin Realty sold this year." Last year it sold 135 homes. There was a 40% increase, which means 54 more homes were sold this year. The total number of homes sold this year was 135 + 54 = 189 homes. Many calculators allow you to calculate 189 with the following keystrokes: [1] [3] [5] [+] [4] [0] [%] [=]. The display will show the answer, 189.

If you need to know the actual amount of the increase, it will usually show in the calculator display immediately after you press the [%] key, but just before you press the [=] key.

Similarly, suppose the original example had said, "The real estate agency sold 40% *fewer* homes this year than it did last year, when it sold 135 homes. Find the total number of homes that it sold this year." The amount of the *decrease* is 54 homes. Therefore, the total number sold this year is 135 − 54 = 81 homes. On the calculator, you would use the following keystrokes: [1] [3] [5] [−] [4] [0] [%] [=]. The display will show the answer, 81.

### CONCEPT CHECK 5.4

A company had sales of $200,000 this month and $160,000 last month *(B)*. Find both the amount of increase *(P)* and the rate of increase *(R)*.

The amount of increase is

$P = \$200{,}000 - \$160{,}000 = \$40{,}000$

The rate of increase is

$R = P \div B = \$40{,}000 \div \$160{,}000 = 0.25 = 25\%$

COMPLETE ASSIGNMENTS 5.2 AND 5.3.

# Using Percents to Allocate Overhead Expenses

**Learning Objective 5**

Use percents to allocate overhead expenses.

Many businesses are organized into divisions or departments. Suppose Cotton's Clothing is a retailer of sportswear. It has three departments: women's clothes, men's clothes, and children's clothes. Management and owners of Cotton's need to measure the profitability of each department. Cotton's also knows the amounts it paid for the merchandise sold and the salaries of employees in each department. Cotton's can subtract these departmental costs from the departmental revenues.

But what about rent and other general costs such as electricity? These costs that are not directly related to the types of merchandise sold are called **overhead costs.** For example, Cotton's monthly rental expense might be $15,000 for the entire building. How should that single amount be divided among the three departments? Should each department be assigned $\frac{1}{3}$, or $5,000, of the total rent?

Businesses can **allocate,** or distribute, the total rent based on a measurement related to the total cost. Rent is a cost of using the building; it could be allocated on the basis of floor space, since each department occupies some of that space.

**STEPS to Allocate an Overhead Expense Based on Total Floor Space (or Some Other Measurement)**

1. Find the total square feet of floor space.
2. Divide the floor space of each department by total floor space, then change the quotients to percents.
3. Multiply each percent (in fractional or decimal form) by the total rent (or other overhead value).

**EXAMPLE W**

The total rent is $15,000. Using the floor space of each department as shown below, determine the amount of rent to allocate to each department of Cotton's.

| | STEP 1 | STEP 2 | STEP 3 |
|---|---|---|---|
| **Department** | **Floor Space** | **Percent of Total** | **Distribution of Rent** |
| Women's | 100 ft × 50 ft = 5,000 sq ft | 5,000 ÷ 10,000 = 50% | 0.5 × $15,000 = $ 7,500 |
| Children's | 50 ft × 60 ft = 3,000 sq ft | 3,000 ÷ 10,000 = 30% | 0.3 × $15,000 = $ 4,500 |
| Men's | 40 ft × 50 ft = 2,000 sq ft | 2,000 ÷ 10,000 = 20% | 0.2 × $15,000 = $ 3,000 |
| | 10,000 sq ft | | $15,000 |

This same method can be used for many other business expenses, such as utilities, fire insurance, and salaries of office personnel. Examples of other bases that might be used for allocation are number of employees, hours worked, and units produced.

## CONCEPT CHECK 5.5

A landscape maintenance company has two different divisions: commercial and residential. Employees spend 1,125 hours working on commercial landscapes and 375 hours working on residential landscapes. The company has a utility expense of $8,000 that it wants to allocate between the two divisions, based on the percent of employee hours used by each division.

Total hours worked: 1,125 + 375 = 1,500

Commercial: 1,125 ÷ 1,500 = 0.75, or 75% of employee hours
75% of $8,000 = 0.75 × $8,000 = $6,000 of office expense

Residential: 375 ÷ 1,500 = 0.25 or 25% of employee hours
25% of $8,000 = 0.25 × $8,000 = $2,000 of office expense

COMPLETE ASSIGNMENT 5.4.

## Chapter Terms for Review

allocate

amount of decrease

amount of increase

Base *(B)*

"of"

overhead costs

percent

Percentage *(P)*

Rate *(R)*

rate of decrease

rate of increase

## Try Microsoft® Excel

Try working the problems using the Microsoft Excel templates found on your student CD. Solutions for the problems are also shown on the CD.

# THE BOTTOM LINE

*Summary of chapter learning objectives:*

| Learning Objective | Example |
|---|---|
| **5.1**<br>Change percents to decimals. | 1. Change 4.25% to a decimal. |
| **5.2**<br>Change fractions and decimals to percents. | 2. Change 0.45 to a percent.<br>3. Change $\frac{7}{8}$ to a percent. |
| **5.3**<br>Find Base, Rate, and Percentage. | 4. Find the Percentage: 35% of 40 $= P$<br>5. Find the Rate: $R$% of 140 = 28<br>6. Find the Base: 80% of $B$ = 220 |
| **5.4**<br>Use percents to measure increase and decrease. | 7. Increase a $5,000 salary by 25%.<br>8. From 300 to 240 is a decrease of what percent? |
| **5.5**<br>Use percents to allocate overhead expenses. | 9. A company has three stores, A, B and C, with 4, 6, and 10 employees, respectively. Based on the number of employees, allocate a $4,000 expense among the stores. |

Answers: 1. 0.0425 2. 45% 3. 87.5% 4. 14 5. 20% 6. 275 7. The increase is $1,250; The new salary is $6,250. 8. 20% 9. Store A, $800; Store B, $1,200; Store C, $2,000

SELF-CHECK

## Review Problems for Chapter 5

1 Change 14.75% to a decimal __________

2 Change 0.625 to a percent __________

3 Change 150% to a decimal __________

4 Change 0.0075 to a percent __________

5 Change 0.06% to a decimal __________

6 Change $\frac{2}{5}$ to a percent __________

7 16% of 70 = __________

8 250% of 60 = __________

9 25% of __________ = 45

10 100% of __________ = 70

11 __________% of 40 = 35

12 __________% of 90 = 144

13 Sales were $100,000 two months ago and increased by 20% last month. How much were sales last month? __________

14 Sales were $120,000 last month and decreased by 20% this month. How much were sales this month? __________

15 Expenses were $200,000 two years ago and $400,000 last year. What was the percent increase last year? __________

16 Expenses were $400,000 last year and $200,000 this year. What was the percent decrease this year? __________

17 Peggy Covey owns a nursery. This year she sold 195 more rose bushes than she did last year. This represents a 12% increase over the previous year. How many rose bushes did Peggy's nursery sell last year? __________

18 Jim Dukes manages Internet sales for a company that started selling its product over the Internet two years ago. Last year, company sales over the Internet were only about $500,000. This year, sales were $1,625,000. Calculate the company's percent increase in Internet sales this year. __________

19 Ken Chard is a bank teller. When he started this morning, his cash drawer had coins worth $86. The coins represented only 2.5% of all the money that Ken had in his cash drawer. What was the total value of all this money? __________

20 Nancy McGraw is an orthopedic surgeon. Last winter, Dr. McGraw performed 50 emergency surgeries. Thirty-two of those surgeries were the result of ski injuries. What percent of Dr. McGraw's emergency surgeries were the result of ski injuries? __________

**Answers to the Self-Check can be found in Appendix B at the back of the text.**

# Assignment 5.1: Base, Rate, and Percentage

Name ______________________________

Date ______________ Score ______________

Learning Objectives 1 2 3

**A (20 points) Change the percents to decimals. Change the nonpercents to percents. (1 point for each correct answer)**

**1.** $31\% =$ ________ **2.** $100\% =$ ________ **3.** $3\frac{1}{3}\% =$ ________

**4.** $0.875 =$ ________ **5.** $3 =$ ________ **6.** $33\frac{2}{3}\% =$ ________

**7.** $0.15 =$ ________ **8.** $0.3 =$ ________ **9.** $1\frac{3}{4} =$ ________

**10.** $5.2\% =$ ________ **11.** $224.5\% =$ ________ **12.** $0.0003\% =$ ________

**13.** $0.52 =$ ________ **14.** $245\% =$ ________ **15.** $0.08\frac{1}{4} =$ ________

**16.** $\frac{1}{2} =$ ________ **17.** $4.0 =$ ________ **18.** $0.000025 =$ ________

**19.** $0.01\% =$ ________ **20.** $1{,}000\% =$ ________

________________
Score for A (20)

**B (30 points) In the following problems, find each Percentage amount. (2 points for each correct answer)**

**21.** 0.375% of 56 = ________ **22.** 0.25% of 1,600 = ________ **23.** 100% of 11.17 = ________

**24.** 87.5% of 48 = ________ **25.** 40% of 0.85 = ________ **26.** 250% of $66 = ________

**27.** 25% of $1.16 = ________ **28.** 120% of $45 = ________ **29.** 2.5% of $66 = ________

**30.** 50% of $162 = ________ **31.** 8% of 200 = ________ **32.** 12% of 0.38 = ________

**33.** 187.5% of 40 = ________ **34.** 1.5% of $86 = ________ **35.** 0.2% of 480 = ________

________________
Score for B (30)

**C (50 points) In each of the following problems, find the Percentage amount, the Rate, or the Base amount. Write rates as percents. Round dollars to the nearest cent. (2 points for each correct answer)**

**36.** 35% of ________ = $14

**37.** ________ of $35 = $7

**38.** ________ of 1.12 = 1.4

**39.** ________ of 14.2 = 28.4

**40.** ________ of 400 = 14

**41.** 80% of ________ = $0.96

**42.** 1.25% of ________ = 1.6

**43.** ________ of 80 = 120

**44.** ________ of 0.056 = 0.014

**45.** 175% of ________ = $84

**46.** 2.5% of $2,820 = ________

**47.** 0.25% of ________ = $20

**48.** ________ of $268.50 = $112.77

**49.** 62.5% of ________ = 35

**50.** 0.025% of $16,400 = ________

**51.** 140% of ________ = 672

**52.** 120% of ________ = $51

**53.** ________ of 5.4 = 2.16

**54.** ________ of $1,480 = $10,064

**55.** 15% of $140 = ________

**56.** 180% of $90 = ________

**57.** ________ of 85 = 136

**58.** 125% of ________ = $520

**59.** 12% of ________ = 3

**60.** ________ of 3.2 = 0.704

________
Score for C (50)

# Assignment 5.2: Rate of Increase and Rate of Decrease

Name ____________________

Date __________ Score __________

Learning Objective 4

**A (40 points) Calculate the missing values. ($2\frac{1}{2}$ points for each correct answer)**

**1.** Decreasing the base value of 280 by 25% gives the new value __________.

**2.** Increasing the base value of 240 by 40% gives the new value __________.

**3.** Start with 75, decrease it by 60%, and end up with __________.

**4.** Start with 80, increase it by 14%, and end up with __________.

**5.** Sales were $8,000 last month and increased by 4% this month. Sales were __________ this month.

**6.** Profits were $67,500 last month, but decreased by 3% this month. Profits were __________ this month.

**7.** Base value = 272; increase = 100%; new (final) value = __________

**8.** Base value = 250; decrease = 100%; new (final) value = __________

**9.** A $17 increase is 10% of the base value of __________.

**10.** A decrease of 45 units is 15% of the base value of __________ units.

**11.** The price decreased from $450 to $378; the percent decrease was __________.

**12.** Production increased from 8,000 units to 10,000 units; the percent increase was __________.

**13.** $300 is what percent less than $400? __________

**14.** 480 is what percent greater than 160? __________

**15.** Sales were $500,000 in June but only $400,000 in July. The rate of decrease was __________.

**16.** Profits were $11,000 last month and $10,000 the previous month. The rate of increase was __________.

__________

Score for A (40)

**B** **(30 points) The following table shows the volumes of various items sold by Thrift's Speed Shop during the past two years. Compute the amount of change and the rate of change between this year and last year. Compute the rates to the nearest tenth of a percent. If the amount and rate are increases, write a + in front of them; if they are decreases, enclose them in parentheses (). (1 point for each correct amount; 2 points for each correct rate)**

**Thrift's Speed Shop**
**Volume Sold (number of units)**

| | Description of Item | This Year | Last Year | Amount of Change | Rate of Change |
|---|---|---|---|---|---|
| **17.** | Batteries | 516 | 541 | ______ | ______ |
| **18.** | Brake fluid (pints) | 1,781 | 1,602 | ______ | ______ |
| **19.** | Coolant (gallons) | 2,045 | 1,815 | ______ | ______ |
| **20.** | Headlight lamps | 5,291 | 5,687 | ______ | ______ |
| **21.** | Oil (quarts) | 13,428 | 14,746 | ______ | ______ |
| **22.** | Mufflers | 639 | 585 | ______ | ______ |
| **23.** | Shock absorbers | 895 | 1,084 | ______ | ______ |
| **24.** | Tires, auto | 6,742 | 5,866 | ______ | ______ |
| **25.** | Tires, truck | 2,115 | 1,805 | ______ | ______ |
| **26.** | Wiper blades | 1,927 | 2,342 | ______ | ______ |

______
Score for B (30)

**C** **(30 points) During May and June, Kalman's Paint Store had sales in the amounts shown in the following table. Compute the amount of change and the rate of change between May and June. Compute the rates of change to the nearest tenth of a percent. If the amount and rate are increases, write a + in front of them; if they are decreases, enclose them in parentheses (). (1 point for each correct amount; 2 points for each correct rate)**

**Kalman's Paint Store**
**Volume Sold (in dollars)**

| | Description of Item | June | May | Amount of Change | Rate of Change |
|---|---|---|---|---|---|
| **27.** | Brush, 2″ wide | $ 611.14 | $ 674.67 | ______ | ______ |
| **28.** | Brush, 3″ wide | 564.20 | 512.51 | ______ | ______ |
| **29.** | Brush, 4″ wide | 429.87 | 374.27 | ______ | ______ |
| **30.** | Drop cloth, 9 × 12 | 143.50 | 175.66 | ______ | ______ |
| **31.** | Drop cloth, 12 × 15 | 174.29 | 151.55 | ______ | ______ |
| **32.** | Paint, latex (gal) | 46,921.64 | 49,075.29 | ______ | ______ |
| **33.** | Paint, latex (qt) | 5,072.35 | 4,878.96 | ______ | ______ |
| **34.** | Paint, oil (gal) | 7,308.44 | 7,564.27 | ______ | ______ |
| **35.** | Paint, oil (qt) | 4,358.35 | 4,574.96 | ______ | ______ |
| **36.** | Paint scraper | 274.10 | 238.82 | ______ | ______ |

______
Score for C (30)

# Assignment 5.3: Business Applications

Name ______________________________

Date ______________ Score ______________

Learning Objectives 3 4

**A (50 points) Solve the following problems. Round dollar amounts to the nearest cent. Round other amounts to the nearest tenth. Write rates as percents to the nearest tenth of a percent. (5 points for each correct answer)**

1. Walter Electric shipped 5,500 capacitors in May. Clients eventually returned 4% of the capacitors. How many of the capacitors shipped in May were eventually returned? __________

2. Jim Walter, CEO of Walter Electric, wants the company to reduce the percent of capacitors that customers return. In June, the company shipped 5,000 capacitors, and 150 were eventually returned. What percent of the June shipment was eventually returned? __________

3. By July of the following year, Walter Electric had reduced the percent of capacitors returned to 2% of the number shipped. If 130 capacitors were returned from that month's shipment, how many had been shipped? __________

4. A European food importer, Fontaine's Food Expo, imports 35% of its vinegars from France, 40% from Italy, and the rest from Spain. The total value of all the vinegars that it imports is $1,216,000. What is the value of the vinegars that are imported from Spain? __________

5. Next year, Fontaine's is planning to import $462,000 worth of vinegars from France, $532,000 worth of vinegars from Italy, and $406,000 worth of vinegars from Spain. If next year's imports occur as currently being planned, what percent of the total imports will be from Italy? __________

6. Rigik Parka Products, Inc., manufactures only parkas for adults and children. Last year, Rigik manufactured all its children's parkas in Asia. Those children's parkas represented 35% of all the Rigik production. If the company made a total of 240,000 parkas, how many children's parkas did it produce? __________

7. This year, Rigik again plans to manufacture all its children's parkas in Asia, and Rigik will expand the children's product line to 40% of the total number of parkas produced. If Rigik plans to produce 112,000 children's parkas, how many parkas does the company plan to produce in total? __________

8. Next year, Rigik plans to keep the percent of children's parkas at 40% but increase the number of children's parkas produced to 125,000. How many parkas does the company plan to produce for adults? (*Hint:* First you need to calculate the total number of all parkas to be produced next year.) __________

9. Manuel Sosa is a single father. He tries to save 15% of his monthly salary for his son's education. In August, Manuel's salary was $4,800. How much should he save to meet his objective? __________

10. In September, Manuel Sosa got a promotion and a raise. Because his monthly expenses did not increase very much, Manuel was able to save more dollars. He saved $1,350, which was 25% of his new salary. How much was Manuel's new salary? __________

__________

Score for A (50)

**B (50 points) Solve the following problems. Round dollar amounts to the nearest cent. Round other amounts to the nearest tenth. Write rates as percents to the nearest tenth of a percent. (5 points for each correct answer)**

**11.** Norman Brewer, a paralegal, will receive a 4% salary increase this month. Hence he will receive $130 more salary this month than he received last month. What was Norman's salary last month? __________

**12.** Roberta Coke works in the marketing research department of a soft-drink company. Yesterday Roberta received a raise of $375 per month. Roberta now earns 6% more than she did before the raise. How much does she earn now? __________

**13.** A farmers' market is held downtown every Saturday. The volume has been increasing by about 3% every week. If the volume was $51,400 this week, what should the volume be next week? __________

**14.** Marcia Almeida works as a sales analyst for a toy manufacturer. She predicts that toy sales will decrease by 5% between May and June. If the amount of the sales decrease is $175,000, what level of sales is she predicting for June? __________

**15.** Last month, Fred Gerhardt started working as an apprentice machinist. One of his first projects was to reduce the diameter of a metal shaft from 0.180 inch to 0.162 inch. By what percent did he reduce the diameter of the shaft? __________

**16.** Judy Gregory, a mechanical engineer, was able to increase the efficiency of a manufacturing facility. By doing so, she decreased the cost to manufacture a commercial quality lawn mower by $18, which was 15% of the former cost. What will be the new reduced cost to manufacture the lawn mower? __________

**17.** Richard Phipps is the purchasing manager for a janitorial service. He orders all the supplies used by his company. Because of new contracts to clean three new office buildings, Richard ordered an additional $5,000 worth of supplies this month. This was an 8% increase from last month. What was the value of the supplies that Richard ordered last month? __________

**18.** Nancy Yamamoto owns a gift shop that had sales of $225,000 in November. Because of the Christmas holiday season, Nancy predicts that the shop will have a 250% increase in sales in December. What total sales is Nancy predicting for December? __________

**19.** Suppose that Yamamoto's Gift Shop had sales of $225,000 in November and then doubled its sales in December to $450,000. What would be the percent increase for December over November? __________

**20.** Because of Father's Day, Martin's Men's Store had sales of $450,000 in June. Sales decreased by $225,000 in July. What was the percent decrease in Martin's sales in July? __________

__________

Score for B (50)

# Assignment 5.4: Allocation of Overhead

Name ______________________________

Date ______________ Score ______________

Learning Objective 5

**A (20 points) Complete the square feet, percent, and allocation columns below. Round percents to the nearest whole number. (1 point for each correct answer in column 1; 2 points for each correct answer in columns 2 and 3)**

**1.** Gerry Sher owns small restaurants in four different towns: (a) Alleghany, (b) Delwood, (c) Bangor, and (d) Lakeside. She manages all four restaurants from a central office that she maintains at the Alleghany restaurant. Monthly office expenses are allocated among the four restaurants based on the floor space of each. In the following table, complete the allocation table for monthly expenses of $15,000.

| Store | Space Occupied | Square Feet | Percent of Total | Allocation of Expense |
|---|---|---|---|---|
| **(a)** Alleghany | 40 ft × 30 ft | ________ | ________ | ________ |
| **(b)** Delwood | 40 ft × 45 ft | ________ | ________ | ________ |
| **(c)** Bangor | 70 ft × 30 ft | ________ | ________ | ________ |
| **(d)** Lakeside | 60 ft × 40 ft | ________ | ________ | ________ |
| Total | | 7,500 | 100% | $15,000 |

______________
Score for A (20)

**B (16 points) Complete the percent and allocation columns in the following table. Before computing the allocation, round each percent to the nearest whole number. (2 points for each correct answer)**

**2.** Diane Kingsley owns a temporary services company. She employs four types of employees whom she places into temporary positions: (a) bookkeepers, (b) secretaries, (c) food service people, and (d) hotel service people. Diane rents office space for $5,200 per month. She allocates the rent among the four labor groups, according to the number of people employed in each group. Calculate the percents and the resulting allocations.

| | Number of Employees | Percent of Total | Allocation of Rent |
|---|---|---|---|
| **(a)** Bookkeepers | 18 | ________ | ________ |
| **(b)** Secretaries | 36 | ________ | ________ |
| **(c)** Food Service | 42 | ________ | ________ |
| **(d)** Hotel Service | 24 | ________ | ________ |
| Total | 120 | 100% | $5,200 |

______________
Score for B (16)

**C** **(64 points) The following situations provide practice in allocating monthly overhead expenses at a central office. From the information given in the following table, complete the allocations indicated in problems 3 through 6. Remember: Answers for each problem should sum to the total monthly overhead expense. (4 points for each correct answer)**

| Monthly Overhead Expense | | Basis of Allocation | Location | | | | |
|---|---|---|---|---|---|---|---|
| | | | East | West | North | South | TOTAL |
| Insurance | $20,000 | Square feet | 19,200 | 9,600 | 14,400 | 16,800 | 60,000 |
| Utilities | 15,000 | Machine hours worked | 18,000 | 14,400 | 10,800 | 28,800 | 72,000 |
| Rent | 26,000 | Units produced | 10,200 | 7,800 | 5,700 | 6,300 | 30,000 |
| Maintenance | 12,000 | Number of employees | 30 | 75 | 105 | 90 | 300 |

**3.** Allocate insurance expense based on the number of square feet at each location.
East __________; West __________; North __________; South __________ Check.

**4.** Allocate utilities expense based on the number of machine hours worked in each location.
East __________; West __________; North __________; South __________ Check.

**5.** Allocate rent expense based on the units produced at each location.
East __________; West __________; North __________; South __________ Check.

**6.** Allocate maintenance expense based on the number of employees at each location.
East __________; West __________; North __________; South __________ Check.

__________
Score for C (64)

# Commissions 6

## Learning Objectives

By studying this chapter and completing all assignments, you will be able to:

Learning Objective 1 Compute sales commissions and gross pay.

Learning Objective 2 Compute graduated sales commissions.

Learning Objective 3 Compute sales and purchases for principals.

A **commission** is a payment to an employee or to an agent for performing a business transaction or service. The most familiar type of commission is that received by a salesperson. Many companies have employees who are paid either totally or partially on a commission basis. People who sell insurance, real estate, and automobiles typically are in this category.

For a business owner, one advantage of using the commission method to pay employees is that the commission is an incentive. Employees are paid on the basis of the volume of business they produce for the company. They can earn more by being more productive.

Besides typical salespeople, other businesspeople provide selling and buying services. These include commission merchants, agents, and brokers, all of whom are paid a commission for their services. The person for whom the services are provided is called the **principal.** A commission merchant will normally take actual possession of the merchandise and make the sales transaction in his or her name. A **broker,** however, will usually make the transaction in the principal's name and will not take possession of the merchandise.

## Computing Sales Commissions and Gross Pay

**Learning Objective 1**

Compute sales commissions and gross pay.

A sales commission paid to a salesperson is usually a stated percent of the dollar value of the goods or services sold. Whether the commission is based on the wholesale or retail value of the goods will depend on the type of business and merchandise sold. The rate used to calculate the commission also will vary among different businesses. In some companies, the salesperson receives both some salary and a commission.

**STEPS to Compute Commission and Total Pay**

1. Multiply the commission rate by the amount sold to get the commission amount.
2. If there is a salary, add it to the commission amount to get the total gross pay.

**EXAMPLE A**

Kay Schiff sells yachts and marine equipment for Delta Marine Sales. She receives a base salary of \$3,000 per month and earns a commission that is 2% of the value of all boating equipment that she sells during the month. Find her commission and total pay during September, a month in which she sold \$132,000 worth of equipment.

STEP 1 $2\% \times \$132{,}000 = 0.02 \times \$132{,}000 = \$2{,}640$ commission

STEP 2 \$2,640 commission + \$3,000 base salary = \$5,640 total pay

Total sales are sometimes called **gross sales.** Commissions are normally paid on **net sales,** which are calculated by subtracting the amount of any returned goods, canceled orders, or other sales expenses. The reason for using net sales is to protect the business from loss or possible fraud. Suppose in example A, that Delta Marine Sales pays a 2% commission whether or not any goods are ever returned. Kay Schiff's commission on \$132,000 worth of merchandise is \$2,640. But if all of the merchandise is returned, or if the orders are all canceled, the company would lose \$2,640 by paying the commission.

## STEPS to Compute Commission When a Sale Involves Returned Goods

1. Subtract the value of the returned goods (or canceled orders) from the total sales to determine net sales.
2. Multiply the commission rate by net sales to get the commission amount.

### EXAMPLE B

Hobart Hamilton is a salesperson for Aggie Office Supply. He works on a commission-only basis—he receives a commission of 2.5% on his monthly sales, but no base salary. What are his commission and total pay during a month when he sells $166,000 worth of office products, but one of his customers cancels an order for $25,000?

STEP 1 $166,000 − $25,000 = $141,000 net sales

STEP 2 2.5% × $141,000 = 0.025 × $141,000 = $3,525 commission

Total Pay = $3,525, as he is paid on a commission-only basis

### CONCEPT CHECK 6.1

Compute the commission and gross pay for a salesperson who is paid a $1,800 salary and earns a 4% commission. Total sales were $88,000, but there were returns of $6,000.

$88,000 − $6,000 = $82,000 net sales

| | | |
|---|---|---|
| 4% × $82,000 = 0.04 × $82,000 = | $3,280 | commission |
| | + 1,800 | salary |
| | $5,080 | gross pay |

# Computing Graduated Sales Commissions

**Learning Objective 2**

Compute graduated sales commissions.

Commission plans provide incentives for employees because employees can earn more money by selling more products. A company can provide additional incentives for even greater productivity by using **graduated commission rates.** As the level of sales increases, so does the commission rate.

## STEPS to Compute Commission Under a Graduated Rate Plan

1. Compute the dollar amount at each rate level by using subtraction.
2. Multiply each level's commission rate by the level's sales dollars.
3. Add the products computed in Step 2 to determine the total commission.

## EXAMPLE C

Donna Chin has a monthly commission plan under which she receives 2% on the first $40,000 of sales during the month and 3% on sales above $40,000 for the month. If Donna has sales of $75,000 during a month, compute her commission for that month.

STEP 1

$$
\begin{array}{rl}
\$75,000 & \text{total sales} \\
-\ 40,000 & \text{at 2\%} \\
\hline
\$35,000 & \text{at 3\%}
\end{array}
$$

STEP 2

STEP 3

$$
\begin{array}{rl}
\$40,000 \times 0.02 = & \$\ \ 800 \\
35,000 \times 0.03 = & +\ 1,050 \\
\hline
\text{Total commission} = & \$1,850
\end{array}
$$

## EXAMPLE D

Assume that Donna has a monthly commission plan under which she receives 2% on the first $40,000 of sales during the month, 3% on sales from $40,000 to $80,000, and 4% on all sales over $80,000. If Donna has sales of $126,000 during a month, compute her commission for that month.

STEP 1

$$
\begin{array}{rl}
\$126,000 & \text{total sales} \\
-\ 40,000 & \text{at 2\%} \\
\hline
\$\ 86,000 & \\
-\ 40,000 & \text{at 3\%} \\
\hline
\$\ 46,000 & \text{at 4\%}
\end{array}
$$

STEP 2

STEP 3

$$
\begin{array}{rl}
\$40,000 \times 0.02 = & \$\ \ 800 \\
40,000 \times 0.03 = & 1,200 \\
46,000 \times 0.04 = & +\ 1,840 \\
\hline
\text{Total commission} = & \$3,840
\end{array}
$$

The same graduated incentive plan can be defined in terms of bonus rates. The calculations are similar.

## EXAMPLE E

Dale Crist has a monthly commission plan under which he receives 2% on all sales during the month. If Dale has sales over $40,000, he receives a bonus of 1% of everything over $40,000. If he sells more than $80,000, he receives a "super bonus" of an additional 1% of everything over $80,000. What is Dale's commission for a month during which he sold $126,000?

| | 0 | $40,000 | | $126,000 | |
|---|---|---|---|---|---|
| Base | | | | $126,000 | $0.02 \times$ $126,000 = \$2,520$ |
| Bonus | | | $126,000 - \$40,000 = \$86,000$ | | $0.01 \times$ $\$\ 86,000 = \ \ \ \ 860$ |
| Super Bonus | | | | $\$126,000 - \$80,000$ $= \$46,000$ | $0.01 \times$ $\$\ 46,000 = +\ 460$ |

Total commission (add the three commission amounts) = $3,840

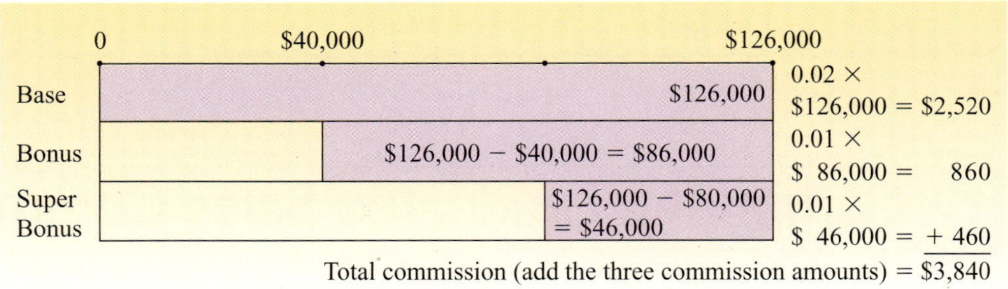

Observe that both example D and example E had a total commission of $3,840 on sales of $126,000. The two graduated incentive plans are identical except for the manner in which they are defined.

## CONCEPT CHECK 6.2

Compute the total commission on sales of $184,000. The commission is graduated: 1% on sales to $50,000, 2% on sales from $50,000 to $100,000, and 3% on sales above $100,000.

$184,000 − $50,000 − $50,000 = $84,000

| | | |
|---|---|---|
| 1% × $50,000 = 0.01 × $50,000 | = | $ 500 |
| 2% × $50,000 = 0.02 × $50,000 | = | 1,000 |
| 3% × $84,000 = 0.03 × $84,000 | = | 2,520 |
| Total commission | = | $4,020 |

# Computing Sales and Purchases for Principals

Learning Objective 3

Compute sales and purchases for principals.

A producer may send goods to an agent, often called a **commission merchant,** for sale at the best possible price. Such a shipment is a **consignment.** The party who sends the shipment is the **consignor;** the party to whom it is sent—that is, the commission merchant—is the **consignee.**

Whatever amount the commission merchant gets for the consignment is the **gross proceeds.** The commission amount is generally a certain percentage of the gross proceeds. Sometimes it is a certain amount per unit of weight or measure of the goods sold. The commission and any other sales expenses (e.g., transportation, advertising, storage, and insurance) are the **charges.** The charges are deducted from the gross proceeds. The resulting amount, which is sent to the consignor, is the **net proceeds.**

### EXAMPLE F

Jack Phelps, owner of Willowbrook Farms, has been trying to sell a used livestock truck and a used tractor. Unsuccessful after 3 months, Phelps consigns the items to Acme Equipment Brokers. They agree on commission rates of 6% of the gross proceeds from the truck and 9% of the gross proceeds from the tractor. Acme sells the truck for $42,500 and the tractor for $78,600. Acme also pays $610 to deliver the truck and $835 to deliver the tractor. What are the net proceeds due Willowbrook Farms from the sale of the equipment?

| | | | | |
|---|---|---|---|---|
| Truck: | Commission: 0.06 × $42,500 = | $2,550 | Gross proceeds: | $42,500 |
| | Freight: | + 610 | less charges | − 3,160 |
| | Total charges | $3,160 | Net Proceeds: | $39,340 |
| Tractor: | Commission: 0.09 × $78,600 = | $7,074 | Gross proceeds: | $78,600 |
| | Freight: | + 835 | less charges | − 7,909 |
| | Total charges | $7,909 | Net proceeds: | $70,691 |

$39,340 + $70,691 = $110,031 Total Net Proceeds

Along with a check for the net proceeds, the commission merchant sends the consignor a form known as an **account sales.** It is a detailed statement of the amount of the sales and the various deductions. Figure 6-1 shows a typical account sales form. Notice that the left side and the right side of the form balance at $121,100. The two sides should always balance.

**Figure 6-1 | Account Sales**

**ACME EQUIPMENT BROKERS**

August 16, 20-- NO. 67324

309 Sule Road, Wilbraham, MA 01095-2073

NAME Willowbrook Farms
ADDRESS 127 N. Kaye
Albany, GA 31704-5606

BELOW ARE ACCOUNT SALES OF Consignment No. 876
RECEIVED August 1, 20--
and sold for account of Same

| DATE | CHARGES | AMOUNT | DATE | SALES | AMOUNT |
|---|---|---|---|---|---|
| Aug. 16 | Freight (truck) | $ 610 | Aug. 10 | Truck | $42,500 |
| | 6% Commission (truck) | 2,550 | | | |
| | Net proceeds (truck) | 39,340 | 13 | Tractor | 78,600 |
| | | | | Gross proceeds | $121,100 |
| 16 | Freight (tractor) | 835 | | | |
| | 9% Commission (tractor) | 7,074 | | | |
| | Net proceeds (tractor) | 70,691 | | | |
| | Total | $121,100 | | | |

When commission merchants purchase goods for their principals, the price they pay for the merchandise is the **prime cost.** The prime cost and all charges are the **gross cost,** which is the cost the principal pays.

**EXAMPLE G**

Asia-Pacific Tours commissioned Specialty Marketing Group to purchase 10,000 vinyl travel bags that will be labeled with Asia-Pacific's logo and used as promotional items. For this size order, Specialty Marketing purchased the bags for $4.29 each. Charges included the commission, which was 6% of the prime cost; storage, $125; and freight, $168. What is the gross cost that Asia-Pacific should pay to Specialty Marketing?

| | | | |
|---|---|---|---|
| $ 4.29 | | $42,900 | prime cost |
| × 10,000 | units | × 0.06 | |
| $ 42,900 | prime cost | $ 2,574 | commission |

$2,574 commission + $125 storage + $168 freight = $2,867 charges
$42,900 prime cost + $2,867 charges = $45,767 gross cost

An **account purchase** is a detailed statement from the commission merchant to the principal. It shows the cost of goods purchased, including charges. Figure 6-2 shows a typical account purchase, for the transaction in example G.

**Figure 6-2** | **Account Purchase**

SPECIALTY MARKETING GROUP

4445 Mission Street
San Francisco, CA 94112

**ACCOUNT PURCHASE**
**NO.** 1311

October 26 20 --

Bought on Consignment for Asia-Pacific Tours
7300 Harbor Place
San Francisco, CA 94104

| DATE | DESCRIPTION | CHARGES | AMOUNT |
|---|---|---|---|
| Oct. 23 | 10,000 units stock #T805 @ $4.29 | | $42,900.00 |
| 23 | 6% commission | $2,574.00 | |
| | Storage | 125.00 | |
| | Freight | 168.00 | 2,867.00 |
| | Gross Cost | | $45,767.00 |

## CONCEPT CHECK 6.3

a. Compute the commission and the net proceeds on a consignment sale of $6,500. The commission rate is 5%, local delivery charges are $328.16, and storage charges are $125.

$5\% \times \$6,500 = 0.05 \times \$6,500 = \$325$ commission

$\$6,500 - \$325 - \$328.16 - \$125 = \$5,721.84$ net proceeds

b. Compute the commission and gross cost on a $12,500 purchase for a principal. The commission rate is 7%, air freight is $138.70, and local delivery charges are $64.60.

$7\% \times \$12,500 = 0.07 \times \$12,500 = \$875$ commission

$\$12,500 + \$875 + \$138.70 + \$64.60 = \$13,578.30$ gross cost

COMPLETE ASSIGNMENTS 6.1 AND 6.2.

## Chapter Terms for Review

account purchase
account sales
broker
charges
commission
commission merchant
consignee
consignment
consignor
graduated commission rates
gross cost
gross proceeds
gross sales
net proceeds
net sales
prime cost
principal

## Try Microsoft® Excel

Try working the problems using the Microsoft Excel templates found on your student CD. Solutions for the problems are also shown on the CD.

# THE BOTTOM LINE

*Summary of chapter learning objectives:*

| Learning Objective | Example |
|---|---|
| **6.1**<br><br>Compute sales commissions and gross pay. | 1. A salesperson gets a $1,750 salary and a 2.5% commission. Find the commission and the gross pay when sales are $58,400 and returns are $6,800. |
| **6.2**<br><br>Compute graduated sales commissions. | 2. A salesperson has a graduated commission rate: 1% on sales up to $100,000; 2% on sales from $100,000 to $200,000; and 2.5% on sales above $200,000. Find the commission when sales are $255,000. |
| **6.3**<br><br>Compute sales and purchases for principals. | 3. A broker sells a principal's merchandise at a gross sales price of $15,600 at a commission rate of 3.5%. There are sales costs of $300 for storage and $119 for delivery. Find the commission and net proceeds.<br>4. A commission merchant purchases merchandise for a principal at a prime cost of $8,400. The commission rate is 8%, air freight is $139, and local delivery is $75. Find the commission and gross cost. |

Answers: 1. Commission: $1,290; Gross pay: $3,040 2. $4,375 3. Commission: $546; Net proceeds: $14,635
4. Commission: $672; Gross cost: $9,286

# Review Problems for Chapter 6

**In problems 1–4, compute both the commission and the total pay based on the information given.**

1 Salary, $3,000; commission rate, 6%; total sales, $58,000; returns, $0

**a.** Commission __________ **b.** Total pay __________

2 Salary, $2,500; commission rate, 5%; total sales, $91,000; returns, $5,000

**a.** Commission __________ **b.** Total pay __________

3 Salary, $3,600; commission rate, 4.5%; total sales, $76,000; returns, $6,800

**a.** Commission __________ **b.** Total pay __________

4 Salary, $0; commission rate, 8%; total sales, $98,000; returns, $11,425

**a.** Commission __________ **b.** Total pay __________

5 Compute the total commission on sales of $160,000 if the commission rates are 3% on the first $100,000 and 5% on everything above $100,000. __________

6 Compute the total commission on sales of $85,000 if the commission rates are 3% on the first $100,000 and 5% on everything above $100,000. __________

7 Compute the total commission on sales of $250,000 if the commission rates are 2% on the first $75,000; then 3% on the next $75,000; and 4% on everything above $150,000. __________

8 Compute the total commission on sales of $135,000 if the commission rates are 2% on the first $75,000; then 3% on the next $75,000; and 4% on everything above $150,000. __________

9 Compute the total commission on sales of $70,000 if the commission rates are 2% on the first $75,000; then 3% on the next $75,000; and 4% on everything above $150,000. __________

10 Compute the total commission on sales of $115,000 if the commission rates are 4% on the first $35,000; then 6% on the next $45,000; and 8% on everything above $80,000. __________

11 Larry Leong is paid 2.5% on all sales. He is also paid a bonus of an additional 1.5% on any sales above $70,000. Calculate Larry's total commission on sales of $120,000. __________

12 Gloria Alvares is paid 4% on all sales. She is also paid a bonus of an additional 2% on any sales above $40,000. Calculate Gloria's total commission on sales of $105,000. __________

13 Charles White sells used logging equipment on consignment. He charges 20% commission plus expenses. Calculate Charles's commission on a log truck he sold for $42,750. __________

14 For the sale in problem 13, Charles also paid an additional $290 to deliver the truck to the new owner. Calculate the net proceeds that Charles's principal should receive. __________

15 Sue Lyon is a designer who purchases furniture for clients. She charges 15% of the price, plus expenses. Calculate Sue's commission on furniture priced at $21,400. __________

16 For the sale in problem 15, calculate the gross cost to the client if Sue also had expenses of $646. __________

**Answers to the Self-Check can be found in Appendix B at the back of the text.**

## Notes

# Assignment 6.1: Commission

Name ______________________________

Date __________ Score __________

Learning Objectives 1 2 3

**A** **(24 points) Find the commission and the total gross pay. (2 points for each correct answer)**

| Employee | Monthly Salary | Commission Rate | Monthly Sales | Commission | Gross Pay |
|---|---|---|---|---|---|
| **1.** Li, Walter | $ 0 | 8% | $45,000 | ______ | ______ |
| **2.** Starr, Karen | 2,000 | 3% | 36,000 | ______ | ______ |
| **3.** Aguire, Luis | 1,500 | 5% | 42,000 | ______ | ______ |
| **4.** Wallace, Fran | 2,650 | 2.5% | 58,000 | ______ | ______ |
| **5.** Rogerro, George | 1,800 | 6% | 64,000 | ______ | ______ |
| **6.** Tang, Suzanne | 2,500 | 4% | 57,000 | ______ | ______ |

______________
Score for A (24)

**B** **(36 points) Compute the total commission for the following commission payment plans. (6 points for each correct answer)**

| Graduated Commission Rates | Sales | Commission |
|---|---|---|
| **7.** 2% on sales to $60,000<br>4% on sales above $60,000 | $106,000 | ______ |
| **8.** 1% on sales to $150,000<br>2% on sales above $150,000 | $188,000 | ______ |
| **9.** 3% on sales to $50,000<br>5% on sales above $50,000 | $ 94,400 | ______ |
| **10.** 1% on sales to $75,000<br>2% on sales from $75,000 to $150,000<br>3% on sales above $150,000 | $240,000 | ______ |
| **11.** 3% on sales to $50,000<br>4% on sales from $50,000 to $100,000<br>5% on sales above $100,000 | $128,000 | ______ |

| | | | |
|---|---|---|---|
| **12.** | 2% on sales to $65,000<br>3% on sales from $65,000 to $130,000<br>4% on sales above $130,000 | $124,800 | ________ |

Score for B (36)

**C** **(20 points) Janet Cronin is a commission merchant. She charges different commission rates to sell different types of merchandise. During May, she completed the following consignment sales for consignors. Find Janet's commission on each sale and the net proceeds sent to each consignor. (2 points for each correct answer)**

| Gross Sales | Comm. Rate | Commission | Local Delivery | Storage | Air Freight | Net Proceeds |
|---|---|---|---|---|---|---|
| **13.** $38,400 | 3% | ________ | $ 68 | $ 0 | $183 | ________ |
| **14.** $1,600 | 4.5% | ________ | 88 | 65 | 0 | ________ |
| **15.** $8,400 | 6% | ________ | 284 | 0 | 0 | ________ |
| **16.** $12,880 | 5% | ________ | 0 | 0 | 148 | ________ |
| **17.** $14,100 | 7% | ________ | 75 | 85 | 112 | ________ |

Score for C (20)

**D** **(20 points) Alvin Guiterez, a commission merchant in Dallas, buys merchandise exclusively for principals. Listed below are five recent transactions. Compute Alvin's commission on each purchase and the gross cost. (2 points for each correct answer)**

| Prime Cost | Comm. Rate | Commission | Local Delivery | Storage | Air Freight | Gross Cost |
|---|---|---|---|---|---|---|
| **18.** $16,600 | 5% | ________ | $89 | $ 88 | $ 0 | ________ |
| **19.** $4,900 | 11% | ________ | 0 | 0 | 195 | ________ |
| **20.** $8,400 | 6% | ________ | 30 | 58 | 196 | ________ |
| **21.** $4,850 | 8% | ________ | 0 | 110 | 108 | ________ |
| **22.** $26,450 | 10% | ________ | 50 | 0 | 246 | ________ |

Score for D (20)

# Assignment 6.2: Applications with Commission

Name ______________________

Date ______________ Score ______________

Learning Objectives 1 2 3

**A** **(56 points) Solve each of the following business application problems involving salespeople who are paid partly or entirely on a commission basis. Solve the problems in order, because some of the questions are sequential. (8 points for each correct answer)**

**1.** Pat Endicot sells memberships to an athletic club. He receives a monthly salary of $2,150 plus a commission of 15% on new membership fees. What was Pat's monthly pay for May, when he sold new memberships valued at $27,500? ________

**2.** Roberta Reavis sells commercial restaurant supplies and equipment. She is paid on a commission-only basis. She receives 2% for her sales up to $60,000. For the next $90,000 of sales, she is paid 3%, and for any sales above $150,000 she is paid 4%. How much commission would Roberta earn in a month when her sales were $175,000? ________

**3.** Roberta Reavis (problem 2) is not paid commission on any restaurant supplies or equipment that are later returned. If an item is returned, its price is deducted from Roberta's total sales to get her net sales. The commission-only rate is applied to her net sales. Suppose that Roberta sold merchandise worth $175,000 but that $40,000 of that was later returned. What would be Roberta's commission on net sales? ________

**4.** Dana Kline works for Southwest Appliance Depot. She receives a monthly salary of $2,500 for which she must sell $20,000 worth of appliances. She also receives a commission of 4% on net sales above $20,000. What will be Dana's pay for October, when her net appliance sales were $42,000? ________

**5.** Southwest Appliance Depot (problem 4) offers service contracts with all appliance sales. To encourage salespeople such as Dana to sell more service contracts, the company pays a commission of 20% on all service contracts. What will be her total pay for a month if she sells $42,000 worth of appliances and $1,500 worth of service contracts? ________

**6.** Stockbrokers for many investment firms are paid a commission on the stocks that they buy and sell for their clients. Suppose that the commission rate is 0.5% of the value of the stock. What will the commission be on 5,000 shares of General Motors stock that is selling for $67.31 per share? ________

**7.** Michelle Sosa works in telemarketing. Her job is to make telephone calls from a computerized list of names and try to convince people to make an appointment with a life insurance salesperson. Michelle receives 40¢ for each completed telephone call, $7.00 for each appointment made and kept, and 1% of any initial revenue that results from the appointment. How much would Michelle earn if she completed 968 calls, 153 persons made and kept appointments, and $37,600 in revenue resulted from the appointments? ________

________
Score for A (56)

**B (24 points) Solve each of the following business applications about consignment sales and commission merchants. (8 points for each correct answer)**

**8.** Theresa Fowler is a commission merchant who charges a 15% commission to sell antique furniture from her showroom. Henry Marshal owns antique furniture, which he transports to her showroom where Theresa sells it for $9,600. Henry agrees to pay Theresa $488 to have the furniture delivered to the buyer from the showroom. What will be Henry's net proceeds from the sale? ________

**9.** Suppose, in problem 8, that payment of the $488 delivery expense was Theresa's responsibility instead of Henry's. Then what would be Theresa's net earnings from the sale? ________

**10.** Sandy McCulloch makes artistic weavings that are used as wall hangings. She sells her weavings primarily at open-air art shows and street fairs through her agent, Ruth Danielson. Ruth charges 20% on all sales, plus the fees to operate the sales booths and transportation expenses. After selling at four art shows, Ruth had total sales of $32,400. Each art show charged a booth fee of $500, and Ruth's total transportation expenses were $425. What were Sandy's net proceeds? ________

________
Score for B (24)

**C (20 points) The following problems involve the purchase of a home. (10 points for each correct answer)**

**11.** JoAnn Ednie has a condominium that she would like to sell and she asks real estate broker Gene Jenkins to sell it. Gene, co-owner of Jenkins/Weekly Real Estate, advises JoAnn that she should be able to sell her condominium for $180,000 and the commission rate for selling it will be 6%. If the condominium sells for the expected price, what will be the total commission amount that JoAnn pays? ________

**12.** See problem 11. To sell her condominium, JoAnn Ednie must also pay some additional fees for inspections, title insurance, and to record the sale. These fees total $3,500 and are added to the 6% commission. What will JoAnn's net proceeds be from the sale of her $180,000 condominium? ________

________
Score for C (20)

# Discounts

# 7

## Learning Objectives

By studying this chapter and completing all assignments, you will be able to:

Learning Objective **1** Compute trade discounts.

Learning Objective **2** Compute a series of trade discounts.

Learning Objective **3** Compute the equivalent single discount rate for a series of trade discounts.

Learning Objective **4** Compute cash discounts and remittance amounts for fully paid invoices.

Learning Objective **5** Compute cash discounts and remittance amounts for partially paid invoices.

When one business sells merchandise to another business, the seller often offers two types of discounts: trade discounts and cash discounts. Trade discounts affect the agreed-upon selling price *before* the sale happens. Cash discounts affect the amount actually paid *after* the transaction.

# Computing Trade Discounts

**Learning Objective 1**

Compute trade discounts.

Businesses that sell products want to attract and keep customers who make repeated, large-volume, more expensive purchases. Manufacturers, distributors, and wholesalers frequently offer **trade discounts** to buyers "in the trade," generally based on the volume purchased. For example, Eastern Restaurant Supply gives a 40% discount to Regal Meals, a local chain of 34 sidewalk sandwich carts that sell hot dogs and sausage sandwiches. Another Eastern customer is Suzi Wilson, founder and owner of Suzi's Muffins. Suzi's business is still small. She bakes her muffins between 11 P.M. and 2 A.M. in oven space that she leases from a bakery. Eastern gives Suzi only a 25% discount because she doesn't do as much business with Eastern as Regal Meals does. Eastern also sells to people who are not "in the trade." These retail customers pay the regular **list price,** or full price without any discount.

Large restaurant chains such as McDonald's and Burger King can go directly to the manufacturer for most items or even do their own manufacturing. They can have items manufactured to their exact specifications for a contracted price. They reduce their costs by eliminating the distributors (the "middle men").

The two traditional methods for computing trade discounts are the discount method and the complement method. You can use both methods to find the **net price** that a distributor will charge the customer after the discount. The **discount method** is useful when you want to know both the net price and the actual amount of the trade discount. The **complement method** is used to find only the net price. It gets its name because you use the **complement rate,** which is 100% minus the discount rate. Each method has only two steps.

**STEPS to Compute Net Price with the Discount Method**

1. Multiply the discount rate by the list price to get the discount amount:
   Discount = Trade discount rate × List price
2. Subtract the discount from the list price to get the net price:
   Net price = List price − Discount

**EXAMPLE A**

Eastern Restaurant Supply sells a set of stainless steel trays to Suzi's Muffins. The list price is $120, and Suzi qualifies for a 25% trade discount. Compute the net price using the discount method.

STEP 1 Discount = 0.25 × $120 = $30

STEP 2 Net price = $120 − $30 = $90

**STEPS to Compute Net Price with the Complement Method**

1. Subtract the discount rate from 100% to get the complement rate:
   Complement rate = 100% − Trade discount rate
2. Multiply the complement rate by the list price to get the net price:
   Net price = Complement rate × List price

**EXAMPLE B**

Using the data in example A, compute the net price, using the complement method.

STEP 1 Complement rate = 100% − 25% = 75%

STEP 2 Net price = 0.75 × $120 = $90

**CONCEPT CHECK 7.1**

a. Compute the trade discount amount and the net price, using the discount method.

List price = $240 Trade discount = 30%
Discount amount = 0.30 × $240 = $72
Net price = $240 − $72 = $168

b. Compute the complement rate and the net price, using the complement method.

List price = $240 Trade discount = 30%
Complement rate = 100% − 30% = 70%
Net price = 0.70 × $240 = $168

## Computing a Series of Trade Discounts

Learning Objective 2

Compute a series of trade discounts.

A distributor or manufacturer may give additional discounts to customers who actually buy larger volumes. Suppose that Eastern Restaurant Supply gives all food preparation businesses a 25% discount for being in the trade. However, if one business buys twice as much from Eastern, it may be rewarded with additional discounts. For example, Suzi's Muffins may receive its first discount of 25% automatically. Then, Suzi's gets an additional 20% discount if its accumulated purchases were between $10,000 and $25,000 during the previous year and another 10% if accumulated purchases were more than $25,000 during the previous year. Therefore, Suzi's Muffins could have discounts of 25%, 20%, and 10%, called a **series of discounts.**

Both the discount method and the complement method can be used to compute the net price for a series of discounts. *The two methods are the same as shown previously, except that the steps are repeated for each discount in the series.* For example, if there are three discounts, repeat the steps three times. Apply the first **discount rate** to the list price. For the second and third discounts, compute intermediate prices and then apply the discount rates to them.

**EXAMPLE C**

Eastern Restaurant Supply sells a set of mixing bowls with a list price of $200. Suzi's Muffins qualifies for the series of discounts: 25%, 20%, 10%. Compute the net price using the discount method.

| | First Discount | Second Discount | Third Discount |
|---|---|---|---|
| STEP 1 | $0.25 \times \$200 = \$50$ | $0.20 \times \$150 = \$30$ | $0.10 \times \$120 = \$12$ |
| STEP 2 | $\$200 - \$50 = \$150$ | $\$150 - \$30 = \$120$ | $\$120 - \$12 = \$108$ |

**EXAMPLE D**

Using the data in example C, calculate the net price using the complement method.

| | First Discount | Second Discount | Third Discount |
|---|---|---|---|
| STEP 1 | $100\% - 25\% = 75\%$ | $100\% - 20\% = 80\%$ | $100\% - 10\% = 90\%$ |
| STEP 2 | $0.75 \times \$200 = \$150$ | $0.80 \times \$150 = \$120$ | $0.90 \times \$120 = \$108$ |

## COMPLEMENT METHOD SHORTCUT

When using complement rates, the buyer may not need to know all of the intermediate prices. If not, an efficient shortcut is to multiply the list price by all of the complement rates successively.

**EXAMPLE E**

Repeat example D, using the shortcut. The list price is $200, and the discounts are 25%, 20%, and 10%. The complement rates are 75%, 80%, and 90%.

Net price $= \$200 \times 0.75 \times 0.80 \times 0.90 = \$108$

*Note:* Remember that there should be *no rounding* until you reach the final net price. Then round it to the nearest cent.

## CONCEPT CHECK 7.2

a. A wholesaler offers a series of trade discounts: 30%, 25%, and 10%. Find each of the discount amounts and the final net price on a $1,500 purchase.

| | |
|---|---|
| First discount amount: | $\$1{,}500 \times 0.30 = \$450$ |
| Second discount amount: | $\$1{,}500 - \$450 = \$1{,}050$; $\$1{,}050 \times 0.25 = \$262.50$ |
| Third discount amount: | $\$1{,}050 - \$262.50 = \$787.50$; $\$787.50 \times 0.10 = \$78.75$ |
| Net price: | $\$787.50 - \$78.75 = \$708.75$ |

b. A series of trade discounts is 30%, 25%, and 10%. Find each of the complement rates, and use the shortcut to calculate the final net price on a purchase of $1,500.

| | |
|---|---|
| First complement rate: | $100\% - 30\% = 70\%$ |
| Second complement rate: | $100\% - 25\% = 75\%$ |
| Third complement rate: | $100\% - 10\% = 90\%$ |
| Net price: | $\$1{,}500 \times 0.70 \times 0.75 \times 0.90 = \$708.75$ |

# Computing the Equivalent Single Discount Rate

Learning Objective 3

Compute the equivalent single discount rate for a series of trade discounts.

Suppose that an Eastern competitor, United Food Services, offers a single discount of 45% to Suzi's Muffins. How does that rate compare to the series of discounts from Eastern, 25%, 20%, and 10%? Suzi or her accountant could check by calculating the **equivalent single discount rate,** which is the single discount rate that can be used in place of two or more trade discount rates to determine the same discount amount.

The most efficient way to find the single discount rate that is equivalent to a series of discounts is similar to the shortcut used in example E.

## STEPS to Compute the Equivalent Single Discount Rate

1. Compute the complement of each rate.
2. Multiply all the complement rates (as decimals), and then write the product as a percent.
3. Subtract the product (Step 2) from 100% to get the equivalent single discount rate.

### EXAMPLE F

Find the equivalent single discount rate for Eastern's series of discounts: 25%, 20%, and 10%.

| | | |
|---|---|---|
| STEP 1 | First complement rate | = 100% − 25% = 75% |
| | Second complement rate | = 100% − 20% = 80% |
| | Third complement rate | = 100% − 10% = 90% |
| STEP 2 | Product of complements | = 0.75 × 0.80 × 0.90 = 54% |
| STEP 3 | Equivalent single discount | = 100% − 54% = 46% |

## CONCEPT CHECK 7.3

A series of trade discounts is 50%, 30%, and 10%. Find the three complement rates and then find the equivalent single trade discount rate.

| | |
|---|---|
| Complement rates: | 100% − 50% = 50%, 100% − 30% = 70%, 100% − 10% = 90% |
| Product of the complement rates: | 0.50 × 0.70 × 0.90 = 0.315, or 31.5% |
| Equivalent single discount rate: | 100% − 31.5% = 68.5% |

COMPLETE ASSIGNMENT 7.1.

# Computing Cash Discounts for Fully Paid Invoices

**Learning Objective 4**

Compute cash discounts and remittance amounts for fully paid invoices.

When a seller sends merchandise to a buyer, the seller usually wants to receive its payment quickly, and some buyers often try to delay payment as long as possible. Sellers can encourage early payment by offering a **cash discount;** they can discourage late payment by assessing an extra interest payment; or they can do both. These stipulations are called the **terms of payment,** or simply the *terms.* The terms describe details about cash discounts and/or penalty periods.

After shipping merchandise to a buyer, the seller usually sends a document called an invoice, requesting payment. An **invoice** lists each item, its cost (including packaging and freight), and the total cost. The invoice also states the terms of payment. The amount the buyer pays is called the **remittance.** The **net purchase amount** is the price of the merchandise actually purchased, including allowances for returns and excluding handling and other costs.

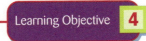

**STEPS to Compute the Remittance**

1. Multiply the discount rate by the net purchase amount to get the cash discount:
   Cash discount = Discount rate × Net purchase amount
2. Subtract the cash discount from the net purchase amount to get the remittance:
   Remittance = Net purchase amount − Cash discount

Figure 7-1 shows an invoice from National Automotive Supply, which sold car wax to Broadway Motors for $528. The wax will be shipped via UPS, and National will pay for the shipping. The invoice lists terms of 2/10, n/30. The **invoice date,** or the beginning of the discount period, is May 23.

**Video**

Cash Discounts

**Figure 7-1** Sales Invoice

NATIONAL AUTOMOTIVE SUPPLY

INVOICE NO. 782535

SOLD TO Broadway Motors
730 W. Columbia Dr.
Peoria, IL 62170-1184

DATE May 23, 20--
TERMS 2/10, n/30
SHIP VIA UPS

| QUANTITY | DESCRIPTION | UNIT PRICE | GROSS AMOUNT | NET AMOUNT |
|---|---|---|---|---|
| 24 gals. | Car wax | $22.00 | $528.00 | $528.00 |

The expression *2/10, n/30* means that Broadway Motors can get a 2% discount if it pays the full invoice within 10 days of the invoice date. Ten days after May 23 is June 2, which is called the **discount date.** The 10-day period between May 23 and June 2 is called the **discount period.** The n/30 is short for net 30, which means that if Broadway Motors does not pay within 30 days, National will charge an interest penalty. Thirty days after May 23 is June 22, which is called the **due date.** (See Figure 7-2.)

**Figure 7-2** **Cash Discount Time Line**

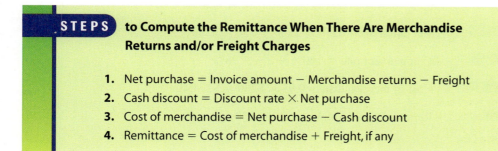

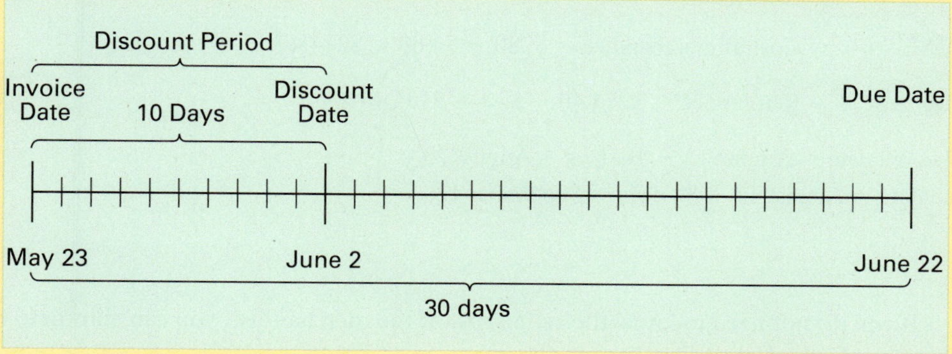


**EXAMPLE G**

Compute the remittance due if Broadway Motors pays National for the $528 invoice amount within the 10-day discount period under the terms 2/10, n/30.

STEP 1 Cash discount = 2% of $528 = 0.02 × $528 = $10.56

STEP 2 Remittance = $528 − $10.56 = $517.44

All companies do not use exactly the same notation for writing their terms; 2/10, n/30 is also written as 2/10, net 30 or as 2-10, n-30. Likewise, there can be more than one discount rate and discount period. For example 2/5, 1/15, n/30 means that the seller gets a 2% discount by paying within 5 days, gets a 1% discount by paying within 6 and 15 days, and must pay a penalty after 30 days. To teach different notations, this book will present cash discounts in various ways.

## RETURNED MERCHANDISE AND FREIGHT CHARGES

The seller gives a discount only on merchandise that is actually purchased—the net purchases. For example, there is no discount on returned items. Likewise, there is no discount on charges from a third party, such as freight.

**STEPS to Compute the Remittance When There Are Merchandise Returns and/or Freight Charges**

1. Net purchase = Invoice amount − Merchandise returns − Freight
2. Cash discount = Discount rate × Net purchase
3. Cost of merchandise = Net purchase − Cash discount
4. Remittance = Cost of merchandise + Freight, if any

**EXAMPLE H**

National Automotive Supply sells merchandise to Broadway Motors. The invoice amount is \$510, which includes \$30 in freight charges. The invoice date is August 13, and the terms are 2/10, n/30. Broadway Motors returns \$200 worth of merchandise and pays the rest of the invoice before the discount date. Compute the cash discount and the remittance. Also, determine the discount date and due date.

STEP 1 Net purchase = \$510 − \$200 − \$30 = \$280

STEP 2 Cash discount = 0.02 × \$280 = \$5.60

STEP 3 Cost of merchandise = \$280 − \$5.60 = \$274.40

STEP 4 Remittance = \$274.40 + \$30 = \$304.40

Discount date = August 13 + 10 days = August 23
Due date = August 13 + 30 days = September 12

© MANCHAN/DIGITALVISION/GETTY IMAGES

If you do not need to know the actual cost of the merchandise, you can eliminate Step 3 and calculate the remittance directly:

Remittance = \$280.00 − \$5.60 + \$30.00 = \$304.40

There is also a complement method for cash discounts. However, it is not used universally because some businesses want to know the amount of the cash discount before deciding whether to pay the invoice early. In the complement method for cash discounts, only Steps 2 and 3 change.

**STEPS to Compute the Remittance with the Complement Method**

1. Net purchase = Invoice amount − Merchandise returns − Freight
2. Complement rate = 100% − Cash discount rate
3. Cost of merchandise = Net purchase × Complement rate
4. Remittance = Cost of merchandise + Freight, if any

**EXAMPLE I**

Solve example H by using the complement method for cash discounts. The invoice amount is \$510, merchandise returns are \$200, and freight is \$30.

STEP 1 Net purchase = \$510 − \$200 − \$30 = \$280

STEP 2 Complement rate = 100% − 2% = 98%

STEP 3 Cost of merchandise = 0.98 × \$280 = \$274.40

STEP 4 Remittance = \$274.40 + \$30 = \$304.40

## CONCEPT CHECK 7.4

a. Use the given information to calculate the discount date, due date, cash discount, and remittance.

| | | |
|---|---|---|
| Terms: | 1/10, n/60 | Discount date = August 24 + 10 days = September 3 |
| Invoice date: | August 24 | Due date = August 24 + 60 days = October 23 |
| Invoice amount: | \$852.43 | Net purchases = \$852.43 − \$187.23 − \$47.20 = \$618.00 |
| Returned goods: | \$187.23 | Cash discount = 0.01 × \$618 = \$6.18 |
| Freight: | \$47.20 | Remittance = \$618 − \$6.18 + \$47.20 = \$659.02 |

b. Calculate the remittance for the problem in part (a), using the complement method.

Net purchases = \$852.43 − \$187.23 − \$47.20 = \$618.00
Complement rate = 100% − 1% = 99%
Cost of merchandise = 0.99 × \$618 = \$611.82
Remittance = \$611.82 + \$47.20 = \$659.02

# Computing Cash Discounts for Partially Paid Invoices

Sometimes a buyer would like to take advantage of a cash discount but can afford to pay only part of the invoice within the discount period. If the seller allows discounts for partial payment, the invoice will be reduced by the amount paid (remittance) plus the amount of the discount. The total of the amount paid plus the amount of cash discount is called the **amount credited** to the buyer's account. To compute the amount credited, you need to know the complement rate: 100% − Discount rate.

**Learning Objective 5**

Compute cash discounts and remittance amounts for partially paid invoices.

### STEPS to Compute the Unpaid Balance

1. Compute the complement of the discount rate (100% − Discount rate).
2. Compute the amount credited by dividing the dollar amount paid (remittance) by the complement rate.
3. Compute the unpaid balance by subtracting the amount credited (Step 2) from the invoice amount.

**EXAMPLE J**

Larry Eickworth operates a shop called Space Savers, a do-it-yourself center for closet and storage materials. Larry buys shelving supplies with an invoice price of \$484 and terms of 2/10, net 60. Within the 10-day discount period, he sends in a check for \$300. With a discount for the partial payment, how much credit should Larry receive, and what will be his new unpaid balance?

STEP 1 Complement rate = 100% − 2% = 98%

STEP 2 Amount credited = \$300 ÷ 0.98 = \$306.1224, or \$306.12

STEP 3 Unpaid balance = \$484.00 − \$306.12 = \$177.88

Note that, in example J, Larry receives \$1.00 credit for every \$0.98 paid. In other words, the \$300 actually remitted is 98% of the total amount credited. We can check this result with multiplication:

Cash discount = 0.02 × \$306.12 = \$6.1224, or \$6.12
Remittance = \$306.12 − \$6.12 = \$300.00

A slightly different situation, which arises less frequently, is when a buyer decides in advance the total amount that he or she wants to have credited to the account. This problem is exactly like the original cash discount problems.

**EXAMPLE K**

Larry Eickworth buys \$484 worth of shelving materials for use in his closet and storage shop. The terms are 2/10, net 60. Larry wants to pay enough within the 10-day discount period to reduce his unpaid balance by exactly \$300. What amount should he remit to the seller? What will be his new unpaid balance?

STEP 1 Cash discount = 2% × \$300 = \$6

STEP 2 Remittance = \$300 − \$6 = \$294

STEP 3 Unpaid balance = \$484 − \$300 = \$184

## CONCEPT CHECK 7.5

a. An invoice for \$476 has terms of 1/15, net 25. How much is the unpaid balance after a \$350 remittance is made within the discount period?
Complement rate = 100% − 1% = 99%
Amount credited = \$350 ÷ 0.99 = \$353.54
Unpaid balance = \$476.00 − \$353.54 = \$122.46

b. An invoice for \$476 has terms of 1/15, net 25. What size remittance should be made in order to have a total of \$350 credited to the account?
Cash discount = \$350 × 0.01 = \$3.50
Remittance = \$350.00 − \$3.50 = \$346.50

COMPLETE ASSIGNMENT 7.2.

## Chapter Terms for Review

amount credited
cash discount
complement method
complement rate
discount date
discount method
discount period
discount rate
due date
equivalent single discount rate
invoice
invoice date
list price
net price
net purchase amount
remittance
series of discounts
terms of payment
trade discounts

## Try Microsoft® Excel

Try working the problems using the Microsoft Excel templates found on your student CD. Solutions for the problems are also shown on the CD.

1. Find the required remittance for goods with a list price of \$240, a trade discount of 25%, and a cash discount of 5%.

   The formula is List Price × (1 − Trade Discount %) × (1 − Cash Discount %) = Remittance. Enter the values in the columns as labeled, and enter the formula in the Remittance cell. Format the Remittance cell for Currency with two digits after the decimal point.

| List Price | Trade Discount | Cash Discount | Remittance |
|---|---|---|---|
| | | | |

2. What is the net price for goods with a list price of \$2,200, a trade discount of 40%, and another trade discount of 25%?

| List Price | Trade Discount | Trade Discount | Net Price |
|---|---|---|---|
| | | | |

3. What is the net price for goods with a list price of \$1,650, a trade discount of 30%, and another trade discount of 20%?

| List Price | Trade Discount | Trade Discount | Net Price |
|---|---|---|---|
| | | | |

# THE BOTTOM LINE

*Summary of chapter learning objectives:*

| Learning Objective | Example |
|---|---|
| **7.1**<br><br>Compute trade discounts. | 1. Find the net price on a list price of $280 with a 25% trade discount, using the discount and the complement methods. |
| **7.2**<br><br>Compute a series of trade discounts. | 2. Find the net price on a list price of $800 with a series of trade discounts of 25% and 10%. Use both the discount method and the complement method. |
| **7.3**<br><br>Compute the equivalent single discount rate for a series of trade discounts. | 3. A series of trade discounts is 25%, 20%, 15%. Use complement rates to find the equivalent single discount rate. |
| **7.4**<br><br>Compute cash discounts and remittance amounts for fully paid invoices. | An invoice is dated May 26 and has terms of 2/10, n/25. The total invoice is $826.44, with $108.12 of returned goods and $67.37 freight.<br><br>4. Compute the discount date, due date, cash discount, and remittance.<br>5. Compute the remittance using the complement rate. |
| **7.5**<br><br>Compute cash discounts and remittance amounts for partially paid invoices. | An invoice for $500 has terms of 3/5, net 45.<br><br>6. Compute the unpaid balance after a $400 payment within the discount period.<br>7. Compute the remittance required within the discount period in order to have $400 credited to the account. |

Answers: 1. Discount method: $280 − $70 = $210; complement method: 0.75 × $280 = $210
2. Discount method: $800 − $200 = $600, $600 − $60 = $540; complement method: 0.75 × 0.90 × $800 = $540
3. 49% 4. Discount date: June 5; due date: June 20; cash discount: $13.02; remittance: $705.30 5. $705.30
6. $87.63 7. $388.00

SELF-CHECK

# Review Problems for Chapter 7

**In problems 1 and 2, use the discount method to compute the missing terms.**

1 List price, $760; trade discount, 25%

a. Discount amount _________

b. Net price _________

2 List price, $1,200; trade discounts, 30% and 20%

a. First discount amount _________

b. Second discount amount _________

c. Net price _________

**In problems 3 and 4, use the complement method to compute the missing terms.**

3 List price, $875; trade discount, 40%

a. Complement rate _________

b. Net price _________

4 List price, $1,800; trade discounts, 30% and 15%

a. First complement rate _________

b. Second complement rate _________

c. Net price _________

5 Patty Duncan is a broker of hotel rooms in Europe. To tour directors, she offers a standard trade discount of 40% off the list price. She has additional discounts of 20% and 10%, which are based on the number of tours in a season and the total number of tourists. Compute the equivalent single discount rate for a major tour organizer, Kristi Atchison, who qualifies for all three discounts.

a. First complement rate _________

b. Second complement rate _________

c. Third complement rate _________

d. Equivalent single discount rate _________

**Use the invoice information given in problems 6 and 7 to compute the missing terms.**

6

| | |
|---|---|
| Terms: | 2/10, n/30 |
| Invoice Date: | July 25 |
| Invoice Amount: | $874.55 |
| Freight: | 0 |
| Returned Goods: | 0 |

a. Discount date _________

b. Due date _________

c. Discount amount _________

d. Remittance _________

7

| | |
|---|---|
| Terms: | 3/5, net 45 |
| Invoice Date: | December 28 |
| Invoice Amount: | $2,480 |
| Freight: | $143 |
| Returned Goods: | $642 |

a. Discount date _________

b. Due date _________

c. Complement rate _________

d. Remittance _________

8 Joyce Thompson purchased some new pieces of office furniture for her Internet consulting firm. The invoice amount was $16,540 with terms of 2/10, net 60 and the discount would apply to any partial payment made within the discount period. Joyce sent in a check for $10,000 by the discount date. Find: (a) the amount credited to Joyce's account _________; and (b) the unpaid balance _________.

**Answers to the Self-Check can be found in Appendix B at the back of the text.**

## Notes

# Assignment 7.1: Trade Discounts

Name

Date Score

Learning Objectives 1 2 3

**A** **(24 points) Problems 1–3: Find the dollar amount of the trade discount and the net price, using the discount method. Problems 4–6: Find the complement rate and the net price, using the complement method. (2 points for each correct answer)**

| Trade Discount | List Price | Discount Amount | Net Price |
|---|---|---|---|
| **1.** 35% | $1,260 | ______ | ______ |
| **2.** 30% | $6,470 | ______ | ______ |
| **3.** 25% | $8,480 | ______ | ______ |

| Trade Discount | List Price | Complement Rate | Net Price |
|---|---|---|---|
| **4.** 30% | $1,670 | ______ | ______ |
| **5.** 20% | $6,990 | ______ | ______ |
| **6.** 35% | $4,720 | ______ | ______ |

Score for A (24)

**B** **(16 points) Find the amount of each discount in the given series of trade discounts. Then find the net price. Where a discount amount doesn't exist write a dash. (2 points for each correct answer)**

| List Price | Trade Discounts | Trade Discount Amounts: First | Second | Third | Net Price |
|---|---|---|---|---|---|
| **7.** $2,400 | 30%, 25% | ______ | ______ | ______ | ______ |
| **8.** $1,600 | 40%, 25%, 20% | ______ | ______ | ______ | ______ |

Score for B (16)

**C** **(20 points) Find the complement rate for each discount in the given series of trade discounts. Then find the net price, using the complement method. Where a complement rate doesn't exist write a dash. (2.5 points for each correct answer)**

| | List Price | Trade Discounts | Complement Rates First | Second | Third | Net Price |
|---|---|---|---|---|---|---|
| **9.** | $1,800 | 40%, 20% | ________ | ________ | ________ | ________ |
| **10.** | $2,000 | 40%, 20%, 10% | ________ | ________ | ________ | ________ |

Score for C (20)

**D** **(20 points) Find the complement rate for each discount in the given series of trade discounts. Then find the equivalent single discount rate, to the nearest $\frac{1}{10}$ of a percent. (2.5 points for each correct answer)**

| | Trade Discounts | Complement Rates First | Second | Third | Equivalent Single Discount Rates |
|---|---|---|---|---|---|
| **11.** | 30%, 20%, 5% | ________ | ________ | ________ | ________ |
| **12.** | 20%, 10%, 5% | ________ | ________ | ________ | ________ |

Score for D (20)

**E** **(20 points) Solve each of the following business applications about trade discounts. Use either the discount method or the complement method. (10 points for each correct answer)**

**13.** Gifford Landscaping, Inc., purchased $425 worth of plants and $180 worth of soil and fertilizer from a garden supply wholesaler. The wholesaler gives Gifford a 20% trade discount on the plants and a 30% trade discount on the other items. Compute the net price that Gifford Landscaping will be required to pay. ______

**14.** Hackett Roofing is purchasing redwood shakes to reroof a house. The shakes have a list price of $15,600. The Pacific Roofing Supply Company gives Hackett the normal trade discount of 25%. In addition, Pacific gives Hackett two further trade discounts of 20% and 10% because of the large volume of business that the company has done with Pacific so far this year. What is Hackett's net price on the order of redwood shakes? ________

Score for E (20)

# Assignment 7.2: Cash Discounts

Name ______________________

Date __________ Score __________

Learning Objectives 4 5

**A** **(64 points) For the following problems, find the discount date, the due date, the amount of the cash discount, and the amount of the remittance. (2 points for each correct date and 6 points for each correct amount)**

**1.**

| | | | |
|---|---|---|---|
| Terms: | 3/5, n/25 | Discount date: | ________ |
| Invoice date: | May 27 | Due date: | ________ |
| Invoice amount: | $2,875.12 | Discount amount: | ________ |
| | | Remittance: | ________ |

**2.**

| | | | |
|---|---|---|---|
| Terms: | 2/10, n/30 | Discount date: | ________ |
| Invoice date: | July 23 | Due date: | ________ |
| Invoice amount: | $484.86 | Discount amount: | ________ |
| Freight: | $45.00 | Remittance: | ________ |

**3.**

| | | | |
|---|---|---|---|
| Terms: | 1.5/15, net 45 | Discount date: | ________ |
| Invoice date: | Aug. 20 | Due date: | ________ |
| Invoice amount: | $692.00 | Discount amount: | ________ |
| Returned goods: | $242.00 | Remittance: | ________ |

**4.**

| | | | |
|---|---|---|---|
| Terms: | 1.5/20, n/60 | Discount date: | ________ |
| Invoice date: | July 26 | Due date: | ________ |
| Invoice amount: | $1,645.55 | Discount amount: | ________ |
| Returned goods: | $498.75 | Remittance: | ________ |
| Freight: | $80.00 | | |

________
Score for A (64)

**B** **(16 points) For the following problems, find the discount date, the complement rate, and the amount of the remittance. (2 points for each date and rate; 4 points for each correct remittance)**

**5.** Terms: 2/10, n/35 — Discount date: ________
Invoice date: March 29 — Complement rate: ________
Invoice amount: $582.50 — Remittance: ________

**6.** Terms: 1/25, net 75 — Discount date: ________
Invoice date: July 9 — Complement rate: ________
Invoice amount: $2,684.92 — Remittance: ________
Returned goods: $171.12
Freight: $45.00

________
Score for B (16)

**C** **(20 points) The following problems involve partial payments made within the discount period. Solve for the items indicated. (5 points for each correct answer)**

**7.** Terms: 4/5, n/20 — Amount credited: ________
Invoice date: Feb. 28 — Remittance: $600
Invoice amount: $981.94 — Unpaid balance: ________

**8.** Terms: 2/15, net 40 — Amount credited: ________
Invoice date: Feb. 15 — Remittance: $500
Invoice amount: $832.90 — Unpaid balance: ________
Returned goods: $186.00

________
Score for C (20)

# Markup

# 8

## Learning Objectives

By studying this chapter and completing all assignments, you will be able to:

Learning Objective **1** Compute the variables in the basic markup formula.

Learning Objective **2** Compute the markup variables when the markup percent is based on cost.

Learning Objective **3** Compute markup percent based on cost.

Learning Objective **4** Compute the markup variables when the markup percent is based on selling price.

Learning Objective **5** Compute markup percent based on selling price.

# Computing Markup Variables

Learning Objective 1

Compute the variables in the basic markup formula.

Some businesses manufacture products and sell them. Other businesses buy products from someone else and then resell them. Both types of businesses must sell their products for more than it costs to produce or purchase them. This price increase is called the **markup.**

Athletes' World is a chain of retail stores that sells athletic equipment and athletic clothing. The store buys shoes directly from a manufacturer. Suppose that the manufacturer charges $43.00 per pair for one particular type of athletic shoe. The prorated amount to deliver one pair to the store is $0.50. The total cost of the shoes, with delivery, is $43.50. $43.50 is called the **cost of goods sold,** or just the cost.

If Athletes' World sells the shoes for exactly the cost, $43.50, it will actually lose money on the sale. The store has many other expenses—such as rent, utilities, and salaries—that are not part of the cost of acquiring the shoes. Athletes' World must mark up the selling price far enough above the cost of the shoes to cover all these additional costs—and also leave some profit for the owners.

The total amount that Athletes' World marks up the selling price is called the **dollar markup.** (*Note:* Markup is expressed both in dollars and in percents. To eliminate confusion, in this book we use two separate terms: *dollar markup* and *markup percent.*)

Suppose that the accountants for Athletes' World estimate that $18.80 of additional expenses should be allocated to each pair of athletic shoes. Also, suppose that the store would like a profit of $16.00 on each pair of shoes. Then the total dollar markup that it should give the shoes is $\$18.80 + \$16.00 = \$34.80$.

To determine the selling price of the shoes, Athletes' World adds the dollar markup to the cost of goods sold (cost), using the basic markup formula:

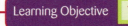

© MICHAEL CONROY/ASSOCIATED PRESS

$$\text{Selling price} = \text{Cost} + \text{Dollar markup} = \$43.50 + \$34.80 = \$78.30$$

Because the dollar markup is the difference between the selling price and the cost of goods sold, it is sometimes useful to rewrite the formula as

$$\text{Dollar markup} = \text{Selling price} - \text{Cost} = \$78.30 - \$43.50 = \$34.80$$

Likewise, cost is the difference between selling price and dollar markup. Thus,

$$\text{Cost} = \text{Selling price} - \text{Dollar markup} = \$78.30 - \$34.80 = \$43.50$$

## CONCEPT CHECK 8.1

Compute the missing terms in the three markup formulas:

a. Cost = $417.82; Dollar markup = $204.20

Selling price = Cost + Dollar markup
= $\$417.82 + \$204.20 = \$622.02$

b. Cost = $154.40; Selling price = $392.12

Dollar markup = Selling price − Cost
= $\$392.12 - \$154.40 = \$237.72$

c. Dollar markup = $41.26; Selling price = $93.20

Cost = Selling price − Dollar markup
= $\$93.20 - \$41.26 = \$51.94$

# Computing Markup Based on Cost

Learning Objective **2**

Compute the markup variables when the markup percent is based on cost.

In the example, Athletes' World computed its markup directly by determining its expenses and the desired profit. However, this method isn't practical when a business has hundreds or thousands of items. Allocating expenses and profit to each item would be too tedious. A more practical method is for the owner, an employee, or an accountant to analyze prior sales of the company or a similar company. The analyst can look at the costs of goods, additional expenses, and desired profit to determine a percent to use to mark up various items, called the **markup percent.**

One company may use different markup percents for different types of items. For example, an appliance store often performs repair services and sells replacement parts for the appliances it sells. The store may have one markup percent for the actual appliance, a second markup percent for repair services, and a third markup percent for replacement parts.

In Chapter 5 on percents, we introduced three terms: rate, base, and percentage. In this chapter, rate is the *markup percent,* or **markup rate.** Percentage is the *dollar markup.* Determining the base is more challenging because sometimes *cost* is the base and sometimes *selling price* is the base. For some businesses, cost may be the more logical base for calculating dollar markup. However, calculating dollar markup based on selling price is an advantageous method for many retail stores.

The accountant for Athletes' World says that, in order to pay all expenses and have a reasonable profit, and based upon a cost of $43.50, the company's markup should be 80% of the cost. When the cost and the markup percent are known, the dollar markup and the selling price can be computed.

**Video**

Markup Based on Cost/Selling Price

**STEPS to Compute the Selling Price Based on Cost**

1. Multiply the cost by the markup percent to get the dollar markup.
2. Add the dollar markup to the cost to get the selling price.

For Athletes' World's athletic shoes:

STEP 1 Dollar markup = Markup percent × Cost = 0.80 × $43.50 = $34.80

STEP 2 Selling price = Cost + Dollar markup = $43.50 + $34.80 = $78.30

**EXAMPLE A**

Using markup based on cost, what are the dollar markup and the selling price for merchandise that costs $60 and has a 35% markup?

STEP 1 Dollar markup = Markup percent × Cost = 0.35 × $60 = $21

STEP 2 Selling price = Cost + Dollar markup = $60 + $21 = $81

## COMPUTING SELLING PRICE DIRECTLY FROM COST

When you know the cost and markup percent (based on cost), you can compute the selling price directly, without computing the dollar markup.

**STEPS to Compute the Selling Price Directly from the Cost**

1. Add the markup percent to 100%.
2. Multiply this sum by the cost to get the selling price.

**EXAMPLE B**

What is the selling price of an item that has a cost of \$250 and a markup percent of 40% based on cost?

STEP 1 100% + Markup percent = 100% + 40% = 140%

STEP 2 Selling price = (100% + Markup percent) × Cost = 1.40 × \$250 = \$350

## COMPUTING COST DIRECTLY FROM SELLING PRICE

Likewise, you can use the reverse procedure to compute the cost directly from the selling price and the markup percent (based on cost), without computing the dollar markup.

**STEPS to Compute the Cost Directly from the Selling Price**

1. Add the markup percent to 100%.
2. Divide the selling price by this sum to get the cost.

**EXAMPLE C**

The selling price of a pair of shoes is \$75. The markup percent based on cost is 25%. Find the cost.

STEP 1 100% + Markup percent = 100% + 25% = 125%

STEP 2 Cost = Selling price ÷ (100% + Markup percent) = \$75 ÷ 1.25 = \$60

You can always check your work in markup problems.
Cost is \$60, and markup percent is 25%.
Dollar markup = Cost × Markup percent = \$60 × 0.25 = \$15
Selling Price = Cost + Dollar markup = \$60 + \$15 = \$75

It checks!

**CONCEPT CHECK 8.2**

Compute the required values when the markup percent is based on cost.

a. Cost = \$1,240; Markup percent = 40%
Find dollar markup, and then find selling price.
Dollar markup = 0.40 × \$1,240 = \$496
Selling price = \$1,240 + \$496 = \$1,736

b. Cost = \$330; Markup percent = 50%
Find 100% + Markup percent, and then find selling price directly.
100% + Markup percent = 100% + 50% = 150%
Selling price = 1.50 × \$330 = \$495

c. Selling price = \$780; Markup percent = 25%
Find 100% + Markup percent, and then find cost directly.
100% + Markup percent = 100% + 25% = 125%
Cost = \$780 ÷ 1.25 = \$624

# Computing Markup Percent Based on Cost

In the illustration for Athletes' World, the accountant determined that the markup percent needed to be 80% of cost, which meant that the selling price needed to be \$78.30. However, management may want to price the shoes at \$79.95. Now, the markup is no longer 80% of cost. The **markup percent based on cost** can be computed in two steps.

**Learning Objective 3**

Compute markup percent based on cost.

**STEPS to Compute the Markup Percent Based on Cost**

1. Subtract the cost from the selling price to get the dollar markup.
2. Divide the dollar markup by the cost to get the markup percent.

For the athletic shoes from Athletes' World, priced at \$79.95:

STEP 1 Dollar markup = Selling price − Cost = \$79.95 − \$43.50 = \$36.45

STEP 2 Markup percent = Dollar markup ÷ Cost = \$36.45 ÷ \$43.50 = 0.838, or 83.8% (rounded to one decimal place)

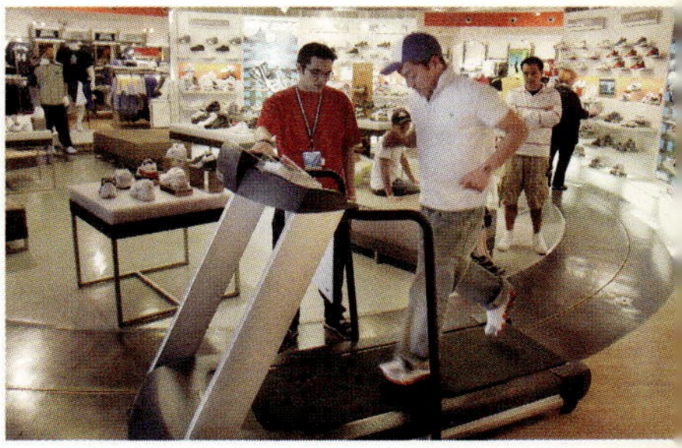

© TED S. WARREN/ASSOCIATED PRESS

**EXAMPLE D**

What is the markup percent based on cost when the selling price is \$120 and the cost is \$80?

STEP 1 Dollar markup = Selling price − Cost = \$120 − \$80 = \$40

STEP 2 Markup percent = Dollar markup ÷ Cost = \$40 ÷ \$80 = 0.50, or 50%

**EXAMPLE E**

What is the markup percent based on cost when the dollar markup is already known to be \$30 and the cost is \$75? (Step 1 is not necessary.)

STEP 2 Markup percent = Dollar markup ÷ Cost = \$30 ÷ \$75 = 0.40, or 40%

**CONCEPT CHECK 8.3**

Cost = \$1,600; Selling price = \$2,560
Find the markup percent based on cost.

Dollar markup = \$2,560 − \$1,600 = \$960
Markup percent = \$960 ÷ \$1,600 = 0.60, or 60%

COMPLETE ASSIGNMENT 8.1.

# Computing Markup Based on Selling Price

Learning Objective 4

Compute the markup variables when the markup percent is based on selling price.

Although many businesses base their markup on cost, many others, often retailers, commonly use a percent of selling price—that is, they use **markup based on selling price.** That doesn't mean that selling price is determined without considering cost or even before considering cost. It merely means that the dollar markup is computed by multiplying the markup percent by the selling price.

Many individuals start their own business when they observe another successful business selling a product. New owners believe that they can acquire the product, pay all expenses, and still sell it for less than the existing business is selling its product. Instead of basing the selling price on costs, expenses, and satisfactory profit, the new owners may price their product just under the competition's price. They base their selling price on the competition's selling price rather than marking up from their own costs.

Basing markup calculations on selling price can be an advantage in a retail store where the salesperson or sales manager has the authority to lower the sales price immediately in order to make a sale. In a larger business, these persons may not even know the exact cost.

**STEPS to Compute the Cost Based on Selling Price**

1. Multiply the selling price by the markup percent to get the dollar markup.
2. Subtract the dollar markup from the selling price to get the cost.

**EXAMPLE F**

Roy Brainard enters Floyd's Appliance Store to buy a washing machine. He finds one with a selling price of $400. He knows that he can buy it for $375 at another store, but he prefers this store because of its reputation for good service. He tells the sales manager, "I would buy it for $375." The manager, Jesse Cullen, knows that the markup percent is 40% based on selling price. What was Jesse's cost for the washing machine?

STEP 1 Dollar markup = Markup percent × Selling price = 0.40 × $400 = $160

STEP 2 Cost = Selling price − Dollar markup = $400 − $160 = $240

Jesse can then decide whether she prefers a sale for which she gets a $135 markup or no sale for which she hopes to have a $160 markup. Although it would be helpful if Jesse knew how much markup she would need to pay for expenses, at least she would know the cost.

**EXAMPLE G**

Find the dollar markup and the cost of an item that sells for $120 and has a markup percent that is 30% based on selling price.

STEP 1 Dollar markup = Markup percent × Selling price = 0.30 × $120 = $36

STEP 2 Cost = Selling price − Dollar markup = $120 − $36 = $84

## COMPUTING COST DIRECTLY FROM SELLING PRICE

When you know the selling price and the markup percent (based on selling price), you can compute the cost directly, wihout computing the dollar markup.

## STEPS to Compute the Cost Directly from the Selling Price

1. Subtract the markup percent from 100%.
2. Multiply this difference by the selling price to get the cost.

### EXAMPLE H

What is the cost of an item that has a selling price of $240 and a markup percent of 60% based on selling price?

STEP 1 100% − Markup percent = 100% − 60% = 40%

STEP 2 Cost = (100% − Markup percent) × Selling price = 0.40 × $240 = $96

## COMPUTING SELLING PRICE DIRECTLY FROM COST

Likewise, you can use the reverse procedure to compute the selling price directly from the cost and the markup percent (based on selling price), without computing the dollar markup.

## STEPS to Compute the Selling Price Directly from the Cost

1. Subtract the markup percent from 100%.
2. Divide the cost by this difference to get the selling price.

### EXAMPLE I

The cost of a mountain bike is $120. The markup percent based on selling price is 40%. Find the selling price.

STEP 1 100% − Markup percent = 100% − 40% = 60%

STEP 2 Selling price = Cost ÷ (100% − Markup percent) = $120 ÷ 0.60 = $200

You can always check your work in markup problems:
Selling price is $200, and markup percent is 40% based on selling price.
Dollar markup = Markup percent × Selling price = 0.40 × $200 = $80
Cost = Selling price − Dollar markup = $200 − $80 = $120

It checks!

## CONCEPT CHECK 8.4

Compute the required values when the markup percent is based on selling price.

| | |
|---|---|
| a. Selling price = $750; Markup percent = 50%<br>Find dollar markup, and then find cost. | Dollar markup = 0.50 × $750 = $375<br>Cost = $750 − $375 = $375 |
| b. Selling price = $40; Markup percent = 30%<br>Find 100% − Markup percent, and then find cost directly. | 100% − Markup percent = 100% − 30% = 70%<br>Cost = 0.70 × $40 = $28 |
| c. Cost = $150; Markup percent = 40%<br>Find 100% − Markup percent, and then find selling price directly. | 100% − Markup percent = 100% − 40% = 60%<br>Selling price = $150 ÷ 0.60 = $250 |

# Computing Markup Percent Based on Selling Price

**Learning Objective 5**

Compute markup percent based on selling price.

In the illustration for Athletes' World, the pair of athletic shoes had a cost of $43.50. The store owner decided that the selling price of the athletic shoes would be $79.95. The markup percent based on selling price can be calculated in two steps.

**STEPS to Compute the Markup Percent from the Selling Price**

1. Subtract the cost from the selling price to get the dollar markup.
2. Divide the dollar markup by the selling price to get the markup percent.

For Athletes' World's athletic shoes,

STEP 1 Dollar markup = Selling price − Cost = $79.95 − $43.50 = $36.45

STEP 2 Markup percent = Dollar markup ÷ Selling price = $36.45 ÷ $79.95 = 0.456, or 45.6% (rounded to one decimal place)

**EXAMPLE J**

What is the markup percent based on selling price when the selling price is $80 and the cost is $50?

STEP 1 Dollar markup = Selling price − Cost = $80 − $50 = $30

STEP 2 Markup percent = Dollar markup ÷ Selling price = $30 ÷ $80 = 0.375, or 37.5%

**EXAMPLE K**

What is the markup percent based on selling price when the dollar markup is already known to be $150 and the selling price is $375? (Step 1 is not necessary.)

STEP 2 Markup percent = Dollar markup ÷ Selling price = $150 ÷ $375 = 0.40, or 40%

**CONCEPT CHECK 8.5**

Cost = $1,600; Selling price = $2,560
Find the markup percent based on selling price.

Dollar markup = $2,560 − $1,600 = $960
Markup percent = $960 ÷ $2,560 = 0.375, or 37.5%

COMPLETE ASSIGNMENT 8.2.

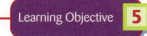

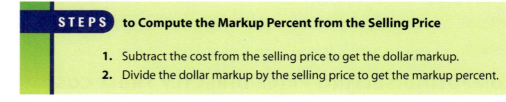

## Chapter Terms for Review

- cost of goods sold
- dollar markup
- markup
- markup based on selling price
- markup percent
- markup percent based on cost
- markup rate

## Try Microsoft® Excel

Try working the problems using the Microsoft Excel templates found on your student CD. Solutions for the problems are also shown on the CD.

# THE BOTTOM LINE

*Summary of chapter learning objectives:*

| Learning Objective | Example |
|---|---|
| **8.1**<br><br>Compute the variables in the basic markup formula. | Find the missing variables in the basic markup formula:<br><br>1. Cost = \$231.50; Dollar markup = \$109.12<br>2. Cost = \$34.20; Selling price = \$59.95<br>3. Dollar markup = \$475; Selling price = \$900 |
| **8.2**<br><br>Compute the markup variables when the markup percent is based on cost. | 4. Cost = \$800; Markup percent = 35%<br><br>a. Find the dollar markup and then find the selling price.<br>b. Find 100% + Markup percent, and then find the selling price.<br><br>5. Selling price = \$2,100; Markup percent = 40%<br><br>Find 100% + Markup percent, and then find the cost. |
| **8.3**<br><br>Compute the markup percent based on cost. | 6. Cost = \$80; Selling price = \$108<br><br>Find the markup percent based on cost. |
| **8.4**<br><br>Compute the markup variables when the markup percent is based on selling price. | 7. Selling price = \$820; Markup percent = 25%<br><br>a. Find the dollar markup and then find the cost.<br>b. Find 100% − Markup percent and then find the cost.<br><br>8. Cost = \$1,350; Markup percent = 40%<br><br>Find 100% − Markup percent, and then find the selling price. |
| **8.5**<br><br>Compute the markup percent based on selling price. | 9. Cost = \$825; Selling price = \$1,100<br><br>Find the markup percent based on the selling price. |

Answers: 1. Selling price = \$340.62 2. Dollar markup = \$25.75 3. Cost = \$425 4. a. \$280; \$1,080 b. 135%; \$1,080 5. 140%; \$1,500 6. 35% 7. a. \$205; \$615 b. 75%; \$615 8. 60%; \$2,250 9. 25%

SELF-CHECK

# Review Problems for Chapter 8

1 Find the missing terms.

| | Cost of Goods Sold | Dollar Markup | Selling Price |
|---|---|---|---|
| **a.** | $28.90 | $14.45 | ______ |
| **b.** | $188.12 | ______ | $399.95 |
| **c.** | ______ | $1,405 | $2,975 |
| **d.** | $426.25 | ______ | $998.88 |

**In problems 2–9, the markup percent is based on cost. Find the missing terms. Round all percents to the nearest one tenth of a percent.**

| | Cost | Markup Percent | Dollar Markup | Selling Price |
|---|---|---|---|---|
| 2 | $500 | 50% | **a.** ______ | **b.** ______ |
| 3 | $36 | 65% | **a.** ______ | **b.** ______ |

| | Cost | Markup Percent | 100% + Markup Percent | Selling Price |
|---|---|---|---|---|
| 4 | $225 | 60% | **a.** ______ | **b.** ______ |
| 5 | $240 | 75% | **a.** ______ | **b.** ______ |

| | Selling Price | Markup Percent | 100% + Markup Percent | Cost |
|---|---|---|---|---|
| 6 | $1,012 | 100% | **a.** ______ | **b.** ______ |
| 7 | $98 | 40% | **a.** ______ | **b.** ______ |

| | Selling Price | Cost | Dollar Markup | Markup Percent |
|---|---|---|---|---|
| 8 | $540 | $240 | **a.** ______ | **b.** ______ |
| 9 | $2,000 | $1,600 | **a.** ______ | **b.** ______ |

**In problems 10–17 the markup percent is based on selling price. Find the missing terms. Round all percents to the nearest one tenth of a percent.**

| | Selling Price | Markup Percent | Dollar Markup | Cost |
|---|---|---|---|---|
| 10 | $240 | 30% | **a.** ______ | **b.** ______ |
| 11 | $144 | 25% | **a.** ______ | **b.** ______ |

| | Selling Price | Markup Percent | 100% − Markup Percent | Cost |
|---|---|---|---|---|
| 12 | $1,240 | 40% | **a.** ______ | **b.** ______ |
| 13 | $528 | 75% | **a.** ______ | **b.** ______ |

| | Cost | Markup Percent | 100% − Markup Percent | Selling Price |
|---|---|---|---|---|
| 14 | $960 | 60% | **a.** ______ | **b.** ______ |
| 15 | $36 | 25% | **a.** ______ | **b.** ______ |

| | Selling Price | Cost | Dollar Markup | Markup Percent |
|---|---|---|---|---|
| 16 | $800 | $480 | **a.** ______ | **b.** ______ |
| 17 | $3,750 | $1,500 | **a.** ______ | **b.** ______ |

18 Carol Wilson sells high-end toys, specializing in all wooden toys for preschool children. She pays $40 for a toy truck. Carol sells the toy truck for $50. a. Find the dollar markup. ______ b. Find the markup percent based on cost. ______ c. Find the markup percent based on selling price. ______

**Answers to the Self-Check can be found in Appendix B at the back of the text.**

## Notes

# Assignment 8.1: Markup Based on Cost

Name ______________________

Date ______________ Score ______________

Learning Objectives 1 2 3

**A** **(12 points) Calculate the missing terms. (2 points for each correct answer)**

| | Cost | Dollar Markup | Selling Price | | Cost | Dollar Markup | Selling Price |
|---|---|---|---|---|---|---|---|
| **1.** | $480.70 | $175.25 | ______ | **2.** | $48.51 | ______ | $69.95 |
| **3.** | ______ | $374.50 | $829.98 | **4.** | $175.50 | $57.50 | ______ |
| **5.** | $629.00 | ______ | $909.99 | **6.** | ______ | $352.49 | $749.49 |

Score for A (12)

**B** **(32 points) In the following problems, the markup percent is based on *cost*. Find the missing terms. (2 points for each correct answer)**

| | Cost | Markup Percent | Dollar Markup | Selling Price | | Cost | Markup Percent | 100% + Markup Percent | Selling Price |
|---|---|---|---|---|---|---|---|---|---|
| **7.** | $850 | 40% | ______ | ______ | **8.** | $160 | 125% | ______ | ______ |
| **9.** | $1,500 | 70% | ______ | ______ | **10.** | $240 | 100% | ______ | ______ |
| **11.** | $640 | 75% | ______ | ______ | **12.** | $800 | 30% | ______ | ______ |
| **13.** | $2,500 | 90% | ______ | ______ | **14.** | $150 | 210% | ______ | ______ |

Score for B (32)

**C** **(32 points) In the following problems, the markup percent is based on cost. Find the missing terms. Round all percents to the nearest tenth of a percent. (2 points for each correct answer)**

| | Selling Price | Markup Percent | 100% + Markup Percent | Cost |
|---|---|---|---|---|
| **15.** | $1,240 | 60% | ________ | ________ |
| **17.** | $110 | 120% | ________ | ________ |
| **19.** | $594 | 35% | ________ | ________ |
| **21.** | $2,250 | 50% | ________ | ________ |

| | Selling Price | Cost | Dollar Markup | Markup Percent |
|---|---|---|---|---|
| **16.** | $48 | $30 | ________ | ________ |
| **18.** | $1,922 | $1,240 | ________ | ________ |
| **20.** | $679 | $388 | ________ | ________ |
| **22.** | $216 | $96 | ________ | ________ |

Score for C (32)

**D** **(24 points) Business Applications. In the following problems, the markup percent is based on cost. Round all percents to the nearest tenth of a percent. (3 points for each correct answer)**

**23.** Susan Chin owns a firm that sells office furniture to local businesses. One set of six matched pieces costs Susan $2,100. To cover her own business expenses and allow a reasonable profit, Susan marks up this set by 75% of the cost. Find the dollar markup and the selling price.

Dollar markup ________

Selling price ________

**24.** Stan Wegner manufactures a handheld heart monitoring device. He sells it for $840, which represents a markup of 275% on his production cost. Stan marks it up this much to cover additional business expenses and profit as well as product development. Find Stan's production cost and the dollar markup.

Cost ________

Dollar markup ________

**25.** Sentry Security Systems sells burglar and fire alarm systems for homes and small businesses. One basic system costs Sentry $720. Sentry marks up the alarm system by $396. Find the selling price, and find the markup percent based on cost.

Selling price ________

Markup percent ________

**26.** After Matt Lord drove his father's car with no oil, the car needed a new engine. A local mechanic charged Matt's father $2,250 for a rebuilt engine that cost the mechanic $1,800. All labor was additional. Compute the dollar markup and the markup percent based on the cost of the engine.

Dollar markup ________

Markup percent ________

Score for D (24)

# Assignment 8.2: Markup Based on Selling Price

Name ______________________

Date ______________ Score ______________

Learning Objectives 1 4 5

**A (12 points) Calculate the missing terms. (2 points for each correct answer)**

| | Cost | Dollar Markup | Selling Price | | Cost | Dollar Markup | Selling Price |
|---|---|---|---|---|---|---|---|
| **1.** | $67.34 | $82.15 | ________ | **2.** | $193.19 | ________ | $458.88 |
| **3.** | ________ | $840 | $2,659 | **4.** | $789.25 | $476.50 | ________ |
| **5.** | $62.50 | ________ | $99.99 | **6.** | ________ | $307.15 | $978.95 |

______________ Score for A (12)

**B (32 points) In the following problems, the markup percent is based on selling price. Find the missing terms. (2 points for each correct answer)**

| | Selling Price | Markup Percent | Dollar Markup | Cost | | Selling Price | Markup Percent | 100% − Markup Percent | Cost |
|---|---|---|---|---|---|---|---|---|---|
| **7.** | $120 | 55% | ________ | ________ | **8.** | $150 | 25% | ________ | ________ |
| **9.** | $360 | 40% | ________ | ________ | **10.** | $1,260 | 35% | ________ | ________ |
| **11.** | $1,998 | 50% | ________ | ________ | **12.** | $75 | 70% | ________ | ________ |
| **13.** | $824 | 60% | ________ | ________ | **14.** | $640 | 65% | ________ | ________ |

______________ Score for B (32)

**C** **(32 points) In the following problems, the markup percent is based on selling price. Find the missing terms. (2 points for each correct answer)**

| | Cost | Markup Percent | 100% − Markup Percent | Selling Price | | Selling Price | Cost | Dollar Markup | Markup Percent |
|---|---|---|---|---|---|---|---|---|---|
| **15.** | $855 | 40% | ______ | ______ | **16.** | $1,040 | $676 | ______ | ______ |
| **17.** | $143 | 45% | ______ | ______ | **18.** | $45 | $27 | ______ | ______ |
| **19.** | $2,520 | 30% | ______ | ______ | **20.** | $1,400 | $924 | ______ | ______ |
| **21.** | $533 | 35% | ______ | ______ | **22.** | $840 | $462 | ______ | ______ |

______

Score for C (32)

**D** **(24 points) Business Applications. In the following problems, the markup percent is based on selling price. Round all percents to the nearest tenth of a percent. (3 points for each correct answer)**

**23.** At the end of summer, Alpine Hardware features garden equipment specials. One rototiller has a selling price of $348. The markup to cover expenses and profit is 50% based on the selling price. Calculate the dollar markup and the cost.

Dollar markup ______

Cost ______

**24.** Parkside Cyclery is a retail bicycle store. For last year's Christmas season, Parkside purchased one model of mountain bike to use in a Christmas promotion. The bicycles cost $156 each. For this promotion, Parkside's markup was 40% of selling price. Find the selling price and the dollar markup.

Selling price ______

Dollar markup ______

**25.** City TV & Stereo sells telephones, along with televisions and stereos. A two-line cordless telephone set with a speaker phone base, two extra remote handsets, and an answering machine is priced at $182.40. This price includes a markup of $109.44. If this set actually sells for $182.40, what are the cost and the markup percent based on selling price?

Cost ______

Markup percent ______

**26.** Teak World, a warehouse superstore, purchased a large volume of teak lounge chairs for $232 each. Upholstered pads were included in the price. To sell the chairs and pads quickly, the store priced the chairs at $320. Compute the dollar markup and the markup percent based on selling price.

Dollar markup ______

Markup percent ______

______

Score for D (24)

## Notes

# Part 3

# Accounting Applications

# Banking

# 9

## Learning Objectives

By studying this chapter and completing all assignments, you will be able to:

Learning Objective 1 — Maintain a checking account.

Learning Objective 2 — Reconcile a bank statement with a checkbook balance.

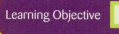

# Using Deposit Slips and Bank Checks

**Learning Objective 1**

Maintain a checking account.

Bank customers usually make deposits to their checking accounts by using **deposit slips.** Figure 9-1 shows a typical deposit slip, with spaces to list cash and checks being deposited.

In most businesses, each deposit will include a number of checks. Each check is individually listed on each deposit slip. Deposits are also made electronically. Many employees have their pay electronically transmitted directly from their employer's bank accounts to their individual bank accounts.

A bank **check** is a written order directing the bank to pay a certain sum to a designated party, called the **payee.** Banks normally provide checkbooks to their members. Figures 9-2 and 9-3 show typical bank checks, one with the stub on the left and the other with the stub on the top.

**Figure 9-1 Deposit Slip**

**WELLS FARGO BANK**

VAN NESS-CALIFORNIA OFFICE 1560 VAN NESS AVENUE SAN FRANCISCO, CA 94109

35-6686
3130

DATE 20

*DEPOSITS MAY NOT BE AVAILABLE FOR IMMEDIATE WITHDRAWAL*

SIGN HERE FOR LESS CASH IN TELLER'S PRESENCE

HART FURNITURE CO.
1039 BROADWAY
SAN FRANCISCO, CA 94103

USE OTHER SIDE FOR ADDITIONAL LISTING. BE SURE EACH ITEM IS PROPERLY ENDORSED.

| | | | |
|---|---|---|---|
| CASH | CURRENCY | 300 | 00 |
| | COIN | 60 | 49 |
| LIST CHECKS SINGLY | 16-30 | 250 | 00 |
| | 18-21 | 125 | 00 |
| | 17-17 | 216 | 00 |
| TOTAL FROM OTHER SIDE | | 209 | 00 |
| TOTAL | | 1,160 | 49 |
| LESS CASH RECEIVED | | | — |
| NET DEPOSIT | | 1,160 | 49 |

Back of Deposit Slip:

PLEASE LIST EACH CHECK SEPARATELY BY BANK NUMBER

| CHECKS | | DOLLARS | CENTS |
|---|---|---|---|
| 1 | 14-36 | 76 | 75 |
| 2 | 13-22 | 13 | 25 |
| 3 | 13-22 | 119 | 00 |
| 4 | | | |
| 5 | | | |
| 6 | | | |
| 7 | | | |
| 8 | | | |
| 9 | | | |
| 10 | | | |
| 11 | | | |
| 12 | | | |
| PLEASE FORWARD TOTAL TO REVERSE SIDE | | 209 | 00 |

**Figure 9-2** Check with Check Stub on Left

No. 2506 $ 124.35
September 24 20 --
To Ace Auto Repair
For Delivery truck

| | $ | ¢ |
|---|---|---|
| Balance Bro't Fwd. | 1,332 | 80 |
| Amount Deposited | 1,160 | 49 |
| Total | 2,493 | 29 |
| Amount This Check | 124 | 35 |
| Balance Car'd Fwd. | 2,368 | 94 |

HART FURNITURE CO.
1039 Broadway
San Francisco, CA 94103

No. 2506

September 24 20 --

35-6686
3130

Pay to the order of Ace Auto Repair $ 124.35

One hundred twenty - four and 35/100 DOLLARS

WELLS FARGO BANK
VAN NESS-CALIFORNIA OFFICE 1560 VAN NESS AVENUE SAN FRANCISCO, CA 94109

For Delivery truck repair Robert S. Hart

⑆313066860⑆ 2506⑈ 117⑈020⑈8

Today, many bank transactions are completed electronically. Funds that are transmitted electronically, primarily via computers, are called **electronic fund transfers (EFTs).** They include **automatic teller machine** (**ATM**) transactions by which customers can check their balances, make deposits, and withdraw funds from their accounts without having to wait for the next available bank teller. Computer programs also initiate many electronic fund transfers. These transactions are processed through the Automated Clearing House Association and include: direct deposits of payroll and Social Security checks, government pension benefits, and other payments specified for direct deposit.

© PHOTODISC/GETTY IMAGES

**Figure 9-3** Check with Check Stub on Top

| | | |
|---|---|---|
| BAL. FWD. | 997 | 03 |
| DEPOSITS | 451 | 04 |
| | 107 | 01 |
| NEW BAL. | 1,555 | 08 |

DATE 10/1/20--
TO: Men's Wearhouse
FOR: Suit-Slacks

3500

| | | |
|---|---|---|
| NEW BAL. | 1,555 | 08 |
| THIS CHECK | 300 | 00 |
| BAL. FWD. | 1,255 | 08 |

VALUED CUSTOMER SINCE 1976

WELLS FARGO BANK

3500

91-119
1221(1)

October 1, 20 --

Pay to the order of Men's Wearhouse $ 300.00

Three hundred no/100---------------------------------- DOLLARS

MARY MAHEW
40 ACELA DR.
TIBURON, CA 94920

For Suit-Slacks Mary Mayhew

⑆122101191⑆3500 0255 355521⑈

## CONCEPT CHECK 9.1

Fill in the total (as necessary) and balance on each check stub. Carry each balance forward to the next stub.

No. 1 $ 65.00
May 1 20--
To Citizens News
For Advertising

| | $ | ¢ |
|---|---|---|
| Balance Bro't Fwd. | 890 | 00 |
| Amount Deposited | | |
| Total | | |
| Amount This Check | 65 | 00 |
| Balance Car'd Fwd. | 825 | 00 |

No. 2 $ 79.00
May 4 20--
To District Utilities
For Gas & electric

| | $ | ¢ |
|---|---|---|
| Balance Bro't Fwd. | 825 | 00 |
| Amount Deposited | | |
| Total | | |
| Amount This Check | 79 | 00 |
| Balance Car'd Fwd. | 746 | 00 |

No. 3 $ 25.00
May 5 20--
To U.S. Postal Service
For Stamps

| | $ | ¢ |
|---|---|---|
| Balance Bro't Fwd. | 746 | 00 |
| Amount Deposited | 100 | 00 |
| Total | 846 | 00 |
| Amount This Check | 25 | 00 |
| Balance Car'd Fwd. | 821 | 00 |

# Using Checkbooks and Check Registers

A bank **checkbook** also provides check stubs or a special page on which to record deposits, withdrawals, check numbers, dates, check amounts, other additions and subtractions, and the account balance.

Figure 9-2 shows that check number 2506 was written against the account of Hart Furniture Co. on September 24 to Ace Auto Repair. The check was for $124.35 for repairs to the delivery truck. The stub shows a balance brought forward of $1,332.80, a deposit

**Figure 9-4** Check Register

| CHECK REGISTER | | | DEDUCT ALL PER CHECK OR SERVICE CHARGES THAT APPLY | | | BALANCE |
|---|---|---|---|---|---|---|
| DATE | | CHECK NUMBER | CHECKS ISSUED TO OR DEPOSITS RECEIVED FROM | AMOUNT OF CHECK | AMOUNT OF DEPOSIT | $1,332.80 |
| Sept | 24 | | Deposit cash receipts | | 1,160.49 | 2,493.29 |
| | 24 | 2506 | Ace Auto Repair | 124.35 | | 2,368.94 |
| | 24 | 2507 | Morton Window Decorators | 450.00 | | 1,918.94 |
| | 24 | 2508 | Donation to Guide Dogs | 100.00 | | 1,818.94 |
| | 25 | 2509 | Secure Alarm Systems | 150.00 | | 1,668.94 |
| | | | | | | |
| Oct | 19 | 2517 | Best Janitorial Service | 325.00 | | 855.94 |
| | 20 | | Deposit cash receipts | | 980.00 | 1,835.94 |
| | | | | | | |
| | | | | | | |

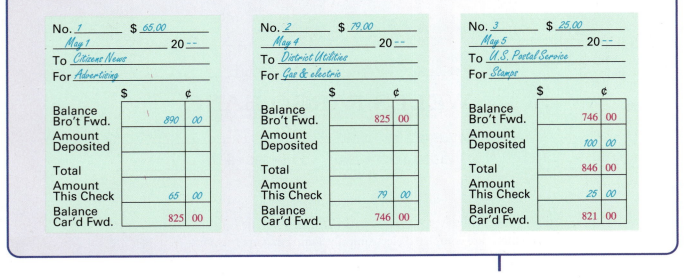

on September 24 of $1,160.49, the amount of this check ($124.35), and a balance carried forward of $2,368.94.

Today, most small businesses and many individuals use a **check register.** Like a check stub, a check register provides a place to record information about each bank transaction. Figure 9-4 shows a typical check register. Note that a continuous balance is maintained.

## CONCEPT CHECK 9.2

In this check register, fill in the cash balance resulting from each transaction.

| CHECK REGISTER | | | DEDUCT ALL PER CHECK OR SERVICE CHARGES THAT APPLY | | | BALANCE |
|---|---|---|---|---|---|---|
| DATE | | CHECK NUMBER | CHECKS ISSUED TO OR DEPOSITS RECEIVED FROM | AMOUNT OF CHECK | AMOUNT OF DEPOSIT | $520.42 |
| Mar | 27 | 123 | Replenish petty cash | $ 65.20 | | 455.22 |
| | 31 | 124 | Jiffy Janitorial Service | 150.00 | | 305.22 |
| Apr | 01 | 125 | Sun County Water District | 96.72 | | 208.50 |
| | 03 | - | Deposit weekly receipts | | $2,470.80 | 2,679.30 |
| | 03 | 126 | Midtown Mortgage Co. | 835.20 | | 1,844.10 |
| | 03 | 127 | Sun Gas and Electric Co. | 72.18 | | 1,771.92 |
| | 04 | 128 | Midtown Weekly Advertiser | 32.80 | | 1,739.12 |
| | 04 | 129 | Trash Disposal, Inc. | 60.00 | | 1,679.12 |
| | 04 | 130 | Pacific Plumbing Supplies | 906.97 | | 772.15 |
| | 10 | - | Deposit weekly receipts | | 2,942.50 | 3,714.65 |

# Reconciling Bank Statements

Learning Objective 2

Reconcile a bank statement with a checkbook balance.

Checking account customers receive a printed **bank statement** every month. The bank statement shows an opening balance; deposits and credits, including EFTs; checks paid; withdrawals, including EFTs; service charges; general information about the account; and the balance at the end of the period. In addition, most banks now provide electronic banking through your personal computer. This allows you to view your current bank statement at any time. Figure 9-5 shows a typical bank statement.

The balance shown in the checkbook or check register is usually different from the balance shown on the bank statement. The items that cause this difference are used in reconciling the two balances. These items are as follows:

An **outstanding check** is one that has been written but hasn't yet cleared the bank. Almost always you will have written and recorded some checks that haven't yet been presented to or processed by the bank for payment and charged to the customer's account.

A **bank charge** is a fee for services performed by the bank. At the time the bank statement is made up, your account may have been charged for bank service fees, printing checks, extra copies of statements, wired funds, traveler's checks, cashier's checks, safe-deposit box rentals, bad checks returned, or EFTs that you haven't yet recorded. These charges would therefore not yet be deducted from your checkbook or check register balance.

**Figure 9-5** **Bank Statement**

WELLS FARGO BANK

VAN NESS-CALIFORNIA #307
1560 VAN NESS AVE.
SAN FRANCISCO CA 94109

HART FURNITURE CO.
1039 BROADWAY
SAN FRANCISCO, CA 94103

CALL (415) 456-9081
24 HOURS/DAY, 7 DAYS/WEEK
FOR ASSISTANCE WITH
YOUR ACCOUNT.

PAGE 1 OF 1 THIS STATEMENT COVERS: 09/21/– – THROUGH 10/20/– –

**WELLS FARGO NEWSLINE**
NEW! GET STAMPS AT EXPRESS ATMS WHEN YOU STOP BY FOR CASH. AND, PLEASE NOTE THAT THE COMBINED TOTAL OF CASH WITHDRAWN AND STAMP PURCHASES CANNOT EXCEED YOUR DAILY CASH LIMIT.

**REWARD ACCOUNT**
31306686

**SUMMARY**

| | |
|---|---|
| PREVIOUS BALANCE | $1,332.80 |
| DEPOSITS | 1,560.49 |
| WITHDRAWALS | 1,081.23 |
| INTEREST | 6.30 |
| MONTHLY CHECKING FEE AND OTHER CHARGES | 13.00 |
| ▸ **NEW BALANCE** | $1,805.36 |

| | |
|---|---|
| MINIMUM BALANCE | $980.17 |
| AVERAGE BALANCE | $1,336.91 |

CHECKS AND WITHDRAWALS

| CHECK | DATE PAID | AMOUNT |
|---|---|---|
| 2506 | 9/26 | 124.35 |
| 2507 | 9/26 | 450.00 |
| 2508 | 9/26 | 100.00 |
| 2509 | 9/27 | 150.00 |
| 2510 | 10/03 | 50.00 |
| 2511 | 10/10 | 132.50 |
| 2512 | 10/20 | 74.38 |

DEPOSITS

| CUSTOMER DEPOSIT | DATE POSTED | AMOUNT |
|---|---|---|
| CUSTOMER DEPOSIT | 9/25 | 1,160.49 |
| EFT CREDIT | 9/26 | 400.00 |

A **credit** is a deposit or addition to a bank account. In many cases, the bank will have credited your account for an item such as an EFT deposited into the account or interest earned on the account. You, the customer, don't know the amount of these credits until the bank statement arrives, so the credits haven't yet been entered in your checkbook or check register.

An **outstanding deposit** is a credit that hasn't yet been recorded by the bank. A deposit that you made near the end of the statement period may have been recorded in your checkbook or check register but not recorded by the bank in time to appear on the statement.

Because these items cause a difference between the bank statement balance and your checkbook or check register balance, you should always reconcile the two balances immediately upon receipt of the statement.

To start the reconciliation, compare the check stubs or check register, all deposit slips, and any company records of ATM transactions with the bank statement. Such a comparison is called a **reconciliation of the bank balance.**

When Hart Furniture Company received its monthly bank statement, the bookkeeper noted that the ending balance was $1,805.36 but that the balance in the company checkbook was $1,835.94. To determine the correct balance, the bookkeeper noted the following differences:

1. An EFT credit for $400 had been made to the account but not recorded by Hart.
2. A bank service charge of $13 had been subtracted from Hart's account by the bank.
3. Interest earnings of $6.30 had been added to Hart's account.
4. A deposit on October 20 of $980 had not yet been recorded by the bank.
5. Checks for $27.92, $10, $48.95, $144.25, and $325 had not yet been processed and deducted by the bank.

Most bank statements have printed on the back of the statement a form that can be used to quickly and easily reconcile the customer's checkbook or check register balance with the statement balance. Figure 9-6 shows this form as completed by the Hart Furniture bookkeeper using the information just noted. Note that the adjusted checkbook balance and the adjusted bank balance now agree, showing the correct cash balance of $2,229.24.

**Figure 9-6** Reconciliation Form

## Balance Your Account

DATE 10/20/--

**Checks Outstanding**

| Check No. | Amount | |
|---|---|---|
| | | |
| 2513 | 27 | 92 |
| 2514 | 10 | 00 |
| 2515 | 48 | 95 |
| 2516 | 144 | 25 |
| 2517 | 325 | 00 |
| | | |
| | | |
| | | |
| | | |
| | | |
| | | |
| | | |
| | | |
| | | |
| | | |
| | | |
| TOTAL | 556 | 12 |

**1** Check off (✓) checks appearing on your statement. Those checks not checked off (✓) should be recorded in the checks outstanding column.

**2**

| | | |
|---|---|---|
| **Enter** your checkbook balance | $ 1,835 | 94 |
| **Add** any credits made to your account through interest, etc. as shown on this statement. (Be sure to enter these in your checkbook). | 6 | 30 |
| | 400 | 00 |
| | | |
| **SUBTOTAL** | 2,242 | 24 |
| **Subtract** any debits made to your account through bank charges, account fees, etc. as shown on this statement. (Be sure to enter these in your checkbook). | − 13 | 00 |
| | | |
| | | |
| **Adjusted** checkbook balance. | $ 2,229 | 24 | **A**

**3**

| | | |
|---|---|---|
| Bank balance shown on this statement. | $ 1,805 | 36 |
| **Add** deposits shown in your checkbook but not shown on this statement, because they were made and received after date on this statement. | 980 | 00 |
| | | |
| | | |
| | | |
| **Subtotal** | 2,785 | 36 |
| **Subtract** checks outstanding | 556 | 12 |
| Adjusted bank balance. | $ 2,229 | 24 | **B**

Your checkbook is in balance if line **A** agrees with line **B**.

### STEPS to Reconcile Bank Balances

1. Reconcile the checkbook (check register) balance. Start with the last balance as recorded in the checkbook.
   a. Add any bank statement credits, such as interest earned or EFT deposits not yet recorded in the checkbook.
   b. Subtract any charges or debits made by the bank, such as service charges, check printing charges, returned check charges, or EFT charges not yet recorded in the checkbook.

   This gives you your **adjusted checkbook balance.**
2. Reconcile the bank balance. Start with the balance as presented on the statement.
   a. Add any deposits or other credits not yet recorded by the bank.
   b. Subtract all outstanding checks.

   This gives you your **adjusted bank balance.**
3. Be sure that the two adjusted balances agree.

## CONCEPT CHECK 9.3

At month end, Johnson Hardware received the following bank statement. Use the forms that follow the statement to reconcile the check register shown in Concept Check 9.2 and the bank statement.

MIDTOWN BANK

**MIDTOWN BANK**

JOHNSON HARDWARE COMPANY
346 POPLAR STREET
MIDTOWN, CA 94872

THIS STATEMENT COVERS: 3/27/-- THROUGH 4/24/--

| SUMMARY | |
|---|---|
| PREVIOUS BALANCE | $ 520.42 |
| DEPOSITS | 2,470.80+ |
| WITHDRAWALS | 2,062.35 |
| INTEREST | 5.60+ |
| SERVICE CHARGES | 7.00- |
| NEW BALANCE | $ 927.47 |

| CHECKS AND WITHDRAWALS | CHECK | DATE PAID | AMOUNT | CHECK | DATE PAID | AMOUNT |
|---|---|---|---|---|---|---|
| | 123 | 3/29 | 65.20 | 130* | 4/06 | 906.97 |
| | 124 | 4/02 | 150.00 | | | |
| | 126* | 4/03 | 835.20 | | | |
| | 127 | 4/05 | 72.18 | | | |
| | 128 | 4/05 | 32.80 | | | |

| DEPOSITS | CUSTOMER DEPOSIT | DATE POSTED | AMOUNT |
|---|---|---|---|
| | CUSTOMER DEPOSIT | 4/05 | 2,470.80 |

* Indicates checks out of sequence

| | | |
|---|---|---|
| **Enter** your checkbook balance | $ 3,714 | 65 |
| **Add** any credits made to your account through interest, etc. as shown on this statement. (Be sure to enter these in your checkbook). | 5 | 60 |
| SUBTOTAL | 3,720 | 25 |
| **Subtract** any debits made to your account through bank charges, account fees, etc. as shown on this statement. (Be sure to enter these in your checkbook). | 7 | 00 |
| **Adjusted** checkbook balance. | $ 3,713 | 25 |

| | | |
|---|---|---|
| Bank balance shown on this statement. | $ 927 | 47 |
| **Add** deposits shown in your checkbook but not shown on this statement, because they were made and received after date on this statement. | 2,942 | 50 |
| **Subtotal** | 3,869 | 97 |
| **Subtract** checks outstanding | 156 | 72 |
| Adjusted bank balance. | $ 3,713 | 25 |

Your checkbook is in balance if line **A** agrees with line **B**.

**Checks Outstanding**

| Check No. | Amount | |
|---|---|---|
| 125 | $ 96 | 72 |
| 129 | 60 | 00 |
| TOTAL | $ 156 | 72 |

COMPLETE ASSIGNMENTS 9.1, 9.2, AND 9.3.

## Chapter Terms for Review

adjusted bank balance
adjusted checkbook balance
automatic teller machine (ATM)
bank charge
bank statement
check
checkbook
check register
credit
deposit slip
electronic fund transfer (EFT)
outstanding check
outstanding deposit
payee
reconciliation of the bank balance

## Try Microsoft® Excel

Try working the following problems using the Microsoft Excel templates found on your student CD. Solutions for the problems are also shown on the CD.

1. Complete the following worksheet by adding formulas in shaded cells to calculate the balance after each transaction in the check register. Formulas should work for either the addition of a deposit or subtraction of a check and be able to be copied down the **Balance** column.

| | A | B | C | D | E | F |
|---|---|---|---|---|---|---|
| 1 | Check Register | | | | | Balance |
| 2 | Date | Check Number | Checks issued to or deposits received from | Amount of Check | Amount of Deposit | 895.42 |
| 3 | May 4 | 237 | Echo Computer Repair Service | 235.00 | | |
| 4 | 5 | | Deposit cash sales | | 1,569.12 | |
| 5 | 6 | 238 | Glendale Gas Co. | 127.90 | | |
| 6 | 6 | 239 | Yellow Pages - ad | 212.33 | | |
| 7 | 8 | 240 | City Stationers - supplies | 582.91 | | |
| 8 | 10 | | Deposit cash sales | | 1,243.32 | |
| 9 | 12 | 241 | Acme Cleaning Service | 450.00 | | |
| 10 | 13 | 242 | General Telephone | 82.57 | | |
| 11 | 15 | | Deposit tax refund | | 750.00 | |

2. Jessica Flint's monthly bank statement balance was $1,753.04. Her checkbook balance was $2,590.24. She noted that the following checks were outstanding: #134 for $17.35, #137 for $128.45, and #138 for $52.00. She also noted that a deposit of $974.50 was not yet recorded by the bank. The bank statement lists a service charge of $15 and a bad check of $45.50 returned to Jessica by the bank from a recent deposit.

Enter the data given above in the appropriate cells and complete the worksheet to reconcile the bank statement and checkbook balances by adding formulas in shaded cells.

| | A | B | C |
|---|---|---|---|
| 1 | Checkbook balance | | |
| 2 | Less bank charges: | | |
| 3 | Service charge | | |
| 4 | Bad check | | |
| 5 | Total subtractions | | |
| 6 | Adjusted checkbook balance | | |
| 7 | | | |
| 8 | Bank statement balance | | |
| 9 | Add unrecorded deposit | | |
| 10 | Subtotal | | |
| 11 | Less outstanding checks: #134 | | |
| 12 | #137 | | |
| 13 | #138 | | |
| 14 | Total outstanding check | | |
| 15 | Adjusted bank balance | | |

# THE BOTTOM LINE

*Summary of chapter learning objectives:*

| Learning Objective | Example |
|---|---|
| **9.1** Maintain a checking account. | 1. Fill in the New Bal. and Bal. Fwd. on each check stub. Carry Bal. Fwd. to the next stub. |

| #1 | | | | #2 | | | |
|---|---|---|---|---|---|---|---|
| Bal. Fwd. | $100.00 | Date | 01/17 | Bal. Fwd. | _______ | Date | 01/22 |
| Deposit | 350.50 | To | AAA | Deposit | 375.00 | To | Longs |
| New Bal. | _______ | | | New Bal. | _______ | | |
| This Ck | 175.09 | For | Ins. | This Ck | 78.88 | For | Misc |
| Bal. Fwd. | _______ | | | Bal. Fwd. | _______ | | |

| Learning Objective | Example |
|---|---|
| **9.2** Reconcile a bank statement with a checkbook balance. | 2. Fill in the cash balance for each date. |

**CHECK REGISTER**

| DATE | CHECK NUMBER | CHECK TO—DEPOSIT INFORMATION | DEPOSIT AMOUNT | CHECK AMOUNT | BALANCE |
|---|---|---|---|---|---|
| | | | | | $453.90 |
| 12/11 | 100 | Albertsons | | $85.92 | |
| 12/12 | | Monthly Salary Check | $1,580.65 | | |
| 12/13 | 101 | C.Dobbs-Rent | | $850.00 | |
| 12/14 | 102 | TJ Max | | $ 99.97 | |
| 12/15 | 103 | Ace Hardware | | $ 107.16 | |
| 12/17 | | Income from Stocks | $212.37 | | |

| Learning Objective | Example |
|---|---|
| **9.2** Reconcile a bank statement with a checkbook balance. | 3. Mike Kent's monthly bank statement balance was $1,418. His checkbook balance was $1,620. He noted the following checks outstanding: #119 for $350 and #125 for $197. He noted a deposit of $1,600 as not recorded by the bank. The bank had charged him $17 for checks and $32 for a bad check he had deposited. The bank had credited his account with an electronic transfer for $900. Reconcile the bank and checkbook balances. |

| | | |
|---|---|---|
| Checkbook balance: | | $1,620 |
| Add electronic transfer: | | ________ |
| Subtotal | | ________ |
| Less bank charges: | ________ | |
| | ________ | ________ |
| Adjusted checkbook balance: | | ________ |
| Bank balance on statement: | | $1,418 |
| Add unrecorded deposit: | | ________ |
| Subtotal | | ________ |
| Less outstanding checks: #119 | ________ | |
| #125 | ________ | ________ |
| Adjusted bank balance | | ________ |

Answers: 1. $450.50; $275.41; $275.41; $650.41; $571.53 2. $367.98; $1,948.63; $1,098.63; $998.66; $891.50; $1,103.87 3. $2,471

SELF-CHECK

# Review Problems for Chapter 9

1 Each of the following items requires an adjustment to either the bank statement balance or the check register balance. Indicate the correct handling of each item by writing the appropriate letter in the blank.

A = add to bank statement balance
B = subtract from bank statement balance
C = add to checkbook balance
D = subtract from checkbook balance

_________ (a) Outstanding check written to the landlord for rent

_________ (b) Bank charge for printing checks

_________ (c) A deposit made at the end of the period that was not included on the bank statement

_________ (d) A customer's check that was returned by the bank for insufficient funds (a bounced check)

_________ (e) An error in recording a check in the check register. A check written to Acme Services for $92.20 was recorded in the check register as $95.50

_________ (f) Interest on the checking account

_________ (g) A bank fee of $20 for the bounced check

_________ (h) Bank fees for ATM withdrawals

2 The balance in Ferndale Construction Company's check register May 31 was $12,583.40. The bank statement for Ferndale Construction Company listed the following information:

| | |
|---|---|
| Previous balance (May 1) | $12,620.10 |
| Deposits | 16,265.00 |
| Checks and withdrawals | 17,805.95 |
| Interest | 52.50 |
| Service charges | 20.00 |
| Check returned for insufficient funds | 150.00 |
| New balance (May 31) | $10,961.65 |

By comparing the bank statement and the check register, the company's bookkeeper determined that a deposit of $1,850.15 was not included on the statement and that the following checks were outstanding:

| | |
|---|---|
| No. 602 | $ 35.80 |
| No. 610 | 212.00 |
| No. 612 | 95.10 |

While preparing the reconciliation, the company's bookkeeper noted that check number 585, which had been written for $82.50, had been recorded in the check register as $85.50.

Prepare a bank reconciliation statement for Ferndale Construction Company.

**Answers to the Self-Check can be found in Appendix B at the back of the text.**

# Assignment 9.1: Check Register and Check Stubs

Name

Date Score

Learning Objective 1

**A (20 points) In the following check register, fill in the cash balance resulting from each transaction. (2 points for each correct answer)**

1.

| CHECK REGISTER | | | DEDUCT ALL PER CHECK OR SERVICE CHARGES THAT APPLY | | | BALANCE |
|---|---|---|---|---|---|---|
| DATE | | CHECK NUMBER | CHECKS ISSUED TO OR DEPOSITS RECEIVED FROM | AMOUNT OF CHECK | AMOUNT OF DEPOSIT | $1,450.00 |
| Apr | 04 | 842 | Alliance Mortgage Company | 865.00 | | |
| | 04 | - | Deposit weekly cash receipts | | 4,197.50 | |
| | 05 | 843 | U.S. Treasury | 1,520.00 | | |
| | 06 | 844 | State Income Tax | 990.00 | | |
| | 07 | 845 | General Telephone | 65.30 | | |
| | 08 | 846 | Maxwell Office Supply | 289.70 | | |
| | 12 | - | Deposit weekly cash receipts | | 3,845.25 | |
| | 12 | 847 | Eastwood Water Co. | 126.42 | | |
| | 12 | 848 | Central Advertising, Inc. | 965.00 | | |
| | 12 | 849 | Johnson Tax Services | 650.00 | | |
| | | | | | | |

Score for A (20)

**B (15 points) Fill in the new balance (New. Bal.) and balance forward (Bal. Fwd.) on each check stub, carrying each balance forward to the next stub. ($1\frac{1}{2}$ points for each correct New Bal. answer)**

2.
#101
Bal. Fwd. 920.15 Date 6-1 New Bal. ______
Deposit 300.00 To ACE This Ck 29.30
New Bal. ______ For REPAIR Bal. Fwd. ______

3.
#102
Bal. Fwd. ______ Date 6-5 New Bal. ______
Deposit ______ To DON This Ck 312.80
New Bal. ______ For NOTE Bal. Fwd. ______

4.
#103
Bal. Fwd. ______ Date 6-8 New Bal. ______
Deposit 862.13 To NEC This Ck 862.42
New Bal. ______ For COMPUTER Bal. Fwd. ______

5.
#104
Bal. Fwd. ______ Date 6-10 New Bal. ______
Deposit 2,160.00 To CHRON This Ck 1,200.27
New Bal. ______ For AD Bal. Fwd. ______

6.
#105
Bal. Fwd. ______ Date 6-15 New Bal. ______
Deposit 907.16 To B/A This Ck 317.77
New Bal. ______ For CAR PAYMENT Bal. Fwd. ______

Score for B (15)

**C** **(20 points) According to the check register of Kyber Electronics, the cash balance on July 1 was $1,335.60. During the month, deposits of $281.75, $681.10, and $385.60 were made. Checks for $98.99, $307.53, $19.56, $212.40, $287.60, and $88.62 were recorded. (15 points for a correct answer in 7; 5 points for a correct answer in 8)**

**7.** What was the cash balance shown in the check register on July 31? __________

**8.** After entering all the items in the check register, the bookkeeper found that the check recorded as $212.40 was actually written as $224.20. What is the correct cash balance? __________

Score for C (20)

**D** **(45 points) The following problems show the deposits and checks that were recorded on a series of check stubs. In each problem, find the bank balance after each deposit or check. (3 points for each correct answer)**

**9.**

| | | |
|---|---|---|
| Balance | $2,420 | 80 |
| Check #1 | 279 | 10 |
| Balance | | |
| Check #2 | 148 | 20 |
| Balance | | |
| Deposit | 976 | 80 |
| Balance | | |
| Check #3 | 814 | 00 |
| Balance | | |
| Check #4 | 285 | 17 |
| Balance | | |

**10.**

| | | |
|---|---|---|
| Balance | $205 | 55 |
| Check #21 | 25 | 00 |
| Balance | | |
| Deposit | 721 | 45 |
| Balance | | |
| Check #22 | 188 | 14 |
| Balance | | |
| Check #23 | 415 | 92 |
| Balance | | |
| Check #24 | 72 | 38 |
| Balance | | |

**11.**

| | | |
|---|---|---|
| Balance | $2,670 | 10 |
| Deposit | 350 | 00 |
| Balance | | |
| Check #31 | 265 | 72 |
| Balance | | |
| Check #32 | 85 | 70 |
| Balance | | |
| Deposit | 935 | 62 |
| Balance | | |
| Check #33 | 1,230 | 14 |
| Balance | | |

Score for D (45)

# Assignment 9.2: Check Register and Bank Statements

Name

Date Score

Learning Objectives 1 2

**A (40 points) Solve the following problems. (10 points for a correct final balance in 1; 30 points for a correct final answer in 2)**

**1.** On October 31, the balance of the account of Hobbies Unlimited at the Citizens Bank was $922.10. This amount was also the balance on the check register at that time. Company checks written and deposits made during November are shown on the check register. Fill in the cash balance for each transaction.

| CHECK REGISTER | | | DEDUCT ALL PER CHECK OR SERVICE CHARGES THAT APPLY | | | BALANCE |
|---|---|---|---|---|---|---|
| DATE | | CHECK NUMBER | CHECKS ISSUED TO OR DEPOSITS RECEIVED FROM | AMOUNT OF CHECK | AMOUNT OF DEPOSIT | $922.10 |
| Nov | 01 | 551 | Muni. Water, Inc. (2 mos) | 119.60 | | |
| | 06 | 552 | Fenton Gas Co. | 49.60 | | |
| | 07 | 553 | Olympia Telephone | 74.19 | | |
| | 07 | - | Deposit cash receipts | | 225.50 | |
| | 21 | 554 | City Trash Disposal (3 mos) | 112.32 | | |
| | 21 | 555 | Jack's Janitorial Service | 33.33 | | |
| | 24 | 556 | United Fund | 12.00 | | |
| | 24 | 557 | Guide Dogs for the Blind | 67.77 | | |
| | 26 | 558 | Wilson Insurance | 212.00 | | |
| | 28 | 559 | Security Systems, Inc. | 138.00 | | |
| | 28 | - | Deposit cash receipts | | 94.00 | |

**2.** On December 3, Hobbies Unlimited, whose check register you completed in problem 1, received the following bank statement. Reconcile the balance on the check register at the end of the month with the final balance on the bank statement. In reconciling the bank statement, you can find which of the checks are outstanding by comparing the list of checks on the statement with the register. Interest and a service charge were recorded on the statement.

CB CITIZEN'S BANK

STATEMENT OF ACCOUNT

HOBBIES UNLIMITED
4617 GILMORE ROAD
WHEATLAND, WI 54828-6075

ACCOUNT NUMBER: 072 4736

DATE OF STATEMENT: 11/30/--

| Balance From Previous Statement | Number of Debits | Amount of Checks and Debits | No. of Credits | Amount of Deposits and Credits | Service Charge | Statement Balance |
|---|---|---|---|---|---|---|
| 922.10 | 8 | 594.81 | 2 | 229.70 | 9.00 | 547.99 |

| DATE | CHECKS - DEBITS | CHECKS - DEBITS | DEPOSITS - CREDITS | BALANCE |
|---|---|---|---|---|
| 11/03 | 119.60 | | | 802.50 |
| 11/05 | 49.60 | | | 752.90 |
| 11/09 | 9.00 SC | | | 743.90 |
| 11/09 | 74.19 | | | 669.71 |
| 11/09 | | | 225.50 ATM | 895.21 |
| 11/23 | 112.32 | 33.33 | | 749.56 |
| 11/26 | 67.77 | | | 681.79 |
| 11/30 | 138.00 | | | 543.79 |
| 11/30 | | | 4.20 INT | 547.99 |

PLEASE EXAMINE AND REPORT ANY DISCREPANCIES WITHIN 10 DAYS    DM-Debit Memo  OD-Overdraft  ATM-Automated Teller Machine  INT-Interest Paid  SC-Service Charge  CM-Credit Memo

HOBBIES UNLIMITED
Reconciliation of Bank Statement
November 30

Bank balance on statement

Plus deposit not recorded by bank

Minus outstanding checks:

Checkbook balance

Plus bank interest

Minus service charge

Score for A (40)

**B (60 points) Solve the following problems. (12 points for each correct answer)**

**3.** Compute the reconciled balance for each of the problems from the information given.

| | Bank Statement Balance | Checkbook Balance | Other Information | Reconciled Balance |
|---|---|---|---|---|
| a. | $ 769.12 | $ 794.47 | Outstanding checks: $9.50, $31.15<br>Automatic transfer to savings: $50.00<br>Automatic charge, safe-deposit box: $16.00 | ________ |
| b. | $1,559.39 | $1,672.00 | Outstanding checks: $84.62, $14.20, $55.00<br>Outstanding deposit: $224.70<br>Automatic transfer to savings: $50.00<br>Bank interest credited: $8.27 | ________ |
| c. | $ 893.17 | $ 944.73 | Outstanding checks: $7.50, $4.18, $62.40<br>Outstanding deposits: $12.32, $120.00<br>Bank interest credited: $24.18<br>Charge for printing new checks: $17.50 | ________ |
| d. | $ 824.90 | $ 739.47 | Outstanding checks: $87.50<br>Deposit of $76.89 shown in check register as $78.96 | ________ |
| e. | $ 710.00 | $1,274.18 | Outstanding checks: $150.00, $37.82<br>Outstanding deposit: $440.00<br>Deposit of $312.00 shown twice in check register | ________ |

________
Score for B (60)

# Assignment 9.3: Bank Balance Reconciliation Statements

Name ______________________________

Date ______________ Score ______________

Learning Objective 2

**A (50 points) Using the data provided, prepare a bank reconciliation statement in each of the following problems. Space is provided for your solutions. (25 points for each correct reconciliation)**

**1.** The balance shown in the bank statement of Cogswell Cooling, Inc., on November 30 was $1,050.82. The balance shown on the check register was $480.77. The following checks were outstanding:

| | | | |
|---|---|---|---|
| No. 148 | $13.90 | No. 161 | $ 96.35 |
| No. 156 | 235.10 | No. 165 | 222.20 |

There was a bank interest credit of $12.00 and a service charge of $9.50 that had not been entered on Cogswell Cooling's check register.

**2.** The June 30 bank statement for Furgison Electric Company shows that a customer's bad check in the amount of $960 was returned and charged against Furgison Electric Company's account by the bank. This is the first knowledge the company had that one of the checks deposited was not good.

The balance shown on Furgison Electric Company's bank statement was $22,367.14. The balance shown on the check register was $24,696.83. The following checks were outstanding:

| | | | |
|---|---|---|---|
| No. 363 | $1,066.20 | No. 396 | $1,544.14 |
| No. 387 | 1,972.81 | No. 397 | 772.86 |

The following items required adjustment on the bank reconciliation statement:

| | |
|---|---|
| Outstanding deposit: | $3,001.87 |
| Automatic transfer to note payment: | $4,000.00 |
| Bad check returned and charged to Furgison Electric Company's account by the bank: | $ 960.00 |
| Bank interest credit: | $ 276.17 |

Score for A (50) ______________

**B (50 points) Using the data provided, prepare a bank reconciliation statement in each of the following problems. Space is provided for your solutions. (25 points for each correct reconciliation)**

**3.** The balance shown on the May 31 bank statement of Linberg Floors was $18,120.16. The balance shown by the check register was $19,512.54. A deposit of $2,004.35 had not been credited by the bank, and the following checks were outstanding:

| | | | | | |
|---|---|---|---|---|---|
| No. 730 | $85.17 | No. 753 | $462.95 | No. 761 | $19.75 |
| No. 749 | 1,216.20 | No. 757 | 512.80 | No. 768 | 982.90 |

The following items required adjustment on the bank reconciliation statement:

| | |
|---|---|
| Charge for printing checks | $ 18.00 |
| Automatic insurance payment charged to depositor's account by the bank | $1,765.00 |
| Check deposited by Linberg Floors, returned by bank as bad check | $ 920.00 |
| Interest on bank account credited by the bank | $ 35.20 |

**4.** The balance shown on the June 30 bank statement of Greenwood Stables was $9,527.72. The balance shown on the check register was $7,124.13. The following checks were outstanding:

| | | | | | |
|---|---|---|---|---|---|
| No. 516 | $621.50 | No. 521 | $93.21 | No. 523 | $144.80 |
| No. 526 | 935.11 | No. 527 | 250.00 | No. 528 | 416.35 |

The following items were listed on the bank statement:

| | |
|---|---|
| Charge made by the bank for safe-deposit box | $ 20.00 |
| Bank error: AA Realty's check was charged in error to Greenwood Stables' account | $ 82.50 |
| Interest on bank account credited by the bank | $ 72.12 |
| Bank charge for printing checks | $ 27.00 |

Score for B (50)

# 10

# Payroll Records

## Learning Objectives

By studying this chapter and completing all assignments, you will be able to:

- **Learning Objective 1** Prepare a payroll register.
- **Learning Objective 2** Compute federal income tax withholding amounts.
- **Learning Objective 3** Compute Social Security, Medicare, and other withholdings.
- **Learning Objective 4** Complete an employee's earnings record.
- **Learning Objective 5** Compute an employer's quarterly federal tax return.
- **Learning Objective 6** Compute an employer's federal and state unemployment tax liability.

Employers must keep payroll records, withhold and pay payroll taxes, and file quarterly and annual reports with state and federal government offices. The payroll records and processes described in this chapter are common to all employers.

Federal taxes paid by all employees include the federal income tax and the two contributions (commonly referred to as taxes) required by the Federal Insurance Contributions Act (FICA): Old-Age, Survivors, and Disability Insurance, commonly called Social Security; and Hospital Insurance, commonly called Medicare.

When hiring new employees, employers must verify each employee's eligibility to work in the United States, get the employee's Social Security number, and have the employee complete a **Form W-4**. The W-4 form shown in Figure 10-1 indicates that Kyle Abrum is married and claims four exemptions, which constitutes his **withholding allowance.**

# Preparing a Payroll Register

**Learning Objective 1**

Prepare a payroll register.

A **payroll register** is a summary of employee status information, wages earned, payroll deductions, and take-home pay. Whether they do it manually or by computer, all employers maintain some form of payroll register.

A payroll register is prepared for each payroll period. Payroll periods are weekly, biweekly, semimonthly, or monthly. Figure 10-2 shows a payroll register for one weekly period ending March 29. The line for Kyle Abrum shows that he is married, claims four withholding allowances, and is paid on an hourly basis at the rate of $11 per hour ($16.50 for overtime hours). For the current week, he worked 40 regular hours and 6 overtime hours, for gross earnings of $539. From his gross pay he had deductions for Social Security ($33.42), Medicare ($7.82), Federal Income Tax ($12.35), Group Medical Insurance ($39), Group Dental Insurance ($12), and Other ($42), totaling $146.59. His net pay was $392.41.

The Fair Labor Standards Act (FLSA), commonly called the federal wage and hour law, requires that nonexempt employees be paid 1½ times their regular hourly rate for all hours worked in excess of 40 per week. Following the FLSA requirements, the calculations for gross pay are as follows:

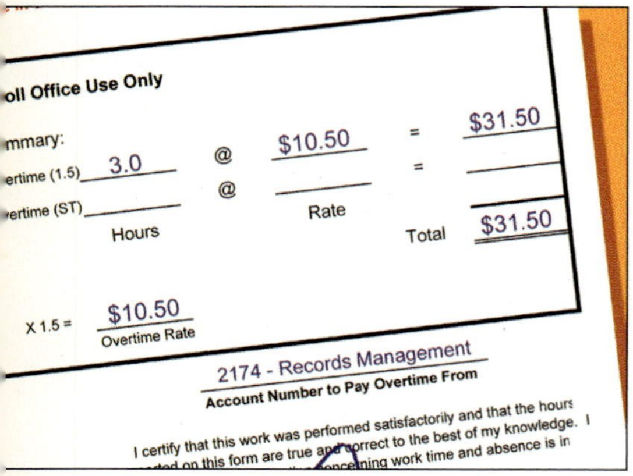


© ROSE ALCORN/THOMSON

STEP 1 Multiply hours worked (up to 40) times the regular rate.

STEP 2 Multiply the regular rate times 1.5 to calculate the overtime rate.

STEP 3 Multiply the hours in excess of 40 times the overtime rate.

STEP 4 Add the results of Steps 1 and 3 to determine gross pay.

Gross pay calculations for Kyle Abrum:

STEP 1 40 hours × $11 = $440 regular pay

STEP 2 $11 × 1.5 = $16.50 overtime rate

STEP 3 6 hours × $16.50 = $99 overtime pay

STEP 4 $440 + $99 = $539 gross pay

**Figure 10-1** | **Form W-4 (2008)**

# Form W-4 (2008)

**Purpose.** Complete Form W-4 so that your employer can withhold the correct federal income tax from your pay. Consider completing a new Form W-4 each year and when your personal or financial situation changes.

**Exemption from withholding.** If you are exempt, complete **only** lines 1, 2, 3, 4, and 7 and sign the form to validate it. Your exemption for 2008 expires February 16, 2009. See Pub. 505, Tax Withholding and Estimated Tax.

**Note.** You cannot claim exemption from withholding if (a) your income exceeds $900 and includes more than $300 of unearned income (for example, interest and dividends) and (b) another person can claim you as a dependent on their tax return.

**Basic instructions.** If you are not exempt, complete the **Personal Allowances Worksheet** below. The worksheets on page 2 adjust your withholding allowances based on itemized deductions, certain credits, adjustments to income, or two-earner/multiple job situations. Complete all worksheets that apply. However, you may claim fewer (or zero) allowances.

**Head of household.** Generally, you may claim head of household filing status on your tax return only if you are unmarried and pay more than 50% of the costs of keeping up a home for yourself and your dependent(s) or other qualifying individuals. See Pub. 501, Exemptions, Standard Deduction, and Filing Information, for information.

**Tax credits.** You can take projected tax credits into account in figuring your allowable number of withholding allowances. Credits for child or dependent care expenses and the child tax credit may be claimed using the **Personal Allowances Worksheet** below. See Pub. 919, How Do I Adjust My Tax Withholding, for information on converting your other credits into withholding allowances.

**Nonwage income.** If you have a large amount of nonwage income, such as interest or dividends, consider making estimated tax payments using Form 1040-ES, Estimated Tax for Individuals. Otherwise, you may owe additional tax. If you have pension or annuity income, see Pub. 919 to find out if you should adjust your withholding on Form W-4 or W-4P.

**Two earners or multiple jobs.** If you have a working spouse or more than one job, figure the total number of allowances you are entitled to claim on all jobs using worksheets from only one Form W-4. Your withholding usually will be most accurate when all allowances are claimed on the Form W-4 for the highest paying job and zero allowances are claimed on the others. See Pub. 919 for details.

**Nonresident alien.** If you are a nonresident alien, see the Instructions for Form 8233 before completing this Form W-4.

**Check your withholding.** After your Form W-4 takes effect, use Pub. 919 to see how the dollar amount you are having withheld compares to your projected total tax for 2008. See Pub. 919, especially if your earnings exceed $130,000 (Single) or $180,000 (Married).

## Personal Allowances Worksheet (Keep for your records.)

**A** Enter "1" for **yourself** if no one else can claim you as a dependent . . . . . . . . . . . . . . . . . . **A** 1

**B** Enter "1" if:
- You are single and have only one job; or
- You are married, have only one job, and your spouse does not work; or
- Your wages from a second job or your spouse's wages (the total of both) are $1,500 or less.

. . **B** ____

**C** Enter "1" for your **spouse.** But, you may choose to enter "-0-" if you are married and have either a working spouse or more than one job. (Entering "-0-" may help you avoid having too little tax withheld.) . . . . . . . . . . **C** 1

**D** Enter number of **dependents** (other than your spouse or yourself) you will claim on your tax return . . . . . . . **D** 2

**E** Enter "1" if you will file as **head of household** on your tax return (see conditions under **Head of household** above) . **E** ____

**F** Enter "1" if you have at least $1,500 of **child or dependent care expenses** for which you plan to claim a credit . . **F** ____
(**Note.** Do **not** include child support payments. See Pub. 503, Child and Dependent Care Expenses, for details.)

**G** **Child Tax Credit** (including additional child tax credit). See Pub. 972, Child Tax Credit, for more information.
- If your total income will be less than $58,000 ($86,000 if married), enter "2" for each eligible child.
- If your total income will be between $58,000 and $84,000 ($86,000 and $119,000 if married), enter "1" for each eligible child plus "1" **additional** if you have 4 or more eligible children.

**G** ____

**H** Add lines A through G and enter total here. (**Note.** This may be different from the number of exemptions you claim on your tax return.) ▶ **H** 4

For accuracy, **complete all worksheets that apply.**
- If you plan to **itemize or claim adjustments to income** and want to reduce your withholding, see the **Deductions and Adjustments Worksheet** on page 2.
- If you have **more than one job** or are **married and you and your spouse both work** and the combined earnings from all jobs exceed $40,000 ($25,000 if married), see the **Two-Earners/Multiple Jobs Worksheet** on page 2 to avoid having too little tax withheld.
- If **neither** of the above situations applies, **stop here** and enter the number from line H on line 5 of Form W-4 below.

**Cut here and give Form W-4 to your employer. Keep the top part for your records.**

Form **W-4** — Department of the Treasury, Internal Revenue Service

## Employee's Withholding Allowance Certificate

▶ **Whether you are entitled to claim a certain number of allowances or exemption from withholding is subject to review by the IRS. Your employer may be required to send a copy of this form to the IRS.**

OMB No. 1545-0074 — **2008**

| | | |
|---|---|---|
| 1 Type or print your first name and middle initial. *Kyle B.* | Last name *Abrum* | 2 Your social security number *123 45 6789* |
| Home address (number and street or rural route) *4052 Oak Avenue* | 3 ☐ Single ☒ Married ☐ Married, but withhold at higher Single rate. **Note.** If married, but legally separated, or spouse is a nonresident alien, check the "Single" box. | |
| City or town, state, and ZIP code *Lawton, OK 12345* | 4 **If your last name differs from that shown on your social security card, check here. You must call 1-800-772-1213 for a replacement card.** ▶ ☐ | |

5 Total number of allowances you are claiming (from line **H** above **or** from the applicable worksheet on page 2) **5** 4

6 Additional amount, if any, you want withheld from each paycheck . . . . . . . . . . . . . **6** $

7 I claim exemption from withholding for 2008, and I certify that I meet **both** of the following conditions for exemption.
- Last year I had a right to a refund of **all** federal income tax withheld because I had **no** tax liability **and**
- This year I expect a refund of **all** federal income tax withheld because I expect to have **no** tax liability.

If you meet both conditions, write "Exempt" here . . . . . . . . . . . . . . . ▶ **7**

Under penalties of perjury, I declare that I have examined this certificate and to the best of my knowledge and belief, it is true, correct, and complete.

**Employee's signature**
(Form is not valid unless you sign it.) ▶ *Kyle B. Abrum* **Date** ▶ *2/16/20--*

| | | |
|---|---|---|
| 8 Employer's name and address (Employer: Complete lines 8 and 10 only if sending to the IRS.) | 9 Office code (optional) | 10 Employer identification number (EIN) |

**For Privacy Act and Paperwork Reduction Act Notice, see page 2.** Cat. No. 10220Q Form **W-4** (2008)

**Figure 10-2** Weekly Payroll Register

| Name | Marital Status | Withholding Allowances | W = Weekly H = Hourly | Rate | Hours Reg. | Hours O/T | Gross Earnings | Deductions: Social Security | Medi-care | Fed. Inc. Tax | Group Med. Ins. | Group Dental Ins. | Other | Total Deduc-tions | Net Earnings |
|---|---|---|---|---|---|---|---|---|---|---|---|---|---|---|---|
| Abrum, Kyle | M | 4 | H | 11.00 | 40 | 6 | 539.00 | 33.42 | 7.82 | 12.35 | 39.00 | 12.00 | 42.00 | 146.59 | 392.41 |
| Garcia, Fran | S | 2 | W | 680.00 | 40 | — | 680.00 | 42.16 | 9.86 | 67.54 | 18.00 | 9.00 | — | 146.56 | 533.44 |
| Parker, Marie | S | 1 | H | 12.10 | 32 | — | 387.20 | 24.01 | 5.61 | 33.42 | 18.00 | — | — | 81.04 | 306.16 |
| Thomas, Robert | M | 3 | H | 9.40 | 40 | 4 | 432.40 | 26.81 | 6.27 | 8.23 | 39.00 | 12.00 | 13.10 | 105.41 | 326.99 |
| Weber, James | S | 1 | H | 16.80 | 40 | — | 672.00 | 41.66 | 9.74 | 76.14 | 18.00 | 9.00 | — | 154.54 | 517.46 |
| TOTALS | | | | | | | 2,710.60 | 168.06 | 39.30 | 197.68 | 132.00 | 42.00 | 55.10 | 634.14 | 2,076.46 |

## CONCEPT CHECK 10.1

After completion of the payroll register entries, one way to check on the accuracy of computations is to subtract the Total Deductions column from the Gross Earnings total; the difference should equal the total of the Net Earnings column. From the payroll register shown in Figure 10-2, check the accuracy of the column totals:

| | |
|---|---|
| Total of Gross Earnings column | $2,710.60 |
| Less Total Deductions column | − 634.14 |
| Total of Net Earnings column | $2,076.46 |

# Computing Federal Income Tax Withholding Amounts

**Learning Objective 2**

Compute federal income tax withholding amounts.

The federal income tax is a payroll tax that the employer must withhold from the employee's pay and turn over to the Internal Revenue Service (IRS). The amount of the deduction varies with the amount of earnings, the employee's marital status, and the number of withholding allowances claimed.

The *Employer's Tax Guide,* published annually by the Internal Revenue Service, gives employers two primary methods to figure how much income tax to withhold from their employees. These two methods are the **percentage method** and the **wage-bracket method.**

Figure 10-2 shows that Kyle Abrum's federal income tax withholding amount was $12.35, computed by the percentage method. With the percentage method, a deduction is granted for each withholding allowance claimed, based on a chart in the *Employer's Tax Guide.* The amount for each withholding allowance is provided in a table labeled Income Tax Withholding Percentage Method Table. Figure 10-3 illustrates a recent table. It shows that, for weekly pay, a deduction of $65.38 is allowed for each withholding allowance. (For monthly pay, a deduction of $283.33 is allowed for each withholding allowance.)

**Figure 10-3** Percentage Method Amount for One Withholding Allowance

| Payroll Period | One Withholding Allowance |
|---|---|
| Weekly | $ 65.38 |
| Biweekly | $130.77 |
| Semimonthly | $141.67 |
| Monthly | $283.33 |

After the total withholding allowance is subtracted from an employee's gross earnings, the amount to be withheld is computed by taking a percentage of the difference. The percentage to be used is given by the IRS in the Tables for Percentage Method of Withholding. Figure 10-4 illustrates a recent table for weekly, biweekly, semimonthly, and monthly payroll periods.

### STEPS to Figure the Amount of Federal Income Tax Withholding, Using the Percentage Method

1. Determine the employee's gross earnings.
2. Multiply the appropriate (weekly/monthly) "one withholding allowance" amount (from the withholding table in Figure 10-3) by the number of allowances the employee claims.
3. Subtract that amount from the employee's gross earnings.
4. From the appropriate (weekly/monthly and single/married) percentage method table, subtract the "of excess over" figure to get the amount subject to the tax.
5. Multiply the amount from Step 4 by the appropriate percentage from the percentage method table.
6. If required, add the base tax amount (if any) shown next to the percentage from the percentage method table. (For example, see Table 1, WEEKLY Payroll Period, Married, the second line of the table: $29.50 plus 15% of excess over $449.)

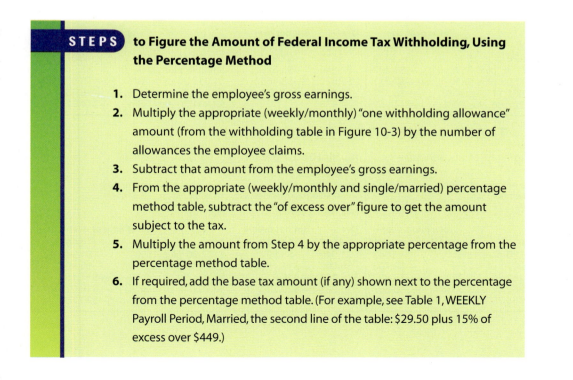

**Figure 10-4** Tables for Percentage Method of Withholding

# Tables for Percentage Method of Withholding

(For Wages Paid in 2007)

## TABLE 1—WEEKLY Payroll Period

**(a) SINGLE person** (including head of household)—

If the amount of wages (after subtracting withholding allowances) is: Not over $51 . . . . . The amount of income tax to withhold is: $0

| Over— | But not over— | | of excess over— |
|---|---|---|---|
| $51 | —$195 . . | 10% | —$51 |
| $195 | —$645 . . | $14.40 plus 15% | —$195 |
| $645 | —$1,482 . . | $81.90 plus 25% | —$645 |
| $1,482 | —$3,131 . . | $291.15 plus 28% | —$1,482 |
| $3,131 | —$6,763 . . | $752.87 plus 33% | —$3,131 |
| $6,763 | . . . . . . | $1,951.43 plus 35% | —$6,763 |

**(b) MARRIED person—**

If the amount of wages (after subtracting withholding allowances) is: Not over $154 . . . . The amount of income tax to withhold is: $0

| Over— | But not over— | | of excess over— |
|---|---|---|---|
| $154 | —$449 . . | 10% | —$154 |
| $449 | —$1,360 . . | $29.50 plus 15% | —$449 |
| $1,360 | —$2,573 . . | $166.15 plus 25% | —$1,360 |
| $2,573 | —$3,907 . . | $469.40 plus 28% | —$2,573 |
| $3,907 | —$6,865 . . | $842.92 plus 33% | —$3,907 |
| $6,865 | . . . . . . | $1,819.06 plus 35% | —$6,865 |

## TABLE 2—BIWEEKLY Payroll Period

**(a) SINGLE person** (including head of household)—

If the amount of wages (after subtracting withholding allowances) is: Not over $102 . . . . The amount of income tax to withhold is: $0

| Over— | But not over— | | of excess over— |
|---|---|---|---|
| $102 | —$389 . . | 10% | —$102 |
| $389 | —$1,289 . . | $28.70 plus 15% | —$389 |
| $1,289 | —$2,964 . . | $163.70 plus 25% | —$1,289 |
| $2,964 | —$6,262 . . | $582.45 plus 28% | —$2,964 |
| $6,262 | —$13,525 . . | $1,505.89 plus 33% | —$6,262 |
| $13,525 | . . . . . . | $3,902.68 plus 35% | —$13,525 |

**(b) MARRIED person—**

If the amount of wages (after subtracting withholding allowances) is: Not over $308 . . . . The amount of income tax to withhold is: $0

| Over— | But not over— | | of excess over— |
|---|---|---|---|
| $308 | —$898 . . | 10% | —$308 |
| $898 | —$2,719 . . | $59.00 plus 15% | —$898 |
| $2,719 | —$5,146 . . | $332.15 plus 25% | —$2,719 |
| $5,146 | —$7,813 . . | $938.90 plus 28% | —$5,146 |
| $7,813 | —$13,731 . . | $1,685.66 plus 33% | —$7,813 |
| $13,731 | . . . . . . | $3,638.60 plus 35% | —$13,731 |

## TABLE 3—SEMIMONTHLY Payroll Period

**(a) SINGLE person** (including head of household)—

If the amount of wages (after subtracting withholding allowances) is: Not over $110 . . . . The amount of income tax to withhold is: $0

| Over— | But not over— | | of excess over— |
|---|---|---|---|
| $110 | —$422 . . | 10% | —$110 |
| $422 | —$1,397 . . | $31.20 plus 15% | —$422 |
| $1,397 | —$3,211 . . | $177.45 plus 25% | —$1,397 |
| $3,211 | —$6,783 . . | $630.95 plus 28% | —$3,211 |
| $6,783 | —$14,652 . . | $1,631.11 plus 33% | —$6,783 |
| $14,652 | . . . . . . | $4,227.88 plus 35% | —$14,652 |

**(b) MARRIED person—**

If the amount of wages (after subtracting withholding allowances) is: Not over $333 . . . . The amount of income tax to withhold is: $0

| Over— | But not over— | | of excess over— |
|---|---|---|---|
| $333 | —$973 . . | 10% | —$333 |
| $973 | —$2,946 . . | $64.00 plus 15% | —$973 |
| $2,946 | —$5,575 . . | $359.95 plus 25% | —$2,946 |
| $5,575 | —$8,465 . . | $1,017.20 plus 28% | —$5,575 |
| $8,465 | —$14,875 . . | $1,826.40 plus 33% | —$8,465 |
| $14,875 | . . . . . . | $3,941.70 plus 35% | —$14,875 |

## TABLE 4—MONTHLY Payroll Period

**(a) SINGLE person** (including head of household)—

If the amount of wages (after subtracting withholding allowances) is: Not over $221 . . . . The amount of income tax to withhold is: $0

| Over— | But not over— | | of excess over— |
|---|---|---|---|
| $221 | —$843 . . | 10% | —$221 |
| $843 | —$2,793 . . | $62.20 plus 15% | —$843 |
| $2,793 | —$6,423 . . | $354.70 plus 25% | —$2,793 |
| $6,423 | —$13,567 . . | $1,262.20 plus 28% | —$6,423 |
| $13,567 | —$29,304 . . | $3,262.52 plus 33% | —$13,567 |
| $29,304 | . . . . . . | $8,455.73 plus 35% | —$29,304 |

**(b) MARRIED person—**

If the amount of wages (after subtracting withholding allowances) is: Not over $667 . . . . The amount of income tax to withhold is: $0

| Over— | But not over— | | of excess over— |
|---|---|---|---|
| $667 | —$1,946 . . | 10% | —$667 |
| $1,946 | —$5,892 . . | $127.90 plus 15% | —$1,946 |
| $5,892 | —$11,150 . . | $719.80 plus 25% | —$5,892 |
| $11,150 | —$16,929 . . | $2,034.30 plus 28% | —$11,150 |
| $16,929 | —$29,750 . . | $3,652.42 plus 33% | —$16,929 |
| $29,750 | . . . . . . | $7,883.35 plus 35% | —$29,750 |

**EXAMPLE A**

Using the six steps given, we compute Kyle Abrum's withholding as follows:

| | | |
|---|---|---|
| STEP 1 | \$539.00 | (gross earnings from payroll register) |
| STEP 2 | \$ 65.38 | (one withholding allowance) |
| | × 4 | (number of withholding allowances) |
| | \$261.52 | (total withholding allowance amount) |
| STEP 3 | \$539.00 | (gross earnings) |
| | −261.52 | (total withholding allowance amount) |
| | \$277.48 | (amount subject to withholding) |
| STEP 4 | \$277.48 | (amount subject to withholding) |
| | −154.00 | (less "excess over" amount in Figure 10-4) |
| | \$123.48 | (amount subject to percentage computation) |
| STEP 5 | \$123.48 | (amount subject to percentage computation) |
| | × 0.1 | (10% computation) |
| | \$ 12.35 | (amount of tax withheld) |
| STEP 6 | The wage range \$154–\$449 doesn't have a base tax amount and therefore doesn't apply in the case of Kyle Abrum. | |

© PHOTODISC/GETTY IMAGES

The second method of figuring the amount of tax to be withheld from an employee's pay, the wage-bracket method, involves use of a series of wage-bracket tables published in the IRS *Employer's Tax Guide*. Figures 10-5 and 10-6 illustrate the tables for single and married persons, respectively, who are paid on a weekly basis.

Using the tables from Figure 10-6, we see that a married employee earning a weekly wage of between \$530 and \$540 and claiming four withholding allowances will have \$12 withheld. Note that the amount of federal income tax withheld from Kyle Abrum's pay, using the wage-bracket method, is approximately the same as the amount withheld using the percentage method: \$12 versus \$12.35. Small differences will frequently result because the wage-bracket method uses tables based on \$10 divisions and rounded amounts. Over a period of a year, these differences tend to be relatively insignificant and are accepted by the IRS.

# **SINGLE** Persons—**WEEKLY** Payroll Period

**(For Wages Paid in 2007)**

| If the wages are– | | And the number of withholding allowances claimed is— | | | | | | | | | | |
|---|---|---|---|---|---|---|---|---|---|---|---|---|
| At least | But less than | 0 | 1 | 2 | 3 | 4 | 5 | 6 | 7 | 8 | 9 | 10 |
| | | The amount of income tax to be withheld is— | | | | | | | | | | |
| $0 | $55 | $0 | $0 | $0 | $0 | $0 | $0 | $0 | $0 | $0 | $0 | $0 |
| 55 | 60 | 1 | 0 | 0 | 0 | 0 | 0 | 0 | 0 | 0 | 0 | 0 |
| 60 | 65 | 1 | 0 | 0 | 0 | 0 | 0 | 0 | 0 | 0 | 0 | 0 |
| 65 | 70 | 2 | 0 | 0 | 0 | 0 | 0 | 0 | 0 | 0 | 0 | 0 |
| 70 | 75 | 2 | 0 | 0 | 0 | 0 | 0 | 0 | 0 | 0 | 0 | 0 |
| 75 | 80 | 3 | 0 | 0 | 0 | 0 | 0 | 0 | 0 | 0 | 0 | 0 |
| 80 | 85 | 3 | 0 | 0 | 0 | 0 | 0 | 0 | 0 | 0 | 0 | 0 |
| 85 | 90 | 4 | 0 | 0 | 0 | 0 | 0 | 0 | 0 | 0 | 0 | 0 |
| 90 | 95 | 4 | 0 | 0 | 0 | 0 | 0 | 0 | 0 | 0 | 0 | 0 |
| 95 | 100 | 5 | 0 | 0 | 0 | 0 | 0 | 0 | 0 | 0 | 0 | 0 |
| 100 | 105 | 5 | 0 | 0 | 0 | 0 | 0 | 0 | 0 | 0 | 0 | 0 |
| 200 | 210 | 16 | 9 | 2 | 0 | 0 | 0 | 0 | 0 | 0 | 0 | 0 |
| 210 | 220 | 17 | 10 | 3 | 0 | 0 | 0 | 0 | 0 | 0 | 0 | 0 |
| 220 | 230 | 19 | 11 | 4 | 0 | 0 | 0 | 0 | 0 | 0 | 0 | 0 |
| 230 | 240 | 20 | 12 | 5 | 0 | 0 | 0 | 0 | 0 | 0 | 0 | 0 |
| 240 | 250 | 22 | 13 | 6 | 0 | 0 | 0 | 0 | 0 | 0 | 0 | 0 |
| 250 | 260 | 23 | 14 | 7 | 1 | 0 | 0 | 0 | 0 | 0 | 0 | 0 |
| 260 | 270 | 25 | 15 | 8 | 2 | 0 | 0 | 0 | 0 | 0 | 0 | 0 |
| 270 | 280 | 26 | 17 | 9 | 3 | 0 | 0 | 0 | 0 | 0 | 0 | 0 |
| 280 | 290 | 28 | 18 | 10 | 4 | 0 | 0 | 0 | 0 | 0 | 0 | 0 |
| 290 | 300 | 29 | 20 | 11 | 5 | 0 | 0 | 0 | 0 | 0 | 0 | 0 |
| 300 | 310 | 31 | 21 | 12 | 6 | 0 | 0 | 0 | 0 | 0 | 0 | 0 |
| 310 | 320 | 32 | 23 | 13 | 7 | 0 | 0 | 0 | 0 | 0 | 0 | 0 |
| 320 | 330 | 34 | 24 | 14 | 8 | 1 | 0 | 0 | 0 | 0 | 0 | 0 |
| 330 | 340 | 35 | 26 | 16 | 9 | 2 | 0 | 0 | 0 | 0 | 0 | 0 |
| 340 | 350 | 37 | 27 | 17 | 10 | 3 | 0 | 0 | 0 | 0 | 0 | 0 |
| 350 | 360 | 38 | 29 | 19 | 11 | 4 | 0 | 0 | 0 | 0 | 0 | 0 |
| 360 | 370 | 40 | 30 | 20 | 12 | 5 | 0 | 0 | 0 | 0 | 0 | 0 |
| 370 | 380 | 41 | 32 | 22 | 13 | 6 | 0 | 0 | 0 | 0 | 0 | 0 |
| 380 | 390 | 43 | 33 | 23 | 14 | 7 | 1 | 0 | 0 | 0 | 0 | 0 |
| 390 | 400 | 44 | 35 | 25 | 15 | 8 | 2 | 0 | 0 | 0 | 0 | 0 |
| 400 | 410 | 46 | 36 | 26 | 17 | 9 | 3 | 0 | 0 | 0 | 0 | 0 |
| 410 | 420 | 47 | 38 | 28 | 18 | 10 | 4 | 0 | 0 | 0 | 0 | 0 |
| 420 | 430 | 49 | 39 | 29 | 20 | 11 | 5 | 0 | 0 | 0 | 0 | 0 |
| 430 | 440 | 50 | 41 | 31 | 21 | 12 | 6 | 0 | 0 | 0 | 0 | 0 |
| 440 | 450 | 52 | 42 | 32 | 23 | 13 | 7 | 0 | 0 | 0 | 0 | 0 |
| 450 | 460 | 53 | 44 | 34 | 24 | 14 | 8 | 1 | 0 | 0 | 0 | 0 |
| 460 | 470 | 55 | 45 | 35 | 26 | 16 | 9 | 2 | 0 | 0 | 0 | 0 |
| 470 | 480 | 56 | 47 | 37 | 27 | 17 | 10 | 3 | 0 | 0 | 0 | 0 |
| 480 | 490 | 58 | 48 | 38 | 29 | 19 | 11 | 4 | 0 | 0 | 0 | 0 |
| 490 | 500 | 59 | 50 | 40 | 30 | 20 | 12 | 5 | 0 | 0 | 0 | 0 |
| 500 | 510 | 61 | 51 | 41 | 32 | 22 | 13 | 6 | 0 | 0 | 0 | 0 |
| 510 | 520 | 62 | 53 | 43 | 33 | 23 | 14 | 7 | 1 | 0 | 0 | 0 |
| 520 | 530 | 64 | 54 | 44 | 35 | 25 | 15 | 8 | 2 | 0 | 0 | 0 |
| 530 | 540 | 65 | 56 | 46 | 36 | 26 | 16 | 9 | 3 | 0 | 0 | 0 |
| 540 | 550 | 67 | 57 | 47 | 38 | 28 | 18 | 10 | 4 | 0 | 0 | 0 |
| 550 | 560 | 68 | 59 | 49 | 39 | 29 | 19 | 11 | 5 | 0 | 0 | 0 |
| 560 | 570 | 70 | 60 | 50 | 41 | 31 | 21 | 12 | 6 | 0 | 0 | 0 |
| 570 | 580 | 71 | 62 | 52 | 42 | 32 | 22 | 13 | 7 | 0 | 0 | 0 |
| 580 | 590 | 73 | 63 | 53 | 44 | 34 | 24 | 14 | 8 | 1 | 0 | 0 |
| 590 | 600 | 74 | 65 | 55 | 45 | 35 | 25 | 16 | 9 | 2 | 0 | 0 |
| 600 | 610 | 76 | 66 | 56 | 47 | 37 | 27 | 17 | 10 | 3 | 0 | 0 |
| 610 | 620 | 77 | 68 | 58 | 48 | 38 | 28 | 19 | 11 | 4 | 0 | 0 |
| 620 | 630 | 79 | 69 | 59 | 50 | 40 | 30 | 20 | 12 | 5 | 0 | 0 |
| 630 | 640 | 80 | 71 | 61 | 51 | 41 | 31 | 22 | 13 | 6 | 0 | 0 |
| 640 | 650 | 82 | 72 | 62 | 53 | 43 | 33 | 23 | 14 | 7 | 1 | 0 |
| 650 | 660 | 84 | 74 | 64 | 54 | 44 | 34 | 25 | 15 | 8 | 2 | 0 |
| 660 | 670 | 87 | 75 | 65 | 56 | 46 | 36 | 26 | 16 | 9 | 3 | 0 |
| 670 | 680 | 89 | 77 | 67 | 57 | 47 | 37 | 28 | 18 | 10 | 4 | 0 |
| 680 | 690 | 92 | 78 | 68 | 59 | 49 | 39 | 29 | 19 | 11 | 5 | 0 |
| 690 | 700 | 94 | 80 | 70 | 60 | 50 | 40 | 31 | 21 | 12 | 6 | 0 |

## Figure 10-6 Married Persons—Weekly Payroll Period

# MARRIED Persons—WEEKLY Payroll Period

**(For Wages Paid in 2007)**

| If the wages are– | | And the number of withholding allowances claimed is— | | | | | | | | | | |
|---|---|---|---|---|---|---|---|---|---|---|---|---|
| At least | But less than | 0 | 1 | 2 | 3 | 4 | 5 | 6 | 7 | 8 | 9 | 10 |
| | | The amount of income tax to be withheld is— | | | | | | | | | | |
| **$0** | **$125** | $0 | $0 | $0 | $0 | $0 | $0 | $0 | $0 | $0 | $0 | $0 |
| **125** | **130** | 0 | 0 | 0 | 0 | 0 | 0 | 0 | 0 | 0 | 0 | 0 |
| **130** | **135** | 0 | 0 | 0 | 0 | 0 | 0 | 0 | 0 | 0 | 0 | 0 |
| **135** | **140** | 0 | 0 | 0 | 0 | 0 | 0 | 0 | 0 | 0 | 0 | 0 |
| **140** | **145** | 0 | 0 | 0 | 0 | 0 | 0 | 0 | 0 | 0 | 0 | 0 |
| **145** | **150** | 0 | 0 | 0 | 0 | 0 | 0 | 0 | 0 | 0 | 0 | 0 |
| **150** | **155** | 0 | 0 | 0 | 0 | 0 | 0 | 0 | 0 | 0 | 0 | 0 |
| **155** | **160** | 0 | 0 | 0 | 0 | 0 | 0 | 0 | 0 | 0 | 0 | 0 |
| **160** | **165** | 1 | 0 | 0 | 0 | 0 | 0 | 0 | 0 | 0 | 0 | 0 |
| **165** | **170** | 1 | 0 | 0 | 0 | 0 | 0 | 0 | 0 | 0 | 0 | 0 |
| **170** | **175** | 2 | 0 | 0 | 0 | 0 | 0 | 0 | 0 | 0 | 0 | 0 |
| **175** | **180** | 2 | 0 | 0 | 0 | 0 | 0 | 0 | 0 | 0 | 0 | 0 |
| **180** | **185** | 3 | 0 | 0 | 0 | 0 | 0 | 0 | 0 | 0 | 0 | 0 |
| **185** | **190** | 3 | 0 | 0 | 0 | 0 | 0 | 0 | 0 | 0 | 0 | 0 |
| **190** | **195** | 4 | 0 | 0 | 0 | 0 | 0 | 0 | 0 | 0 | 0 | 0 |
| **195** | **200** | 4 | 0 | 0 | 0 | 0 | 0 | 0 | 0 | 0 | 0 | 0 |
| **200** | **210** | 5 | 0 | 0 | 0 | 0 | 0 | 0 | 0 | 0 | 0 | 0 |
| **210** | **220** | 6 | 0 | 0 | 0 | 0 | 0 | 0 | 0 | 0 | 0 | 0 |
| **220** | **230** | 7 | 1 | 0 | 0 | 0 | 0 | 0 | 0 | 0 | 0 | 0 |
| **230** | **240** | 8 | 2 | 0 | 0 | 0 | 0 | 0 | 0 | 0 | 0 | 0 |
| **240** | **250** | 9 | 3 | 0 | 0 | 0 | 0 | 0 | 0 | 0 | 0 | 0 |
| **250** | **260** | 10 | 4 | 0 | 0 | 0 | 0 | 0 | 0 | 0 | 0 | 0 |
| **260** | **270** | 11 | 5 | 0 | 0 | 0 | 0 | 0 | 0 | 0 | 0 | 0 |
| **270** | **280** | 12 | 6 | 0 | 0 | 0 | 0 | 0 | 0 | 0 | 0 | 0 |
| **280** | **290** | 13 | 7 | 0 | 0 | 0 | 0 | 0 | 0 | 0 | 0 | 0 |
| **290** | **300** | 14 | 8 | 1 | 0 | 0 | 0 | 0 | 0 | 0 | 0 | 0 |
| **300** | **310** | 15 | 9 | 2 | 0 | 0 | 0 | 0 | 0 | 0 | 0 | 0 |
| **310** | **320** | 16 | 10 | 3 | 0 | 0 | 0 | 0 | 0 | 0 | 0 | 0 |
| **320** | **330** | 17 | 11 | 4 | 0 | 0 | 0 | 0 | 0 | 0 | 0 | 0 |
| **330** | **340** | 18 | 12 | 5 | 0 | 0 | 0 | 0 | 0 | 0 | 0 | 0 |
| **340** | **350** | 19 | 13 | 6 | 0 | 0 | 0 | 0 | 0 | 0 | 0 | 0 |
| **350** | **360** | 20 | 14 | 7 | 1 | 0 | 0 | 0 | 0 | 0 | 0 | 0 |
| **360** | **370** | 21 | 15 | 8 | 2 | 0 | 0 | 0 | 0 | 0 | 0 | 0 |
| **370** | **380** | 22 | 16 | 9 | 3 | 0 | 0 | 0 | 0 | 0 | 0 | 0 |
| **380** | **390** | 23 | 17 | 10 | 4 | 0 | 0 | 0 | 0 | 0 | 0 | 0 |
| **390** | **400** | 24 | 18 | 11 | 5 | 0 | 0 | 0 | 0 | 0 | 0 | 0 |
| **400** | **410** | 25 | 19 | 12 | 6 | 0 | 0 | 0 | 0 | 0 | 0 | 0 |
| **410** | **420** | 26 | 20 | 13 | 7 | 0 | 0 | 0 | 0 | 0 | 0 | 0 |
| **420** | **430** | 27 | 21 | 14 | 8 | 1 | 0 | 0 | 0 | 0 | 0 | 0 |
| **430** | **440** | 28 | 22 | 15 | 9 | 2 | 0 | 0 | 0 | 0 | 0 | 0 |
| **440** | **450** | 29 | 23 | 16 | 10 | 3 | 0 | 0 | 0 | 0 | 0 | 0 |
| **450** | **460** | 30 | 24 | 17 | 11 | 4 | 0 | 0 | 0 | 0 | 0 | 0 |
| **460** | **470** | 32 | 25 | 18 | 12 | 5 | 0 | 0 | 0 | 0 | 0 | 0 |
| **470** | **480** | 33 | 26 | 19 | 13 | 6 | 0 | 0 | 0 | 0 | 0 | 0 |
| **480** | **490** | 35 | 27 | 20 | 14 | 7 | 0 | 0 | 0 | 0 | 0 | 0 |
| **490** | **500** | 36 | 28 | 21 | 15 | 8 | 1 | 0 | 0 | 0 | 0 | 0 |
| **500** | **510** | 38 | 29 | 22 | 16 | 9 | 2 | 0 | 0 | 0 | 0 | 0 |
| **510** | **520** | 39 | 30 | 23 | 17 | 10 | 3 | 0 | 0 | 0 | 0 | 0 |
| **520** | **530** | 41 | 31 | 24 | 18 | 11 | 4 | 0 | 0 | 0 | 0 | 0 |
| **530** | **540** | 42 | 33 | 25 | 19 | 12 | 5 | 0 | 0 | 0 | 0 | 0 |
| **540** | **550** | 44 | 34 | 26 | 20 | 13 | 6 | 0 | 0 | 0 | 0 | 0 |
| **550** | **560** | 45 | 36 | 27 | 21 | 14 | 7 | 1 | 0 | 0 | 0 | 0 |
| **560** | **570** | 47 | 37 | 28 | 22 | 15 | 8 | 2 | 0 | 0 | 0 | 0 |
| **570** | **580** | 48 | 39 | 29 | 23 | 16 | 9 | 3 | 0 | 0 | 0 | 0 |
| **580** | **590** | 50 | 40 | 30 | 24 | 17 | 10 | 4 | 0 | 0 | 0 | 0 |
| **590** | **600** | 51 | 42 | 32 | 25 | 18 | 11 | 5 | 0 | 0 | 0 | 0 |
| **600** | **610** | 53 | 43 | 33 | 26 | 19 | 12 | 6 | 0 | 0 | 0 | 0 |
| **610** | **620** | 54 | 45 | 35 | 27 | 20 | 13 | 7 | 0 | 0 | 0 | 0 |
| **620** | **630** | 56 | 46 | 36 | 28 | 21 | 14 | 8 | 1 | 0 | 0 | 0 |
| **630** | **640** | 57 | 48 | 38 | 29 | 22 | 15 | 9 | 2 | 0 | 0 | 0 |
| **640** | **650** | 59 | 49 | 39 | 30 | 23 | 16 | 10 | 3 | 0 | 0 | 0 |
| **650** | **660** | 60 | 51 | 41 | 31 | 24 | 17 | 11 | 4 | 0 | 0 | 0 |
| **660** | **670** | 62 | 52 | 42 | 32 | 25 | 18 | 12 | 5 | 0 | 0 | 0 |
| **670** | **680** | 63 | 54 | 44 | 34 | 26 | 19 | 13 | 6 | 0 | 0 | 0 |
| **680** | **690** | 65 | 55 | 45 | 35 | 27 | 20 | 14 | 7 | 1 | 0 | 0 |
| **690** | **700** | 66 | 57 | 47 | 37 | 28 | 21 | 15 | 8 | 2 | 0 | 0 |
| **700** | **710** | 68 | 58 | 48 | 38 | 29 | 22 | 16 | 9 | 3 | 0 | 0 |
| **710** | **720** | 69 | 60 | 50 | 40 | 30 | 23 | 17 | 10 | 4 | 0 | 0 |
| **720** | **730** | 71 | 61 | 51 | 41 | 32 | 24 | 18 | 11 | 5 | 0 | 0 |
| **730** | **740** | 72 | 63 | 53 | 43 | 33 | 25 | 19 | 12 | 6 | 0 | 0 |

## ✔ CONCEPT CHECK 10.2

Using the percentage method steps given, verify the federal income tax withholding for Fran Garcia as recorded in the payroll register.

| | |
|---|---|
| \$680.00 | (gross earnings from payroll register) |
| \$ 65.38 | (one withholding allowance) |
| × 2 | (number of withholding allowances) |
| \$130.76 | (total withholding allowance amount) |
| \$680.00 | (gross earnings) |
| −130.76 | (total withholding allowance amount) |
| \$549.24 | (amount subject to withholding) |
| \$549.24 | (amount subject to withholding) |
| −195.00 | (less "excess over" amount in Figure 10-4) |
| \$354.24 | (amount subject to percentage computation) |
| \$354.24 | (amount subject to percentage computation) |
| × 0.15 | (15% computation) |
| \$53.14 | (amount of tax withheld on percentage computation) |
| \$53.14 | (amount of tax withheld on percentage computation) |
| +14.40 | (base tax amount) |
| \$67.54 | (total amount of tax withheld) |

Use the wage-bracket method to find the federal income tax withholding for Fran Garcia. Then compute the difference between the percentage method and the wage-bracket method.

| | |
|---|---|
| Wage-bracket method (Figure 10-5 because she is single) | \$68.00 |
| Percentage method | −67.54 |
| Difference | \$ 0.46 |

# Computing Social Security, Medicare, and Other Withholdings

**Learning Objective 3**

Compute Social Security, Medicare, and other withholdings.

The **Federal Insurance Contributions Act (FICA)** provides for a federal system of old-age, survivors, disability, and hospital insurance. The old-age, survivors, and disability insurance part of FICA is financed by the *Social Security tax*. The hospital insurance part of FICA is financed by the *Medicare tax*. These taxes are reported separately and are levied on both the employer and the employee. These taxes have different rates, but only the Social Security tax has a wage base, which is the *maximum* wage that is subject to the tax for the year.

The Social Security tax rate of 6.2% is levied on both the employer and the employee. For 2007, the wage base was \$97,500.

The Medicare tax rate of 1.45% is levied on both the employer and the employee. There is no wage-base limit for Medicare; all covered wages are subject to the Medicare tax.

Although both rates are subject to change by legislation, they were current when we compiled the payroll register illustrated in this chapter. All amounts are rounded to the nearest cent. The amounts for Kyle Abrum were $33.42 for Social Security and $7.82 for Medicare.

**EXAMPLE B**

Social Security deduction:

| | |
|---|---|
| $539.00 | (gross earnings) |
| × 0.062 | (Social Security rate) |
| $ 33.42 | (Social Security amount) |

**EXAMPLE C**

Medicare deduction:

| | |
|---|---|
| $539.00 | (gross earnings) |
| × .0145 | (Medicare rate) |
| $ 7.82 | (Medicare amount) |

Many employers today provide some form of group medical insurance for their employees. Frequently, the employee is asked to pay a portion of the premium charged for such insurance, based on the number of dependents the employee has named to be insured. For the payroll register shown in Figure 10-2, we assumed the weekly rates for medical and dental plans shown in Figure 10-7.

**Figure 10-7 Weekly Medical and Dental Plan Rates**

| | Weekly Medical Plan Premium Paid by Employee | Weekly Dental Plan Premium Paid by Employee |
|---|---|---|
| Employee only | $18.00 | $9.00 |
| Employee plus one dependent | $22.00 | $10.00 |
| Employee plus 2 or more dependents | $39.00 | $12.00 |

The payroll register presented in Figure 10-2 showed that Kyle Abrum subscribed to both the medical and the dental programs. Because of his three dependents, the amounts of his deductions were $39 and $12, respectively.

Frequently, employees will arrange to have special payroll deductions made by the employer to pay union dues, put money into special retirement or savings plans, or make contributions to charitable organizations.

In addition, 42 of the 50 states have some form of state income tax, which normally requires withholding in the same manner as the federal income tax. In such states, state income tax withholding columns are added to the payroll register and withholdings are made according to wage-bracket or percentage charts established by the state, in the same manner as federal income tax withholdings.

The payroll register illustrated in Figure 10-2 reflects a $42 weekly deduction that Kyle Abrum requested be made for payment of his union dues (other).

## ✔ CONCEPT CHECK 10.3

Using the format in examples B and C, compute Social Security and Medicare amounts for Fran Garcia, based on her gross weekly earnings of $680.

| Social Security deduction: | | Medicare deduction: | |
|---|---|---|---|
| $ 680 | (gross earnings) | $ 680 | (gross earnings) |
| × 0.062 | (Social Security rate) | × 0.0145 | (Medicare rate) |
| $42.16 | (Social Security amount) | $9.86 | (Medicare amount) |

# Completing an Employee's Earnings Record

**Learning Objective 4**

Complete an employee's earnings record.

An employer must submit quarterly and annual reports to the federal government and appropriate state government and pay the amount of taxes withheld from employees' earnings for the period. To obtain the necessary information, most employers keep an **employee's earnings record** for each employee. The employee's earnings record summarizes by quarter the employee's gross earnings, deductions, and net pay.

**EXAMPLE D**

**Figure 10-8 Employee's Earnings Record**

Name Kyle Abrum Social Security No. 123-45-6789

Address 4052 Oak Ave. No. of Allowances 4 Marital Status Married

| | | | Deductions | | | | | | |
|---|---|---|---|---|---|---|---|---|
| Period Ending | Total Wages | Cumulative Wages | Social Security | Medicare | Federal Inc. Tax | Other Deductions | Total | Net Pay |
| 1/4 | $ 550.00 | $ 550.00 | $ 34.10 | $ 7.98 | $ 13.45 | $ 93.00 | $ 148.53 | $ 401.47 |
| 1/11 | 550.00 | 1,100.00 | 34.10 | 7.98 | 13.45 | 93.00 | 148.53 | 401.47 |
| 3/29 | 539.00 | 7,250.00 | 33.42 | 7.82 | 12.35 | 93.00 | 146.59 | 392.41 |
| Quarter Totals | $7,250.00 | | $449.50 | $ 105.13 | $172.86 | $ 1,209 | $1,936.49 | $5,313.51 |

The employee's earnings record presented in Figure 10-8 shows that Kyle Abrum is married, claims four allowances, and for the first quarter of the year earned total wages of $7,250. His net pay was $5,313.51 after first-quarter withholdings as follows:

| | |
|---|---|
| Federal income tax withholding | $ 172.86 |
| Social Security withholding | 449.50 |
| Medicare withholding | 105.13 |
| Other deductions | +1,209.00 |
| Total deductions | $1,936.49 |

## CONCEPT CHECK 10.4

Assuming that Fran Garcia's weekly earnings and deductions have remained constant for each of the 13 weeks in the first quarter of the year, compute the following totals, which would appear on her employee's earnings record for the first quarter:

| | | |
|---|---|---|
| Total wages | $8,840.00 | ($680.00 × 13) |
| Federal income tax withholding | 878.02 | ($67.54 × 13) |
| Social Security withholding | 548.08 | ($42.16 × 13) |
| Medicare withholding | 128.18 | ($9.86 × 13) |
| Group medical insurance deductions | 234.00 | ($18.00 × 13) |
| Group dental insurance deductions | 117.00 | ($9.00 × 13) |
| Total deductions | $1,905.28 | |
| Net pay | $6,934.72 | |

# Computing an Employer's Quarterly Federal Tax Return

Learning Objective 5

Compute an employer's quarterly federal tax return.

Every employer who withholds federal income tax and FICA taxes (Social Security and Medicare) must file a quarterly return, Form 941—**Employer's Quarterly Federal Tax Return.** Figure 10-9 shows the data that the employer must include on Form 941 (the completed form is slightly abbreviated here). The return must be filed with the IRS within one month after the end of the quarter.

The employer obtains Social Security and Medicare amounts by multiplying the taxable wages paid by 12.4% for the first $97,500 for Social Security and by 2.9% for all wages for Medicare. These amounts represent the employees' deductions and matching amounts required to be paid by the employer.

### EXAMPLE E

For the first quarter of 2007, Yeager Manufacturing paid total wages of $2,132,684.27. The company withheld $372,486.20 for federal income tax. Since no employee earned more than $97,500 in taxable wages, all wages paid were subject to Social Security and Medicare taxes. If during the quarter Yeager had deposited $680,000 toward its taxes due, how much would it be required to send in with itsfirst-quarter Form 941?

| | |
|---|---|
| Gross wages $2,132,684.27 × 12.4% (Social Security) | $264,452.85 |
| Gross wages $2,132,684.27 × 2.9% (Medicare) | + 61,847.84 |
| Subtotal | 326,300.69 |
| Income taxes withheld | +372,486.20 |
| Total | 698,786.89 |
| Less deposit | −680,000.00 |
| Balance due | $ 18,786.89 |

## Figure 10-9 Form 941 Employer's Quarterly Federal Tax Return (extract)

| Line | Description | | Amount |
|---|---|---|---|
| 1 | Number of employees who received wages, tips, or other compensation for the pay period including: *Mar. 12* (Quarter 1), *June 12* (Quarter 2), *Sept. 12* (Quarter 3), *Dec. 12* (Quarter 4) | 1 | 5 |
| 2 | Wages, tips, and other compensation | 2 | 60,138 . 12 |
| 3 | Total income tax withheld from wages, tips, and other compensation | 3 | 4,997 . 45 |
| 4 | If no wages, tips, and other compensation are subject to social security or Medicare tax | | ☐ Check and go to line 6. |
| 5 | Taxable social security and Medicare wages and tips: | | |

| | Column 1 | | Column 2 |
|---|---|---|---|
| 5a Taxable social security wages | 60,138 . 12 | × .124 = | 7,457 . 13 |
| 5b Taxable social security tips | . | × .124 = | . |
| 5c Taxable Medicare wages & tips | 60,138 . 12 | × .029 = | 1,744 . 01 |

| Line | Description | | Amount |
|---|---|---|---|
| 5d | Total social security and Medicare taxes (*Column 2,* lines 5a + 5b + 5c = line 5d) | 5d | 9,201 . 14 |
| 6 | Total taxes before adjustments (lines 3 + 5d = line 6) | 6 | 14,198 . 59 |
| 7 | TAX ADJUSTMENTS (read the instructions for line 7 before completing lines 7a through 7g): | | |
| 7a | Current quarter's fractions of cents | . | |
| 7b | Current quarter's sick pay | . | |
| 7c | Current quarter's adjustments for tips and group-term life insurance | . | |
| 7d | Current year's income tax withholding (attach Form 941c) | . | |
| 7e | Prior quarters' social security and Medicare taxes (attach Form 941c) | . | |
| 7f | Special additions to federal income tax (attach Form 941c) | . | |
| 7g | Special additions to social security and Medicare (attach Form 941c) | . | |
| 7h | TOTAL ADJUSTMENTS (combine all amounts: lines 7a through 7g) | 7h | 0 . 00 |
| 8 | Total taxes after adjustments (combine lines 6 and 7h) | 8 | 14,198 . 59 |
| 9 | Advance earned income credit (EIC) payments made to employees | 9 | . |
| 10 | Total taxes after adjustment for advance EIC (line 8 – line 9 = line 10) | 10 | 14,198 . 59 |
| 11 | Total deposits for this quarter, including overpayment applied from a prior quarter | 11 | 14,107 . 58 |
| 12 | Balance due (If line 10 is more than line 11, write the difference here.) For information on how to pay, see the instructions. | 12 | 91 . 01 |
| 13 | Overpayment (If line 11 is more than line 10, write the difference here.) | . | Check one ☐ Apply to next return. ☐ Send a refund. |

▶ You **MUST** fill out both pages of this form and **SIGN** it. Next ➔

For Privacy Act and Paperwork Reduction Act Notice, see the back of the Payment Voucher. Cat. No. 17001Z Form **941** (Rev. 1-2008)

## CONCEPT CHECK 10.5

As displayed in Figure 10-9, the total taxes due the IRS consist of the $4,997.45 in federal income taxes withheld from employees, plus $7,457.13 and $1,744.01 for Social Security and Medicare taxes, respectively, half of which is withheld from the employees' paychecks and half of which is paid by the employer. Although the employer files Form 941 quarterly, the amount of taxes due is usually deposited in a qualified depository (bank) monthly or more often, and it is only the difference between the monthly deposits and the total taxes due that is sent with the Form 941 report.

# Computing an Employer's Federal and State Unemployment Tax Liability

In the preceding section, you learned that the employer must match the employee's contributions to Social Security and Medicare taxes. In addition, employers must pay two payroll taxes for federal and state unemployment programs.

The **Federal Unemployment Tax Act (FUTA)** annually requires the employer to pay a 6.2% tax on the first $7,000 paid to each employee to fund the federal unemployment compensation program for those who have lost their jobs. Most states have also passed a **State Unemployment Tax Act (SUTA),** requiring the employer to pay 5.4% tax on the first $7,000 paid to each employee to fund state programs for the unemployed. This 5.4% state tax is *deductible* from the federal tax payment. Thus, in most cases, employers pay the federal government just 0.8% FUTA tax: 6.2% FUTA − 5.4% SUTA = 0.8% requirement.

**Learning Objective 6**

Compute an employer's federal and state unemployment tax liability.

**EXAMPLE F**

During the first quarter, Johnson and Johnson paid wages of $976,550.80. Of this amount, $172,400.60 was paid to employees who had been paid $7,000 earlier in the quarter. What was the employer's liability for FUTA and SUTA taxes, assuming that the state rate was 5.4%?

$976,550.80 − $172,400.60 = $804,150.20 subject to FUTA and SUTA taxes
$804,150.20 × 0.008 = $6,433.20 FUTA tax payment
$804,150.20 × 0.054 = $43,424.11 SUTA tax payment
$6,433.20 + $43,424.11 = $49,857.31

**CONCEPT CHECK 10.6**

Warner-Lambert Company employed Rojas Perez for 13 weeks during the period January 1 through March 31, 2007. His salary was $1,350 per week. At the end of the quarter, how much in FUTA and SUTA taxes did the company have to pay to the federal and state governments based on Rojas's income?

$1,350 per week × 13 weeks = $17,550 total wage
$7,000 maximum × 0.008 = $56 FUTA tax
$7,000 maximum × 0.054 = $378 SUTA tax
$56 + $378 = $434 total federal and state unemployment taxes

COMPLETE ASSIGNMENTS 10.1 AND 10.2.

## Chapter Terms for Review

employee's earnings record

Employer's Quarterly Federal Tax Return

Federal Insurance Contributions Act (FICA)

Federal Unemployment Tax Act (FUTA)

Form W-4

payroll register

percentage method

State Unemployment Tax Act (SUTA)

wage-bracket method

withholding allowance

## Try Microsoft® Excel

Try working the following problems using the Microsoft Excel templates found on your Student CD. Solutions for the problems are also shown on the CD.

1. Brighton Company pays its employees at the regular hourly rate for all hours worked up to 40 hours per week. Hours in excess of 40 are paid at $1\frac{1}{2}$ times the regular rate. Set up the following spreadsheet in Excel and add formulas to calculate **Overtime Hours, Regular Pay, Overtime Pay,** and **Total Gross Pay** for each employee in the shaded cells.

   *Hint: Use the IF function to determine overtime hours.*

| Employees | Total Hours Worked | Regular Hourly Rate | Overtime Hours | Regular Pay | Overtime Pay | Total Gross Pay |
|---|---|---|---|---|---|---|
| Baker, Jason | 42 | $12.80 | | | | |
| Castro, Jill | 38 | 15.70 | | | | |
| Dobson, Jack | 40 | 12.00 | | | | |
| Ellis, Jennifer | 45 | 14.50 | | | | |

2. Set up the following worksheet and add formulas in the shaded cells to calculate the **Social Security**, **Medicare**, **Total Deductions**, and **Net Pay** for each employee. Assume all wages are taxable and use the following rates: Social Security = 6.2%, Medicare = 1.45%.

| Employees | Wages | Social Security | Medicare | Income Tax | Total Deductions | Net Pay |
|---|---|---|---|---|---|---|
| Carter, Janes | $460.35 | | | $45.80 | | |
| Edison, Alice | 289.50 | | | 25.00 | | |
| Garcia, Joseph | 375.00 | | | 36.90 | | |
| Kilmer, Martha | 450.70 | | | 52.00 | | |

# THE BOTTOM LINE

*Summary of chapter learning objectives:*

| Learning Objective | Example |
|---|---|
| **10.1** Prepare a payroll register. | Based on the data presented, complete the following payroll register. Fill out the total wages section and then compute the federal income tax, Social Security, Medicare, and other withholdings. Total all columns and check. Use the percentage method for federal income tax. |
| **10.2** Compute federal income tax withholding amounts. | 1. G. Lee is paid $14.20 per hour. He worked 40 regular hours and 6 overtime hours during the week ending January 7. He is single and claims one withholding allowance. He takes a weekly medical deduction of $7.<br>2. E. Berg is paid $13 per hour. He worked 40 regular hours and 8 overtime hours during the week of January 7. He is married and claims four withholding allowances. He takes a weekly medical deduction of $15. |
| **10.3** Compute Social Security, Medicare, and other withholdings. | |

| Name | Marital Status | W/H Allow | Total Hours | Regular Earnings | | Overtime Earnings | | | Total Wages | Deductions | | | | | Net Pay |
|---|---|---|---|---|---|---|---|---|---|---|---|---|---|---|---|
| | | | | Rate per Hour | Amt | Hours Worked | Rate per Hour | Amt | | Social Security | Medi-care | Fed. Inc. Tax | Med. Insurance | Total | |
| Lee, G. | | | | | | | | | | | | | | | |
| Berg, E. | | | | | | | | | | | | | | | |
| | | | | | | | | | | | | | | | |

| Learning Objective | Example |
|---|---|
| **10.4** Complete an employee's earnings record. | 3. Complete the earnings record for D. Chan. Use 6.2% for Social Security and 1.45% for Medicare taxes. Use the percentage method for federal income tax withholding, on the monthly wages. |

Name D. Chan  Social Security No. 125-11-3296

Address 7821 Oak Ave.  No. of Allowances 1  Marital Status Married

| Period Ending | Total Wages | Cumulative Total | Deductions | | | | | Net Pay |
|---|---|---|---|---|---|---|---|---|
| | | | Social Security | Medicare | Federal Inc. Tax | Other Deductions | Total | |
| 1/31 | $3,100 | $3,100 | | | | $18.00 | | |
| 2/28 | 3,000 | 6,100 | | | | 18.00 | | |
| 3/31 | 3,450 | $9,550 | | | | 18.00 | | |
| Quarter Total | $9,550 | | | | | $54.00 | | |

# THE BOTTOM LINE

*Summary of chapter learning objectives:*

| Learning Objective | Example |
|---|---|
| **10.5**<br>Compute an employer's quarterly federal tax return. | 4. The Frazer Company had a total payroll of $279,440 for the first quarter of the year. It withheld $29,700 for federal income tax. It made monthly tax deposits of $24,100. Frazer is now filing its quarterly Form 941. Complete the following to determine the amount of the check that Frazer must send to the IRS for undeposited taxes due.<br>a. Social Security tax due for the quarter _____<br>b. Medicare tax due for the quarter _____<br>c. Total taxes due for the quarter _____<br>d. Total deposits for the quarter _____<br>e. Undeposited taxes due IRS _____ |
| **10.6**<br>Compute an employer's federal and state unemployment tax liability. | 5. Miller Outfitters employed R. Rehnquist for the period from January 1 through March 31, 13 weeks, at a salary of $1,230 per week. At the end of the quarter, how much in FUTA and SUTA taxes are owed to the federal and state governments if the state had a 0.8% FUTA rate and a 5.4% SUTA rate?<br>a. Total wages<br>b. FUTA tax<br>c. SUTA tax<br>d. Total federal and state unemployment taxes paid |

**Answers:** 1, 2 and 3. Lee: Regular Earnings $568.00; O/T Earnings $127.80; Total $695.80; Deductions: SS-$43.14; MC-$10.09; FIT-$79.71; MI-$7.00. Total Deductions $139.94; Net pay $555.86 Berg: Regular Earnings $520.00; O/T Earnings $156.00; Total $676.00; Deductions: SS-$41.91; MC-$9.80; FIT-$26.05; MI-$15.00. Total Deductions $92.76; net Pay $583.24. 4. 1/31: $192.20; $44.95; $301.00; $556.15; $2,543.85 2/28: $186.00; $43.50; $286.00; $533.50; $2,466.50 3/31: $213.90; $50.03; $353.50; $635.43; $2,814.57 5. a. $34,650.56 b. $8,103.76 c. $72,454.32 d. $72,300.00 e. $154.32 6. a. $15,990.00 b. $56.00 c. $378.00 d. $434.00

SELF-CHECK

# Review Problems for Chapter 10

1 Alex Muñoz is paid $15 per hour for the first 40 hours and $1\frac{1}{2}$ times his regular rate for all hours worked over 40 per week.

**a.** Determine Alex's gross pay for the week if he works 45 hours.

**b.** Calculate the amount to be deducted for Social Security and Medicare taxes for the week.

**c.** Determine the amount to be withheld for federal income tax, using the percentage method, if Alex is single and claims one withholding allowance.

**d.** What is Alex's net pay for the week, assuming that his only payroll deductions are for Social Security, Medicare, and federal income tax?

2 Determine the amount to be withheld for federal income tax for each of the following, using both the percentage and the wage-bracket methods.

**a.** A married employee, claiming two allowances, has weekly gross pay of $650.

**b.** A single employee, with one allowance, has weekly gross pay of $525.

3 Calculate the employer's payroll taxes for each of the first three months of the year for three employees who are paid as follows:

| | |
|---|---|
| Albertson, K. | $3,000 per month |
| Becket, W. | $4,000 per month |
| Jones, C. | $2,100 per month |

Include FUTA (0.8%), SUTA (5.4%), Social Security (6.2%), and Medicare (1.45%) taxes. Be sure to consider the maximum taxable amount for unemployment taxes ($7,000) per employee.

4 Determine the taxes to be reported on the quarterly 941 form for an employer who paid total gross wages of $62,000 and withheld $7,800 for federal income tax.

| | |
|---|---|
| Social Security | ________ |
| Medicare | ________ |
| Federal income tax | ________ |
| Total | ________ |

5 Determine the amount to be withheld from the current period's gross pay of $7,600 for Social Security and Medicare for an employee whose cumulative wages were $92,300, not including pay for the current period. Use the rates and taxable maximum given in the chapter.

6 Employees of Xper Co. are paid at their regular rate for the first 40 hours, at $1\frac{1}{2}$ times their regular rate for hours worked between 40 and 48, and double their regular rate for all hours worked over 48, per week. Calculate each employee's gross pay for the week.

John Kowalski, regular rate $12.16, worked 47 hours

Martha Madison, regular rate $9.50, worked 50 hours

Joy Weston, regular rate $10.80, worked 42 hours

**Answers to the Self-Check can be found in Appendix B at the back of the text.**

## Notes

# Assignment 10.1: Payroll Problems

Name

Date Score

Learning Objectives 1 2

**A (52 points) Complete the payroll. (1 point for each correct answer)**

**1.** In this company, employees are paid $1\frac{1}{2}$ times their regular rate for overtime hours between 40 and 48 and 2 times their regular rate for overtime hours over 48, per week.

| Name | Total Hours | Regular Rate Per Hour | Regular Earnings | | Time and a Half | | Double Time | | Total Earnings |
|---|---|---|---|---|---|---|---|---|---|
| | | | Hours | Amount | Hours | Amount | Hours | Amount | |
| Avila, Susan | 49 | 9.00 | 40 | | 8 | | 1 | | |
| Carter, Dale | 40 | 8.00 | 40 | | — | | — | | |
| Kula, Mary | 50 | 10.00 | 40 | | 8 | | 2 | | |
| Murphy, Tom | 45 | 9.00 | 40 | | 5 | | — | | |
| Norton, Alice | 40 | 8.80 | 40 | | — | | — | | |
| Payton, Alan | 35 | 8.00 | 35 | | — | | — | | |
| Perry, Lance | 47 | 8.00 | 40 | | 7 | | — | | |
| Polar, Barbara | 41 | 9.00 | 40 | | 1 | | — | | |
| Quinn, Carl | 49 | 8.80 | 40 | | 8 | | 1 | | |
| Reston, Sally | 40 | 8.80 | 40 | | — | | — | | |
| Sacco, Dom | 50 | 9.50 | 40 | | 8 | | 2 | | |
| Warren, Bill | 44 | 10.00 | 40 | | 4 | | — | | |
| TOTALS | | | | | | | | | |

Score for A (52)

**B (28 points) Solve the following problems. (7 points for each correct answer)**

**2.** Mark Johnston is employed at a monthly salary of $2,980. How much is deducted from his monthly salary for FICA taxes (Social Security and Medicare)? ________

**3.** Joleen Dole is employed by a company that pays her $3,600 a month. She is single and claims one withholding allowance. What is her net pay after Social Security, Medicare, and federal income tax withholding? Use the percentage method for federal income tax. ________

**4.** On April 1, the company in problem 3 changed its pay plan from monthly to weekly and began paying Joleen $830.77 per week. What is her net weekly pay after Social Security, Medicare, and income tax deductions? Use the percentage method. ________

**5.** William Diggs is married and claims four withholding allowances. His weekly wages are $725. Calculate his Social Security and Medicare deductions and, using the wage-bracket method, his federal income tax withholding. Find his weekly net pay. ________

________
Score for B (28)

**C** **(20 points) Compute and compare the federal income tax withholding amounts for each of the following individuals using the percentage method and the wage-bracket method. (Follow the steps in Section 10.2 for the percentage method.) (5 points for each correct difference)**

**6.** Martha Gail: weekly wages, $412; single; 1 withholding allowance
Percentage method: ________
Wage-bracket method: ________
Difference: ________

**7.** George Wilson: weekly wages, $445; married; 3 withholding allowances
Percentage method: ________
Wage-bracket method: ________
Difference: ________

**8.** Fred Greys: weekly wages, $387; single; 2 withholding allowances
Percentage method: ________
Wage-bracket method: ________
Difference: ________

**9.** Josephine Creighton: weekly wages, $595; married; 1 withholding allowance
Percentage method: ________
Wage-bracket method: ________
Difference: ________

________
Score for C (20)

# Assignment 10.2: Payroll, Earnings Record, Payroll Tax Returns

Name

Date Score

Learning Objectives 1 2 3 4 5 6

**A (40 points) Solve the following problems. (1 point for each correct answer in the Total Wages column in 1; 2 points for each correct answer in the Net Pay column in 1 and 2)**

**1.** Complete the following weekly payroll register. Workers receive overtime pay for any time worked in excess of 40 hours per week at the rate of 1 1/2 their regular rate per hour. There is a 6.2% deduction for Social Security and a 1.45% deduction for Medicare taxes. Use the wage-bracket method for federal income tax withholding. Be sure to use the correct table based on the marital status of each employee.

| Name | Marital Status | W/H Allow. | Total Hours | Regular Earnings: Rate Per Hour | Regular Earnings: Amount | Overtime Earnings: Hours Worked | Overtime Earnings: Rate Per Hour | Overtime Earnings: Amount | Total Wages | Deductions: Social Security | Deductions: Medicare | Deductions: Fed. Inc. Tax | Deductions: Med. Ins. | Deductions: Total | Net Pay |
|---|---|---|---|---|---|---|---|---|---|---|---|---|---|---|---|
| Baker, C. | S | 1 | 40 | $14.80 | | | | | | | | | $ 15.00 | | |
| Dillon, W. | M | 2 | 45 | 15.00 | | | | | | | | | 12.00 | | |
| Garcia, L. | S | 0 | 32 | 13.50 | | | | | | | | | 12.00 | | |
| Ingle, F. | M | 3 | 40 | 15.00 | | | | | | | | | 18.00 | | |
| Jung, S. | M | 2 | 48 | 12.40 | | | | | | | | | 18.00 | | |
| Kent, P. | M | 4 | 43 | 14.80 | | | | | | | | | 18.00 | | |
| Masters, T. | S | 1 | 40 | 10.60 | | | | | | | | | 12.00 | | |
| Ohm, R. | M | 5 | 42 | 14.28 | | | | | | | | | 12.00 | | |
| Valdez, M. | S | 1 | 40 | 12.50 | | | | | | | | | 15.00 | | |
| TOTALS | | | | | | | | | | | | | $132.00 | | |

**2.** The total monthly wages of four employees are listed below. Determine the amount of the deductions and the net pay due to each employee. Use 6.2% for Social Security and 1.45% for Medicare tax deductions, and use the percentage method for federal income tax withholding. Determine the deductions and totals.

| Name | Marital Status | W/H Allow. | Total Wages | Deductions: Social Security | Deductions: Medicare | Deductions: Federal Income Tax | Deductions: Total | Net Pay |
|---|---|---|---|---|---|---|---|---|
| Ali, Kyber | S | 1 | $1,750.00 | | | | | |
| Dawson, William | M | 3 | 2,100.00 | | | | | |
| Henson, Gail | S | 0 | 2,820.00 | | | | | |
| Johns, Mary | M | 2 | 2,665.00 | | | | | |
| TOTALS | | | | | | | | |

Score for A (40)

**B** **(20 points) Solve the following problems. (1 point for each correct answer in the Net Pay column and 2 points for the correct Net Pay quarter total in 3; 1 point for each correct answer in 4)**

**3.** Complete the employee's earnings record for Michelle Lee. Use 6.2% for Social Security and 1.45% for Medicare taxes. Use the percentage method for federal income tax withholding.

Name Michelle Lee    Social Security No. 125-55-1254

Address 645 Abby Ln.    No. of Allowances 2    Marital Status Married

| Period Ending | Total Wages | Cumulative Wages | Deductions: Social Security | Medicare | Federal Inc. Tax | United Fund | Total | Net Pay |
|---|---|---|---|---|---|---|---|---|
| 1/6 | $ 450.60 | $ 450.60 | | | | $ 4.00 | | |
| 1/13 | 412.00 | 862.60 | | | | 4.00 | | |
| 1/20 | 412.00 | 1,274.60 | | | | 4.00 | | |
| 1/27 | 475.50 | 1,750.10 | | | | 4.00 | | |
| 2/3 | 415.20 | 2,165.30 | | | | 4.00 | | |
| 2/10 | 490.25 | 2,655.55 | | | | 4.00 | | |
| 2/17 | 427.50 | 3,083.05 | | | | 4.00 | | |
| 2/24 | 435.90 | 3,518.95 | | | | 4.00 | | |
| 3/3 | 510.00 | 4,028.95 | | | | 4.00 | | |
| 3/10 | 505.60 | 4,534.55 | | | | 4.00 | | |
| 3/17 | 516.00 | 5,050.55 | | | | 4.00 | | |
| 3/24 | 498.50 | 5,549.05 | | | | 4.00 | | |
| 3/31 | 535.80 | 6,084.85 | | | | 4.00 | | |
| Quarter Totals | $6,084.85 | | | | | $52.00 | | |

**4.** The following is a summary of quarterly earnings of a company's employees. Determine the information requested for the employer's quarterly federal tax return.

| Name | Total Wages | Taxes Withheld: Social Security | Medicare | Fed. Inc. Tax |
|---|---|---|---|---|
| Carter, M. | $ 6,084.85 | $ 377.27 | $ 88.22 | $ 451.42 |
| Davis, L. | 5,368.00 | 332.82 | 77.84 | 437.50 |
| Gordon, J. | 4,266.35 | 264.51 | 61.86 | 398.65 |
| McBride, C. | 7,230.00 | 448.26 | 104.84 | 595.80 |
| Taggert, L. | 6,240.50 | 386.91 | 90.49 | 465.50 |
| Walton, N. | 5,285.92 | 327.73 | 76.65 | 566.00 |
| TOTALS | | | | |

**a.** Total earnings paid ________

**b.** Federal income tax withheld ________

**c.** Total Social Security tax paid ________

**d.** Total Medicare tax paid ________

**e.** Total taxes withheld ________

________

Score for B (20)

**C (40 points) Solve the following problems. (4 points for each correct answer in 5 and 6; 1 point for each correct answer in 7)**

**5.** The quarterly earnings of the employees of the Alpha Company are listed in the following table. Determine the employee information needed for the employer's quarterly federal tax return (Form 941).

| | | Taxes Withheld | | |
|---|---|---|---|---|
| Name | Total Wages | Social Security | Medicare | Fed. Inc. Tax |
| Caldwell, Janice | $ 3,420.00 | $ 212.04 | $ 49.59 | $ 423.90 |
| Dorman, J.A. | 3,600.00 | 223.20 | 52.20 | 473.67 |
| Eagie, T.W. | 4,016.50 | 249.02 | 58.24 | 433.33 |
| Fortune, Mark | 3,774.90 | 234.04 | 54.74 | 410.05 |
| Morris, Regina | 3,605.40 | 223.53 | 52.28 | 399.83 |
| Tracy, Joseph | 4,111.60 | 254.92 | 59.62 | 360.17 |
| TOTALS | | | | |

**a.** Total earnings paid ________

**b.** Employee's contribution of Social Security tax ________

**c.** Employee's contribution of Medicare tax ________

**d.** Federal income tax withheld from wages ________

**e.** Total taxes withheld ________

**6.** The Primo Company had a total payroll of $148,600.34 for the first quarter of the current year. It withheld $28,531.27 from the employees for federal income tax during this quarter. The company made the following deposits in a qualified bank depository for the amount of the income and Social Security and Medicare taxes withheld from the employees and for the company's contribution to the FICA tax: $17,050 on February 6; $17,050 on March 4; and $17,050 on April 5. Primo Company's bookkeeper is now filling out Form 941 (quarterly return), which is due by the end of April. Complete the following to determine the amount of the check that the company must send to the IRS for the undeposited taxes due.

**a.** Total Social Security and Medicare taxes to be paid for quarter ________

**b.** Total taxes ________

**c.** Total deposits for quarter (sent to qualified bank depository) ________

**d.** Undeposited taxes due IRS ________

**7.** Jordan Mills employed Ruth Liebowitz for the period January 1 through March 31 (13 weeks) at a salary of $1,500 per week. At the end of the first quarter of the year, how much in FUTA and SUTA taxes did the company owe to the federal and state governments if the state had an 0.8% FUTA rate and a 5.4% SUTA rate?

**a.** Total wages and taxable wages ______ ______

**b.** FUTA tax ________

**c.** SUTA tax ________

**d.** Total federal and state unemployment taxes paid ________

________

Score for C (40)

## Notes

# 11

# Taxes

## Learning Objectives

By studying this chapter and completing all assignments, you will be able to:

Learning Objective 1 — Compute sales taxes, using rate tables and percents.

Learning Objective 2 — Compute assessed valuations and property taxes based on assessed valuation.

Learning Objective 3 — Compute tax rates in percents and mills.

Learning Objective 4 — Compute property tax payments involving special assessments, prorations, and exemptions.

Learning Objective 5 — Make basic computations to determine taxable income for taxpayers who use the standard federal income tax Form 1040.

Learning Objective 6 — Make basic computations to determine the tax liability for taxpayers who use the standard federal income tax Form 1040.

Most retail businesses collect a sales tax from customers when a sale occurs. The tax money must be turned over to the government. People and companies owning property usually pay taxes on the property's value. In this chapter we explain calculations involving sales, property, and income taxes.

## Computing Sales Taxes

**Learning Objective 1**

Compute sales taxes, using rate tables and percents.

A **sales tax** is a government **levy,** or charge, on retail sales of certain goods and services. Most states and many cities and other local government entities levy sales taxes. State **tax rates**—the percent used to compute the amount of sales tax—currently range from 3% to 7%, and city and county rates range from 0.925% to 7%.

Retail sales taxes, which usually are a combination of state and local taxes, are calculated as a single percent of taxable sales. For example, a sale is subject to a state sales tax of 5% and a local sales tax of 1%. The combined rate of 6% is applied to all taxable sales in that locality.

### SALES TAX AS A PERCENT OF PRICE

Sales taxes generally are rounded to the nearest cent. For example, sales taxes of 4% and 5% on amounts of up to $1 are charged as shown in Figure 11-1.

**Figure 11-1** Sales Taxes

| 4% on Sales of | Tax Due | 5% on Sales of | Tax Due |
|---|---|---|---|
| $0.01 to $0.12 | none | $0.01 to $0.09 | none |
| $0.13 to $0.37 | $0.01 | $0.10 to $0.29 | $0.01 |
| $0.38 to $0.62 | $0.02 | $0.30 to $0.49 | $0.02 |
| $0.63 to $0.87 | $0.03 | $0.50 to $0.69 | $0.03 |
| $0.88 to $1.00 | $0.04 | $0.70 to $0.89 | $0.04 |
| | | $0.90 to $1.00 | $0.05 |

**STEPS to Compute Sales Tax and Total Sales Amount**

1. Multiply the taxable sales amount by the tax rate.
2. Add the sales tax amount to the taxable sales amount to get the total sales amount.

**EXAMPLE A**

If taxable merchandise of $60.39 is sold in a state with a 5% sales tax, what are the amount of tax and the total amount to be paid?

Amount of tax: $60.39 × 0.05 = $3.0195, which rounds to $3.02
Total amount to be paid: $60.39 + $3.02 = $63.41

Most retail stores have cash registers that recognize a code such as the Uniform Product Code (UPC) to determine taxable sales and to calculate the sales tax automatically. The sales receipt usually shows the total taxable sales as a subtotal, the sales tax, and the total sales plus tax. Usually, discounts on a sale are subtracted from the sale price before the tax is figured. Shipping and installation labor charges are generally not taxed.

**EXAMPLE B**

A customer living in a city with a 6% state sales tax and a 1.5% city sales tax purchased a refrigerator regularly priced at $850. He was given a 10% discount. Delivery charges were $45. What were the amount of tax and the total cost to the buyer?

Discount amount: $850 × 10% = $850 × 0.10 = $85
Price after discount: $850 − $85 = $765, or $850 × 0.90 = $765
Sales tax: $765 × (0.06 + 0.015) = $57.38
Cost to buyer: $765 + $57.38 tax + $45 delivery = $867.38

State laws regarding the items subject to sales tax vary. Most states do not tax groceries; however, most do tax meals served in restaurants. Certain nonfood items also sold in grocery stores (such as laundry detergent) are generally taxed. When nontaxable and taxable items are purchased together, the register usually computes the total price of items purchased and automatically adds the correct amount of tax for each taxable item. The taxable items are clearly marked on the register tape along with the total amount of tax charged.

**EXAMPLE C**

A customer living in a state in which the tax rate is 7% went to a grocery store and purchased a quart of milk for $1.15, a loaf of bread for $2.79, potatoes for $2.25, and two taxable items—laundry detergent for $8.49 and fabric softener for $5.30. What was her total charge at the checkout counter?

Taxable items: $8.49 + $5.30 = $13.79
Tax: $13.79 × 0.07 = $0.9653 = $0.97
Total: $1.15 + $2.79 + $2.25 + $8.49 + $5.30 + $0.97 = $20.95

## SALES TAX AS AN AMOUNT PER UNIT

All of the states and the District of Columbia levy special taxes on gasoline and cigarettes, usually stated in cents per unit (gallon or pack). State taxes on gasoline vary widely, from $0.075 in Georgia to $0.285 in Wisconsin; in addition, the federal tax is currently $0.184 per gallon. State taxes on cigarettes currently range from $0.07 (South Carolina) to $2.575 (New Jersey) per pack; the federal tax is currently $0.39 per pack.

## EXCISE TAX AS AN AMOUNT PER UNIT

An **excise tax** is a tax assessed on each unit. In some states both the excise tax and the general sales tax apply to items such as gasoline, cigarettes, and alcoholic beverages. In such instances, the excise tax may be part of the taxable sales price for general sales tax purposes. For example, in a certain locality gasoline costs $3.40 per gallon, plus state and federal excise taxes of $0.48, and is subject to a general sales tax of 6%. The total price per gallon is $4.11 ($3.40 + $0.48 excise tax + $0.23 general sales tax). The general sales tax is calculated as 6% of $3.88.

## CONCEPT CHECK 11.1

In a state in which the combined state and city sales tax rate is 6%, a customer went to a convenience store and purchased the following items: bread, $1.95; ground meat, $6.79; cheese, $4.79; lightbulbs, $4.25; and motor oil, $1.79. Only the last two items are taxable. Rounding the tax to the nearest cent, compute the total cost of all items and tax.

| | | |
|---|---|---|
| Nontaxable items: | $1.95 + $6.79 + $4.79 = $13.53 | |
| Taxable items: | $4.25 + $1.79 = $6.04 | |
| Total tax: | $6.04 × 0.06 tax rate = $0.36 | |
| | $13.53 | Nontaxable items |
| | 6.04 | Taxable items |
| | + 0.36 | Tax |
| | $19.93 | Total |

# Computing Assessed Valuations and Property Taxes

**Learning Objective 2**

Compute assessed valuations and property taxes based on assessed valuation.

A **property tax** for a business is a tax on real estate or other property, such as machinery, owned by the business. Businesses usually pay property tax bills semiannually. Taxes are based on a value, known as the **assessed valuation,** determined by a representative of the local or state government.

Assessed valuation ordinarily is based on the current **market value** of the property (what the property could be sold for). In many states it is fixed by law at 100%, but it is a fraction of that value in other states. Thus a particular community may use 60% of property values as the basis for tax billing. In most instances, land and buildings are assessed separately.

**EXAMPLE D**

The Kinsey family lives in a town in which assessed valuation is 60% of market value. The Bailey family lives in a town in which assessed valuation is 75% of market value. Each home has a market value of $260,000. What is the assessed valuation of each home?

Kinsey: $260,000 × 0.60 = $156,000
Bailey: $260,000 × 0.75 = $195,000

Assessed valuation often is increased by improvements to the property, such as the addition of an enclosed porch, a pool, or landscaping: Ordinary maintenance—a new coat of paint, for instance, or repairs to the roof—isn't justification for an increased assessment.

**EXAMPLE E**

The Lee family and the Kelly family live in a town in which assessed valuation is set by law at 80% of market value. They live in identical houses having a market value of \$220,000. The Lee family added an enclosed deck costing \$10,500 and a family room costing \$23,000. The Kelly family made extensive repairs and repainted the house a new color at a total cost of \$15,000. What was the assessed valuation on each home the following year?

Lee: \$220,000 + \$10,500 + \$23,000 = \$253,500 × 0.8 = \$202,800

Kelly: \$220,000 × 0.8 = \$176,000 (repairs and painting are not considered improvements)

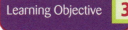

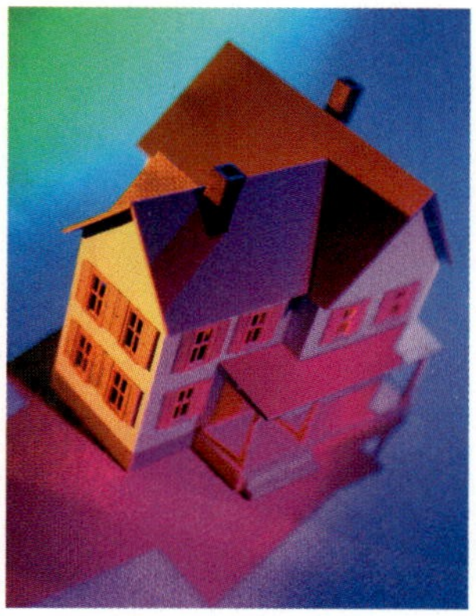



**CONCEPT CHECK 11.2**

a. The Coles family owns a home with a market value of \$300,000 in a community that assesses property at 100% of market value. The Jensen family owns a home with a market value of \$400,000 in a community that assesses property at 60% of market value. What is the difference between the actual assessments of the two homes?
   Coles: \$300,000 × 1 = \$300,000
   Jensen: \$400,000 × 0.6 = \$240,000
   Difference = \$60,000

b. The Bay family home has a present market value of \$280,000 in a community that assesses property at 80% of market value. If they add a family room and an additional bathroom at a cost of \$42,000, what will be the new assessed valuation?
   Revised market value: \$280,000 + \$42,000 = \$322,000
   New assessed value: \$322,000 × 0.80 = \$257,600

# Computing Tax Rates in Percents and Mills

## PERCENTS

Learning Objective 3

Compute tax rates in percents and mills.

For a city, county, or special district, the tax rate is found by dividing the amount of money the government unit needs to raise by the total assessed valuation of the particular unit.

**EXAMPLE F**

The town of Lakeside has a total assessed valuation of \$570,000,000. The amount to be raised by taxation is \$9,975,000. What is the tax rate?

The tax rate is

\$9,975,000 ÷ \$570,000,000 = 0.0175, or 1.75%.

This rate is usually written as 1.75% of value, or \$1.75 on each \$100 of value.

**EXAMPLE G**

If a property in Lakeside is assessed for \$160,000, what is the tax?

The tax can be found by multiplying the amount by the rate:

$\$160,000 \times 0.0175 = \$2,800$

## MILLS

Tax rates sometimes are expressed in a unit of measure called mills. A **mill** is a tenth of a cent, or \$0.001 (one thousandth of a dollar). To convert mills to dollars, divide by 1,000 (move the decimal three places to the left). To convert cents to mills, multiply by 10. Thus a tax rate can be converted from mills to cents or dollars or vice versa by using the following relationships:

| | |
|---|---|
| mills ÷ 10 = cents | 150 mills ÷ 10 = 15¢ |
| mills ÷ 1,000 = dollars | 150 mills ÷ 1,000 = \$0.15 |
| cents × 10 = mills | 15¢ × 10 = 150 mills |
| dollars × 1,000 = mills | \$0.15 × 1,000 = 150 mills |

**EXAMPLE H**

Davis County assesses property at the rate of 182 mills per \$100 of assessed value. How much tax would be due on property assessed at \$620,000?

\$620,000 ÷ 100 = \$6,200 to assess millage
182 mills = \$0.182
0.182 × \$6,200 = \$1,128.40 tax

**CONCEPT CHECK 11.3**

a. A town has a total assessed valuation of \$960,000,000. A total of \$12,000,000 must be raised by taxation for the operating expenses of the town. What will be the tax rate?
\$12,000,000 ÷ \$960,000,000 = 0.0125, or 1.25%

b. Convert \$0.57 into mills: 57¢ × 10 = 570 mills, or \$0.57 × 1,000 = 570 mills

c. If property in a town is assessed at the rate of 140 mills per \$100 of assessed value, how much tax will be due on property assessed at \$475,000?
\$475,000 ÷ 100 = \$4,750 to assess millage
140 mills = \$0.14
\$4,750 × \$0.14 = \$665 tax due

# Computing Special Assessments, Prorations, and Exemptions

Learning Objective 4

Compute property tax payments involving special assessments, prorations, and exemptions.

Communities can levy special assessments for improvements such as sewers, roads, or sidewalks. Sometimes the cost is spread over a period of years and added to the annual property tax bill of each property owner.

**EXAMPLE I**

The residents of Sonora voted to widen their roads and add sidewalks at a cost of $480 per residence, with the cost to be spread over a 12-year period. The Walker family had an annual tax bill of $630 before the improvements. If they pay their property taxes semiannually, what will be the amount of their next tax payment?

Annual cost for improvement: $\$480 \div 12 = \$40$

Annual property tax and improvement payment:

$\$630 + \$40 = \$670$

Next semiannual tax payment: $\$670 \div 2 = \$335$

Whenever property is sold, it is customary to *prorate,* or distribute, the taxes between seller and buyer as of the date of the settlement.

**EXAMPLE J**

A home having an annual tax bill of $720 was sold at the end of the seventh month of the taxable year. The seller had already paid the tax for the full year. How much tax was the seller reimbursed on proration of taxes at the time of the sale?

Months prepaid by seller: $12 - 7 = 5$

Tax reimbursed by buyer: $\$720 \times \frac{5}{12} = \$300$

In almost all states, property used exclusively by nonprofit organizations, such as schools, churches, governments, and charities, is exempt from taxation. Some states also allow partial exemptions for veterans and the elderly.

**EXAMPLE K**

The town of Hillton assesses property at 75% of market value. The tax rate is 1.2%. A church has a total market value of $560,000. How much does the church save each year by being exempt from property taxes?

$\$560{,}000 \times 0.75 = \$420{,}000$ $\quad$ $\$420{,}000 \times 0.012 = \$5{,}040$ saved

## EXAMPLE L

A veteran living in Conton receives a partial exemption of 15% of regular property taxes. The veteran owns property valued at \$380,000. If the property is assessed at 80% of value and the current rate is 1.3%, how much tax is due each six months?

Assessed value: $\$380,000 \times 0.80 = \$304,000$

Regular taxes: $\$304,000 \times 0.013 = \$3,952$

Taxes due after exemption: $\$3,952 \times 0.85\ (100\% - 15\%) = \$3,359.20$

Taxes due each six months: $\$3,359.20 \div 2 = \$1,679.60$

## CONCEPT CHECK 11.4

a. The city of Belton voted to build a new library at a cost of \$540 per residence, to be spread over a period of 15 years. If the Douglas family presently has a yearly tax bill of \$730, paid semiannually, what will be the amount of their next tax payment?

$\$540$ per residence $\div$ 15 years $=$ \$36 per year

$\$730$ present yearly tax amount $+$ \$36 $=$ \$766 new yearly tax amount

$\$766 \div 2 = \$383$ new semiannual tax amount

b. If a home with an annual tax bill of \$780 is sold at the end of the third month of the tax year, after taxes have already been paid for the full year, how much will the buyer reimburse the seller when taxes are prorated?

$12 - 3 = 9$ months prepaid by seller

$\$780 \times \frac{9}{12} = \$585$ reimbursed by buyer

c. A 70-year-old man lives in a state that grants senior citizens a 10% exemption from property taxes. If his home has a market value of \$250,000 and the tax rate is 1.3%, how much will his yearly taxes be? The county in which he resides assesses property at 70% of market value.

$\$250,000$ market value $\times 0.7 = \$175,000$ assessed valuation

$\$175,000$ assessed valuation $\times 0.013 = \$2,275$ regular taxes

$\$2,275$ regular taxes $\times 0.10 = \$227.50$ reduction

$\$2,275$ regular taxes $- \$227.50$ reduction $= \$2,047.50$ revised taxes

COMPLETE ASSIGNMENTS 11.1 AND 11.2.

Personal income taxes provide 37% of all income of the federal government. Social Security and Medicare taxes, which you studied in Chapter 10, provide another 33%. Together, these three taxes make up 70% of all federal government income.

Outlays for Social Security, Medicare, and retirement programs constitute 37% of all government expenditures. Payment of interest on government debt represents 7% of all government expenditures.

Figure 11-2 shows the breakdown of federal government income and the allocation of federal government spending.

**Figure 11-2** **Income and Outlays. These pie charts show the relative sizes of the major categories of federal income and outlays for fiscal year 2007.**

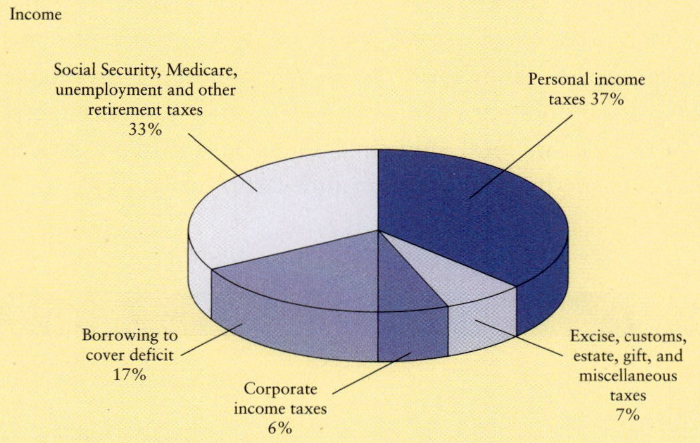


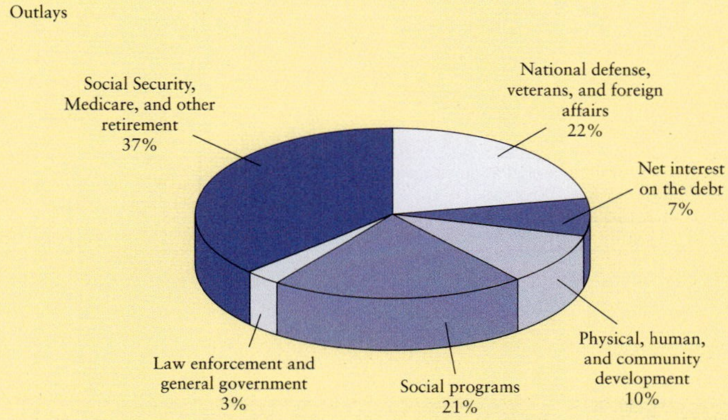


# Determining Taxable Income, Using Standard Form 1040

**Learning Objective 5**

Make basic computations to determine taxable income for taxpayers who use the standard federal income tax Form 1040.

**Form 1040** is the basic form filed by the majority of taxpayers. There are two simplified variations of this form: Form 1040A and Form 1040EZ. The income tax calculation process is illustrated for Form 1040 in Figures 11-3 through 11-8. The label in Figure 11-3 contains spaces for names, address, and Social Security numbers, as well as boxes to check to designate $3 to finance presidential elections.

A taxpayer's current **filing status** is indicated in the second section of Form 1040, shown in Figure 11-4. Five choices are given. The one selected determines the tax rate the taxpayer uses, as well as many of the taxpayer's deductions.

**Personal exemptions**, shown in Figure 11-5, are reductions to taxable income for the primary taxpayer and a spouse. One **dependency exemption** is granted for each dependent. Exemptions are phased out for individuals with higher incomes. The amount deducted for each exemption is currently $3,400. This amount is usually adjusted for inflation each year.

**Taxable income**, shown in Figure 11-6, includes wages, salaries, tips, dividends, interest, commissions, back pay, bonuses and awards, refunds of state and local taxes, alimony received, property received for services, severance pay, accrued leave payments, sick pay, unemployment compensation payments, capital gains, and any other income not specifically exempted by statute. Taxable income may include a portion of Social Security payments, IRA distributions, and pensions and annuities. It also includes income from businesses, professions, farming, partnerships, rents, royalties, estates, trusts, and other sources. It does not include income from gifts, inheritances, bequests, interest on tax-exempt state and local municipal bonds, life insurance proceeds at death, workers' compensation benefits, and certain income items for veterans.

**Figure 11-3 Form 1040 Label Section**

Form **1040** Department of the Treasury—Internal Revenue Service **U.S. Individual Income Tax Return** **2007** IRS Use Only—Do not write or staple in this space.

| | | | |
|---|---|---|---|
| **Label** (See instructions on page 12.) **Use the IRS label.** Otherwise, please print or type. LABEL HERE | For the year Jan. 1–Dec. 31, 2007, or other tax year beginning , 2007, ending , 20 | | OMB No. 1545-0074 |
| | Your first name and initial: *John S.* | Last name: *Sample* | **Your social security number** *345 67 8901* |
| | If a joint return, spouse's first name and initial: *Mary M.* | Last name: *Sample* | **Spouse's social security number** *456 78 9012* |
| | Home address (number and street). If you have a P.O. box, see page 12. *210 Elm Street* | Apt. no. | ▲ You **must** enter your SSN(s) above. ▲ |
| | City, town or post office, state, and ZIP code. If you have a foreign address, see page 12. *Anytown, MO 83817-2402* | | Checking a box below will not change your tax or refund. |

**Presidential Election Campaign** ▶ Check here if you, or your spouse if filing jointly, want $3 to go to this fund (see page 12) ▶ ☐ **You** ☒ **Spouse**

**Figure 11-4 Form 1040 Filing Status Section**

**Filing Status**

Check only one box.

1 ☐ Single
2 ☒ Married filing jointly (even if only one had income)
3 ☐ Married filing separately. Enter spouse's SSN above and full name here. ▶
4 ☐ Head of household (with qualifying person). (See page 13.) If the qualifying person is a child but not your dependent, enter this child's name here. ▶
5 ☐ Qualifying widow(er) with dependent child (see page 14)

**Figure 11-5 Form 1040 Exemptions Section**

**Exemptions**

6a ☒ **Yourself.** If someone can claim you as a dependent, **do not** check box 6a . . . .
b ☒ **Spouse** . . . . . . . . . . . . . . . . . . . .

Boxes checked on 6a and 6b: *2*

c **Dependents:**

| (1) First name | Last name | (2) Dependent's social security number | (3) Dependent's relationship to you | (4) ✓ if qualifying child for child tax credit (see page 15) |
|---|---|---|---|---|
| *Johnny* | *Sample* | *567 89 0123* | *Son* | ☑ |
| *Maria* | *Sample* | *678 90 1234* | *Daughter* | ☐ |
| | | | | ☐ |
| | | | | ☐ |

If more than four dependents, see page 15.

No. of children on 6c who:
- lived with you: *2*
- did not live with you due to divorce or separation (see page 16):

Dependents on 6c not entered above:

d Total number of exemptions claimed . . . . . . . . . . . . Add numbers on lines above ▶ *4*

**Figure 11-6** | **Form 1040 Income Section**

| | | | | |
|---|---|---|---|---|
| **Income** | 7 | Wages, salaries, tips, etc. Attach Form(s) W-2 | 7 | 65,000 00 |
| | 8a | **Taxable** interest. Attach Schedule B if required | 8a | 500 00 |
| **Attach Form(s) W-2 here. Also attach Forms W-2G and 1099-R if tax was withheld.** | b | **Tax-exempt** interest. **Do not** include on line 8a . . . 8b | | |
| | 9a | Ordinary dividends. Attach Schedule B if required | 9a | |
| | b | Qualified dividends (see page 19) . . . 9b | | |
| | 10 | Taxable refunds, credits, or offsets of state and local income taxes (see page 20) | 10 | |
| | 11 | Alimony received | 11 | |
| | 12 | Business income or (loss). Attach Schedule C or C-EZ | 12 | |
| | 13 | Capital gain or (loss). Attach Schedule D if required. If not required, check here ▶ ☐ | 13 | |
| If you did not get a W-2, see page 19. | 14 | Other gains or (losses). Attach Form 4797 | 14 | |
| | 15a | IRA distributions . . 15a / b Taxable amount (see page 21) | 15b | |
| | 16a | Pensions and annuities 16a / b Taxable amount (see page 22) | 16b | |
| Enclose, but do not attach, any payment. Also, please use **Form 1040-V.** | 17 | Rental real estate, royalties, partnerships, S corporations, trusts, etc. Attach Schedule E | 17 | |
| | 18 | Farm income or (loss). Attach Schedule F | 18 | |
| | 19 | Unemployment compensation | 19 | 1,300 00 |
| | 20a | Social security benefits . 20a / b Taxable amount (see page 24) | 20b | |
| | 21 | Other income. List type and amount (see page 24) | 21 | |
| | 22 | Add the amounts in the far right column for lines 7 through 21. This is your **total income** ▶ | 22 | 66,800 00 |

**Figure 11-7** | **Form 1040 Adjustments to Income Section/Adjusted Gross Income**

| | | | | | | |
|---|---|---|---|---|---|---|
| **Adjusted Gross Income** | 23 | Educator expenses (see page 26) | 23 | | | |
| | 24 | Certain business expenses of reservists, performing artists, and fee-basis government officials. Attach Form 2106 or 2106-EZ | 24 | | | |
| | 25 | Health savings account deduction. Attach Form 8889 | 25 | | | |
| | 26 | Moving expenses. Attach Form 3903 | 26 | | | |
| | 27 | One-half of self-employment tax. Attach Schedule SE | 27 | | | |
| | 28 | Self-employed SEP, SIMPLE, and qualified plans | 28 | | | |
| | 29 | Self-employed health insurance deduction (see page 26) | 29 | | | |
| | 30 | Penalty on early withdrawal of savings | 30 | | | |
| | 31a | Alimony paid b Recipient's SSN ▶ | 31a | | | |
| | 32 | IRA deduction (see page 27) | 32 | 3,000 00 | | |
| | 33 | Student loan interest deduction (see page 30) | 33 | | | |
| | 34 | Tuition and fees deduction. Attach Form 8917 | 34 | | | |
| | 35 | Domestic production activities deduction. Attach Form 8903 | 35 | | | |
| | 36 | Add lines 23 through 31a and 32 through 35 | | | 36 | 3,000 00 |
| | 37 | Subtract line 36 from line 22. This is your **adjusted gross income** ▶ | | | 37 | 63,800 00 |

**For Disclosure, Privacy Act, and Paperwork Reduction Act Notice, see page 83.** Cat. No. 11320B Form **1040** (2007)

The Adjustments to Income section, shown in Figure 11-7, allows the taxpayer to list certain items that are allowed as reductions to the total income. These adjustments include payments by the taxpayer or spouse to an individual retirement account (IRA), student loan interest, payments into a health savings account, moving expenses, one half of self-employment tax paid, and payments to a retirement plan for the self-employed, penalty on early withdrawal of savings, and alimony paid. **Adjusted gross income (AGI)** is a taxpayer's income after subtraction of adjustments to income from total income. (See line 37 of Adjusted Gross Income in Figure 11-7.)

After the adjusted gross income figure is computed, *deductions*—either the standard deduction or itemized deductions—are subtracted in order to figure taxable income (see Figure 11-8). The standard deductions for most taxpayers are shown in Figure 11-9. There are higher standard deductions for individuals who are 65 or over and for individuals who are blind; these are shown in Figure 11-10.

**Figure 11-8** Form 1040 Taxable Income and Income Tax Section

Form 1040 (2007) Page **2**

**Tax and Credits**

| Line | | | Amount |
|---|---|---|---|
| 38 | Amount from line 37 (adjusted gross income) | 38 | 63,800 00 |
| 39a | Check if: ☐ **You** were born before January 2, 1943, ☐ Blind. ☐ **Spouse** was born before January 2, 1943, ☐ Blind. **Total boxes checked** ▶ **39a** ☐ | | |
| b | If your spouse itemizes on a separate return or you were a dual-status alien, see page 31 and check here ▶**39b** ☐ | | |
| 40 | **Itemized deductions** (from Schedule A) **or** your **standard deduction** (see left margin) | 40 | 10,700 00 |
| 41 | Subtract line 40 from line 38 | 41 | 53,700 00 |
| 42 | If line 38 is $117,300 or less, multiply $3,400 by the total number of exemptions claimed on line 6d. If line 38 is over $117,300, see the worksheet on page 33 | 42 | 13,600 00 |
| 43 | **Taxable income.** Subtract line 42 from line 41. If line 42 is more than line 41, enter -0- | 43 | 39,500 00 |
| 44 | **Tax** (see page 33). Check if any tax is from: **a** ☐ Form(s) 8814 **b** ☐ Form 4972 **c** ☐ Form(s) 8889 | 44 | 5,142 50 |

**Figure 11-9** Standard Deduction Chart for Most People

**Standard Deduction for—**

- People who checked any box on line 39a or 39b **or** who can be claimed as a dependent, see page 31.
- All others:

Single or Married filing separately, $5,350

Married filing jointly or Qualifying widow(er), $10,700

Head of household, $7,850

**b** If your spouse itemizes on a separate return or you were a dual-status alien, see page 31 and check here ▶**39b** ☐

**40** **Itemized deductions** (from Schedule A) **or** your **standard deduction** (see left margin) . . **40**

**Figure 11-10** Standard Deduction Chart for People Age 65 and Older or Blind (line 40)

**Standard Deduction Chart for People Who Were Born Before January 2, 1943, or Were Blind—Line 40**

**Do not** use this chart if someone can claim you, or your spouse if filing jointly, as a dependent. Instead, use the worksheet above.

Enter the number from the box on Form 1040, line 39a . . . . . . . . . . . . . . . ▶ ☐

CAUTION: Do not use the number of exemptions from line 6d.

| IF your filing status is . . . | AND the number in the box above is . . . | THEN your standard deduction is . . . |
|---|---|---|
| Single | 1<br>2 | $6,650<br>7,950 |
| Married filing jointly or Qualifying widow(er) | 1<br>2<br>3<br>4 | $11,750<br>12,800<br>13,850<br>14,900 |
| Married filing separately | 1<br>2<br>3<br>4 | $6,400<br>7,450<br>8,500<br>9,550 |
| Head of household | 1<br>2 | $9,150<br>10,450 |

Some taxpayers choose to itemize deductions rather than use the IRS-approved standard deduction. **Itemized deductions** are deductions allowed for specific payments made by the taxpayer during the tax year. These deductions include charitable contributions, certain interest payments, state and local income (or sales) and property taxes, a portion of medical and dental expenses, casualty and theft losses, tax preparation fees, and other annually identified deductions. Illustrations, examples, and problems in this book are based on the assumption that all state and local taxes and all donations to charity are deductible.

## COMPUTING TAXABLE INCOME

Line 43 of Form 1040 shows "taxable income." Taxable income is the amount of income on which the income tax is based. Taxable income for most taxpayers is computed as follows (amounts from the preceding figures):

| | |
|---|---|
| Total income (income from all sources) (line 22) | $66,800 |
| Less adjustments to income (reductions of Total Income) (line 36) | − 3,000 |
| Adjusted gross income (line 37) | 63,800 |
| Less deductions (line 40)(from Figure 11-9 or 11-10) | 10,700 |
| Less exemptions (line 6d × $3,400, per line 42) | −13,600 |
| Taxable income (the amount on which taxes are computed) (line 43) | $39,500 |

### CONCEPT CHECK 11.5

Catherine, a 72-year-old blind widow, had an annual adjusted gross income of $29,000. She filed a return claiming a single exemption and standard deduction. What is her taxable income?

| | |
|---|---|
| Adjusted gross income | $29,000 |
| Less standard deduction: single, over 65, blind | − 7,950 |
| | 21,050 |
| Less 1 exemption | − 3,400 |
| Taxable income | $17,650 |

# Determining Taxes Due, Using Standard Form 1040

Taxes are computed from taxable income (line 43). **Tax Rate Schedules** (Figure 11-11) show the tax rate for (1) single, (2) married filing joint return (even if only one had income), (3) married filing separate returns, (4) head of household, and (5) qualifying widow or widower. The Tax Rate Schedules shown are used for all illustrations, examples, and problems in this book.

The remaining sections of Form 1040 permit listing of special credits, other taxes, and payments to arrive at the final refund or amount owed, and have spaces for signatures of the taxpayers and of paid preparers.

**Learning Objective 6**

Make basic computations to determine the tax liability for taxpayers who use the standard federal income tax Form 1040.

## Figure 11-11 Tax Rate Schedules

**Schedule X—**If your filing status is **Single**

| If your taxable income is: Over— | But not over— | The tax is: | of the amount over— |
|---|---|---|---|
| $0 | $7,825 | .......... 10% | $0 |
| 7,825 | 31,850 | $782.50 + 15% | 7,825 |
| 31,850 | 77,100 | 4,386.25 + 25% | 31,850 |
| 77,100 | 160,850 | 15,698.75 + 28% | 77,100 |
| 160,850 | 349,700 | 39,148.75 + 33% | 160,850 |
| 349,700 | -------- | 101,469.25 + 35% | 349,700 |

**Schedule Y-1—**If your filing status is **Married filing jointly** or **Qualifying widow(er)**

| If your taxable income is: Over— | But not over— | The tax is: | of the amount over— |
|---|---|---|---|
| $0 | $15,650 | .......... 10% | $0 |
| 15,650 | 63,700 | $1,565.00 + 15% | 15,650 |
| 63,700 | 128,500 | 8,772.50 + 25% | 63,700 |
| 128,500 | 195,850 | 24,972.50 + 28% | 128,500 |
| 195,850 | 349,700 | 43,830.50 + 33% | 195,850 |
| 349,700 | --------- | 94,601.00 + 35% | 349,700 |

**Schedule Y-2—**If your filing status is **Married filing separately**

| If your taxable income is: Over— | But not over— | The tax is: | of the amount over— |
|---|---|---|---|
| $0 | $7,825 | .......... 10% | $0 |
| 7,825 | 31,850 | $782.50 + 15% | 7,825 |
| 31,850 | 64,250 | 4,386.25 + 25% | 31,850 |
| 64,250 | 97,925 | 12,486.25 + 28% | 64,250 |
| 97,925 | 174,850 | 21,915.25 + 33% | 97,925 |
| 174,850 | --------- | 47,300.50 + 35% | 174,850 |

**Schedule Z—**If your filing status is **Head of household**

| If your taxable income is: Over— | But not over— | The tax is: | of the amount over— |
|---|---|---|---|
| $0 | $11,200 | .......... 10% | $0 |
| 11,200 | 42,650 | $1,120.00 + 15% | 11,200 |
| 42,650 | 110,100 | 5,837.50 + 25% | 42,650 |
| 110,100 | 178,350 | 22,700.00 + 28% | 110,100 |
| 178,350 | 349,700 | 41,810.00 + 33% | 178,350 |
| 349,700 | --------- | 98,355.50 + 35% | 349,700 |

© PHOTODISC

**EXAMPLE M**

For the Form 1040 illustrated in the text, the tax is computed as follows:

| | |
|---|---|
| Line 43—Taxable income | $39,500.00 |
| From Schedule Y-1 (married filing jointly): | |
| Tax on the first $15,650 | $1,565.00 |
| Plus 15% of amount over $15,650 | |
| $39,500 − $15,650 = $23,850 × 0.15 | +3,577.50 |
| Total tax | $5,142.50 |

**EXAMPLE N**

Filing as head of household, Dave has an adjusted gross income of $110,000. He itemizes the following deductions: $700 to Salvation Army, $900 to his church, $8,200 interest on his mortgage, and $3,300 state taxes. He claims two exemptions. Compute his federal tax.

| | |
|---|---|
| Adjusted gross income | $110,000 |
| Minus itemized deductions | − 13,100 |
| | 96,900 |
| Minus 2 exemptions | − 6,800 |
| Taxable income | $ 90,100 |

| | |
|---|---|
| From Schedule Z Head of Household: | |
| Tax on the first $42,650 | $ 5,837.50 |
| Plus 25% (0.25) of excess over $42,650 | |
| $90,100 − $42,650 = $47,450 × 0.25 | + 11,862.50 |
| Total tax | $ 17,700.00 |

## TAX CREDITS AND NET TAX

Credits allowed are subtracted from the tax to calculate the net tax. One of the most common credits is the **Child Tax Credit** (line 52). Taxpayers with dependent children under age 17 can receive a credit of $1,000 per qualifying child. The credit phases out at higher income levels.

Figure 11-12 shows that John and Mary Sample received a Child Tax Credit of $1,000. Look back at Figure 11-5 and note a check mark in the "qualifying child" box for Johnny Sample but not for Maria Sample. This distinction means that the son qualified for the credit because he was under age 17. The daughter qualifies as a dependent for exemption purposes, but no Child Tax Credit is allowed because she is age 17 or older.

**Figure 11-12** **Form 1040 Credits Section**

| | | | | | |
|---|---|---|---|---|---|
| 47 | Credit for child and dependent care expenses. Attach Form 2441 | 47 | | | |
| 48 | Credit for the elderly or the disabled. Attach Schedule R . | 48 | | | |
| 49 | Education credits. Attach Form 8863 . . . . . . | 49 | | | |
| 50 | Residential energy credits. Attach Form 5695 . . . . | 50 | | | |
| 51 | Foreign tax credit. Attach Form 1116 if required . . . | 51 | | | |
| 52 | Child tax credit (see page 39). Attach Form 8901 if required | 52 | 1,000 00 | | |
| 53 | Retirement savings contributions credit. Attach Form 8880. | 53 | | | |
| 54 | Credits from: a ☐ Form 8396 b ☐ Form 8859 c ☐ Form 8839 | 54 | | | |
| 55 | Other credits: a ☐ Form 3800 b ☐ Form 8801 c ☐ Form______ | 55 | | | |
| 56 | Add lines 47 through 55. These are your **total credits** . . . . . . . . . . . . | | | 56 | 1,000 00 |
| 57 | Subtract line 56 from line 46. If line 56 is more than line 46, enter -0- . . . . . . . ▶ | | | 57 | 4,142 50 |

## EXAMPLE O

Eric and Audrey Vaughn file a joint return. Their adjusted gross income is $48,900, and they take the standard deduction. They have three children, aged 12, 15, and 17, and claim five exemptions. Compute their net federal income tax after credits.

| | |
|---|---|
| Adjusted gross income | $48,900 |
| Standard deduction (joint) | −10,700 |
| | 38,200 |
| Minus 5 exemptions × $3,400 | −17,000 |
| Taxable income | $21,200 |
| From Schedule Y-1: | |
| Tax on the first $15,650 | $ 1,565.00 |
| Plus 15% on amount over $15,650 | |
| ($21,200 − $15,650) = $5,550 × 0.15 | + 832.50 |
| Total | 2,397.50 |
| Minus child tax credit ($1,000 × 2) | −2,000 |
| Net tax after credit | $ 397.50 |

## CONCEPT CHECK 11.6

Brian and Margaret Lee had wages of $33,200 and interest income of $2,400. They put $3,000 into a deductible IRA. They filed a joint return—claiming three exemptions (Brian, Margaret, and their daughter, aged 5)—and used the standard deduction. During the year, $950 in federal income tax had been withheld from their wages. What was the refund or tax due with the return?

| | |
|---|---|
| Total income | $35,600 |
| Adjustments to income: IRA deduction | − 3,000 |
| Adjusted gross income | 32,600 |
| Standard deduction: married, filing jointly | −10,700 |
| | 21,900 |
| Minus 3 exemptions: 3 × $3,400 | −10,200 |
| Taxable income | $11,700 |
| From Schedule Y-1: | |
| $11,700 × 0.10 | $ 1,170 |
| Minus child tax credit for one child | −1,000 |
| Net tax due after credits | $ 170 |
| Minus federal income tax withheld | −950 |
| Refund | $ 780 |

## Chapter Terms for Review

adjusted gross income (AGI)
assessed valuation
Child Tax Credit
dependency exemption
excise tax
filing status
Form 1040
itemized deductions
levy
market value
mill
personal exemptions
property tax
sales tax
tax rate
Tax Rate Schedules
taxable income

## Try Microsoft® Excel

Try working the following problems using the Microsoft Excel templates found on your Student CD. Solutions for the problems are also shown on the CD.

1. Set up the following table and complete using Excel formulas to calculate the values in the **Sales Tax Amount** and **Total Sale with Tax** columns using the sales tax rate indicated.

*Hint:* Use an absolute cell reference for the sales tax rate so that the formula can be copied. Cell references are changed to absolute by adding a $ before both the column letter and the row number. Example: $D$9

| Sales tax rate: | 7.25% |
|---|---|

| Taxable sale | Sales tax amount | Total sale with tax |
|---|---|---|
| $12.83 | | |
| $81.91 | | |
| $20.11 | | |
| $111.92 | | |
| $0.55 | | |
| $7.20 | | |
| $328.90 | | |
| $1,552.44 | | |
| $62.00 | | |

Try Microsoft® Excel is continued on page 226.

# THE BOTTOM LINE

*Summary of chapter learning objectives:*

| Learning Objective | Example |
|---|---|
| **11.1**<br><br>Compute sales taxes, using rate tables and percents. | 1. The Denver family lives in a state in which the sales tax rate is 6%. When they purchased a dining room table and chairs regularly priced at $990, they were given a discount of 15%. Shipping charges were $50. What was the total cost to the Farleys?<br><br>2. Wanda Green lives in a state in which the state tax on gasoline is $0.22 a gallon. Federal tax is $0.19 a gallon. If she purchased an average of 12 gallons per week during the 52-week year, how much did she pay in state and federal taxes combined? |
| **11.2**<br><br>Compute assessed valuations and property taxes based on assessed valuation. | 3. The Nguyen family lives in a town in which the assessed valuation on property is 65% of market value. The Parker family lives in a town in which the assessed valuation on property is 80% of market value. Each home has a market value of $162,000. How much is the assessed valuation of each home? |
| **11.3**<br><br>Compute tax rates in percents and mills. | 4. The town of Tyler has a total assessed valuation of $850,000,000. For the coming year the city must raise $11,730,000 for operating expenses.<br>a. What will the tax rate be?<br>b. What will the semiannual taxes be on a home with an assessed valuation of $135,000?<br><br>5. a. Convert 650 mills to its dollar equivalent.<br>b. Convert $0.12 to mills. |
| **11.4**<br><br>Compute property tax payments involving special assessments, prorations, and exemptions. | 6. A home with annual tax payments of $510 was sold at the end of the tenth month of the taxable year. What was the amount of tax prorated to the buyer?<br><br>7. A veteran living in Alameda receives a partial exemption of 10% of regular property taxes. The veteran owns property valued at $312,000. If the property is assessed at 70% of value and the current rate is 1.5%, how much tax is due each six months? |

Answers: 1. $941.99 2. $255.84 3. $105,300 (Nguyen), $129,600 (Parker) 4. a. 1.38% b. $931.50
5. a. $0.65 b. 120 mills 6. $85 7. $1,474.20

# THE BOTTOM LINE

*Summary of chapter learning objectives:*

| Learning Objective | Example |
|---|---|
| **11.5**<br><br>Make basic computations to determine taxable income for taxpayers who use the standard federal income tax Form 1040. | 8. Gilbert Black is 28 years old and single. He claimed one exemption. In 200X he earned $47,000 in wages and $675 in taxable interest income. During the year he invested $1,800 in an individual retirement account. Because of a change of jobs, he also had $1,200 in moving expenses, which qualified as an adjustment to income. He had qualifying deductions of $1,000 in deductible medical bills, $300 in church donations, and $9,600 in interest on the condominium he owned. He also paid $150 in state taxes. He had $2,500 in federal income tax withheld during the year. What was the amount of tax due with his return?<br><br>Income:<br>Less adjustments to income:<br>Adjusted gross income<br>Less deductions:<br><br>Less exemption:<br>Taxable income<br>Tax computation<br><br>Less tax withheld during the year<br>Tax due with return |
| **11.6**<br><br>Make basic computations to determine the tax liability for taxpayers who use the standard federal income tax Form 1040. | 9. Donald and Judy Mason are 72 and 70 years of age, respectively. Judy is blind. They filed as married, filing jointly. Last year they had a total income of $35,000 from investments. They filed a return and claimed the standard deduction. During the year they made quarterly payments of estimated tax totalling $1,000. What was the amount of tax due with their return?<br><br>Adjusted gross income<br>Less standard deduction<br><br>Less exemptions:<br>Taxable income<br>Tax computation<br><br>Less payments made during the year on estimated tax<br>Tax due with return |

Answers: 8. $1,643 9. $435

SELF-CHECK

## Review Problems for Chapter 11

1 The Dupree Company is considering the purchase of some equipment from two different suppliers. If the sales tax rate is 6%, which of the following offers should Johnson Company accept?

Company A: Equipment price of $65,000 plus installation and shipping costs of $1,200.

Company B: Equipment price of $73,500 less 10% discount, no additional charge for installation or shipping.

2 Georgetown needs to raise $7,800,000 in property taxes on property with a total market value of $650,000,000.

**a.** What will the tax rate be if property is assessed at 80% of market value?

**b.** Determine the amount of semiannual property tax to be paid by each of the following property owners who live in Georgetown:

Juan Garcia's home in Georgetown has a market value of $350,000.

Margaret Smith is a senior citizen who receives a 10% exemption from property tax. Her home in Georgetown has a market value of $215,000.

3 The residents of Hunterville voted to add street lights and sidewalks to their city at a cost per residence of $324 to be spread over 12 years.

**a.** If Mary Nowitski, a resident of Hunterville, had an annual tax bill of $860 before the special assessment, how much must she now pay semiannually for her property taxes?

**b.** If Mary Nowitski sells her home at the end of the eighth month of the tax year and has already paid the property taxes for the full year, including the special assessment, how much of the prepaid property tax should be allocated to the purchaser?

4 Samantha Jones works as a waitress. Last year she earned $15,800 in wages, $8,600 in tips, and $1,500 catering on weekends. She also received $600 interest from her credit union, $800 from a corporate bond, and an inheritance of $10,000. What was her gross income for federal income tax purposes?

5 Pete and Angel Romero are married and have two children aged 5 and 8. They also support Pete's sister, who lives with them. How much can Pete and Angel subtract from their gross income for exemptions?

6 Jan and Kirsten Bjorg, aged 63 and 66, are married filing a joint tax return. They have itemized deductions totaling $8,500. Should they itemize or use the standard deduction?

7 Eva Jung files as a head of household, has an adjusted gross income of $38,000, claims two exemptions, and uses the standard deduction on her federal return. What is her taxable income?

8 Brad and Justine O'Riley are married, filing a joint return, and have taxable income of $65,000. What is the amount of their income tax?

**Answers to the Self-Check can be found in Appendix B at the back of the text.**

# Assignment 11.1: Sales Tax

Name

Date                    Score

Learning Objective 1

**A (50 points) Solve the following problems. (1 point for each correct answer)**

**1.** The Country Corner store is in a state with a sales tax rate of 7%. Compute the sales tax, the total sale, and the change given for each transaction.

| Amount of Sale | Sales Tax | Total Sale | Cash Paid | Amount of Change |
|---|---|---|---|---|
| $8.37 | ________ | ________ | $10.00 | ________ |
| 2.35 | ________ | ________ | 5.01 | ________ |
| 34.85 | ________ | ________ | 40.00 | ________ |
| 19.56 | ________ | ________ | 25.00 | ________ |
| 5.12 | ________ | ________ | 10.00 | ________ |
| 16.50 | ________ | ________ | 20.00 | ________ |
| 18.55 | ________ | ________ | 20.00 | ________ |
| 0.98 | ________ | ________ | 1.25 | ________ |
| 9.98 | ________ | ________ | 15.00 | ________ |
| 17.78 | ________ | ________ | 20.00 | ________ |

**2.** Bill's Hardware is in a city where the state sales tax is 3.5% and the city tax is 2%. Determine the sales tax, the total sale, and the change given for each transaction. Then compute the total sales taxes and total sales.

| Amount of Sale | Sales Tax | Total Sale | Cash Paid | Amount of Change |
|---|---|---|---|---|
| $189.50 | ________ | ________ | $200.00 | ________ |
| 54.21 | ________ | ________ | 60.00 | ________ |
| 22.89 | ________ | ________ | 25.00 | ________ |
| 289.44 | ________ | ________ | 320.00 | ________ |
| 17.00 | ________ | ________ | 20.00 | ________ |
| 99.98 | ________ | ________ | 120.00 | ________ |
| Total | ________ | ________ | | ________ |

Score for A (50)

**B (30 points) Solve the following problems. Use Figure 11-1 for problems 3 and 4. (points for correct answers as marked)**

**3.** A candy store, operating in a state with a sales tax of 4%, made 658 sales at 10¢, 935 sales at 35¢, 720 sales at 49¢, 985 sales at 65¢, 612 sales at 75¢, and 865 sales at 90¢. How much did the store receive in sales taxes? (8 points) ________

**4.** If the candy store in problem 3 computed the amount of state sales tax submitted to the state based on 4% of gross sales, what would be the difference between the amount of tax the store collected and the amount it submitted to the state? (8 points) ________

**5.** Discount Carpets Company and Oriental Rugs, Inc., each purchased a new delivery van. Discount Carpets is located in a state that has a 5% sales tax and paid the regular price of $21,800 plus tax. Oriental Rugs is located in a state that has a 6% sales tax and received a special discount of $500 off the regular $21,800 price.

a. Including sales tax, which company paid more for its van? (8 points) ____________

b. How much more? (6 points) ________

________
Score for B (30)

**C** **(20 points) Solve the following problems. (points for correct answers as marked)**

**6.** Calico Books has stores in four states. Sales tax rates for the four states are as follows: state A, 8%; state B, 6.2%; state C, $5\frac{1}{2}$%; state D, 3%. Annual sales for the four states last year were as follows: state A, $865,000; state B, $925,000; state C, $539,000; state D, $632,000.

a. How much did Calico Books pay in sales taxes during the year? (10 points) ________

b. If all four states had the same lower sales tax rate of 3%, how much would Calico Books have collected in sales taxes during the year? (5 points) ________

c. If all four states had the same higher tax rate of 8%, how much would Calico Books have collected in sales taxes during the year? (5 points) ________

________
Score for C (20)

# Assignment 11.2: Property Taxes

Name ______________________________

Date ______________ Score ______________

Learning Objectives 2 3 4

**A (40 points) Solve the following problems. (4 points for each correct answer)**

**1.** Find the assessed valuation for each of the following towns.

| Town | Property Value | Basis for Tax Billing | Assessed Valuation |
|---|---|---|---|
| A | $625,000,000 | 100% | ____________ |
| B | $862,350,000 | 85% | ____________ |
| C | $516,800,000 | 70% | ____________ |

**2.** Find the tax rate for each of the following towns. Show your answer as a percent.

| Town | Assessed Valuation | Amount to Be Raised | Tax Rate |
|---|---|---|---|
| F | $860,000,000 | $13,932,000 | ____________ |
| G | $645,000,000 | 10,965,000 | ____________ |
| H | $732,000,000 | 9,150,000 | ____________ |

**3.** Convert the following percentage tax rates into dollars and cents per $100 of assessed valuation.

| Tax Rate | Dollars and cents |
|---|---|
| 1.3% | ____________ |
| 0.98% | ____________ |

**4.** Convert the following tax rates per $100 of assessed valuation into mills.

| Tax Rate | Mills |
|---|---|
| $1.30 | ____________ |
| $0.98 | ____________ |

____________

Score for A (40)

**B** **(24 points) Solve the following problems. (6 points for each correct answer)**

**5.** The Griffin Company is located in a state in which assessed valuation is 100% of market value. The tax rate this year is $1.35 on each $100 of market value. The market value of the company building is $190,000. How much property tax will Griffin pay this year? ________

**6.** The Balford Corp. is located in an area in which assessed valuation is 80% of market value. The tax rate this year is 1.7%. The market value of Balford's property is $635,000. How much property tax will Balford pay this year? ________

**7.** Next year, the assessed valuation in Balford's area (problem 6) will decrease to 75% of market value and the tax rate will remain the same as this year. How much less tax will Balford pay next year than it paid this year? ________

**8.** Perez, Inc., is headquartered in an area in which assessed valuation is 80% of market value. The tax rate this year is $1.40 on each $100 of assessed valuation. Its property has a market value of $320,000. How much property tax will Perez pay this year? ________

________
Score for B (24)

**C** **(24 points) Solve the following problems. Round to the nearest dollar. (3 points for each correct answer)**

**9a.** There are four towns in Hogan county: Lawton, Johnsville, Dover, and Gault. Using the total assessed valuations given and the amount of money the town must raise for operating expenses, compute the necessary tax rate for each town.

| Town | Total Assessed Valuation | Money That Must Be Raised | Tax Rate as a Percent |
|---|---|---|---|
| Lawton | $200,000,000 | $3,400,000 | ________ |
| Johnsville | $340,000,000 | $5,100,000 | ________ |
| Dover | $280,000,000 | $3,780,000 | ________ |
| Gault | $620,000,000 | $12,400,000 | ________ |

**b.** Convert each of the percentage rates in part a to mills per dollar of assessed valuation.

Lawton ________
Johnsville ________
Dover ________
Gault ________

________
Score for C (24)

**D (12 points) Solve the following problems. Round to the nearest dollar. (6 points for each correct answer)**

**10.** A home with annual tax payments of $624 was sold at the end of the fifth month of the taxable year. The seller had already paid the entire tax for the year. How much tax was the seller reimbursed on proration of taxes at the time of the sale? ________

**11.** A senior citizen lives in a state that grants a 20% exemption on property taxes. Her property is valued at $290,000 and is assessed at 75% of value. The current tax rate is 1.6%. How much tax is due each six months? ________

________________
Score for D (12)

## Try Microsoft® Excel *(Continued from page 217.)*

2. Adams Company purchased a new copy machine priced at $2,650 less a 10% discount plus delivery and setup charges of $150. Determine the amount of the discount, the sales tax at 6.5%, and the total amount of the sale including delivery and setup costs. Set up the table below on an Excel worksheet and complete by adding formulas for calculations. *Hint:* Discounts are subtracted before and delivery costs are added after calculating sales tax.

| | |
|---|---|
| Original price of copy machine | |
| Discount amount | |
| Net price after discount | |
| Sales tax at 6.5% | |
| Delivery and setup | |
| Total sale amount | |

3. Kingstrom Corporation is located in an area in which assessed valuation is 70% of market value. The current tax rate is 1.35%. Determine Kingstrom's property tax for the year on property with a market value of $652,000. Enter the data below into an Excel worksheet and complete by adding formulas for calculations.

| | |
|---|---|
| Market value of property | |
| Assessed valuation at 70% | |
| Property tax at 1.35% | |

# Assignment 11.3: Federal Income Tax

Name

Date Score

Learning Objectives 5 6

**A** **(52 points) Complete all problems, using the exemptions, deductions, and tax rates given in the chapter. Round all amounts to the nearest dollar. (Rounding is allowed so long as it is done consistently.) (12 points for correct answers to 2a and 3a; 4 points for other correct answers)**

**1.** Determine the taxable income for each of the following taxpayers.

| Adjusted Gross Income | Number of Exemptions | Type of Return | Deductions | Taxable Income |
|---|---|---|---|---|
| **a.** $28,700 | 1 | Single | Standard | ________ |
| **b.** $52,450 | 4 | Head of household | Standard | ________ |
| **c.** $34,700 | 2 | Joint | Standard | ________ |
| **d.** $16,452 | 1 | Single | $5,960 | ________ |
| **e.** $43,700 | 6 | Joint | $12,218 | ________ |

**2.** Sadie Gilford is a single, 70-year-old blind person who lives alone. She takes the standard deduction. Her income during the year was $28,700.

**a.** What is Sadie's taxable income? ________

**b.** What is Sadie's tax? ________

**3.** George Sampson is 82 years old. His wife Marcia is 83 and is blind. They have $21,000 total income. They file a joint return and take the standard deduction.

**a.** What is the Sampsons' taxable income? ________

**b.** What is the Sampsons' income tax? ________

________

Score for A (52)

**B** **(48 points) Solve the following problems. (12 points for correct taxable income; 4 points for correct income tax)**

**4.** Alfred Wild is 66 years old; his wife Silvia is 64. They file a joint return. Alfred's salary for the year was $45,000. Silvia's salary was $47,000. They paid mortgage interest of $12,600 and property tax of $1,200 on their home. They paid state income tax of $3,800 during the year. They itemize their deductions.

**a.** What is their taxable income? ________ **b.** What is their income tax? ________

**5.** Michael and Martha Miller are married and have three dependents living with them: their children, aged 17 and 19, and Martha's mother. Michael's salary for the year was $30,000, and Martha's salary was $32,000. They received taxable interest of $1,250 and $500 interest from a state bond. They take the standard deduction and file a joint return.

**a.** What is their taxable income? ________ **b.** What is their net tax after credits? ________

**6.** Renaldo and Rita Hernandez have three children aged 17, 18, and 12. Renaldo's father lives with them and has no income. Renaldo earned a salary of $46,000 during the year. Rita is not employed. They paid $3,100 property tax and $6,200 mortgage interest on their home. They paid $2,600 principal on their mortgage. They paid state income tax of $2,175. They donated $500 to their church and $500 to the Salvation Army. They spent $5,600 on groceries and $1,100 on utilities. They itemize their deductions.

**a.** What is their taxable income? ________ **b.** What is their net income tax after credits? ________

________

Score for B (48)

# Insurance

# 12

## Learning Objectives

By studying this chapter and completing all assignments, you will be able to:

Learning Objective **1** Compute costs and savings for auto insurance.

Learning Objective **2** Compute auto insurance premium rates for high- and low-risk drivers.

Learning Objective **3** Compute short-rate refunds.

Learning Objective **4** Compute coinsurance on property losses.

Learning Objective **5** Compute life insurance premiums.

Learning Objective **6** Compute cash surrender and loan values.

Learning Objective **7** Compute medical insurance contributions and reimbursements.

# Computing Auto Insurance Costs

**Learning Objective 1**

Compute costs and savings for auto insurance.

Auto insurance falls into three categories: liability and property damage, comprehensive, and collision. A policy that fully protects the insured will contain all three types.

**Auto liability and property damage insurance** protects the insured against claims resulting from personal injuries and property damage. Some states require all drivers to carry auto liability and property damage insurance. The amount of protection generally ranges from $50,000 to $1,000,000 per accident.

**Auto comprehensive insurance** protects the vehicle of the insured against water, theft, vandalism, falling objects, and other damage not caused by collision.

**Auto collision insurance** protects the vehicle of the insured against collision damage. Such damage may result from a collision with another vehicle or a one-car accident, such as hitting a tree.

The payment for an insurance policy is called a **premium.** Premium rates for auto insurance depend primarily on the coverage included in the policy, the driving record of the insured, the geographical area where the driver lives, and government laws and regulations.

Auto collision insurance policies usually contain a **deductible clause,** which stipulates that the insured will pay the first portion of collision damage, usually $50 to $500, and that the insurance company will pay the remainder up to the value of the insured vehicle. A deductible clause not only reduces the amount of damages for which the insurance company must pay but also keeps the insurance company from having to get involved in and do paperwork for small repairs costing less than the deductible. Therefore, a deductible clause lowers the premium for collision insurance.

**EXAMPLE A**

A car was insured for collision damage with a $250 deductible. The premium was $1,750 per year. The insured hit a tree, causing $2,530 damage to his car. How much more did the insured receive than he paid in premiums for that year?

$2,530 damage − $250 deductible = $2,280 paid by insurance
$2,280 received by insured − $1,750 premium paid = $530.

**EXAMPLE B**

The driver of car A carried auto liability and property damage insurance only. She struck car B, causing $1,400 damage to car B and $700 in injuries to the driver. Car A suffered $940 damage.

a. How much did the insurance company pay for this accident?
   $1,400 for damage to car B + $700 for injuries to driver = $2,100

b. How much did this accident cost the driver of car A?
   $940 in uncovered damage to her own car

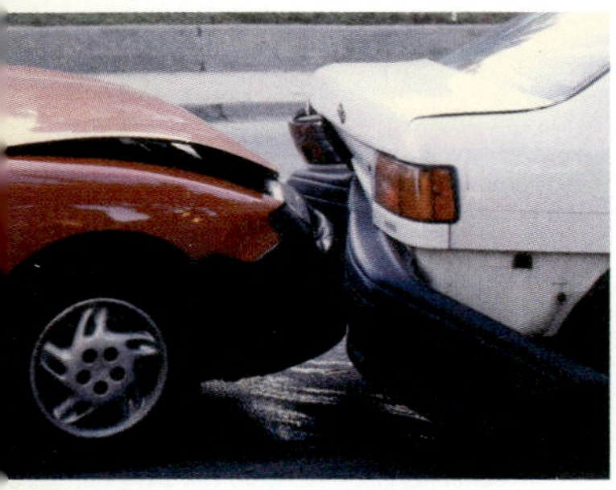


**No-fault insurance** is a term that is used to describe an auto insurance system that requires drivers to carry insurance for their own protection and that limits their ability to sue other drivers for damages. No-fault insurance requires that the driver of each vehicle involved in an injury accident submit a claim to *his or her own insurance company* to cover medical costs for injuries to the driver and passengers in that person's own vehicle. No-fault insurance is mandatory in some states. No-fault insurance doesn't cover damage to either vehicle involved in an accident.

**EXAMPLE C**

Drivers A and B live in a state in which no-fault insurance is mandatory. Their two cars collided. Driver A and his passengers incurred medical expenses of $3,500. Driver B and her passengers incurred $1,700 in medical expenses. Car A required $1,400 in repairs. Car B required $948 in repairs. How much did the insurance companies pay under the no-fault insurance coverage?

Driver A's insurance company paid $3,500 in medical expenses.
Driver B's insurance company paid $1,700 in medical expenses.
Car repairs are not covered under no-fault insurance.

**CONCEPT CHECK 12.1**

Driver A lives in a state in which no-fault insurance is mandatory. He carries all three classifications of insurance to be fully protected. His total insurance premium is $2,400, with a collision deductible of $500. Driver A is involved in a major accident when he loses control of his car and hits two parked cars (cars B and C) before colliding with an oncoming car (car D) containing a driver and three passengers. Driver A is alone.

Damage to driver A's car is $3,200.
Damages to cars B, C, and D total $8,600.
Medical expenses for driver A are $2,800.
Medical expenses for the driver and passengers of car D are $7,300.

a. How much does driver A's insurance company pay?
   Damage to car A: $3,200 − $500 deductible = $2,700 covered by collision
   Damage to cars B, C, and D: $8,600 covered by liability
   Medical expenses for driver A under no-fault: $2,800
   $2,700 + $8,600 + $2,800 = $14,100 paid by driver A's insurance
b. How much does driver D's insurance company pay?
   Medical expenses paid for driver D and passengers (no-fault): $7,300
c. How much more did driver A's insurance company pay to him and on his behalf for this accident than he paid in insurance expenses for the year? (This is the amount driver A saved this year by being fully insured.)
   $2,400 premium + $500 deductible for repairs in this accident = $2,900 paid by driver A
   $14,100 from insurance − $2,900 = $11,200
   Driver A saved $11,200 this year by being fully insured with a $500 deductible clause.

# Computing Low-Risk and High-Risk Rates

Learning Objective 2

Compute auto insurance premium rates for high- and low-risk drivers.

Auto insurance premium rates reflect the risk involved. Insurance companies study the statistics on automobile accidents relative to driving records. Premium rates are adjusted according to the driving record of the insured. A driver with a clear record of long standing is considered to be a **low-risk driver** and may be rewarded with a discount in the premium rate. Conversely, a driver with a record of numerous citations or accidents is considered to be a **high-risk driver** and may pay double, triple, or even a higher multiple than the normal premium rate.

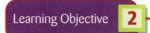

### EXAMPLE D

Drivers A and B have identical automobiles and amounts of insurance coverage. The normal premium rate for each is $2,000 per year. Driver A is a low-risk driver and receives a 15% discount on the premium rate. Driver B is a high-risk driver and must pay double the normal rate. How much more does driver B pay for insurance than driver A?

Driver A pays $2,000 × 85% = $1,700 (100% − 15% discount)
Driver B pays $2,000 × 2 = $4,000
Driver B pays $4,000 − $1,700 = $2,300 more

### CONCEPT CHECK 12.2

Driver A, a very careful driver, has had the same insurance company for 5 years and has not had a ticket during that 5-year period. Each year, driver A has received a 10% reduction in her premium. Driver B has a record of speeding tickets. He has had one or more every year for 5 years. His premium for year 1 was normal, for years 2 and 3 it was 150%, and for years 4 and 5 it was 200%. The normal annual premium rate for each driver would be $980.

a. How much did driver A pay in premiums over the 5-year period?
   $980 × 90% = $882
   $882 × 5 = $4,410
b. How much did driver B pay in premiums over the 5-year period?
   Year 1: $980
   Years 2 and 3: $980 × 1.5 × 2 = $2,940
   Years 4 and 5: $980 × 2 × 2 = $3,920
   $980 + $2,940 + $3,920 = $7,840
c. How much more did driver B pay during the 5-year period than driver A?
   $7,840 − $4,410 = $3,430

## Computing Short Rates

**Learning Objective 3**

Compute short-rate refunds.

**Short rates** are rates charged for less than a full term of insurance. If an insurance policy is canceled by the **insured** (the person who receives the benefit of the insurance) before the policy's full term is complete, the insured will receive a short-rate return of premium. If a policy is canceled by the insurance company rather than by the insured, the company must refund the entire unused premium.

### EXAMPLE E

A driver paid an annual premium of $1,960 for auto insurance. After 3 months, the vehicle was sold and the insurance canceled. The insurance company refunded the remaining portion of the premium at the short rate, based on a penalty of 10% of the full-year premium. What was the refund?

Unused premium: $\$1{,}960 \times \frac{3}{4} = \$1{,}470$ (9 months canceled $= \frac{9}{12} = \frac{3}{4}$ year)

Penalty: $1,960 × 10% = $196
Short-rate refund: $1,470 − $196 = $1,274

## CONCEPT CHECK 12.3

A company purchased two cars. Each car was insured at an annual premium of $1,780. At the end of 6 months, the company sold one car and canceled the insurance on that car. At the end of 9 months, the insurance company decided to cancel the insurance on the second car. The insurance company imposes a 10% penalty for short-rate premiums. Compute the refunds the insurance company paid for car 1 and car 2.

Car 1: $\$1{,}780 \times \frac{1}{2}$ year $= \$890$ unused premium

$\$1{,}780 \times 10\% = \$178$ penalty

$\$890 - \$178 = \$712$ refunded

Car 2: $\$1{,}780 \times \frac{1}{4}$ year $= \$445$ unused and refunded premium

COMPLETE ASSIGNMENT 12.1.

# Computing Coinsurance on Property Losses

Learning Objective 4

Compute coinsurance on property losses.

**Property insurance** is insurance against loss of or damage to property. A policy can be written to protect the insured against loss from fire, casualty, liability, and theft.

Premium rates, which are quoted in terms of dollars per $1,000 of insurance, depend on the nature of the risk, the location of the property, and the length of time covered by the policy. Short rates and short-rate penalties for less than a full term of insurance apply to property insurance as they do to auto insurance.

### EXAMPLE F

A building worth $350,000 is insured for $210,000. The annual premium for the policy is $5,000. A fire causes $80,000 in damage.

a. How much does the insurance company pay?
$80,000 in damage is less than the $210,000 policy. The insurance company pays the entire $80,000.

b. How much does the property owner pay?
The property owner does not pay for damages.

c. How much does the property owner pay that year in damages and insurance?
$5,000 for the insurance premium only.

In an ordinary fire insurance policy, the insured will be paid for the loss up to the amount of the insurance. Policies may be obtained at lower rates if they contain a **coinsurance clause.** This clause specifies that if a property is not insured up to a specified percentage of its value, the owner is responsible for part of the loss and will not be covered for the full amount of damages.

It is common practice for a fire insurance policy to have an 80% coinsurance clause. Under this clause, the full amount of the loss will be paid by the insurance company only if the policy amount equals 80% of the property value.

**STEPS to Determine the Owner's Share of Property Loss Under Coinsurance**

1. Compute the amount of insurance required by multiplying the entire value of the property by the percentage of coinsurance specified.
2. Compute the **recovery amount,** the maximum amount the insurance company will pay, by using the formula
$$\frac{\text{Amount of insurance carried}}{\text{Amount of insurance required}} \times \text{Loss} = \text{Recovery amount.}$$
3. Compare the recovery amount with the amount of the insurance policy.
   a. If the recovery amount is greater than the amount of the policy, the insurance company will limit its payment to the amount of the policy.
   b. If the recovery amount is less than the amount of the policy, the insurance company will pay the recovery amount.

   *Note:* The insurance company will never pay more than the amount of the loss.
4. Determine the owner's share of the property loss by subtracting the amount the insurance company will pay from the loss amount.

## EXAMPLE G

A building valued at $400,000 is insured for $200,000 under a policy with an 80% coinsurance clause. The annual premium is $2,800. A fire causes $100,000 damage to the building.

a. How much will the insurance company pay the insured?

STEP 1 $\quad \$400{,}000 \times 80\% = \$320{,}000$ insurance required

STEPS 2 & 3 $$\frac{\$200{,}000 \text{ amount of insurance carried}}{\$320{,}000 \text{ amount of insurance required}} \times \$100{,}000 = \$62{,}500 \text{ insurance pays}$$

b. How much must the owner pay if the building is repaired for $100,000?

STEP 4 $\quad \$100{,}000 - \$62{,}500 = \$37{,}500$ paid by owner

c. How much does the property owner pay that year for damages and insurance?
$37,500 damages + $2,800 premium = $40,300

d. How much would the insurance company pay if the fire caused $300,000 damage to the building?

$$\frac{\$200{,}000}{\$320{,}000} \times \$300{,}000 = \$187{,}500 \text{ recovery amount}$$

The insurance company would pay $187,500 (because the recovery amount is within the policy's coverage).

**EXAMPLE H**

If the amount of insurance carried in example G had been $320,000, how much would the insured have paid for damages and insurance that year?

$2,800 premium only (the 80% coinsurance requirement would have been met)

**CONCEPT CHECK 12.4**

A building worth $100,000 is insured for $60,000 with an 80% coinsurance clause. A fire causes $70,000 in damage. How much of the repair cost will the insurance company pay, and how much will the insured pay?

$\$100{,}000 \times 80\% = \$80{,}000$ insurance required

$$\frac{\$60{,}000}{\$80{,}000} \times \$70{,}000 = \$52{,}500 \text{ insurance pays}$$

$\$70{,}000 - \$52{,}500 = \$17{,}500$ insured pays

COMPLETE ASSIGNMENT 12.2.

# Computing Life Insurance Premiums

Learning Objective 5

Compute life insurance premiums.

The policies most commonly issued by life insurance companies are term insurance, straight life (sometimes called ordinary life), limited-payment life, endowment, and annuity.

**Term insurance** is protection issued for a limited time. A certain premium is paid every year *during the specified time period,* or term. The policy is payable only in case of death of the insured during the term. Otherwise, neither the insured nor the specified beneficiaries receive any payment, and the protection stops at the end of the term.

For **straight (ordinary) life insurance** coverage, a certain premium, or fee, is paid every year *until the death of the insured.* The policy then becomes payable to the **beneficiary.** A policy beneficiary can be a person, a company, or an organization.

**Limited-payment life insurance** (such as 20-payment life) requires the payment of a specified premium each year for a certain number of years or until the death of the insured, whichever comes first. Should the insured live longer than the specified number of years, the policy requires no further payments for the remainder of the insured's life and is payable to the beneficiary on the death of the insured.

**Endowment insurance** provides insurance payable on the insured's death if it occurs within a specified period. If the insured is alive at the end of the specified period, an endowment of the same amount as the policy is payable.

**Annuity insurance** pays a certain sum of money to the insured every year after the insured reaches a specified age, until the insured's death.

An **additional death benefit (ADB)**, sometimes referred to as an *accidental death benefit*, accompanies some policies. ADB allows the insured to purchase, at a low rate per thousand dollars of coverage, additional insurance up to the full face value of the policy. In case of death of the insured by accident, both the full value of the policy and the ADB are paid to the beneficiaries. If death occurs other than by accident, the full value of the policy is paid, but no ADB is paid.

© BRONWYN KIDD/PHOTODISC/GETTY IMAGES

Figure 12-1 shows typical annual, semiannual, and quarterly premiums (ages 25–28) for straight life, 20-payment life, and 20-year endowment policies.

**Figure 12-1** Insurance Premium per $1,000

| | Straight Life | | | 20-Payment Life | | | 20-Year Endowment | | |
|---|---|---|---|---|---|---|---|---|---|
| Age | Annual | Semi-annual | Quarterly | Annual | Semi-annual | Quarterly | Annual | Semi-annual | Quarterly |
| 25 | $17.20 | $ 8.94 | $4.73 | $31.20 | $16.26 | $8.26 | $52.00 | $27.04 | $14.30 |
| 26 | 17.85 | 9.28 | 4.91 | 31.81 | 16.52 | 8.45 | 52.60 | 27.35 | 14.47 |
| 27 | 18.60 | 9.67 | 5.11 | 32.41 | 16.83 | 8.64 | 53.20 | 27.66 | 14.63 |
| 28 | 19.30 | 10.04 | 5.31 | 33.06 | 17.31 | 8.85 | 53.86 | 28.01 | 14.81 |

**EXAMPLE I**

Using the premiums shown in Figure 12-1, determine the yearly premiums for each of the following $50,000 life insurance policies purchased at age 27.

| Type of Insurance | Method of Payment | Premium Computation |
|---|---|---|
| Straight Life | Annual | $18.60 × 50 = $930 |
| 20-Year Endowment | Quarterly | $14.63 × 4 × 50 = $2,926 |
| 20-Payment Life | Semiannual | $16.83 × 2 × 50 = $1,683 |
| 20-Year Endowment | Semiannual | $27.66 × 2 × 50 = $2,766 |
| Straight Life | Quarterly | $ 5.11 × 4 × 50 = $1,022 |

**CONCEPT CHECK 12.5**

(Use the premiums in Figure 12-1.)

a. If a person at age 28 purchases a straight life insurance policy having a face value of $150,000 with quarterly premiums, what is the yearly premium?
$5.31 × 4 × 150 = $3,186

b. If a person at age 25 purchases a 20-payment life insurance policy having a face value of $100,000 with semiannual premiums, what is the yearly premium?
$16.26 × 2 × 100 = $3,252

c. If a person at age 25 purchases a 20-year endowment insurance policy having a face value of $75,000 with annual premiums, what is the yearly premium?
$52 × 75 = $3,900

# Computing Cash Surrender and Loan Values

**Learning Objective 6**

Compute cash surrender and loan values.

Except for term insurance, insurance usually has a **cash surrender value,** which is the amount of cash that the company will pay the insured on the surrender, or "cashing in," of the policy. The **loan value** of a policy is the amount that the insured may borrow on the policy from the insurance company. Interest is charged on such loans. The values, often quoted after the third year of the policy, are stated in the policy and increase every year. Figure 12-2 shows typical cash surrender and loan values for policies issued at age 25 per $1,000 of life insurance.

**Figure 12-2** Insurance Values per $1,000

| End of Policy Year | Cash Surrender and Loan Values | | |
|---|---|---|---|
| | Straight Life | 20-Payment Life | 20-Year Endowment |
| 3 | $ 10 | $ 43 | $ 88 |
| 4 | 22 | 68 | 130 |
| 5 | 35 | 93 | 173 |
| 10 | 104 | 228 | 411 |
| 15 | 181 | 380 | 684 |
| 20 | 264 | 552 | 1,000 |

**EXAMPLE J**

Use the values shown in Figure 12-2 to determine the cash surrender or loan value for each of the following policies.

| Policy Year | Type of Policy | Amount of Policy | Cash Surrender or Loan Value |
|---|---|---|---|
| 10 | Straight Life | $ 75,000 | 75 × $104 = $ 7,800 |
| 5 | 20-Year Endowment | $ 15,000 | 15 × $173 = $ 2,595 |
| 10 | 20-Payment Life | $ 50,000 | 50 × $228 = $11,400 |
| 20 | Straight Life | $200,000 | 200 × $264 = $52,800 |
| 15 | 20-Year Endowment | $ 50,000 | 50 × $684 = $34,200 |

**CONCEPT CHECK 12.6**

Use the values shown in Figure 12-2 to determine the cash surrender or loan value for each of the following policies.

a. Third policy year of a $50,000 20-year endowment policy
   50 × $88 = $4,400
b. Twentieth policy year of a $100,000 straight life policy
   100 × $264 = $26,400
c. Tenth policy year of a $25,000 20-payment life policy
   25 × $228 = $5,700

# Computing Medical Insurance Contributions and Reimbursements

**Learning Objective 7**

Compute medical insurance contributions and reimbursements.

Most large employers and many small employers subscribe to a group plan on behalf of their employees. **Group insurance** plans provide medical insurance coverage to large numbers of people at lower premium rates than individuals could obtain separately. Employers generally pay all the premium for employees and a portion of the premium for family members of employees. Many employers now use group plans known as a **health maintenance organization** (HMO) or a **preferred provider organization** (PPO).

## EXAMPLE K

Employer A selected a basic health care plan to cover employees who want to participate. Monthly premiums are as follows: employee only, \$350; employee with one dependent, \$450; and employee with multiple dependents, \$530. Employees pay a portion of the premium as follows: employee only, \$0; employee with one dependent, \$80; and employee with multiple dependents, \$120. How much does the employer pay during the year for each category of employee?

Employee only: \$350 × 12 = \$4,200
Employee with one dependent: (\$450 − \$80) × 12 = \$4,440
Employee with multiple dependents: (\$530 − \$120) × 12 = \$4,920

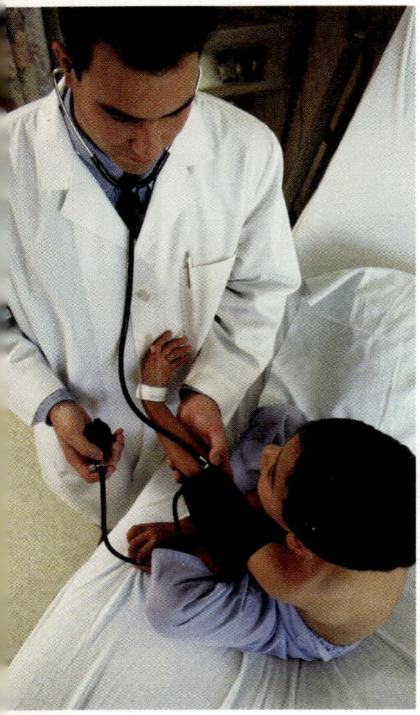

© PHOTODISC/GETTY IMAGES

## EXAMPLE L

Employer B selected a total care health plan to cover employees who want to participate. Monthly premiums are as follows: employee only, \$300; employee with one dependent, \$400; and employee with multiple dependents, \$480. The employer pays most of the premium, but employees pay a portion as follows: employee only, \$30; employee with one dependent, \$80; and employee with multiple dependents, \$120. What percent of the premium will be paid by a single employee, an employee with one dependent, and an employee with six dependents?

A single employee: \$30 ÷ 300 = 0.10, or 10%
An employee with 1 dependent: \$80 ÷ 400 = 0.20, or 20%
An employee with 6 dependents: \$120 ÷ 480 = 0.25, or 25%

Many group plans include a provision for an annual deductible, which is the cost that must be paid by the employee before any cost is paid by the insurance company. Group medical plans also frequently provide for the payment by the insurance company of a percent of costs over the deductible, usually 70% to 90%, with the remaining 30% to 10% paid by the insured.

## EXAMPLE M

Employer C provides group health coverage that includes a \$500 annual deductible per family and payment of 70% of the medical charges exceeding the deductible. How much would an employee with three dependents pay if her medical bills for the year were \$1,500?

\$1,500 − \$500 deductible = \$1,000
\$1,000 × 30% paid by employee = \$300
\$500 deductible + \$300 payments = \$800 paid by the employee

## CONCEPT CHECK 12.7

An employer provides group health coverage that includes a $300 annual deductible per family and payment of 80% of costs over the deductible.

a. How much would an employee with two dependents pay if his medical bills for the year were $460?
   $460 − $300 deductible = $160
   $160 × 20% = $32
   $300 deductible + $32 = $332 paid by the employee

b. How much would that employee have paid if his total medical bills for the year had been $4,300?
   $4,300 medical costs − $300 deductible = $4,000
   $4,000 × 20% = $800
   $300 deductible + $800 = $1,100

c. How much of the $4,300 in medical bills would that employee have paid if his employer did not provide medical insurance and he did not have other coverage?
   $4,300

d. How much would the employer pay if the monthly premium for an employee with multiple dependents was $480?
   $480 × 12 = $5,760

COMPLETE ASSIGNMENT 12.3.

## Chapter Terms for Review

- additional death benefit (ADB)
- annuity insurance
- auto collision insurance
- auto comprehensive insurance
- auto liability and property damage insurance
- beneficiary
- cash surrender value
- coinsurance clause
- deductible clause
- endowment insurance
- group insurance
- health maintenance organization (HMO)
- high-risk driver
- insured
- limited-payment life insurance
- loan value
- low-risk driver
- no-fault insurance
- preferred provider organization (PPO)
- premium
- property insurance
- recovery amount
- short rates
- straight (ordinary) life insurance
- term insurance

## Try Microsoft® Excel

Try working the problems using the Microsoft Excel templates found on your student CD. Solutions for the problems are also shown on the CD.

# THE BOTTOM LINE

*Summary of chapter learning objectives:*

| Learning Objective | Example |
|---|---|
| **12.1**<br><br>Compute costs and savings for auto insurance. | Drivers A and B live in a state in which no-fault insurance is mandatory. Both drivers carry all three classifications of insurance. Driver A has a deductible of $500; driver B has a deductible of $200. Driver A crashes into driver B. Neither auto has any passengers. Car A has $1,800 in damages; car B has $2,000 in damages. Driver A is not hurt; driver B has $900 in medical bills.<br><br>1. How much does driver A's insurance company pay?<br>2. How much does driver B's insurance company pay? |
| **12.2**<br><br>Compute auto insurance premium rates for high- and low-risk drivers. | 3. Juan has an excellent driving record and receives a 20% discount on his annual premium. Dave has a record of numerous tickets and must pay 2 times the normal annual premium rate. If the normal premium for each driver is $1,500, how much more does Dave pay for his insurance than Juan pays? |
| **12.3**<br><br>Compute short-rate refunds. | 4. XYZ company purchased a delivery truck and paid an annual insurance premium of $3,600. XYZ company sold the truck at the end of 8 months and canceled the policy. The insurance company charges a 10% penalty for short-rate refunds. What was the amount of the short-rate refund to XYZ company? |
| **12.4**<br><br>Compute coinsurance on property losses. | 5. A building worth $400,000 is insured for $300,000 with an 80% coinsurance clause. Fire causes $200,000 in damage. How much does the insurance company pay? |
| **12.5**<br><br>Compute life insurance premiums. | 6. Premiums per $1,000 of straight life insurance at the age of 25 are as follows: annual, $17.20; semiannual, $8.94; and quarterly, $4.73. What will be the cumulative yearly premiums for the following three policies: $50,000, annual; $25,000, semiannual; and $20,000, quarterly? |

Answers: 1. $3,300 2. $900 3. $1,800 4. $840 5. $187,500 6. $1,685.40

| Learning Objective | Example |
| --- | --- |
| **12.6**<br><br>Compute cash surrender and loan values. | 7. If cash surrender values for year 15 of a policy are $200 per thousand dollars of coverage for straight life and $380 per thousand dollars of coverage for 20-payment life, what is the total cash surrender value of these two policies: $50,000 straight life and $50,000 20-payment life? |
| **12.7**<br><br>Compute medical insurance contributions and reimbursements. | 8a. An employer provides group health coverage that includes a $200 annual deductible per family and payment of 80% of costs over deductible. How much would an employee with four dependents pay if his medical bills for the year were as follows: self, $240; dependent 1, $170; dependent 2, $30; dependent 3, $460; and dependent 4, $2,200?<br><br>b. How much would the employee pay if the annual deductible were $50 per person? |

Answers: 7. $29,000 8a. $780 8b. $804

SELF-CHECK

## Review Problems for Chapter 12

1. Drivers Jim Olson and Joshua Stein live in a state having no-fault auto insurance. Joshua causes an accident by hitting Jim's car. Joshua isn't hurt. Jim spends 3 days in the hospital at a cost of $5,300. Compute the amount that each driver's insurance company pays toward medical expenses. ___________

2. IXP insured an office building for $290,000 for 1 year at a premium rate of $7.20 per thousand. At the end of 9 months, IXP sold the building and canceled the policy. If the insurance company has a short-rate refund policy that includes a 10% penalty, how much refund did IXP receive? ___________

3. Driver Devon Cooper has a poor driving record and pays double the usual premium as a high-risk driver. The regular premium would be $490 for a year. If Devon must pay the high-risk premium every year for 5 years, how much more will he pay for insurance premiums than a low-risk driver receiving a 10% discount over the same 5-year period? ___________

4. Insurance company A has a standard 90% coinsurance clause for all fire insurance coverage. Insurance company B has a standard 75% coinsurance clause for all fire insurance coverage. A building is valued at $195,000. How much more insurance coverage would insurance company A require than insurance company B for full coinsurance coverage? ___________

5. The Morgan Company warehouse was valued at $425,000. The building was insured for $170,000. The policy contained an 80% coinsurance clause. A fire caused $60,000 in damages. Compute the amount of the fire damage The Morgan Company had to pay. ___________

6. Mike Jankowski, age 27, purchased a $35,000, 20-payment life policy with premiums payable annually. John Jamison, also age 27, purchased a $35,000 straight life policy with premiums payable semiannually. Both Mike and John lived 40 more years. How much more in premiums did John pay the insurance company during his lifetime than Mike paid during his? (Use values from Figure 12-1.) ___________

7. Sally Munson, age 25, purchased a $35,000, 20-payment life policy. Five years later she needed cash. Compute the maximum amount she could borrow on the policy. (Use values from Figure 12-2.) ___________

8. An employer provides group health coverage that includes a $600 annual deductible per family and payment of 80% of costs exceeding the deductible amount. An employee with no dependents incurs $4,800 in medical expenses during the year. How much of the medical costs must the employee pay? ___________

**Answers to the Self-Check can be found in Appendix B at the back of the text.**

# Assignment 12.1: Auto Insurance

Name ______________________________

Date ______________ Score ______________

Learning Objectives **1** **2**

**A (50 points) Solve the following problems. (5 points for each correct answer)**

**1.** Mary Johnson had full insurance coverage. Her liability and property damage coverage was $100,000 per accident. Her collision insurance had a $500 deductible clause. She struck two cars. Damages to the cars were $640 and $320. Damage to her own car was $470. Her annual insurance premium was $1,180.

**a.** What are the total costs to the insurance company for Mary's accident? __________

**b.** If this was the only accident that Mary had this year, did the insurance company profit after paying for Mary's accident? __________

**c.** What are Mary's total costs this year for insurance and the accident? __________

**d.** What would Mary's total costs for the accident have been without insurance? __________

**2.** Renaldo Garcia paid an annual premium of $3,200 for auto collision insurance with a $500 deductible clause. His steering went out and he hit a tree, causing $4,000 damage to his car. How much did he save this year by having insurance? __________

**3.** Sean O'Day received his driver's license 1 year ago. He has had three citations for speeding, but no accidents. His insurance premium last year was $1,800. This year his premium will be 100% higher because of his driving record.

**a.** What will be the amount of his premium this year? __________

**b.** Four months into the next year, Sean has continued his unsafe driving habits. The insurance company is canceling his policy. What will be the amount of the refund? __________

**c.** Sean O'Day has found an insurance company that will insure him as a high-risk driver at triple the standard annual rate of $1,600. What will be his average monthly insurance premium for the first 28 months of his driving career? (Round your answer to the nearest dollar.) __________

**d.** If Sean had been a careful driver and kept the amount of his premium unchanged, how much would he have saved in these first 28 months? (Round your computations to the nearest dollar.) __________

**4.** Drivers A and B have identical insurance coverage. Driver A has an excellent driving record and receives a 15% discount on the standard premium. Driver B has numerous citations and pays 50% above the standard rate. The standard rate in both cases is $1,600. How much more does driver B pay for insurance than driver A? __________

__________

Score for A (50)

**B** **(50 points) Solve the following problems. (5 points for each correct answer)**

**5.** Tom Barton carries liability and property damage insurance coverage up to $50,000 per accident, comprehensive insurance, and collision insurance with a $100 deductible clause. He lost control of his car and drove through the display window of a furniture store. Damage to the building was $17,200 and the damage to the inventory was $34,300. Damage to a bike rack on the sidewalk and three bicycles in the rack was $1,840. Damage to his own car was $6,100.

**a.** What was the total property damage, excluding damage to Tom's car? __________

**b.** How much did the insurance company pay for property damage, excluding damage to Tom's car? __________

**c.** How much did the insurance company pay for damage to Tom Barton's car? __________

**d.** How much did the accident cost Tom Barton? __________

**e.** If Tom Barton had been in a previous accident this year in which there had been property damage to a parked car of $12,700, how much would the insurance company have paid for damages to everything in the current accident, including Tom Barton's car? __________

**6.** Amy Tan and John Rogers live in a state in which no-fault insurance is mandatory. They have identical full coverage of $50,000 liability and property damage per accident, comprehensive insurance, and collision insurance with a $350 deductible. John lost control of his car on an icy street and struck Amy's car, a parked motorcycle, and a fence. Amy had medical expenses of $780. John had medical expenses of $560. Amy's car had damages of $1,350. John's car had damages of $1,750. Damage to the parked motorcycle was $650 and damage to the fence was $320.

**a.** What did Amy's insurance company pay under the no-fault provision? __________

**b.** What did John's insurance company pay under the no-fault provision? __________

**c.** How much did John's insurance company pay under his liability and property damage coverage? __________

**d.** How much did John's insurance company pay under his comprehensive coverage? __________

**e.** How much would John's insurance company have paid under his liability and property damage if he had hit Amy's car and five parked cars, with total damage to the six cars of $56,700? __________

__________

Score for B (50)

# Assignment 12.2: Property Insurance

Name ______________________________

Date ______________ Score ______________

Learning Objectives 3 4

**A (42 points) Solve the following problems. (6 points for each correct answer)**

**1.** A building valued at $380,000 is insured for its full value. The annual premium is $9.80 per thousand dollars of coverage.

**a.** How much does the insured pay to insure his building? __________

**b.** If the insurance company cancels the policy at the end of 3 months, how much refund does the insured receive? __________

**c.** If the insurance company has a 10% penalty clause for short-rate refunds and the insured cancels the policy after 9 months, how much refund does the insured receive? __________

**2.** If a company pays an annual premium of $6,000 and the insurance company charges $30 per thousand dollars of insurance, how much insurance does the company carry? __________

**3.** A company carries property insurance of $200,000 with no coinsurance clause. A fire causes $210,000 in damage. How much does the insurance company pay the insured? __________

**4.** A company carries property insurance of $300,000 with a premium of $13.10 per thousand dollars of coverage. A fire causes $120,000 in damage.

**a.** How much does the insurance company pay the insured? __________

**b.** What is the amount of the company's benefits after its annual premium payment? __________

__________

Score for A (42)

**B (58 points) Solve the following problems. (points for correct answers as marked)**

**5.** A building worth $300,000 is insured for $180,000, and the policy carries an 80% coinsurance clause. A fire causes $220,000 in damage.

**a.** How much will the insurance company pay? (10 points) __________

**b.** How much will the insured pay if the building is repaired for $220,000? (6 points) __________

**c.** How much would the insurance company pay if damage to the building totaled $300,000? (10 points)

__________

**d.** If the damage totaled $300,000, how much would the insured pay if the building were rebuilt for $300,000? (6 points) __________

**6.** A building worth $1,800,000 is insured for $1,200,000, and the policy carries an 80% coinsurance clause. A fire causes $300,000 in damage. (Round to the nearest dollar.)

**a.** How much does the insurance company pay if the building is repaired for $300,000? (10 points) __________

**b.** How much does the insured pay? (6 points) __________

**7.** If an insurance company issues insurance on property valued at $400,000 with a 90% coinsurance clause, what is the amount required to be carried by the insured? (5 points) __________

**8.** If an insurance company issues insurance on property valued at $3,000,000 with a 75% coinsurance clause, what is the amount required to be carried by the insured? (5 points) __________

__________

Score for B (58)

# Assignment 12.3: Life and Medical Insurance

Name ______________________________

Date ______________ Score ______________

Learning Objectives 5 6 7

**A** **(50 points) Refer to Figures 12-1 and 12-2 for the premium and surrender rates in solving the following problems. Assume that every year is a full 12 months long. (points for correct answers as marked)**

**1.** Find the rates per thousand dollars and the premiums for the following policies. (1 point for each correct answer)

| Age | Type | Payments Made | Face Value of Policy | Rate per $1,000 | Premium Paid Each Year |
|---|---|---|---|---|---|
| 28 | Straight Life | Annually | $200,000 | ________ | ________ |
| 25 | 20-Payment Life | Quarterly | 80,000 | ________ | ________ |
| 25 | 20-Year Endowment | Semiannually | 10,000 | ________ | ________ |
| 26 | Straight Life | Quarterly | 120,000 | ________ | ________ |
| 27 | 20-Payment Life | Semiannually | 100,000 | ________ | ________ |
| 28 | 20-Year Endowment | Annually | 85,000 | ________ | ________ |

**2.** Find the cash surrender or loan value for each of the following policies issued at age 25. (1 point for each correct answer)

| Policy Year | Type of Policy | Amount of Policy | Cash Surrender or Loan Value |
|---|---|---|---|
| 10 | Straight Life | $50,000 | ________ |
| 15 | 20-Payment Life | $25,000 | ________ |
| 10 | 20-Year Endowment | $50,000 | ________ |
| 3 | Straight Life | $20,000 | ________ |
| 5 | 20-Payment Life | $75,000 | ________ |
| 4 | 20-Year Endowment | $60,000 | ________ |

**3.** When Sue Adams was 27 years old, she took out a $75,000, 20-year endowment policy. She paid the premiums annually and survived the endowment period. How much more did she pay in annual premiums than she received from the insurance company at the end of 20 years? (4 points) ________

**4.** Roger Johnson purchased a $50,000 ordinary life policy and an ADB for 50% of the value of the policy. In addition, he purchased a 5-year, $50,000 term policy. He died in an accident 3 years later.

**a.** How much money did Roger's beneficiaries receive? (4 points) ________

**b.** How much money would Roger's beneficiaries have received if he had died in an accident 7 years after purchasing the policies? (4 points) ________

**c.** How much money would Roger's beneficiaries have received if he had died of natural causes 10 years after purchasing the policies? (4 points) ________

**5.** At the age of 25, Carlos Baker purchased a $50,000 straight life policy, with premiums payable annually. He also purchased a $25,000 20-payment life policy, with premiums payable semiannually. At the end of 15 years, he decided to cash in both policies.

**a.** How much did Carlos receive for the straight life policy? (4 points) __________

**b.** How much did Carlos receive for the 20-payment life policy? (4 points) __________

**c.** How much more did Carlos pay in premiums than the total amount received for both policies? (8 points) __________

__________

Score for A (50)

**B** **(50 points) Solve the following problems. (10 points for a correct answer to problem 6; 8 points for each other correct answer)**

**6.** An employer provides group health coverage that includes a $250 annual deductible per family and payment of 80% of costs exceeding the deductible. How much would an employee with two dependents pay if her medical bills for the year were $550 for herself; $920 for dependent 1; and $230 for dependent 2? __________

**7.** An employer provides group health coverage that includes a $500 annual deductible per family and 80% of costs over the deductible.

**a.** How much would an employee with no dependents pay if his medical bills were $1,000 this year? __________

**b.** How much would that employee have paid this year if his medical bills were $7,480? __________

**8.** An employer provides group health coverage with the following monthly premiums: employee only, $350; employee with one dependent, $450; and employee with multiple dependents, $550.

**a.** How much does the employer pay over a 5-year period for an employee with multiple dependents? __________

**b.** If that employee had a dependent with a catastrophic illness that cost $97,000 for hospitalization and treatments during that 5-year period, how much would the insurance company lose on that employee, assuming that she had no other medical claims? __________

**c.** If an employee with no dependents had no illnesses during that same 5-year period, how much would the insurance company make on that employee? __________

__________

Score for B (50)

# Notes

# Part 4

# Interest Applications

# 13

# Simple Interest

## Learning Objectives

By studying this chapter and completing all assignments, you will be able to:

Learning Objective 1 Compute simple interest with time in years or months.

Learning Objective 2 Compute ordinary simple interest, using a 360-day year.

Learning Objective 3 Compute exact simple interest, using a 365-day year.

Learning Objective 4 Compare ordinary simple interest and exact simple interest.

Learning Objective 5 Estimate exact simple interest computations.

Learning Objective 6 Compute the Principal, Rate, and Time from the basic interest formula.

Most businesses and individuals buy at least some assets without making full payment at the time of the purchase. The seller gives immediate possession to the buyer but does not require payment until some later date. For example, large retailers such as Macy's Department Store may receive merchandise for the Christmas season but may not be required to pay the seller until January. The seller, who *extends credit* to the buyer, may or may not charge for this privilege. The charge is called **interest,** and it is usually quoted as a percent of the amount of credit extended (the principal). When part of the price is paid at the time of purchase, that part is called a **down payment.**

If the seller charges too much interest or does not extend credit, the buyer might borrow money from a third party, such as a bank. The buyer would then sell the merchandise to repay the bank loan. The amount borrowed is called the **principal,** and the interest charged is a percent of the principal. The bank will charge interest between the loan date and the repayment date. This period of **time** is called the **interest period** or the **term of the loan.**

The promise to repay a loan or pay for merchandise may be oral or written. If it is written, it may be in the form of a letter or it could be one of several special documents known collectively as **commercial paper. Short-term credit** transactions are those whose term is between 1 day and 1 year. **Long-term credit** transactions are those for longer than 1 year. Normally, long-term credit transactions involve major items such as new buildings or equipment rather than supplies or merchandise for sale.

# Computing Simple Interest

Learning Objective 1

Compute simple interest with time in years or months.

The easiest type of interest to calculate is called **simple interest.** The calculations are the same for both a loan and a purchase on credit. The interest rate is a percent of the principal for the period of the loan or credit. The quoted percent usually is an *annual* (yearly) rate. A rate of 10% means that the interest payment for 1 year will be 10% of the principal.

To compute the amount of simple interest on a 1-year loan, simply multiply the Principal by the Rate.

**EXAMPLE A**

Stan McSwain borrowed \$1,000 for 1 year at a rate of 8% simple interest. Compute the interest.

The principal is \$1,000. The interest for 1 year is 8% of \$1,000, or $0.08 \times \$1{,}000 = \$80$.

Most loans, however, are not for a period of exactly 1 year. Loans for longer periods will require the borrower to pay more interest. Likewise, loans for shorter periods will require less interest. To compute the simple interest on loans of any period, multiply the Principal by the Rate and then multiply by the Time, with Time stated in years or in fractions of years. The fundamental formula for simple interest is

Interest = Principal × Rate × Time
abbreviated as $I = P \times R \times T$ or, even more simply, $I = PRT$.

**EXAMPLE B**

Find the amounts of simple interest on loans of \$1,200 when the rate is 6% and the loan periods are $\frac{3}{4}$ year and 4 years.

**$\frac{3}{4}$ year**

$I = P \times R \times T$

$= \$1{,}200 \times 0.06 \times \frac{3}{4}$

$= \$54$

**4 years**

$I = P \times R \times T$

$= \$1{,}200 \times 0.06 \times 4$

$= \$288$

The time period often will be measured in months instead of years. Before computing the interest, change the time into years by dividing the number of months by 12 (the number of months in 1 year).

**EXAMPLE C**

Compute the interest on credit purchases of \$3,000 at 5% for periods of 8 months and 30 months.

**8 months**

$I = P \times R \times T$

$= \$3{,}000 \times 0.05 \times \frac{8}{12}$

$= \$100$

**30 months**

$I = P \times R \times T$

$= \$3{,}000 \times 0.05 \times \frac{30}{12}$

$= \$375$

## USING CALCULATORS

Today, calculators or computers are used in almost every interest application. The numbers are often large and are always important. The steps are performed on the calculator in the same order as they are written in the formula.

**EXAMPLE D**

Write the calculator steps for computing the simple interest on \$8,000,000 at 9% for 18 months.

$I = P \times R \times T = \$8{,}000{,}000 \times 0.09 \times \frac{18}{12}$

8 000 000 [×] .09 [×] 18 [÷] 12 [=]

The display will show 1,080,000, which means \$1,080,000.

With the percent key [%], the steps would be

8 000 000 [×] 9 [%] [×] 18 [÷] 12 [=]

The display will show 1,080,000, which means \$1,080,000.

**CONCEPT CHECK 13.1**

The Principal is \$2,500, the Rate is 10%, and Interest = Principal × Rate × Time, or $I = P \times R \times T$. Find the interest both for 5 years and for 6 months.

a. If Time is 5 years: $I = P \times R \times T = \$2{,}500 \times 0.10 \times 5 = \$1{,}250$

b. If Time is 6 months: $I = P \times R \times T = \$2{,}500 \times 0.10 \times \frac{6}{12} = \$125$

# Computing Ordinary Interest

**Learning Objective 2**

Compute ordinary simple interest, using a 360-day year.

If the term of the loan is stated as a certain number of days, computing interest involves dividing the number of days by the number of days in 1 year—either 360 or 365. Before computers and calculators, interest was easier to compute by assuming that every year had 360 days and that every month had 30 days. The 360-day method, called the **ordinary interest method,** is still used by some businesses and individuals.

© KEITH BROFSKY/PHOTODISC/GETTY IMAGES

**EXAMPLE E**

Compute the ordinary simple interest on \$900 at 9% for 120 days.

$$I = P \times R \times T$$

$$= \$900 \times 0.09 \times \frac{120}{360}$$

$$= \$27$$

**CONCEPT CHECK 13.2**

The Principal is \$4,000, the Rate is 7%, and the Time is 180 days. Compute the ordinary simple interest.

Use a 360-day year: $I = P \times R \times T = \$4{,}000 \times 0.07 \times \frac{180}{360} = \$140$

# Computing Exact Interest

**Learning Objective 3**

Compute exact simple interest, using a 365-day year.

Banks, savings and loan institutions, credit unions, and the federal government use a 365-day year (366 days for leap years) to compute interest. This method is called the **exact interest method.** The computations are the same as for ordinary simple interest, except that 365 days is used instead of 360 days.

**EXAMPLE F**

Compute the exact simple interest on \$900 at 9% for 120 days.

$$I = P \times R \times T$$

$$= \$900 \times 0.09 \times \frac{120}{365}$$

$$= \$26.6301, \text{ or } \$26.63$$

## CONCEPT CHECK 13.3

The Principal is \$4,000, the Rate is 7%, and the Time is 180 days. Compute the exact simple interest.

Use a 365-day year: $I = P \times R \times T = \$4{,}000 \times 0.07 \times \frac{180}{365} = \$138.0822$, or \$138.08

# Comparing Ordinary Interest and Exact Interest

**Learning Objective 4**

Compare ordinary simple interest and exact simple interest.

The 360-day year was very useful before the advent of calculators and computers, so there is a long tradition of using it. However, the 365-day year is more realistic than the 360-day year. Also, the 365-day year is financially better for the borrower because the interest amounts are always smaller. (Why? Because a denominator of 365 gives a smaller quotient than a denominator of 360.)

Reexamine examples E and F. The difference between ordinary interest and exact interest is only \$27.00 − \$26.63, or \$0.37. When businesses borrow money, the principal may be very large and then the difference will be more significant. Example G is similar to examples E and F, except that the principal is in millions of dollars rather than hundreds.

### EXAMPLE G

Find the difference between ordinary interest and exact interest on \$8,000,000 at 9% for 120 days.

**Ordinary Interest**

$I = P \times R \times T$

$= \$8{,}000{,}000 \times 0.09 \times \dfrac{120}{360}$

$= \$240{,}000$

**Exact Interest**

$I = P \times R \times T$

$= \$8{,}000{,}000 \times 0.09 \times \dfrac{120}{365}$

$= \$236{,}712.3288$, or \$236,712.33

The difference is \$240,000.00 − \$236,712.33 = \$3,287.67.

## CONCEPT CHECK 13.4

The Principal is \$6,000, the Rate is 12%, and the Time is 120 days. Find the difference between the amounts of simple interest calculated by using the ordinary method (360-day year) and the exact method (365-day year).

Ordinary interest: $I = P \times R \times T = \$6{,}000 \times 0.12 \times \frac{120}{360} = \$240.00$

Exact interest: $I = P \times R \times T = \$6{,}000 \times 0.12 \times \frac{120}{365} = \$236.7123$, or \$236.71

Difference = Ordinary interest − Exact interest = \$240.00 − \$236.71 = \$3.29

# Estimating Exact Simple Interest

Learning Objective 5

Estimate exact simple interest computations.

Although calculators are used to compute exact interest, approximation remains very useful. The following calculator solution requires a minimum of 20 key entries.

8 000 000 [×] .09 [×] 120 [÷] 365 [=]
The display will show 236,712.3288.

Pressing any one of the 20 keys incorrectly could result in a large error. By making an estimate of the interest in advance, you may spot a significant calculator error.

## COMBINATIONS OF TIME AND INTEREST THAT YIELD 1%

To simplify mental approximations, you can round the rate and time to numbers that are easy to compute mentally. Also, use 360 days instead of 365 because it cancels more often. For ordinary interest, several combinations of rate and time are easy to use because their product is 1%. For example, $12\% \times \frac{30}{360} = 12\% \times \frac{1}{12} = 1\%$ and $6\% \times \frac{60}{360} = 6\% \times \frac{1}{6} = 1\%$.

**EXAMPLE H**

Approximate the ordinary simple interest on $2,500 at 6.15% for 59 days. Then calculate the actual ordinary simple interest.

| | |
|---|---|
| Round | 6.15% to 6% and 59 days to 60 days. |
| Estimate: | $\$2{,}500 \times 0.06 \times \frac{60}{360} = \$2{,}500 \times 0.01 = \$25.00$ |
| Actual interest: | $\$2{,}500 \times 0.0615 \times \frac{59}{360} = \$25.1979$, or \$25.20 |

## OTHER RATES AND TIMES

Table 13-1 shows several combinations of Rate and Time whose products are useful for estimating interest.

**Table 13-1:** Rate and Time

| | |
|---|---|
| $4\% \times \frac{90}{360} = 4\% \times \frac{1}{4} = 1\%$ | $10\% \times \frac{36}{360} = 10\% \times \frac{1}{10} = 1\%$ |
| $6\% \times \frac{60}{360} = 6\% \times \frac{1}{6} = 1\%$ | $12\% \times \frac{30}{360} = 12\% \times \frac{1}{12} = 1\%$ |
| $8\% \times \frac{45}{360} = 8\% \times \frac{1}{8} = 1\%$ | $18\% \times \frac{20}{360} = 18\% \times \frac{1}{18} = 1\%$ |
| $9\% \times \frac{40}{360} = 9\% \times \frac{1}{9} = 1\%$ | $6\% \times \frac{120}{360} = 6\% \times \frac{1}{3} = 2\%$ |
| $12\% \times \frac{60}{360} = 12\% \times \frac{1}{6} = 2\%$ | $12\% \times \frac{90}{360} = 12\% \times \frac{1}{4} = 3\%$ |
| $8\% \times \frac{90}{360} = 8\% \times \frac{1}{4} = 2\%$ | $9\% \times \frac{120}{360} = 9\% \times \frac{1}{3} = 3\%$ |

## ESTIMATING EXACT INTEREST

The goal in approximating interest is just to get an estimate. Even though exact interest requires 365 days in a year, you can make a reasonable estimate by assuming that the number of days in a year is 360. This permits the use of all of the shortcut combinations from Table 13-1.

**EXAMPLE I**

First, compute the actual exact simple interest on \$1,200 at 11.8% for 62 days.

Actual interest: $\$1{,}200 \times 0.118 \times \frac{62}{365} = \$24.0526$, or \$24.05

Second, estimate the amount of interest by using 12% instead of 11.8%, 60 days instead of 62 days, and 360 instead of 365.

Estimate: $\$1{,}200 \times 0.12 \times \frac{60}{360} = \$1{,}200 \times 0.02 = \$24$

The difference is $\$24.05 - \$24 = \$0.05$.

**CONCEPT CHECK 13.5**

The Principal is \$3,750, the Rate is 9.1%, and the Time is 39 days. Calculate the actual exact simple interest. Then make an estimate by using a 360-day year and simpler values for *R* and *T*. Compare the results.

Actual interest: $I = P \times R \times T = \$3{,}750 \times 0.091 \times \frac{39}{365} = \$36.4623$, or \$36.46

Estimate: $I = P \times R \times T = \$3{,}750 \times 0.09 \times \frac{40}{360} = \$3{,}750 \times 0.01 = \$37.50$

Difference: Estimate − Actual = $\$37.50 - \$36.46 = \$1.04$

# Computing the Interest Variables

**Learning Objective 6**

Compute the Principal, Rate, and Time from the basic interest formula.

Every simple interest problem has four variables: Interest, Principal, Rate, and Time. Thus far, you have solved for the Interest Amount $(I)$ when the Principal $(P)$, Rate $(R)$, and Time $(T)$ were all given. However, as long as any three variables are given, you can always compute the fourth by just changing the formula $I = P \times R \times T$ into one of its possible variations, as shown in Table 13-2.

**Table 13-2:** PRT formulas

| To find | You must know | Use this formula |
|---|---|---|
| *I* | *P*, *R*, and *T* | $I = P \times R \times T$ |
| *P* | *I*, *R*, and *T* | $P = \frac{I}{(R \times T)}$ |
| *R* | *I*, *P*, and *T* | $R = \frac{I}{(P \times T)}$ |
| *T* | *I*, *P*, and *R* | $T = \frac{I}{(P \times R)}$ |

Assume the use of ordinary interest (a 360-day year) unless the use of exact interest (a 365-day year) is indicated. The stated or computed interest rate is the rate for 1 full year. Also, the length of time used for computing interest dollars must be stated in terms of all or part of a year.

## FINDING THE INTEREST AMOUNT, PRINCIPAL, RATE, OR TIME

When any three variables are known, you can solve for the fourth variable, using a formula from Table 13-2. All rates are ordinary simple interest (360-day year).

**EXAMPLE J**

Find the Principal if the Interest is \$75, the Rate is 6%, and the Time is 30 days.

$$P = ?; \quad I = \$75; \quad R = 6\%; \quad T = \frac{30}{360} \text{ year}$$

$$P = \frac{I}{(R \times T)} = \frac{\$75}{\left(0.06 \times \frac{30}{360}\right)} = \frac{\$75}{0.005} = \$15{,}000$$

**EXAMPLE K**

Find the Rate if the Interest is \$22, the Principal is \$2,000, and the Time is 30 days.

$$R = ?; \quad I = \$22; \quad P = \$2{,}000; \quad T = \frac{30}{360} \text{ year}$$

$$R = \frac{I}{(P \times T)} = \frac{\$22}{\left(\$2{,}000 \times \frac{30}{360}\right)} = \frac{\$22}{\$166.67} = 0.132, \text{ or } 13.2\%$$

**EXAMPLE L**

Find the Time if the Interest is \$324, the Principal is \$4,800, and the Rate is 9%. Express Time in days, based on a 360-day year.

$$T = ?; \quad I = \$324; \quad P = \$4{,}800; \quad R = 9\%$$

$$T = \frac{I}{(P \times R)} = \frac{\$324}{(\$4{,}800 \times 0.09)} = \frac{\$324}{\$432} = 0.75 \text{ year}$$

Based on a 360-day year, 0.75 year = 0.75 × 360 days = 270 days.

## CONCEPT CHECK 13.6

Each of the following problems gives three of the four variables. Compute the missing variable. All rates are ordinary simple interest (360-day year). Round $P$ and $I$ to the nearest cent; round $R$ to the nearest $\frac{1}{10}$%; round $T$ to the nearest whole day, assuming that 1 year has 360 days. Use one of the four formulas:

$$I = P \times R \times T, \quad P = \frac{I}{(R \times T)}, \quad R = \frac{I}{(P \times T)}, \quad \text{and} \quad T = \frac{I}{(P \times R)}$$

a. Principal = $1,240; Rate = 6%; Time = 270 days
Find Interest:

$$I = P \times R \times T = \$1{,}240 \times 0.06 \times \frac{270}{360} = \$55.80$$

b. Principal = $8,000; Interest = $50;
Time = 45 days
Find Rate:

$$R = \frac{I}{(P \times T)} = \frac{\$50}{\left(\$8{,}000 \times \frac{45}{360}\right)} = 0.05, \text{ or } 5\%$$

c. Principal = $1,280; Interest = $64; Rate = 10%
Find Time:

$$T = \frac{I}{(P \times R)} = \frac{\$64}{(\$1{,}280 \times 0.10)} = 0.5 \text{ year}$$

In a 360-day year, $T = 0.5$ year $= 0.5 \times 360$ days $= 180$ days.

d. Interest = $90; Rate = 9%; Time = 60 days
Find Principal:

$$P = \frac{I}{(R \times T)} = \frac{\$90}{\left(0.09 \times \frac{60}{360}\right)} = \$6{,}000$$

COMPLETE ASSIGNMENTS 13.1 AND 13.2.

## Chapter Terms for Review

commercial paper
down payment
exact interest method
interest
interest period
long-term credit
ordinary interest method
principal
short-term credit
simple interest
term of the loan
time

## Try Microsoft® Excel

Try working the problems using the Microsoft Excel templates found on your student CD. Solutions for the problems are also shown on the CD.

# THE BOTTOM LINE

*Summary of chapter learning objectives:*

| Learning Objective | Example |
|---|---|
| **13.1**<br>Compute simple interest with time in years or months. | Find the simple interest using the basic formula:<br>**Interest = Principal × Rate × Time,** or $I = P \times R \times T$<br>1. Principal = \$3,500; Rate = 9%; Time = 2.5 years<br>2. Principal = \$975; Rate = 8%; Time = 9 months |
| **13.2**<br>Compute ordinary simple interest, using a 360-day year. | 3. Find the ordinary simple interest for a 360-day year: Principal = \$5,000; Rate = 6%; Time = 150 days |
| **13.3**<br>Compute exact simple interest, using a 365-day year. | 4. Find the exact simple interest for a 365-day year: Principal = \$2,800; Rate = 7%; Time = 75 days |
| **13.4**<br>Compare ordinary simple interest and exact simple interest. | 5. Find the difference between ordinary simple interest and exact simple interest: Principal = \$5,000; Rate = 6%; Time = 75 days |
| **13.5**<br>Estimate exact simple interest computations. | 6. Estimate the exact interest by using a 360-day year and simpler values for Rate and Time: Principal = \$2,100; Rate = 5.8%; Time = 62 days |
| **13.6**<br>Compute the Principal, Rate, and Time from the basic interest formula. | Solve for Principal, Rate, and Time using a 360-day year and the formulas<br>$P = \frac{I}{(R \times T)}$, $R = \frac{I}{(P \times T)}$, and $T = \frac{I}{(P \times R)}$<br>7. Interest = \$42; Rate = 6%; Time = 105 days<br>8. Principal = \$1,600; Interest = \$30; Time = 75 days<br>9. Principal = \$7,200; Interest = \$135; Rate = 15% (express Time in days) |

Answers: 1. \$787.50 2. \$58.50 3. \$125.00 4. \$40.27 5. \$62.50 − \$61.64 = \$0.86
6. \$2,100 × 0.06 × $\frac{60}{360}$ = \$21 7. \$2,400 8. 0.09, or 9% 9. 45 days

## SELF-CHECK

# Review Problems for Chapter 13

**In problems 1 and 2, compute the amount of (a) ordinary simple interest and (b) exact simple interest. Then compute (c) the difference between the two interest amounts.**

| | Principal | Rate | Time | | Ordinary Interest | | Exact Interest | | Difference |
|---|---|---|---|---|---|---|---|---|---|
| 1 | $1,680 | 6% | 270 Days | **a.** | ________ | **b.** | ________ | **c.** | ________ |
| 2 | $10,500 | 8% | 60 Days | **a.** | ________ | **b.** | ________ | **c.** | ________ |

**In problems 3 and 4, first compute (a) the actual exact simple interest. Then, change each rate and time to the closest numbers that permit use of the shortcuts shown in Table 13-1 and compute (b) the *estimated* amount of exact interest. Finally, compute (c) the difference between the actual and estimated exact interest.**

| | Principal | Rate | Time | | Actual Exact Interest | | Estimated Exact Interest | | Difference |
|---|---|---|---|---|---|---|---|---|---|
| 3 | $12,000 | 3.8% | 92 Days | **a.** | ________ | **b.** | ________ | **c.** | ________ |
| 4 | $2,000 | 9.2% | 117 Days | **a.** | ________ | **b.** | ________ | **c.** | ________ |

5 Dick Liebelt borrowed money for 240 days at a rate of 9% ordinary simple interest. How much did Dick borrow if he paid $90 in interest? ________

6 Linda Rojas loaned $1,000 to one of her employees for 90 days. If the employee's interest amount was $12.50, what was the ordinary simple interest rate? ________

7 Tessa O'Leary loaned $8,000 to a machine shop owner who was buying a piece of used equipment. The interest rate was 6% ordinary simple interest, and the interest amount was $360. Compute the number of days of the loan. ________

8 Kaye Mushalik loaned $2,500 to Fay Merritt, a good friend since childhood. Because of their friendship, Kaye charged only 3% ordinary simple interest. Two months later, when Fay received her annual bonus, she repaid the entire loan and all the interest. What was the total amount that Fay paid? ________

9 Katherine Wu and her sister Madeline have a home decorating and design business. They often buy antiques and fine art objects and then resell the items to their clients. They have a line of credit at their bank to provide short-term financing for these purchases. The bank always charges exact simple interest, but the rate varies depending on the economy. Katherine and Madeline need to borrow $22,400 for 90 days to buy a collection of antique furniture at an estate sale. If the bank charges 5.25%, how much interest would they pay? ________

**Answers to the Self-Check can be found in Appendix B at the back of the text.**

## Notes

# Assignment 13.1: Simple Interest

Name

Date Score

Learning Objectives 1 2 3 4 5 6

**A** **(20 points) Compute the simple interest. If the time is given in months, let 1 month be $\frac{1}{12}$ of a year. If the time is in days, let 1 year be 360 days. (2 points for each correct answer)**

| | Principal | Rate | Time | Interest | | Principal | Rate | Time | Interest |
|---|---|---|---|---|---|---|---|---|---|
| **1.** | $500 | 6.0% | 1 year | ______ | **2.** | $4,000 | 8% | 3 years | ______ |
| **3.** | $1,800 | 8% | 4 months | ______ | **4.** | $840 | 9% | 15 months | ______ |
| **5.** | $7,500 | 5% | 180 days | ______ | **6.** | $3,600 | 12% | 30 months | ______ |
| **7.** | $12,800 | 7% | 2.5 years | ______ | **8.** | $450 | 5% | $3\frac{1}{2}$ years | ______ |
| **9.** | $5,200 | 10% | 90 days | ______ | **10.** | $20,000 | 7.5% | 8 months | ______ |

______

Score for A (20)

**B** **(30 points) Compute the ordinary interest, the exact interest, and their difference. Round answers to the nearest cent. (2 points for each correct interest; 1 point for each correct difference)**

| | Principal | Rate | Time | Ordinary Interest | Exact Interest | Difference |
|---|---|---|---|---|---|---|
| **11.** | $2,400 | 4% | 180 days | ______ | ______ | ______ |
| **12.** | $960 | 7% | 45 days | ______ | ______ | ______ |
| **13.** | $12,000 | 6% | 240 days | ______ | ______ | ______ |
| **14.** | $1,400 | 15% | 60 days | ______ | ______ | ______ |
| **15.** | $7,500 | 8% | 225 days | ______ | ______ | ______ |
| **16.** | $365 | 4% | 30 days | ______ | ______ | ______ |

______________
Score for B (30)

**C** **(20 points) In each problem, first find the actual exact simple interest. Then, estimate the interest by assuming a 360-day year and round each rate and time to the nearest numbers that will permit the shortcuts in Table 13-1. Finally, find the difference. Round answers to the nearest cent. (2 points for each correct estimate and actual interest; 1 point for each correct difference)**

| | Principal | Rate | Time | Actual Exact Interest | Estimate | Difference |
|---|---|---|---|---|---|---|
| **17.** | $925 | 8.1% | 47 days | ______ | ______ | ______ |
| **18.** | $5,600 | 3.99% | 92 days | ______ | ______ | ______ |
| **19.** | $2,000 | 8.95% | 123 days | ______ | ______ | ______ |
| **20.** | $7,500 | 6.2% | 58 days | ______ | ______ | ______ |

______
Score for C (20)

**D** **(30 points) Determine the missing variable by using one of the following formulas:**

$$I = P \times R \times T, \quad P = \frac{I}{(R \times T)}, \quad R = \frac{I}{(P \times T)}, \quad \text{or} \quad T = \frac{I}{(P \times R)}$$

**For problems 21–25, use a 360-day year. For problems 26–30, use a 365-day year. Round dollar amounts to the nearest cent. Round interest rates to the nearest $\frac{1}{10}$ of a percent. Find the time in days, rounded to the nearest whole day. (3 points for each correct answer)**

| | Principal | Rate | Time | Interest |
|---|---|---|---|---|
| **21.** | ______ | 11% | 240 days | $352.00 |
| **22.** | $12,500 | 5% | ______ | $50.00 |

| | Principal | Rate | Time | Interest |
|---|---|---|---|---|
| **23.** | $600 | ________ | 45 days | $6.00 |
| **24.** | $4,260 | 5.6% | 90 days | ________ |
| **25.** | $25,000 | 4% | ________ | $625.00 |
| **26.** | ________ | 8% | 270 days | $510.00 |
| **27.** | $3,650 | 6.75% | 136 days | ________ |
| **28.** | $34,950 | 5.5% | ________ | $395.00 |
| **29.** | $16,000 | ________ | 90 days | $296.00 |
| **30.** | ________ | 4.9% | 270 days | $50.00 |

________

Score for D (30)

# Assignment 13.2: Simple Interest Applications

Name ____________________

Date ____________ Score ____________

Learning Objectives 1 2 3

**A** **(50 points) Solve each of the following ordinary simple interest problems by using a 360-day year. Find both the interest dollars and the total amount (i.e., principal plus interest) of the loan. (7 points for each correct interest; 3 points for each correct amount)**

**1.** Tom Titus plans to lend $850 to his friend Bill White so that Bill can fly with him to Canada for vacation. Tom is charging Bill only 3% ordinary simple interest. Bill repays everything, interest plus principal, to Tom 180 days later. How much does Bill pay?

Interest ________

Amount ________

**2.** Tony Woo and Helen Lee are planning to start a business that will export American food to China. They estimate that they will need $75,000 to pay for organizational costs, get product samples, and make three trips to Shanghai. They can borrow the money from their relatives for 4 years. Tony and Helen are willing to pay their relatives 9% ordinary simple interest. Compute the total amount that Tony and Helen will owe their relatives in 4 years.

Interest ________

Amount ________

**3.** Carolyn Wilfert owns a temporary services employment agency. Businesses call her when they need to hire various types of workers for a short period of time. The businesses pay a fee to Carolyn, who pays the salaries and benefits to the employees. One benefit is that Carolyn will make small, short-term loans to her employees. After a flood, employee Judy Hillstrom needed to borrow $3,600 to have her house cleaned and repainted. Judy repaid the loan in 6 months. If Carolyn charged 5% ordinary simple interest, how much did Judy repay?

Interest ________

Amount ________

**4.** Several years ago, Dick Shanley and Karl Coke formed a partnership to rent musical instruments to school districts that do not want to own and maintain the instruments. In the spring, they investigate borrowing $80,000 to buy trumpets and trombones. Because they collect their rental fees in advance, they anticipate being able to repay the loan in 135 days. How much will they need to repay if the ordinary simple interest rate is 6.5%?

Interest ________

Amount ________

**5.** Along with her husband, Ruby Williams owns and manages a video game arcade. A manufacturer developed a new line of games and offered very low interest financing to encourage arcade operators such as Ruby to install the new games. Ruby was able to finance $60,000 worth of games for 8 months for 5.2% ordinary simple interest. Calculate how much Ruby will repay.

Interest ________

Amount ________

________

Score for A (50)

**B** **(50 points) Solve each of the following exact simple interest problems by using a 365-day year. Find both the interest dollars and the total amount (i.e., principal plus interest) of the loan. (7 points for each correct interest; 3 points for each correct amount)**

**6.** Robert Burke, managing partner of a local transportation company, thinks that the company should borrow money to upgrade its truck repair facility. After investigating several sources of short-term loans, Robert determines that the company can borrow $400,000 for 200 days at 5.5% exact simple interest. If the company agrees to take out this loan, how much will it need to repay at the end of the 200 days?

Interest ________

Amount ________

**7.** Dave Engle, a former teacher, now has a business selling supplemetary educational materials such as books and computer software to parents and schools. In June, he borrowed $45,000 from his bank to buy some new educational computer games that he hopes to sell during August and September. The bank's rate is 6.25% exact simple interest as long as the time does not exceed half a year. If Dave pays the principal plus the interest in 120 days, how much will he pay?

Interest ________

Amount ________

**8.** After working in construction for 5 years, Jerry Weekly had saved almost enough money to buy a fishing boat and move to Alaska to become a commercial fisherman. He still needed $9,500, which his wife could borrow from her parents until the end of the first fishing season. The parents charged 5% exact simple interest, and Jerry repaid them after 95 days. How much interest did he pay, and what was the total amount?

Interest ________

Amount ________

**9.** Bill and Carol Campbell need to purchase two new saws for their retail lumber yard. The company that sells the saws offers them some short-term financing at the relatively high rate of 11% exact simple interest. They decide to accept the financing offer, but only for $5,000 and only for 45 days. How much will Bill and Carol repay at the end of the 45 days?

Interest ________

Amount ________

**10.** After working for a large accounting firm for 10 years, Bette Ryan, C.P.A., decided to open her own office. She borrowed $50,000 at 6.7% exact simple interest. She made enough during the first income tax season to repay the loan in 219 days. How much did Bette repay?

Interest ________

Amount ________

____________

Score for B (50)

# 14

# Installment Purchases

## Learning Objectives

By studying this chapter and completing all assignments, you will be able to:

**Learning Objective 1** Convert between annual and monthly interest rates.

**Learning Objective 2** Compute simple interest on a monthly basis.

**Learning Objective 3** Compute finance charges for credit account purchases.

**Learning Objective 4** Compute costs of installment purchases.

**Learning Objective 5** Compute effective rates.

**Learning Objective 6** Amortize a loan.

**Learning Objective 7** Compute the monthly payment on a home mortgage.

Most individuals today can purchase goods or services on credit if they choose. The buyer gets immediate possession or immediate service but delays payment. Either the seller extends the credit or the buyer uses a **credit card,** or loan, from a third party.

Credit is usually offered for an interest charge, which is usually computed each month. A summary of the purchases, payments, and interest charges is sent to the borrower (credit purchaser) each month. It may not be simple to compare the methods used to compute interest by competing lenders. Some lenders may charge interest on the **average daily balance.** Although it is a simple concept, and easy for a computer to calculate, it may be difficult for the purchaser to reconcile when he or she makes many purchases and/or merchandise returns in a single month.

In addition to interest, a lender may charge additional fees to extend credit or loan money. These might include items such as loan origination fees, membership fees, credit check fees, administrative fees, and insurance premiums. All of the fees together are called **finance charges.** These additional fees, whether one-time, annual, or monthly, also make it difficult to compare lenders because each lender could be slightly different. It is of some help to consumers that there are laws that mandate that lenders must explain their various fees and rates.

## Converting Interest Rates

**Learning Objective 1**

Convert between annual and monthly interest rates.

The general concept behind charging for credit purchases is to compute finance charges on the unpaid balance each month. The formula is still $I = P \times R \times T$, where $P$ is the unpaid balance. However, $T$ is not years or a fraction of a year (as in Chapter 13)—$T$ is in months, and $R$, the rate, is a monthly rate. For example, the rate might be 1.5% *per month.*

Understanding the relationship between monthly and annual rates is important.

**Rule: To convert an annual rate to a monthly rate, divide the annual rate by 12; to convert a monthly rate to an annual rate, multiply the monthly rate by 12.**

**EXAMPLE A**

a. Convert 9% per year to the equivalent monthly rate.
   9% annually ÷ 12 = 0.75% monthly

b. Convert 0.5% per month to the equivalent annual rate.
   0.5% monthly × 12 = 6% annually

**CONCEPT CHECK 14.1**

a. Convert an 18% annual rate to the equivalent monthly rate.
   Divide the annual rate by 12 to get the monthly rate: 18% ÷ 12 = 1.5% per month

b. Convert a 1.25% monthly rate to the equivalent annual rate.
   Multiply the monthly rate by 12 to get the annual rate: 1.25% × 12 = 15% per year

# Computing Simple Interest on a Monthly Basis

In terms of single-payment simple interest, 1.5% *per month* is identical to 18% *per year.*

**Rule: If the rate is annual, the time must be in years; if the rate is monthly, the time must be in months.**

Learning Objective 2

Compute simple interest on a monthly basis.

**EXAMPLE B**

Compute the simple interest on \$1,000 for 2 months at 18% per year, on an annual basis and on a monthly basis.

Annual: $I = P \times R \times T = \$1{,}000 \times 0.18 \text{ per year} \times \frac{2}{12} \text{ year} = \$30$

Monthly: $18\% \text{ per year} = 18\% \div 12 = 1.5\% \text{ per month}$

$$I = P \times R \times T = \$1{,}000 \times 0.015 \text{ per month} \times 2 \text{ months} = \$30$$

*Reminder:* Both computations differ from most of those in Chapter 13, where you counted the exact number of days and divided by either 360 or 365.

**CONCEPT CHECK 14.2**

Compute the simple interest on \$800 for 3 months at 0.5% per month.

$I = P \times R \times T = \$800 \times 0.5\% \text{ per month} \times 3 \text{ months} = \$800 \times 0.005 \times 3 = \$12$

# Computing Finance Charges

Learning Objective 3

Compute finance charges for credit account purchases.

To enable consumers to compute the total cost of credit, Congress has passed several laws, beginning with the Consumer Credit Protection Act of 1968 (CCPA). Title I of the CCPA is known as the **Truth in Lending Act (TILA).** TILA is administered by the Federal Reserve Board. Among other major legislation, Congress also passed the Consumer Leasing Act of 1976, administered by the Federal Trade Commission, and the Home Ownership and Equity Protection Act of 1994, administered by the Department of Housing and Urban Development. All of these require lenders to make certain disclosures to consumers.

Among several mandates, TILA requires creditors to tell consumers these three things:

1. The total of all finance charges, including interest, carrying charges, insurance, and special fees
2. The annual percentage rate (APR) of the total finance charge
3. The method by which they compute the finance charge

As noted in the previous section, an annual interest rate is a monthly interest rate multiplied by 12. However, as the term is used in TILA, the **annual percentage rate (APR)** is a specific, defined term that must include all finance charges, not just interest.

Furthermore, under TILA, lenders are permitted to use more than one method to compute the APR. Lenders may even use either a 360-day year or a 365-day year. TILA does not set limits on rates.

As mentioned, TILA does require that total finance charges be stated clearly, that the finance charges also be stated as an annual percentage rate, and that the method of computation be given. Although the method that is mentioned may be stated clearly, it may not always be simple for a consumer to calculate. One difficulty might be to determine the account balance that is to be used in the calculation. A wide variety of methods may be applied. For example:

1. The finance charge may be based on the amount owed at the beginning of the current month, ignoring payments and purchases.
2. The finance charge may be based on the amount owed at the beginning of the month, after subtracting any payments during the month and ignoring purchases.
3. The finance charge may be based on the average daily balance. (Add the unpaid balance each day; divide the total by the number of days in the month.) Payments are usually included; new purchases may or may not be included.
4. A variation of the average daily balance method is to compute the interest charge each day, on a daily basis, and then add all the daily interest charges for the month.

Although the total finance charges, and the annual percentage rate, and the method of calculation may all be clearly stated, some consumers will have difficulty reconstructing the interest and finance charges on their bills. A consumer who wants to understand more can write to the creditor to request a more detailed explanation and even an example of how to do the calculations.

Figure 14-1 is the lower portion of a typical statement from a retail store. Examples C and D illustrate two simple methods used to compute finance charges.

**Figure 14-1 Retail Statement of Account**

| PREVIOUS BALANCE | FINANCE CHARGE | PAYMENTS | CREDITS | PURCHASES | NEW BALANCE | MINIMUM PAYMENT | CLOSING DATE |
|---|---|---|---|---|---|---|---|
| 624.12 | 9.36 | 500.00 | 62.95 | 364.45 | 434.98 | 45.00 | 10-16-09 |

IF WE RECEIVE PAYMENT OF THE FULL AMOUNT OF THE NEW BALANCE BEFORE THE NEXT CYCLE'S CLOSING DATE, SHOWN ABOVE, YOU WILL AVOID A FINANCE CHARGE NEXT MONTH. THE FINANCE CHARGE, IF ANY, IS CALCULATED ON THE PREVIOUS BALANCE BEFORE DEDUCTING ANY PAYMENTS OR CREDITS SHOWN ABOVE. THE PERIODIC RATES USED ARE 1.5% OF THE BALANCE ON AMOUNTS UNDER $1,000 AND 1% OF AMOUNTS IN EXCESS OF $1,000, WHICH ARE ANNUAL PERCENTAGE RATES OF 18% AND 12%, RESPECTIVELY.

### EXAMPLE C

Compute the finance charge and the new balance for the statement shown in Figure 14-1 based on the previous balance, $624.12, ignoring all payments, credits, and purchases.

Finance charge = $\$624.12 \times 1.5\% \times 1$ month = $\$9.3618$, or $\$9.36$

New balance = $\$624.12 + \$9.36 - \$500.00 - \$62.95 + \$364.45 = \$434.98$

**EXAMPLE D**

Assume that the finance charge in Figure 14-1 is based on the previous balance, less any payments or credits, but ignores subsequent purchases. Compute the finance charge and the new balance.

The finance charge is based on $624.12 − $500.00 − $62.95 = $61.17
Finance charge = $61.17 × 1.5% × 1 month = $0.91575, or $0.92
New balance = $624.12 + $0.92 − $500.00 − $62.95 + $364.45 = $426.54

**CONCEPT CHECK 14.3**

The finance terms given in the charge account statement of Figure 14-1 indicate that the finance charge, if any, is charged on the previous balance, before deducting payments or credits or adding purchases. Calculate the finance charge and the unpaid balance if the previous balance was $2,425.90, the payment was $1,200, there were no credits, and there were $572.50 in new purchases.

An interest rate of 1.5% applies to the first $1,000 and 1% applies to the excess:
$2,425.90 − $1,000 = $1,425.90.

0.015 × $1,000 = $15.00
0.01 × $1,425.90 = $14.26
Finance charge = $15.00 + $14.26 = $29.26
New balance = $2,425.90 − $1,200 + $29.26 + $572.50 = $1,827.66

COMPLETE ASSIGNMENT 14.1.

# Computing Costs of Installment Purchases

Learning Objective **4**

Compute costs of installment purchases.

In a credit sale, the buyer pays the purchase price plus credit charges. Usually, the buyer makes monthly payments called **installments.** Just as you saw in the previous section, the method of computing the interest is just as important as the interest rate. Most often, the interest is based on the unpaid balance and is calculated each month using a monthly interest rate. Sometimes, the interest may be calculated only once at the beginning using an annual interest rate, but the interest might be paid in equal installments along with the principal installments.

**EXAMPLE E**

Nancy Bjonerud purchases $4,000 worth of merchandise. She will repay the principal in four equal monthly payments of $1,000 each. She will also pay interest each month on the unpaid balance for that month, which is calculated at an annual rate of 12%. First, calculate each of the monthly interest payments. Then, display the results in a table.

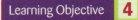

© VIKING RANGE CORPORATION/PRNEWSFOTO (ASSOCIATED PRESS)

Given the annual interest of 12%, the monthly rate is 12% ÷ 12 = 1% per month.

Month 1: \$4,000 × 1% = \$40

Month 2: \$3,000 × 1% = \$30

Month 3: \$2,000 × 1% = \$20

Month 4: \$1,000 × 1% = \$10

Total interest = \$40 + \$30 + \$20 + \$10 = \$100

| Month | Unpaid Balance | Interest Payment | Principal Payment | Total Payment | New Balance |
|---|---|---|---|---|---|
| 1 | \$ 4,000 | \$ 40 | \$1,000 | \$1,040 | \$3,000 |
| 2 | 3,000 | 30 | 1,000 | 1,030 | 2,000 |
| 3 | 2,000 | 20 | 1,000 | 1,020 | 1,000 |
| 4 | 1,000 | +10 | +1,000 | +1,010 | 0 |
| | | \$100 | \$4,000 | \$4,100 | |

**EXAMPLE F**

Carmel Dufault purchases \$4,000 worth of merchandise. She will pay interest of 12% on \$4,000 for four months. First, calculate the total amount of interest. Carmel will repay one-fourth of the interest amount each month. In addition, she will repay the \$4,000 in four equal monthly amounts of \$1,000 each. Display the results in a table.

$\$4{,}000 \times 12\% \times \frac{4}{12} = \$160$

\$160 ÷ 4 = \$40 per month for interest

| Month | Unpaid Balance | Interest Payment | Principal Payment | Total Payment | New Balance |
|---|---|---|---|---|---|
| 1 | \$ 4,000 | \$ 40 | \$1,000 | \$1,040 | \$3,000 |
| 2 | 3,000 | 40 | 1,000 | 1,040 | 2,000 |
| 3 | 2,000 | 40 | 1,000 | 1,040 | 1,000 |
| 4 | 1,000 | + 40 | +1,000 | +1,040 | 0 |
| | | \$160 | \$4,000 | \$4,160 | |

## CONCEPT CHECK 14.4

A kitchen stove is priced at \$600 and is purchased with a \$100 down payment. The \$500 remaining balance is paid in two successive monthly payments of \$250 each. Compute the total interest using the following methods:

a. Interest of 1.5% is calculated on the unpaid balance each month (18% annual rate).
   Month 1: \$500 × 0.015 = \$7.50
   Month 2: New balance is \$250. \$250 × 0.015 = \$3.75
   Total interest = \$7.50 + \$3.75 = \$11.25

b. Simple interest is calculated on the entire \$500 for 2 months at 1.5% per month (18% annual rate).
   \$500 × 0.015 per month × 2 months = \$15.00

# Computing Effective Interest Rates

Learning Objective 5

Compute effective rates.

Examples E and F are very similar, but not quite identical. The numbers are the same: Both purchases are for \$4,000; both repay the \$4,000 principal in four equal monthly payments; both use a 12% annual interest rate. The only difference is the method of calculating the interest. In example E, the total amount of interest is \$100; in example F, it is \$160. In example F, it is more expensive to borrow the same money than in example E. In example F, interest is calculated as if the entire \$4,000 were borrowed for 4 months (\$4,000 × 0.12 × 4/12). But Carmel repays \$1,000 of the money after only 1 month.

The true interest rate, or the **effective interest rate,** cannot be the same in each example because it costs more in example F to borrow the same amount of money for the same length of time. To calculate the effective interest rate, we use the familiar formula from Chapter 13, $R = \frac{I}{P \times T}$, where $I$ is the amount of interest in dollars, $T$ is the time of the loan in years, and $P$ is the **average unpaid balance** (or the **average principal**) over the period of the loan. The average unpaid balance is the sum of all of the unpaid monthly balances divided by the number of months. (*Note:* The term *effective interest rate* is also used in other contexts where a different formula is used to find the effective rate.)

## EXAMPLE G

Use the formula $R = \frac{I}{P \times T}$ to compute the effective interest rates for (a) example E and (b) example F. In both examples, the time of the loan is $T = \frac{4}{12}$ of a year. Using the preceding tables, for each example, the average unpaid balance is $P = \frac{\$4{,}000 + \$3{,}000 + \$2{,}000 + \$1{,}000}{4} = \frac{\$10{,}000}{4} = \$2{,}500$. But in example E, $I = \$100$ and in example F, $I = \$160$.

a. Example E: $T = \frac{4}{12}$; $P = \$2{,}500$; $I = \$100$; so that

$$R = \frac{I}{P \times T} = \frac{\$100}{\$2{,}500 \times \frac{4}{12}} = \frac{\$100}{\$833.33} = 0.120000\text{, or } 12\%$$

b. Example F: $T = \frac{4}{12}$; $P = \$2{,}500$; $I = \$160$; so that

$$R = \frac{I}{P \times T} = \frac{\$160}{\$2{,}500 \times \frac{4}{12}} = \frac{\$160}{\$833.33} = 0.1920008\text{, or } 19.2\%$$

**Rule: When the interest is calculated on the unpaid balance each month, the quoted rate and the effective rate will always be the same. When interest is computed only once on the original principal, but the principal is repaid in installments, then the effective interest rate will always be higher than the quoted rate.**

The preceding rule is true even when the principal is not repaid in equal installments each month.

**EXAMPLE H**

Look back at example E where Nancy Bjonerud made four equal principal payments of \$1,000 each. Suppose instead that she repays the principal in four monthly payments of \$900, \$1,200, \$1,100, and \$800. As in example E, she will also pay interest each month on the unpaid balance for that month, which is calculated at an annual rate of 12%. Compute the interest amount for each month and display the results in a table. Then, compute the average unpaid balance and the effective interest rate using the formula $R = \frac{I}{P \times T}$.

Given annual interest of 12%, the monthly rate is 12% ÷ 12 = 1% per month.

Month 1: \$4,000 × 1% = \$40 Month 3: \$1,900 × 1% = \$19

Month 2: \$3,100 × 1% = \$31 Month 4: \$800 × 1% = \$8

Total interest = \$40 + \$31 + \$19 + \$8 = \$98

| Month | Unpaid Balance | Interest Payment | Principal Payment | Total Payment | New Balance |
|---|---|---|---|---|---|
| 1 | \$4,000 | \$40 | \$ 900 | \$ 940 | \$3,100 |
| 2 | 3,100 | 31 | 1,200 | 1,231 | 1,900 |
| 3 | 1,900 | 19 | 1,100 | 1,119 | 800 |
| 4 | 800 | + 8 | + 800 | + 808 | 0 |
| | | \$98 | \$4,000 | \$4,098 | |

$$P = \frac{\$4{,}000 + \$3{,}100 + \$1{,}900 + \$800}{4} = \frac{\$9{,}800}{4} = \$2{,}450$$

$$R = \frac{I}{P \times T} = \frac{\$98}{\$2{,}450 \times \frac{4}{12}} = \frac{\$98}{\$816.67} = 0.11999951, \text{ or } 12\%$$

## INCREASING THE EFFECTIVE RATE

Example F shows how the effective rate in an installment sale can be increased by using a different method to calculate interest. Of course, a reputable lender should indicate the true interest rate in the terms of the agreement. But in installment sales, the interest rate may be only one of several variables in the total cost of purchasing. Any additional fees to make the installment purchase increase the actual cost of borrowing.

Naturally, some businesses will attempt to attract buyers by offering very low purchase prices, even "guaranteeing to match all competitors' advertised prices for 30 days." Others may offer installment purchases at low or even 0% interest rates and no additional fees—but they will charge a higher base price. Different consumers are attracted by different things—some by low prices, some by favorable terms of purchase. For many consumers, buying is simply an emotional response with very little thought given to actual costs.

Lenders and sellers "effectively" increase the cost of borrowing money or buying in installments by charging or suggesting additional fees. If it is a purchase of merchandise, the lender could require that the merchandise be insured for the term of purchase. Or the lender could charge a credit application fee.

Consider the following modification to example G, part a, which had an effective rate of 12%.

**EXAMPLE I**

Look back at example G, part a, where we used $R = \frac{I}{P \times T}$ to calculate the effective rate for example E, with $I$ equal to the total interest charge of \$100. Suppose instead that the lender had charged Nancy the interest of \$100, and a loan origination fee of 1% of the purchase price, and an insurance premium of \$1 per month for the term of the loan. Use the formula $R = \frac{I}{P \times T}$ to compute the effective interest rate, but let $I$ be the total finance charge.

The average unpaid balance is still $P = \frac{\$4{,}000 + \$3{,}000 + \$2{,}000 + \$1{,}000}{4} = \frac{\$10{,}000}{4} = \$2{,}500$.

$I$ = Total finance charge = Interest + Loan origination fee + Insurance

Interest only = \$40 + \$30 + \$20 + \$10 = \$100

Loan origination fee = 1% of \$4,000 = 0.01 × \$4,000 = \$40

Insurance = \$1 × 4 months = \$4

Therefore, $I$ = \$100 + \$40 + \$4 = \$144

$$R = \frac{I}{P \times T} = \frac{\$144}{\$2{,}500 \times \frac{4}{12}} = \frac{\$144}{\$833.33} = 0.17280069, \text{ or } 17.3\%$$

Because the interest in example E was paid on the unpaid balance, the effective rate was 12%, the same as the quoted interest rate. If the same additional finance charges from example I were applied to example F, the results would be even more dramatic.

## CONCEPT CHECK 14.5

From Concept Check 14.4, a kitchen stove priced at \$600 is purchased with a \$100 down payment. The remaining balance of \$500 may be financed over 2 months with either of the following installment payment plans:

Plan 1: Two monthly principal payments of \$250 each and a total interest amount of \$11.25

Plan 2: Two monthly principal payments of \$250 each and a total interest amount of \$15.00

Calculate the effective annual rate of each plan, using $R = \frac{I}{(P \times T)}$, where $P$ is the average unpaid monthly balance and $T$ is $\frac{2}{12}$ year. In each plan, the monthly unpaid balances are \$500 in month 1 and \$250 in month 2.

The average unpaid balance is $\frac{(\$500 + \$250)}{2} = \frac{\$750}{2} = \$375$, so $P = \$375$.

Plan 1: $R = \frac{I}{(P \times T)} = \frac{\$11.25}{(\$375 \times \frac{2}{12})} = \frac{\$11.25}{\$62.50} = 0.18$, or 18% effective annual rate

Plan 2: $R = \frac{I}{(P \times T)} = \frac{\$15.00}{(\$375 \times \frac{2}{12})} = \frac{\$15.00}{\$62.50} = 0.24$, or 24% effective annual rate

COMPLETE ASSIGNMENT 14.2.

# Amortizing a Loan

Learning Objective 6

Amortize a loan.

In example E, interest was calculated on the unpaid balance, but the total payments were different each month: $1,040, $1,030, $1,020, and $1,010. Equal monthly payments are usually simpler, especially for the borrower. In example F, the total payments were the same each month, always $1,040. However, the interest was not calculated on the unpaid balance. In example E, the effective interest rate was equal to the quoted interest rate of 12%. But in example F, the effective rate was much higher, 19.2%.

Taking the best features of each example, consider a loan where the total payments are equal each month and the interest is calculated on the unpaid balance each month. Such a loan is said to be *amortized;* the method is called **amortization.** (The word *amortize* is also used in different contexts and there is more than one way to amortize a loan.) Although possible for purchases of any length of time, amortization is especially relevant for larger purchases made over longer periods of time. Loans to pay for homes and automobiles are usually amortized. There may or may not be a down payment.

## COMPUTING THE MONTHLY PAYMENT

The basic concept to amortize a loan is to multiply the loan amount by an **amortization payment factor.** The product is the amount of the monthly payment. This factor may be derived from a calculator or computer or from a book of financial tables. When lenders amortize loans today, they use computers to do the final calculations. Initial calculations, however, are often made using calculators or tables. Chapter 23 will describe how to use a calculator to make amortization calculations. In this chapter we will use tables. Both methods are still used, and both lead to the same results. (You can also go to the Internet, search on "amortization calculations," and find Websites that help you do the calculations.)

Table 14-1 illustrates the concept of tables for amortization payment factors. Actual tables would have many pages and would be much more detailed. If you study other courses in business mathematics, accounting or finance, you may use tables that are slightly different than Table 14-1. In Chapter 23, we will encounter one such table. Regardless of the exact format of the table, the concepts are the same. And, to repeat, financial calculators and computers will eventually completely eliminate the need for any of these tables.

Notice that the title of Table 14-1 is "Amount of Monthly Payment per $1,000 Borrowed." Therefore, you must first determine the amount of the loan in "thousands of dollars," not in the number of dollars. The annual interest rates in Table 14-1 were selected because they are evenly divisible by 12. This will eliminate the necessity to round off interest rates when you convert an annual rate into a monthly rate.

### STEPS to Find the Monthly Payment of an Amortized Loan Using Table 14-1

1. Divide the loan amount by $1,000 to get the number of thousands of dollars.
2. Locate the amortization payment factor in Table 14-1.
3. Multiply the quotient in Step 1 by the amortization payment factor. The product is the amount of the monthly payment.

**Table 14-1:** Amortization Payment Factors—Amount of Monthly Payment per $1,000 Borrowed

| Term of Loan | | Annual Interest Rate | | | | | |
|---|---|---|---|---|---|---|---|
| | | 4.5% | 6% | 7.5% | 9% | 10.5% | 12% |
| 1 | month | 1003.75000 | 1005.00000 | 1006.25000 | 1007.50000 | 1008.75000 | 1010.00000 |
| 2 | months | 502.81425 | 503.75312 | 504.69237 | 505.63200 | 506.57203 | 507.51244 |
| 3 | months | 335.83645 | 336.67221 | 337.50865 | 338.34579 | 339.18361 | 340.02211 |
| 4 | months | 252.34814 | 253.13279 | 253.91842 | 254.70501 | 255.49257 | 256.28109 |
| 5 | months | 202.25561 | 203.00997 | 203.76558 | 204.52242 | 205.28049 | 206.03980 |
| 6 | months | 168.86099 | 169.59546 | 170.33143 | 171.06891 | 171.80789 | 172.54837 |
| 1 | year | 85.37852 | 86.06643 | 86.75742 | 87.45148 | 88.14860 | 88.84879 |
| 2 | years | 43.64781 | 44.32061 | 44.99959 | 45.68474 | 46.37604 | 47.07347 |
| 3 | years | 29.74692 | 30.42194 | 31.10622 | 31.79973 | 32.50244 | 33.21431 |
| 4 | years | 22.80349 | 23.48503 | 24.17890 | 24.88504 | 25.60338 | 26.33384 |
| 5 | years | 18.64302 | 19.33280 | 20.03795 | 20.75836 | 21.49390 | 22.24445 |
| 10 | years | 10.36384 | 11.10205 | 11.87018 | 12.66758 | 13.49350 | 14.34709 |
| 15 | years | 7.64993 | 8.43857 | 9.27012 | 10.14267 | 11.05399 | 12.00168 |
| 20 | years | 6.32649 | 7.16431 | 8.05593 | 8.99726 | 9.98380 | 11.01086 |
| 25 | years | 5.55832 | 6.44301 | 7.38991 | 8.39196 | 9.44182 | 10.53224 |
| 30 | years | 5.06685 | 5.99551 | 6.99215 | 8.04623 | 9.14739 | 10.28613 |

**EXAMPLE J**

Find the monthly payment required to amortize a $4,000 loan over 4 months at 12% (1% per month).

STEP 1 $4,000 ÷ $1,000 = 4 (thousands)

STEP 2 Find the intersection of the 12% column and the 4-month row in Table 14-1. The amortization payment factor is $256.28109 per each one thousand dollars.

STEP 3 Multiply the 4 (from Step 1) by the amortization payment factor.
4 × $256.28109 = $1,025.12436, or $1,025.12 monthly.

**EXAMPLE K**

Judith Kranz agrees to purchase an automobile for $18,300. Judith will make a $2,000 down payment and amortize the balance with monthly payments over 4 years at 9% (0.75% per month). Determine Judith's monthly payment.

$18,300 − $2,000 = $16,300 amount financed

STEP 1 $16,300 ÷ $1,000 = 16.3 (thousands)

STEP 2 Find the intersection of the 9% column and the 4-year row in Table 14-1. The amortization payment factor is $24.88504 per thousand.

STEP 3 Multiply the 16.3 (from Step 1) by the amortization payment factor.
16.3 × $24.88504 = $405.62615, or $405.63 monthly.

## LOAN PAYMENT SCHEDULE

After determining the amount of the monthly payments, a lender can prepare a schedule of loan payments called an **amortization schedule.** The payment for the last month is determined in the schedule, and it may be slightly different from the payment in the other months.

**STEPS to Create an Amortization Schedule**

For each row except the last:

1. Interest payment = Unpaid balance × Monthly interest rate
2. Principal payment = Monthly payment − Interest payment
3. New unpaid balance = Old unpaid balance − Principal payment

For the last row (the final payment):

1. Interest payment = Unpaid balance × Monthly interest rate
2. Monthly payment = Unpaid balance + Interest payment
3. Principal payment = Unpaid balance

**EXAMPLE L**

Create an amortization schedule for the loan in example J, a $4,000 loan amortized at 12% over 4 months. The interest rate is 1% per month.

| Month | Unpaid Balance | Interest Payment | Principal Payment | Total Payment | New Balance |
|---|---|---|---|---|---|
| 1 | $ 4,000.00 | $ 40.00 | $ 985.12 | $1,025.12 | $3,014.88 |
| 2 | 3,014.88 | 30.15 | 994.97 | 1,025.12 | 2,019.91 |
| 3 | 2,019.91 | 20.20 | 1,004.92 | 1,025.12 | 1,014.99 |
| 4 | 1,014.99 | +10.15 | +1,014.99 | +1,025.14 | 0 |
| Totals | | $100.50 | $4,000.00 | $4,100.50 | |

*Note:* In example L, the last monthly payment is 2 cents larger than the others. Because the interest payments need to be rounded, the final payment usually will be slightly different from the previous payments.

Since amortization implies that interest is paid on the unpaid balance, the formula $R = \frac{I}{P \times T}$ should show that the effective rate is the same as the quoted rate of 12%. Looking at the table for example L, the average unpaid balance is

$$P = \frac{\$4{,}000.00 + \$3{,}014.88 + \$2{,}019.91 + \$1{,}014.99}{4} = \frac{\$10{,}049.78}{4}$$
$$= \$2{,}512.445, \text{ or } \$2{,}512.45$$

The total interest paid is $I = \$40.00 + \$30.15 + \$20.20 + \$10.15 = \$100.50$. Therefore,

$$R = \frac{I}{P \times T} = \frac{\$100.50}{\$2{,}512.45 \times \frac{4}{12}} = \frac{\$100.50}{\$837.48} = 0.1200029, \text{ or } 12\%$$

The reason that the result was 12.00029% instead of 12% is that all of the payments were rounded to the nearest cent. You can easily verify that if you round all payments to five decimal places, $R = 12.00007$. However, also be sure to calculate the monthly payment to five decimal places, or $1,025.12436.

## CONCEPT CHECK 14.6

A $2,000 purchase is amortized over 2 months at an annual rate of 9%. First use Table 14-1 to calculate the monthly payment for month 1. Then show the calculations to construct a 2-month amortization schedule. *(Remember: In this problem, month 2 is the last month.)*

$2,000 ÷ $1,000 = 2 (thousands)

Amortization payment factor from Table 14-1 is $505.63200.

2 × $505.63200 = $1,011.264, or $1,011.26 for month 1

| Month | 1 | | 2 | |
|---|---|---|---|---|
| Unpaid balance | Original principal: | $2,000.00 | From end of month 1: | $1,003.74 |
| Monthly rate | 0.09 ÷ 12 = 0.0075 | | | |
| Interest payment | $2,000.00 × 0.0075 = | $ 15.00 | $1,003.74 × 0.0075 = | $ 7.53 |
| Total payment | From above: | $1,011.26 | $1,003.74 + $7.53 = | $1,011.27 |
| Principal payment | $1,011.26 − $15.00 = | $ 996.26 | | $1,003.74 |
| New balance | $2,000.00 − $996.26 = | $1,003.74 | $1,003.74 − $1,003.74 = | $ 0.00 |

# Finding the Monthly Payment of a Home Mortgage

Learning Objective 7

Compute the monthly payment on a home mortgage.

Persons who decide to purchase a home usually borrow the majority of the money. The amount that is borrowed is usually amortized, and usually for a long time, such as 15, 20, or 30 years. Such a home loan is called a **mortgage.** The interest rate may be **fixed,** which means that it stays the same for the entire length of the loan. Other mortgages are **variable-rate loans,** which permit the lender to periodically adjust the interest rate depending on current financial market conditions. Whether a borrower decides on a fixed or variable rate loan depends on several factors, such as how long he or she plans to remain in that home.

A mortgage loan is still a loan. And amortizing a mortgage is the same as amortizing any other loan: Look up the amortization payment factor in Table 14-1 and multiply by the number of thousands of dollars that are borrowed.

**EXAMPLE M**

George and Kathy Jarvis bought a condominium priced at $190,000. They made a $20,000 down payment and took out a 30-year, 6% mortgage on the balance. Find the size of their monthly payment.

$190,000 − $20,000 = $170,000 amount borrowed

STEP 1 Divide $170,000 by $1,000 to get 170 (thousands)

STEP 2 Find the amortization factor in the 6% column and 30-year row of Table 14-1. It is $5.99551.

STEP 3 Multiply the 170 from Step 1 by $5.99551 to get $1,019.2367. The monthly payment will be $1,019.24.

## AMORTIZATION SCHEDULE FOR A MORTGAGE

An amortization schedule for a mortgage is computed line by line, just as the amortization schedules are for other loans such as the one in example L. However, a 30-year home mortgage will have 360 lines, one for each month of the loan. This could be about six or seven pages of paper with three calculations per line, or 1,080 calculations. Today, these tables are always produced with a computer. You can create an amortization schedule using Excel or you can find several sources on the Internet to do the calculations for you. However, to review the concept manually, examine example N.

**EXAMPLE N**

Construct the first three lines of an amortization schedule for the Jarvis's home mortgage loan in example M.

The Jarvis's $170,000 mortgage has a monthly payment of $1,019.24.
For a 6% annual interest rate, the monthly rate is 6% ÷ 12 = 0.5%.
For each row,
1. Monthly interest = Unpaid balance × 0.005
2. Principal payment = Total payment − Monthly interest
3. New balance = Unpaid balance − Principal payment

| Month | Unpaid Balance | Interest Payment | Principal Payment | Total Payment | New Balance |
|---|---|---|---|---|---|
| 1 | $170,000.00 | $850.00 | $169.24 | $1,019.24 | $169,830.76 |
| 2 | 169,830.76 | 849.15 | 170.09 | 1,019.24 | 169,660.67 |
| 3 | 169,660.67 | 848.30 | 170.94 | 1,019.24 | 169,489.73 |

In problems 6 and 7, Lelia McDaniel has an account at Lakeside Furniture Store. Compute the missing values in Lelia's account summary for the months of August and September. The previous balance in September is the same as the new balance in August.

| | Cycle Closing | Previous Balance | Payment Amount | Credits | Finance Charge | Purchases | New Balance |
|---|---|---|---|---|---|---|---|
| **6.** | 8/20/20-- | $1,636.55 | $900.00 | $ 36.00 | ________ | $966.75 | ________ |
| **7.** | 9/20/20-- | ________ | $1,200.00 | $109.75 | ________ | $589.41 | ________ |

________

Score for B (33)

**C (48 points) Devlin's Feed & Fuel offers the credit terms shown below to its retail customers. In problems 8-12 compute the missing values in the charge accounts shown. Assume that all payments are made within 30 days of the billing date. (3 points for each correct answer)**

TERMS: Finance Charge is based on the Net Balance, if any payment is received within 30 days of the billing date. If payment is made after 30 days, then the Finance Charge is based on the Previous Balance. Net Balance equals Previous Balance less Payments and Credits. In either case, the monthly rate is 1.25% on the first $500 and 1% on any amount over $500. These are annual percentage rates of 15% and 12%, respectively.

| | Billing Date | Previous Balance | Payment Amount | Credit | Net Balance | Finance Charge | New Purchases | New Balance |
|---|---|---|---|---|---|---|---|---|
| **8.** | 4/25/20-- | $2,621.05 | $1,700.00 | $0.00 | ________ | ________ | $751.16 | ________ |

| | Billing Date | Previous Balance | Payment Amount | Credit | Net Balance | Finance Charge | New Purchases | New Balance |
|---|---|---|---|---|---|---|---|---|
| **9.** | 3/25/20-- | $1,827.15 | $700.00 | $28.75 | ________ | ________ | $672.39 | ________ |
| **10.** | 11/25/20-- | $1,019.63 | $325.00 | $26.50 | ________ | ________ | $218.75 | ________ |

In problems 11 and 12 compute the missing values in Jimmy Petrasek's charge account summary at Devlin's for the months of June and July. The previous balance in July is the same as the new balance in June.

| | | | | | | | | |
|---|---|---|---|---|---|---|---|---|
| **11.** | 6/25/20-- | $1,352.12 | $500.00 | $62.00 | ________ | ________ | $772.35 | ________ |
| **12.** | 7/25/20-- | ________ | $600.00 | $67.77 | ________ | ________ | $743.95 | ________ |

________

Score for C (48)

# Assignment 14.2 Installment Sales and Effective Rates

Name

Date Score

Learning Objectives 4 5

**A** **(60 points) Hal Layer needed to purchase office equipment costing $4,800. He was able to finance his purchase over 3 months at a 9% annual interest rate. Following are three different payment options under these conditions. Complete the installment purchase table for each payment option. (2 points for each correct answer)**

**1.** Hal pays $1,600 per month on the principal and pays interest of 0.75% on the unpaid balance each month (9% annual rate).

| Month | Unpaid Balance | Interest Payment | Principal Payment | Total Payment | New Balance |
|---|---|---|---|---|---|
| 1 | $4,800.00 | ______ | $1,600.00 | ______ | ______ |
| 2 | ______ | ______ | 1,600.00 | ______ | ______ |
| 3 | ______ | ______ | +1,600.00 | ______ | 0.00 |
| | | | $4,800.00 | | |

**2.** Hal makes monthly payments of $1,400, $1,400, and $2,000 on the principal and pays interest of 0.75% on the unpaid balance each month (9% annual rate).

| Month | Unpaid Balance | Interest Payment | Principal Payment | Total Payment | New Balance |
|---|---|---|---|---|---|
| 1 | $4,800.00 | ______ | $1,400.00 | ______ | ______ |
| 2 | ______ | ______ | 1,400.00 | ______ | ______ |
| 3 | ______ | ______ | +2,000.00 | ______ | 0.00 |
| | | | $4,800.00 | | |

**3.** Hal pays $1,600 per month on the principal. The total interest charge is 9% of the original principal for 3 months. Bob pays $\frac{1}{3}$ of the total interest each month.

| Month | Unpaid Balance | Interest Payment | Principal Payment | Total Payment | New Balance |
|---|---|---|---|---|---|
| 1 | $4,800.00 | ______ | $1,600.00 | ______ | ______ |
| 2 | ______ | ______ | 1,600.00 | ______ | ______ |
| 3 | ______ | ______ | +1,600.00 | ______ | 0.00 |
| | | | $4,800.00 | | |

______
Score for A (60)

**B** **(40 points) For each of the following problems calculate the effective rate using the formula $R = \frac{I}{P \times T}$.**
**(Points for each correct answer as shown)**

**4.** Compute $R$ = effective rate for the table in problem 1 in part A, with $P$ = average unpaid balance, $I$ = total interest charge and $T = \frac{3}{12}$ year.

**a.** $P$ = Average unpaid balance __________ (3 pts)
**b.** $I$ = Total interest charge __________ (3 pts)
**c.** $R$ = Effective interest rate __________ (4 pts)

**5.** Compute $R$ = effective rate for the table in problem 1 in part A, with $P$ = average unpaid balance, $I$ = total finance charge, and $T = \frac{3}{12}$ year. The finance charge is the total interest, plus a loan origination fee of $\frac{3}{4}$% of the original principal, plus $7.50 of insurance premiums ($2.50 per month).

**a.** $P$ = Average unpaid balance __________ (3 pts)
**b.** $I$ = Total finance charge __________ (3 pts)
**c.** $R$ = Effective interest rate __________ (4 pts)

**6.** Compute $R$ = effective rate for the table in problem 2 in part A, with $P$ = average unpaid balance, $I$ = total interest charge, and $T = \frac{3}{12}$ year.

**a.** $P$ = Average unpaid balance __________ (3 pts)
**b.** $I$ = Total interest charge __________ (3 pts)
**c.** $R$ = Effective interest rate __________ (4 pts)

**7.** Compute $R$ = effective rate for the table in problem 3 in part A, with $P$ = average unpaid balance, $I$ = total interest charge, and $T = \frac{3}{12}$ year.

**a.** $P$ = Average unpaid balance __________ (3 pts)
**b.** $I$ = Total interest charge __________ (3 pts)
**c.** $R$ = Effective interest rate __________ (4 pts)

__________
Score for B (40)

# Assignment 14.3 Amortization and Mortgages

Name ______________________

Date ______________ Score ______________

Learning Objectives 6 7

**A** **(16 points) Lincoln Lending Corp. amortizes all of its mortgage loans and many of its personal loans on a monthly basis. The total monthly payments are equal each month and include both interest and principal. Use Table 14-1 to find the amortization payment factor for each loan. Then compute the monthly payment. (2 points for each correct answer)**

| Loan and Terms of Amortization | Amortization Payment Factor | Monthly Payment |
|---|---|---|
| **1.** $18,000 over 5 months at 9% | ________ | ________ |
| **2.** $27,000 over 3 years at 7.5% | ________ | ________ |
| **3.** $275,000 over 20 years at 4.5% | ________ | ________ |
| **4.** $150,000 over 15 years at 6% | ________ | ________ |

________________

Score for A (16)

**B** **(32 points) On April 13, Braunda Johannesen borrowed $6,000 from her bank to help pay her federal income taxes for the previous year. The bank amortized her loan over 4 months at an annual rate of 9%. Braunda paid interest of 0.75% of the unpaid balance each month. Find the amortization payment factor in Table 14-1. This factor makes a total payment of $1,528.23 each month except the last. For the last month, the total payment is the interest payment plus the unpaid balance. Complete the following amortization schedule. (2 points for each correct answer)**

**5.** Amortization factor from Table 14-1: ________

Multiply the amortization factor by 6 to get the total payment shown for months 1, 2, and 3.

| | Month | Unpaid Balance | Interest Payment | Total Payment | Principal Payment | New Balance |
|---|---|---|---|---|---|---|
| **6.** | 1 | $6,000.00 | ________ | $1,528.23 | ________ | ________ |
| **7.** | 2 | ________ | ________ | 1,528.23 | ________ | ________ |
| **8.** | 3 | ________ | ________ | 1,528.23 | ________ | ________ |
| **9.** | 4 | ________ | ________ | ________ | ________ | 0.00 |

________________

Score for B (32)

**C** **(30 points) Refer to part B, in which Braunda Johannesen borrowed $6,000 to help pay her federal income taxes. Now suppose that Braunda agreed to make payments of $1,200 in months 1, 2, and 3. The bank will compute the interest on the unpaid balance at a rate of 0.75% (9%/12) each month and will deduct the interest from the $1,200. In the last (fourth) month, Braunda will pay all of the remaining unpaid balance plus the interest for the last month. Complete the table, using the same procedure as in part B. (2 points for each correct answer)**

| | Month | Unpaid Balance | Interest Payment | Total Payment | Principal Payment | New Balance |
|---|---|---|---|---|---|---|
| **10.** | 1 | $6,000.00 | ______ | $1,200.00 | ______ | ______ |
| **11.** | 2 | ______ | ______ | 1,200.00 | ______ | ______ |
| **12.** | 3 | ______ | ______ | 1,200.00 | ______ | ______ |
| **13.** | 4 | ______ | ______ | ______ | ______ | 0.00 |

______
Score for C (30)

**D** **(22 points) Mr. and Mrs. Paul Yeiter sold their previous home and used the profits as a down payment to buy a new home. They took out a $160,000, 25-year mortgage from Colonial Home Finance. The mortgage had an annual interest rate of 6%. From Table 14-1, the amortization payment factor is $6.44301 and the monthly payment is $1,030.88. Complete the first three rows of the amortization schedule for the Yeiters' mortgage. (2 points for each correct answer)**

Amortization Schedule for Mortgage

| | Month | Unpaid Balance | Interest Payment | Total Payment | Principal Payment | New Balance |
|---|---|---|---|---|---|---|
| **14.** | 1 | $160,000.00 | ______ | $1,030.88 | ______ | ______ |
| **15.** | 2 | ______ | ______ | 1,030.88 | ______ | ______ |
| **16.** | 3 | ______ | ______ | 1,030.88 | ______ | ______ |

______
Score for D (22)

# 15

# Promissory Notes and Discounting

## Learning Objectives

By studying this chapter and completing all assignments, you will be able to:

Learning Objective 1 Compute the number of interest days of a promissory note.

Learning Objective 2 Determine the due date of a promissory note.

Learning Objective 3 Compute the maturity value of a promissory note.

Learning Objective 4 Discount a promissory note.

Learning Objective 5 Compute the proceeds and actual interest rate on a bank discount loan.

Learning Objective 6 Compute the savings from borrowing money to take a cash discount.

Businesses and individuals both use long-term loans (more than 1 year) to purchase large items such as equipment or buildings. Likewise, businesses and individuals also use short-term loans when they are convenient. Long-term and short-term loans are written in the form of various financial documents, one of which is called a **promissory note.** It is a promise by a borrower to repay a certain amount of money on a certain date. Sometimes the promissory note can be sold to a third party, in which case the note is called a **negotiable promissory note.** Because the buyer of the note is assuming some risk that the borrower will not repay, he or she will not likely pay the entire value of the note. Such a note is called a **discounted note.** Similarly, an individual may go to a bank to borrow money, and the bank may deduct the entire amount of the interest in advance. This is called bank discounting, and the loan is called a **bank discount loan.**

Unlike individuals, however, businesses may borrow large amounts of money for only a few days. For example, a retail business buys merchandise from manufacturers and wholesalers. But the retailer may know immediately that it cannot sell enough merchandise in time to pay the supplier's invoice. Perhaps the supplier also offers a cash discount if the buyer pays the invoice within a few days (see Chapter 7). The retailer can usually save money by borrowing enough cash to pay the invoice and take advantage of the cash discount. If the amounts are large, the savings can be significant.

## Promissory Notes

A promissory note is an unconditional promise by the **maker** of the note (the borrower) to repay money to the **bearer** of the note (the lender) at some time in the future. This date is called the **due date** or the **maturity date.** The dollar amount written on the note is called the **face value** (*FV*) of the note. It is usually the same as the principal (***P*** in Chapter 13). Most promissory notes are **interest-bearing,** especially if one or both parties is a business. This means that the maker must also pay interest to the bearer on the maturity date. The sum of the face value and the **interest dollars** (***I***) is the **maturity value** (*MV*) of the note. Figure 15-1 illustrates a simple promissory note.

**Figure 15-1** **Promissory Note**

$ 2,000.00 ATLANTA, GEORGIA March 15 20 --

— Sixty days — AFTER DATE I, Sylvia Cometta, PROMISE TO PAY TO

THE ORDER OF William Dale Crist

PAYABLE AT Bank of the South

Two thousand and 00/100 DOLLARS

VALUE RECEIVED WITH EXACT INTEREST AT 10% PER ANNUM

NO. 47 DUE May 14, 20--

Sylvia Cometta

# Computing the Number of Interest Days of a Note

To define the interest period, or term, of a promissory note, the lender either specifies the due date of the note or states the number of interest days. When the due date is given, the number of interest days must be computed before the interest charge can be computed.

To do so you need the number of days in each month, as shown in Table 15-1. February has 29 days in leap years. A leap year is any year that is evenly divisible by 4, except for certain years ending in 00 (e.g., 1900). In order to be leap years, years ending in 00 must be evenly divisible by 400; thus 2000 was a leap year, but 1900 was not.

**Learning Objective 1**

Compute the number of interest days of a promissory note.

**STEPS to Compute the Number of Interest Days Between Two Dates**

1. Determine the number of interest days in the beginning month.
2. Determine the number of interest days in the middle months.
3. Add the numbers from Steps 1 and 2 to the number of interest days in the final month. (For the final month, the number of interest days is equal to the number of the due date.)

**Table 15-1 Days in Each Month (non-leap years)**

| Month | Number of Days | Month | Number of Days | Month | Number of Days |
|---|---|---|---|---|---|
| January | 31 days | May | 31 days | September | 30 days |
| February | 28 days | June | 30 days | October | 31 days |
| March | 31 days | July | 31 days | November | 30 days |
| April | 30 days | August | 31 days | December | 31 days |

**EXAMPLE A**

A promissory note is made on July 25. The due date is October 8. Use Table 15-1 to help you determine the number of interest days between July 25 and October 8.

STEP 1

| | |
|---|---|
| 31 | days in July |
| − 25 | date of note |
| 6 | days of interest |

STEP 2

August has 31 days
September has 30 days

STEP 3

| | |
|---|---|
| 6 | days in July |
| 31 | days in August |
| 30 | days in September |
| + 8 | days in October (due date) |
| 75 | total interest days in the promissory note |

## CONCEPT CHECK 15.1

A promissory note is dated October 20. The maturity date (due date) is February 20. Determine the number of interest days.

As October has 31 days and the note is dated October 20, there are $31 - 20 = 11$ days of interest in October. Since the note is due on February 20, there are 20 interest days in February. The total can be expressed as

| October | | November | | December | | January | | February | | Total Interest Days |
|---|---|---|---|---|---|---|---|---|---|---|
| 11 | + | 30 | + | 31 | + | 31 | + | 20 | = | 123 |

# Determining the Due Date of a Note

**Learning Objective 2**

Determine the due date of a promissory note.

When the promissory note explicitly states the number of interest days, then you must determine the due date. The procedure is somewhat the reverse of finding the number of interest days.

**STEPS to Determine the Due Date**

1. Determine the number of interest days in the beginning month.
2. Determine the number of interest days that remain after the first month.
3. Determine the number of interest days remaining at the end of each succeeding month by subtracting. Continue subtracting until less than 1 month remains. The due date is the number of interest days remaining in the final month.

## EXAMPLE B

A promissory note is made on July 25. The note is for 75 days. Determine the due date.

© R. ALCORN/CENGAGE LEARNING

STEP 1

| | |
|---|---|
| 31 | days in July |
| −25 | date of note |
| 6 | days of interest in July |

STEP 2

| | |
|---|---|
| 75 | days of interest in the note |
| − 6 | days of interest in July |
| 69 | days left in term after end of July |

STEP 3

| | |
|---|---|
| 69 | days of interest left after July |
| −31 | days in August |
| 38 | days of interest left after August |
| −30 | days in September |
| 8 | days of interest left after end of September, or 8 days of interest in October |

The due date is October 8.

Although the procedure looks somewhat cumbersome on paper, it goes very quickly on a calculator. You can subtract repeatedly to deduct the days of each month, and after each subtraction, the calculator will display the number of interest days remaining. You don't need to write down all the intermediate results.

When the length of the interest period is expressed in months, the date is advanced by the number of months given. The due date is the same date of the month as the date of the note. For example, a 2-month note dated July 3 will be due on September 3. The exact number of interest days must then be computed, as shown previously. If the note is dated the 31st of a month and the month of maturity is April, June, September, or November, the due date is the 30th. If the month of maturity is February, the due date is the 28th (or 29th in a leap year).

## EXAMPLE C

Find the due date of a 3-month note dated January 31 (the last day of the month).

Maturity month: April (count "February, March, April")
Last day: 30 (last day of April)
Therefore the due date is April 30.

## CONCEPT CHECK 15.2

a. A 90-day promissory note is dated February 5 in a non-leap year. Determine the due date.

| | |
|---|---|
| 28 | days in February |
| − 5 | date of note |
| 23 | days of interest in February |
| 90 | days of interest in the note |
| − 23 | days of interest in February |
| 67 | days of interest left after February |

| | |
|---|---|
| 67 | days of interest left after February |
| − 31 | days in March |
| 36 | days of interest left after March |
| − 30 | days in April |
| 6 | days of interest left after April |

The due date is May 6.

b. A 4-month promissory note is dated April 30. Determine the due date.
Four months after April 30 is August 30. The due date is August 30.

# Computing the Maturity Value of a Note

Learning Objective 3

Compute the maturity value of a promissory note.

The maturity value ($MV$) of a promissory note is the sum of the face value (principal) of the note and the interest:

$$\text{Maturity Value} = \text{Principal} + \text{Interest}, \quad \text{or} \quad MV = P + I$$

**EXAMPLE D**

Compute the maturity value of the interest-bearing promissory note illustrated in Figure 15-1.

The face value ($P$) of the note is \$2,000. The interest rate ($R$) is 10% exact interest per year. The loan period of the note is 60 days, so the time in years ($T$) is $\frac{60}{365}$.

$$I = P \times R \times T = \$2{,}000 \times 0.10 \times \frac{60}{365} = \$32.88$$

$$MV = P + I = \$2{,}000 + \$32.88 = \$2{,}032.88$$

**CONCEPT CHECK 15.3**

A 90-day promissory note has a face value of \$2,800 and an exact simple interest rate of 7.5%. Compute the maturity value.

$$I = P \times R \times T = \$2{,}800 \times 0.075 \times \frac{90}{365} = \$51.78 \qquad MV = P + I = \$2{,}800 + \$51.78 = \$2{,}851.78$$

COMPLETE ASSIGNMENT 15.1.

# Discounting Promissory Notes

Learning Objective 4

Discount a promissory note.

Often, when a lender holds a promissory note as security for a loan to a borrower, the lender may need cash before the maturity date of the note. One option is for the lender to "sell" the note to a third party. Such a note is said to be *negotiable.*

However, now the third party is assuming the risk that the original borrower might not pay everything on the maturity date. Therefore, to acquire the note, the third party will pay the original lender less money than the maturity value. The note is said to "sell at a discount."

There are several vocabulary terms involved in discounting promissory notes. The calculations, however, are straightforward and very similar to simple interest calculations. These can be explained by using examples.

**EXAMPLE E**

On August 19, Telescan Medical Instruments borrows \$75,000 from a private investor, Margaret Wegner. In return, Telescan gives Margaret a 120-day promissory note at an ordinary simple interest rate of 8% (360-day year). Compute the due date and the maturity value of the promissory note.

Due date: August 19 + 120 days = December 17

Interest: $I = P \times R \times T = \$75{,}000 \times 0.08 \times \frac{120}{360} = \$2{,}000$

Maturity value: $MV = P + I = \$75{,}000 + \$2{,}000 = \$77{,}000$

In example E, Telescan Medical must pay \$77,000 to Margaret Wegner on December 17. During the 120 days, Margaret has only the promissory note—no cash. If the note is negotiable, Margaret can sell the note to a third party at any time before December 17. Suppose that Margaret sells the note on October 5 to Auburn Financial Corporation. October 5 is called the **discount date.** The time between October 5 and December 17 is the **discount period.** The length of the discount period is the number of days between October 5 and December 17. Since the original 8% interest rate was ordinary simple interest (360-day year), we will also use a 360-day year in the discount calculation.

Auburn Financial agrees to buy the note at a discount of 12% of the maturity value. 12% is the **discount rate.** The **discount amount** is calculated using a formula similar to ordinary simple interest:

Discount Amount = Maturity value × Discount rate × Time (Discount period)

Maturity value: \$77,000
Discount rate: 12%
Discount period: October 5 to December 17 = (31 − 5) + 30 + 17 = 73 days

$$\text{Discount Amount} = \$77{,}000 \times 0.12 \times \frac{73}{360} = \$1{,}873.67$$

The difference between the maturity value and the discount amount is called the **proceeds.** It is the amount that Auburn Financial will pay to Margaret Wegner for her promissory note from Telescan Medical Systems.

Proceeds = Maturity value − Discount amount
= \$77,000 − \$1,873.67 = \$75,126.33

**STEPS to Discount a Promissory Note**

1. Compute the interest amount ($I$) and maturity value ($MV$) of the promissory note.
2. Determine the maturity (due) date of the note.
3. Compute the number of days in the discount period. The time, $T$, is the number of days in the discount period divided by 360, or by 365.
4. Compute the discount amount, using $D = MV \times R \times T$, where $R$ is the discount rate.
5. Compute the proceeds by subtracting the discount amount from the maturity value.

## NON-INTEREST-BEARING PROMISSORY NOTES

Sometimes the original lender may not charge any interest at all. In this situation, the maturity value of the note is equal to the face value. Similarly, the original lender may require that all of the interest must be completely paid in advance. Therefore, this is another type of promissory note that does not have any interest dollars in the maturity value, so the maturity value is equal to the face value. To find the proceeds of a **non-interest-bearing promissory note,** follow the same steps that were listed above. But, in Step 1, the amount of interest is $0 and the maturity value is the face value.

### EXAMPLE F

Willie Smith, owner of a True-Value Hardware Store, is holding a 75-day, non-interest-bearing note for $3,500. The note is dated June 21. On August 10, Willie sells the note to the Marshfield Lending Company, which discounts the note at 11%. Find the discount amount and the proceeds using a 365-day year.

STEP 1 Interest amount = $0; Maturity value = Face value = $3,500

STEP 2 Due date: June 21 + 75 days = September 4

STEP 3 Discount period: August 10 to September 4 = 25 days

STEP 4 Discount amount: Maturity value × Discount rate × Time

$$= \$3{,}500 \times 0.11 \times \frac{25}{365}$$

$$= \$26.3697, \text{ or } \$26.37$$

STEP 5 Proceeds: Maturity value − Discount amount

$$= \$3{,}500 - \$26.37$$

$$= \$3{,}473.63$$

### CONCEPT CHECK 15.4

A 75-day promissory note, bearing interest at 10%, is dated December 11 and has a face value of $5,000. On January 24, the note is discounted at 14%. Find the discount amount and the proceeds. *Note:* The interest amount, the maturity value, the maturity date, and the days of discount must first be determined. Use a 365-day year for all interest and discount calculations.

Interest amount: $\$5{,}000 \times 0.10 \times \frac{75}{365} = \$102.7397, \text{ or } \$102.74$

Maturity value: $5,000 + $102.74 = $5,102.74

Maturity date: Dec. 11 + 75 days = Feb. 24

Days of discount: Jan. 24 to Feb. 24 = 31 days

Discount amount: $\$5{,}102.74 \times 0.14 \times \frac{31}{365} = \$60.6737, \text{ or } \$60.67$

Proceeds: $5,102.74 − $60.67 = $5,042.07

COMPLETE ASSIGNMENT 15.2.

# Bank Discounting

In Chapter 13 and at the beginning of this chapter, we studied the simple procedure to borrow and repay money: Determine the Principal, Rate, and Time; compute the interest amount; the maturity value (amount due) is the principal plus the interest.

**Learning Objective 5**

Compute the proceeds and actual interest rate on a bank discount loan.

**EXAMPLE G**

Rueben Cortez, owner/operator of a fast-food restaurant, borrows $50,000 from his bank for 60 days at 9% ordinary simple interest. Using a 360-day year, compute the interest and the maturity value.

$P = \$50{,}000;\ R = 9\%;\ T = \frac{60}{360}$

$\text{Interest } (I) = P \times R \times T = \$50{,}000 \times 0.09 \times \frac{60}{360} = \$750$

$\text{Maturity value } (MV) = P + I = \$50{,}000 + \$750 = \$50{,}750$

Please observe: Rueben will keep the entire $50,000 for the entire 60 days and then repay a total of $50,750 on the due date.

In the previous section, we studied promissory notes that were discounted at some date between the date of the loan and the due date. Similarly, sometimes banks will discount loans immediately, at the time they are written. The steps to discount a loan are the same as discounting promissory notes, but even simpler because (a) the face value is equal to the maturity value, (b) the discount date is the same as the loan date, and (3) the number of discount days is the same as the period of the loan.

**STEPS to Discount a Bank Loan**

1. Compute the discount amount, using $D = FV \times R \times T$, where $R$ is the discount rate.
2. Compute the proceeds by subtracting the discount amount from the face value.

**EXAMPLE H**

Rueben Cortez, owner/operator of a fast-food restaurant, goes to his bank to borrow money. Rueben signs a 60-day note with a $50,000 face value at a 9% discount rate. Using a 360-day year, compute the discount amount and the proceeds of the loan.

$FV = \$50{,}000;\ R = 9\%;\ T = \frac{60}{360}$

STEP 1 $\text{Discount amount } (D) = FV \times R \times T = \$50{,}000 \times 0.09 \times \frac{60}{360} = \$750$

STEP 2 $\text{Proceeds} = \text{Face value} - \text{Discount amount} = \$50{,}000 - \$750 = \$49{,}250$

Please observe: In example H, Rueben will keep \$49,250 for the entire 60 days and then repay a total of \$50,000 on the due date.

As mentioned earlier, some persons refer to this type of discounted loan as "non-interest-bearing" because the amount to be repaid is the "face value." However, the term *non-interest-bearing* is misleading because the loan is *not* "interest-free." There is a charge of \$750 to borrow \$49,250 for 60 days.

## COMPARING A DISCOUNT RATE TO AN INTEREST RATE

Discount rates are less familiar to those consumers who have encountered only interest rates. There is the possibility of misunderstanding or confusion. In example G, Rueben Cortez borrowed \$50,000 for 60 days and paid \$750. The ordinary simple interest rate was 9%. In example H, Rueben borrowed \$49,250 for 60 days and paid \$750. Although a discount rate (9%) was given, a simple interest rate was not given. To compute Rueben's actual simple interest rate in example H, use the formula from Chapter 13:

$$R = \frac{I}{P \times T}, \text{ letting } I = \$750,\ P = \$49{,}250, \text{ and } T = \frac{60}{360}$$

$$R = \frac{I}{P \times T} = \frac{\$750}{\$49{,}250 \times \frac{60}{360}} = \frac{\$750}{\$8{,}208.33} = 0.09137, \text{ or } 9.14\%$$

The interest rate in example H is actually 9.14%; the discount rate is 9%. They are different rates, but both lead to a \$750 fee to borrow \$49,250 for 60 days. A borrower must understand the difference between interest rates and discount rates and how each is used in loan calculations.

### CONCEPT CHECK 15.5

A bank made a 90-day loan on a discount basis. The face value was \$64,000, and the discount rate was 11%. Compute the discount amount and the proceeds. Then compute the actual interest rate, using the proceeds as the principal of the loan instead of the face value. Use a 360-day year in all calculations.

$$\text{Discount amount} = FV \times R \times T = \$64{,}000 \times 0.11 \times \frac{90}{360} = \$1{,}760$$

$$\text{Proceeds} = \text{Face value} - \text{Discount amount} = \$64{,}000 - \$1{,}760 = \$62{,}240$$

$$\text{Actual interest rate} = \frac{I}{(P \times T)} = \frac{\$1{,}760}{\left(\$62{,}240 \times \frac{90}{360}\right)} = 0.1131, \text{ or } 11.31\%$$

## Borrowing Money to Take a Cash Discount

Learning Objective 6

Compute the savings from borrowing money to take a cash discount.

In Chapter 7, we described how manufacturers and wholesalers use cash discounts to encourage their customers to pay their invoices early. Recall that the terms "2/10, net 30" mean that the buyer will receive a 2% discount by paying the invoice within 10 days and that the entire invoice is due within 30 days. However, it would be normal that a buyer would not have the immediate cash to pay the invoice early. The buyer may need to sell the merchandise to get the cash to pay the invoice. Normally, a buyer can save money by borrowing money to pay the invoice early and earn the cash discount.

**EXAMPLE I**

DVD Central purchased $100,000 worth of CDs and DVDs. The invoice was dated October 4 with terms of 2/10, net 30. Compute the due date, the (cash) discount date, the cash discount, and the total remittance required to get the cash discount. (Review Chapter 7 if necessary. Notice that the terms "discount date" and "due date" had different meanings in Chapter 7 than they have had here in Chapter 15.)

Due date = October 4 + 30 days = November 3
Discount date = October 4 + 10 days = October 14
If paid by October 14:
Cash discount = $100,000 × 0.02 = $2,000
Total remittance = $100,000 − $2,000 = $98,000

Regardless of whether it takes the discount, DVD Central needs to pay $100,000 by November 3. The company may want to save the $2,000, but perhaps it doesn't have the $98,000 now. Or maybe it has the money but wants to spend it on something else. In either situation, DVD Central might be able to borrow the money from October 14 until November 3. Before borrowing, DVD Central should compare the savings from the cash discount with the interest on a loan.

**EXAMPLE J**

DVD Central can borrow $98,000 for 20 days (October 14 to November 3) by paying 10% exact simple interest (365-day year). Compute the interest on the loan and the savings for DVD Central if it borrows to take the cash discount.

$$\text{Interest} = P \times R \times T = \$98{,}000 \times 0.10 \times \frac{20}{365} = \$536.99$$

Savings = $2,000 cash discount − $536.99 interest = $1,463.01

The reason for borrowing only between the (cash) discount date and the due date is to delay making payments as long as possible, whether to get cash discounts or to avoid penalties. The (cash) discount date is the latest possible date to pay and get the cash discount; the due date is the latest possible date to pay and avoid a penalty.

Although borrowing and taking the cash discount is almost always cheaper, the actual dollar amount may determine what DVD Central decides. If the original purchase were only $1,000, the savings would be only $14.63. Such an amount may not be worth the effort of getting a loan. However, for borrowing small amounts regularly, businesses often have "revolving lines of credit." These allow them to borrow and repay frequently, without always making a new loan application.

## CONCEPT CHECK 15.6

A retailer purchases merchandise under the terms 1.5/20, net 45. The invoice is for $45,000 and is dated July 22. For the cash discount, calculate the due date, the (cash) discount date, the amount of the cash discount, and the total remittance required. The retailer borrows enough money to pay the entire remittance. The interest rate is 12% exact simple interest, and the loan is for the length of time between the last date to take advantage of the cash discount and the due date. Calculate the amount of the interest and the savings gained by borrowing the remittance to take the discount.

| | | |
|---|---|---|
| Discount: | Due date: | July 22 + 45 days = September 5 |
| | Discount date: | July 22 + 20 days = August 11 |
| | Cash discount: | $45,000 × 0.015 = $675 |
| | Remittance: | $45,000 − $675 = $44,325 |
| Loan: | Interest days: | August 11 to September 5 = 25 days |

$$\text{Interest} = P \times R \times T = \$44{,}325 \times 0.12 \times \frac{25}{365} = \$364.32$$

Savings: $675 cash discount − $364.32 interest = $310.68

COMPLETE ASSIGNMENT 15.3.

## Chapter Terms for Review

- bank discount loan
- bearer
- discounted note
- discount amount
- discount date
- discount period
- discount rate
- due date
- face value
- interest-bearing note
- interest dollars
- maker
- maturity date
- maturity value
- negotiable promissory note
- non-interest-bearing promissory note
- proceeds
- promissory note

# THE BOTTOM LINE

*Summary of chapter learning objectives:*

| Learning Objective | Example |
|---|---|
| **15.1** Compute the number of interest days of a promissory note. | 1. Find the number of days between December 10 and February 27. |
| **15.2** Determine the due date of a promissory note. | 2. Find the due date of a 90-day note written on May 20. |
| **15.3** Compute the maturity value of a promissory note. | 3. Find the maturity value of a 90-day promissory note with a face value of $6,500 and an exact interest rate of 8%. |
| **15.4** Discount a promissory note. | 4a. A 30-day note, bearing an interest rate of 9%, is dated November 6 and has a face value of $8,000. On November 15, the note is discounted at 12%. Use a 365-day year to find the interest amount, the discount amount, and the proceeds.<br>4b. A 60-day, non-interest-bearing note has a face value of $2,500 and is dated May 13. On June 3, the note is discounted at 11%. Use a 365-day year to find the discount amount and the proceeds. |
| **15.5** Compute the proceeds and actual interest rate on a bank discount loan. | 5. A 60-day bank loan with a face value of $3,900 is made on a discount basis at a discount rate of 12%. Use the 360-day year to compute the discount amount and the proceeds. Then find the actual interest rate, based on the proceeds rather than on the face value. |
| **15.6** Compute the savings from borrowing money to take a cash discount. | 6. A $20,000 invoice dated March 15 has terms of 2/5, net 25. Find the due date, (cash) discount date, cash discount, and required remittance. Next, calculate the interest amount of borrowing the remittance at 9% exact interest for the time between the last date to take advantage of the cash discount and the due date. Finally, calculate the savings. |

Answers: 1. 79 days 2. August 18 3. $6,628.22 4a. Interest, $59.18; discount, $55.64; proceeds, $8,003.54; 4b. Discount, $29.38; proceeds, $2,470.62 5. Discount, $78; proceeds, $3,822; interest rate, 12.24% 6. Due date, April 9; discount date, March 20; cash discount, $400; remittance, $19,600; interest, $96.66; savings, $303.34

SELF-CHECK

# Review Problems for Chapter 15

1 A 75-day promissory note for $3,400 is dated November 24, 2010. Find (a) the due date and (b) the maturity value, if the rate is 9% ordinary simple interest.

2 A promissory note for $4,400 is dated December 11, 2009, and has a due date of May 11, 2010. Find (a) the number of interest days and (b) the maturity value, if the rate is 7.2% ordinary simple interest.

3 A 135-day promissory note for $15,000 is dated August 24, 2011. Find (a) the due date and (b) the maturity value, if the rate is 4.6% exact simple interest.

4 A promissory note for $2,980 is dated May 21, 2012, and has a due date of September 21, 2012. Find (a) the number of interest days and (b) the maturity value, if the rate is 6.5% exact simple interest.

5 Vernon Lee holds a 120-day, interest-bearing note for $2,960 that is dated May 15 and has a rate of 8% exact simple interest. On July 15, Vernon sells it at a discount rate of 15%. Using a 365-day year, calculate (a) the interest amount, (b) the maturity value, (c) the maturity date, (d) the days of discount, (e) the discount amount, and (f) the proceeds.

6 Contractor Allen Kimmel is holding a 90-day, non-interest-bearing note for $3,100 dated November 10. On December 10, Mr. Kimmel sells the note to Thrift's Financing, Inc., at a discount rate of 12%. Using a 365-day year, calculate (a) the maturity value, (b) the maturity date, (c) the days of discount, (d) the discount amount, and (e) the proceeds.

7 Eastside Bank & Trust Co. made a 120-day loan for $4,500 on a discount basis, using a discount rate of 9%. Using a 360-day year, calculate (a) the discount amount, (b) the proceeds, and (c) the actual interest rate (to two decimal places).

8 Jankowski Corporation just received an invoice for $1,600 that has cash discount terms of 2/10, net 30. Jankowski borrows enough money from Eastside Bank & Trust Co. at 10% exact simple interest (365-day year) to take advantage of the cash discount. It borrows the money only for the time period between the due date and the last day to take advantage of the discount. Calculate (a) the amount of the cash discount, (b) the number of interest days, (c) the amount of interest on the loan, and (d) the amount of its savings.

**Answers to the Self-Check can be found in Appendix B at the back of the text.**

# Assignment 15.1: Dates, Times, and Maturity Value

Name ______________________

Date ______________ Score ______________

Learning Objectives 1 2 3

**A** **(36 points) Problems 1–6: Find the number of interest days. Problems 7–12: Find the due date. Be sure to check for leap years. (3 points for each correct answer)**

| | Date of Note | Due Date | Days of Interest |
|---|---|---|---|
| 1. | April 6, 2010 | October 11, 2010 | ________ |
| 2. | June 29, 2012 | October 5, 2012 | ________ |
| 3. | February 8, 2011 | June 10, 2011 | ________ |
| 4. | June 15, 2009 | September 14, 2009 | ________ |
| 5. | November 8, 2010 | March 9, 2011 | ________ |
| 6. | July 17, 2012 | October 5, 2012 | ________ |

| | Date of Note | Days of Interest | Due Date |
|---|---|---|---|
| 7. | November 1, 2011 | 90 days | ________ |
| 8. | August 18, 2010 | 180 days | ________ |
| 9. | September 21, 2012 | 75 days | ________ |
| 10. | April 29, 2010 | 60 days | ________ |
| 11. | November 9, 2009 | 120 days | ________ |
| 12. | October 31, 2011 | 4 months | ________ |

________
Score for A (36)

**B** **(64 points) For each of the following promissory notes, find the missing entry for days of interest or maturity date (due date). Then compute the amount of interest due at maturity and the maturity value. For problems 13–16, use a 360-day year; for problems 17–20, use a 365-day year. (Points indicated at the top of each column)**

| | Face Value | Date of Note | Days of Interest (3 pts) | Maturity Date (3 pts) | Rate | Interest Amount (3 pts) | Maturity Value (2 pts) |
|---|---|---|---|---|---|---|---|
| **13.** | $26,000 | Oct. 12, 2010 | 90 | ______ | 6.2% | ______ | ______ |
| **14.** | $12,500 | Mar. 29, 2010 | ______ | July 8, 2010 | 8.5% | ______ | ______ |
| **15.** | $35,750 | July 15, 2009 | 105 | ______ | 5.6% | ______ | ______ |
| **16.** | $950 | Jan. 25, 2011 | ______ | April 1, 2011 | 7.2% | ______ | ______ |
| **17.** | $41,800 | Nov. 24, 2009 | ______ | Mar. 29, 2010 | 5.1% | ______ | ______ |
| **18.** | $18,420 | May 6, 2011 | ______ | Sept. 19, 2011 | 6.75% | ______ | ______ |
| **19.** | $52,000 | Feb. 11, 2009 | 180 | ______ | 8.25% | ______ | ______ |
| **20.** | $31,860 | June 4, 2012 | 105 | ______ | 7.5% | ______ | ______ |

______

Score for B (64)

# Assignment 15.2: Discounting Promissory Notes

Name ______________________________

Date ______________ Score ______________

Learning Objective 4

**A (50 points) Compute the missing information to discount the following interest-bearing and non-interest-bearing promissory notes. Use a 360-day year for all interest and discount calculations. (Points for each correct answer are shown in parentheses)**

**1.** Sharon Wilder had been holding a 75-day note for $2,500. The note had a 6% interest rate and had been written on March 1. To pay income taxes, Sharon sold the note on April 13 to a loan company. The loan company discounted the note at 11%.

Interest amount (3 pts) __________
Maturity value (2 pts) __________
Maturity date (2 pts) __________
Days of discount (2 pts) __________
Discount amount (3 pts) __________
Proceeds (2 pts) __________

**2.** On September 10, Carol Swift Financial Services bought a $12,500 promissory note. The note had been written on July 10, was for 150 days, and had an interest rate of 9%. Carol's company discounted the note at 12%.

Interest amount (3 pts) __________
Maturity value (2 pts) __________
Maturity date (2 pts) __________
Days of discount (2 pts) __________
Discount amount (3 pts) __________
Proceeds (2 pts) __________

**3.** Jim Walter was holding a 105-day, non-interest-bearing note for $4,500. The note was dated October 9. To raise Christmas cash, Jim sold the note to a local finance company on December 14. The company discounted the note at 10%.

Interest amount (1 pt) __________
Maturity value (1 pt) __________
Maturity date (2 pts) __________
Days of discount (2 pts) __________
Discount amount (3 pts) __________
Proceeds (2 pts) __________

**4.** Barbara Finell owned a finance company. On July 19 she purchased a 180-day, non-interest-bearing promissory note. The note had been written on May 23 for $7,100. Because of the high financial risk involved, Barbara discounted the note at 14%.

Interest amount (1 pt) __________
Maturity value (1 pt) __________
Maturity date (2 pts) __________
Days of discount (2 pts) __________
Discount amount (3 pts) __________
Proceeds (2 pts) __________

______________
Score for A (50)

**B** **(50 points) Compute the missing information to discount the following interest-bearing and non-interest-bearing promissory notes. Use a 365-day year for all interest and discount calculations. (Points for each correct answer are shown in parentheses)**

**5.** As payment for services, Pat Chard held a 90-day, 8% note for $3,600 that was dated April 20. On June 5, Pat took the note to a financial services company, which bought the note at a 13% discount rate.

Interest amount (3 pts)__________
Maturity value (2 pts)__________
Maturity date (2 pts)__________
Days of discount (2 pts)__________
Discount amount (3 pts)__________
Proceeds (2 pts)__________

**6.** Joslin Builders received a 135-day, 7% note dated October 10. The face value was $12,450, which was for remodeling a client's garage. On December 19, Joslin sold the note to McGraw Lending Corp., which discounted the note at 12%.

Interest amount (3 pts) __________
Maturity value (2 pts) __________
Maturity date (2 pts) __________
Days of discount (2 pts) __________
Discount amount (3 pts) __________
Proceeds (2 pts) __________

**7.** Teri Chung loaned $4,000 to a client who gave Teri a non-interest-bearing note dated August 1. The note was for 75 days. On August 31, Teri sold the note to her finance company, which discounted it at 10%.

Interest amount (1 pt) __________
Maturity value (1 pt) __________
Maturity date (2 pts) __________
Days of discount (2 pts) __________
Discount amount (3 pts) __________
Proceeds (2 pts) __________

**8.** Patti Gentry was holding a 60-day, non-interest-bearing note for $1,700. The note was dated June 22. On July 16, Patti sold the note to a lender who discounted the note at 15%.

Interest amount (1 pt) __________
Maturity value (1 pt) __________
Maturity date (2 pts) __________
Days of discount (2 pts) __________
Discount amount (3 pts) __________
Proceeds (2 pts) __________

__________
Score for B (50)

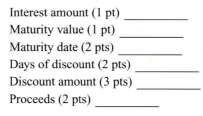

# Assignment 15.3: Bank Discounting and Cash Discounts

Name ____________________

Date ____________ Score ____________

Learning Objectives 5 6

**A** **(36 points) The Citizens' Bank of New England made six new loans on a discount basis. Compute the discount amount and the proceeds. Then compute the actual interest rate based on the proceeds rather than the face value. Use a 360-day year for problems 1–3 and use a 365-day year for problems 4–6. Round the actual interest rates to the nearest 1/100 of a percent. (2 points for each correct answer)**

| | Face Value | Discount Rate | Time | Discount Amount | Proceeds | Actual Interest Rate |
|---|---|---|---|---|---|---|
| **1.** | $7,500 | 10% | 120 days | ________ | ________ | ________ |
| **2.** | $4,450 | 6% | 90 days | ________ | ________ | ________ |
| **3.** | $16,500 | 12% | 150 days | ________ | ________ | ________ |
| **4.** | $22,500 | 6.5% | 60 days | ________ | ________ | ________ |
| **5.** | $980 | 7.5% | 135 days | ________ | ________ | ________ |
| **6.** | $18,250 | 9.6% | 105 days | ________ | ________ | ________ |

____________________

Score for A (36)

**B** **(64 points) William Bros. Home Builders made several purchases from vendors who offered various terms of payment. How much can William Bros. save on each invoice if it borrows the money to pay the invoice early and receive the cash discount? The loan interest rates are all exact simple interest (365-day year). Assume that the number of interest days is the time between the due date and the last day to take advantage of the cash discount. (2 points for each correct answer)**

| | Invoice | Terms | Cash Discount | Interest Rate on Loan | Days of Interest | Interest Amount | Savings |
|---|---|---|---|---|---|---|---|
| **7.** | $5,000 | 2/10, n/30 | ______ | 10% | ______ | ______ | ______ |
| **8.** | $8,500 | 1.5/15, n/30 | ______ | 6.25% | ______ | ______ | ______ |
| **9.** | $32,575 | 1.25/7, n/40 | ______ | 8.75% | ______ | ______ | ______ |
| **10.** | $18,600 | 1/15, n/45 | ______ | 9% | ______ | ______ | ______ |
| **11.** | $9,200 | 1/30, n/60 | ______ | 9.6% | ______ | ______ | ______ |
| **12.** | $12,500 | 2/10, n/45 | ______ | 8% | ______ | ______ | ______ |
| **13.** | $26,000 | 2.5/5, n/25 | ______ | 8.5% | ______ | ______ | ______ |
| **14.** | $88,960 | 2.25/10, n/30 | ______ | 10.5% | ______ | ______ | ______ |

______

Score for B (64)

# 16

# Compound Interest

### Learning Objectives

By studying this chapter and completing all assignments, you will be able to:

**Learning Objective 1** Compute future values from tables and formulas.

**Learning Objective 2** Compute present values from future value tables.

**Learning Objective 3** Compute using present value tables and formulas.

Most Americans will buy at least one item that is financed over 1 or more years. The product will probably be expensive, such as a car or a home. Likely, the interest on the loan will not be the simple interest you studied in Chapter 13; it will be *compound* interest. Interest on car loans or home loans is normally compounded monthly. Most banks offer savings accounts and certificates of deposit (CDs) for which interest is compounded daily. Credit unions may pay interest that is compounded quarterly (four times a year). To evaluate the value of corporate bonds, an investor uses calculations on interest that is compounded semiannually (twice a year).

To understand even the most fundamental financial decisions in today's world, you need to understand the basic concepts of compound interest, future values, and present values.

## Compute Future Values from Tables and Formulas

Learning Objective 1

Compute future values from tables and formulas.

Simple interest is computed with the formula $I = P \times R \times T$, which you learned in Chapter 13. For example, the simple interest on \$2,000 invested at 6% for 2 years is $I = P \times R \times T = \$2{,}000 \times 0.06 \times 2 = \$240$. The amount, or future value, of the investment is $A = P + I = \$2{,}000 + \$240 = \$2{,}240$.

**Compound interest** means that the computations of the simple interest formula are performed every period during the term of the investment. The money from the previous interest computation is added to the principal before the next interest computation is performed. If an investment is *compounded annually for 2 years,* the simple interest is computed once at the end of each year. The simple interest earned in year 1 is added to the principal for the beginning of year 2. The total value of an investment is the principal plus all of the compound interest. The total is called the **future value** or the **compound amount.** In finance, the original principal is usually called the present value.

**EXAMPLE A**

Don Robertson invests \$2,000 for 2 years in an account that pays 6% compounded annually. Compute the total compound interest and future value (compound amount).

| | |
|---|---|
| \$2,000.00 | Original principal |
| × 0.06 | Interest rate |
| \$120.0000 | First-year interest |
| +2,000.00 | First-year principal |
| \$2,120.00 | Second-year principal |
| × 0.06 | Interest rate |
| \$127.2000 | Second-year interest |
| +2,120.00 | Second-year principal |
| \$2,247.20 | Final compound amount (future value) |
| −2,000.00 | Original principal |
| \$247.20 | Total compound interest |

On the \$2,000 investment in example A, the total amount of compound interest paid is \$247.20, compared to \$240 simple interest over the same 2 years.

The computations in example A are time-consuming and become more tedious with each compounding. Twice as many computations would be required for a 4-year investment. In actual practice, compound interest is computed using calculators, computers, or compound interest tables.

Table 16-1, on pages 338 and 339, is part of a future value table. The numbers in the table are called **future value factors** or **compound amount factors.** The columns (vertical) represent interest rates, and the rows (horizontal) represent the number of times that interest is compounded. The following steps explain how to use Table 16-1 to find future values (compound amounts) and compound interest.

**STEPS to Use the Future Value Table**

1. Locate the factor in the proper row and column of Table 16-1.
2. Multiply the principal (present value) by the factor. The product is the future value.
3. Subtract the principal (present value) from the future value. The difference is the total amount of compound interest.

**EXAMPLE B**

Use Table 16-1 to compute the future value and total amount of compound interest of a 2-year, $2,000 investment at 6% compounded annually.

STEP 1 The interest rate is 6%. Interest is compounded twice—once each year for 2 years. Locate the intersection of the 6.00% column and row 2. The future value factor is 1.12360.

STEP 2 Future value = $2,000 × 1.12360 = $2,247.20

STEP 3 Compound interest = $2,247.20 − $2,000 = $247.20

These results are identical to the results in example A.

**EXAMPLE C**

Mary Simmons loans $5,000 to her son for 6 years at 4% compounded annually. Compute the future value and total compound interest. Use Table 16-1.

STEP 1 The interest rate is 4%. Interest is computed six times, once each year for 6 years. The future value factor in the 4.00% column and row 6 is 1.26532.

STEP 2 Future value = $5,000 × 1.26532 = $6,326.60

STEP 3 Compound interest = $6,326.60 − $5,000 = $1,326.60

## FUTURE VALUE FORMULA

If you prefer, Step 2 may be summarized as a formula in words or symbols:

Future value = Principal (Present value) × Future value factor (from Table 16-1)
or, $FV = PV \times FVF$

## VARIOUS COMPOUNDING PERIODS

In examples A, B, and C, the compounding was annual (i.e., done once each year). Compounding is also done daily (every day), monthly (every month), quarterly (every quarter), or semiannually (every half-year). The word **period** is the unit of time of the compounding. The period will be a day, a month, a quarter, a half-year, or a year. You can use Table 16-1 with some interest rates for all these compounding periods except 1 day. Daily compounding requires the use of a calculator with an exponent key.

To do monthly, quarterly, or semiannual compounding using Table 16-1, follow the same steps you used to do annual compounding. The only differences are that the column will be the **periodic interest rate** ($i$) and that the row will be the **number of compounding periods** ($n$). Sometimes the periodic rate and the number of periods will be stated clearly. Usually, however, the interest rate will be given as an annual rate ($r$) and the time will be stated in years ($t$). When that happens, find the row and column as described in the steps below. The letter $m$ is the number of compounding periods in one year.

### STEPS to Determine the Periodic Rate and the Number of Compounding Periods

**i.** Determine ***m***, the compounding periods in one year: $\boldsymbol{m = 1, 2, 4, 12, 365}$. ($m = 1$ for annual compounding; $m = 2$ for semiannual; $m = 4$ for quarterly; $m = 12$ for monthly; $m = 365$ for daily)

**ii.** Determine ***i***, the periodic interest rate: $i = \frac{r}{m}$ (or, $\boldsymbol{i = r \div m}$). (Divide the stated annual rate, $r$, by $m$.) ***i*** is the correct column.

**iii.** Determine ***n***, the total number of compounding periods: $\boldsymbol{n = m \times t}$. (Multiply the periods per year, $m$, by the number of years, $t$.) ***n*** is the correct row.

### EXAMPLE D

Find the periodic interest rate and the number of compounding periods in 2 years when 12% is compounded (a) semiannually ($m = 2$ times per year), (b) quarterly ($m = 4$ times per year), and (c) monthly ($m = 12$ times per year). Then find the future value factors in Table 16-1.

Each term is for 2 years; each rate is 12%, but compounded differently:

| STEP i<br>**Periods per Year** | STEP ii<br>**Periodic Interest Rate** | STEP iii<br>**Total Compounding Periods** |
|---|---|---|
| a. $m = 2$ | $i = 12\% \div 2 = 6\%$ | $n = 2 \times 2$ years $= 4$ periods |
| b. $m = 4$ | $i = 12\% \div 4 = 3\%$ | $n = 4 \times 2$ years $= 8$ periods |
| c. $m = 12$ | $i = 12\% \div 12 = 1\%$ | $n = 12 \times 2$ years $= 24$ periods |

Future value factors from Table 16-1 are as follows:

| | | |
|---|---|---|
| a. Semiannually | 6.00% column and row 4 | Factor = 1.26248 |
| b. Quarterly | 3.00% column and row 8 | Factor = 1.26677 |
| c. Monthly | 1.00% column and row 24 | Factor = 1.26973 |

To compute the future value and the compound interest, first determine the periodic rate and the number of compounding periods using Steps i, ii, and iii. Then do Steps 1, 2, and 3, as illustrated in examples B and C previously.

## Calculators and Exponents

*Note:* This is an optional section that describes how to use a calculator to compute future value factors. It requires some knowledge of exponents and exponential notation, and it requires a calculator that has an exponent key. Some persons will prefer to use Table 16-1, but others may prefer to use a calculator or to use a calculator just to check their work.

The expression $2^3$ means $2 \times 2 \times 2 = 8$. The 3 is called an **exponent,** or we can say that "2 is raised to the 3rd **power.**" Many calculators have a key labeled [$y^x$] that is used for exponents. To compute $2^3$, enter the following keystrokes: 2 [$y^x$] 3 [=]. The answer on the calculator display is 8.

The future value factors in Table 16-1 can be calculated directly by anyone who has a calculator that will compute exponents. For the periodic interest rate of $i$ (decimal) and for the number of compounding periods equal to $n$, the future value factor is $FVF = (1 + i)^n$. *Note: The interest rate must be entered as a decimal, not as a percent.*

**EXAMPLE E**

Use a calculator with an exponent key to compute the future value factor for each of the following:

a. 12% compounded semiannually for 2 years: $i = 0.12 \div 2 = 0.06$; $n = 2 \times 2 =$ 4 periods

$FVF = (1 + i)^n = (1 + 0.06)^4 = 1.26247696$

The calculator keystrokes might be 1.06 [$y^x$] 4 [=]

The exact calculator keystrokes will depend upon your own calculator. Refer to your calculator's manual. It is usually faster to mentally add the 1 and 0.06 because the sum is just 1.06, but many calculators also have keys for "parentheses."

b. 12% compounded quarterly for 2 years: $i = 0.12 \div 4 = 0.03$; $n = 2 \times 4 = 8$ periods

$FVF = (1 + i)^n = (1 + 0.03)^8 = 1.26677008$ 1.03 [$y^x$] 8 [=]

c. 12% compounded monthly for 2 years: $i = 0.12 \div 12 = 0.01$; $n = 2 \times 12 = 24$ periods

$FVF = (1 + i)^n = (1 + 0.01)^{24} = 1.26973465$ 1.01 [$y^x$] 24 [=]

In the example, we wrote each future value factor with eight decimal places. The factors in Table 16-1 have only five decimal places. Throughout this chapter, factors that have five decimal places come from the tables, and factors with eight decimal places come from the formula using a calculator. If you use a calculator and more than five decimal places, usually you will get a slightly different answer than if you use only five decimal places. The more decimal places you use, the more accurate the answers will be. In this book, all of the solutions assume the use of the tables and only five decimal places.

Throughout the remainder of this chapter, the calculator solutions will be shown in blue in the margins.

**EXAMPLE F**

Barbara Scoble and her husband deposit $20,000 in her credit union, which pays interest of 8% compounded quarterly. Find the future value and the total compound interest after 2 years. (Use Table 16-1, or a calculator.)

$m = 4$

$i = \dfrac{0.08}{4} = 0.02$

$n = 4 \times 2 = 8$

$FVF = (1 + i)^n = (1.02)^8$

$= 1.17165938$

$FV = PV \times FVF$

$= \$20{,}000 \times 1.17165938$

$= \$23{,}433.1876$

or $23,433.19

**STEP i** There are $m = 4$ compounding periods in 1 year.

**STEP ii** Periodic interest rate = 8% ÷ 4 = 2% per period

**STEP iii** Number of periods = 4 × 2 years = 8 periods

**STEP 1** Using Table 16-1, the 2.00% column and row 8:
Future value factor ($FVF$) = 1.17166

**STEP 2** Future value = Present value × Future value factor
= $20,000.00 × 1.17166 = $23,433.20

**STEP 3** Total compound interest = $23,433.20 − $20,000.00 = $3,433.20

Thus, using Table 16-1 to find the *FVF*, $20,000 invested at 8% compounded quarterly will be worth $23,433.20 in 2 years. If you use a calculator to find the *FVF*, the future value is $23,433.19. You should use whichever method seems more clear to you.

## Effective Rates

In Chapter 14, we said that the term "effective rate" is used in more than one context. In Chapter 14, "effective rate" was related to the interest rate paid on the "average unpaid balance" in an installment purchase. Here in Chapter 16, "effective rate" refers to the true annual yield an investor earns when her/his money is compounded more than once per year.

In example F, Barbara Scoble and her husband earned 8% compounded quarterly. Their $20,000 deposit was worth $23,433.20 after 2 years. 8% is an *annual* rate, not a *quarterly* rate. But 8% was not really used in the compounding; the rate that was actually compounded was 2% per quarter. Thus, 8% is not the true annual rate, or the effective rate. The 8% in example F is called a "nominal" rate because the full *name* of the rate is "8% compounded quarterly."

The effective rate is the rate that the Scobles would earn if their money had been compounded annually instead of quarterly. You can either use Table 16-1 or use a calculator to compute the effective rate.

To use Table 16-1, find the future value factor of 2% for 4 quarters (1 year). It is 1.08243. Subtract 1 to get 0.08243, or 8.243%. The effective rate is 8.243% per year. What this means is that the Scobles are actually earning 8.243% per year on an investment that has been quoted as earning "8% compounded quarterly."

The formula for the effective rate is $R = (1 + \frac{0.08}{4})^4 - 1$. In example F, $R = (1 + \frac{0.08}{4})^4 - 1 = (1 + 0.02)^4 - 1 = 1.08243216 - 1 = 0.08243216$, or 8.243216%. Rounded to four decimal places, the effective rate is $R = 8.2432\%$.

## DAILY COMPOUNDING

Most banks today offer daily compounding on several different savings accounts and certificates of deposit. Tables to do daily compounding would be cumbersome and impractical. However, using a calculator with an exponent key, the computation is just as simple as other compounding computations. Assume that there are 365 days in a year.

**EXAMPLE G**

Use a calculator to find the future value of $20,000 invested for 2 years at 8% compounded daily. First find the periodic interest rate ($i$) as a decimal, and find the number of days ($n$) in two years. Then find the future value factor to eight decimal places.

STEP i — Compounding periods in one year: $m = 365$

STEP ii — Periodic interest rate: $i = r \div m = 0.08 \div 365 = 0.00021918$

STEP iii — Number of compounding periods: $n = m \times t = 365 \times 2 = 730$

STEP 1 — $FVF = (1 + i)^n = (1 + 0.00021918)^{730} = 1.17349194$

STEP 2 — Future value $= \$20{,}000 \times 1.17349194 = \$23{,}469.84$

Compare the two future values from examples F and G. The future value using quarterly compounding is $23,433.19 (using a calculator to find the FVF). With daily compounding, the future value is $23,469.84, a difference of $36.65.

## CONCEPT CHECK 16.1

a. If $2,600 is invested for 5 years at 6% compounded semiannually, compute the future value of the investment. (Use Table 16-1 or a calculator.)

*Semiannually* means $m = 2$ periods per year.
Periodic rate = 6% ÷ 2 = 3% per half-year
Number of periods = 2 × 5 years = 10 periods
The FVF from row 10 of the 3.00% column in Table 16-1 is 1.34392.

$FV = PV \times FVF = \$2{,}600 \times 1.34392 = \$3{,}494.192$, or $3,494.19

b. If $3,200 is invested for 1 year at 9% compounded monthly, what is the compound interest on the investment?

*Monthly* means $m = 12$ periods per year.
Periodic rate = 9% ÷ 12 = 0.75% per month
Number of periods = 12 × 1 year = 12 periods
The FVF from row 12 of the 0.75% column in Table 16-1 is 1.09381.

$FV = PV \times FVF = \$3{,}200 \times 1.09381 = \$3{,}500.192$, or $3,500.19
Compound interest = Future value − Present value (Principal)
= $3,500.19 − $3,200 = $300.19

COMPLETE ASSIGNMENT 16.1.

$m = 2$

$i = \dfrac{0.06}{2} = 0.03$

$n = 2 \times 5 = 10$

$FVF = (1 + 0.03)^{10} = 1.34391638$

$FV = \$2{,}600 \times 1.34391638 = \$3{,}494.18$

$m = 12$

$i = \dfrac{0.09}{12} = 0.0075$

$n = 12 \times 1 = 12$

$FVF = (1 + 0.0075)^{12} = 1.09380690$

$FV = \$3{,}200 \times 1.09380690 = \$3{,}500.18$

# Compute Present Values from Future Value Tables

**Learning Objective 2**

Compute present values from future value tables.

The basic investment problem is to compute what a given sum of money invested today will be worth in the future. Example F was a future value problem. There we found that $20,000 original principal (or present value) invested today at 8% compounded quarterly will have a future value of $23,433.20 in 2 years.

Some savers and investors want to compute future values; others want to compute present values. Consider the following present value problem.

**EXAMPLE H**

Polly Layer has a 12-year-old son and a 10-year-old daughter. Polly inherits $100,000. Friends tell Polly that she should plan to have $60,000 cash available for her son's education when he turns 18. She should also have $70,000 cash available for her daughter's education when she turns 18. Polly wants to put enough money in an investment for each child so that in 6 and 8 years the two accounts will be worth $60,000 and $70,000, respectively. If Polly can earn interest at 5% compounded annually, how much money should she put into each investment today?

Polly knows the future value of the investments—$60,000 and $70,000. What she wants to compute is the **present value**—the amounts that she needs to invest today for each child. We will solve this problem later, in example L.

Businesses make investments in the present to provide future revenues. Sometimes a business will estimate its future revenues and costs (future values). Then the business might use these numbers to compute the required amounts to invest at the beginning (present values).

As given earlier, the formula for future value is

Future value = Present value × Future value factor (from Table 16-1 or a calculator)

$FV = PV \times (1 + i)^n$

Using symbols, $FV = PV \times FVF$

Rewriting the formula to solve for present value gives

Present value = Future value ÷ Future value factor (from Table 16-1 or a calculator)

$$PV = \frac{FV}{(1 + i)^n}$$

Using symbols, $PV = FV \div FVF$, or $PV = \dfrac{FV}{FVF}$

**EXAMPLE I**

How much money must be invested today to end up with $6,326.60 in 3 years? The interest rate is 8% compounded semiannually. (Use Table 16-1 or a calculator.)

$m = 2$

$i = \dfrac{0.08}{2} = 0.04$

$n = 2 \times 3 = 6$

$FVF = (1 + 0.04)^6$
$= 1.26531902$

The $6,326.60 is the future value for which we want to find the present value. Interest is computed six times—twice each year for 3 years. The future value factor in Table 16-1 in the 4.00% column and row 6 is 1.26532. Substitute these values into the formula to solve for present value.

Present value = Future value ÷ Future value factor (from Table 16-1)
= $6,326.60 ÷ 1.26532 = $5,000

Compare this result to that of example C, in which $5,000 was invested for 6 years at 4% compounded annually. The future value was $6,326.60.

**EXAMPLE J**

Edison Motors estimates that in 2 years it will cost $20,000 to repair a diagnostic machine. How much must Edison invest today to have $20,000 in 2 years, if the interest rate is 6% compounded monthly? How much interest will Edison Motors earn on its investment?

$20,000 is the given future value and Edison wants to know the present value.

**STEP i** There are 12 compounding periods in 1 year (monthly).

**STEP ii** Periodic rate = 6% ÷ 12 = 0.5%

**STEP iii** Number of compounding periods = 12 × 2 years = 24
The future value factor in the 0.5% column and row 24 of Table 16-1 is 1.12716.

Substitute these values into the formula to solve for present value:

Present value = Future value ÷ Future value factor (from Table 16-1)
= $FV \div FVF$ = $20,000 ÷ 1.12716 = $17,743.71 to the nearest cent

If Edison Motors invests $17,743.71 today at 6% compounded monthly, it will have $20,000 at the end of 2 years.

The $20,000 is the sum of the amount invested plus the total compound interest earned. To find the interest, subtract the amount invested from $20,000.

Interest = Future value − Present value = $20,000 − $17,743.71 = $2,256.29

$m = 12$

$i = \frac{0.06}{12} = 0.005$

$n = 12 \times 2 = 24$

$FVF = (1 + 0.005)^{24} = 1.12715978$

$PV = \frac{FV}{FVF} = \frac{\$20{,}000}{1.12715978} = \$17{,}743.71$

## CONCEPT CHECK 16.2

What present value (principal) invested for 4 years at 6% compounded quarterly will result in a total future value of $8,000? (Use Table 16-1 or a calculator.)

*Quarterly* means 4 periods per year.
Periodic rate = 6% ÷ 4 = 1.5% per quarter
Number of periods = 4 years × 4 = 16 periods
The future value factor from row 16 of the 1.50% column in Table 16-1 is 1.26899.

Present value = Future value ÷ Future value factor
= $8,000 ÷ 1.26899 = $6,304.226, or $6,304.23

$m = 2$

$i = \frac{0.06}{4} = 0.015$

$n = 4 \times 4 = 16$

$FVF = (1 + 0.015)^{16} = 1.26898555$

$PV = \frac{\$8{,}000}{1.26898555} = \$6{,}304.25$

# Compute Using Present Value Tables and Formulas

**Learning Objective 3**

Compute using present value tables and formulas.

You may prefer to solve for present values by using **present value factors (PVF)** rather than future value factors, as in the preceding formula. Table 16-2, on pages 340 and 341, is a table of present value factors. Use exactly the same procedure (Steps i, ii, and iii) to find present value factors as you used to find future value factors.

## PRESENT VALUE FORMULA

With a calculator,

$$PVF = \frac{1}{FVF} = \frac{1}{(1+i)^n}$$

If you use the present value factors (Table 16-2 or a calculator), you use a different formula, the present value formula,

> Present value = Future value × Present value factor (from Table 16-2 or a calculator)
> or, $PV = FV \times PVF$

### EXAMPLE K

$m = 12$

$i = \frac{0.06}{12} = 0.005$

$n = 12 \times 2 = 24$

$PVF = \frac{1}{(1+0.005)^{24}} = 0.88718567$

$PV = FV \times PVF = \$20{,}000 \times 0.88718567 = \$17{,}743.71$

Rework example J using Table 16-2 and the present value formula. How much must Edison Motors invest today to have $20,000 in 2 years if the interest rate is 6% compounded monthly?

$20,000 is the future value, for which Edison wants to know the present value.

**STEP i** There are 12 compounding periods in 1 year (monthly).

**STEP ii** Periodic rate = 6% ÷ 12 = 0.5%

**STEP iii** Number of compounding periods = 12 × 2 years = 24
The present value factor in the 0.5% column and row 24 of Table 16-2 is 0.88719.

Substitute these values into the present value formula.

Present value = Future value × Present value factor (from Table 16-2)
$= FV \times PVF = \$20{,}000 \times 0.88719 = \$17{,}743.80$

The answer to example J was $17,743.71. The discrepancy between that result and $17,743.80 in example K is due to rounding. If the two tables had more decimal places instead of just five, this discrepancy would disappear. In fact, using the calculator PVF from the margin, we get $PV = \$20{,}000 \times 0.88718567 = \$17{,}743.7134$, which is identical to the nearest cent.

### EXAMPLE L

Son

$m = 1$

$i = \frac{0.05}{1} = 0.05$

$n = 1 \times 6 = 6$

$PVF = \frac{1}{(1+0.05)^{6}} = 0.74621540$

$PV = \$60{,}000 \times 0.74621540 = \$44{,}772.92$

Daughter

$m = 1$

$i = \frac{0.05}{1} = 0.05$

$n = 1 \times 8 = 8$

$PVF = \frac{1}{(1+0.05)^{8}} = 0.67683936$

$PV = \$70{,}000 \times 0.67683936 = \$47{,}378.76$

Solve the present value problem from example H. If Polly Layer can earn 5% compounded annually, how much should she deposit today in investments for her son and daughter so that the investments will be worth $60,000 and $70,000 in 6 and 8 years, respectively?

| | | Son | Daughter |
|---|---|---|---|
| | Future value: | $60,000 | $70,000 |
| | Term: | 6 years | 8 years |
| | Rate: | 5% compounded annually | 5% compounded annually |
| STEP i | Periods per year: | 1 (annual) | 1 (annual) |
| STEP ii | Periodic rate: | 5% ÷ 1 = 5% | 5% ÷ 1 = 5% |
| STEP iii | Compounding periods: | 1 × 6 years = 6 | 1 × 8 years = 8 |
| | PV factor (Table 16-2): | 0.74622 | 0.67684 |
| | Present value: | $60,000 × 0.74622 = $44,773.20 | $70,000 × 0.67684 = $47,378.80 |

The reason for two formulas and two tables is historical, predating handheld calculators. Without a calculator, a multiplication problem is typically easier than a long division problem with the same two large numbers.

Theoretically, we need only one formula and one table. The second present value formula and the table of present value factors permit us to solve present value problems by using multiplication instead of division. Look at example J. To solve the problem requires that we divide $20,000 by 1.12716, which is extremely time-consuming to do without a calculator. (The answer is $17,743.71.) Using Table 16-2, we can solve the same problem by multiplying $20,000 by 0.88719, a relatively easy calculation even without a calculator. (The answer is $17,743.80; the difference is due to rounding in the creation of the table.)

## NOTES ABOUT THE FUTURE VALUE AND PRESENT VALUE TABLES

The numbers in the future value table (Table 16-1) are actually just the future value of $1.00 at a specific interest rate and for a specific period of time. For example, suppose that you invest $1.00 for 2 years at 6% compounded annually. This is the same problem as example A, except that the principal is only $1.00 instead of $2,000.00

The calculations shown at the right have not been rounded off. The answer, which is $1.1236, is the future value of the $1.00 investment. Now, find row 2 and the 6.00% column of Table 16-1. The future value factor is 1.12360—exactly the same as $1.1236, without the dollar sign and with five decimal places.

| | |
|---:|---|
| $1.00 | Original principal |
| × 0.06 | Interest rate |
| $0.0600 | First-year interest |
| + 1.00 | First-year principal |
| $1.0600 | Second-year principal |
| × 0.06 | Interest rate |
| $0.0636 | Second-year interest |
| + 1.06 | Second-year principal |
| $1.1236 | Final compound amount |

Each number in the present value table (Table 16-2) can be calculated directly from the corresponding number in the future value table. The corresponding numbers are *reciprocals* of each other. The reciprocal of a number is found by dividing the number into 1.

Look back at examples J and K, which showed two different ways to solve the same problem. In example J we used a future value factor, which was 1.12716. In example K we used a present value factor, which was 0.88719. Each factor is in row 24 and the 0.50% column of its respective table. With your calculator, divide 1 by 1.12716 to get 0.88718549, which, rounded to five places, is 0.88719. And dividing 1 by 0.88719 gives 1.12715427.

$1 \div 1.12716 = 0.88718549$, or 0.88719
$1 \div 0.88719 = 1.12715427$, or 1.12716

Examine your calculator. You may have a reciprocal key, labeled "1/x." If you have this key, enter 1.12716 and press the $y^x$. The calculator will display 0.88718549. Press the $y^x$ again and the calculator will display 1.12716, or perhaps 1.12716000.

## CONCEPT CHECK 16.3

a. What present value (principal) invested for 3 years at 10% compounded semiannually will result in a total future value of $4,000? (Use Table 16-2 or a calculator.)

*Semiannually* means 2 periods per year.

Periodic rate = 10% ÷ 2 = 5% per half-year

Number of periods = 2 × 3 years = 6 periods

The present value factor from row 6 of the 5.00% column in Table 16-2 is 0.74622.

$PV = FV \times PVF$ = $4,000 × 0.74622 = $2,984.88

$m = 2$

$i = \frac{0.10}{2} = 0.05$

$n = 2 \times 3 = 6$

$PVF = \frac{1}{(1 + 0.05)^6} = 0.74621540$

$PV$ = $4,000 × 0.74621540 = $2,984.86

b. Four years ago, a woman invested money at 9% compounded monthly. If the investment is now worth $12,000, how much compound interest did she earn in the 4 years? (Use Table 16-2 or a calculator.)

*Monthly* means 12 periods per year.

Periodic rate = 9% ÷ 12 = 0.75% per month

Number of periods = 12 × 4 years = 48 periods

The present value factor from row 48 of the 0.75% column in Table 16-2 is 0.69861.

$PV = FV \times PVF$ = $12,000 × 0.69861 = $8,383.32

Compound interest = Future value − Present value
= $12,000 − $8,383.32 = $3,616.68

$m = 12$

$i = \frac{0.09}{12} = 0.0075$

$n = 12 \times 4 = 48$

$PVF = \frac{1}{(1 + 0.0075)^{48}} = 0.69861414$

$PV$ = $12,000 × 0.69861414 = $8,383.37

COMPLETE ASSIGNMENT 16.2.

## Chapter Terms for Review

compound amount

compound amount factors

compound interest

exponent

future value

future value factor

number of compounding periods

period (compounding period)

periodic interest rate

power

present value

present value factor

# THE BOTTOM LINE

*Summary of chapter learning objectives:*

| Learning Objective | Example |
|---|---|
| **16.1** Compute future values from tables and formulas. | 1. Compute the future value of $8,000 invested at 9% compounded monthly for 3 years.<br>2. Compute the compound interest earned on $5,000 invested at 6% compounded quarterly for 5 years. |
| **16.2** Compute present values from future value tables. | 3. Compute the present value that has to be invested at 10% compounded semiannually for 6 years to result in $8,000. |
| **16.3** Compute using present value tables and formulas. | 4. If $6,000 is the future value after 13 years at 9% compounded annually, compute the principal (present value).<br>5. An investment made 16 months ago is worth $5,634.95 today. If the interest rate was 9% compounded monthly, what was the amount of compound interest? |

Answers: 1. $10,469.20 2. $1,734.30 3. $4,454.69 4. $1,957.08 5. $634.95

SELF-CHECK

# Review Problems for Chapter 16

1. Calculate the future value (compound amount) and compound interest. (Use Table 16-1 or a calculator.)

| Principal | Rate | Time | Future Value | Interest |
|---|---|---|---|---|
| $ 4,000 | 6% compounded monthly | 3 yr | a. ________ | b. ________ |
| $12,000 | 8% compounded quarterly | 7 yr | c. ________ | d. ________ |
| $30,000 | 10% compounded annually | 16 yr | e. ________ | f. ________ |
| $ 8,000 | 10% compounded semiannually | 10 yr | g. ________ | h. ________ |

2. Calculate the present value (principal) and compound interest. (Use Table 16-2 or a calculator.)

| Future Value | Rate | Time | Present Value | Interest |
|---|---|---|---|---|
| $25,000 | 6% compounded annually | 9 yr | a. ________ | b. ________ |
| $ 6,000 | 8% compounded semiannually | 12 yr | c. ________ | d. ________ |
| $15,000 | 9% compounded monthly | 4 yr | e. ________ | f. ________ |
| $40,000 | 6% compounded quarterly | 5 yr | g. ________ | h. ________ |

3. Vernon Lee received a $6,000 bonus from his employer. He can invest it safely in his credit union at 4% compounded quarterly. What will be the value of the investment in 7 years?

4. Kathy Shutter inherited $26,760. She invested it immediately in an investment fund paying 8% compounded semiannually. How much interest would Kathy earn if she left principal and interest invested for 9 years?

5. Sandy Hopkins was planning to buy a new car in 3 years. She has some money today that she can invest for 3 years in an account that will pay 6% compounded quarterly. How much of it would she need to deposit today so that she will have $8,000 in her account in 3 years?

6. Doug Jurgensen will need to buy a $25,000 wood lathe in 2 years. He can deposit excess profits from this year in an investment that should pay 9% compounded monthly. If Doug earns the $25,000 in 2 years, how much will he earn in interest?

**Answers to the Self-Check can be found in Appendix B at the back of the text.**

# Assignment 16.1: Future Value (Compound Amount)

Name ______

Date ______ Score ______

Learning Objective 1

**A** **(28 points) Find the future value (compound amount) and the compound interest, as indicated, for each of the following investments. Round answers to the nearest cent. Use Table 16-1 or a calculator. (2 points for each correct answer)**

| | Principal | Rate | Term | Future Value | Compound Interest |
|---|---|---|---|---|---|
| **1.** | $6,000 | 6% compounded monthly | 4 years | ______ | ______ |
| **2.** | $750 | 8% compounded semiannually | 13 years | ______ | ______ |
| **3.** | $20,000 | 8% compounded quarterly | 8 years | ______ | ______ |
| **4.** | $12,500 | 12% compounded annually | 30 years | ______ | ______ |
| **5.** | $5,000 | 9% compounded monthly | 18 months | ______ | ______ |
| **6.** | $14,450 | 6% compounded quarterly | 4 years | ______ | ______ |
| **7.** | $4,000 | 4% compounded semiannually | 9 years | ______ | ______ |

______

Score for A (28)

**B** **(32 points) Find the future value (compound amount) or the compound interest, as indicated, for each of the following investments or loans. Round answers to the nearest cent. Use Table 16-1 or a calculator. (4 points for each correct answer)**

**8.** Compute the future value (compound amount) of $4,500 invested for 10 years at 5% compounded quarterly.

________

**9.** How much compound interest will you pay if you borrow $25,000 for 13 months at 15% compounded monthly?

________

**10.** Calculate the future value (compound amount) on a loan of $38,260 at 8% compounded annually for 13 years.

________

**11.** How much compound interest will you earn if you invest $7,900 for 16.5 years at 12% compounded semiannually?

________

**12.** What total amount (principal and interest) must be repaid in $2\frac{1}{2}$ years on a loan of $15,000 at 9% compounded monthly?

________

**13.** Determine the total compound interest that you will have to pay if you borrow $1,780 at 16% compounded semiannually and don't pay it back for 5 years.

________

**14.** How much compound interest will you earn if you invest $10,000 for 17 years at 9% compounded annually?

________

**15.** Compute the future value (compound amount) of $18,000 invested for 4.5 years at 5% compounded quarterly.

________

____________

Score for B (32)

**C (40 points) Business Applications. Find the future value (compound amount) or the compound interest, as indicated. Round answers to the nearest cent. Use Table 16-1 or a calculator. (4 points for each correct answer)**

**16.** Karen Wilson thinks that she needs to borrow $7,600 for 2 years. She doesn't have a very good credit rating, so most finance companies want to charge her a high interest rate. She finally finds a lender that will loan her the money at 12% compounded monthly. How much interest will Karen have to pay to this particular lender?

__________

**17.** Mary Sousa receives a telephone call from a salesperson who describes "an incredible investment opportunity." The investment promises a return of 16% compounded semiannually for investments of $5,000 or more. One disadvantage is that no money will be paid out for a long time. Another disadvantage is that the investment is very risky. Mary doesn't think that she will need the money for 6 years, so she decides to invest $5,000. If the investment pays what it promises, how much interest will Mary earn in the 6 years?

__________

**18.** William Wang wants to borrow money from his father to buy a car. William's father is trying to teach him how to manage money, so he agrees to loan him the money, but at 5% compounded quarterly. William borrows $11,200 and repays everything—principal plus all of the interest—in $3\frac{1}{2}$ years. How much does William pay back to his father?

__________

**19.** Don Hildebrand is trying to decide whether to invest money in a bank or in something a little riskier that will pay a higher return. One very simple investment promises to pay a minimum of 8% compounded annually, but he must leave all of the money and interest invested for 9 years. How much interest will Don earn during the 9 years if he invests $7,150 and the investment pays the minimum?

__________

**20.** Marcia Juarez and her brother-in-law have a successful business with several employees. They decide to borrow $15,000 to pay their quarterly deposits for payroll taxes and federal income tax. They get the money at 9% compounded monthly and repay all interest and principal after 9 months. How much do they repay?

__________

**21.** Sammie Crass inherited $16,780. She wants to invest it in something relatively safe so that she can transfer all the money to her children's college fund in about 8 years. One investment brochure (called a prospectus) states that it will pay a return of 8% compounded quarterly. How much will Sammie have total, principal plus interest, after 8 years?

__________

**22.** To help his daughter and son-in-law purchase their first new car, Robert Chiu loans them $24,500. They agree on an interest rate of 4% compounded annually, and Mr. Chiu tells them that they can pay it all back, the $24,500 plus the interest, in 6 years. How much interest will Mr. Chiu receive from them?

__________

**23.** Sandee Millet owns and operates an art supply store in a suburban shopping center. Sandee learns about an investment that claims to pay a return of 8% compounded semiannually for 4 years. Sandee decides to invest $4,750. Compute the amount of interest that she will earn in the 4 years.

__________

**24.** Ken Ortman is a student at medical school. He borrowed $32,000 for 26 months at the rate of 6% compounded monthly. How much total, principal plus compound interest, must Ken repay at the end of the 26 months?

__________

**25.** The County Employees Credit Union pays an interest rate of 8% compounded quarterly on savings accounts of $1,000 or more, with the requirement that the money be deposited for at least 6 months. How much interest will Marilyn Bunnell earn if she deposits $1,800 and leaves it in the credit union for 2 years?

__________

__________

Score for C (40)

# Assignment 16.2: Present Value

Name ______________________

Date ______________ Score ______________

Learning Objectives 2 3

**A** **(28 points) Find the present value (principal) and the compound interest, as indicated, for each of the following investments. (*Hint:* Subtract the present value from the future value to find the compound interest.) Use Table 16-1, Table 16-2, or a calculator. Round answers to the nearest cent. (2 points for each correct answer)**

| | Future Value | Rate | Term | Present Value | Compound Interest |
|---|---|---|---|---|---|
| **1.** | $3,900 | 6% compounded semiannually | 3 years | ______ | ______ |
| **2.** | $15,000 | 8% compounded quarterly | 7 years | ______ | ______ |
| **3.** | $23,000 | 6% compounded annually | 11 years | ______ | ______ |
| **4.** | $6,800 | 9% compounded monthly | 4 years | ______ | ______ |
| **5.** | $10,000 | 6% compounded quarterly | 10 years | ______ | ______ |
| **6.** | $50,000 | 8% compounded semiannually | 6 years | ______ | ______ |
| **7.** | $2,500 | 6% compounded monthly | 18 months | ______ | ______ |

______________
Score for A (28)

**B** **(32 points) Find the present value (principal) or the compound interest, as indicated, for each of the following investments or loans. Use Table 16-1, Table 16-2, or a calculator. Round answers to the nearest cent. (4 points for each correct answer)**

**8.** Compute the present value (principal) if the future value 20 years from now is $25,000 and if the interest rate is 8% compounded semiannually.

__________

**9.** How much compound interest would you pay if you repay a total of $8,425 one and a half years after borrowing the principal at 9% compounded monthly?

__________

**10.** Calculate the present value (principal) of a loan made 4 years ago at 12% compounded quarterly if the borrower repays a total of $9,600.

__________

**11.** Compute the amount that a company must invest (the present value) at 10% compounded annually if it wants to have $100,000 available (the future value) in 25 years.

__________

**12.** How much compound interest is earned on a 6.5-year investment that has a rate of return of 6% compounded quarterly and repays a total compound amount (future value) of $9,600?

__________

**13.** Determine the present value (principal) of a single deposit that is worth exactly $4,750 after 15 months at 6% compounded monthly.

__________

**14.** Calculate the amount of compound interest that has accrued on an investment that is now worth $15,000 after 14 years at 10% compounded semiannually.

__________

**15.** Compute the present value (principal) if the future value is $50,000 after 50 years at 6% compounded annually.

______

______

Score for B (32)

**C** **(40 points) Business Applications. Find the present value (principal) or the compound interest, as indicated. Use either Table 16-1, Table 16-2, or a calculator. Round answers to the nearest cent. (4 points for each correct answer)**

**16.** Ben Mahaffy needs to buy another used logging truck. His mother will loan him part of the money at only 4% compounded quarterly. If Ben estimates that he will be able to repay his mother a total of $27,400 in $1\frac{1}{2}$ years, how much can he borrow from her today?

______

**17.** Six years ago, Eleanor Baker invested money at 8% compounded annually. Today she received a check for $6,000 that represented her total payment of principal and interest. Compute the amount of the interest that she earned.

______

**18.** Lee Oman wants to have $30,000 available at the end of 3 years to help purchase a computerized metal lathe for his machine shop. If he can invest money at 6% compounded semiannually, how much should he invest?

______

**19.** As part of their financial planning, Janice Garcia's grandparents made monetary gifts to each of their grandchildren. In addition, Janice's grandfather told her that, if she would save part of her gift for at least a year, he would pay her interest of 9% compounded monthly. Janice decided to save just enough so that she would have $5,000 at the end of 21 months, when she will be 16 years old. How much should she save?

______

**20.** Erin Blackstone estimated that she would need $11,100 in $4\frac{1}{2}$ years to buy new equipment for her pottery shop. Having extra cash, she invested money in an extremely safe investment that advertised a return of 8% compounded semiannually. Erin invested just enough money to end up with the $11,100. How much of the $11,100 did Erin earn on her investment?

______

**21.** Keith Smith is a financial advisor. A client would like to have $25,000 in 5 years for possible weddings for her twin daughters who are now 18 years old. After comparing the projected returns with the risk, Keith recommends an investment that will pay 6% compounded quarterly. To end up with the $25,000, how much must the client invest today?

__________

**22.** A small company estimates that a modest investment today would realize a return of 10% compounded annually. The company wants a total sum of $20,000 in 5 years. If the company invests the appropriate amount to reach the $20,000 objective, how much of the $20,000 will be earned by the investment?

__________

**23.** Linda Anderson inherited $10,000. She knew that she would need $8,000 in 3 years to pay additional tuition for her children's education. Linda wanted to save enough to have the $8,000 three years from now. She found an incredible, relatively safe investment that would pay 15% compounded monthly for the entire 3 years—if she agreed to leave the money untouched for 3 years. Linda invests just enough of her inheritance to create the $8,000. How much does she have left over from the $10,000?

__________

**24.** Charles Peterson owns an antique store in New England. He is planning a buying trip to France for next spring—in 9 months. Charles estimates the cost of the trip will be $8,000 in 9 months. How much should Charles set aside today to have $8,000 in 9 months? He can earn 8% compounded quarterly.

__________

**25.** Technology advances so rapidly that printers for higher-end computer systems are obsolete almost before they come onto the market. Frances Leung thinks that it would be reasonable to budget $2,600 for a high-speed color printer. Frances can make a safe investment paying 12% compounded monthly for 15 months. If she invests the necessary amount of money now, how much of the $2,600 will be paid by the investment at the end of the 15 months?

__________

__________

Score for C (40)

## Notes

**Table 16-1:** Future Value (Compound Amount) Factors

| Period | 0.50% | 0.75% | 1.00% | 1.25% | 1.50% | 2.00% | 3.00% | 4.00% | 5.00% | 6.00% | 8.00% | 9.00% | 10.00% | 12.00% |
|---|---|---|---|---|---|---|---|---|---|---|---|---|---|---|
| **1** | 1.00500 | 1.00750 | 1.01000 | 1.01250 | 1.01500 | 1.02000 | 1.03000 | 1.04000 | 1.05000 | 1.06000 | 1.08000 | 1.09000 | 1.10000 | 1.12000 |
| **2** | 1.01003 | 1.01506 | 1.02010 | 1.02516 | 1.03023 | 1.04040 | 1.06090 | 1.08160 | 1.10250 | 1.12360 | 1.16640 | 1.18810 | 1.21000 | 1.25440 |
| **3** | 1.01508 | 1.02267 | 1.03030 | 1.03797 | 1.04568 | 1.06121 | 1.09273 | 1.12486 | 1.15763 | 1.19102 | 1.25971 | 1.29503 | 1.33100 | 1.40493 |
| **4** | 1.02015 | 1.03034 | 1.04060 | 1.05095 | 1.06136 | 1.08243 | 1.12551 | 1.16986 | 1.21551 | 1.26248 | 1.36049 | 1.41158 | 1.46410 | 1.57352 |
| **5** | 1.02525 | 1.03807 | 1.05101 | 1.06408 | 1.07728 | 1.10408 | 1.15927 | 1.21665 | 1.27628 | 1.33823 | 1.46933 | 1.53862 | 1.61051 | 1.76234 |
| **6** | 1.03038 | 1.04585 | 1.06152 | 1.07738 | 1.09344 | 1.12616 | 1.19405 | 1.26532 | 1.34010 | 1.41852 | 1.58687 | 1.67710 | 1.77156 | 1.97382 |
| **7** | 1.03553 | 1.05370 | 1.07214 | 1.09085 | 1.10984 | 1.14869 | 1.22987 | 1.31593 | 1.40710 | 1.50363 | 1.71382 | 1.82804 | 1.94872 | 2.21068 |
| **8** | 1.04071 | 1.06160 | 1.08286 | 1.10449 | 1.12649 | 1.17166 | 1.26677 | 1.36857 | 1.47746 | 1.59385 | 1.85093 | 1.99256 | 2.14359 | 2.47596 |
| **9** | 1.04591 | 1.06956 | 1.09369 | 1.11829 | 1.14339 | 1.19509 | 1.30477 | 1.42331 | 1.55133 | 1.68948 | 1.99900 | 2.17189 | 2.35795 | 2.77308 |
| **10** | 1.05114 | 1.07758 | 1.10462 | 1.13227 | 1.16054 | 1.21899 | 1.34392 | 1.48024 | 1.62889 | 1.79085 | 2.15892 | 2.36736 | 2.59374 | 3.10585 |
| **11** | 1.05640 | 1.08566 | 1.11567 | 1.14642 | 1.17795 | 1.24337 | 1.38423 | 1.53945 | 1.71034 | 1.89830 | 2.33164 | 2.58043 | 2.85312 | 3.47855 |
| **12** | 1.06168 | 1.09381 | 1.12683 | 1.16075 | 1.19562 | 1.26824 | 1.42576 | 1.60103 | 1.79586 | 2.01220 | 2.51817 | 2.81266 | 3.13843 | 3.89598 |
| **13** | 1.06699 | 1.10201 | 1.13809 | 1.17526 | 1.21355 | 1.29361 | 1.46853 | 1.66507 | 1.88565 | 2.13293 | 2.71962 | 3.06580 | 3.45227 | 4.36349 |
| **14** | 1.07232 | 1.11028 | 1.14947 | 1.18995 | 1.23176 | 1.31948 | 1.51259 | 1.73168 | 1.97993 | 2.26090 | 2.93719 | 3.34173 | 3.79750 | 4.88711 |
| **15** | 1.07768 | 1.11860 | 1.16097 | 1.20483 | 1.25023 | 1.34587 | 1.55797 | 1.80094 | 2.07893 | 2.39656 | 3.17217 | 3.64248 | 4.17725 | 5.47357 |
| **16** | 1.08307 | 1.12699 | 1.17258 | 1.21989 | 1.26899 | 1.37279 | 1.60471 | 1.87298 | 2.18287 | 2.54035 | 3.42594 | 3.97031 | 4.59497 | 6.13039 |
| **17** | 1.08849 | 1.13544 | 1.18430 | 1.23514 | 1.28802 | 1.40024 | 1.65285 | 1.94790 | 2.29202 | 2.69277 | 3.70002 | 4.32763 | 5.05447 | 6.86604 |
| **18** | 1.09393 | 1.14396 | 1.19615 | 1.25058 | 1.30734 | 1.42825 | 1.70243 | 2.02582 | 2.40662 | 2.85434 | 3.99602 | 4.71712 | 5.55992 | 7.68997 |
| **19** | 1.09940 | 1.15254 | 1.20811 | 1.26621 | 1.32695 | 1.45681 | 1.75351 | 2.10685 | 2.52695 | 3.02560 | 4.31570 | 5.14166 | 6.11591 | 8.61276 |
| **20** | 1.10490 | 1.16118 | 1.22019 | 1.28204 | 1.34686 | 1.48595 | 1.80611 | 2.19112 | 2.65330 | 3.20714 | 4.66096 | 5.60441 | 6.72750 | 9.64629 |
| **21** | 1.11042 | 1.16989 | 1.23239 | 1.29806 | 1.36706 | 1.51567 | 1.86029 | 2.27877 | 2.78596 | 3.39956 | 5.03383 | 6.10881 | 7.40025 | 10.80385 |
| **22** | 1.11597 | 1.17867 | 1.24472 | 1.31429 | 1.38756 | 1.54598 | 1.91610 | 2.36992 | 2.92526 | 3.60354 | 5.43654 | 6.65860 | 8.14027 | 12.10031 |
| **23** | 1.12155 | 1.18751 | 1.25716 | 1.33072 | 1.40838 | 1.57690 | 1.97359 | 2.46472 | 3.07152 | 3.81975 | 5.87146 | 7.25787 | 8.95430 | 13.55235 |
| **24** | 1.12716 | 1.19641 | 1.26973 | 1.34735 | 1.42950 | 1.60844 | 2.03279 | 2.56330 | 3.22510 | 4.04893 | 6.34118 | 7.91108 | 9.84973 | 15.17863 |
| **25** | 1.13280 | 1.20539 | 1.28243 | 1.36419 | 1.45095 | 1.64061 | 2.09378 | 2.66584 | 3.38635 | 4.29187 | 6.84848 | 8.62308 | 10.83471 | 17.00006 |

**Table 16-1:** Future Value (Compound Amount) Factors *(continued)*

| Period | 0.50% | 0.75% | 1.00% | 1.25% | 1.50% | 2.00% | 3.00% | 4.00% | 5.00% | 6.00% | 8.00% | 9.00% | 10.00% | 12.00% |
|---|---|---|---|---|---|---|---|---|---|---|---|---|---|---|
| **26** | 1.13846 | 1.21443 | 1.29526 | 1.38125 | 1.47271 | 1.67342 | 2.15659 | 2.77247 | 3.55567 | 4.54938 | 7.39635 | 9.39916 | 11.91818 | 19.04007 |
| **27** | 1.14415 | 1.22354 | 1.30821 | 1.39851 | 1.49480 | 1.70689 | 2.22129 | 2.88337 | 3.73346 | 4.82235 | 7.98806 | 10.24508 | 13.10999 | 21.32488 |
| **28** | 1.14987 | 1.23271 | 1.32129 | 1.41599 | 1.51722 | 1.74102 | 2.28793 | 2.99870 | 3.92013 | 5.11169 | 8.62711 | 11.16714 | 14.42099 | 23.88387 |
| **29** | 1.15562 | 1.24196 | 1.33450 | 1.43369 | 1.53998 | 1.77584 | 2.35657 | 3.11865 | 4.11614 | 5.41839 | 9.31727 | 12.17218 | 15.86309 | 26.74993 |
| **30** | 1.16140 | 1.25127 | 1.34785 | 1.45161 | 1.56308 | 1.81136 | 2.42726 | 3.24340 | 4.32194 | 5.74349 | 10.06266 | 13.26768 | 17.44940 | 29.95992 |
| **31** | 1.16721 | 1.26066 | 1.36133 | 1.46976 | 1.58653 | 1.84759 | 2.50008 | 3.37313 | 4.53804 | 6.08810 | 10.86767 | 14.46177 | 19.19434 | 33.55511 |
| **32** | 1.17304 | 1.27011 | 1.37494 | 1.48813 | 1.61032 | 1.88454 | 2.57508 | 3.50806 | 4.76494 | 6.45339 | 11.73708 | 15.76333 | 21.11378 | 37.58173 |
| **33** | 1.17891 | 1.27964 | 1.38869 | 1.50673 | 1.63448 | 1.92223 | 2.65234 | 3.64838 | 5.00319 | 6.84059 | 12.67605 | 17.18203 | 23.22515 | 42.09153 |
| **34** | 1.18480 | 1.28923 | 1.40258 | 1.52557 | 1.65900 | 1.96068 | 2.73191 | 3.79432 | 5.25335 | 7.25103 | 13.69013 | 18.72841 | 25.54767 | 47.14252 |
| **35** | 1.19073 | 1.29890 | 1.41660 | 1.54464 | 1.68388 | 1.99989 | 2.81386 | 3.94609 | 5.51602 | 7.68609 | 14.78534 | 20.41397 | 28.10244 | 52.79962 |
| **36** | 1.19668 | 1.30865 | 1.43077 | 1.56394 | 1.70914 | 2.03989 | 2.89828 | 4.10393 | 5.79182 | 8.14725 | 15.96817 | 22.25123 | 30.91268 | 59.13557 |
| **37** | 1.20266 | 1.31846 | 1.44508 | 1.58349 | 1.73478 | 2.08069 | 2.98523 | 4.26809 | 6.08141 | 8.63609 | 17.24563 | 24.25384 | 34.00395 | 66.23184 |
| **38** | 1.20868 | 1.32835 | 1.45953 | 1.60329 | 1.76080 | 2.12230 | 3.07478 | 4.43881 | 6.38548 | 9.15425 | 18.62528 | 26.43668 | 37.40434 | 74.17966 |
| **39** | 1.21472 | 1.33831 | 1.47412 | 1.62333 | 1.78721 | 2.16474 | 3.16703 | 4.61637 | 6.70475 | 9.70351 | 20.11530 | 28.81598 | 41.14478 | 83.08122 |
| **40** | 1.22079 | 1.34835 | 1.48886 | 1.64362 | 1.81402 | 2.20804 | 3.26204 | 4.80102 | 7.03999 | 10.28572 | 21.72452 | 31.40942 | 45.25926 | 93.05097 |
| **41** | 1.22690 | 1.35846 | 1.50375 | 1.66416 | 1.84123 | 2.25220 | 3.35990 | 4.99306 | 7.39199 | 10.90286 | 23.46248 | 34.23627 | 49.78518 | 104.21709 |
| **42** | 1.23303 | 1.36865 | 1.51879 | 1.68497 | 1.86885 | 2.29724 | 3.46070 | 5.19278 | 7.76159 | 11.55703 | 25.33948 | 37.31753 | 54.76370 | 116.72314 |
| **43** | 1.23920 | 1.37891 | 1.53398 | 1.70603 | 1.89688 | 2.34319 | 3.56452 | 5.40050 | 8.14967 | 12.25045 | 27.36664 | 40.67611 | 60.24007 | 130.72991 |
| **44** | 1.24539 | 1.38926 | 1.54932 | 1.72735 | 1.92533 | 2.39005 | 3.67145 | 5.61652 | 8.55715 | 12.98548 | 29.55597 | 44.33696 | 66.26408 | 146.41750 |
| **45** | 1.25162 | 1.39968 | 1.56481 | 1.74895 | 1.95421 | 2.43785 | 3.78160 | 5.84118 | 8.98501 | 13.76461 | 31.92045 | 48.32729 | 72.89048 | 163.98760 |
| **46** | 1.25788 | 1.41017 | 1.58046 | 1.77081 | 1.98353 | 2.48661 | 3.89504 | 6.07482 | 9.43426 | 14.59049 | 34.47409 | 52.67674 | 80.17953 | 183.66612 |
| **47** | 1.26417 | 1.42075 | 1.59626 | 1.79294 | 2.01328 | 2.53634 | 4.01190 | 6.31782 | 9.90597 | 15.46592 | 37.23201 | 57.41765 | 88.19749 | 205.70605 |
| **48** | 1.27049 | 1.43141 | 1.61223 | 1.81535 | 2.04348 | 2.58707 | 4.13225 | 6.57053 | 10.40127 | 16.39387 | 40.21057 | 62.58524 | 97.01723 | 230.39078 |
| **49** | 1.27684 | 1.44214 | 1.62835 | 1.83805 | 2.07413 | 2.63881 | 4.25622 | 6.83335 | 10.92133 | 17.37750 | 43.42742 | 68.21791 | 106.71896 | 258.03767 |
| **50** | 1.28323 | 1.45296 | 1.64463 | 1.86102 | 2.10524 | 2.69159 | 4.38391 | 7.10668 | 11.46740 | 18.42015 | 46.90161 | 74.35752 | 117.39085 | 289.00219 |

**Table 16-2: Present Value Factors**

| Period | 0.50% | 0.75% | 1.00% | 1.25% | 1.50% | 2.00% | 3.00% | 4.00% | 5.00% | 6.00% | 8.00% | 9.00% | 10.00% | 12.00% |
|---|---|---|---|---|---|---|---|---|---|---|---|---|---|---|
| 1 | 0.99502 | 0.99256 | 0.99010 | 0.98765 | 0.98522 | 0.98039 | 0.97087 | 0.96154 | 0.95238 | 0.94340 | 0.92593 | 0.91743 | 0.90909 | 0.89286 |
| 2 | 0.99007 | 0.98517 | 0.98030 | 0.97546 | 0.97066 | 0.96117 | 0.94260 | 0.92456 | 0.90703 | 0.89000 | 0.85734 | 0.84168 | 0.82645 | 0.79719 |
| 3 | 0.98515 | 0.97783 | 0.97059 | 0.96342 | 0.95632 | 0.94232 | 0.91514 | 0.88900 | 0.86384 | 0.83962 | 0.79383 | 0.77218 | 0.75131 | 0.71178 |
| 4 | 0.98025 | 0.97055 | 0.96098 | 0.95152 | 0.94218 | 0.92385 | 0.88849 | 0.85480 | 0.82270 | 0.79209 | 0.73503 | 0.70843 | 0.68301 | 0.63552 |
| 5 | 0.97537 | 0.96333 | 0.95147 | 0.93978 | 0.92826 | 0.90573 | 0.86261 | 0.82193 | 0.78353 | 0.74726 | 0.68058 | 0.64993 | 0.62092 | 0.56743 |
| 6 | 0.97052 | 0.95616 | 0.94205 | 0.92817 | 0.91454 | 0.88797 | 0.83748 | 0.79031 | 0.74622 | 0.70496 | 0.63017 | 0.59627 | 0.56447 | 0.50663 |
| 7 | 0.96569 | 0.94904 | 0.93272 | 0.91672 | 0.90103 | 0.87056 | 0.81309 | 0.75992 | 0.71068 | 0.66506 | 0.58349 | 0.54703 | 0.51316 | 0.45235 |
| 8 | 0.96089 | 0.94198 | 0.92348 | 0.90540 | 0.88771 | 0.85349 | 0.78941 | 0.73069 | 0.67684 | 0.62741 | 0.54027 | 0.50187 | 0.46651 | 0.40388 |
| 9 | 0.95610 | 0.93496 | 0.91434 | 0.89422 | 0.87459 | 0.83676 | 0.76642 | 0.70259 | 0.64461 | 0.59190 | 0.50025 | 0.46043 | 0.42410 | 0.36061 |
| 10 | 0.95135 | 0.92800 | 0.90529 | 0.88318 | 0.86167 | 0.82035 | 0.74409 | 0.67556 | 0.61391 | 0.55839 | 0.46319 | 0.42241 | 0.38554 | 0.32197 |
| 11 | 0.94661 | 0.92109 | 0.89632 | 0.87228 | 0.84893 | 0.80426 | 0.72242 | 0.64958 | 0.58468 | 0.52679 | 0.42888 | 0.38753 | 0.35049 | 0.28748 |
| 12 | 0.94191 | 0.91424 | 0.88745 | 0.86151 | 0.83639 | 0.78849 | 0.70138 | 0.62460 | 0.55684 | 0.49697 | 0.39711 | 0.35553 | 0.31863 | 0.25668 |
| 13 | 0.93722 | 0.90743 | 0.87866 | 0.85087 | 0.82403 | 0.77303 | 0.68095 | 0.60057 | 0.53032 | 0.46884 | 0.36770 | 0.32618 | 0.28966 | 0.22917 |
| 14 | 0.93256 | 0.90068 | 0.86996 | 0.84037 | 0.81185 | 0.75788 | 0.66112 | 0.57748 | 0.50507 | 0.44230 | 0.34046 | 0.29925 | 0.26333 | 0.20462 |
| 15 | 0.92792 | 0.89397 | 0.86135 | 0.82999 | 0.79985 | 0.74301 | 0.64186 | 0.55526 | 0.48102 | 0.41727 | 0.31524 | 0.27454 | 0.23939 | 0.18270 |
| 16 | 0.92330 | 0.88732 | 0.85282 | 0.81975 | 0.78803 | 0.72845 | 0.62317 | 0.53391 | 0.45811 | 0.39365 | 0.29189 | 0.25187 | 0.21763 | 0.16312 |
| 17 | 0.91871 | 0.88071 | 0.84438 | 0.80963 | 0.77639 | 0.71416 | 0.60502 | 0.51337 | 0.43630 | 0.37136 | 0.27027 | 0.23107 | 0.19784 | 0.14564 |
| 18 | 0.91414 | 0.87416 | 0.83602 | 0.79963 | 0.76491 | 0.70016 | 0.58739 | 0.49363 | 0.41552 | 0.35034 | 0.25025 | 0.21199 | 0.17986 | 0.13004 |
| 19 | 0.90959 | 0.86765 | 0.82774 | 0.78976 | 0.75361 | 0.68643 | 0.57029 | 0.47464 | 0.39573 | 0.33051 | 0.23171 | 0.19449 | 0.16351 | 0.11611 |
| 20 | 0.90506 | 0.86119 | 0.81954 | 0.78001 | 0.74247 | 0.67297 | 0.55368 | 0.45639 | 0.37689 | 0.31180 | 0.21455 | 0.17843 | 0.14864 | 0.10367 |
| 21 | 0.90056 | 0.85478 | 0.81143 | 0.77038 | 0.73150 | 0.65978 | 0.53755 | 0.43883 | 0.35894 | 0.29416 | 0.19866 | 0.16370 | 0.13513 | 0.09256 |
| 22 | 0.89608 | 0.84842 | 0.80340 | 0.76087 | 0.72069 | 0.64684 | 0.52189 | 0.42196 | 0.34185 | 0.27751 | 0.18394 | 0.15018 | 0.12285 | 0.08264 |
| 23 | 0.89162 | 0.84210 | 0.79544 | 0.75147 | 0.71004 | 0.63416 | 0.50669 | 0.40573 | 0.32557 | 0.26180 | 0.17032 | 0.13778 | 0.11168 | 0.07379 |
| 24 | 0.88719 | 0.83583 | 0.78757 | 0.74220 | 0.69954 | 0.62172 | 0.49193 | 0.39012 | 0.31007 | 0.24698 | 0.15770 | 0.12640 | 0.10153 | 0.06588 |
| 25 | 0.88277 | 0.82961 | 0.77977 | 0.73303 | 0.68921 | 0.60953 | 0.47761 | 0.37512 | 0.29530 | 0.23300 | 0.14602 | 0.11597 | 0.09230 | 0.05882 |

**Table 16-2:** Present Value Factors *(continued)*

| Period | 0.50% | 0.75% | 1.00% | 1.25% | 1.50% | 2.00% | 3.00% | 4.00% | 5.00% | 6.00% | 8.00% | 9.00% | 10.00% | 12.00% |
|---|---|---|---|---|---|---|---|---|---|---|---|---|---|---|
| **26** | 0.87838 | 0.82343 | 0.77205 | 0.72398 | 0.67902 | 0.59758 | 0.46369 | 0.36069 | 0.28124 | 0.21981 | 0.13520 | 0.10639 | 0.08391 | 0.05252 |
| **27** | 0.87401 | 0.81730 | 0.76440 | 0.71505 | 0.66899 | 0.58586 | 0.45019 | 0.34682 | 0.26785 | 0.20737 | 0.12519 | 0.09761 | 0.07628 | 0.04689 |
| **28** | 0.86966 | 0.81122 | 0.75684 | 0.70622 | 0.65910 | 0.57437 | 0.43708 | 0.33348 | 0.25509 | 0.19563 | 0.11591 | 0.08955 | 0.06934 | 0.04187 |
| **29** | 0.86533 | 0.80518 | 0.74934 | 0.69750 | 0.64936 | 0.56311 | 0.42435 | 0.32065 | 0.24295 | 0.18456 | 0.10733 | 0.08215 | 0.06304 | 0.03738 |
| **30** | 0.86103 | .079919 | 0.74192 | 0.68889 | 0.63976 | 0.55207 | 0.41199 | 0.30832 | 0.23138 | 0.17411 | 0.09938 | 0.07537 | 0.05731 | 0.03338 |
| **31** | 0.85675 | 0.79324 | 0.73458 | 0.68038 | 0.63031 | 0.54125 | 0.39999 | 0.29646 | 0.22036 | 0.16425 | 0.09202 | 0.06915 | 0.05210 | 0.02980 |
| **32** | 0.85248 | 0.78733 | 0.72730 | 0.67198 | 0.62099 | 0.53063 | 0.38834 | 0.28506 | 0.20987 | 0.15496 | 0.08520 | 0.06344 | 0.04736 | 0.02661 |
| **33** | 0.84824 | 0.78147 | 0.72010 | 0.66369 | 0.61182 | 0.52023 | 0.37703 | 0.27409 | 0.19987 | 0.14619 | 0.07889 | 0.05820 | 0.04306 | 0.02376 |
| **34** | 0.84402 | 0.77565 | 0.71297 | 0.65549 | 0.60277 | 0.51003 | 0.36604 | 0.26355 | 0.19035 | 0.13791 | 0.07305 | 0.05339 | 0.03914 | 0.02121 |
| **35** | 0.83982 | 0.76988 | 0.70591 | 0.64740 | 0.59387 | 0.50003 | 0.35538 | 0.25342 | 0.18129 | 0.13011 | 0.06763 | 0.04899 | 0.03558 | 0.01894 |
| **36** | 0.83564 | 0.76415 | 0.69892 | 0.63941 | 0.58509 | 0.49022 | 0.34503 | 0.24367 | 0.17266 | 0.12274 | 0.06262 | 0.04494 | 0.03235 | 0.01691 |
| **37** | 0.83149 | 0.75846 | 0.69200 | 0.63152 | 0.57644 | 0.48061 | 0.33498 | 0.23430 | 0.16444 | 0.11579 | 0.05799 | 0.04123 | 0.02941 | 0.01510 |
| **38** | 0.82735 | 0.75281 | 0.68515 | 0.62372 | 0.56792 | 0.47119 | 0.32523 | 0.22529 | 0.15661 | 0.10924 | 0.05369 | 0.03783 | 0.02673 | 0.01348 |
| **39** | 0.82323 | 0.74721 | 0.67837 | 0.61602 | 0.55953 | 0.46195 | 0.31575 | 0.21662 | 0.14915 | 0.10306 | 0.04971 | 0.03470 | 0.02430 | 0.01204 |
| **40** | 0.81914 | 0.74165 | 0.67165 | 0.60841 | 0.55126 | 0.45289 | 0.30656 | 0.20829 | 0.14205 | 0.09722 | 0.04603 | 0.03184 | 0.02209 | 0.01075 |
| **41** | 0.81506 | 0.73613 | 0.66500 | 0.60090 | 0.54312 | 0.44401 | 0.29763 | 0.20028 | 0.13528 | 0.09172 | 0.04262 | 0.02921 | 0.02009 | 0.00960 |
| **42** | 0.81101 | 0.73065 | 0.65842 | 0.59348 | 0.53509 | 0.43530 | 0.28896 | 0.19257 | 0.12884 | 0.08653 | 0.03946 | 0.02680 | 0.01826 | 0.00857 |
| **43** | 0.80697 | 0.72521 | 0.65190 | 0.58616 | 0.52718 | 0.42677 | 0.28054 | 0.18517 | 0.12270 | 0.08163 | 0.03654 | 0.02458 | 0.01660 | 0.00765 |
| **44** | 0.80296 | 0.71981 | 0.64545 | 0.57892 | 0.51939 | 0.41840 | 0.27237 | 0.17805 | 0.11686 | 0.07701 | 0.03383 | 0.02255 | 0.01509 | 0.00683 |
| **45** | 0.79896 | 0.71445 | 0.63905 | 0.57177 | 0.51171 | 0.41020 | 0.26444 | 0.17120 | 0.11130 | 0.07265 | 0.03133 | 0.02069 | 0.01372 | 0.00610 |
| **46** | 0.79499 | 0.70913 | 0.63273 | 0.56471 | 0.50415 | 0.40215 | 0.25674 | 0.16461 | 0.10600 | 0.06854 | 0.02901 | 0.01898 | 0.01247 | 0.00544 |
| **47** | 0.79103 | 0.70385 | 0.62646 | 0.55774 | 0.49670 | 0.39427 | 0.24926 | 0.15828 | 0.10095 | 0.06466 | 0.02686 | 0.01742 | 0.01134 | 0.00486 |
| **48** | 0.78710 | 0.69861 | 0.62026 | 0.55086 | 0.48936 | 0.38654 | 0.24200 | 0.15219 | 0.09614 | 0.06100 | 0.02487 | 0.01598 | 0.01031 | 0.00434 |
| **49** | 0.78318 | 0.69341 | 0.61412 | 0.54406 | 0.48213 | 0.37896 | 0.23495 | 0.14634 | 0.09156 | 0.05755 | 0.02303 | 0.01466 | 0.00937 | 0.00388 |
| **50** | 0.77929 | 0.68825 | 0.60804 | 0.53734 | 0.47500 | 0.37153 | 0.22811 | 0.14071 | 0.08720 | 0.05429 | 0.02132 | 0.01345 | 0.00852 | 0.00346 |

Part 5

# Business Applications

# 17

# Inventory and Turnover

## Learning Objectives

By studying this chapter and completing all assignments, you will be able to:

**Learning Objective 1** Account for inventory by inventory sheets and reports from a perpetual inventory system.

**Learning Objective 2** Compute inventory value by the average cost, LIFO, and FIFO methods.

**Learning Objective 3** Compute inventory by using the lower of cost or market value.

**Learning Objective 4** Estimate inventory by using cost of goods sold.

**Learning Objective 5** Compute inventory turnover.

A company's inventory is the amount of goods it has on hand at any particular time. Retailers and wholesalers have only one kind of inventory—*merchandise,* which are the goods they sell.

# Accounting for Inventory

**Learning Objective 1**

Account for inventory by inventory sheets and reports from a perpetual inventory system.

## INVENTORY SHEETS

At least once each year, businesses undertake a **physical inventory**—an actual counting of the merchandise on hand. Some stores that require close control take a physical inventory every six months, quarterly, or even monthly. Sometimes retail stores use outside firms that specialize in taking inventory.

When inventory is counted, a description of each item, the quantity, the unit cost or retail price, and the **extension** (quantity × price) are recorded on an **inventory sheet,** as shown in Figure 17-1. The inventory value is then compared with accounting records, and any needed adjustments are made.

**Figure 17-1** Inventory Sheet

**WARREN'S AUTO PARTS**
**Inventory Sheet**
**April 30, 20—**

| Description | Quantity | Unit Price (Average Cost) | Extension |
|---|---|---|---|
| Ignition terminals—#746083 | 318 | $36.14 | $11,492.52 |
| Odometer cables—#007614 | 73 | 9.97 | 727.81 |
| Wiper blades, compact—#417654 | 38 | 4.71 | 178.98 |
| Spark plugs, 0.14—#772034 | 354 | 2.34 | 828.36 |
| Hood/truck latches—#476508 | 58 | 13.42 | + 778.36 |
| Total | | | $14,006.03 |

## PERPETUAL INVENTORY SYSTEMS

Some firms keep a **perpetual inventory**—a running count of all inventory items, based on tracking each item as it comes into and goes out of inventory. In businesses that handle high-cost items, such as cars or large appliances, the perpetual system keeps track of each item by serial number and price.

Businesses that handle small items, such as candy bars or shoes, have difficulty identifying each specific item. Their perpetual inventory systems keep a count of the number of units on hand, not individual prices and serial numbers.

Data for a perpetual inventory system are usually kept on a computer. Figure 17-2 illustrates a computer printout of an inventory record sheet. The last item in the Balance on Hand column shows how many units are on hand on the 4/30 recording date—354 Quickstart spark plugs: 0.14, part number 772034.

### THE LIFO METHOD

The **last-in, first-out (LIFO) costing method** is based on the assumption that the cost of the inventory remaining is determined by the cost of the units purchased the earliest.

**EXAMPLE C**

Under the LIFO method, the 354 units would consist of the 350 units on hand on 1/01 plus 4 units from the first purchase on 3/02.

| Date | | | |
|---|---|---|---|
| 1/01 | 350 units × $2.10 = | $735.00 | |
| 3/02 | + 4 units × $2.36 = | + 9.44 | |
| | 354 | $744.44 | Ending inventory at LIFO cost |

**CONCEPT CHECK 17.2**

The inventory record sheets for hairbrushes at Debbie's Beauty Supply show 5,000 units purchased (or on hand) at a total cost of $10,240. The inventory at year's end was 1,500 units. Compute the value of the ending inventory by each of the three methods: average cost, FIFO, and LIFO.

| Date | Units Purchased | Cost | Extension |
|---|---|---|---|
| 1/01 | 2,000 | $2.00 | $ 4,000 |
| 1/30 | 200 | 2.10 | 420 |
| 2/20 | 700 | 2.10 | 1,470 |
| 3/17 | 1,100 | 2.00 | 2,200 |
| 10/30 | 500 | 2.20 | 1,100 |
| 11/17 | +500 | 2.10 | +1,050 |
| | 5,000 | | $10,240 |

Average Cost: $10,240 ÷ 5,000 = $2.048
1,500 × $2.05 (rounded) = $3,075

FIFO: (500 × $2.10) + (500 × $2.20) + (500 × $2.00) = $3,150

LIFO: (1,500 × $2.00) = $3,000

## Computing Inventory at the Lower of Cost or Market Value

Financial statements usually present the ending inventory at its cost value, computed by using the average, FIFO, or LIFO costing method. However, in some cases the **market value** (current replacement cost) of goods is lower than the original or average cost of those goods. Most companies prefer to show the **lower of cost or market value** in their inventories. When market value exceeds the cost, the cost is used; when the cost exceeds market value, market value is used.

**Learning Objective 3**

Compute inventory by using the lower of cost or market value.

**STEPS to Determine the Lower of Cost or Market (LCM) Inventory Value**

1. Compute the unit or total cost for each type of inventory item using the average, FIFO, or LIFO costing method.
2. Determine the market value for each inventory item.
3. Compare the cost value from Step 1 with the market value from Step 2 and choose the lower of the two.
4. Compute the extension amount for each item based on the lower amount.
5. Sum the amounts in Step 4 to determine the total inventory value under LCM.

**EXAMPLE D**

Under LCM, using the average cost method illustrated in example A, the total inventory shown in Figure 17-1 would be valued at $13,802.13.

| Description | (A) Quantity | STEP 1 (B) Unit Price (Average Cost) | STEP 2 (C) Unit Price at Market | STEP 3 (D) Lower of (B) or (C) | STEP 4 Extension (A × D) | |
|---|---|---|---|---|---|---|
| Ignition terminals—#746083 | 318 | $36.14 | $35.50 | $35.50 | $11,289.00 | Market |
| Odometer cables—#007614 | 73 | 9.97 | 11.00 | 9.97 | 727.81 | Cost |
| Wiper blades, compact—#417654 | 38 | 4.71 | 4.70 | 4.70 | 178.60 | Market |
| Spark plugs, 0.14—#772034 | 354 | 2.34 | 2.64 | 2.34 | 828.36 | Cost |
| Hood/trunk latches—#476508 | 58 | 13.42 | 14.10 | 13.42 | + 778.36 | Cost |
| Total | | | | | $13,802.13 | STEP 5 |

**EXAMPLE E**

Under LCM, using the FIFO cost method illustrated in example B, the FIFO cost for the inventory for Quickstart spark plugs would be $897.60. Combining LCM with FIFO for the Quickstart spark plugs illustrated in example B, the ending inventory for this one item would be valued at $897.60 because the market value ($934.56) is higher than the FIFO cost.

| | | | Market Value | | | |
|---|---|---|---|---|---|---|
| Description | (A) Quantity | (B) FIFO Cost | (C) Unit Price at Market | (D) Total (A × C) | Lower of (B) or (D) | |
| Spark plugs | 354 | $897.60 | $2.64 | $934.56 | $897.60 | Cost |

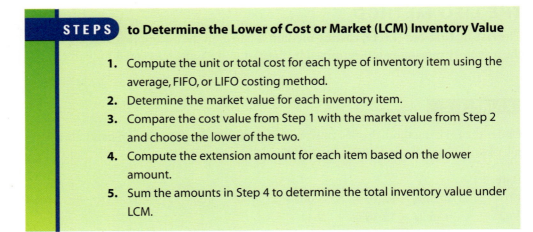

## CONCEPT CHECK 17.3

L & L Records' inventory shows the following. Compute the inventory value at the lower of cost or market value.

| Description | Quantity | Cost | Market | Extension | |
|---|---|---|---|---|---|
| Classical #3 | 300 | $ 7.07 | $10.10 | $2,121.00 | Cost |
| Western #8 | 180 | 9.10 | 8.07 | 1,452.60 | Market |
| Modern—light #11 | 410 | 11.17 | 12.08 | 4,579.70 | Cost |
| Rock—new #4 | 89 | 12.10 | 12.10 | +1,076.90 | Cost/market |
| Total | | | | $9,230.20 | |

# Estimating Inventory Value

Learning Objective 4

Estimate inventory by using cost of goods sold.

For monthly financial statements, inventory frequently is estimated without a physical count or a perpetual inventory system. The method usually used to estimate month-end inventory is called the **gross profit method.** This method involves estimating the **cost of goods sold** and subtracting this amount from the sum of the opening inventory and purchases made during the month. Note that **beginning inventory (BI)** is the ending inventory from the month before and **purchases (P)** are those goods for sale that have been purchased during the current month. The gross profit method is based on the formula

| |
|---|
| Beginning inventory (BI) |
| + Purchases (P) |
| Cost of goods available for sale |
| − Cost of goods sold (CGS) (estimated) |
| Ending inventory (EI) (estimate) |

Without a physical inventory, a precise cost of goods sold can't be determined. In this case, it is estimated by applying a markup percentage rate to **net sales** (total sales less sales returned and adjustments for the period). The net sales (100%) less this markup rate (percent) equals the cost of goods sold (percent). For instance, if the markup rate were 30%, the cost of goods sold would be 100% − 30% = 70%. If the rate of markup were 40%, the cost of goods sold would be 100% − 40% = 60%.

**EXAMPLE F**

Assume that Warren's Auto Parts had a beginning inventory of $80,000. During the month, the company purchased and received $50,000 in goods and had net sales of $90,000. Throughout the month, Warren's maintained a 40% markup on all sales. Its cost of goods sold would be computed as follows:

| | | |
|---|---|---|
| Net sales for the month | $90,000 | |
| Cost of goods sold (estimated) | $54,000 | [$90,000 × (100% − 40%) = $90,000 × 0.60] |

Warren's Auto Parts would then determine its ending inventory (estimated) as follows:

| | |
|---|---|
| Inventory, beginning of month | $ 80,000 |
| Purchases for month | + 50,000 |
| Goods available for sale | $130,000 |
| Cost of goods sold (estimated) | − 54,000 |
| Ending inventory (estimated) | $ 76,000 |

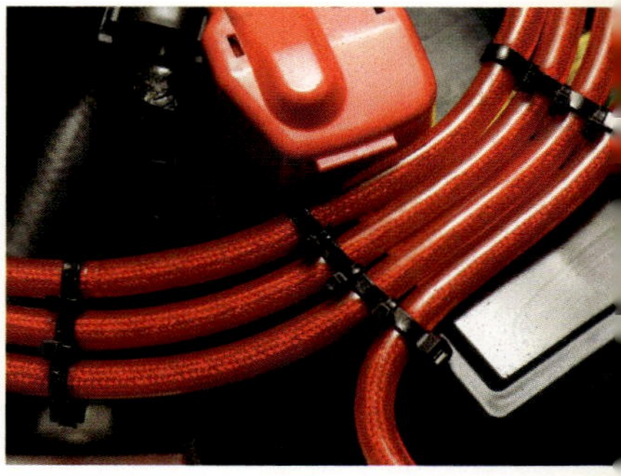
© JEREMY WEE/ISTOCKPHOTO INTERNATIONAL

Sometimes a company's markup rate is based on cost rather than selling price. In this case, if the markup on cost were 30%, the cost of goods sold would be net sales divided by 130%. If the markup on cost were 40%, the cost of goods sold would be net sales divided by 140%.

**EXAMPLE G**

Assume that Warren's Auto Parts had a beginning inventory of $80,000. During the month, it had purchases of $50,000 and net sales of $90,000. Throughout the month, Warren's maintained a markup of 50% based on cost. What were Warren's cost of goods sold and ending inventory?

| | | |
|---|---|---|
| Beginning inventory | $80,000 | |
| Purchases | + 50,000 | |
| Cost of goods available for sale | $130,000 | |
| Cost of goods sold (estimated) | − 60,000 | ($90,000 ÷ 150%) |
| Ending inventory (estimated) | $70,000 | |

**CONCEPT CHECK 17.4**

C & S Electronics' records show the following. Compute the estimated ending inventory at cost.

| | | | |
|---|---|---|---|
| Beginning inventory | $24,000 | Net sales for period | $60,000 |
| Purchases for period | $33,000 | Markup based on retail | 40% |

$24,000 + $33,000 = $57,000 cost of goods available
$60,000 × 60% = $36,000 cost of goods sold
$57,000 − $36,000 = $21,000 ending inventory

# Computing Inventory Turnover

**Learning Objective 5**

Compute inventory turnover.

**Inventory turnover** is the number of times the average inventory is converted into sales during the year. Inventory turnover is very high for a grocery store or ice cream parlor; it is very low for a specialty jewelry store or an antique shop. Standard turnover rates for corporate businesses are published. Some standard rates are 3.5 for hardware stores, 12.7 for grocery stores, 3.3 for nurseries, and 39.3 for stations and mini-marts.

Before turnover can be determined, average inventory must be calculated. **Average inventory** is the average of the inventories taken over a specific period of time—annually, semiannually, quarterly, or monthly.

| Inventory is taken | Average inventory (at retail or cost) |
|---|---|
| Annually (once a year) | (BI + EI) ÷ 2 |
| Semiannually (every six months) | (BI + end of 6 months + EI) ÷ 3 |
| Quarterly (every three months) | (BI + 3 quarterly + EI) ÷ 5 |
| Monthly (every month) | (BI + 11 monthly + EI) ÷ 13 |

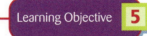

Computation of inventory turnover can be based on either retail (selling) price or cost. **Inventory turnover at retail** is net sales divided by average inventory.

**STEPS to Compute Inventory Turnover at Retail**

1. Determine net sales.
2. Compute average inventory using retail price.
3. Compute inventory turnover at retail: Net sales ÷ Average inventory at retail.

**EXAMPLE H**

Assume that inventories for the year, based on selling price, are as follows: beginning, \$90,000; end of month 3, \$80,000; end of month 6, \$100,000; end of month 9, \$70,000; and end of month 12 (ending), \$60,000. Net sales for the year are \$520,000. Compute the inventory turnover at retail.

STEP 2 Average inventory = (\$90,000 + \$80,000 + \$100,000 + \$70,000 + \$60,000) ÷ 5
= \$400,000 ÷ 5 = \$80,000

STEP 3 Inventory turnover at retail = \$520,000 net sales ÷ \$80,000 average inventory = 6.5 times

*Note*: The value of net sales and average inventory must both be figured at retail.

Some retailers prefer to express their rate of inventory turnover in terms of cost. **Inventory turnover at cost** is obtained by dividing the cost of goods sold (CGS) during a period by the average inventory for the same period computed at cost prices. (CGS is simply net sales at cost.)

**STEPS to Compute Inventory Turnover at Cost**

1. Compute the cost of goods sold using the formula BI + P − EI = CGS.
2. Compute the average inventory at cost.
3. Compute inventory turnover at cost: Cost of goods sold ÷ Average inventory at cost.

## EXAMPLE I

Assume that beginning inventory cost $60,000, purchases cost $300,000, and ending inventory cost $80,000. Compute the inventory turnover at cost.

**STEP 1** Cost of goods sold:

| | | |
|---|---|---|
| Cost of goods sold: | Inventory at beginning of year | $ 60,000 |
| | Purchases during year | + 300,000 |
| | Goods available for sale | $ 360,000 |
| | Inventory at end of year | − 80,000 |
| | Cost of goods sold | $ 280,000 |

**STEP 2** Average inventory = ($60,000 BI + $80,000 EI) ÷ 2
= $140,000 ÷ 2 = $70,000

**STEP 3** Inventory turnover at cost = $280,000 cost of goods sold
÷ $70,000 average inventory = 4.0 times

*Note:* The value of goods sold and average inventory must both be figured at cost.

## CONCEPT CHECK 17.5

Brinkman Scooter Shop has two branches (A and B), each using a markup of 50% of retail. Compute ending inventory, average inventory, and inventory turnover based on retail for each branch from the following data. Round answers to the nearest hundredth.

| | Branch A | Branch B |
|---|---|---|
| Net sales | $1,400,000 | $1,200,000 |
| Beginning inventory | 220,000 | 300,000 |
| Inventory (March 31) | 190,000 | 400,000 |
| Inventory (June 30) | 280,000 | 350,000 |
| Inventory (September 30) | 280,000 | 360,000 |
| Inventory (December 31) | 200,000 | 300,000 |

Average inventory: A—($220,000 + 190,000 + 280,000 + 280,000 + 200,000) ÷ 5 = $234,000
B—($300,000 + 400,000 + 350,000 + 360,000 + 300,000) ÷ 5 = $342,000

Retail turnover: A—$1,400,000 ÷ $234,000 = 5.98
B—$1,200,000 ÷ $342,000 = 3.51

COMPLETE ASSIGNMENTS 17.1 and 17.2.

## Chapter Terms for Review

- average cost method
- average inventory
- beginning inventory (BI)
- cost of goods sold (CGS)
- ending inventory (EI)
- extension
- first-in, first-out (FIFO) costing method
- gross profit method
- inventory sheet
- inventory turnover
- inventory turnover at cost
- inventory turnover at retail
- last-in, first-out (LIFO) costing method
- lower of cost or market value (LCM)
- market value
- net sales
- perpetual inventory
- physical inventory
- purchases (P)

# THE BOTTOM LINE

*Summary of chapter learning objectives:*

| Learning Objective | Example |
|---|---|
| **17.1**<br><br>Account for inventory by inventory sheets and reports from a perpetual inventory system. | 1. Compute the balance on hand after each transaction: |

| Date | Units In | Units Out | Balance on Hand |
|---|---|---|---|
| 12/01 | | | 34,768 |
| 12/17 | 7,732 | | ________ |
| 12/19 | | 16,500 | ________ |
| 12/20 | 9,700 | | ________ |
| 12/31 | | 12,030 | ________ |

| Learning Objective | Example |
|---|---|
| **17.2**<br><br>Compute inventory value by the average cost, LIFO, and FIFO methods. | 2. From the data shown, compute the ending inventory by the average cost, FIFO, and LIFO methods for Redwood Stove Company's stove part #717. The ending inventory, by physical count, was 300. |

**Stove Part #717**

| Date | Units In | Cost | Extension | Ending Inventory Value: |
|---|---|---|---|---|
| 1/12 | 200 | $3.00 | $600 | |
| 1/14 | 300 | 3.20 | 960 | Average cost: ________ |
| 1/15 | 500 | 3.00 | 1,500 | FIFO: ________ |
| 1/17 | 200 | 3.10 | 620 | LIFO: ________ |
| 1/18 | +400 | 3.00 | +1,200 | |
| Total | 1,600 | | $4,880 | |

| Learning Objective | Example |
|---|---|
| **17.3**<br><br>Compute inventory by using the lower of cost or market value. | 3. Compute Redwood Stove Company's inventory value at the lower of cost or market value. |

| Description | Quantity | Cost | Market | Extension |
|---|---|---|---|---|
| Stoves | 20 | $277.50 | $350.50 | ________ |
| Piping | 60 | 34.50 | 27.00 | ________ |
| Hearths | 65 | 78.00 | 78.00 | ________ |
| Screens | 105 | 105.00 | 125.00 | ________ |
| Tool Sets | 16 | 65.50 | 55.00 | ________ |
| Total | | | | ________ |

Answers: 1. 42,500; 26,000; 35,700; 23,670 2. Average cost, $915; FIFO, $900; LIFO, $920 3. $5,550; $1,620; $5,070; $11,025; $880; $24,145

# THE BOTTOM LINE

*Summary of chapter learning objectives:*

| Learning Objective | Example |
|---|---|
| **17.4**<br>Estimate inventory by using cost of goods sold. | 4. Redwood Stove Company has a markup of 50% of retail. Last year it had total sales of $400,000. It had a beginning inventory of $150,000 based on cost. It purchased merchandise for $180,000 during the year. Compute the ending inventory at cost. |
| **17.5**<br>Compute inventory turnover. | 5. Two years ago Redwood Stove Company used a markup of 65% of cost. That year's data are shown. Compute ending inventory, average inventory, and inventory turnover at retail.<br>Net sales $800,000 Purchases (cost) $600,000<br>Beginning inventory—retail 300,000 Inventory—retail (June 30) 440,000 |

Answers: 4. Inventory $130,000 5. Ending inventory at retail, $490,000; average inventory, $410,000; turnover, 1.95

SELF-CHECK

# Review Problems for Chapter 17

1 The D&D Company has 45 units on hand January 1. During the month, units in total 320 and units out total 285. What is the balance on hand January 31? ______________

2 According to physical count, Dawson Lumber had 3,250 units in inventory March 31. Dawson Lumber's beginning inventory and purchases for the first quarter were as follows:

| | | |
|---|---|---|
| Jan. 1 | Beginning Inventory | 2,500 units @ $25.00 |
| Jan. 15 | Purchased | 5,000 units @ $27.50 |
| Feb. 5 | Purchased | 6,000 units @ $26.25 |
| Mar. 10 | Purchased | 3,000 units @ $27.00 |

Calculate the value of the inventory March 31 and cost of goods sold for the quarter based on the average, FIFO, and LIFO costing methods.

| | Inventory Value | Cost of Goods Sold |
|---|---|---|
| **a.** Average cost: | ______________ | ______________ |
| **b.** FIFO cost: | ______________ | ______________ |
| **c.** LIFO cost: | ______________ | ______________ |

3 Lansky Company's inventory January 1 was valued at $41,000. During the first quarter, $365,000 of goods were purchased and sales totaled $550,000. Estimate the inventory March 31 if Lansky's markup is 40% based on selling price. ______________

4 Compute the average inventory, cost of goods sold, and turnover based on cost using the following data. Kelly Pet Supplies takes inventory every 6 months and had inventory of $35,000 on January 1, $42,600 on June 30, and $38,200 on December 31. Kelly's purchased goods totaling $275,000 during the year and had sales of $390,000.

**a.** Average inventory: ______________

**b.** Cost of goods sold: ______________

**c.** Turnover: ______________

**Answers to the Self-Check can be found in Appendix B at the back of the text.**

# Assignment 17.1: Inventory Cost

Name

Date Score

Learning Objectives 1 2 3

**A (40 points) Compute the extensions and totals. (1 point for each correct answer)**

**1.** The inventory of Michelle's Clock Shop shows the following items, at both cost and market prices. Determine the total value of the inventory at the lower of cost or market price for each item.

| Description | Quantity | Unit Cost Price | Unit Market Price | Extension at Lower of Cost or Market |
|---|---|---|---|---|
| Quartz clock and pen set | 20 | $36.00 | $34.80 | |
| Travel alarm clock | 35 | 15.60 | 19.20 | |
| Ultrasonic travel clock | 24 | 23.00 | 23.70 | |
| Digital alarm clock | 42 | 19.80 | 18.60 | |
| AM/FM clock radio | 60 | 21.00 | 21.00 | |
| Digital clock radio | 12 | 54.00 | 57.50 | |
| Total | | | | |

**2.** A retail furniture dealer counted the following goods in inventory on December 31. An accountant recommended that the inventory items be valued at the lower of cost or market price. Compute the total value of the inventory based on the lower of cost or market price.

| Article | Quantity | Unit Cost Price | Extension at Cost | Unit Market Price | Extension at Market | Inventory Value at Lower of Cost or Market |
|---|---|---|---|---|---|---|
| Armchairs, wood | 24 | $60.00 | | $ 68.50 | | |
| Armchairs, tapestry | 6 | 85.00 | | 105.00 | | |
| Armchairs, Windsor | 12 | 90.00 | | 85.00 | | |
| Beds, bunk | 8 | 85.00 | | 75.00 | | |
| Bedroom suites | 3 | 297.50 | | 410.00 | | |
| Tables, coffee | 30 | 63.00 | | 62.00 | | |
| Chairs, kitchen | 24 | 23.00 | | 32.00 | | |
| Dining tables | 8 | 117.40 | | 95.70 | | |
| Dining suites | 5 | 288.80 | | 395.00 | | |
| Sofa sets | 9 | 330.00 | | 325.00 | | |
| Total | | | | | | |

Score for A (40)

**B (60 points) Compute the value of ending inventory. (10 points for each correct answer)**

**3.** Garcia Manufacturing Company made purchases of a material as shown in the following listing. The inventory at the end of the year was 3,500 units. Compute the value of the inventory by each of the three methods: (a) average cost; (b) first-in, first-out; and (c) last-in, first-out.

| Date | Units | Unit Cost | Total Cost |
|---|---|---|---|
| Jan. 5 | 3,600 | $6.20 | $ 22,320 |
| Mar. 11 | 3,000 | 5.80 | 17,400 |
| May 14 | 5,300 | 6.00 | 31,800 |
| July 8 | 1,600 | 6.30 | 10,080 |
| Sept. 7 | 4,000 | 6.20 | 24,800 |
| Nov. 10 | +2,500 | 6.40 | +16,000 |
| Total | 20,000 | | $122,400 |

**a.** Average cost: __________

**b.** First-in, first-out: __________

**c.** Last-in, first-out: __________

**4.** The Willand Company had 320 units on hand at the beginning of the year, with a unit cost of $4.20. The number of units purchased and the unit cost and the number of units sold during the year are shown. What would be the value of the ending inventory of 380 units based on the (a) average cost; (b) first-in, first-out; and (c) last-in, first-out costing methods?

| Date | Units Purchased | Unit Cost | Units Sold | Units on Hand |
|---|---|---|---|---|
| Jan. 1 | | $4.20 | | 320 |
| Feb. 2 | | | 190 | 130 |
| Apr. 16 | 200 | $4.32 | | 330 |
| June 10 | 300 | $4.40 | | 630 |
| Aug. 5 | | | 280 | 350 |
| Oct. 12 | 250 | $4.48 | | 600 |
| Nov. 27 | | | 220 | 380 |

**a.** Average cost: __________

**b.** First-in, first-out: __________

**c.** Last-in, first-out: __________

__________

Score for B (60)

# Assignment 17.2: Inventory Estimating and Turnover

Name

Date Score

Learning Objectives 4 5

**A (50 points) Solve the following problems. (2 points for each correct answer)**

**1.** Fill in the blanks in each of the following calculations with the correct amount. Use the formulas

Beginning inventory + Purchases = Goods available for sale

Goods available for sale − Cost of goods sold = Ending inventory

| | Store A | Store B | Store C | Store D | Store E |
|---|---|---|---|---|---|
| Beginning inventory | $ 80,000 | ______ | $ 37,000 | ______ | $42,000 |
| Purchases | ______ | 90,000 | ______ | 21,000 | ______ |
| Goods available for sale | 200,000 | 210,000 | 109,000 | 117,000 | 135,000 |
| Less cost of goods sold | 125,000 | 128,000 | ______ | 30,000 | 74,000 |
| Ending inventory | ______ | ______ | $ 23,000 | ______ | ______ |

**2.** Each of the five stores in problem 1 had the net sales shown. What was the average percent of markup, based on cost, for each of the five stores? What was the average percent of markup, based on selling price, for each of the five stores?

| | Store A | Store B | Store C | Store D | Store E |
|---|---|---|---|---|---|
| Net sales | $200,000 | $150,000 | $172,000 | $40,000 | $100,000 |
| Markup—cost | ______ | ______ | ______ | ______ | ______ |
| Markup—selling price | ______ | ______ | ______ | ______ | ______ |

**3.** The Country Kitchen takes inventory at retail sales price every 3 months. Its inventory at the beginning of last year was $68,500; at 3 months, $55,500; at 6 months, $69,000; at 9 months, $70,000; and at the end of the year, $44,000. Net sales for the year were $352,000.

**a.** What was the average inventory? __________

**b.** What was the turnover? __________

**4.** Steve's Auto Shop began the year with an inventory of $33,500. Purchases during the year totaled $194,200. The inventory at the end of the year was $36,400.

**a.** What was the cost of goods sold? __________

**b.** What was the average inventory? __________

**c.** What was the turnover? __________

__________

Score for A (50)

**B** **(50 points) Solve the following problems. (Points for each correct answer as marked)**

**5.** Jackson Wholesalers' records showed these figures:

| | Cost | Retail Price | | |
|---|---|---|---|---|
| Beginning inventory | $19,793 | $32,990 | Net sales for the year | $61,450 |
| Purchases for the year | $47,200 | $78,665 | Markup based on sales | 40% |

Compute the ending inventory:

**a.** At cost (2 1/2 points): __________

**b.** At retail price (2 1/2 points): __________

**6.** The JM Clothing store kept all merchandise records in terms of selling price. On July 1, the JM books showed the following information:

| | |
|---|---|
| Beginning inventory, January 1: | $23,500 |
| 6-month purchases: | 99,000 |
| 6-month net sales: | 87,800 |

What was the estimated ending inventory on July 1? (5 points) ________

**7.** The Kid's Land Clothing Store kept all purchase and inventory records on a cost basis. The owner marked up all goods at 40.0% of the cost price. On July 1, the Kid's Land books showed the following information:

| | |
|---|---|
| Beginning inventory, January 1: | $1,126,000 |
| 6-month purchases: | 2,221,400 |
| 6-month net sales: | 2,508,200 |

What was the estimated inventory, at cost, on July 1? (5 points) ________

**8.** Amy's Art Shop kept all inventory and sales records on the basis of retail prices. It recorded purchases at cost and marked up its merchandise at 120% of cost. On January 1, its inventory of art was $260,000. During the year, its purchases were $300,000 and net sales were $730,000. What was its ending inventory? (5 points) ________

**9.** From the information given, calculate the estimated cost of goods sold and ending inventory. Round to the nearest dollar. (1 point for each correct answer)

| | Cost of Goods Available for Sale | Net Sales | Markup Based on Cost | Markup Based on Sales | Estimated Cost of Goods Sold | Estimated Ending Inventory |
|---|---|---|---|---|---|---|
| a. | $204,000 | $260,000 | 30% | | ______ | ______ |
| b. | 268,000 | 260,000 | | 30% | ______ | ______ |
| c. | 444,000 | 350,000 | | 27% | ______ | ______ |
| d. | 444,000 | 350,000 | 27% | | ______ | ______ |
| e. | 37,500 | 36,000 | 50% | | ______ | ______ |
| f. | 368,000 | 400,000 | | 60% | ______ | ______ |
| g. | 420,000 | 600,000 | | 40% | ______ | ______ |
| h. | 440,000 | 360,000 | 15% | | ______ | ______ |
| i. | 125,000 | 180,000 | 60% | | ______ | ______ |
| j. | 130,000 | 200,000 | 100% | | ______ | ______ |

**10.** Maurice Company sells hair products. From the following inventory record sheets for Baby Soft Shampoo, determine the total units in, total amount, and the value of the ending inventory of 300 bottles based on average cost, FIFO, and LIFO. (2 points for each correct answer)

| Date | Units In | Cost | Amount |
|---|---|---|---|
| 1/11 | 400 | $3.40 | $1,360 |
| 1/23 | 50 | 3.00 | 150 |
| 2/10 | 100 | 3.20 | 320 |
| 2/20 | 200 | 3.30 | 660 |
| 2/25 | +80 | 3.50 | +280 |
| | ______ | | ______ |

Average cost: ______

FIFO: ______

LIFO: ______

______

Score for B (50)

# Depreciation 18

## Learning Objectives

By studying this chapter and completing all assignments, you will be able to:

Learning Objective 1 — Compute depreciation using the straight-line method.

Learning Objective 2 — Compute depreciation using the units-of-production method.

Learning Objective 3 — Compute depreciation using the declining-balance method.

Learning Objective 4 — Compute depreciation using the sum-of-the-years-digits method.

Learning Objective 5 — Compute depreciation for income tax purposes using the Modified Accelerated Cost Recovery System (MACRS).

Learning Objective 6 — Compute partial-year depreciation using the five different primary depreciation methods covered.

**Depreciation** is the decrease in the value of assets owned by a business, such as automobiles, buildings, and computers. Depreciation is caused by wear or by **obsolescence** (becoming out-of-date). In the toy manufacturing industry, some dies and tools last only 1 or 2 years because of changing fads. An automobile will wear out after a number of years or miles of use. Buildings lose value as wood, electrical wiring, and fixtures deteriorate and as design characteristics and owners' needs change. A business computer frequently becomes obsolete in 3 to 5 years.

In business, depreciation is figured on almost all physical assets owned and in use. Depreciation is deducted from gross profits as an expense. In this chapter, we present five common methods of calculating depreciation: the straight-line, units-of-production, declining-balance, sum-of-the-years-digits, and Modified Accelerated Cost Recovery System methods.

# Computing Depreciation with the Straight-Line Method

Learning Objective 1

Compute depreciation using the straight-line method.

The **straight-line (SL) method** of determining depreciation is the easiest method. It distributes depreciation evenly over the useful life of an asset, assigning equal amounts to designated units (miles, number of items made, etc.) or periods (usually months or years). It is based on the assumption that wear and obsolescence occur evenly over the life of the property. The three factors used to compute depreciation by the straight-line method are

1. The **original cost,** which includes the price paid for an item and any freight charges and expenses for installation. Cost includes anything necessary to get the asset to where it is to be used and in a condition to be used.
2. The **estimated service life,** which is the length of time the buyer expects to be able to use an asset. The estimated service life may be stated in terms of years or months that normally may be expected during the life of the asset.
3. The estimated **scrap value (SV),** which is the amount the owner of an asset expects to receive upon disposing of it at the end of its estimated service life.

The basic formula for computing the amount of depreciation under the straight-line method is

(Original cost − Scrap value) ÷ Estimated service life in periods of time
= Depreciation amount for one unit or period

**EXAMPLE A**

An office computer costing $12,500 has an estimated life of 5 years and an estimated scrap value of $900. What is the annual depreciation amount?

$12,500 cost − $900 SV = $11,600 estimated total depreciation
$11,600 ÷ 5 estimated total years = $2,320 annual depreciation

# Computing Depreciation with the Units-of-Production Method

The **units-of-production method** of determining depreciation distributes depreciation based on how much the asset is used. It is usually expressed in miles driven, hours used, tons hauled, or units produced. Calculation is like that used in the straight-line method except that miles, hours, tons, or units are used rather than months or years. The basic formula for computing the amount of depreciation under the units-of-production method is

Learning Objective 2

Compute depreciation using the units-of-production method.

(Original cost − Scrap value) ÷ Estimated life in service units
= Depreciation amount for one unit

Example B shows depreciation of an asset based on the number of hours it is used. First you must find the hourly depreciation and then multiply it by the number of hours operated during a particular month or year.

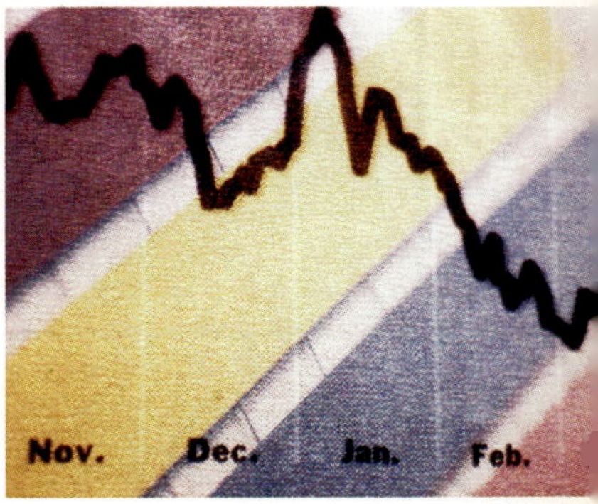


© RYAN MCVAY/PHOTODISC/GETTY IMAGES

**EXAMPLE B**

A machine costing \$10,000 has an estimated life of 60,000 hours of operation and an estimated scrap value of \$400. If it was operated for 2,800 hours during the first year, how much depreciation expense will be shown for the first year?

\$10,000 cost − \$400 SV = \$9,600 estimated total depreciation
\$9,600 ÷ 60,000 estimated total hours = \$0.16 hourly depreciation
2,800 hours operated × \$0.16 = \$448 first year's depreciation.

Example C shows depreciation in terms of the number of units that it will produce during its lifetime: Divide the number of units into the estimated total depreciation amount to get the depreciation per unit.

**EXAMPLE C**

A press that costs \$145,000 will produce an estimated 3,500,000 units in its life and has an estimated scrap value of \$5,000. If it produced 235,000 units this year, how much depreciation will be shown for the year?

\$145,000 cost − \$5,000 SV = \$140,000 estimated total depreciation
\$140,000 ÷ 3,500,000 estimated total units = \$0.04 depreciation per unit
235,000 units produced × \$0.04 = \$9,400 first year's depreciation

## BOOK VALUE

The **book value** of an asset is the original cost minus the **accumulated depreciation,** or the total of all depreciation to that time.

**EXAMPLE D**

At the end of the first year, the book value of the press in example C would be

\$145,000 cost − \$9,400 accumulated depreciation = \$135,600

The book value can be determined at any time in the life of an asset.

**EXAMPLE E**

At the end of the third year, the book value of the computer in example A would be computed as follows:

\$2,320 annual depreciation × 3 years = \$6,960 accumulated depreciation
\$12,500 cost − \$6,960 = \$5,540.

**CONCEPT CHECK 18.1**

On January 1, Oakdale Appliances bought a new delivery truck for \$48,000. Oakdale's accountant estimated a truck life of 200,000 miles and a scrap (trade-in) value of \$4,000. In the first year, the truck was driven 38,000 miles; in the second year, it was driven 46,000 miles. Compute the depreciation and book value for the first 2 years.

\$48,000 cost − \$4,000 SV = \$44,000 estimated total depreciation
\$44,000 ÷ 200,000 miles = \$0.22 depreciation per mile

Year 1: 38,000 miles × \$0.22 per mile = \$8,360 depreciation
\$48,000 cost − \$8,360 = \$39,640 book value

Year 2: 46,000 miles × \$0.22 per mile = \$10,120 depreciation
\$39,640 year 1 book value − \$10,120 = \$29,520 new book value
or
\$48,000 cost − (\$8,360 + \$10,120) accumulated depreciation = \$29,520 book value

# Computing Depreciation with the Declining-Balance Method

**Learning Objective 3**

Compute depreciation using the declining-balance method.

The **declining-balance (DB) method** is based on the theory that depreciation is greatest in the first year and less in each succeeding year.

**STEPS to Compute Depreciation, Using the DB Method**

1. Divide 100% by the estimated years of useful life to determine the **basic depreciation rate**.
2. Multiply the basic depreciation rate by 2 **(double-declining-balance)** or by 1.5 **(150%-declining-balance)** to determine the **declining-balance depreciation rate.**
3. Multiply the declining-balance depreciation rate by the book value of the asset at the beginning of the year to determine the depreciation amount for that year. (For the first year, the book value at the beginning of the year equals the asset cost. Do not subtract the scrap value.)

Step 3 is repeated each year, using the new (declined) book value (last year's beginning book value minus last year's depreciation amount). The same rate is used each year. The declining-balance rate continues to apply until the scrap value is reached. The item may not be depreciated below its scrap value.

## EXAMPLE F

Use the declining-balance method with an annual double-declining balance to depreciate the office computer in example A.

STEP 1 $100\% \div 5 \text{ years} = 20\%$

STEP 2 $20\% \times 2 = 40\%$ annual double-declining-balance rate.

| Year | | Beginning Book Value | Rate | STEP 3 Depreciation |
|---|---|---|---|---|
| 1 | | $12,500 | ×40% = | $5,000 |
| 2 | $12,500 − $5,000 = | 7,500 | ×40% = | 3,000 |
| 3 | 7,500 − 3,000 = | 4,500 | ×40% = | 1,800 |
| 4 | 4,500 − 1,800 = | 2,700 | ×40% = | 1,080 |
| 5 | 2,700 − 1,080 = | 1,620 | ×40% = | 648 |
| 6 | 1,620 − 648 = | 972 | ×40% = | 388.80 $72* |

*As book value ($972) is larger than estimated scrap value ($900), there is some depreciation in the sixth year. However, the calculated depreciation ($388.80) is greater than book value minus scrap value ($972 − $900 = $72). Thus, depreciation is limited to the smaller amount, $72.

## CONCEPT CHECK 18.2

On January 1, Oakdale Appliances bought a new delivery truck for $60,000. Oakdale's accountant estimated a truck life of 4 years and a scrap value of $6,000. Compute the depreciation for the first 2 years using the 150%-declining-balance method.

$60,000 cost

$100\% \div 4 \text{ years} = 25\%$

$25\% \times 1.5 = 37.5\%$ annual 150%-declining-balance rate

Year 1: $60,000 × 37.5% = $22,500 depreciation

$60,000 − $22,500 = $37,500 book value

Year 2: $37,500 × 37.5% = $14,062.50 depreciation

# Computing Depreciation with the Sum-of-the-Years-Digits Method

Learning Objective **4**

Compute depreciation using the sum-of-the-years-digits method.

The **sum-of-the-years-digits (SYD) method** also is used to compute a greater depreciation amount in the earlier years of an asset's life. The book value decreases more slowly than under the declining-balance method. This method's name comes from the calculation done in Step 1.

**STEPS to Compute Depreciation Using the SYD method**

1. Compute the sum of all the year's digits in the estimated life of the asset. Use this shortcut formula:

   $$\frac{(n + 1) \times n}{2},$$

   where $n$ = number of years in the estimated life.
2. Determine the current year's depreciation fraction by using this formula: Estimated years of life remaining at the beginning of the current year ÷ Sum of all digits from Step 1.
3. Multiply the total depreciation amount (Cost − SV) of the asset by the depreciation fraction from Step 2 to determine depreciation for the current year.

Note that each year a new depreciation fraction from Step 2 is determined and Step 3 is repeated. The sum of all digits in Step 1 and the total depreciation amount in Step 3 are the same every year.

**EXAMPLE G**

Under the sum-of-the-years-digits method, the office computer in example A would be depreciated as follows:

STEP 1 $$\frac{(5 + 1) \times 5}{2} = 15 \text{ (or } 1 + 2 + 3 + 4 + 5 = 15\text{)}$$

| Year | STEP 2<br>Fraction | | Depreciation<br>Total Amount | | STEP 3<br>Depreciation |
|---|---|---|---|---|---|
| 1 | $\frac{5}{15}$ | × | \$11,600 | = | \$ 3,866.67 |
| 2 | $\frac{4}{15}$ | × | 11,600 | = | 3,093.33 |
| 3 | $\frac{3}{15}$ | × | 11,600 | = | 2,320.00 |
| 4 | $\frac{2}{15}$ | × | 11,600 | = | 1,546.67 |
| 5 | $\frac{1}{15}$ | × | 11,600 | = | + 773.33 |
| | | | | Total depreciation | \$11,600.00 |

## CONCEPT CHECK 18.3

On January 1, Oakdale Appliances bought a new delivery truck for $48,000. Oakdale's accountant estimated a truck life of 4 years and a scrap value of $4,000. Compute the depreciation for the first 2 years using the sum-of-the-years-digits method.

$48,000 cost − $4,000 SV = $44,000 to be depreciated

$$\frac{(4 + 1) \times 4}{2} = 10 \text{ (or } 1 + 2 + 3 + 4 = 10)$$

Year 1: $\frac{4}{10} \times \$44,000 = \$17,600$ depreciation

Year 2: $\frac{3}{10} \times \$44,000 = \$13,200$ depreciation

# Computing Depreciation with the Modified Accelerated Cost Recovery System

**Learning Objective 5**

Compute depreciation for income tax purposes using the Modified Accelerated Cost Recovery System (MACRS).

Businesses use the depreciation methods previously described for financial reporting. However, federal tax laws regulate how depreciation must be taken for income tax purposes. The IRS requires that the **Modified Accelerated Cost Recovery System (MACRS)** be used for depreciation of property purchased and put into service after 1986. MACRS "recovers" the entire cost of depreciable property over the allowable period. No scrap value is permitted.

For common business assets, MACRS provides depreciation periods of 3, 5, 7, 10, 15, and 20 years. Examples of assets from each of these categories are as follows:

*3 years:* Property with a life of 4 years or less—some types of equipment used for research and development, some machine tools, some tractors, and racehorses more than 2 years old when placed in service

*5 years:* Property with a life of 4 to 10 years—computers, automobiles and taxis, office machines, certain telephone equipment, and trucks and buses

*7 years:* Property with a life of 10 to 15 years—office furniture and fixtures, some agricultural and horticultural structures, and commercial airplanes

*10 years:* Property with a life of 16 to 19 years—tugboats, vessels, and barges

*15 years:* Property with a life of 20 to 24 years—this category usually contains certain municipal, public utility, and telephone distribution plants

*20 years:* Property with a life of 25 or more years—farm buildings and certain municipal infrastructure items such as sewers

Figure 18-1 shows IRS annual percentages used to compute depreciation by MACRS.

**Figure 18-1** **MACRS Depreciation Schedule**

| | Appropriate Percentage | | | | | |
|---|---|---|---|---|---|---|
| Year | 3-Year Class | 5-Year Class | 7-Year Class | 10-Year Class | 15-Year Class | 20-Year Class |
| 1 | 33.33 | 20.00 | 14.29 | 10.00 | 5.00 | 3.750 |
| 2 | 44.45 | 32.00 | 24.49 | 18.00 | 9.50 | 7.219 |
| 3 | 14.81 | 19.20 | 17.49 | 14.40 | 8.55 | 6.677 |
| 4 | 7.41 | 11.52 | 12.49 | 11.52 | 7.70 | 6.177 |
| 5 | | 11.52 | 8.93 | 9.22 | 6.93 | 5.713 |
| 6 | | 5.76 | 8.92 | 7.37 | 6.23 | 5.285 |
| 7 | | | 8.93 | 6.55 | 5.90 | 4.888 |
| 8 | | | 4.46 | 6.55 | 5.90 | 4.522 |
| 9 | | | | 6.56 | 5.91 | 4.462 |
| 10 | | | | 6.55 | 5.90 | 4.461 |
| 11 | | | | 3.28 | 5.91 | 4.462 |
| 12 | | | | | 5.90 | 4.461 |
| 13 | | | | | 5.91 | 4.462 |
| 14 | | | | | 5.90 | 4.461 |
| 15 | | | | | 5.91 | 4.462 |
| 16 | | | | | 2.95 | 4.461 |
| 17 | | | | | | 4.462 |
| 18 | | | | | | 4.461 |
| 19 | | | | | | 4.462 |
| 20 | | | | | | 4.461 |
| 21 | | | | | | 2.231 |

*Note:* The MACRS percentage for the first year is applicable to a partial or full year.

**EXAMPLE H**

Use the MACRS Depreciation Schedule shown in Figure 18-1 to depreciate the office computer in example A for tax purposes.

| Year | Rate (%) | Cost | Depreciation (Rounded) | Beginning Book Value | Current Depreciation | Ending Book Value |
|---|---|---|---|---|---|---|
| 1 | 20.00 | × $12,500 = | $2,500 | $12,500 | − $2,500 | = $10,000 |
| 2 | 32.00 | × 12,500 = | 4,000 | 10,000 | − 4,000 | = 6,000 |
| 3 | 19.20 | × 12,500 = | 2,400 | 6,000 | − 2,400 | = 3,600 |
| 4 | 11.52 | × 12,500 = | 1,440 | 3,600 | − 1,440 | = 2,160 |
| 5 | 11.52 | × 12,500 = | 1,440 | 2,160 | − 1,440 | = 720 |
| 6 | 5.76 | × 12,500 = | 720 | 720 | − 720 | = 0 |

## CONCEPT CHECK 18.4

On April 10, Oakdale Appliances bought a new delivery truck for $48,000. Compute the depreciation for the first year and for the second year using the MACRS table (5-year class).

MACRS depreciation first year: $\$48{,}000 \times 20.00\% = \$9{,}600$ (MACRS percentage for the first year is applicable to a partial or full year.)

MACRS depreciation second year: $\$48{,}000 \times 32.00\% = \$15{,}360$

# Computing Partial-Year Depreciation

**Learning Objective 6**

Compute partial-year depreciation using the five different primary depreciation methods covered.

Frequently, businesses are faced with the need to compute depreciation for only part of the year. Partial-year depreciation can be computed with any of the methods described in this chapter.

With the straight-line method, compute the depreciation amount for a partial year by dividing the annual depreciation amount by 12 and then multiplying that result by the number of months of use.

With the units-of-production method, simply multiply the number of units (miles or hours) used by the per-unit amount.

With the declining-balance method, find the current year's annual depreciation and then divide by 12; multiply that result by the number of months of use.

With the sum-of-the-years-digits method, first consider the overlapping years. To find the annual depreciation for the first partial year, divide by 12 and multiply the result by the number of months of use. From then on, every year will include the remaining fraction of the prior year's depreciation and the partial-year depreciation for the remainder of the current year.

MACRS tables automatically consider partial-year depreciation for the first and last years regardless of the date the item was placed in service.

**EXAMPLE I**

Office furniture costing $18,000 and put in use on May 1 is expected to have a useful life of 10 years. Its estimated resale value is $1,500. Using each of the four appropriate methods, compute the depreciation expense for May 1 through December 31 of the first tax year and all 12 months of the second year.

| Method | Year | Calculation (rounded to the nearest dollar) |
|---|---|---|
| SL | 1st | $(\$18{,}000 - \$1{,}500) \div 10 \times \frac{8}{12} = \$1{,}100$ |
| | 2nd | $(\$18{,}000 - \$1{,}500) \div 10 = \$1{,}650$ |
| DB (200%) | 1st | $\left(\frac{100\%}{10}\right) \times 2 \times \$18{,}000 \times \frac{8}{12} = \$2{,}400$ |
| | 2nd | $(\$18{,}000 - \$2{,}400) \times 20\% = \$3{,}120$ |

| Method | Year | Calculation (rounded to the nearest dollar) |
|---|---|---|
| SYD | 1st | $\frac{(10 + 1) \times 10}{2} = 55$ |
| | | $(\$18{,}000 - \$1{,}500) \times \frac{10}{55} \times \frac{8}{12} = \$2{,}000$ |
| | 2nd | $(\$18{,}000 - \$1{,}500) \times \frac{10}{55} \times \frac{4}{12} = \$1{,}000$ } \$2,800 |
| | | $(\$18{,}000 - \$1{,}500) \times \frac{9}{55} \times \frac{8}{12} = \$1{,}800$ |
| MACRS | 1st | $\$18{,}000 \times 14.29\% = \$2{,}572.20$ |
| (7-year class) | 2nd | $\$18{,}000 \times 24.49\% = \$4{,}408.20$ |

## CONCEPT CHECK 18.5

In October, Oakdale Appliances bought a new mid-size van for \$34,000. It had an estimated scrap value of \$4,000 and a useful life of 5 years. Compute the depreciation expense for the 3 months of the first year and for the full second year, using the 150%-declining-balance and the sum-of-the-years-digits methods.

\$34,000 cost − \$4,000 scrap value = \$30,000 to be depreciated

**Declining Balance**

$100\% \div 5 \text{ years} \times 1.5 = 30\%$

$30\% \times \$34{,}000 = \$10{,}200$

Year 1: $\$10{,}200 \times \frac{3}{12} = \$2{,}550$ (3 months)

Year 2: $(\$34{,}000 - \$2{,}550) \times 30\% = \$9{,}435$ (full year)

**Sum of the Years Digits**

$\frac{(5 + 1) \times 5}{2} = 15$ (or $1 + 2 + 3 + 4 + 5 = 15$)

$\frac{5}{15} \times \$30{,}000 = \$10{,}000$

Year 1: $\$10{,}000 \times \frac{3}{12} = \$2{,}500$ (3 months)

Year 2: $\$10{,}000 \times \frac{9}{12} = \$7{,}500$ (9 months)

$\frac{4}{15} \times \$30{,}000 = \$8{,}000$

$\$8{,}000 \times \frac{3}{12} = \$2{,}000$ (3 months)

$\$7{,}500 + \$2{,}000 = \$9{,}500$ in year 2

COMPLETE ASSIGNMENTS 18.1 AND 18.2.

## Chapter Terms for Review

- accumulated depreciation
- basic depreciation rate
- book value
- declining-balance (DB) method
- declining-balance depreciation rate
- depreciation
- double-declining-balance
- estimated service life
- Modified Accelerated Cost Recovery System (MACRS)
- obsolescence
- 150%-declining-balance
- original cost
- scrap value (SV)
- straight-line (SL) method
- sum-of-the-years-digits (SYD) method
- units-of-production method

# THE BOTTOM LINE

*Review of chapter learning objectives:*

| Learning Objective | Example |
|---|---|
| **18.1**<br>Compute depreciation using the straight-line method. | 1. On January 1, 2008, the local Pepsi-Cola bottling franchise purchased a bottling machine for $320,000. Freight was added for $12,000. The cost of installation was $68,000. It was estimated that the machine had a useful life span of five years, after which there would be no resale value. Using the straight-line method, determine the annual amount of depreciation. |
| **18.2**<br>Compute depreciation using the units-of-production method. | 2. The Yellow Cab Company bought a new taxi for $42,000 and estimated its useful life to be 200,000 miles, after which it would have a scrap value of $2,000. Compute the depreciation for the first 7 months if the vehicle had been driven 37,600 miles. |
| **18.3**<br>Compute depreciation using the declining-balance method. | 3. For $56,000, a Gap clothing store bought display racks with an estimated life of 20 years and a scrap value of $4,000. After 3 years, this store closed and sold the display racks for $32,000. If the racks were depreciated by the declining-balance method (150% annual rate), how much less than the book value did the company receive? Round to the nearest dollar. |
| **18.4**<br>Compute depreciation using the sum-of-the-years-digits method. | 4. A local Ford dealership purchased, for $60,000, a hydraulic lift unit with an estimated life of 7 years and a scrap value of $4,000. Compute the depreciation for each of the first 2 years using the sum-of-the-digits method. Round to the nearest dollar. |
| **18.5**<br>Compute depreciation for income tax purposes, using the Modified Accelerated Cost Recovery System (MACRS). | 5. Bank One bought new calculators in July for $12,000. Using the MACRS method (5-year class), show the rate, depreciation, and ending book value for the first 2 years. |
| **18.6**<br>Compute partial-year depreciation using the five different primary depreciation methods covered. | 6. On October 1, 2008, Corner Grocery bought and installed a new cash register for $1,400. It has an estimated service life of 6 years and an estimated scrap value of $200. The company decided to use the straight-line method of depreciation. What was the depreciation for 2008? What was it for 2009? |

Answers: 1. $80,000 2. $7,520 3. $12,321 4. First year: $14,000; Second year: $12,000 5. First year: 20.00% rate, $2,400 depreciation, $9,600 EBV; Second year: 32.00% rate, $3,840 depreciation, $5,760 EBV 6. 2008: $50; 2009: $200

# Review Problems for Chapter 18

1. Determine the annual declining-balance depreciation rate to be used for each of the following:

   **a.** 150% declining balance, 12-year life __________

   **b.** 200% declining balance, 8-year life __________

   **c.** 125% declining balance, 5-year life __________

   **d.** 200% declining balance, 5-year life __________

2. What fraction is to be used each year for sum-of-the-years-digits depreciation for an asset with a useful life of 4 years? __________

3. For which depreciation method(s) is salvage value *not* subtracted to calculate depreciation? __________

4. Lopez Construction Company purchased construction equipment for $116,000 at the beginning of the year. It is estimated that the equipment will have a useful life of 12 years and will have a scrap value of $8,000.

   **a.** Calculate the annual depreciation if Lopez uses straight-line depreciation. __________

   **b.** Calculate the book value of the equipment at the end of 5 years, assuming that Lopez uses straight-line depreciation. __________

   **c.** Compute the depreciation for the first year ending December 31 if Lopez purchased the equipment September 1. __________

   **d.** Determine the depreciation per hour if Lopez uses the straight-line method based on 120,000 hours of useful life and an $8,000 scrap value. __________

   **e.** Using the rate determined in (d), what is the depreciation for the year if the equipment is used for 2,360 hours? __________

5. Jurgenson Manufacturing uses the double-declining-balance method of depreciation. A piece of equipment costing $37,500 has an estimated useful life of 5 years and an estimated scrap value of $2,700.

   **a.** Compute the amount of depreciation taken in the second year. __________

   **b.** What is the book value at the end of the second year? __________

6. Young Manufacturing uses the sum-of-the-years-digits method of depreciation. Equipment costing $37,500 has an estimated life of 5 years and an estimated scrap value of $2,700.

   **a.** Compute the amount of depreciation expense for the second year. __________

   **b.** What is the book value at the end of the second year? __________

7. Calculate the depreciation expense for tax purposes using MACRS for each asset. Use Figure 18-1 on page 370 to determine the proper life and rate for each asset. (Round to the nearest dollar.)

   **a.** Computer equipment purchased this year for $5,200. __________

   **b.** Office furniture purchased 2 years ago for $8,500. (This is the third year.) __________

**Answers to the Self-Check can be found in Appendix B at the back of the text.**

## Notes

# Assignment 18.1: Business Depreciation

Name ______________________

Date ______________ Score ______________

Learning Objectives 1 2 3 4

**A (30 points) Solve the following depreciation problems. (points for correct answers as marked)**

**1.** A pharmaceutical company has testing machines on which it estimates depreciation by the straight-line method. The following table shows cost, estimated life, years used, and scrap value for each machine. Find the annual depreciation, total depreciation, and book value after the indicated number of years of use. ($\frac{1}{2}$ point for each correct answer)

| | Original Cost | Estimated Life (years) | Years Used | Scrap Value | Annual Depreciation | Total Depreciation to Date | Book Value |
|---|---|---|---|---|---|---|---|
| **a.** | $30,000 | 10 | 8 | $3,000 | ________ | ________ | ________ |
| **b.** | 48,000 | 7 | 6 | $5,300 | ________ | ________ | ________ |
| **c.** | 84,000 | 8 | 5 | none | ________ | ________ | ________ |
| **d.** | 34,600 | 6 | 1 | $1,000 | ________ | ________ | ________ |

**2.** Ace Delivery Service bought two new trucks. The following table shows the cost, scrap value, estimated life (in miles), and mileage for the first year. Using the straight-line method based on mileage driven, compute the first year's depreciation and the book value at the end of the first year for each truck. (2 points for each correct depreciation amount and 1 point for each correct book value)

| | Original Cost | Scrap Value | Estimated Life (miles) | Mileage for First Year | Depreciation for First Year | Book Value after 1 Year |
|---|---|---|---|---|---|---|
| **a.** | $49,500 | $1,500 | 150,000 | 21,700 | ________ | ________ |
| **b.** | $23,000 | $ 600 | 80,000 | 9,500 | ________ | ________ |

**3.** Dole Fruit Company's equipment cost $214,000. Its useful life is estimated to be 15 years, and its scrap value is $4,000. The company uses straight-line depreciation. (2 points for each correct answer)

**a.** What is the annual depreciation? ________

**b.** What is the book value of the equipment at the end of 14 years? ________

**4.** Carlucci and sons purchased a machine for $13,645 at the beginning of the year. Additional costs included $250 freight and $175 for installation. It was estimated that the machine could be operated for 30,000 hours, after which its resale value would be $570. Determine the straight-line depreciation based on hours of operation and the book value at the end of each of the first 7 years. (1 point for each correct answer)

| Year | Hours of Operation | Depreciation | Book Value |
|---|---|---|---|
| 1 | 2,300 | ________ | ________ |
| 2 | 2,750 | ________ | ________ |
| 3 | 2,500 | ________ | ________ |
| 4 | 2,480 | ________ | ________ |
| 5 | 2,800 | ________ | ________ |
| 6 | 3,100 | ________ | ________ |
| 7 | 2,950 | ________ | ________ |

________

Score for A (30)

**B** **(56 points) Solve the following depreciation problems. Round dollar amounts to two decimal places. (points for correct answers as marked)**

**5.** Anderson Tool and Die Company owns a group of machines, the details of which are shown in the following table. Anderson uses the double-declining-balance method of calculating depreciation. Compute the depreciation for the specific years indicated. (2 points for each correct answer)

| | Original Cost | Estimated Life (years) | Scrap Value | Year | Depreciation | Year | Depreciation |
|---|---|---|---|---|---|---|---|
| **a.** | $32,000 | 16 | $1,200 | 1 | ________ | 3 | ________ |
| **b.** | $25,800 | 5 | $3,000 | 3 | ________ | 5 | ________ |
| **c.** | $ 8,000 | 4 | $ 300 | 2 | ________ | 3 | ________ |
| **d.** | $15,000 | 10 | — | 3 | ________ | 5 | ________ |
| **e.** | $12,600 | 8 | $1,200 | 2 | ________ | 4 | ________ |
| **f.** | $95,000 | 20 | — | 3 | ________ | 5 | ________ |

6. Machinery purchased from Telecom, Inc., by Blazedales cost $69,800. Depreciation was determined by the double-declining-balance method for an estimated life of 16 years. Compute the following:

a. Book value after 4 years (8 points): __________

b. Total depreciation after 6 years (4 points): __________

7. The Dugan Manufacturing Company bought an engine for $31,500. The engine had an estimated life of 20 years and a scrap value of $5,250. After 6 years, the company went out of business and sold the engine for $15,200. If the machine was depreciated by the double-declining-balance method, how much did the company lose on the sale (the difference between the book value and the selling price)? (20 points) __________

__________

Score for B (56)

**C (14 points) Solve the following depreciation problems. (1 point for each correct answer)**

**8.** The Western Salvage Service bought three trucks. The following table shows the cost, estimated life, and resale estimate for each truck. Use the sum-of-the-years-digits method to find each truck's depreciation for the first and second years of use. Round answers to the nearest dollar.

| | Original Cost | Estimated Life | Resale Estimate | Depreciation for First Year | Depreciation for Second Year |
|---|---|---|---|---|---|
| **a.** | $36,000 | 6 yr | $6,000 | ________ | ________ |
| **b.** | $48,000 | 5 yr | 8,000 | ________ | ________ |
| **c.** | $60,000 | 7 yr | 12,000 | ________ | ________ |

**9.** Use the information in problem 8b to compute the amount of depreciation for years 3–5.

Year 3: ________

Year 4: ________

Year 5: ________

**10.** Use the information in problem 8 to compute the amount of depreciation for each vehicle for the first 2 years using the straight-line method. Round to the nearest dollar.

**a.** ________ **b.** ________ **c.** ________

**11.** Which method of depreciation would give the smaller amount of write-off, and how much less would it be for the three vehicles for the first 2 years? ________ ________

________

Score for C (14)

# Assignment 18.2: Business Depreciation

______________________________
Name

______________________________
Date                    Score

Learning Objectives 1 4 5 6

**A (43 points) Solve the following depreciation problems. Round dollar amounts to two decimal places. (points for correct answers as marked)**

**1.** An architect bought drafting equipment for $7,500. Its estimated life was 6 years, and its scrap value was $300. At the end of 4 years, the equipment wears out and is sold for scrap for $225. (4 points for each correct answer)

**a.** By the straight-line method, how much difference is there between the book value and the cash value of the equipment on the date of the sale? __________

**b.** In April 2000, a computer and software costing $18,000 are purchased. Its estimated life is 5 years. What is the book value of the new computing equipment on December 31, 2001? Use MACRS. __________

**2.** E, F, and G were partners in a small textile company. They spent $54,000 for equipment that they agreed would last 8 years and have a resale value of 5% of cost. The three partners couldn't agree on the depreciation method to use. E was in favor of using the double-declining-balance system, F insisted on the 150%-declining-balance method, and G was sure that the sum-of-the-years-digits method would be better. Show the depreciation for the first 4 years for each method in the following table. At the end of 4 years, what would be the book value under each of the three methods? (2 points for each correct depreciation amount, 1 point for each correct total, and 1 point for the correct book value)

| Year | Double-DB | 150%-DB | SYD |
|---|---|---|---|
| 1 | __________ | __________ | __________ |
| 2 | __________ | __________ | __________ |
| 3 | __________ | __________ | __________ |
| 4 | __________ | __________ | __________ |
| Total | __________ | __________ | __________ |
| Book value | __________ | __________ | __________ |

**3.** Baxter Company owned assets that cost $240,000. Depreciation was figured at a straight-line rate of 6.5% per year. After 12 years, the company sold the assets for $150,000. How much greater was the selling price than the book value at the time of the sale? (5 points) __________

______________
Score for A (43)

**B (57 points) Solve the following depreciation problems. (points for correct answers as marked)**

**4.** On March 1, Jarvis Realty spent $16,000 for a new company car with an estimated life of 4 years and an estimated scrap value of $4,000. Jarvis Realty elected to use the straight-line method for depreciation. On the same date, Carter Realty bought an identical car at the same price and also estimated the car's life and scrap value to be 4 years and $4,000, respectively. Carter Realty, however, chose the sum-of-the-years-digits method for depreciation.

**a.** At the end of the first year (10 months of use) and second year, how much depreciation did each company calculate? (3 points for each correct answer)

| | | | | | |
|---|---|---|---|---|---|
| Jarvis: | Year 1 | ________ | Carter: | Year 1 | ________ |
| | Year 2 | ________ | | Year 2 | ________ |

**b.** At the end of the second year, which company had more recorded accumulated depreciation, and what was the difference in the amounts? (5 points) ____________________

**c.** True or false: At the end of the fourth year, Carter Realty will have recorded more accumulated depreciation than Jarvis Realty. Explain your answer. (4 points) ________

**5.** In May 2001, Jian & Ming bought a light-duty truck for $20,800. One year later, they bought an additional truck for $21,800. In June 2003, a third truck was purchased for $23,500. Use MACRS (5-year class) to determine the total allowable cost recovery for 2003. (12 points) ________

**6.** David Marcus purchased new office furniture July 15, 2008, for $28,100. Use MACRS (7-year class) to show the rate, depreciation, and beginning and ending book values for 2008, 2009, and 2010. Round to the nearest dollar. (2 points for each correct answer)

| Year | Rate | | Cost | | Depreciation | Beginning Book Value | Ending Book Value |
|---|---|---|---|---|---|---|---|
| 2008 | ________ | × | $28,100 | = | ________ | ________ | ________ |
| 2009 | ________ | × | $28,100 | = | ________ | ________ | ________ |
| 2010 | ________ | × | $28,100 | = | ________ | ________ | ________ |

________
Score for B (57)

# 19

# Financial Statements

## Learning Objectives

By studying this chapter and completing all assignments, you will be able to:

Learning Objective **1** Analyze balance sheets, comparing items and periods.

Learning Objective **2** Analyze income statements, comparing items and periods.

Learning Objective **3** Compute commonly used business operating ratios.

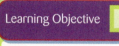

**Financial statements** provide information that allows owners, managers, and others interested in a business to evaluate its current condition and past operating results. Two important financial statements are the balance sheet and income statement. The **balance sheet** shows the current condition of a business at a definite point in time. It lists what a business owns **(assets)**, how much it owes **(liabilities)**, and the difference between the two **(net worth)**, usually referred to as owners' or shareholders' equity. The **income statement** shows the past operating results for a given period of time. It lists the revenues, the expenses, and the net income or loss for the period.

Financial statement data are typically analyzed three ways. The first, called *horizontal analysis*, is a comparison of data from year to year. This analysis shows the dollar amount of change and the percent of change for each item on the statement from one year to the next. The second, called *vertical analysis*, compares all other data on a statement with one figure for that same year. On the balance sheet, for example, each asset, liability, and equity amount is calculated as a percent of total assets (or total liabilities and owners' equity). The third type of analysis compares selected related data for the year such as current assets to current liabilities. These analyses are used by managers, owners, investors, creditors, and others to help them analyze data and make decisions concerning the business.

# Analyzing Balance Sheets

Learning Objective 1

Analyze balance sheets, comparing items and periods.

On a balance sheet, total assets must always equal total liabilities plus owners' or shareholders' equity. Balance sheets are analyzed to compare individual items with other items and with the same item on different dates, usually 1 year apart. Many businesses use the form of balance sheet illustrated in Figure 19-1.

**Figure 19-1** Balance Sheet

**THE SKI CHALET**

**Balance Sheet as of December 31, 2008 and 2007**

| | 2008 Amount | 2008 Percent | 2007 Amount | 2007 Percent | Increase/Decrease Amount | Increase/Decrease Percent |
|---|---|---|---|---|---|---|
| ASSETS | | | | | | |
| Current assets: | | | | | | |
| Cash | $ 90,000 | 12.64% | $ 86,000 | 13.15% | $ 4,000 | 4.65% |
| Accounts receivable | 134,000 | 18.82% | 98,000 | 14.98% | 36,000 | 36.73% |
| Notes receivable | 28,000 | 3.93% | 32,000 | 4.89% | (4,000) | −12.50% |
| Merchandise inventory | 180,000 | 25.28% | 148,000 | 22.63% | 32,000 | 21.62% |
| Total current assets | $432,000 | 60.67% | $364,000 | 55.66% | $ 68,000 | 18.68% |
| Fixed assets: | | | | | | |
| Equipment | $220,000 | 30.90% | $190,000 | 29.05% | $ 30,000 | 15.79% |
| Less depreciation | (60,000) | −8.43% | (50,000) | −7.65% | (10,000) | 20.00% |
| Equipment net | $160,000 | 22.47% | $140,000 | 21.41% | $ 20,000 | 14.29% |
| Buildings | 300,000 | 42.13% | 300,000 | 45.87% | — | 0.00% |
| Less depreciation | (180,000) | −25.28% | (150,000) | −22.94% | (30,000) | −20.00% |
| Buildings net | $120,000 | 16.85% | $150,000 | 22.94% | $(30,000) | −20.00% |
| Total fixed assets | $280,000 | 39.33% | $290,000 | 44.34% | $(10,000) | −3.45% |
| TOTAL ASSETS | $712,000 | 100.00% | $654,000 | 100.00% | $ 58,000 | 8.87% |

**Figure 19-1** **Balance Sheet *(continued)***

| | 2008 Amount | 2008 Percent | 2007 Amount | 2007 Percent | Increase/Decrease Amount | Increase/Decrease Percent |
|---|---|---|---|---|---|---|
| LIABILITIES AND SHAREHOLDERS' EQUITY | | | | | | |
| Current liabilities: | | | | | | |
| Accounts payable | $ 18,000 | 2.53% | $ 24,000 | 3.67% | $ (6,000) | −25.00% |
| Accrued payroll | 38,000 | 5.34% | 30,000 | 4.59% | 8,000 | 26.67% |
| Payroll taxes payable | 6,000 | 0.84% | 4,000 | 0.61% | 2,000 | 50.00% |
| Notes payable | 42,000 | 5.90% | 48,000 | 7.34% | (6,000) | −12.50% |
| Total current liabilities | $104,000 | 14.61% | $106,000 | 16.21% | $ (2,000) | −1.89% |
| Long-term liabilities: | | | | | | |
| Mortgage payable | $ 90,000 | 12.64% | $120,000 | 18.35% | $(30,000) | −25.00% |
| Notes payable (over 1 year) | 36,000 | 5.06% | 30,000 | 4.59% | 6,000 | 20.00% |
| Total long-term liabilities | $126,000 | 17.70% | $150,000 | 22.94% | $(24,000) | −16.00% |
| Total liabilities | $230,000 | 32.30% | $256,000 | 39.14% | $(26,000) | −10.16% |
| Shareholders' equity: | | | | | | |
| Common stock | $359,000 | 50.42% | $359,000 | 54.89% | — | 0.00% |
| Retained earnings | 123,000 | 17.28% | 39,000 | 5.96% | 84,000 | 215.38% |
| Total shareholders' equity | $482,000 | 67.70% | $398,000 | 60.86% | $ 84,000 | 21.11% |
| TOTAL LIABILITIES AND SHAREHOLDERS' EQUITY | $712,000 | 100.00% | $654,000 | 100.00% | $ 58,000 | 8.87% |

In Figure 19-1, the amounts for various items such as cash and accounts payable are compared to total assets and total liabilities and shareholders' equity. Also, the amounts for 2008 are compared to the corresponding amounts for 2007, and the amounts and percents of increase or decrease are shown. When two statements are compared, the earlier period, usually the prior year, is *always* used as the base. The changes in balance sheet items between two periods measure the growth or decline of the business.

© RYAN MCVAY/PHOTODISC/GETTY IMAGES

The first step in analyzing a balance sheet is to compute the percent each item is of the total assets or of the total liabilities and shareholders' equity (net worth). For example, the percent of cash for 2008 is calculated by dividing the amount of cash for 2008 by the total assets for 2008 and then converting the resulting decimal answer to a percent ($90,000 ÷ $712,000 = 0.1264 = 12.64%).

The second step is to compute the amount and percent of change between the two dates being compared. The amount of change in cash from 2007 to 2008 is calculated by subtracting the cash amounts for the two years ($90,000 − $86,000 = $4,000 increase). Increases are shown as positive numbers. Decreases, negative changes, are shown in parentheses. The percent of change in cash is calculated by dividing the amount of change by the prior year's amount ($4,000 ÷ $86,000 = 0.0465 = 4.65%).

Note three facts:

1. The totals for assets equal the totals for liabilities and shareholders' equity.
2. The percent listed for each item under assets is of the total assets; the percent listed for each item under liabilities and shareholders' equity is of the total liabilities and shareholders' equity.
3. The percent of increase or decrease between the two years is based on 2007, the *earlier* year.

## CONCEPT CHECK 19.1

In its next year, 2009, The Ski Chalet had total assets of $720,000, total liabilities of $245,000, cash of $123,000, and mortgage payable of $60,000. Determine the following amounts and percents:

a. What was its total shareholders' equity in 2009?
$720,000 − $245,000 = $475,000

b. What was its balance sheet percent of cash?
$123,000 ÷ $720,000 = 17.08%

c. What was its balance sheet percent of mortgage payable?
$60,000 ÷ $720,000 = 8.33%

d. What was its percent of increase in cash?
($123,000 − $90,000) ÷ $90,000 = 36.67%

e. What was its percent of decrease in mortgage payable?
($90,000 − $60,000) ÷ $90,000 = 33.33%

# Analyzing Income Statements

**Learning Objective 2**

Analyze income statements, comparing items and periods.

The income statement shows revenue, expenses, and the difference between the two, or net income. Income statements are analyzed by comparing all other statement items with the **net revenue,** which is total revenue less any returns and allowances. Net revenue (frequently called net sales) is always 100%. All other items on the income statement are reported as a percent of net revenue/sales. The resulting percents are extremely important for all businesspeople. They are compared to budgeted amounts, to percents for competing businesses, and to percents for past periods.

Figure 19-2 shows a typical income statement for 1 year, in which dollar amounts are converted to percents based on net sales. Percents are rounded to two decimal places, and dollar amounts are rounded to the nearest whole dollar. Cents are seldom used in reporting annual figures.

**Figure 19-2 Income Statement**

**THE SKI CHALET**
**Income Statement for Year Ended December 31, 2008**

| | 2008 Amount | 2008 Percent |
|---|---|---|
| Revenue from sales: | | |
| Sales | $988,900 | 101.43% |
| Less returns | 13,900 | 1.43% |
| NET SALES | $975,000 | 100.00% |

**Figure 19-2** **Income Statement (continued)**

| | 2008 Amount | 2008 Percent |
|---|---|---|
| Cost of goods sold: | | |
| Inventory, January 1 | $148,000 | 15.18% |
| Purchases | 440,000 | 45.13% |
| Available for sale | $588,000 | 60.31% |
| Inventory, December 31 | 180,000 | 18.46% |
| Cost of goods sold | $408,000 | 41.85% |
| Gross profit on sales | $567,000 | 58.15% |
| Operating expenses: | | |
| Salary and benefits | $290,000 | 29.74% |
| Rent and utilities | 62,000 | 6.36% |
| Advertising | 32,400 | 3.32% |
| Depreciation | 40,000 | 4.10% |
| Equipment and supplies | 15,800 | 1.62% |
| Administrative | 12,500 | 1.28% |
| Total operating expense | $452,700 | 46.43% |
| Income before tax | $114,300 | 11.72% |
| Income tax | 30,300 | 3.11% |
| NET INCOME | $ 84,000 | 8.62% |

Most businesses want to compare the operations of the current year with those of the preceding year. The statement shown in Figure 19-3 has information for both the current year and the preceding year. It also shows the amount and percent of increase or decrease from the preceding year.

**Figure 19-3** **Comparative Income Statement**

**THE SKI CHALET**

**Income Statement for the Years Ended December 31, 2008 and 2007**

| | 2008 Amount | 2008 Percent | 2007 Amount | 2007 Percent | Difference Amount | Difference Percent |
|---|---|---|---|---|---|---|
| Revenue from sales: | | | | | | |
| Sales | $988,900 | 101.43% | $850,000 | 104.81% | $138,900 | 16.34% |
| Less returns | 13,900 | 1.43% | 39,000 | 4.81% | (25,100) | −64.36% |
| NET SALES | $975,000 | 100.00% | $811,000 | 100.00% | $164,000 | 20.22% |
| Cost of goods sold: | | | | | | |
| Inventory, January 1 | $148,000 | 15.18% | $152,000 | 18.74% | $ (4,000) | −2.63% |
| Purchases | 440,000 | 45.13% | 379,000 | 46.73% | 61,000 | 16.09% |
| Available for sale | $588,000 | 60.31% | $531,000 | 65.47% | $ 57,000 | 10.73% |
| Inventory, December 31 | 180,000 | 18.46% | 148,000 | 18.25% | 32,000 | 21.62% |
| Cost of goods sold | $408,000 | 41.85% | $383,000 | 47.23% | $ 25,000 | 6.53% |
| Gross profit on sales | $567,000 | 58.15% | $428,000 | 52.77% | $139,000 | 32.48% |

**Figure 19-3** Comparative Income Statement (continued)

| | 2008 Amount | 2008 Percent | 2007 Amount | 2007 Percent | Difference Amount | Difference Percent |
|---|---|---|---|---|---|---|
| Operating expenses: | | | | | | |
| Salary and benefits | $290,000 | 29.74% | $242,000 | 29.84% | $ 48,000 | 19.83% |
| Rent and utilities | 62,000 | 6.36% | 61,400 | 7.57% | 600 | 0.98% |
| Advertising | 32,400 | 3.32% | 25,700 | 3.17% | 6,700 | 26.07% |
| Depreciation | 40,000 | 4.10% | 32,000 | 3.95% | 8,000 | 25.00% |
| Equipment and supplies | 15,800 | 1.62% | 10,300 | 1.27% | 5,500 | 53.40% |
| Administrative | 12,500 | 1.28% | 14,200 | 1.75% | (1,700) | −11.97% |
| Total operating expense | $452,700 | 46.43% | $385,600 | 47.55% | $ 67,100 | 17.40% |
| Income before tax | $114,300 | 11.72% | $42,400 | 5.23% | $ 71,900 | 169.58% |
| Income tax | 30,300 | 3.11% | 24,400 | 3.01% | 5,900 | 24.18% |
| NET INCOME | $ 84,000 | 8.62% | $18,000 | 2.22% | $ 66,000 | 366.67% |

Another analysis carried out by many businesses is a comparison between actual results and budgeted figures. Owners and managers note differences between budgeted and actual amounts and make adjustments where necessary. Most businesses and virtually all government entities use monthly and annual budgets to guide and monitor their operations. Figure 19-4 illustrates a monthly and year-to-date budget comparison at the end of June, the sixth month of the year.

To find the percent change, the budgeted amount is subtracted from the actual amount and the difference is divided by the *budgeted* amount.

**Figure 19-4** Monthly/Year-to-Date Budget Comparison

**THE SKI CHALET**

**Income Statement for the Month and the Six-Month Period Ended June 30, 2008**

| | June 2008 | | | | Six Months Year-to-Date | | | |
|---|---|---|---|---|---|---|---|---|
| | Budget | Actual | Amount Difference | Percent Difference | Budget | Actual | Amount Difference | Percent Difference |
| Revenue from sales: | | | | | | | | |
| Sales | $85,000 | $86,500 | $ 1,500 | 1.76% | $510,000 | $480,000 | $(30,000) | −5.88% |
| Sales returns | 5,000 | 3,500 | (1,500) | −30.00% | 10,000 | 6,000 | (4,000) | −40.00% |
| NET SALES | $80,000 | $83,000 | $ 3,000 | 3.75% | $500,000 | $474,000 | $(26,000) | −5.20% |
| Cost of goods sold | 35,000 | 38,000 | 3,000 | 8.57% | 225,000 | 230,000 | 5,000 | 2.22% |
| Gross profit | $45,000 | $45,000 | $ — | 0.00% | $275,000 | $244,000 | $(31,000) | −11.27% |
| Operating expenses | 31,000 | 39,000 | 8,000 | 25.81% | 185,000 | 196,000 | 11,000 | 5.95% |
| Income before tax | $14,000 | $ 6,000 | $(8,000) | −57.14% | $ 90,000 | $ 48,000 | $(42,000) | −46.67% |
| Income tax | 6,000 | 1,000 | (5,000) | −83.33% | 40,000 | 16,000 | (24,000) | −60.00% |
| NET INCOME | $ 8,000 | $ 5,000 | $(3,000) | −37.50% | $ 50,000 | $ 32,000 | $(18,000) | −36.00% |

## CONCEPT CHECK 19.2

In its next year, 2009, The Ski Chalet had total sales of $1,480,000, net sales of $1,320,000, gross profit of $710,000, and advertising expense of $45,000. In 2009, the company budgeted gross profit of $800,000. Determine the following amounts and percents:

a. Amount of sales returns in 2009
$1,480,000 − $1,320,000 = $160,000

b. Amount of cost of goods sold in 2009
$1,320,000 − $710,000 = $610,000

c. Percent of net sales increase from 2008 to 2009
($1,320,000 − $975,000) ÷ $975,000 = 35.38%

d. Percent of advertising expense in 2009
$45,000 ÷ $1,320,000 = 3.41%

e. Difference between percent gross profit and 2009 budgeted amount
($710,000 − $800,000) ÷ $800,000 = −11.25%

# Computing Business Operating Ratios

**Learning Objective 3**

Compute commonly used business operating ratios.

In addition to comparing dollar amounts and percents on financial statements, business managers and owners frequently want to study relationships between various items on their income statements and balance sheets. These relationships generally are expressed by ratios. A **ratio** is the relation of one amount to another. Thus the ratio of one dollar to one quarter, or $1 to $0.25, is a ratio of 4 to 1, or 4:1, showing that a dollar is 4 times the value of a quarter.

In analyzing financial statements, six important financial analysis ratios are commonly used: the working capital ratio, the acid test ratio, the ratio of accounts receivable to net sales, the inventory turnover rate, the relation of net income to net sales, and the rate of return on investment (equity).

## WORKING CAPITAL RATIO

Working capital and the working capital ratio come from the balance sheet. **Working capital** is the amount of current assets less current liabilities. It tells the amount of current assets that would remain if all the company's current liabilities were paid immediately. The **working capital ratio** shows the relationship between current assets and current liabilities. It calculates the amount of current assets per dollar of current liabilities. The working capital ratio helps the reader of the balance sheet understand how well the company is able to pay its current debts.

Working capital ratio = Total current assets ÷ Total current liabilities

**EXAMPLE A**

The working capital ratio for The Ski Chalet for 2008 from Figure 19-1 is

$432,000 ÷ $104,000 = 4.2 = 4.2:1

The ratio 4.2 to 1, or 4.2:1, means that the business has $4.20 in current assets to pay for each $1 in current liabilities.

## ACID TEST RATIO

The **acid test ratio** is used to determine the relationship between assets that can be quickly turned into cash and current liabilities. Usually, these assets are cash and accounts receivable. **Accounts receivable** are amounts owed to a business for services performed or goods delivered.

Acid test ratio = (Total of cash + Accounts receivable) ÷ Total current liabilities

**EXAMPLE B**

The acid test ratio for The Ski Chalet for 2008 from Figure 19-1 is computed as follows:

| | |
|---|---|
| Cash | $ 90,000 |
| Accounts receivable | +134,000 |
| Total cash and receivables | $224,000 |

$224,000 ÷ $104,000 = 2.2 = 2.2:1

## RATIO OF ACCOUNTS RECEIVABLE TO NET SALES

When businesses sell on credit, they need to be alert to the amount and quality of their accounts receivable. They need to compare the amount of their current receivables to the amounts for prior years and compare the extent of their receivables to those of similar companies. By computing the **ratio of accounts receivable to net sales** every year, management and investors can keep track of the percent of sales that have not yet been paid for by customers. An increasing ratio over the years can indicate problems with collecting payments and should be investigated.

Ratio of accounts receivable to net sales = Accounts receivable ÷ Net sales

**EXAMPLE C**

The Ski Chalet ratio for 2008 is

| Figure 19-1 | | Figure 19-3 |
|---|---|---|
| $134,000 | ÷ | $975,000 = 0.137 = 0.14:1 |

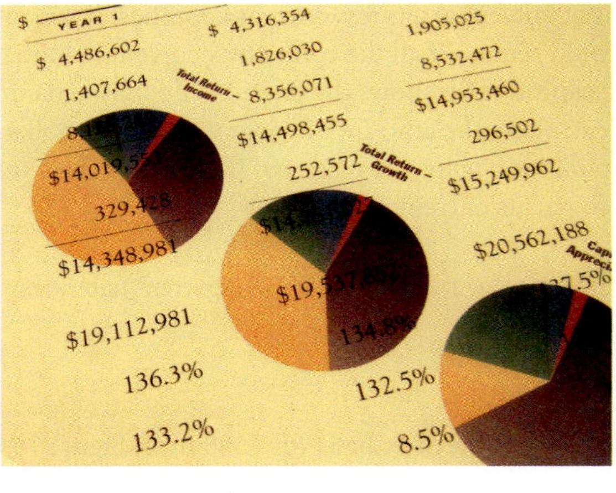


© BRAND X/GETTY IMAGES

## INVENTORY TURNOVER

In retail stores, the cost of inventory often is very high. One way to control inventory costs and increase profit is to maintain a high level of inventory turnover. Recall from Chapter 17 that *inventory turnover* lets management and others know the number of times average inventory is sold during the year. The higher the turnover number, the better is the movement of inventory. Recall also that *average inventory,* found by averaging monthly, quarterly, or yearly inventory amounts, must be computed first. Inventory turnover is given as the number of times instead of as a ratio to 1.

Average inventory = (Beginning inventory + Ending inventory) ÷ 2 (annual)
Inventory turnover = Cost of goods sold ÷ Average inventory

**EXAMPLE D**

Based on the information given in Figures 19-3 and 19-1, the 2008 inventory turnover for The Ski Chalet is found as follows:

| 01-Jan | | 31-Dec | |
|---|---|---|---|
| ($148,000 | + | $180,000) | ÷ 2 = $328,000 ÷ 2 = $164,000 average inventory |

$408,000 cost of merchandise sold ÷ $164,000 = 2.5 times inventory turnover rate

## RELATIONSHIP OF NET INCOME TO NET SALES

An increase in total sales volume doesn't necessarily mean that a business is improving because expenses may be increasing at an equal or greater rate than revenues. Thus, looking at the **relationship of net income to net sales** is important. The relationship is given as a percentage.

Relationship of net income to net sales = Net income ÷ Net sales

**EXAMPLE E**

Based on information from Figure 19-3, The Ski Chalet's 2008 relationship of net income to net sales is $84,000 ÷ $975,000 = 8.6%. Comparison with the relationship for 2007 of 2.2% ($18,000 ÷ $811,000) indicates an improvement.

## RATE OF RETURN ON INVESTMENT

Shareholders and owners want a reasonable return on their investment (equity). A ratio that measures the **rate of return on investment** is the ratio of net income to shareholders'/owners' equity. The rate is given as a percentage.

Rate of return on investment = Net income ÷ Shareholders'/owners' equity

**EXAMPLE F**

Based on Figures 19-3 and 19-1, the rate of return on the shareholders' investment for The Ski Chalet for 2008 is

$84,000 ÷ $482,000 = 0.1742 = 17.4% rate of return

## CONCEPT CHECK 19.3

Boswell Designs' financial statements showed the following:

| | | | | | |
|---|---|---|---|---|---|
| Cash | $ 85,000 | Current liabilities | $320,000 | Net sales | $950,000 |
| Accounts receivable | 260,000 | Total liabilities | 560,000 | Inventory 1/1/2008 | 240,000 |
| Total current assets | 580,000 | Net income | 80,000 | Inventory 12/31/2008 | 200,000 |
| Total assets | 990,000 | Shareholders' equity | 430,000 | Purchases for 2008 | 630,000 |

Using the above numbers, compute the following ratios:

a. Working capital ratio $580,000 ÷ $320,000 = 1.81:1

b. Acid test ratio ($85,000 + $260,000) ÷ $320,000 = 1.08:1

c. Average inventory ($240,000 + $200,000) ÷ 2 = $220,000

d. Inventory turnover $240,000 + $630,000 − $200,000 = $670,000
$670,000 ÷ $220,000 = 3.05 turnovers

e. Net income to net sales ratio $80,000 ÷ $950,000 = 0.084, or 8.4%

f. Rate of return on investment $80,000 ÷ $430,000 = 0.186, or 18.6%

COMPLETE ASSIGNMENTS 19.1, 19.2, AND 19.3.

## Chapter Terms for Review

accounts receivable

acid test ratio

assets

balance sheet

financial statements

income statement

liabilities

net revenue

net worth

rate of return on investment

ratio

ratio of accounts receivable to net sales

relationship of net income to net sales

working capital

working capital ratio

# THE BOTTOM LINE

*Summary of chapter learning objectives:*

| Learning Objective | Example |
|---|---|
| **19.1**<br><br>Analyze balance sheets, comparing items and periods. | 1. A modified balance sheet for The Ski Chalet for December 2008 and 2007 is shown. Compute the percents for 2008 and the percents of increase/decrease between 2008 and 2007. |

**THE SKI CHALET**
**Balance Sheet as of**
**December 31, 2008 and 2007**

| | 2008 Amount | 2008 Percent | 2007 Amount | 2007 Percent | Increase/Decrease Amount | Increase/Decrease Percent |
|---|---|---|---|---|---|---|
| ASSETS | | | | | | |
| Current assets: | | | | | | |
| Cash | $ 90,000 | ______ | $ 86,000 | 15.03% | $ 4,000 | ______ |
| Accounts receivable | 134,000 | ______ | 98,000 | 17.13% | 36,000 | ______ |
| Merchandise inventory | 180,000 | ______ | 148,000 | 25.87% | 32,000 | ______ |
| Total current assets | $404,000 | ______ | $332,000 | 58.04% | $ 72,000 | ______ |
| Fixed assets: | | | | | | |
| Equipment | $220,000 | ______ | $190,000 | 33.22% | $ 30,000 | ______ |
| Less depreciation | (60,000) | ______ | (50,000) | −8.74% | (10,000) | ______ |
| Equipment net | $160,000 | ______ | $140,000 | 24.48% | $ 20,000 | ______ |
| Buildings | 100,000 | ______ | 100,000 | 17.48% | — | ______ |
| Total fixed assets | $260,000 | ______ | $240,000 | 41.96% | $ 20,000 | ______ |
| TOTAL ASSETS | $664,000 | ______ | $572,000 | 100.00% | $ 92,000 | ______ |
| LIABILITIES AND SHAREHOLDERS' EQUITY | | | | | | |
| Current liabilities: | | | | | | |
| Accounts payable | $ 18,000 | ______ | $ 24,000 | 4.20% | $ (6,000) | ______ |
| Accrued payroll | 38,000 | ______ | 30,000 | 5.24% | 8,000 | ______ |
| Payroll taxes payable | 6,000 | ______ | 4,000 | 0.70% | 2,000 | ______ |
| Total current liabilities | $ 62,000 | ______ | $ 58,000 | 10.14% | $ 4,000 | ______ |
| Long-term liabilities: | | | | | | |
| Mortgage payable | 90,000 | ______ | 120,000 | 20.98% | (30,000) | ______ |
| Total liabilities | $152,000 | ______ | $178,000 | 31.12% | $(26,000) | ______ |
| Shareholders' equity: | | | | | | |
| Common stock | $359,000 | ______ | $359,000 | 62.76% | — | ______ |
| Retained earnings | 153,000 | ______ | 35,000 | 6.12% | 18,000 | ______ |
| Total shareholders' equity | $512,000 | ______ | $394,000 | 68.88% | $118,000 | ______ |
| TOTAL LIABILITIES AND SHAREHOLDERS' EQUITY | $664,000 | ______ | $572,000 | 100.00% | $ 92,000 | ______ |

Answers: 1. 2008 percent: 13.55%; 20.18%; 27.11%; 60.84%; 33.13%; −9.04%; 24.10%; 15.06%; 39.16%; 100.00%; 2.71%; 5.72%; 0.90%; 9.34%; 13.55%; 22.89%; 54.07%; 7.98%; 77.11%; 100.00%. Increase/decrease percent: 4.65%; 36.73%; 21.62%; 21.69%; 15.79%; 20.00%; 14.29%; 0%; 8.33%; 16.08%; −25.00%; 26.67%; 50.00%; 6.90%; −25.00%; −14.61%; 0%; 51.43%; 29.95%; 16.08%

# THE BOTTOM LINE

*Summary of chapter learning objectives:*

| Learning Objective | Example |
|---|---|
| **19.2**<br>Analyze income statements, comparing items and periods. | 2. A modified income statement for The Ski Chalet for the years 2008 and 2007 is shown. Compute the percents for 2008 and the percents of difference between 2008 and 2007. |

**THE SKI CHALET**

**Income Statement for the Years Ended December 31, 2008 and 2007**

| | 2008 Amount | 2008 Percent | 2007 Amount | 2007 Percent | Difference Amount | Difference Percent |
|---|---|---|---|---|---|---|
| Revenue from sales: | | | | | | |
| Sales | $ 988,900 | ______ | $ 850,000 | 104.81% | $138,900 | ______ |
| Less returns | 13,900 | ______ | 39,000 | 4.81% | (25,100) | ______ |
| NET SALES | $ 975,000 | ______ | $ 811,000 | 100.00% | $164,000 | ______ |
| Cost of goods sold: | | | | | | |
| Inventory, January 1 | $ 148,000 | ______ | $ 152,000 | 18.74% | $ (4,000) | ______ |
| Purchases | 440,000 | ______ | 379,000 | 46.73% | 61,000 | ______ |
| Available for sale | $ 588,000 | ______ | $ 531,000 | 65.47% | $ 57,000 | ______ |
| Inventory, December 31 | 180,000 | ______ | 148,000 | 18.25% | 32,000 | ______ |
| Cost of goods sold | $ 408,000 | ______ | $ 383,000 | 47.23% | $ 25,000 | ______ |
| Gross profit on sales | $(408,000) | ______ | $(383,000) | 52.77% | $(25,000) | ______ |
| Operating expenses: | | | | | | |
| Salary and benefits | $ 221,000 | ______ | $ 225,000 | 27.74% | $ (4,000) | ______ |
| Rent and utilities | 62,000 | ______ | 61,400 | 7.57% | 600 | ______ |
| Advertising | 32,400 | ______ | 25,700 | 3.17% | 6,700 | ______ |
| Depreciation | 40,000 | ______ | 32,000 | 3.95% | 8,000 | ______ |
| Equipment and supplies | 15,800 | ______ | 10,300 | 1.27% | 5,500 | ______ |
| Administrative | 12,500 | ______ | 14,200 | 1.75% | (1,700) | ______ |
| Total operating expense | $ 383,700 | ______ | $ 368,600 | 45.45% | $ 15,100 | ______ |
| Income before tax | $ 183,300 | ______ | $ 59,400 | 7.32% | $123,900 | ______ |
| Income tax | 30,300 | ______ | 24,400 | 3.01% | 5,900 | ______ |
| NET INCOME | $ 153,000 | ______ | $ 35,000 | 4.32% | $118,000 | ______ |

| Learning Objective | Example |
|---|---|
| **19.3**<br>Compute commonly used business operating ratios. | Using the Balance Sheet and Income Statement for 2008 from The Bottom Line problems 1 and 2, compute the following ratios:<br>3. Acid test<br>4. Average inventory<br>5. Net income to net sales<br>6. Rate of return on investment |

Answers: 2. 2008 percent: 101.43%; 1.43%; 100%; 15.18%; 45.13%; 60.31%; 18.46%; 41.85%; 58.15%; 22.67%; 6.36%; 3.32%; 4.10%; 1.62%; 1.28%; 39.35%; 18.80%; 3.11%; 15.69%. Difference percent: 16.34%; −64.36%; 20.22%; −2.63%; 16.09%; 10.73%; 21.62%; 6.53%; 32.48%; −1.78%; 0.98%; 26.07%; 25.00%; 53.40%; −11.97%; 4.10%; 208.59%; 24.18%; 337.14% 3. 3.61 4. $218,500 5. 15.7% 6. 29.9%

SELF-CHECK

# Review Problems for Chapter 19

1 Quality Construction Company, Inc., had total assets of $620,000 and total liabilities of $335,000 on December 31, 2008. On December 31, 2009, Quality Construction has total assets of $712,000 and total liabilities of $330,000.

**a.** What was the amount of the owners' equity as of December 31, 2008?

**b.** What is the amount of the owners' equity as of December 31, 2009?

**c.** Calculate the percent of increase or decrease in total assets, total liabilities, and owners' equity. (Round to two decimal places.)

2 Quality Construction Company, Inc., had net sales of $460,250 and cost of merchandise sold of $320,600. Compute the gross profit amount and the percent of gross profit based on net sales.

3 The comparative income statement of Benson Electronics, Inc., showed sales of $425,000 in 2007 and $494,450 in 2008. Compute the percent of change in sales. (Round answer to one decimal place.)

4 Calculate the percent of increase or decrease for each of the following balance sheet items. If any percent cannot be calculated, give a brief explanation. (Answers correct to two decimal places.)

| Item | 2009 | 2008 | Percent of Increase/Decrease |
|---|---|---|---|
| **a.** Cash | $35,000 | $30,000 | ____________ |
| **b.** Supplies | 1,200 | 1,600 | ____________ |
| **c.** Notes Receivable | 2,000 | 1,000 | ____________ |
| **d.** Merchandise Inventory | 16,500 | 16,500 | ____________ |
| **e.** Accounts Receivable | 1,000 | 1,500 | ____________ |

5 Selected figures from the Balance Sheet and the Income Statement of Multimedia, Inc., follow. Use the data to calculate the ratios listed. (Give answers accurate to two decimal places.)

| From the Balance Sheet | | From the Income Statement | |
|---|---|---|---|
| Cash | $210,734 | Net Sales | $244,750 |
| Accounts Receivable | $138,126 | Cost of Merchandise Sold | $190,000 |
| Merchandise Inventory: | | Net Income | $26,406 |
| End of this year | $184,500 | | |
| End of last year | $178,300 | | |
| Total Current Assets | $533,360 | | |
| Total Current Liabilities | $324,152 | | |
| Total Stockholders' Equity | $149,000 | | |

**a.** Working capital ratio ____________

**b.** Acid test ratio ____________

**c.** Inventory turnover ____________

**d.** Rate of return on investment ____________

**e.** Net income as a percent of sales ____________

**f.** Ratio of accounts receivable to net sales ____________

**Answers to the Self-Check can be found in Appendix B at the back of the text.**

## Notes

# Assignment 19.1: Balance Sheet Analysis

Name

Date Score

Learning Objective 1

**A** **(50 points) Solve the following balance sheet problems. (points for correct answers as marked)**

**1.** In the following balance sheet, find the percent for each 2008 and 2007 item. Then find the amount and percent of change. Round percents to two decimal places. (1/2 point for each correct answer)

**Milwaukee Manufacturing Corporation**
**Balance Sheet**
**As of December 31, 2008 and 2007**

| | 2008 Amount | 2008 Percent | 2007 Amount | 2007 Percent | Increase/Decrease Amount | Increase/Decrease Percent |
|---|---|---|---|---|---|---|
| ASSETS | | | | | | |
| Current assets: | | | | | | |
| Cash | $ 850,000 | | $ 750,000 | | | |
| Accounts receivable | 1,300,000 | | 1,050,000 | | | |
| Inventory | 780,000 | | 650,500 | | | |
| Total current assets | $2,930,000 | | $2,450,500 | | | |
| Fixed assets: | | | | | | |
| Machinery | $1,020,000 | | $ 970,000 | | | |
| (Less depreciation) | −360,000 | | −295,800 | | | |
| Machinery net | $ 660,000 | | $ 674,200 | | | |
| Building | 3,110,000 | | 3,000,000 | | | |
| Land parcel holdings | 500,000 | | 472,800 | | | |
| Total fixed assets | $4,270,000 | | $4,147,000 | | | |
| TOTAL ASSETS | $7,200,000 | | $6,597,500 | | | |
| LIABILITIES | | | | | | |
| Current liabilities: | | | | | | |
| Accounts payable | $ 38,000 | | $ 62,000 | | | |
| Accrued payroll | 110,030 | | 87,500 | | | |
| Payroll taxes payable | 23,600 | | 19,600 | | | |
| Total current liabilities | $ 171,630 | | $ 169,100 | | | |
| Long-term liabilities: | | | | | | |
| Mortgages payable | $1,750,300 | | $1,574,100 | | | |
| Notes payable long term | 180,000 | | 210,000 | | | |
| Total long-term liabilities | $1,930,300 | | $1,784,100 | | | |
| Total liabilities | $2,101,930 | | $1,953,200 | | | |
| Shareholders' equity: | | | | | | |
| Common stock | $4,500,000 | | $4,070,800 | | | |
| Preferred stock | 450,000 | | 440,000 | | | |
| Retained earnings | 148,070 | | 133,500 | | | |
| Total shareholders' equity | $5,098,070 | | $4,644,300 | | | |
| TOTAL LIABILITIES AND SHAREHOLDERS' EQUITY | $7,200,000 | | $6,597,500 | | | |

**2.** Milwaukee Manufacturing Corporation's bookkeeper overlooked the fact that, in 2008, $15,000 cash had been paid to employees but not deducted from the cash account. Assume that the balance sheet in problem 1 was adjusted to reflect the correction. (1 point for each correct answer)

**a.** What would be the adjusted amount for 2008 cash? ________

**b.** What would be the adjusted amount for 2008 accrued payroll? ________

Score for A (50)

**B (50 points) Solve the following balance sheet problems. (points for correct answers as marked)**

**3.** In the following balance sheet, find the percent for each 2008 and 2007 item. Then find the amount and percent of change. Round percents to one decimal place. Note that totals will sometimes be different from individual amounts because of rounding. (1/2 point for each correct answer)

**Stardoe Coffee Corporation**
**Balance Sheet**
**As of December 31, 2008 and 2007**

| | 2008 Amount | 2008 Percent | 2007 Amount | 2007 Percent | Increase/Decrease Amount | Increase/Decrease Percent |
|---|---|---|---|---|---|---|
| ASSETS | | | | | | |
| Current assets: | | | | | | |
| Cash | $ 7,800,778 | | $ 6,872,000 | | | |
| Accounts receivable | 1,307,777 | | 1,278,444 | | | |
| Inventory | 427,888 | | 350,000 | | | |
| Total current assets | $ 9,536,443 | | $ 8,500,444 | | | |
| Fixed assets: | | | | | | |
| Machinery | $ 1,737,130 | | $ 1,680,727 | | | |
| (Less depreciation) | −785,222 | | −690,455 | | | |
| Machinery net | $ 951,908 | | $ 990,272 | | | |
| Buildings | 4,770,385 | | 4,168,020 | | | |
| Land parcel holdings | 2,786,444 | | 2,786,400 | | | |
| Total fixed assets | $ 8,508,737 | | $ 7,944,692 | | | |
| TOTAL ASSETS | $18,045,180 | | $16,445,136 | | | |
| LIABILITIES | | | | | | |
| Current liabilities: | | | | | | |
| Accounts payable | $ 3,728,415 | | $ 4,073,888 | | | |
| Accrued payroll | 2,853,888 | | 2,278,222 | | | |
| Payroll taxes payable | 768,415 | | 694,732 | | | |
| Total current liabilities | $ 7,350,718 | | $ 7,046,842 | | | |
| Long-term liabilities: | | | | | | |
| Mortgages payable | $ 3,780,050 | | $ 3,740,777 | | | |
| Note payable long term | 1,283,888 | | 978,285 | | | |
| Total long-term liabilities | $ 5,063,938 | | $ 4,719,062 | | | |
| Total liabilities | $12,414,656 | | $11,765,904 | | | |
| Shareholders' equity: | | | | | | |
| Common stock | $ 4,745,742 | | $ 4,078,222 | | | |
| Preferred stock | 502,000 | | 461,628 | | | |
| Retained earnings | 382,782 | | 139,382 | | | |
| Total shareholders' equity | $ 5,630,524 | | $ 4,679,232 | | | |
| TOTAL LIABILITIES AND SHAREHOLDERS' EQUITY | $18,045,180 | | $16,445,136 | | | |

**4.** Show what changes would have been made in the cash and preferred stock amount in 2008 if Stardoe Coffee Corporation had sold an additional $6,000 in preferred stock. (1/2 point for each correct answer)

| | Amount | Percent |
|---|---|---|
| Cash | | |
| Preferred stock | | |

Score for B (50)

# Assignment 19.2: Income Statement Analysis

Name

Date Score

Learning Objective 2

**A (50 points) Solve the following income statement problems. (points for correct answers as marked)**

**1.** In the following income statement, find the percent for each 2008 and 2007 item. Then find the amount and percent of change. Round percents to two decimal places. (1/2 point for each correct answer)

**Georgia Textiles**
**Income Statement**
**For the Years Ended December 31, 2008 and 2007**

| | 2008 Amount | 2008 Percent | 2007 Amount | 2007 Percent | Increase/Decrease Amount | Increase/Decrease Percent |
|---|---|---|---|---|---|---|
| Revenue from sales: | | | | | | |
| Sales | $920,000 | | $827,000 | | | |
| Less returns | 35,000 | | 30,000 | | | |
| NET SALES | $885,000 | | $797,000 | | | |
| Cost of goods sold: | | | | | | |
| Inventory, January 1 | $210,000 | | $197,000 | | | |
| Purchases | 460,000 | | 395,000 | | | |
| Available for sale | $670,000 | | $592,000 | | | |
| Inventory, December 31 | 240,000 | | 210,000 | | | |
| Cost of goods sold | $430,000 | | $382,000 | | | |
| Gross profit | $455,000 | | $415,000 | | | |
| Operating expenses: | | | | | | |
| Wages | $132,600 | | $120,000 | | | |
| Rent | 84,000 | | 80,000 | | | |
| Advertising | 18,000 | | 20,000 | | | |
| Insurance | 4,500 | | 4,200 | | | |
| Depreciation | 3,600 | | 3,100 | | | |
| Equipment rental | 1,200 | | 1,400 | | | |
| Administrative | 7,000 | | 5,200 | | | |
| Miscellaneous | 3,200 | | 2,100 | | | |
| Total operating expenses | $254,100 | | $236,000 | | | |
| Income before tax | $200,900 | | $179,000 | | | |
| Income tax | 32,000 | | 28,000 | | | |
| NET INCOME | $168,900 | | $151,000 | | | |

**2.** Assume that the ending inventory was $220,000 in 2008. Compute the following items. (2 points for each correct answer)

2008 Gross profit amount ________ 2008 Gross profit percent ________

2008 NET INCOME amount ________ 2008 NET INCOME percent ________

Score for A (50)

**B** **(100 points) Solve the following income statement problems. (points for correct answers as marked)**

**3.** In the following income statement, find the percent for each 2008 and 2007 item, then find the amount and percent of change. Round percents (no decimal places). (84 points, 1 point for each correct answer)

**Baldwin Field Enterprises**
**Income Statement**
**For the Years Ended December 31, 2008 and 2007**

| | 2008 Amount | 2008 Percent | 2007 Amount | 2007 Percent | Difference Amount | Difference Percent |
|---|---|---|---|---|---|---|
| Revenue from sales: | | | | | | |
| Sales | $ 87,000 | | $ 74,800 | | | |
| Less returns | 2,000 | | 1,800 | | | |
| NET SALES | $ 85,000 | | $ 73,000 | | | |
| Cost of goods sold: | | | | | | |
| Inventory, January 1 | $ 22,000 | | 17,500 | | | |
| Purchases | 38,000 | | 35,000 | | | |
| Available for sale | $ 60,000 | | 52,500 | | | |
| Inventory, December 31 | 24,100 | | 22,000 | | | |
| Cost of goods sold | $ 35,900 | | 30,500 | | | |
| Gross profit | $ 49,100 | | $ 42,500 | | | |
| Operating expenses: | | | | | | |
| Salary | $ 11,200 | | 10,900 | | | |
| Rent | 7,500 | | 6,000 | | | |
| Advertising | 1,400 | | 1,200 | | | |
| Delivery | 450 | | 380 | | | |
| Depreciation | 650 | | 600 | | | |
| Equipment rental | 350 | | 420 | | | |
| Administrative | 1,900 | | 1,700 | | | |
| Miscellaneous | 190 | | 220 | | | |
| Total operating expenses | $ 23,640 | | $ 21,420 | | | |
| Income before tax | $ 25,460 | | 21,080 | | | |
| Income tax | 2,200 | | 2,000 | | | |
| NET INCOME | $ 23,260 | | $ 19,080 | | | |

**4.** Assume that the beginning inventory was $18,000 in 2007 and $20,500 in 2008 and that the rent was $6,400 in 2007 and $8,800 in 2008. Compute the following amounts and percents to reflect the revised beginning inventory and rent numbers. (8 points for each correct row)

| | 2008 Amount | 2008 Percent | 2007 Amount | 2007 Percent | Difference Amount | Difference Percent |
|---|---|---|---|---|---|---|
| Gross profit | | | | | | |
| NET INCOME | | | | | | |

Score for B (100)

# Assignment 19.3: Financial Statement Ratios

Name

Date Score

Learning Objectives 1 2 3

**A (26 points) Solve the following financial statement ratio problems. (1/2 point for each correct answer)**

**1.** Alice Anderson was considering investing in a business. She used the following statement in analyzing the Dover Clock Shop. Compute the net changes in the balance sheet and income statement. Round to one decimal place.

**Dover Clock Shop**
**Comparative Balance Sheet**
**As of December 31, 2008 and 2007**

| | 2008 | 2007 | Increase/Decrease | |
|---|---|---|---|---|
| | **Amount** | **Amount** | **Amount** | **Percent** |
| ASSETS | | | | |
| Current assets: | | | | |
| Cash | $110,000 | $104,600 | ______ | ______ |
| Accounts receivable | 135,000 | 115,900 | ______ | ______ |
| Merchandise inventory | 185,000 | 145,000 | ______ | ______ |
| Total current assets | $430,000 | $365,500 | ______ | ______ |
| Fixed assets: | | | | |
| Building improvements | $ 45,000 | $ 48,500 | ______ | ______ |
| Equipment | 145,000 | 132,000 | ______ | ______ |
| Total fixed assets | $190,000 | $180,500 | ______ | ______ |
| TOTAL ASSETS | $620,000 | $546,000 | ______ | ______ |
| LIABILITIES | | | | |
| Current liabilities: | | | | |
| Salaries payable | $ 33,000 | $ 28,200 | ______ | ______ |
| Accounts payable | 120,000 | 112,900 | ______ | ______ |
| Total current liabilities | $153,000 | $141,100 | ______ | ______ |
| Long-term liabilities: | | | | |
| Note payable | $100,000 | $120,000 | ______ | ______ |
| Total liabilities | $253,000 | $261,100 | ______ | ______ |
| Owner's equity: | | | | |
| J. C. Dover, capital | 367,000 | 284,900 | ______ | ______ |
| TOTAL LIABILITIES AND OWNER'S EQUITY | $620,000 | $546,000 | ______ | ______ |

**Dover Clock Shop**
**Comparative Income Statement**
**For the Years Ended December 31, 2008 and 2007**

| | | | Difference | |
|---|---|---|---|---|
| | **2008** | **2007** | **Amount** | **Percent** |
| NET SALES | $780,000 | $835,000 | | |
| Cost of goods sold: | | | | |
| Merchandise inventory, January 1 | $145,000 | $138,000 | | |
| Purchases | 585,000 | 620,000 | | |
| Merchandise available for sale | $730,000 | $758,000 | | |
| Merchandise inventory, December 31 | 185,000 | 145,000 | | |
| Cost of goods sold | $545,000 | $613,000 | | |
| Gross profit on sales | $235,000 | $222,000 | | |
| Expenses: | | | | |
| Selling | $ 82,000 | $ 78,600 | | |
| Other | 29,200 | 30,200 | | |
| Total expenses | $111,200 | $108,800 | | |
| NET INCOME | $123,800 | $113,200 | | |

Score for A (26)

**B (24 points) Solve the following problems. (2 points for each correct answer)**

**2.** Provide the following information for Alice Anderson's consideration. When the ratio is less than 1, give the ratio to three decimal places; otherwise, round to one decimal place.

| | **2008** | **2007** |
|---|---|---|
| **a.** Working capital ratio | | |
| **b.** Acid test ratio | | |
| **c.** Ratio of accounts receivable to net sales | | |
| **d.** Inventory turnover | | |
| **e.** Ratio of net income to net sales | | |
| **f.** Rate of return on investment | | |

Score for B (24)

**C (26 points) Solve the following problems. (1/2 point for each correct answer)**

**3.** Alice Anderson was offered a second business. She received the following statements for 2008 and 2007. Complete calculations for a comparative balance sheet and a comparative income statement for the Grandfather Clock Shop, showing the amount and percent of change.

**Grandfather Clock Shop**
**Comparative Balance Sheet**
**As of December 31, 2008 and 2007**

| | 2008 | | 2007 | | Increase/Decrease | |
|---|---|---|---|---|---|---|
| | **Amount** | **Percent** | **Amount** | **Percent** | **Amount** | **Percent** |
| ASSETS | | | | | | |
| Current assets: | | | | | | |
| Cash | $ 25,000 | 18.2% | $ 16,000 | 14.7% | ______ | ______ |
| Accounts receivable | 12,000 | 8.8% | 8,000 | 7.3% | ______ | ______ |
| Merchandise inventory | 46,000 | 33.6% | 31,000 | 28.4% | ______ | ______ |
| Total current assets | $ 83,000 | 60.6% | $ 55,000 | 50.5% | ______ | ______ |
| Fixed assets: | | | | | | |
| Store fixtures | $ 39,000 | 28.5% | $ 43,000 | 39.4% | ______ | ______ |
| Office equipment | 15,000 | 10.9% | 11,000 | 10.1% | ______ | ______ |
| Total fixed assets | $ 54,000 | 39.4% | $ 54,000 | 49.5% | ______ | ______ |
| TOTAL ASSETS | $137,000 | 100.0% | $109,000 | 100.0% | ______ | ______ |
| LIABILITIES | | | | | | |
| Current liabilities: | | | | | | |
| Sales tax payable | $ 4,500 | 3.3% | $ 5,500 | 5.0% | ______ | ______ |
| Accounts payable | 9,500 | 6.9% | 6,000 | 5.5% | ______ | ______ |
| Total current liabilities | $ 14,000 | 10.2% | $ 11,500 | 10.6% | ______ | ______ |
| Long-term liabilities: | | | | | | |
| Note payable | $ 30,000 | 21.9% | $ 38,000 | 34.9% | ______ | ______ |
| Total liabilities | $ 44,000 | 32.1% | $ 49,500 | 45.4% | ______ | ______ |
| Owner's equity | | | | | | |
| R. A. Banner, capital | $ 93,000 | 67.9% | $ 59,500 | 54.6% | ______ | ______ |
| TOTAL LIABILITIES AND OWNER'S EQUITY | $137,000 | 100.0% | $109,000 | 100.0% | ______ | ______ |

**Grandfather Clock Shop**
**Comparative Income Statement**
**For the Years Ended December 31, 2008 and 2007**

| | 2008 | | 2007 | | Difference | |
|---|---|---|---|---|---|---|
| | Amount | Percent | Amount | Percent | Amount | Percent |
| NET SALES | $205,000 | 100.0% | $120,000 | 100.0% | | |
| Cost of goods sold: | | | | | | |
| Merchandise inventory, January 1 | $ 31,000 | 15.1% | $ 27,500 | 22.9% | | |
| Purchases | 154,000 | 75.1% | 84,500 | 70.4% | | |
| Merchandise available for sale | $185,000 | 90.2% | $112,000 | 93.3% | | |
| Merchandise inventory, December 31 | 46,000 | 22.4% | 31,000 | 25.8% | | |
| Cost of goods sold | $139,000 | 67.8% | $ 81,000 | 67.5% | | |
| Gross profit on sales | $ 66,000 | 32.2% | $ 39,000 | 32.5% | | |
| Expenses: | | | | | | |
| Selling | $ 31,000 | 15.1% | $ 21,500 | 17.9% | | |
| Other | 13,000 | 6.3% | 7,250 | 6.0% | | |
| Total expenses | $ 44,000 | 21.5% | $ 28,750 | 24.0% | | |
| NET INCOME | $ 22,000 | 10.7% | $ 10,250 | 8.5% | | |

Any differences of 0.1% from individual items are due to rounding.

Score for C (26)

# International Business 20

## Learning Objectives

By studying this chapter and completing all assignments, you will be able to:

**Learning Objective 1** Compute currency exchange rates.

**Learning Objective 2** Compute the effects of exchange rate changes.

**Learning Objective 3** Compute duties on imports.

**Learning Objective 4** Convert between U.S. weights and measures and metric weights and measures.

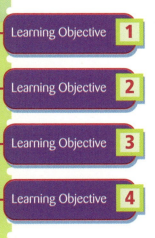

Businesses in the United States **import** goods made in other countries and **export** domestic goods made in the United States. International business transactions amount to billions of dollars annually and constitute an important part of the economies of most nations in the world.

International trade between U.S. companies and those in other countries is under the jurisdiction of the International Trade Administration (ITA), a branch of the Department of Commerce. All international trade is subject to a set of ITA rules and regulations known as the **Export Administration Regulations.** Any company in the United States planning to sell goods to companies in other countries must have an ITA export license for the transactions.

## Computing Currency Exchange Rates

**Learning Objective 1**

Compute currency exchange rates.

In order to conduct international trade, U.S. companies must exchange U.S. dollars for other currencies and vice versa. Figure 20-1 lists the names of the currency units used in the major countries, the U.S. dollars per unit, and the number of units per U.S. dollar.

**Figure 20-1** Foreign Currency–U.S. Dollar Exchange Rates

**CURRENCY EXCHANGE RATES**

| | Per US Dollar | In US Dollars |
|---|---|---|
| Argentine Peso | 3.15622 | 0.316835 |
| Australian Dollar | 1.10681 | 0.903497 |
| Brazilian Real | 1.7438 | 0.57346 |
| British Pound | 0.507949 | 1.9687 |
| Canadian Dollar | 0.9939 | 1.00614 |
| Chinese Yuan | 7.1845 | 0.139189 |
| Danish Krone | 5.0183 | 0.199271 |
| Euro | 0.673355 | 1.4851 |
| Hong Kong Dollar | 7.7971 | 0.128253 |
| Hungarian Forint | 173.443 | 0.00576559 |
| Indian Rupee | 39.12 | 0.0255624 |
| Israel New Shekel | 3.57988 | 0.279339 |
| Japanese Yen | 106.3 | 0.009407 |
| Malaysian Ringgit | 3.231 | 0.309502 |
| Mexican Peso | 10.812 | 0.09248 |
| New Zealand Dollar | 1.25818 | 0.794799 |
| Norwegian Kroner | 5.4046 | 0.185028 |
| Russian Ruble | 24.502 | 0.040813 |
| Singapore Dollar | 1.4136 | 0.707414 |
| South African Rand | 7.45705 | 0.134101 |
| South Korean Won | 944.5 | 0.00105876 |
| Sri Lanka Rupee | 107.65 | 0.00928936 |
| Swedish Krona | 6.3512 | 0.157451 |
| Swiss Franc | 1.0821 | 0.924129 |
| Taiwan Dollar | 32.03 | 0.0312207 |
| Thai Baht | 31.05 | 0.0322061 |

Four other governments call their currency the dollar—Australia, Canada, Hong Kong, and New Zealand. These dollars are not U.S. dollars; each is a separate currency. Several currencies share names, such as the franc, mark, peso, pound, and euro.

**EXAMPLE A**

A person planning a trip to Denmark wants to change $100 U.S. to Danish kroner. How many kroner will the person get for the $100 U.S.? (Round answer to nearest krone.)

$5.0183 \times 100 = 502$ kroner

**EXAMPLE B**

A traveler from Argentina is planning a trip to the United States and wants to change 1,000 Argentine pesos to U.S. dollars. How many U.S. dollars will the traveler receive for the 1,000 pesos? (Round answer to nearest dollar.)

$1{,}000 \div 3.15622 = \$317$

**EXAMPLE C**

An American tourist shopping in a Canadian store purchased an item for 100 Canadian dollars. How much did his purchase cost him in U.S. dollars? (Round answer to nearest U.S. penny.)

100 Canadian dollars × 1.00614 U.S. dollars per Canadian dollar = $100.61

**CONCEPT CHECK 20.1**

Using the "Per US Dollar" column from Figure 20-1, compute the number of *euros* one would receive for $300 U.S. (Round answer to nearest euro.)

$\$300 \times 0.673355 = 202$ euros

Using the "In US Dollars" column from Figure 20-1, compute the number of U.S. dollars one would receive for 400 *Japanese yen*. (Round answer to nearest U.S. penny.)

$400 \times 0.009407 = \$3.76$

# Computing the Effects of Exchange Rate Changes

One hazard of foreign trade is the uncertainty of future exchange rates between currencies. The relationship between the values of the U.S. dollar and a foreign currency can change between the time a contract is signed and the time payment is received. If a U.S. exporter agrees to accept foreign currency, a devaluation in the foreign currency could cause the exporter to lose money on the transaction.

**Learning Objective 2**

Compute the effects of exchange rate changes.

© PHOTOLINK/PHOTODISC/GETTY IMAGES

## EXAMPLE D

Global Industries, a U.S. company, sold merchandise to Europa, a company in Hungary. Europa agreed to pay 500,000 Hungarian forint for the goods. On the date of the sale, the Hungarian forint was valued at 173.443 per U.S. dollar, as noted in Figure 20-1. Global Industries expected to receive $2,882.79. (500,000 Hungarian forint ÷ 173.443 per U.S. dollar = $2,882.79.)

Between the date the sale was made and the date the goods were shipped and paid for by Europa, the value of the forint changed to 177.022 per U.S. dollar. How much did Global Industries lose by accepting the forint as the medium of payment?

Value of merchandise at time of sale: 500,000 Hungarian forint ÷ 173.443 per U.S. dollar = $2,882.79. Value of merchandise at time shipped and paid for: 500,000 Hungarian forint ÷ 177.022 = $2,824.51. Value of 500,000 forint at time of sale $2,882.79 − value of 500,000 forint at time shipped and paid $2,824.51 = loss to Global Industries $58.28.

## EXAMPLE E

Global Industries investigated a purchase of raw materials from a company in England. The price of the materials was 150,000 British pounds. At the time, the value of the British pound was $1.652. Ten months later, when Global actually made the purchase, the value of the British pound was as shown in Figure 20-1. How many more dollars did Global have to pay as a result of the change in the value of the British pound?

150,000 × $1.652 = $247,800 cost when investigated
150,000 × $1.9687 = $295,305 cost when purchase was made
$295,305 − $247,800 = $47,505 more dollars at time of purchase

## CONCEPT CHECK 20.2

Global Industries contracts to sell a printing press to a company in Denmark. The Danish company agreed to pay $300,000 U.S. dollars for the press.

On the date the agreement was made, the Danish krone was worth 0.199271 U.S. dollars. On the date payment was made, the krone had changed to 0.1972 U.S. dollars. How many more or less Danish kroner did the Danish company pay by stipulating a purchase price of $300,000 U.S. dollars?

$300,000 ÷ 0.199271 = 1,505,487.50 kroner at time of agreement
$300,000 ÷ 0.1972 = 1,521,298.17 kroner at time of payment
1,521,298.17 − 1,505,487.50 = 15,810.67 more kroner at time of payment

If the Danish company had agreed to pay 1,505,487.50 kroner instead of $300,000 for the purchase, how many U.S. dollars would it have saved between the time of agreement and the time of payment?

1,505,487.50 kroner to be paid × 0.1972 value of krone at payment = $296,882.14
$300,000 value of kroner at time of agreement − $296,882.14 = $3,117.86 saved

# Computing Duties on Imports

Learning Objective 3

Compute duties on imports.

All items imported into the United States must go through the U.S. Customs Agency. Many imported items have a **duty** (charge or tax) imposed by the Customs Agency to protect U.S. manufacturers against foreign competition in domestic markets. Duties vary widely from item to item. A duty may be a set amount—such as $0.50 per item—or an **ad valorem duty,** which is a percent of the value of the item.

**EXAMPLE F**

Assume that a wristwatch in a leather case with a metal band has four duty rates imposed: $0.40 per wristwatch + 6% of the value of the case + 14% of the value of the metal band + 5% of the value of the battery. Anderson Jewelry Company imported four dozen wristwatches. The value of the case was $16; the metal band, $10; and the battery, $6. How much duty did the Anderson Jewelry Company pay for the four dozen wristwatches? (Round answer to nearest cent.)

| | | |
|---|---|---|
| Duty per wristwatch: | | $0.40 |
| Ad valorem duty on case: $16 × 0.06 | = | 0.96 |
| Ad valorem duty on metal band: $10 × 0.14 | = | 1.40 |
| Ad valorem duty on battery: $6 × 0.05 | = | + 0.30 |
| Total duty per watch | | $3.06 |

$3.06 per watch × 48 watches = $146.88 total duty paid

**EXAMPLE G**

A computer printer costs $150 whether purchased from Country A or Country B. However, it has an ad valorem duty rate of 3.5% if purchased from Country A and an ad valorem duty rate of 28% if purchased from Country B. How much more would it cost a company to purchase the printer from Country B than from Country A?

Country A: $150 × 0.035 = $5.25
$150 + $5.25 = $155.25 total cost

Country B: $150 × 0.28 = $42
$150 + $42 = $192 total cost

$192 Country B − $155.25 Country A = $36.75 more

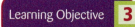

**Foreign trade zones** are domestic sites in the United States considered to be outside U.S. Customs territory. These foreign trade zones are used for import and export activities. No duty or federal excise taxes are charged on foreign goods moved into the zone until the goods or products made from them are moved into U.S. Customs territory. No duty is charged on imports that later are exported for sale, because they never entered U.S. Customs territory. Recently, there were more than 150 foreign trade zones in port communities in the United States. Operations in them include storage, repacking, inspection, exhibition, assembly, and manufacturing.

**EXAMPLE H**

A U.S. company located in a foreign trade zone imported \$500,000 worth of goods. The duty rate on the goods is 5%. If 30% of the goods were moved into U.S. Customs territory for sale and 70% were exported for sale, how much money did the company save by being located in a foreign trade zone?

\$500,000 × 70% for export = \$350,000 in goods
\$350,000 × 5% duty = \$17,500 saved

**CONCEPT CHECK 20.3**

a. Downtown Toy Store ordered from a foreign country 400 dolls on which an ad valorem duty of 4.5% is charged. Payment is to be made in U.S. dollars. The price of each doll is \$23. What is the total cost to Downtown Toy Store?

400 × \$23 = \$9,200 cost before duty
\$9,200 × 0.045 duty = \$414
\$9,200 + \$414 = \$9,614 total cost to buyer

b. A company located in a foreign trade zone purchased \$1 million worth of electronic equipment having an ad valorem duty of 4.1%. Forty percent of the products were moved into U.S. Customs territory for sale, and 60% were repackaged and exported. How many dollars did the company save by being located in a foreign trade zone?

\$1,000,000 × 60% = \$600,000
\$600,000 × 4.1% = \$24,600 saved

# Converting Between U.S. Weights and Measures and Metric Weights and Measures

**Learning Objective 4**

Convert between U.S. weights and measures and metric weights and measures.

Some businesses, especially in the area of import–export activities, must convert U.S. customary units of weights and measures to the **metric system** of weights and measures used in most other countries. Figure 20-2 shows the conversion values for the U.S./metric units used most frequently in business.

**Figure 20-2** U.S./Metric Unit Conversions

| To Convert U.S. | to Metric | Multiply by Number of Metric in U.S. | To Convert Metric | to U.S. | Multiply by Number of U.S. in Metric |
|---|---|---|---|---|---|
| Inches | Meters | 0.0254 | Meters | Inches | 39.37 |
| Feet | Meters | 0.305 | Meters | Feet | 3.281 |
| Yards | Meters | 0.914 | Meters | Yards | 1.09 |
| Miles | Kilometers | 1.609 | Kilometers | Miles | 0.621 |
| Ounces | Grams | 28.35 | Grams | Ounces | 0.035 |
| Pounds | Grams | 454 | Grams | Pounds | 0.0022 |
| Pounds | Kilograms | 0.454 | Kilograms | Pounds | 2.2 |
| Pints | Liters | 0.473 | Liters | Pints | 2.113 |
| Quarts | Liters | 0.946 | Liters | Quarts | 1.057 |
| Gallons | Liters | 3.785 | Liters | Gallons | 0.264 |

**EXAMPLE I**

Convert the following U.S. measures to metric measures.

a. Convert 30 inches to meters.
30 in. × 0.0254 = 0.7620 m

b. Convert 15 feet to meters.
15 ft × 0.305 = 4.5750 m

c. Convert 10 yards to meters.
10 yd × 0.914 = 9.14 m

d. Convert 20 miles to kilometers.
20 mi × 1.609 = 32.18 km

e. Convert 15 ounces to grams.
15 oz × 28.35 = 425.25 g

f. Convert 20 pounds to grams.
20 lb × 454 = 9,080 g

g. Convert 10 pounds to kilograms.
10 lb × 0.454 = 4.54 kg

h. Convert 20 pints to liters.
20 pt × 0.473 = 9.46 L

i. Convert 40 quarts to liters.
40 qt × 0.946 = 37.84 L

j. Convert 20 gallons to liters.
20 gal × 3.785 = 75.7 L

**EXAMPLE J**

Convert the following metric measures to U.S. measures.

a. Convert 20 meters to inches.
20 m × 39.37 = 787.4 in.

b. Convert 20 meters to feet.
20 m × 3.281 = 65.62 ft

c. Convert 30 meters to yards.
30 m × 1.09 = 32.7 yd

d. Convert 15 kilometers to miles.
15 km × 0.621 = 9.315 mi

e. Convert 20 grams to ounces.
20 g × 0.035 = 0.7 oz

f. Convert 20 grams to pounds.
20 g × 0.0022 = 0.044 lb

g. Convert 40 kilograms to pounds.
40 kg × 2.2 = 88 lb

h. Convert 30 liters to pints.
30 L × 2.113 = 63.39 pt

i. Convert 20 liters to quarts.
20 L × 1.057 = 21.14 qt

j. Convert 20 liters to gallons.
20 L × 0.264 = 5.28 gal

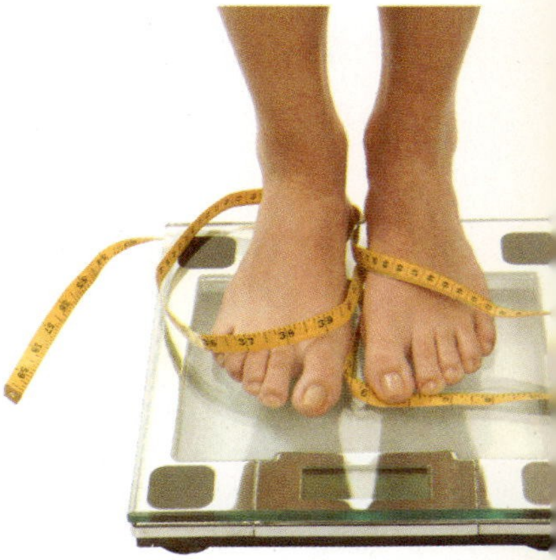

## CONCEPT CHECK 20.4

Using Figure 20-2, make the following conversions:

a. Convert 28 inches to meters.
   28 in. × 0.0254 = 0.7112 m

b. Convert 17 feet to meters.
   17 ft × 0.305 = 5.185 m

c. Convert 3 meters to inches.
   3 m × 39.37 = 118.11 in.

d. Convert 18 meters to feet.
   18 m × 3.281 = 59.058 ft

e. Convert 3 ounces to grams.
   3 oz × 28.35 = 85.05 g

f. Convert 7 pounds to grams.
   7 lb × 454 = 3,178 g

g. Convert 36 grams to pounds.
   36 g × 0.0022 = 0.0792 lb

h. Convert 18 kilograms to pounds.
   18 kg × 2.2 = 39.6 lb

i. Convert 8 pints to liters.
   8 pt × 0.473 = 3.784 L

j. Convert 2 quarts to liters.
   2 qt × 0.946 = 1.892 L

COMPLETE ASSIGNMENT 20.2.

## Chapter Terms for Review

ad valorem duty
duty
export
Export Administration Regulations
foreign trade zones
import
metric system

## Notes

# THE BOTTOM LINE

*Summary of chapter learning objectives:*

| Learning Objective | Example |
|---|---|
| **20.1**<br><br>Compute currency exchange rates. | 1. Using the In US Dollars column in Figure 20-1, compute the value in U.S. dollars of 5,000 units of each of the following foreign currencies. Round answers to the nearest cent.<br>a. Chinese yuan _______ b. Russian ruble _______<br>c. Brazilian real _______ d. Thailand's baht _______<br><br>2. Using the Per US Dollar column in Figure 20-1, compute the amount of U.S. dollars necessary to buy 5,000 units of each of the following foreign currencies. Round answers to the nearest cent.<br>a. Sweden's krona _______ b. Hungary's forint _______<br>c. Taiwan dollar _______ d. Mexican peso _______ |
| **20.2**<br><br>Compute the effects of exchange rate changes. | 3. A U.S. company has contracted to sell certain goods to a company in Mexico. The Mexican company has contracted to pay 700,000 pesos for the goods. At the time the contract was signed, the In US Dollars column in the newspaper showed that the Mexican peso was worth $0.0883. On the date payment was due, the peso changed to a value of $0.09248 U.S. How much did the U.S. company gain or lose by having agreed to accept payment in pesos instead of U.S. dollars? |
| **20.3**<br><br>Compute duties on imports. | 4. Broadway Department Store ordered from a foreign country 300 sets of dishes on which an ad valorem duty of 5.8% is charged. The price of each set of dishes is $72. Payment is to be made in U.S. currency. What is the total cost to Broadway? |
| **20.4**<br><br>Convert between U.S. weights and measures and metric weights and measures. | 5. Using Figure 20-2, make the following conversions.<br>a. Convert 100 inches to meters. b. Convert 1,000 meters to feet.<br>c. Convert 6 miles to kilometers. d. Convert 100 grams to ounces.<br>e. Convert 3 gallons to liters. f. Convert 7 liters to quarts. |

Answers: 1a. $695.95 b. $204.07 c. $2,867.30 d. $161.03 2a. $787.25 b. $28.83 c. $156.10 d. $462.45
3. $61,810 expected; $64,736 received; $2,926 gain 4. $22,852.80 5a. 2.54 m b. 3,281 ft c. 9.654 km d. 3.5 oz
e. 11.355 L f. 7.399 qt

SELF-CHECK

# Review Problems for Chapter 20

**(In all cases, round to the nearest hundredth.)**

1. How many Thai baht can a person get for $15 U.S. dollars?
2. How many U.S. dollars can a person get for 15 Thai baht?
3. How many South African rand can a person get for $540 U.S. dollars?
4. How many U.S. dollars can a person get for 540 South African rand?
5. A U.S. exporter agrees to accept 300,000 South African rand in payment for goods. The South African rand is valued as shown in Figure 20-1. Compute the value in U.S. dollars that the U.S. exporter will receive. (Round to nearest dollar.)
6. In problem 5, suppose that the value of the South African rand changes to 7.777 per U.S. dollar. How much will the exporter gain or lose in this transaction? (Round to nearest dollar.)
7. Tonaka Manufacturing, Inc., contracted to sell goods to a company in Sweden for 630,000 Swedish kronor. Using the data in Figure 20-1, compute the U.S. dollar value that Tonaka expects to receive. (Round to nearest dollar.)
8. Assume that the value of the Swedish krona decreased by 20%; compute the U.S. dollar value that Tonaka would then expect to receive.
9. Princess Jewelry contracted to purchase 144 bracelets from a foreign manufacturer. The price of each bracelet is $40. An ad valorem duty of 17% is charged on each bracelet. Compute the duty Princess Jewelry will pay for the shipment.
10. ABC, Inc., plans to purchase 250 units of computer components. ABC can buy the components from country Y at a price of $60 each plus an ad valorem duty of 35% or from country YY at a price of $64 plus an ad valorem duty of 13%. Compute the amount ABC will save by purchasing from the lowest-cost source.
11. Convert 8 pints to liters.
12. The length of trip A is stated as 300 miles. The length of trip B is stated as 300 kilometers. In miles, how much farther is trip A than trip B?

**Answers to the Self-Check can be found in Appendix B at the back of the text.**

## Notes

# Assignment 20.1: Trading with Other Countries

Name ______

Date ______ Score ______

Learning Objectives 1 2

**A** **(44 points) Solve the following problems. (4 points for each correct answer)**

**1.** Using the data in Figure 20-1, find the amount of U.S. dollars needed to buy 300 units of each foreign currency listed.

| Foreign Currency | Price of 300 Units |
|---|---|
| **a.** Australian dollar | ______ |
| **b.** Euro | ______ |
| **c.** Israel new shekel | ______ |
| **d.** Brazilian real | ______ |
| **e.** Canadian dollar | ______ |
| **f.** Chinese yuan | ______ |
| **g.** South African rand | ______ |

**2.** Using the data in Figure 20-1, determine the value in U.S. dollars of 4,500 units of each foreign currency listed below. (Round answers to the nearest cent.)

| Foreign Currency | Value of 4,500 units |
|---|---|
| **a.** Argentinean peso | ______ |
| **b.** British pound | ______ |
| **c.** Danish krone | ______ |
| **d.** Indian rupee | ______ |

______
Score for A (44)

**B (56 points) Solve the following problems. Round pennies to the nearest dollar. (8 points for each correct answer)**

**3.** Hadley Enterprises has contracted to sell certain goods to a company in Britain. The price agreed on for the goods is 80,000 British pounds. On the date the contract was signed, the financial section of the local paper showed that the British pound was valued at $1.9501.

**a.** How much in U.S. dollars does Hadley Enterprises expect to receive for the goods? __________

**b.** If the value of the British pound fell from 1.9501 to 1.8932 on the date of payment, how much would Hadley Enterprises lose by having contracted in British pounds instead of U.S. dollars? __________

**c.** If the British pound rose to 1.9688 on the date of payment, how much would Hadley Enterprises gain by having contracted in British pounds instead of U.S. dollars? __________

**4.** Miller Furniture Company imported 150 chairs from a Danish firm. Each chair is valued at 890 Danish kroner. What is the value of the chairs in U.S. dollars if the Danish krone is currently valued at 0.199271? __________

**5.** Oldtown Industries, Inc., is contracting to sell its product to a country whose currency is unstable and difficult to convert to U.S. currency. The value of the goods is $20,000 U.S. The currency of the country to which the goods will be shipped is currently valued at 0.0040 per U.S. dollar. Oldtown Industries is willing to accept the currency of a third country. The Singapore dollar is agreed on. The Singapore dollar is shown as 0.707414 on the date the contract is signed.

**a.** How many Singapore dollars does Oldtown Industries expect to receive? (Round the answer to the nearest dollar.) __________

**b.** If the Singapore dollar does not change before the date of payment, but the value of the currency of the receiving country falls from 0.0040 to 0.0003, how much would Oldtown Industries save by using the Singapore dollar? __________

**6.** If the British pound is valued at 1.9000 per U.S. dollar and the Egyptian pound at 0.3700, how many more Egyptian pounds than British pounds could a U.S. citizen buy for $1,000 U.S.? (Round the answer to the nearest pound.) (10 points) __________

__________
Score for B (56)

# Assignment 20.2: Duties and Metric Conversion

Name

Date Score

Learning Objectives 3 4

**A** **(56 points) Solve the following problems. (points for correct answers as marked)**

**1.** Benjamin's Department Store ordered from a foreign country 150 music boxes on which an ad valorem duty rate of 3.2% is charged. Payment is to be made in U.S. dollars. The price of each music box is $18. (2 points for each correct answer)

**a.** What is the price of the 150 music boxes before duty is added? ________

**b.** What is the amount of duty charged on the shipment? ________

**c.** What is the total cost to Benjamin's? ________

**2.** Gems International Company is purchasing from a foreign country one gross (144) of 20-inch gold necklaces at $75 each and six dozen 18-inch silver necklaces at $55 each. The ad valorem duty rate for gold and silver jewelry is 7%. What is the total cost of the shipment to the buyer? (8 points) ________

**3.** Sutter's Department Store is going to buy four gross (one gross = 144) of vases for the next Christmas season. It can buy porcelain vases or lead crystal vases for $45 each. The duty on porcelain vases is 9%. The duty on lead crystal vases is 4%. How much will Sutter's save in total cost by purchasing lead crystal instead of porcelain? (8 points) ________

**4.** Melody Piano Store can purchase pianos domestically for $1,360 each. It can purchase pianos from a foreign country for $1,300 plus 5.3% ad valorem duty.

**a.** Melody Piano Store purchases the pianos with the lower total cost. Does it purchase from a domestic or a foreign manufacturer? (6 points) ________

**b.** How much does it save on each piano? (2 points) ________

**5.** Broadway Office Equipment Company purchased the following equipment from a foreign country:

72 automatic typewriters at $150 each + 2.2% duty

24 addressing machines at $30 each + 4.2% duty

144 pencil sharpeners at $12 each + 6% duty

24 check-writing machines at $60 each, duty free

80 calculators at $24 each + 3.9% duty

**a.** What was the cost of the order before duty? (8 points) __________

**b.** What was the cost of the order after duty? (Round each calculation to the nearest cent.) (8 points) __________

**c.** If the 144 pencil sharpeners had been purchased at $12 each from a country with which trade was discouraged and the ad valorem duty rate was 50%, how much would the pencil sharpeners have cost? (4 points) __________

**d.** How much more duty would a buyer pay on the pencil sharpeners at the ad valorem rate of 50% than at an ad valorem duty rate of 6%? (2 points) __________

**6.** Adams Industries could purchase $30,000 worth of textiles from country A with an ad valorem duty rate of 2.5% or from country B with an ad valorem duty rate of 1.2%.

**a.** How much would the shipment cost if purchased from country A? (2 points) __________

**b.** How much would Adams Industries save by purchasing from country B? (2 points) __________

__________

Score for A (56)

**B (24 points) Solve the following problems. (points for correct answers as marked)**

**7.** The Allied Computer Company imports some computer components and manufactures other components and then assembles computers for sale within the United States or for export to foreign countries. The company is located in a district that has been designated by the International Trade Administration as a foreign trade zone. The company imported $250,000 worth of monitors having an ad valorem duty rate of 3.7%, $300,000 worth of power supplies having an ad valorem duty rate of 3.0%, and $500,000 worth of printers having an ad valorem duty rate of 3.7%. All products were finished and sold 1 year later.

**a.** If all products were sold within U.S. Customs territories, how much duty—in U.S. dollars—would the company pay at the end of the year? (2 points) __________

**b.** If 40% of each of the finished products were moved into U.S. Customs territories for sale and 60% were exported for sale in foreign countries, how many dollars of duty would the company pay at the end of the year? (8 points)

__________

**c.** If all products were exported for sale, how much duty would the company pay at the end of the year? (2 points) __________

**8.** The Allied Computer Company imported $260,000 worth of portable computers having an ad valorem duty rate of 3.9% and kept 20% of them for exhibition and company use on the premises.

**a.** If the company repackaged and sold the remaining portable computers in U.S. Customs territories, how many dollars of duty would the company pay on the portable computers? (4 points) __________

**b.** If the company repackaged and exported 50% of the portable computers for sale in foreign countries and moved the remaining 30% into U.S. Customs territories for sale, how many dollars would the company pay in duty on the portable computers? (4 points) __________

**9.** A company imported $5 million worth of laptop computers having an ad valorem duty rate of 3.9%. The company repackaged and exported all the computers for resale. How many dollars did the company save by being located in a foreign trade zone? (4 points) __________

__________

Score for B (24)

**C (20 points) Solve the following problems using Figure 20-2. (1 point for each correct answer)**

**10.** Make the following conversions from U.S. measures to metric:

**a.** Convert 15 inches to meters: __________

**b.** Convert 15 feet to meters: __________

**c.** Convert 15 yards to meters: __________

**d.** Convert 15 miles to kilometers: __________

**e.** Convert 25 ounces to grams: __________

**f.** Convert 25 pounds to grams: __________

**g.** Convert 25 pounds to kilograms: __________

**h.** Convert 30 pints to liters: __________

**i.** Convert 30 quarts to liters: __________

**j.** Convert 30 gallons to liters: __________

**11.** Make the following conversions from metric to U.S. measures:

**a.** Convert 15 meters to inches: __________

**b.** Convert 15 meters to feet: __________

**c.** Convert 15 meters to yards: __________

**d.** Convert 15 kilometers to miles: __________

**e.** Convert 25 grams to ounces: __________

**f.** Convert 25 grams to pounds: __________

**g.** Convert 25 kilograms to pounds: __________

**h.** Convert 30 liters to pints: __________

**i.** Convert 30 liters to quarts: __________

**j.** Convert 30 liters to gallons: __________

__________________

Score for C (20)

Notes

# Part 6

# Corporate and Special Applications

# 21

# Corporate Stocks

## Learning Objectives

By studying this chapter and completing all assignments, you will be able to:

**Learning Objective 1** Compute the costs and proceeds of stock buy-and-sell transactions.

**Learning Objective 2** Compute the costs and proceeds of round and odd lots.

**Learning Objective 3** Compute rates of yield and gains or losses on the purchase and sale of stocks.

**Learning Objective 4** Compute comparative earning potential of the major classes of corporate stocks.

Many companies operate as corporations. A **corporation** is a body that is granted a charter by a state legally recognizing it as a separate entity, having its own rights, privileges, and liabilities distinct from those of its owners. A corporation acquires assets, enters into contracts, sues or is sued, and pays taxes in its own name. Two primary reasons for forming a corporation are to limit liability and facilitate broadening the ownership base. A corporation raises capital by selling shares of ownership, which increases its assets without increasing its debt.

The general term applied to the shares of a corporation is **capital stock.** Each share of capital stock is a share of the ownership of the company's net assets (assets minus liabilities). The number of shares that a corporation is authorized to *issue,* or offer for sale, is set forth in its **charter,** the basic approval document issued by the state, under which the corporation operates. Ownership of stock is evidenced by a **stock certificate.**

Frequently, the shares of capital stock are assigned a value known as **par**, which is stated on the stock certificate. For example, a company incorporated with capital stock of $1,000,000 and 100,000 shares has a par value of $10 per share. Stock issued without par value is known as **no-par stock.** The par value may differ from the market price. In the marketplace, stock may be sold for any amount agreed upon by the buyer and seller.

# Computing the Costs and Proceeds of Stock Transactions

**Learning Objective 1**

Compute the costs and proceeds of stock buy-and-sell transactions.

After purchasing stock, a buyer may sell that stock at any price on the open market, regardless of the par value. Stocks are usually bought and sold on **stock exchanges**, the formal marketplaces set up for the purpose of trading stocks. Major exchanges in the United States are the New York Stock Exchange (NYSE), the American Stock Exchange (AMEX), and the National Association of Securities Dealers Automated Quotations (NASDAQ). A **stockbroker** usually handles **stock transactions**—the purchase and sale of stocks for clients. Today, many people also trade via the Internet.

The trading of shares of stock is published daily in newspapers. Figure 21-1 shows a sample stock market report, in which stocks are quoted in the traditional manner—dollars and fractions of a dollar. The NYSE, NASDAQ, and AMEX quote prices in hundredths. Consequently, the smallest increase or decrease in a stock price that will be reported is .01.

Both the buyer and the seller of stock pay commissions to the stockbroker. The total amount paid by a buyer to purchase a stock includes the market price of the stock and the stockbroker's commission (charge). The **total cost** paid by the purchaser is equal to the purchase price plus a broker's commission. The **proceeds** received by the seller are equal to the selling price minus the commission.

Broker commissions may be a flat rate per transaction, a percent of the value of the stock, an amount per share traded, or an amount negotiated between the client and the broker. Generally, commissions for brokers are less than 1% of the value of the stock, ranging from $0.02 to $0.50 per share bought or sold. A number of discount brokerages operating on the Internet now charge $7.00 to $22.99 per transaction, normally for up to 5,000 shares. Figure 21-2 shows a broker's confirmation report of a stock purchase with a commission rate of $50 and a transaction fee of $3.

We use a transaction charge of $0.20 per share or a flat fee of $19.95 per transaction in computing the cost of commissions in this chapter.

## Figure 21-1 Daily Stock Report from the NYSE

| 52 weeks | | | | Day's Activity | | | | | | | |
|---|---|---|---|---|---|---|---|---|---|---|---|
| Hi | Low | Stock | Sym | Div | Yld-% | PE | Vol. (000) | High | Low | Close | Change |
| 54.21 | 33.12 | Bank of America | BAC | $0.64 | 0.64% | 12.79 | 37,700 | 43.33 | 43.21 | 42.33 | −0.04 |
| 107.38 | 74.12 | Boeing | BA | $0.40 | 1.96% | 15.4 | 22,838 | 81.90 | 80.54 | 80.54 | 0.33 |
| 87.00 | 59.60 | Caterpillar | CAT | $0.36 | 2.13% | 12.57 | 7,304 | 69.05 | 67.55 | 67.90 | −0.46 |
| 65.59 | 45.56 | Coca-Cola Co | KO | $0.34 | 2.37% | 24.84 | 8,408 | 58.19 | 57.57 | 57.70 | 0.31 |
| 94.77 | 51.06 | Deere Inc | DE | $0.25 | 1.20% | 21.01 | 3,897 | 86.24 | 82.89 | 83.30 | −0.18 |
| 46.30 | 26.30 | Disney | DIS | $0.35 | 1.16% | 14.49 | 3,578 | 31.18 | 31.10 | 31.50 | 1.43 |
| 9.70 | 5.50 | Ford Motor Co | F | $ - | 0.00% | 0 | 6,160 | 6.42 | 6.25 | 6.31 | −0.12 |
| 43.20 | 21.34 | General Motors | GM | $0.25 | 3.78% | 0 | 18,165 | 26.30 | 25.29 | 25.71 | −0.76 |
| 56.89 | 46.25 | Kellogg's | KO | $0.31 | 2.58% | 17.45 | 4,740 | 49.33 | 48.30 | 49.09 | 0.94 |
| 78.79 | 61.89 | PepsiCo | PEP | $0.38 | 2.21% | 18.21 | 14,149 | 68.38 | 66.32 | 66.73 | −1.22 |
| 38.31 | 30.10 | Safeway | SWY | $0.07 | 0.89% | 15.41 | 2,569 | 31.97 | 30.98 | 31.03 | 0.23 |
| 195.58 | 84.72 | Sears | SHLD | $ - | 0.00% | 12.93 | 1,933 | 104.74 | 97.28 | 97.67 | −4.63 |
| 59.34 | 42.80 | Sony | SNE | $0.12 | 0.52% | 18.08 | 1,323 | 43.89 | 42.50 | 43.82 | −0.46 |
| 23.42 | 8.07 | Sprint | S | $0.03 | 1.01% | 21.53 | 20,042 | 10.02 | 9.53 | 9.62 | −0.25 |
| 138.00 | 91.21 | Toyota Motor Co | TM | $1.20 | 2.27% | 9.76 | 1,096 | 110.63 | 107.73 | 107.78 | 2.41 |
| 45.57 | 10.73 | Washington Mu | WM | $0.15 | 3.32% | 0 | 44,220 | 18.31 | 16.71 | 17.12 | −0.96 |

[1] The highest price per share in the previous 52 weeks.
[2] The lowest price per share in the previous 52 weeks.
[3] Company names, often abbreviated to fit in stock tables, are listed alphabetically.
[4] The symbol is a stock's designation on databases and quote machines.
[5] The dividend shown usually is the annual rate based on the company's last payout.
[6] The dividend divided by the closing share price gives the stock's yield.
[7] One measure of a stock's value is its **price/earnings ratio (P/E)**. It is based on the per-share earnings as reported by the company for the four most recent quarters. The PE number is found by dividing the current price by those most recent four-quarter earnings.
[8] Volume is the number of shares traded that day, shown in hundreds of shares.
[9] The high for the day's trading range.
[10] The low for the day's trading range.
[11] The closing price on that day.
[12] The net change in price lets you calculate something that isn't in the stock table: the previous day's closing price.

### EXAMPLE A

Jennifer Low bought 200 shares of Sears (SHLD) stock at $103. What was her cost, including commission of $0.20 per share?

| | | |
|---|---|---|
| 200 shares × $103 price | = $20,600 | purchase price |
| 200 shares × $0.20 commission | = + 40 | commission |
| | $20,640 | total cost |

### EXAMPLE B

Ken Yeager sold 800 shares of Verizon at $36.17, less commission of $0.20 per share. What were the proceeds of the sale?

| | | |
|---|---|---|
| 800 shares × $36.17 | = $28,936 | selling price |
| 800 shares × $0.20 commission | = − 160 | commission |
| | $28,776 | proceeds |

© FEATURE NEWS SERVICE (ASSOCIATED PRESS)

**Figure 21-2** Confirmation Report of a Stock Purchase

*Wachovia*

WE CONFIRM THE FOLLOWING TRANSACTION SUBJECT TO THE AGREEMENT ON THE REVERSE SIDE

| YOU | QUANTITY | PRICE | SECURITY DESCRIPTION | CUSIP NUMBER |
|---|---|---|---|---|
| BOUGHT | 50 | 35.47 | GENERAL ELECTRIC CO | 369604103 |

| ACCOUNT NUMBER | IB | T | TRF | MKT | OFFICE PHONE NUMBER |
|---|---|---|---|---|---|
| | 47 | 1 | 4 | 3 | |

| SYMBOL |
|---|
| GE |

WHEN COMMUNICATING WITH US PLEASE REFER TO YOUR ACCOUNT NUMBER

| TRADE DATE | | | SETTLEMENT DATE | | |
|---|---|---|---|---|---|
| 12 | 31 | 08 | 01 | 08 | 09 |

PLEASE PAY OR DELIVER BY THIS DATE

| PRINCIPAL | STATE TAX | ACCRUED INTEREST | COMMISSION | SEC FEE | TRANSACTION CHARGE | AMOUNT |
|---|---|---|---|---|---|---|
| 1,773.50 | | | 50.00 | | 3.00 | 1,720.50 |

**EXAMPLE C**

Juan Hernandez bought 500 shares of PepsiCo stock at \$68.30. What was his cost, including a flat fee of \$19.95?

| | | | |
|---|---|---|---|
| 500 shares × \$68.30 price | = | \$34,150.00 | purchase price |
| commission | = | + 19.95 | flat fee |
| | | \$34,169.95 | total cost |

**CONCEPT CHECK 21.1**

David Cooper purchased 300 shares of Safeway at \$31.02. He later sold the stock at \$33.10. What was his gain/loss on the purchase and sale, after counting commissions of \$0.20 per share on both the purchase and the sale?

| | | | |
|---|---|---|---|
| Purchase: 300 shares × \$31.02 price | = | \$9,306 | purchase price |
| 300 shares × \$0.20 commission | = | + 60 | commission |
| | | \$9,366 | total cost |
| Sale: 300 shares × \$33.10 price | = | \$9,930 | selling price |
| 300 shares × \$0.20 commission | = | − 60 | commission |
| | | \$9,870 | proceeds |

\$9,870 proceeds − \$9,366 cost = \$504 gain

# Computing the Costs and Proceeds of Round and Odd Lots

Learning Objective 2

Compute the costs and proceeds of round and odd lots.

Stocks are sold in round lots, odd lots, or a combination of the two. A **round lot** usually is 100 shares. An **odd lot** consists of any number of shares less than 100 (1 to 99 shares is an odd lot for a stock with a 100-share round lot). When odd lots are purchased, a small extra charge, or **odd-lot differential,** is commonly added to the round-lot price. The differential is added to the price for a purchaser and deducted from the price for the seller. In this book, we use a differential of 12.5 cents as the odd-lot rate.

**EXAMPLE D**

Carson Grant bought 160 shares of U.S. Steel at $43. What was his cost?

Odd-lot purchase price = $43 + $0.125 = $43.125 per odd-lot share

| | | | |
|---|---|---|---|
| 100 shares × $43.00 round-lot price | = | $4,300.00 | round-lot total cost |
| 60 shares × $43.125 odd-lot price | = | 2,587.50 | odd-lot total cost |
| 160 shares × $0.20 commission | = | + 32.00 | commission |
| | | $6,919.50 | total cost |

**EXAMPLE E**

Carson sold 160 shares of U.S. Steel at $43. What was the amount of his net proceeds?

Odd-lot selling price = $43 − $0.125 = $42.875

| | | | |
|---|---|---|---|
| 100 shares × $43.00 round-lot price | = | $4,300.00 | round-lot price |
| 60 shares × $42.875 odd-lot price | = | 2,572.50 | odd-lot price |
| 160 shares × $0.20 commission | = | − 32.00 | commission |
| | | $6,840.50 | net proceeds |

**CONCEPT CHECK 21.2**

James O'Brien bought 160 shares of Kelloggs at $48. What was his total cost?

Odd-lot purchase price = $48 + $0.125 = $48.125

| | | |
|---|---|---|
| 100 shares × $48 round-lot price | = | $4,800.00 |
| 60 shares × $48.125 odd-lot price | = | $2,887.50 |
| 160 shares × $0.20 commission | = | + 32.00 |
| Total cost | | $7,719.50 |

Sarah Loeb sold 220 shares of Aetna at $153.25. What was the amount of her net proceeds?

Odd-lot selling price = $153.25 − $0.125 = $153.125

| | | |
|---|---|---|
| 200 shares × $153.25 round-lot price | = | $30,650.00 |
| 20 shares × $153.125 odd-lot price | = | + 3,062.50 |
| 220 shares × $0.20 commission | = | − 44.00 |
| Net proceeds | | $33,668.50 |

# Computing the Rate of Yield and Gains or Losses

**Learning Objective 3**

Compute rates of yield and gains or losses on the purchase and sale of stocks.

## THE RATE OF YIELD

The **board of directors** is a group of people elected by shareholders to oversee the operations of the corporation. The board has sole authority to distribute earnings to shareholders. When such action is taken, the directors are said to **declare a dividend.** The rate of dividend is either a certain percent of the par value of the stock or a flat amount of money per share. Thus, a dividend of 8% on a stock with a par value of $100 would be $8.00 per share. Most large corporations pay dividends quarterly.

The **rate of yield** from an investment in stock is the ratio of the dividend to the total cost of the stock.

### EXAMPLE F

Aaron Ramos bought 300 shares of Wells Fargo stock at $32 and paid a $19.95 commission. A dividend of $2.15 per share was paid this year. What was the rate of yield?

| | | |
|---|---|---|
| 300 × $32 = | $9,600.00 | purchase price |
| | + 19.95 | commission |
| | $9,619.95 | total cost |

300 × $2.15 = $645 dividend for first year

$645 ÷ $9,619.95 = 6.7% rate of yield

## GAIN OR LOSS ON SALE OF STOCK

For income tax and accounting purposes, the amount of gain or loss on a sale of stock is determined by comparing the sale proceeds to the total cost.

### EXAMPLE G

Refer back to example F. If Aaron sold his stock after 3 years at $36.50, less $19.95 commission, what were the amount and the percent of gain or loss?

| | | |
|---|---|---|
| 300 × $36.50 = | $10,950.00 | selling price |
| | − 19.95 | commission |
| | $10,930.05 | proceeds |

$10,930.05 proceeds − $9,619.95 cost (example F) = $1,310.10 net gain

$1,310.10 ÷ $9,619.95 = 13.6% gain on sale

### EXAMPLE H

Suppose that Aaron held his stock for 3 years and received a $645 dividend each year. Then to determine the total change in value (example G) he would need to add to his proceeds the $1,935 in dividends received.

| Proceeds | Total Dividends | Total Cost | |
|---|---|---|---|
| ($10,930.05 | + $1,935) | − $9,619.95 | = $3,245.10 total gain in value |

$3,245.10 total gain ÷ $9,619.95 initial cost = 33.7% gain in value

## CONCEPT CHECK 21.3

a. Maria Sanchez owns 700 shares of stock with a par value of \$100. If she receives a dividend of 5%, how much will her total dividend be?

\$100 par value × 5% per share = \$5.00 per-share dividend
700 shares × \$5.00 per share = \$3,500 total dividend

b. Maria also owns 300 shares of a stock without a stated par value. If she receives a dividend of \$2.00 per share, what will her total dividend be?

300 shares × \$2.00 per share = \$600 total dividend

c. Magdalena Kaur bought 200 shares of Clorox at \$32.25. A dividend of \$0.45 per share was paid this year. What was the rate of yield?

| | | |
|---|---|---|
| 200 shares × \$32.25 = | \$6,450 | purchase price |
| 200 shares × \$0.20 = | + 40 | commission |
| | \$6,490 | total cost |

200 shares × \$0.45 dividend = \$90 for first year
\$90 dividend ÷ \$6,490 total cost = 1.39% rate of yield

d. After 4 years, Magdalena sold the Clorox stock for \$32.50. What were the amount and percent of gain or loss on the sale?

| | | |
|---|---|---|
| 200 shares × \$32.50 selling price = | \$6,500 | selling price |
| 200 shares × \$0.20 commission = | − 40 | commission |
| | \$6,460 | proceeds |

\$6,460 proceeds − \$6,490 total cost = \$(30) loss
\$(30) loss ÷ \$6,490 total cost = 0.46% loss

e. If Magdalena held the Clorox stock for 4 years, receiving the same \$90 dividend each year, what was the total change in the value over the 4 years?

| **Proceeds** | **+** | **Total Dividends (4 years)** | **−** | **Total Cost** | **=** | **Gain in Value** |
|---|---|---|---|---|---|---|
| (\$6,460 | + | \$360) | − | \$6,490 | = | \$330 |

\$330 gain in value ÷ \$6,490 total cost = 5.08% gain

# Computing Comparative Earning Potential

Learning Objective 4

Compute comparative earning potential of the major classes of corporate stocks.

**Common stock** is the usual type of stock issued by a corporation. Another type frequently issued, **preferred stock,** gives holders a right to share in earnings and liquidation before common shareholders do. For example, a company that has a 7% preferred stock must first pay dividends of 7% of the par value to the holders of preferred stock before anything is paid to the holders of common stock. Preferred stock may be designated as **cumulative**—that is, if the corporation doesn't pay the specified percentage, the unpaid amount, called a **dividend in arrears**, carries over to the following year or years. If dividends aren't paid on noncumulative preferred stock during one year, the unpaid amount doesn't carry over to the next year.

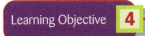

**EXAMPLE I**

The ABC Company earned $48,000 last year. The capital stock of the company consists of 10,000 shares of 7% preferred stock, with a par value of $40 per share, and 50,000 shares of no-par common stock. If the board of directors declared a dividend of the entire earnings, what amount would be paid in total to the preferred and common shareholders and how much would each common shareholder receive?

Preferred: 10,000 shares × $40 par value = $400,000 total value
$400,000 value × 0.07 = $28,000 paid to preferred

Common: $48,000 total earnings − $28,000 paid to preferred = $20,000
$20,000 ÷ 50,000 shares = $0.40 paid per share to common

**EXAMPLE J**

© DIGITALVISION/GETTY IMAGES

Assume in example I that the preferred stock is cumulative and that for the preceding year the company had declared a dividend of only $16,000, or enough to pay a 4% dividend on preferred stock. The earnings of $48,000 for this year would be divided as follows:

| | |
|---|---|
| Unpaid dividend from preceding year: 7% − 4% | = 3% |
| $400,000 preferred par value × 0.03 | = $12,000 cumulative (dividend in arrears) |
| $400,000 × 0.07 dividend for current year | = $28,000 |
| Total paid on preferred stock | = $40,000 |
| $48,000 total earnings − $40,000 paid to preferred | = $ 8,000 |
| $8,000 ÷ 50,000 common shares | = $0.16 dividend per common share |

Another feature that sometimes makes preferred stock an attractive investment is the possibility of converting the preferred stock into common stock. **Convertible preferred stock** gives the owner the option of converting those preferred shares into a stated number of common shares. For example, a stated conversion of 1 to 3 means that 1 share of preferred stock could be changed into 3 shares of common stock. The conversion feature combines the safety of preferred stock with the possibility of growth through conversion to common stock.

**EXAMPLE K**

Joel Turner owned 200 shares of GM convertible preferred stock at $20 par value. He converted each share of preferred into 3 shares of common. How many shares of common stock did Joel receive when he converted?

200 × 3 = 600 shares of common stock

If common stock was selling at $22 per share on the date of conversion, how much was Joel's common stock worth?

$22 × 600 shares = $13,200 common stock value

If Joel paid $42 per share for his preferred stock, how much had his investment increased?

$42 × 200 preferred = $8,400 preferred stock value
$13,200 − $8,400 = $4,800 increase in value

If the convertible stock pays 7% annually and the common stock usually pays \$0.60 per share, how much more dividend might Joel expect to receive annually?

\$20 par value × 200 shares = \$4,000
\$4,000 × 0.07 = \$280 preferred stock dividend
600 shares × \$0.60 = \$360 common stock dividend
\$360 − \$280 = \$80 more dividend annually

## CONCEPT CHECK 21.4

a. The XYZ Corporation had a net profit of \$120,000 in the fiscal year just ended. The capital stock consists of 8,000 shares of 8% convertible preferred stock with a par value of \$50 per share and 20,000 shares of no-par common stock. If the board of directors declared a dividend of the entire earnings, what amount would be paid to preferred and common shareholders?

Preferred: 8,000 shares × \$50 per share = \$400,000 total par value
\$400,000 par value × 8% = \$32,000 paid to preferred shareholders
Common: \$120,000 total earnings − \$32,000 paid to preferred = \$88,000 to be paid to common shareholders

b. Seth Ames owns 1,000 shares of convertible preferred stock in the XYZ Corporation, with a current market price of \$52.00 per share. The preferred stock is convertible to common stock at the rate of 2 shares of common for each share of preferred. After the end of the year in part (a), common stock was selling for \$32 per share. What would be the current market value of his stock before and after a conversion?

Preferred: 1,000 shares × \$52 per share = \$52,000 current value
Common: 1,000 shares preferred × 2 = 2,000 shares common
2,000 shares × \$32 per share = \$64,000 current value

COMPLETE ASSIGNMENTS 21.1 AND 21.2.

## Chapter Terms for Review

- board of directors
- capital stock
- charter
- common stock
- convertible preferred stock
- corporation
- cumulative preferred stock
- declare a dividend
- dividend in arrears
- no-par stock
- odd lot
- odd-lot differential
- par
- preferred stock
- price/earnings ratio (P/E)
- proceeds (from sale of stock)
- rate of yield
- round lot
- stockbroker
- stock certificate
- stock exchanges
- stock transactions
- total cost (for purchaser of stock)



Answers: 1. \$2,679 2. \$1,224 3. \$83,200 4. \$31,348 5. Total cost, \$25,986.50; net proceeds, \$29,485.50; gain \$3,499.00 6. \$60,000 7. \$5.50 per share 8. 750 shares 9. \$19,875

**Try Microsoft® Excel**

SELF-CHECK

# Review Problems for Chapter 21

1 Use the following stock quotes from the NYSE to answer questions (a) through (e) below.

| 52 Weeks | | | | | | | | | | | |
|---|---|---|---|---|---|---|---|---|---|---|---|
| High | Low | Stock | Div | % Yld | PE | Vol 1,000s | Hi | Low | Close | Chg |
| 107.38 | 74.12 | Boeing | 0.40 | 1.96 | 15.4 | 37,700 | 81.90 | 80.54 | 80.54 | −0.04 |
| 43.20 | 21.34 | GM | 0.25 | 3.78 | 0 | 18,165 | 26.30 | 25.59 | 25.71 | −0.76 |

**a.** How many shares of Boeing were traded?
**b.** What was the closing price per share of GM in dollars and cents?
**c.** What was the previous day's closing price for each stock?
**d.** By how much has the price of 1 share of Boeing stock changed over the last 52 weeks?
**e.** Use the P/E ratio to calculate the earnings per share for the last four quarters for Boeing.

2 Determine the total cost or proceeds of each purchase or sale. Include regular commission of $0.20 per share and an odd-lot differential of $0.125 per share.

**a.** Purchased 300 shares of Caterpillar at $67.80.
**b.** Purchased 550 shares of Sprint at $9.66.
**c.** Sold 200 shares of Washington Mutual at $18.07.

3 Jason purchased 500 shares of XYZ stock at $17.12. One year later he sold the 500 shares at $18. He paid a transaction fee of $19.95 for each transaction.

**a.** What was the amount of gain or loss on the sale?
**b.** What was the rate of gain or loss?

4 Jason from question 3 received dividends of $0.65 per share during the year that he owned the stock.

**a.** What was the rate of dividend yield?
**b.** What was the total rate of gain or loss including the dividend?

5 Audrey owned 400 shares of Znix convertible preferred stock with a $20 par value. She converted all 400 shares into common stock at the rate of 4 to 1 (4 shares of common stock for each share of preferred). How many shares of common stock did she receive?

6 The Znix preferred stock from question 5 paid an annual dividend of 8%. Znix paid annual dividends on its common stock of $0.60 per share. How much more will Audrey receive each year in dividends by converting her stock from preferred to common?

7 Alpha Company's capital consists of 8,000 shares of $50 par 7.5% preferred stock and 50,000 shares of no-par common stock. The board of directors declared a dividend of $85,000. What is the dividend per share for preferred and common stock?

8 Assume the preferred stock in question 7 is cumulative and no dividends were declared the year before. Determine the dividend to be paid for each share of preferred and common if the board declares a total dividend of $90,000 the current year.

**Answers to the Self-Check can be found in Appendix B at the back of the text.**

# Assignment 21.1: Buying and Selling Stock

Name ______________________________

Date ______________ Score ______________

Learning Objectives 1 2

**A (41 points) For calculations, use $0.20 a share for commissions unless the problem gives a flat fee and $0.125 for the odd-lot differential. Round all percents to two places. (5 points for a correct answer to problem 3; 4 points for each other correct answer)**

**1.** Gail Sanders purchased 2,000 shares of Bank of America (BAC) common stock at $42.50 and 180 shares of preferred stock at $60.

**a.** What was the total cost of the purchase of common stock? ________

**b.** What was the total cost of the purchase of preferred stock? ________

**2.** Three months later, Gail sold her 2,000 shares of BAC common stock at $44 and her 180 shares of preferred stock at $58.50.

**a.** What were the proceeds on the sale of common stock? ________

**b.** What were the proceeds on the sale of preferred stock? ________

**c.** How much did Gail gain or lose on the purchase and sale of all of her BAC stock? ________

**3.** Susan Lu purchased 200 shares of Telmart common stock at $88.50 and paid a $19.95 transaction fee. A dividend of $7.00 per share was paid the first year. What was the rate of yield? ________

**4.** Sheri Jeffers purchased stock for a total cost of $12,600, including commission. She sold the stock a month later for $13,960, after commission.

**a.** What was her net gain on the sale? ________

**b.** What was her percent of gain on the sale? ________

**c.** If Sheri had held her stock another week and sold for $12,280 after commission, what would her percent of loss on the sale have been? ________

**5.** If Sheri hadn't sold her stock for $12,280 but had waited another 3 months while the stock fell to a price where she could have realized net proceeds of $11,275, what would have been her percent of loss? ________

________

Score for A (41)

**B** **(59 points) Solve the following problems. (points for correct answers as marked)**

**6.** Peter Roncalio, Paul Stevens, and Mary Petrakas each invested $10,000 in different areas. Calculate the value of each $10,000 investment at the end of 2 years. (5 points for each correct answer)

**a.** Peter put his $10,000 in a savings account that paid 6.2% interest annually. (Add interest on the savings account the first year to the principal before figuring interest for the second year.) ________

**b.** Paul bought 9%, $50 par value preferred stock at $62.50 a share, including commission. He received his full dividend at the end of each year. He sold his stock at the end of the second year. The sales proceeds, after commission, were $62.50 a share. ________

**c.** Mary bought common stock at $40 a share, including commission. Her stock paid quarterly dividends of 90 cents per share. In 2 years, the stock decreased to a value of $38.50 a share. ________

**7.** Find the amount of the dividend per share and the rate of yield per share for each of the following preferred stocks. The cost per share includes all commissions. (2 points for each correct answer)

**a.** Cost per share $32; dividend declared $2.10.

Amount of dividend ________

Rate of yield ________

**b.** Cost per share $80; par value $100; dividend declared 6%.

Amount of dividend ________

Rate of yield ________

**c.** Cost per share $44.50; dividend declared $2.00.

Amount of dividend ________

Rate of yield ________

**d.** Cost per share $90; par value $100; dividend declared 5.5%.

Amount of dividend ________

Rate of yield ________

**e.** Cost per share $58; par value $50; dividend declared 6.5%.

Amount of dividend ________

Rate of yield ________

**8.** Determine the amount and percent of gain or loss for each of the following transactions. Show an amount of loss in parentheses ( ). The purchase costs and the sale proceeds include commissions. Round percents to two decimal places. (3 points for each correct answer)

| | Number of Shares | Per-Share Purchase Cost | Per-Share Sale Proceeds | Amount of Gain or Loss | Percent of Gain or Loss |
|---|---|---|---|---|---|
| **a.** | 100 | $47.20 | $52.85 | ________ | ________ |
| **b.** | 250 | 12.00 | 14.50 | ________ | ________ |
| **c.** | 140 | 22.30 | 20.70 | ________ | ________ |
| **d.** | 640 | 17.00 | 12.75 | ________ | ________ |

________________

Score for B (59)

# Assignment 21.2: Capital Stock

Name ______________________

Date ____________ Score ____________

Learning Objectives 3 4

**A** **(34 points) The information in problem 1 also applies to problems 2 and 3. (2 points for each correct answer)**

**1.** The Duval Company was incorporated with 7% preferred capital stock of $500,000 and common stock of $1,800,000. The par value of the preferred stock was $100, and the par value of the common stock was $20. How many shares of each kind of stock were there?

Preferred stock __________

Common stock __________

**2.** Last year, dividends were declared by the Duval Company, which had earnings totaling $359,000.

**a.** What was the total amount of the preferred stock dividend? __________

**b.** What amount would have been paid on each share of common stock if all the earnings had been distributed?

__________

**3.** The directors of the Duval Company actually declared four quarterly dividends of $0.75 a share on the common stock and $\frac{1}{4}$ of the amount due annually on the preferred stock.

**a.** What was the total amount paid by Duval to all common shareholders for each quarterly dividend? __________

**b.** What was the total amount paid to preferred shareholders each quarter? __________

**c.** What was the quarterly per-share payment to preferred shareholders? __________

**d.** What was the year's total amount of the common stock dividends? __________

**e.** What was the total amount of all dividends paid by Duval during the year? __________

**f.** How much more in dividends was paid to each share of preferred than to each share of common? __________

4. The capital stock of the Shubert Company consists of 300,000 shares of preferred stock and 5,500,000 shares of common stock. Last year, a dividend of $3.60 a share was declared on preferred stock and four quarterly dividends of $0.35 a share on common stock. How much was the total dividend for the year on each class of stock?

Preferred stock ___________

Common stock ___________

5. ComputerMart has 150,000 shares of 6.5% preferred stock at $1 par value and 1,500,000 shares of common stock. ComputerMart declared total dividends of $250,000 for the current year. How much was the total dividend for preferred stock and how much was the dividend per share on the common stock?

Preferred stock ___________

Common stock ___________

(per share)

6. Michael Wu bought 300 shares of XRT 8% preferred stock, $10 par value, when it was selling at $11 per share, including commission.

a. What was Michael's stock worth at the time of purchase? ___________

b. What was the amount of Michael's quarterly dividend? ___________

c. What was Michael's dividend yield? ___________

___________

Score for A (34)

**B (66 points) Do not consider commission in the following problems. (points for correct answers as marked)**

7. Inland Sales, Inc., has issued 25,000 shares of 8%, $20 par, cumulative preferred stock and 50,000 shares of common stock. The board of directors declares 50% of net income each year as dividends. Inland Sales had net income of $76,000 for 2000, $112,000 for 2001, and $130,000 for 2002. Compute the annual dividends per share for preferred and common stock for each of the 3 years. (2 points for each correct answer)

| Year | Preferred Dividends/Share | Common Dividends/Share |
|---|---|---|
| 2000 | ___________ | ___________ |
| 2001 | ___________ | ___________ |
| 2002 | ___________ | ___________ |

**8.** Dan Baxter owned 200 shares of Sony 6.5% convertible preferred stock, $50 par value, for which he paid $56 per share, including commission. Two years later, after receiving preferred dividends each year, he converted to 600 shares of Sony common stock, valued at $23.50 a share at the time of conversion. (4 points for each correct answer)

**a.** What was the cost to Dan of the preferred stock? __________

**b.** How much did Dan receive in dividends from the preferred stock? __________

**c.** What was the value of the common stock that Dan received? __________

**d.** If he sells the 600 common shares immediately, how much gain will Dan realize, including his dividend?

__________

**e.** What would be Dan's percent of gain? __________

**9.** Texas Air Corporation issued 5,000,000 shares of 7% preferred stock at $100 par value and 10,000,000 shares of no-par common stock. Bob Thruston owned 100 shares of preferred. Barbara Beck owned 500 shares of common. In 2009, Texas Air paid $25,000,000 in dividends to its common shareholders. How much more than Bob did Barbara receive? (10 points) __________

**10.** Sonia Revas owned 700 shares of PIE 6% convertible stock, $50 par value, for which she paid $42 a share. She received a dividend for 1 year. She then converted the preferred stock to 400 shares of common stock valued at $98.50 a share. (4 points for each correct answer)

**a.** What was the cost to Sonia for her preferred stock? __________

**b.** How much did Sonia receive as a dividend for her preferred stock? __________

**c.** What was the value of her common stock at the time of conversion? __________

**d.** If the common stock paid an annual dividend of $6.00 a share, how much more dividend would she receive annually? __________

**e.** What was Sonia's percent of increase in annual return as a result of conversion to common stock? __________

**11.** Determine the price/earnings ratio (P/E) of each of the following stocks: (2 points for each correct answer)

**a.** JBC common stock has a current market price of $49 and has had earnings per share of $0.72 each quarter for the last four quarters. __________

**b.** The current market price of Cannon common stock is $72.88. Cannon has paid dividends of $1.20 per quarter for each of the last four quarters. __________

__________________

Score for B (66)

# 22

# Corporate and Government Bonds

## Learning Objectives

By studying this chapter and completing all assignments, you will be able to:

**Learning Objective 1** Compute gains and losses on convertible and callable corporate bond transactions.

**Learning Objective 2** Compute annual interest on bonds.

**Learning Objective 3** Compute accrued interest on bond transactions made between interest payment dates.

**Learning Objective 4** Compute annual yield on bonds selling at a premium or a discount.

**Learning Objective 5** Compute a rate of yield to maturity.

When a corporation or government entity needs cash for a long period of time, usually 10 years or more, it often will issue long-term notes known as **bonds.** Bonds are bought and sold on the open market, much like stocks.

Two main types of **government bonds** are treasury bonds and municipal bonds. **Treasury bonds** are issued by the United States government. These bonds are fully guaranteed by the full faith and credit of the United States government. Bondholders are protected against default unless the federal government becomes insolvent. **Municipal bonds** are issued by states, cities, school districts, and other public entities. Unlike treasury bonds, municipal bonds pose a risk that the issuer might fail to repay the principal. Interest paid on municipal bonds generally is exempt from federal and state income taxes.

There are many kinds of **corporate bonds,** two of which are convertible bonds and callable bonds. **Convertible bonds** have a provision that they may be converted to a designated number of shares or a designated value of the corporation's stock. **Callable bonds** have a provision that the issuer can repurchase, or call in, the bonds at specified dates if the board of directors authorizes the retirement (payoff) of the bonds before their maturity date. Such action by the board of directors would be appropriate if interest rates fell significantly below the interest rate of the callable bond.

## Computing Gains and Losses on Corporate Bonds

**Learning Objective 1**

Compute gains and losses on convertible and callable corporate bond transactions.

**EXAMPLE A**

Steve Bando bought one ABC Corporation convertible bond for $1,000. The bond was convertible to 100 shares of stock. At the time of the purchase, the stock was selling for $10 per share. At the end of 1 year, the stock was selling for $15 per share. Steve converted his bond. Assuming that the market value of the bond hadn't changed, how much profit did Steve realize by converting?

100 shares of stock × $15 per share = $1,500
$1,500 stock value − $1,000 bond value = $500 profit

**EXAMPLE B**

XYZ Corporation issued $1,000,000 worth of callable bonds paying 8% interest. The maturity date for the bonds was in 10 years. Two years later, interest rates fell to 6%. The bonds were called, and new bonds were sold at the 6% rate. How much did XYZ Corporation save by calling the bonds?

10 years to maturity at issue − 2 years = 8 years remaining to maturity
8% − 6% = 2% savings per year
$1,000,000 × 2% = $20,000 interest saved per year
$20,000 × 8 years = $160,000 saved

## CONCEPT CHECK 22.1

a. What would be the "stock" value of a bond that was convertible to 40 shares of stock if the stock was priced at $37.62?

40 shares × $37.62 = $1,504.80

b. If a company issued a callable bond at $7\frac{1}{2}\%$ interest, would it be likely to call the bond if the current rate of interest was 8%?

No, because it could invest the cash at an extra $\frac{1}{2}\%$ interest.

# Computing Annual Interest on Corporate and Government Bonds

**Learning Objective 2**

Compute annual interest on bonds.

When first issued, bonds are sold either through brokerage houses or directly to investors at or near the price of $1,000, called face value. **Face value** represents the amount that will be paid to the holder when the bonds are redeemed at maturity. If the market value becomes less than the face value, the bond sells at a **discount.** If the market value becomes more than the face value, the bond sells at a **premium.** (The discount or premium amount is the difference between the market value and the face value.)

Bonds are rated. By checking a bond's rating, buyers can have some indication of how safe their bond investment is. **Bond ratings** are information based on experience and research; they are not a guarantee. One major firm rating bonds is Standard & Poor's.

In Standard & Poor's system, the ratings include AAA (the highest rating), AA, A, BBB, BB, B, CCC, CC, C, and D. A bond with a low rating is a higher-risk bond and sometimes is known as a **junk bond.** The lower a bond's rating, the higher are its yield and its risk.

### EXAMPLE C

Kiley Moore purchased a $1,000 bond with a rating of B, paying 14% per year. Mary Baker purchased a $1,000 bond with a rating of AAA, paying 5% per year. Jean Carlson purchased a $1,000 junk bond, paying 25% per year. Each bond was to mature in 10 years.

Kiley's B-rated bond paid faithfully for 4 years. Then the company filed for bankruptcy and paid 60 cents on the dollar. Mary's AAA-rated bond paid interest during its entire 10-year life and paid face value on maturity. Jean's junk bond paid interest for 3 years. Then the company filed for bankruptcy and paid 30 cents on the dollar.

Compute how much each investor received for her $1,000 investment.

Kiley: $1,000 × 14% = $140 annual interest
$140 × 4 years = $560 interest
$560 interest + (0.60 × $1,000) redemption = $1,160 total

© COMSTOCK IMAGES/JUPITERIMAGES

Mary: $1,000 × 5% = $50 annual interest
$50 × 10 years = $500 interest
$500 interest + $1,000 redemption = $1,500 total

Jean: $1,000 × 25% = $250 annual interest
$250 × 3 years = $750 interest
$750 interest + (0.30 × $1,000) redemption = $1,050 total

How much would Kiley and Jean have received on their investments if the bonds had paid full interest for the 10-year period and face value on maturity?

Kiley: $1,000 × 14% × 10 years = $1,400
$1,400 + $1,000 = $2,400

Jean: $1,000 × 25% × 10 years = $2,500
$2,500 + $1,000 = $3,500

## NEWSPAPER INFORMATION ON BONDS

Information about the market value and sale of bonds on the major exchanges is reported daily in financial newspapers. Figure 22-1 shows information usually included in a bond report.

**Figure 22-1** **Bond Market Report**

| Bonds | Current Yield | Volume | Close | Net Change |
|---|---|---|---|---|
| ATT $7\frac{1}{2}$s09 | 7.2 | 10 | 104 | +1 |
| Aetna $6\frac{3}{8}$s12 | 6.6 | 25 | 96.80 | . . . |
| ClrkOil $9\frac{1}{2}$s06 | 9.1 | 33 | 104.25 | +.25 |
| Hertz 7s12 | 7.0 | 13 | 99.70 | +.70 |
| IBM 7s25 | 7.4 | 102 | 94.50 | +.80 |
| RJR Nb 8s10 | 7.9 | 15 | 101.50 | . . . |

Prices of bonds are quoted in percents of face value. For example, a $1,000 bond quoted at 104 would sell at a premium price of $1,040 ($1,000 × 104%). If quoted at 87, the bond would sell at a discounted price of $870 ($1,000 × 87%).

**Rule: Prices over 100 (100%) include a premium. Those under 100 (100%) include a discount.**

The two main factors that influence the market price are the interest rate and the bond rating. For example, if a bond pays 8% interest and the current market rate of interest is greater than 8% for similarly rated bonds, the bonds will sell at a discount sufficient to make up for the difference in interest rates over the term of the bond.

Printed bond reports generally give a letter abbreviation for the company, the interest rate, a small s to designate *semiannual* (every 6 months) interest payments, and the maturity date, followed by the current yield, the number of bonds sold that day, the closing price of the bond, and the net change in price from the prior day.

The first line of the bond market report in Figure 22-1 would be interpreted as ATT (designating American Telephone and Telegraph), a $7\frac{1}{2}$ interest rate based on the face value of the bond, and interest paid semiannually. The bond matures in 2009. The current yield (average annual interest rate based on the current price of the bond) is 7.2%. The day's volume of bonds sold was 10. The closing price was 104, up 1 from the prior day.

**EXAMPLE D**

Calculate the amount of the semiannual interest check for a $1,000 bond reported in a financial paper as R&S Corp $7\frac{1}{2}$s21.

$1,000 face value × $7\frac{1}{2}$% = $75; $75 ÷ 2 = $37.50 semiannual interest payment

## COMMISSIONS FOR BUYING AND SELLING BONDS

The charge for buying and selling bonds varies among brokers, but there is no standard commission. Commissions are very small and thus comprise only a negligible part of the bond transaction. We do not use commission costs for problems in this textbook.

**CONCEPT CHECK 22.2**

If James Kun purchased 27 triple-A bonds that pay 7.1% and mature in 8 years, what amount of interest income could he expect annually?

$1,000 × 0.071 × 27 = $1,917

If James holds the bonds until maturity, how much will he receive on redemption of the bonds?

$1,000 × 27 = $27,000 total face value

# Computing Accrued Interest on Bond Transactions

Learning Objective 3

Compute accrued interest on bond transactions made between interest payment dates.

Most bonds specify that interest is payable quarterly, semiannually, or annually. The interest payment dates—such as January 1 (for interest through December 31) and July 1 (for interest through June 30)—are stated on the bond. When a bond is purchased between these dates, it is customary to add the **accrued interest** (interest earned from the last payment date to the purchase date). This interest is calculated by finding the number of days from the day on which interest was last paid through the day before the purchase and dividing this number by 360.

The buyer pays the seller for the interest accumulated or accrued on the bond since the last interest payment date. On the next regular interest payment date, the new owner receives the interest for the full interest period. This procedure allocates the interest correctly between the buyer and the seller for the split interest period because the corporation that issued the bond will pay the entire amount to whomever owns the bond as of each interest date.

**EXAMPLE E**

A $1,000 bond, with interest at 8% payable semiannually on January 1 and July 1, was purchased on October 8 at 104 plus accrued interest. What is the number of days for which the accrued interest is paid?

Purchase date: October 8

Days of accrued interest: (July) 31 + (August) 31 + (September) 30 + (October) 7 = 99

What is the purchase payment for the bond?

$\$1{,}000 \times 104\% = \$1{,}040$ market value

$\$1{,}000 \times 0.08$ interest $\times \frac{99}{360}$ accrued days $= \$22$ accrued interest

$\$1{,}040 + \$22 = \$1{,}062$ purchase payment for bond

In example E, although the accrued interest is an additional payment by the buyer, the buyer will get it back in the $40 ($\$1{,}000 \times 8\% \times \frac{1}{2}$) interest payment on January 1.

**CONCEPT CHECK 22.3**

Ann Ahn purchased two Hertz 7s08 bonds at 95.6 on March 15. What amount did she pay her broker?

$\$2{,}000 \times 0.956 = \$1{,}912.00$

Purchase date: March 15

(January) 31 + (February) 28 + (March) 14 = 73 days

$\$2{,}000 \times 0.07 \times \frac{73}{360} = \$28.39$ accrued interest

$\$1{,}912.00 + \$28.39 = \$1{,}940.39$ paid to her broker

## Computing the Rate of Yield for Bonds

**Learning Objective 4**

Compute annual yield on bonds selling at a premium or a discount.

Interest on bonds provides income to bondholders. This income is referred to as **yield.** Newspapers and bond brokers refer to the annual yield of a bond as its **current yield.** Many newspaper bond reports include a column showing current yield. To calculate the current yield from an investment in bonds, use the following formula:

Annual interest ÷ Current purchase price = Current yield

When a bond is purchased at a discount, the current yield is greater than the face rate. For example, a $1,000 bond, purchased at 90, pays 7% interest and matures in 10 years. Interest of $70 ($\$1{,}000 \times 7\%$) is paid annually, but as the bond was purchased for $900 ($\$1{,}000 \times 90\%$), the effective rate, or yield, as a percent of cost is 7.8% ($\$70 \div \$900$).

When a bond is purchased at a premium, the current yield is less than the face rate. The reason is that the interest paid is calculated on the face value, and the yield is based on the higher market price.

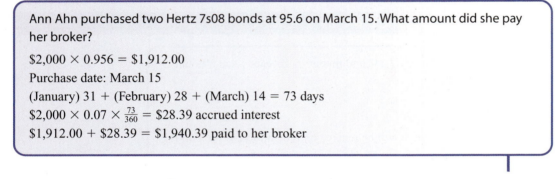

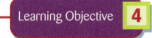

**EXAMPLE F**

Five \$1,000 Levi Strauss $9\frac{1}{2}$s19 bonds were purchased at 80. What was the current yield on the bonds?

\$1,000 × 5 = \$5,000 face value
\$5,000 × 80% = \$4,000 purchase price
\$5,000 × 0.095 = \$475 annual interest
\$475 ÷ \$4,000 = 0.11875 = 11.9 % current yield
or 9.5 ÷ 0.80 = 11.875 = 11.9% current yield

In example F, the bonds sold at a discount of \$1,000 (\$5,000 − \$4,000) because the investor paid that much less for them than the maturity (face) value. Therefore, the current yield of 11.8% is more than the stated interest rate of $9\frac{1}{2}$%.

**CONCEPT CHECK 22.4**

The RJR Nb bonds listed in Figure 22-1 recently rose to a price of 109. Zelda Morantz purchased four at 109. What will be her annual current yield?

\$4,000 × 109% = \$4,360 purchase price
\$4,000 × 0.08 = \$320 annual interest
\$320 ÷ \$4,360 = 0.0734, or 7.34%,
or 0.08 ÷ 1.09 = 0.0734, or 7.34%

# Computing the Rate of Yield to Maturity

Careful investors calculate the **rate of yield to maturity,** or the rate of interest they will earn if they hold the bond to its maturity date. The yield to maturity calculation involves use of the true annual interest by adding a part of the discount or subtracting a part of the premium and basing the rate on the average principal invested (the average of the investor's purchase price and the bond's maturity value).

Learning Objective 5

Compute a rate of yield to maturity.

**STEPS to Compute the Rate of Yield to Maturity**

1. Compute the annual interest: Multiply the face value by the stated (face) rate.
2. Determine the **annual discount** (or **premium**) **amortization:** Divide the discount (or premium) by the number of years from purchase to maturity.
3. Determine the **average principal invested:** Add the maturity value and the cost price and then divide by 2.
4. The following formula computes the rate:

$$\frac{\text{Annual interest} + \text{Annual discount amortization (or} - \text{Annual premium amortization)}}{\text{Average principal invested}}$$

Again, because brokerage charges are such a small part of the cost, they usually are omitted from the calculations of yield to maturity.

**EXAMPLE G**

Assume that the Levi Strauss bonds in example F matured 20 years after the purchase date.

STEP 1 $\$5{,}000 \times 0.095 = \$475$ annual interest

STEP 2 $\$1{,}000 \div 20$ years $= \$50$ annual discount amortization

STEP 3 $(\$5{,}000 + \$4{,}000) \div 2 = \$4{,}500$ average principal invested

STEP 4 $(\$475 + \$50) \div \$4{,}500 = 0.1167 = 11.67\%$ yield to maturity

This rate is somewhat less than the 11.9% current yield, but it is more accurate with respect to actual income if the bond is held to maturity.

**EXAMPLE H**

To calculate the yield to maturity on bonds sold at a premium, assume that five IntTT $9\frac{1}{2}$s20 bonds were bought at a premium price of 124 and that the bonds will mature in 15 years. The market value of the five bonds is \$6,200 ($\$5{,}000 \times 124\%$).

STEP 1 $\$5{,}000 \times 0.095 = \$475$ annual interest

STEP 2 $(\$6{,}200 - \$5{,}000) \div 15$ years $= \$80$ annual premium amortization

STEP 3 $(\$5{,}000 + \$6{,}200) \div 2 = \$5{,}600$ average principal invested

STEP 4 $(\$475 - \$80) \div \$5{,}600 = 0.0705 = 7.05\%$ yield to maturity

This rate is less than the stated rate of $9\frac{1}{2}\%$ on the premium bonds.

## CONCEPT CHECK 22.5

If the four RJR Nb 8s10 bonds Zelda Morantz purchased at 109 (Concept Check 22.4) had 5 years to maturity, what would be her rate of yield to maturity?

$\$4{,}000 \times 0.08 = \$320$ annual interest
$\$360$ premium $\div 5$ years $= \$72$ annual premium amortization
$(\$4{,}000 + \$4{,}360) \div 2 = \$4{,}180$ average principal invested
$(\$320 - \$72) \div \$4{,}180 = 0.0593 = 5.93\%$ yield to maturity

COMPLETE ASSIGNMENTS 22.1 and 22.2.

## Chapter Terms for Review

accrued interest
annual discount amortization
annual premium amortization
average principal invested
bond ratings
bonds
callable bonds
convertible bonds
corporate bonds
current yield
discount
face value
government bonds
junk bond
municipal bonds
premium (bond)
rate of yield to maturity
treasury bonds
yield

## Try Microsoft® Excel

Try working the following problems using the Microsoft Excel templates found on your Student CD. Solutions for the problems are also found on the CD.

1. Complete the following Excel worksheet by entering formulas in the shaded cells to calculate the **Total Cost** and **Premium** or (**Discount**) for each bond purchase. *Hint: Remember that each bond has a face value of $1,000.*

| Number Purchased | Price Paid | Total Cost | Premium (Discount) |
|---|---|---|---|
| 5 | 92 | | |
| 12 | 108 | | |
| 8 | 112 | | |
| 2 | 88 | | |
| 16 | 92 | | |

2. Complete the following Excel worksheet by entering formulas in the shaded cells to calculate the **Annual Interest, Current Purchase Price,** and **Current Yield** for each bond.
*Hint: Calculations are for one bond (face value $1,000). Current yield should be shown as a percent.*

| Bond | Price | Annual Interest | Current Purchase Price | Current Yield |
|---|---|---|---|---|
| IBM 7s12 | 90 | | | |
| SBC 9s08 | 107 | | | |
| CXL 6.2s09 | 86.5 | | | |

3. Complete the following Excel worksheet by entering formulas in the shaded cells to calculate the Yield to Maturity for six InTT 8.2s18 bonds purchased at a premium price of 120. The bonds will mature in 12 years.
*Hint: Use parentheses to do addition or subtraction before multiplication or division. Yield to maturity should be shown as a percent.*

| | |
|---|---|
| Market Value of Bonds | |
| Annual Interest | |
| Annual Premium Amortization | |
| Average Principal Invested | |
| Yield to Maturity | |

# THE BOTTOM LINE

*Summary of chapter learning objectives:*

| Learning Objective | Example |
|---|---|
| **22.1**<br>Compute gains and losses on convertible and callable corporate bond transactions. | 1. John Jacobs bought five DVC bonds at $1,000 per bond. Each bond was convertible after 3 years to 50 shares of stock. At the end of 3 years, shares of DVC stock were selling at $32. The bond price had risen to 120. Should Mark exercise his option to convert?<br>2. Colton Mfg. Corp. issued $2,000,000 worth of callable bonds paying 9% interest. The maturity date for the bonds was in 20 years. Four years later, interest rates fell to $7\frac{1}{2}$%. The bonds were called, and new bonds sold at the $7\frac{1}{2}$% rate. How much did Colton Mfg. Corp. save by calling the bonds? |
| **22.2**<br>Compute annual interest on bonds. | 3. Amy Coles purchased three 12-year, $1,000 bonds: one Boeing at 7%, one U.S. Treasury at 4.5%, and one Water World Sports at 12%. If the Water World Sports bond defaulted after 5 years and paid holders 60%, which bond produced the most income in the 5-year period, assuming that the $400 loss on the WWS bond was considered to be a reduction in income? How much did it produce? |
| **22.3**<br>Compute accrued interest on bond transactions made between interest payment dates. | 4. One BLM 9s18 bond was purchased at 102 on February 12. What was the amount of accrued interest if interest is paid January 1 and July 1? |
| **22.4**<br>Compute annual yield on bonds selling at a premium or a discount. | 5. Six Khol 7.4s25 bonds were purchased at 92. What was the current yield? |
| **22.5**<br>Compute a rate of yield to maturity. | 6. Three NYR 8s20 bonds were purchased at 120. The bonds will mature in 14 years. What is the rate of yield to maturity? |

**Answers:** 1. The stock has $2,000 greater value; yes, he should convert 2. $480,000 3. Boeing; $350 4. $10.50 5. 8.04% 6. 5.97%

SELF-CHECK

# Review Problems for Chapter 22

1. Alfred Tennyson purchased 15 IBM 7½s18 bonds at 104.
   - **a.** What was the cost of the bonds?
   - **b.** How often will interest be paid?
   - **c.** How much interest will Alfred receive each interest period?
   - **d.** Assuming the bonds pay interest on April 1 and October 1, calculate the accrued interest if the bonds were purchased June 6.
   - **e.** What is the total amount Alfred paid for the bonds including accrued interest?
   - **f.** Were the bonds purchased at a premium or a discount?
   - **g.** What was the amount of the premium or discount?
   - **h.** When do the bonds mature?
   - **i.** What is the current yield on the bonds?
   - **j.** Assume the bonds mature in 12 years. Calculate the yield to maturity.

2. Marta Samuals purchased six Xerox $1,000 convertible bonds at 95. Each bond was convertible into 30 shares of common stock. After 5 years, when the stock was selling at $42, Marta converted all six bonds.
   - **a.** How many shares of stock did she receive?
   - **b.** What was the value of the stock upon conversion?
   - **c.** What was Marta's gain upon conversion of the bonds?
   - **d.** Should Marta convert her bonds into stock if the stock's current market price is $35 per share? Why or why not?

3. Avis, Inc., issued $50,000,000 of 9½%, 20-year, callable bonds. After 6 years, the interest rate fell to 8%. How much interest would Avis save by calling the bonds and reissuing bonds at the lower rate?

4. Ron Nelson is considering purchasing one of the following bonds:

   MCD 7s15 at a market price of 90
   AOC 8s15 at a market price of 100
   JBC 9s15 at a market price of 110

   Calculate the annual yield and yield to maturity for each bond assuming there are 10 years to maturity for each bond. Which bond would you recommend Ron purchase based on your computations?

**Answers to the Self-Check can be found in Appendix B at the back of the text.**

# Assignment 22.1: Corporate and Government Bonds

Name ______________________________

Date ______________ Score ______________

Learning Objectives 1 2 3

**A (38 points) Solve the following problems. (points for correct answers as marked)**

**1.** Jean Francis purchased seven IBM $1,000 convertible bonds at $1.05. Each bond was convertible to 25 shares of IBM stock in 5 years. At the end of 5 years, IBM stock was selling at $97. If Jean converted, what would be her 5-year capital gain? (4 points) __________

**2.** Return to problem 1 and assume that the stock price after 5 years was $38. How much more money would Jean get by cashing in the bonds rather than converting to stock? (4 points) __________

**3.** The city of Jamestown, Virginia, issued $27,000,000 worth of callable bonds at 9% on January 1, 2008. The bonds were due in 2023. If interest rates were to fall to 6.5% on January 1, 2015, how much could Jamestown save by reissuing the bonds at the 6.5% rate on January 1, 2015? (4 points) __________

**4.** Assume that an investor had purchased $500,000 worth of the Jamestown bonds referred to in problem 3. How much interest would he lose from having the bonds called if he reinvested in the new bond issue? (4 points) __________

**5.** Devi Sharma purchased 22 corporate bonds, as shown. What was her total cost, and how much interest income would she realize annually? (1 point for each correct answer)

| Bond | Number Purchased | Price | Total Cost | Annual Interest |
|---|---|---|---|---|
| **a.** Apex $7\frac{1}{2}$s09 | 4 | 100 | __________ | __________ |
| **b.** DukeP $7\frac{7}{8}$s02 | 3 | 98 | __________ | __________ |
| **c.** PGE $10\frac{1}{8}$s12 | 9 | 86 | __________ | __________ |
| **d.** IBM $9\frac{3}{8}$s08 | 6 | 109 | __________ | __________ |
| Total | 22 | | __________ | __________ |

**6.** What is the dollar amount of interest per year and the maturity date for each of the following $1,000 bonds? (1 point for each correct answer)

| Bond | Interest | Maturity Date | Bond | Interest | Maturity Date |
|---|---|---|---|---|---|
| **a.** PGE 6s08 | ________ | ________ | **d.** Fldcst $12\frac{1}{2}$ s12 | ________ | ________ |
| **b.** Avnet 8s13 | ________ | ________ | **e.** OwCor 12s10 | ________ | ________ |
| **c.** CPoWV 9s15 | ________ | ________ | **f.** Cisco $7\frac{1}{2}$ s09 | ________ | ________ |

________

Score for A (38)

**B** **(50 points) Solve the following problems. (points for correct answers as marked)**

**7.** In each of the following problems, determine the number of days for which accrued interest is paid and the total purchase payment made for the bonds. (5 points for each correct answer)

**a.** On September 12, Tracy Dean bought, at 103 plus accrued interest, two IBM 9s10 bonds with interest paid on January 1 and July 1.

Number of days accrued interest: ________ Total payment: ________

**b.** On October 9, Ben Blue bought, at 93 plus accrued interest, three IBM $7\frac{1}{2}$s09 bonds with interest paid on January 1 and July 1.

Number of days accrued interest: ________ Total payment: ________

**8.** Jack Mueller purchased a $1,000 corporate bond with a rating of AAA, paying 8% per year. Tom Bronkowski purchased a $1,000 junk bond paying 20%. Each bond was to mature in 10 years. Jack's bond paid interest for the 10-year period and face value at maturity. Tom's junk bond paid interest for 3 years before the company filed for bankruptcy and paid 45 cents on the dollar to its bondholders. How much more did Jack receive from his investment than Tom received from his? (10 points)

**9.** Compute the current yield for the following bonds. (5 points for each correct answer)

| Bond | Price | Current Yield |
|---|---|---|
| **a.** PepsiCo 9s08 | 108 | ________ |
| **b.** IBM $7\frac{3}{8}$s08 | 93.5 | ________ |
| **c.** Avitar 10s12 | 112 | ________ |
| **d.** ABM 6s08 | 82 | ________ |

________

Score for B (50)

# Assignment 22.2: Bond Rate of Yield

Name ______________________________

Date ______________ Score ______________

Learning Objectives 4 5

**A (52 points) Solve the following problems. (points for correct answers as marked)**

**1.** An investor bought a 7.4% bond at 90. The bond would mature in 8 years. Round answers to two decimal places. (4 points for each correct answer)

**a.** What was the average annual yield? ________ **b.** What was the rate of yield to maturity? ________

**2.** In 2008, Jim Ayers bought six LTV 5s23 bonds for which he paid 82. Three years later, he sold the bonds at 84 and bought six Southern Electric $9\frac{1}{2}$s30 bonds at 93. Did he increase or decrease the original rate of yield to maturity, and, if so, by how much? Round yields to one decimal place. (14 points) ________

**3.** On July 29, Ann McCoy purchased four GMC $8\frac{1}{2}$s09 bonds at 88. Interest was payable March 1 and September 1. Included in Ann's cost was accrued interest for 150 days. (4 points for each correct answer)

**a.** What was the total purchase cost? ________ **b.** What was the average annual yield? Do not consider accrued interest when calculating this rate of yield. ________

**4.** In 2008, Benito Cooper planned to purchase 20 $1,000 bonds and hold them to maturity. He had two choices: The first was EM&E $8\frac{1}{2}$s21 at 106.50. The second was Standard of California 6s18 at 80. Benito purchased the issue that provided the higher rate of yield to maturity.

**a.** Which issue did Benito purchase? (12 points) ________________

**b.** How much income would Benito have earned monthly if Standard of California had been purchased? (3 points)

________

**c.** If, in 2011, Benito had purchased EM&E $8\frac{1}{2}$s21 bonds at a price of 97.5, what would have been the yield to maturity? (6 points) ________

**d.** Which company's bonds would be the better buy: EM&E at 97.5 or Standard of California? (1 point)

________________________________

Score for A (52)

**5.** (48 points) Complete the following table. Show yield to maturity to one decimal place. (2 points for each correct answer)

| | Number Purchased | Price Paid | Discount or Premium | Years to Maturity | Interest Rate | Annual Interest | +Discount −Premium Amortization | Average Principal Invested | Yield to Maturity |
|---|---|---|---|---|---|---|---|---|---|
| **a.** | 8 | 105 | $−400 | 5 | 8% | ______ | ______ | ______ | ______ |
| **b.** | 10 | 97 | +300 | 10 | 6% | ______ | ______ | ______ | ______ |
| **c.** | 12 | 86 | +1,680 | 8 | 7.50% | ______ | ______ | ______ | ______ |
| **d.** | 5 | 112 | −600 | 3 | 10.20% | ______ | ______ | ______ | ______ |
| **e.** | 1 | 90 | +100 | 5 | 7% | ______ | ______ | ______ | ______ |
| **f.** | 20 | 102.5 | −500 | 8 | 9.75% | ______ | ______ | ______ | ______ |

Score for 5 (48)

# Annuities

23

## Learning Objectives

By studying this chapter and completing all assignments, you will be able to:

Learning Objective 1 — Compute the future value of an annuity.

Learning Objective 2 — Compute the regular payments of an annuity from the future value.

Learning Objective 3 — Compute the present value of an annuity.

Learning Objective 4 — Compute the regular payments of an annuity from the present value.

Learning Objective 5 — Compute the loan payment required to amortize a loan.

Learning Objective 6 — Create a loan amortization schedule.

John and Joan Popplewell just won their state's lottery and the prize was listed as $5,000,000. When they purchased the winning ticket, they had a choice of taking the prize over 20 years or taking one cash payment now. The $5,000,000 represents the sum of 20 annual payments of $250,000 each. The series of equal payments is called an **annuity.** Because they chose the single cash payment, they do not actually receive $5,000,000 in cash. The amount that they receive is the **present value of an annuity.**

In Chapter 22, we discussed corporate and government bonds. When a corporation issues $10,000,000 worth of 8%, 20-year bonds, the corporation is simply borrowing money from the public for 20 years. Each $1,000 bond pays 8% (or $80) each year. The $80 is paid out in two $40 payments every 6 months for 20 years. The series of $40 interest payments is an annuity. The amount that someone pays for the bond is the present value of the annuity. Some investors may worry that the corporation won't have $10,000,000 available in 20 years to repay the bonds. Therefore, the corporation may decide to make 20 equal annual payments into a separate account managed by a neutral third party. At the end of the 20 years, the deposits plus accumulated interest will be worth the $10,000,000. This fund of deposits is called a **sinking fund.** Equal deposits into a sinking fund form an annuity. The total amount is the **future value of an annuity.**

# Computing the Future Value of an Annuity

**Learning Objective 1**

Compute the future value of an annuity.

An annuity is made up of a series of equal payments that occur at regular time intervals. The payments go into—or come out of—an interest-bearing account or investment. The constant interest rate is compounded at the same time the payments are made. (Perhaps obviously, the number of periods in an annuity is the same as the number of payments.)

We can illustrate an annuity by drawing a straight line, called a **time line.** On the time line, we insert equal marks and the payment dates, and write in the payment amounts.

**EXAMPLE A**

An annuity has four annual payments of $1,000, always on December 31. The date of the first $1,000 payment is December 31, 2010. Draw a time line showing the four years—2010, 2011, 2012, and 2013—and the four payments.

The annuity illustrated in Figure 23-1, with the payments occurring at the end of each period, is called an **ordinary annuity.** In this book, every annuity will have its payments at the end of each period. The date December 31, 2009, is the *beginning of the annuity,* and the date December 31, 2013, is the *end of the annuity.*

**Figure 23-1 Diagram of an Ordinary Annuity**

| Date | 12/31/09 | | 12/31/10 | | 12/31/11 | | 12/31/12 | | 12/31/13 |
|---|---|---|---|---|---|---|---|---|---|
| Period | | 1 | | 2 | | 3 | | 4 | |
| Payment | $0 | | $1,000 | | $1,000 | | $1,000 | | $1,000 |

Again, the value of the annuity at the end of the annuity is called the *future value of the annuity.* In example A, it is the total value of all payments plus the compound interest from the date of each payment until December 31, 2013. When a business or individual decides to deposit the same amount of money every year (or month or quarter) into an interest-bearing account for a specified amount of time, the future value of the annuity is the amount that will be in the account when the last deposit is made.

**EXAMPLE B**

In December, 2009, Mary Currie accepted a job with a manufacturing company. Mary decided to save \$1,000 at the end of each year for 4 years. The company credit union allowed Mary to open a savings account on December 31, 2009, but Mary will not make any deposit until December 31, 2010. She also will make deposits on December 31 of 2011, 2012, and 2013. The credit union pays interest of 10% compounded annually. How much will be in the account after the last deposit? (*Hint:* Make a time line diagram and compute the future value of each of the four deposits.)

To find the future value of the annuity on December 31, 2013, first use Table 16-1 (see Chapter 16) to determine the future value of each of the four payments as of December 31, 2013. Then compute the total.

| Amount of Payment | Date of Payment | Years of Interest | Future Value on 12/31/13 |
|---|---|---|---|
| \$1,000 | 12/31/10 | 3 | \$1,000 × 1.33100 = \$ 1,331 |
| \$1,000 | 12/31/11 | 2 | \$1,000 × 1.21000 = \$ 1,210 |
| \$1,000 | 12/31/12 | 1 | \$1,000 × 1.10000 = \$ 1,100 |
| \$1,000 | 12/31/13 | 0 | \$1,000 × 1.00000 = +1,000 |
| | | | Total = \$ 4,641 |

Figure 23-2 illustrates how each of the four payments moves *forward* in time to December 31, 2013.

**Figure 23-2** Future Value of an Ordinary Annuity

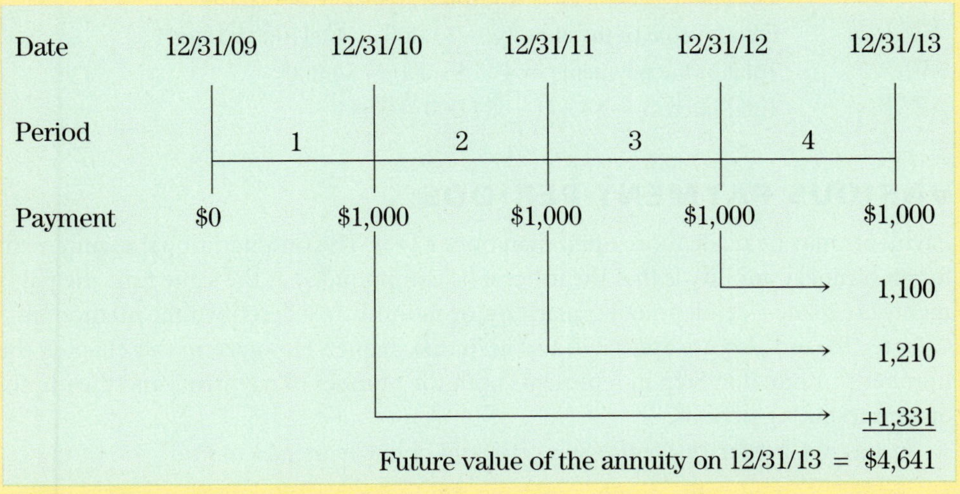


## ANNUITY TABLES

Annuity calculations can be time-consuming, even with just four payments. With 20 or 30 payments, the calculations could be tiresome. Computers, financial calculators, and tables eliminate tedious computations. Table 23-1, on pages 488–489, is an abbreviated sample of a table of **future value of annuity factors (FVAFs).** It is used the same way as Table 16-1. As in Table 16-1, the columns in Table 23-1 indicate the periodic interest rate and the rows indicate the number of periods.

**STEPS to Use Table 23-1 to Compute Future Value and Total Interest Earned**

1. Locate the annuity factor (FVAF) in the correct row and column of Table 23-1, on pages 488–489.
2. Multiply the payment amount by the annuity factor (FVAF). The product is the future value of the annuity (FVA).
3. Multiply the payment amount by the number of payments. The product is the total of all payments.
4. Subtract the total of all payments from the future value of the annuity. The difference is the total interest earned.

## FUTURE VALUE OF AN ANNUITY FORMULA

If you prefer, Step 2 above may be summarized as a formula, in words or in symbols:

Future value of an annuity = Periodic payment × Future value of annuity factor (Table 23-1) or $FVA = Pmt \times FVAF$

**EXAMPLE C**

Find the future value of an annuity of four annual payments of $1,000. Each payment is made at the end of the year, and 10% interest is compounded each year. Also find the total interest earned over the 4 years.

STEP 1 The annuity factor (FVAF) from Table 23-1 is 4.64100.

STEP 2 Future value of the annuity = $1,000 × 4.64100 = $4,641

STEP 3 Total of the payments = 4 × $1,000 = $4,000

STEP 4 Total interest = $4,641 − $4,000 = $641

## VARIOUS PAYMENT PERIODS

Payments may be made more often than once a year. The only additional requirement for an ordinary annuity is that the interest be compounded at the same time the payments are made—semiannually, quarterly, or monthly. We described the method in Chapter 16, and also use Steps i, ii, and iii in this chapter. However, in this chapter, the number computed in Step iii represents both the number of payments and the number of compounding periods.

Just as in Chapter 16, we use Steps i, ii, and iii in Chapter 23 to find

STEP i $m$ = the number of compounding periods (and payments) in one year

STEP ii $i$ = periodic interest rate = *annual rate* ÷ $m$

STEP iii $n$ = number of periods (payments) in the entire annuity = $m$ × *number of years*

These three steps are required whether we use Table 23-1 or a calculator to find the FVAF.

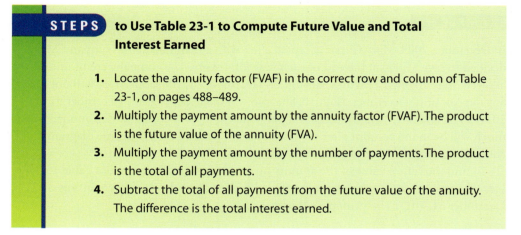

## EXAMPLE D

Find the future value of an annuity in which $2,600 is deposited at the end of each quarter for 4 years. Interest is 8% compounded quarterly.

STEP i — There are $m = 4$ compounding periods in 1 year.

STEP ii — Periodic interest rate $i = 8\% \div 4 = 2\%$ per period

STEP iii — Number of payments $n = 4 \times 4$ years $= 16$ payments

STEP 1 — Use Table 23-1, 2% column and row 16: annuity factor = 18.63929

STEP 2 — Future value = \$2,600 × 18.63929 = \$48,462.154, or \$48,462.15

$m = 4$

$$i = \frac{0.08}{4} = 0.02$$

$n = 4 \times 4 = 16$

## CONCEPT CHECK 23.1

Assume that $5,000 is invested every 6 months for 5 years in an account that pays 6% compounded semiannually. Compute the future value of the investment. Then compute the total interest earned by the investment.

Semiannual means $m = 2$ periods per year.

Periodic rate = 6% ÷ 2 = 3% per period

Number of payments 2 × 5 years = 10 payments

The future value annuity factor from row 10 of the 3.00% column in Table 23-1 is 11.46388.

Future value of the annuity = \$5,000 × 11.46388 = \$57,319.40

Total of all payments = \$5,000 × 10 payments = \$50,000.00

Total interest earned = Future value − Total payments = \$57,319.40 − \$50,000.00
= \$7,319.40

$m = 2$

$$i = \frac{0.06}{4} = 0.03$$

$n = 2 \times 5 = 10$

## USING A CALCULATOR TO COMPUTE ANNUITY FACTORS (OPTIONAL)

Recall from Chapter 16 on Compound Interest that Tables 16-1 and 16-2 showed the "future value factors" (FVF) and the "present value factors" (PVF), respectively. Recall also that you could use a calculator to find the FVF and PVF with these simple formulas: $\mathbf{FVF} = (1 + i)^n$ and $\mathbf{PVF} = 1 \div (1 + i)^n$ (or $\mathbf{PVF} = (1 + i)^{-n}$), where $\boldsymbol{i}$ is the *periodic* interest rate and $\boldsymbol{n}$ is the total number of *periods*. To find the future value of \$5,000 invested at 8% compounded quarterly for 3 years, you used either Table 16-1 or a calculator to find **FVF** = 1.26824. The future value is FV = PV × FVF = \$5,000 × 1.26824 = \$6,341.20.

We defined the terms in Table 23-1 as "future value of annuity factors (**FVAF**s)." Just as there was a calculator formula for **FVF,** there is a calculator formula for **FVAF.** It is

$$\text{FVAF} = \frac{(1 + i)^n - 1}{i}$$

where $i$ is the periodic interest rate *written as a decimal* (as in Chapter 16)
$n$ is the total number of payments (or the number of periods).

Applying the formula to example C where $n = 4$ years and $i = 10\%$ compounded annually, we find the same FVAF = 4.46100 as in row 4, column 10%, of Table 23-1:

$$FVAF = \frac{(1+i)^n - 1}{i} = \frac{(1+0.10)^4 - 1}{0.10} = \frac{1.46410000 - 1}{0.10}$$

$$= \frac{0.46410000}{0.10} = 4.6410000$$

Depending on your calculator, one set of calculator keystrokes to calculate this **FVAF** is

1 [+] .1 [=] [$y^x$] 4 [=] [−] 1 [=] [÷] .1 [=]

To compute the future value of an annuity with a calculator, the formula is

$$FVA = Pmt \times FVAF \quad \text{or} \quad FVA = Pmt \times \left[\frac{(1+i)^n - 1}{i}\right]$$

In example C, $FVA = Pmt \times FVAF = \$1{,}000 \times 4.64100 = \$4{,}641.$

In example D, Steps i, ii, and iii give $m = 4$, $i = 6\% \div 4 = 1.5\%$ or 0.015, and $n = 4 \times 5$ years $= 20$. Using the formula and a calculator, we get

$$FVA = Pmt \times FVAF = Pmt \times \left[\frac{(1+i)^n - 1}{i}\right] = \$200 \times \left[\frac{(1+0.015)^{20} - 1}{0.015}\right]$$

$$= \$200 \times 23.1236671 = \$4{,}624.73$$

After first calculating $i = 0.015$ and $n = 20$, one typical set of calculator keystrokes to find the future value is

1 [+] .015 [=] [$y^x$] 20 [=] [−] 1 [=] [÷] .015 [=] [×] 200 [=]

Calculators differ. If your calculator has parentheses, you could use one or more pairs of parentheses to make an expression that you think is simpler. Use the keystrokes that seem simplest to you.

## Computing Regular Payments of an Annuity from the Future Value

**Learning Objective 2**

Compute the regular payments of an annuity from the future value.

In examples A–D, the amounts of the payments were known and the future values were unknown. But when the future value is known, you can compute the amount of each payment. The procedure is identical whether you use Table 23-1 or a calculator to find the FVAF.

**STEPS to Find the Size of the Payment in an Annuity, Given Its Future Value**

1. Determine the annuity factor (FVAF) using Table 23-1 or a calculator.
2. Divide the future value by the annuity factor. The quotient is the amount of each payment in the annuity.

As a formula, Step 2 could be written as $Pmt = FVA \div FVAF$.

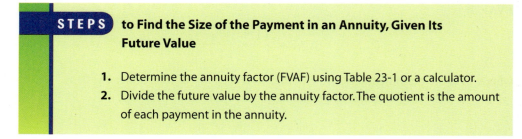

### EXAMPLE E

Nate and Nan Roth want to have \$85,000 in their credit union account when their son Danny starts college. They will make equal payments every month for 4 years. The credit union will pay 6% compounded monthly. What should their payment amount be?

The value of the annuity at the end, or the future value of the annuity, is \$85,000. Use Table 23-1.

STEP i   There are $m = 12$ compounding periods in 1 year.

$m = 12$

STEP ii   Periodic interest rate = 6% ÷ 12 = 0.5% per period

$i = \frac{0.06}{12} = 0.005$

STEP iii   Number of deposits = 12 × 4 years = 48 deposits

$n = 12 \times 4 = 48$

STEP 1   Use Table 23-1, 0.5% column and row 48: annuity factor = 54.09783

$$\text{FVAF} = \frac{(1 + 0.005)^{48} - 1}{0.005} = 54.09783222$$

STEP 2   Future value of the annuity = \$85,000

Payment amount = \$85,000 ÷ 54.09783 = \$1,571.2275, or \$1,571.23

## SINKING FUNDS

At the beginning of this chapter, we mentioned that a \$10,000,000 corporate bond issue may include a sinking fund feature. Sometimes a sinking fund means that the corporation will set aside an equal amount of money each year so that by the end of the 20 years, the corporation will have accumulated the \$10,000,000. At other times, perhaps, a sinking fund may be used by the corporation to buy back \$500,000 worth of the bonds each year.

Although the term *sinking fund* may be most often associated with the repayment of a bond issue, its use isn't restricted to bonds. A corporation may set up a sinking fund to save money for an expensive piece of equipment that it knows it must replace in the future. The college fund set up by Nate and Nan Roth in example E was essentially a sinking fund.

### EXAMPLE F

Micromedia Corporation is preparing a \$20,000,000 bond issue. The company wants to make 25 equal annual payments into a sinking fund so that it will have a total of \$20,000,000 available in 25 years to repay the bonds. What size should each of the payments be if the company can earn 6% per year on the payments?

STEP i   There is $m = 1$ compounding period in 1 year.

$m = 1$

STEP ii   Periodic interest rate = 6% ÷ 1 = 6% per period

$i = \frac{0.06}{1} = 0.06$

STEP iii   Number of deposits = 1 × 25 years = 25 deposits

$n = 1 \times 25 = 25$

STEP 1   Use Table 23-1, 6% column and row 25: annuity factor = 54.86451

$$\text{FVAF} = \frac{(1 + 0.06)^{25} - 1}{0.06} = 54.86451100$$

STEP 2   Future value of the annuity = \$20,000,000

Payment amount = \$20,000,000 ÷ 54.86451 = \$364,534.38

## CONCEPT CHECK 23.2

Assume that an equal amount is invested every quarter for 7 years. After the last payment, the future value is $75,000. If the interest rate is 8% compounded quarterly, compute the size of each regular quarterly payment.

Quarterly means $m = 4$ periods per year.
Periodic rate = 8% ÷ 4 = 2% per period
Number of payments is 4 × 7 years = 28 payments
The future value annuity factor from row 28 of the 2% column in Table 23-1 is 37.05121.

Regular quarterly payment = $75,000 ÷ 37.05121 = $2,024.2254, or $2,024.23

$m = 4$

$i = \frac{0.08}{4} = 0.02$

$n = 4 \times 7 = 28$

$\text{FVAF} = \frac{(1 + 0.02)^{28} - 1}{0.02}$

$= 37.05121031$

COMPLETE ASSIGNMENT 23.1.

# Computing the Present Value of an Annuity

**Learning Objective 3**

Compute the present value of an annuity.

The annuity shown in Figure 23-3 begins December 31, 2009. Again, the value of the annuity on this date is called the present value of the annuity. For example, when a person deposits a large amount in a bank account and then makes a series of equal withdrawals from the account until it is empty, the series of withdrawals (the equal payments) is the annuity, and the amount deposited is the present value. The interest earned equals the difference between the total amount withdrawn and the amount deposited.

**Figure 23-3** Present Value of an Ordinary Annuity

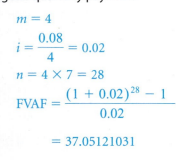

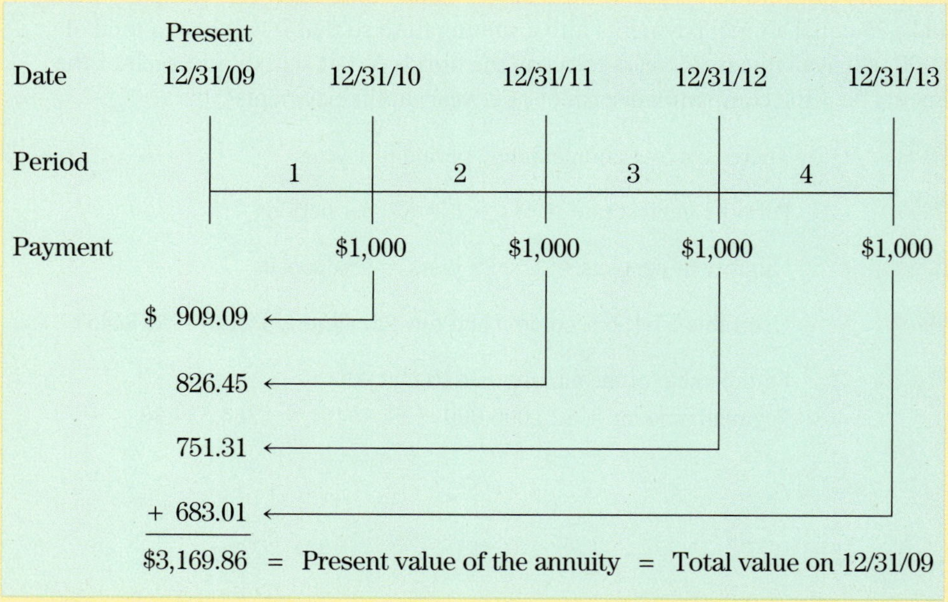

**EXAMPLE G**

In November 2009, Ashley Hamilton inherited some money. She planned to donate part of the money immediately to the American Cancer Society and then to make four equal donations of $1,000 each on December 31 of 2010, 2011, 2012, and 2013. To prepare for the four future payments, Ashley went to her bank on December 31, 2009, and deposited money into a new account. The account paid 10% compounded annually. Ashley would withdraw $1,000 each year always on December 31. After the last withdrawal on December 31, 2013, the account would be empty.

How much must Ashley deposit on December 31, 2009? (*Hint:* Make a time line diagram, and compute the present value of each of the four withdrawals.)

To find the present value of the annuity on December 31, 2009, first use Table 16-2 to find the present value of each of the four payments on December 31, 2009. Then compute the total.

| Amount of Payment | Date of Payment | Years of Interest | Present Value on 12/31/09 |
|---|---|---|---|
| $1,000 | 12/31/10 | 1 | $1,000 × 0.90909 = $ 909.09 |
| $1,000 | 12/31/11 | 2 | $1,000 × 0.82645 = 826.45 |
| $1,000 | 12/31/12 | 3 | $1,000 × 0.75131 = 751.31 |
| $1,000 | 12/31/13 | 4 | $1,000 × 0.68301 = + 683.01 |
| | | | Present value of the annuity on 12/31/09 = $3,169.86 |

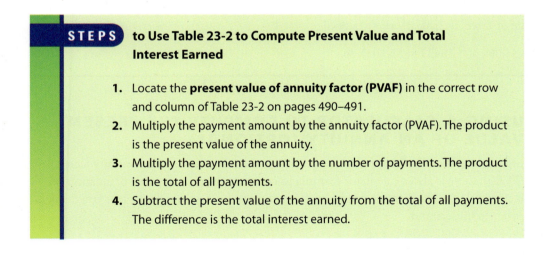

Figure 23-3 illustrates example G. The time line shows the equal withdrawals as each payment is moved from the future backward to the present (to December 31, 2009). Compare Figure 23-3 with Figure 23-2 where each payment was projected forward into the future.

The method shown in Figure 23-3 aids instruction but is too time-consuming to be practical. To get the same solution quickly, use Table 23-2 on pages 490–491.

**STEPS to Use Table 23-2 to Compute Present Value and Total Interest Earned**

1. Locate the **present value of annuity factor (PVAF)** in the correct row and column of Table 23-2 on pages 490–491.
2. Multiply the payment amount by the annuity factor (PVAF). The product is the present value of the annuity.
3. Multiply the payment amount by the number of payments. The product is the total of all payments.
4. Subtract the present value of the annuity from the total of all payments. The difference is the total interest earned.

## PRESENT VALUE OF AN ANNUITY FORMULA

If you prefer, Step 2 may be summarized as a formula, in words or in symbols:

Present value of an annuity = Periodic payment × Present value of annuity factor (Table 23-2), or $PVA = Pmt \times PVAF$.

For example G, the factor in the 10.00% column and row 4 of Table 23-2 is 3.16987 (Step 1), and $1,000 × 3.16987 = $3,169.87 (Step 2).

The application in example H may not sound complicated, but it would be tedious to compute without Table 23-2. Because the payments and compounding are quarterly, use Steps i, ii, and iii to find the periodic rate and the number of periods.

**EXAMPLE H**

Nanda Cerrado just won first prize in a fund-raising raffle. Nanda has a choice: She can receive quarterly payments of $750 each for 6 years, with the first payment 3 months (one quarter) from now, or she can receive 1 lump sum today. Assuming an interest rate of 6% compounded quarterly, what lump sum today equals the future payments? (*Hint:* The series of $750 payments is an annuity, and the lump sum is the present value of the annuity.)

$m = 4$

$i = \frac{0.06}{4} = 0.015$

$n = 4 \times 6 = 24$

**STEP i** There are $m = 4$ compounding periods in 1 year.

**STEP ii** Periodic interest rate = 6% ÷ 4 = 1.5% per period

**STEP iii** Number of payments 4 × 6 years = 24

**STEP 1** Using Table 23-2, 1.50% column and row 24: the PVAF = 20.03041

**STEP 2** Present value = $750 × 20.03041 = $15,022.8075, or $15,022.81

## CONCEPT CHECK 23.3

What present value (principal) must be invested today in an account to provide for 7 equal annual withdrawals (an annuity) of $5,000 each? The interest rate is 8% compounded annually.

Annual means $m = 1$ period per year.
Periodic rate = 8% ÷ 1 = 8% per year
Number of payments = 1 × 7 years = 7 payments
From row 7 of the 8.00% column of Table 23-2, the PVAF = 5.20637.

Present value of the annuity = $5,000 × 5.20637 = $26,031.85

$m = 1$

$i = \frac{0.08}{1} = 0.08$

$n = 1 \times 7 = 7$

## USING A CALCULATOR TO COMPUTE THE PRESENT VALUE OF AN ANNUITY (OPTIONAL)

Just as there is a calculator formula to compute the future value of an annuity factor (FVAF), there is also a calculator formula to compute the present value of an annuity factor (PVAF). The formula can be written several ways. Use whichever one you think is easier to understand.

$$\text{PVAF} = \frac{1 - (1 + i)^{-n}}{i} \quad \text{or} \quad \text{PVAF} = \frac{1 - (1 \div (1 + i)^n)}{i}$$

$$\text{or} \quad \text{PVAF} = \frac{1 - \dfrac{1}{(1 + i)^n}}{i}$$

where $i$ is the periodic interest rate *written as a decimal* (as in Chapter 16)
$n$ is the number of payments (or the number of periods)

To compute the present value of an annuity (**PVA**) with a calculator, the formula is

$$PVA = Pmt \times PVAF \quad \text{or} \quad PVA = Pmt \times \left[\frac{1 - (1 + i)^{-n}}{i}\right]$$

where $Pmt$ is the periodic payment
$i$ is the periodic interest rate written as a decimal
$n$ is the number of payments (or the number of periods)
$PVA$ is the present value of the annuity

Return to example H and use the formulas for PVA and PVAF to compute the present value of the annuity in example H: Quarterly payments of \$750 each for 6 years at an interest rate of 6% compounded quarterly.

$Pmt = \$750$
$m = 4$ compounding periods in 1 year
$i = 6\% \div 4 = 1.5\%$, or 0.015, is the periodic interest rate
$n = 4 \times 6$ years $= 24$ is the number of compounding periods

$$PVA = Pmt \times \left[\frac{1 - (1 + i)^{-n}}{i}\right] = \$750 \times \left[\frac{1 - (1 + 0.015)^{-24}}{0.015}\right]$$

$$= \$750 \times \left[\frac{1 - 0.69954392}{0.015}\right] = \$750 \times \left[\frac{0.30045608}{0.015}\right]$$

$$= \$750 \times (20.03040537) = \$15{,}022.80402, \text{ or } \$15{,}022.80$$

After first calculating $i = 0.015$ and $n = 24$, one typical set of calculator keystrokes to find the present value is 1 [+] .015 [=] [$y^x$] 24 [+/−] [=] [+/−] [+] 1 [=] [÷] .015 [=] [x] 750 [=].

And remember: Your calculator may be different. You may have to use different keystrokes and you may be able to find a more efficient sequence of keystrokes.

# Computing Regular Payments of an Annuity from the Present Value

Learning Objective 4

Compute the regular payments of an annuity from the present value.

In examples G and H, the amounts of the payments were known and the present values were unknown. If, however, the present value is known, then you can compute the amount of the payments. The procedure is identical whether you use Table 23-2 or a calculator to find the **PVAF**.

**STEPS to Find the Size of the Payment in an Annuity, Given the Present Value**

1. Determine the annuity factor (PVAF) using Table 23-2 or a calculator.
2. Divide the present value by the annuity factor (PVAF). The quotient is the amount of the payments in the annuity.

## EXAMPLE I

Jim Schremp received a $25,000 bonus from his employer. Rather than spend it all at once, he decided to deposit it in a bank account that pays 9% compounded monthly. He will make equal monthly withdrawals for 4 years. After the last withdrawal, the account will be empty. How much will he withdraw each month?

The value of the annuity in the beginning (present value of the annuity) is $25,000. Use Table 23-2.

$m = 12$

$$i = \frac{0.09}{12} = 0.0075$$

$n = 12 \times 4 = 48$

$$\text{PVAF} = \frac{1 - (1 + 0.0075)^{-48}}{0.0075} = 40.18478189$$

**STEP i** There are $m = 12$ compounding periods in 1 year

**STEP ii** Periodic interest rate = 9% ÷ 12 = 0.75% per period

**STEP iii** Number of withdrawals = 12 × 4 years = 48 withdrawals

**STEP 1** Using Table 23-2, 0.75% column and row 48: the PVAF = 40.18478

**STEP 2** Each withdrawal = $25,000 ÷ 40.18478 = $622.126, or $622.13

## CONCEPT CHECK 23.4

Assume that $75,000 is deposited today (the present value) to provide for 36 equal quarterly withdrawals (an annuity) over the next 9 years. If the interest rate is 6% compounded quarterly, what is the size of each regular quarterly payment (a withdraw)? What is the total interest earned during the term of the annuity?

Quarterly means $m = 4$ periods per year.
Periodic rate = 6% ÷ 4 = 1.5% per quarter
Number of payments = 4 × 9 years = 36 payments
From row 36 of the 1.50% column in Table 23-2, the PVAF = 27.66068

Regular quarterly payment = $75,000 ÷ 27.66068 = $2,711.43

Total of all payments = $2,711.43 × 36 payments = $97,611.48
Total interest earned = Total payments − Present value
= $97,611.48 − $75,000.00 = $22,611.48

$m = 4$

$$i = \frac{0.06}{4} = 0.015$$

$n = 4 \times 9 = 36$

$$\text{PVAF} = \frac{1 - (1 + 0.015)^{-36}}{0.015} = 27.66068431$$

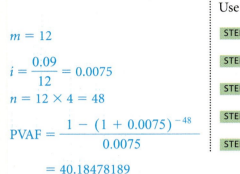

# Computing the Payment to Amortize a Loan

Learning Objective 5

Compute the loan payment required to amortize a loan.

Recall from your study of loan amortization in Chapter 14 that the borrower repays the loan by making equal monthly payments and that the interest is computed on the unpaid balance each month. Loan amortization creates an annuity because there is a series of equal periodic payments. Computing the interest each month makes it compound interest. The amount of the loan is the present value of the annuity.

Stated another way, in amortization, when the amount of the loan is known, the present value of the annuity is known. As illustrated in example J, you can use Table 23-2 to compute the amount of the monthly payments.

**STEPS to Find the Size of the Payment to Amortize a Loan**

1. Determine the annuity factor (PVAF) using Table 23-2 or a calculator.
2. Divide the loan amount by the annuity factor (PVAF). The quotient is the amount of the monthly loan payments.

**EXAMPLE J**

Barbara Luzardi buys a new piano. Barbara pays $2,200 cash and also trades in her old piano. The balance is $4,100 and the piano dealer will amortize the $4,100 over 9 months at 15%. Find the size of her required monthly payments.

STEP i There are 12 compounding periods in 1 year

STEP ii Periodic interest rate = 15% ÷ 12 = 1.25% per period

STEP iii Number of monthly payments = 9

STEP 1 Because the borrowing occurs at the *beginning* of the annuity, this is a present value problem and $4,100 is the present value of the annuity; use Table 23-2. In the 1.25% column and row 9, the PVAF = 8.46234.

STEP 2 Size of each payment = $4,100 ÷ 8.46234 = $484.4996, or $484.50

$m = 12$

$i = \dfrac{0.15}{12} = 0.0125$

$n = 9$

$$\text{PVAF} = \frac{1 - (1 + 0.0125)^{-9}}{0.0125}$$

$= 8.46234498$

**CONCEPT CHECK 23.5**

A bank loans $40,000 at an interest rate of 9% compounded monthly. Find the loan payment necessary to amortize the loan with monthly payments over 3 years.

Loan amortization involves an annuity. The amount borrowed is the present value of the annuity, and the monthly loan payment is the regular annuity payment.

Monthly means 12 periods per year.
Periodic rate = 9% ÷ 12 = 0.75% per period
Number of payments = 12 × 3 years = 36 payments
From row 36 of the 0.75% column of Table 23-2, the PVAF = 31.44681.

Loan payment = $40,000 ÷ 31.44681 = $1,271.98911, or $1,271.99

$m = 12$

$i = \dfrac{0.09}{12} = 0.0075$

$n = 12 \times 3 = 36$

$$\text{PVAF} = \frac{1 - (1 + 0.0075)^{-36}}{0.0075}$$

$= 31.44680525$

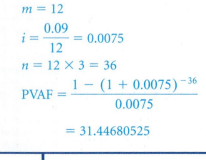

# Creating a Loan Amortization Schedule

**Learning Objective 6**

Create a loan amortization schedule.

Recall from Chapter 14 that the following procedure is used to create an amortization schedule.

© RYAN MCVAY/PHOTODISC/GETTYIMAGES

**STEPS to Create an Amortization Schedule**

For each row except the last:

1. Interest payment = Unpaid balance × Monthly interest rate
2. Principal payment = Monthly payment − Interest payment
3. New unpaid balance = Old unpaid balance − Principal payment

For the last row:

1. Interest payment = Unpaid balance × Monthly interest rate
2. (Then ADD) Monthly payment = Unpaid balance + Interest payment
3. Principal payment = Unpaid balance

**EXAMPLE K**

Mike Ward borrows $2,400. The loan is amortized over 4 months at 12% compounded monthly (1% per month on the unpaid balance). The PVAF (Table 23-2) is 3.90197 and the first three monthly payments will be $615.07. Create the amortization schedule for the loan. 1% interest is charged on the unpaid balance each month.

| Month | Unpaid Balance | STEP 1 Interest Payment | STEP 2 Principal Payment | Total Payment | STEP 3 New Balance |
|---|---|---|---|---|---|
| 1 | $2,400.00 | $24.00 | $591.07 | $615.07 | $1,808.93 |
| 2 | 1,808.93 | 18.09 | 596.98 | 615.07 | 1,211.95 |
| 3 | 1,211.95 | 12.12 | 602.95 | 615.07 | 609.00 |
| 4 | 609.00 | 6.09 | 609.00 | 615.09 | 0 |

**Month 1**

$2,400.00 × 0.01 = $24.00
$615.07 − $24.00 = $591.07
$2,400.00 − $591.07 = $1,808.93

**Month 2**

$1,808.93 × 0.01 = $18.09
$615.07 − $18.09 = $596.98
$1,808.93 − $596.98 = $1,211.95

**Month 3**

$1,211.95 × 0.01 = $12.12
$615.07 − $12.12 = $602.95
$1,211.95 − $602.95 = $609.00

**Month 4**

$609.00 × 0.01 = $6.09
$609.00 + $6.09 = $615.09
$609.00 − $609.00 = $0.00

In example K, note that each month's beginning unpaid balance is multiplied by the monthly interest rate (1%) and rounded to the nearest cent.

## CONCEPT CHECK 23.6

Amortize a $1,500 purchase over 3 months at an annual rate of 12%. First, use Table 23-2 or a calculator to calculate the first two monthly payments. Then show the calculations to construct a 3-month amortization schedule.

The periodic interest rate is 12% ÷ 12 = 1%, and the number of periods is 3. The present value annuity factor from row 3 of the 1.00% column of Table 23-2 is 2.94099. The first two loan payments are $1,500 ÷ 2.94099 = $510.03.

$m = 12$

$i = \dfrac{0.12}{12} = 0.01$

$n = 3$

$\text{PVAF} = \dfrac{1 - (1 + 0.01)^{-3}}{0.01}$

$= 2.94098521$

| | **Month 1** | | **Month 2** | | **Month 3** | |
|---|---|---|---|---|---|---|
| Unpaid balance: | Purchase price | $1,500.00 | From month 1 | $1,004.97 | From month 2 | $504.99 |
| Interest payment: | $1,500.00 × 0.01 = | $15.00 | $1,004.97 × 0.01 = | $10.05 | $504.99 × 0.01 = | $5.05 |
| Total payment: | From above | $510.03 | From above | $510.03 | $504.99 + $5.05 = | $510.04 |
| Principal payment: | $510.03 − $15.00 = | $495.03 | $510.03 − $10.05 = | $499.98 | (Unpaid balance) | $504.99 |
| New balance: | $1,500 − $495.03 = | $1,004.97 | $1,004.97 − $499.98 = | $504.99 | $504.99 − $504.99 = | $0.00 |

COMPLETE ASSIGNMENT 23.2.

## Chapter Terms for Review

annuity

future value of an annuity

future value of an annuity factor (FVAF)

ordinary annuity

present value of an annuity

present value of an annuity factor (PVAF)

sinking fund

time line

## Try Microsoft® Excel

Try working the problems using the Microsoft Excel templates found on your student CD. Solutions for the problems are also shown on the CD.

## Notes

# THE BOTTOM LINE

*Summary of chapter learning objectives:*

| Learning Objective | Example |
|---|---|
| **23.1** Compute the future value of an annuity. | 1. Compute the future value of $900 invested every month for 2.5 years, with interest at 6% compounded monthly. |
| **23.2** Compute the regular payments of an annuity from the future value. | 2. Compute the regular annuity payment that is required to accumulate $6,000 after 17 quarterly payments at an interest rate of 8% compounded quarterly. |
| **23.3** Compute the present value of an annuity. | 3. Compute the present value of $4,750 withdrawn every half-year for $6\frac{1}{2}$ years, with interest at 10% compounded semiannually. |
| **23.4** Compute the regular payments of an annuity from the present value. | 4. An account starts at $4,000. Compute the regular, equal annual withdrawal that is required to empty the account in 6 years if the interest is 10% compounded annually. |
| **23.5** Compute the loan payment required to amortize a loan. | 5. Compute the loan payment that is required to amortize a $20,000 loan in 24 monthly payments, with an interest rate of 9% compounded monthly. |
| **23.6** Create a loan amortization schedule. | 6. A $10,000 loan at a rate of 12% compounded monthly is amortized in 15 monthly payments of $721.24. Compute the entries for the first row of the amortization schedule. |

Answers: 1. $29,052.02 2. $299.82 3. $44,619.46 4. $918.43 5. $913.69
6. $10,000; $100.00; $621.24; $721.24; $9,378.76

# Review Problems for Chapter 23

1 For each annuity, find either the future value (compound amount) or the payment, as indicated. Then compute the compound interest earned by the annuity. (Use Table 23-1)

| Payment | Rate | Period | Time | Future Value | Interest |
|---|---|---|---|---|---|
| $13,600 | 12% | monthly | 10 mo | a. ________ | b. ________ |
| $ 5,000 | 8% | semiannually | 20 yr | c. ________ | d. ________ |

| Future Value | Rate | Period | Time | Payment | Interest |
|---|---|---|---|---|---|
| $30,000 | 5% | annually | 18 yr | e. ________ | f. ________ |
| $28,000 | 6% | quarterly | 6 yr | g. ________ | h. ________ |

2 For each annuity, find either the present value or the payment, as indicated. Then compute the compound interest earned by the annuity. (Use Table 23-2)

| Payment | Rate | Period | Time | Present Value | Interest |
|---|---|---|---|---|---|
| $1,750 | 12% | semiannually | 2 yr | a. ________ | b. ________ |
| $8,400 | 16% | quarterly | 3 yr | c. ________ | d. ________ |

| Present Value | Rate | Period | Time | Payment | Interest |
|---|---|---|---|---|---|
| $24,000 | 10% | annually | 17 yr | e. ________ | f. ________ |
| $60,000 | 9% | monthly | 2.5 yr | g. ________ | h. ________ |

3 Sharon Wilder planned to save money for retirement. She put $750 every month in an investment that paid a return of 6% compounded monthly. How much would Sharon have in her account after 4 years?

4 Med-West wanted to set up a sinking fund to have $15,000,000 in 20 years. The company would make annual payments that would pay a return of 6% per year. What size should the payments be?

5 Nancy Duncan received a payment of $75,000 from a life insurance company. She put it in an account that would pay 6% compounded quarterly. Nancy wanted to make equal quarterly withdrawals from the account for 10 years, when the account would be empty. What size withdrawals can Nancy make?

6 Wayne Runn read about an investment opportunity on the Internet. The Website explained that Wayne would receive payments of $1,000 every 6 months for 14 years. If the returns are based on 8% compounded semiannually, what is the present value of this investment opportunity?

**Answers to the Self-Check can be found in Appendix B at the back of the text.**

# Assignment 23.1: Annuities—Future Value

Name ______________________

Date ______________ Score ______________

Learning Objectives 1 2

**A** **(28 points) For each of the following annuities, find the future value or the amount of the periodic payment. Round answers to the nearest cent. (4 points for each correct answer)**

| | Payment Amount | Payment Periods | Interest Rate | Length of Annuity | Future Value |
|---|---|---|---|---|---|
| 1. | $2,200 | monthly | 9% compounded monthly | 2 years | ________ |
| 2. | ________ | quarterly | 6% compounded quarterly | 7 years | $24,000 |
| 3. | $3,500 | semiannually | 8% compounded semiannually | 10 years | ________ |
| 4. | ________ | annually | 8% compounded annually | 25 years | $200,000 |
| 5. | $500 | monthly | 15% compounded monthly | 3 years | ________ |
| 6. | ________ | quarterly | 5% compounded quarterly | 10 years | $30,000 |
| 7. | $1,000 | semiannually | 10% compounded semiannually | 16 years | ________ |

______________

Score for A (28)

**B** **(32 points) For each of the following annuities, find the future value, the amount of the periodic payment, or the total amount of interest paid. Round answers to the nearest cent. (4 points for each correct answer)**

**8.** Calculate the future value of a 25-year annuity with payments of $3,000 each year and an interest rate of 5% compounded annually.

______

**9.** How much total interest is earned on an annuity with payments of $300 per month for 4 years and an interest rate of 6% compounded monthly?

______

**10.** An annuity consists of quarterly payments of $1,600 each for 10 years at an interest rate of 6% compounded quarterly. Compute the future value of the annuity.

______

**11.** A 7-year annuity has semiannual payments of $8,000 each and an interest rate of 8% compounded semiannually. What will be the total amount of interest earned?

______

**12.** A sinking fund has 10 annual payments, has an interest rate of 10% compounded annually, and has a future value of $75,000. Compute the amount of each annual payment.

______

**13.** An 8-year annuity with quarterly payments and an interest rate of 5% compounded quarterly has a future value of $45,000. How much total interest does the annuity earn?

______

**14.** Calculate the amount of each monthly payment in a 1-year annuity that has a future value of $5,000 and an interest rate of 9% compounded monthly.

______

**15.** Determine the total interest earned by an annuity with semiannual payments for 18 years, an interest rate of 10% compounded semiannually, and a future value of $25,000.

__________

__________

Score for B (32)

**C** **(40 points) In each of the following applications, find the future value of the annuity, the amount of the periodic payment, or the total amount of interest earned. Round answers to the nearest cent. (4 points for each correct answer)**

**16.** Jim Walter decides to make semiannual deposits in his credit union account because it is guaranteeing a rate of 8% compounded semiannually for the next 5 years. How much will Jim have after making equal semiannual deposits of $2,500 for 5 years?

__________

**17.** Calvin White is planning for his daughter's college education. An investment advisor recommends an investment whose prospectus claims it will return 9% compounded monthly. If the investment does return 9% compounded monthly, how much must Calvin invest each month for 4 years if he wants to have a total of $50,000 after the last deposit?

__________

**18.** Maxfield International is raising $25,000,000 by selling bonds that will mature in 20 years. Maxfield plans to make equal annual payments in a sinking fund to repay the bonds. If Maxfield can earn 6% per year, what amount should it deposit each year in order to have $25,000,000 at the end of 20 years?

__________

**19.** Luis Garza is quite certain he will need to replace some construction equipment in 3 years. He decides to set up a sinking fund now to help buy the equipment. Luis estimates that he can deposit $1,400 each month for 3 years in a sinking fund that will pay 6% compounded monthly. How much will Luis' sinking fund be worth after the last deposit?

__________

**20.** Bill Starnes is planning that his twin daughters could get married in 6 years. He thinks that he should start saving now to try to accumulate $30,000 by the end of the 6 years. Assuming that Bill can find an investment that will pay 8% compounded quarterly, what amount must Bill deposit each quarter to have the necessary $30,000 at the end of the 6 years?

__________

**21.** Joseph Woo imports patio furniture from various countries. He prefers to have cash available when he goes on buying trips. Suppose that Joseph makes equal monthly deposits into a risky investment that promises to pay 12% compounded monthly. If he deposits enough each month to accumulate $60,000 by the end of 2 years, and if the investment pays as promised, how much of the $60,000 will the bank have paid in interest?

______________

**22.** Jeanne Knowles will graduate from high school in a few months. She has found a part-time job and is trying to determine how much money she can save in 6 years. Calculate the future value after 6 years if Jeanne makes semiannual deposits of $600 each into an investment account that promises a return of 8% compounded semiannually.

______________

**23.** Musical Instrument Manufacturing, Inc., (MIMI) just sold $40,000,000 in bonds. The bonds will mature in 20 years. MIMI will make equal semiannual payments into a sinking fund that will earn 10% compounded semiannually. If MIMI has the $40,000,000 after 20 years, what amount of the total was earned from the interest?

______________

**24.** Every three months, Katie Webb sends $1,600 to her granddaughter, Jenny. To encourage Jenny to save more money, Jenny's father promises to give her interest of 12% compounded quarterly on everything that she saves. If Jenny always saves the entire $1,600 each quarter, and receives these payments every quarter for 5 years, how much money will Jenny's father have to pay her in interest?

______________

**25.** This year, Doug McCombs charged all his family's Christmas gifts on a credit card, and the result was a minor financial disaster. Planning for next year, Doug decides to save money each month from February through November and put it into an account that will pay 12% compounded monthly. He plans to make 10 equal deposits, and he wants to have accumulated $3,500 once he makes the tenth deposit. Calculate the size of each deposit.

______________

______________

Score for C (40)

# Assignment 23.2: Annuities—Present Value

Name ______________________________

Date ______________ Score ______________

Learning Objectives 3 4 5 6

**A** **(28 points) For each of the following annuities, find the present value or the amount of the periodic payment. Round answers to the nearest cent. (4 points for each correct answer)**

| | Payment Amount | Payment Periods | Interest Rate | Length of Annuity | Present Value |
|---|---|---|---|---|---|
| **1.** | $1,500 | semiannually | 8% compounded semiannually | 9 years | ________ |
| **2.** | ________ | quarterly | 6% compounded quarterly | 12 years | $35,000 |
| **3.** | $800 | monthly | 6% compounded monthly | 4 years | ________ |
| **4.** | ________ | annually | 10% compounded annually | 27 years | $86,000 |
| **5.** | $2,500 | quarterly | 8% compounded quarterly | 8 years | ________ |
| **6.** | ________ | semiannually | 6% compounded semiannually | 25 years | $100,000 |
| **7.** | $750 | monthly | 9% compounded monthly | 3 years | ________ |

________________
Score for A (28)

**B** **(32 points) For each of the following annuities, find the present value, the amount of the periodic payment, or the total amount of interest paid. Round answers to the nearest cent. (4 points for each correct answer)**

**8.** An annuity consists of quarterly payments of $1,200 each for 10 years at an interest rate of 5% compounded quarterly. Determine the present value of the annuity.

__________

**9.** Compute the amount of each payment in an annuity that has a present value of $10,000 with 9 years of semiannual payments at an interest rate of 16% compounded semiannually.

__________

**10.** In a 40-year annuity, the annual payments are $10,000 each and the interest rate is 6% compounded annually. What is the present value of the annuity?

__________

**11.** What is the total interest earned by an annuity that has a present value of $16,000 with monthly payments over a 2-year period at an interest rate of 9% compounded monthly?

__________

**12.** Calculate the size of the regular quarterly payments in a 10-year annuity that has a present value of $100,000 and an interest rate of 8% compounded quarterly.

__________

**13.** An annuity has a present value of $75,000. Compute the total interest earned by the annuity if there are annual payments over 10 years at an interest rate of 12% compounded annually.

__________

**14.** Find the present value of a 15-year annuity with semiannual payments of $8,000 each, which earns interest at a rate of 6% compounded semiannually.

__________

**15.** Compute the amount of the regular monthly payments in a 1-year annuity that has a present value of $20,000 and an interest rate of 12% compounded monthly.

__________

__________

Score for B (32)

**C (28 points) In each of the following applications, find the present value of the annuity, the amount of the periodic payment, or the total amount of interest earned. Round answers to the nearest cent. (4 points for each correct answer)**

**16.** Walt Pierce is making a budget for the next 18 months. He estimates that his rent will be about $650 per month. For calculations, Walt considers his housing expense to be an annuity of 18 payments. If he uses an interest rate of 9% compounded monthly, what will be the present value of the annuity?

__________

**17.** After their children moved away from home, Barbara Cain and her husband sold their large house and bought a smaller condominium. Barbara invested $25,000 of their after-tax profit in an annuity that would give them equal quarterly payments for 10 years. The fund will pay a return of 8% compounded quarterly. At the end of the 10 years, their annuity will be finished. What amount will they receive each quarter?

__________

**18.** Joe Littrell is considering an investment that is somewhat like a bond. The investment is an annuity that would pay Joe $2,400 every 6 months for 16 years. He is trying to determine how much the investment is worth today. If he uses an interest rate of 10% compounded semiannually, what is the present value of the annuity?

__________

**19.** Bonnie Bomar will receive a retirement bonus of $80,000. She has the option of either receiving the $80,000 now in one lump sum or having it invested and then receiving 15 equal annual annuity payments, the first payment arriving 1 year after retirement. If she selects payments over 15 years, the $80,000 is invested at a guaranteed rate of 8% compounded annually. Compute the amount of interest that Bonnie would earn by choosing the payments over 15 years instead of the lump sum.

__________

**20.** Nellie Van Calcar inherited money from her grandfather. Nellie's daughter is in her second year of college, and Nellie wants to give her $1,600 every quarter for 3 years. Nellie can invest the money for her daughter at 6% compounded quarterly. How much should she invest now to provide for all the quarterly withdrawals and have an empty account after the last withdrawal?

__________

**21.** Joyce Bodley plans to buy a pre-owned car. She can either finance the car through the dealer or borrow the money from the bank. Either way, the amount borrowed will be amortized in equal payments over 4 years. If the bank's 12% annual interest rate for pre-owned cars is compounded monthly, compute Joyce's monthly payments for a bank loan of $15,000.

__________

**22.** Sonny Hansen wanted to protect his home from fire and burglars, so he purchased a home security system. The total price including installation was $4,460. The alarm company convinced Sonny to amortize the cost over 30 months at an interest rate of 9% compounded monthly. Determine the amount of each of the equal monthly payments.

__________

__________

Score for C (28)

**D** **(12 points) Gary Robinson purchased some new equipment and furniture for his office. Instead of charging it on a credit card, which had an 18% interest rate, Gary negotiated financing with the office supply dealer. The total purchase amount was $6,450 and it was amortized over 4 months. The interest rate was 6% per year, or 0.5% per month. The first three monthly payments were each $1,632.70. Complete the first three lines of the following amortization schedule. Round answers to the nearest cent. (1 point for each correct answer)**

| | Month | Unpaid Balance | Interest Payment | Principal Payment | Total Payment | New Balance |
|---|---|---|---|---|---|---|
| **23.** | 1 | ________ | ________ | ________ | $1,632.70 | ________ |
| **24.** | 2 | ________ | ________ | ________ | $1,632.70 | ________ |
| **25.** | 3 | ________ | ________ | ________ | $1,632.70 | ________ |

__________

Score for D (12)

## Notes

**Table 23-1** Future Value Annuity Factors

| Period | 0.50% | 0.75% | 1.00% | 1.25% | 1.50% | 2.00% | 3.00% | 4.00% | 5.00% | 6.00% | 8.00% | 9.00% | 10.00% | 12.00% |
|---|---|---|---|---|---|---|---|---|---|---|---|---|---|---|
| **1** | 1.00000 | 1.00000 | 1.00000 | 1.00000 | 1.00000 | 1.00000 | 1.00000 | 1.00000 | 1.00000 | 1.00000 | 1.00000 | 1.00000 | 1.00000 | 1.00000 |
| **2** | 2.00500 | 2.00750 | 2.01000 | 2.01250 | 2.01500 | 2.02000 | 2.03000 | 2.04000 | 2.05000 | 2.06000 | 2.08000 | 2.09000 | 2.10000 | 2.12000 |
| **3** | 3.01502 | 3.02256 | 3.03010 | 3.03766 | 3.04522 | 3.06040 | 3.09090 | 3.12160 | 3.15250 | 3.18360 | 3.24640 | 3.27810 | 3.31000 | 3.37440 |
| **4** | 4.03010 | 4.04523 | 4.06040 | 4.07563 | 4.09090 | 4.12161 | 4.18363 | 4.24646 | 4.31013 | 4.37462 | 4.50611 | 4.57313 | 4.64100 | 4.77933 |
| **5** | 5.05025 | 5.07556 | 5.10101 | 5.12657 | 5.15227 | 5.20404 | 5.30914 | 5.41632 | 5.52563 | 5.63709 | 5.86660 | 5.98471 | 6.10510 | 6.35285 |
| **6** | 6.07550 | 6.11363 | 6.15202 | 6.19065 | 6.22955 | 6.30812 | 6.46841 | 6.63298 | 6.80191 | 6.97532 | 7.33593 | 7.52333 | 7.71561 | 8.11519 |
| **7** | 7.10588 | 7.15948 | 7.21354 | 7.26804 | 7.32299 | 7.43428 | 7.66246 | 7.89829 | 8.14201 | 8.39384 | 8.92280 | 9.20043 | 9.48717 | 10.08901 |
| **8** | 8.14141 | 8.21318 | 8.28567 | 8.35889 | 8.43284 | 8.58297 | 8.89234 | 9.21423 | 9.54911 | 9.89747 | 10.63663 | 11.02847 | 11.43589 | 12.29969 |
| **9** | 9.18212 | 9.27478 | 9.36853 | 9.46337 | 9.55933 | 9.75463 | 10.15911 | 10.58280 | 11.02656 | 11.49132 | 12.48756 | 13.02104 | 13.57948 | 14.77566 |
| **10** | 10.22803 | 10.34434 | 10.46221 | 10.58167 | 10.70272 | 10.94972 | 11.46388 | 12.00611 | 12.57789 | 13.18079 | 14.48656 | 15.19293 | 15.93742 | 17.54874 |
| **11** | 11.27917 | 11.42192 | 11.56683 | 11.71394 | 11.86326 | 12.16872 | 12.80780 | 13.48635 | 14.20679 | 14.97164 | 16.64549 | 17.56029 | 18.53117 | 20.65458 |
| **12** | 12.33556 | 12.50759 | 12.68250 | 12.86036 | 13.04121 | 13.41209 | 14.19203 | 15.02581 | 15.91713 | 16.86994 | 18.97713 | 20.14072 | 21.38428 | 24.13313 |
| **13** | 13.39724 | 13.60139 | 13.80933 | 14.02112 | 14.23683 | 14.68033 | 15.61779 | 16.62684 | 17.71298 | 18.88214 | 21.49530 | 22.95338 | 24.52271 | 28.02911 |
| **14** | 14.46423 | 14.70340 | 14.94742 | 15.19638 | 15.45038 | 15.97394 | 17.08632 | 18.29191 | 19.59863 | 21.01507 | 24.21492 | 26.01919 | 27.97498 | 32.39260 |
| **15** | 15.53655 | 15.81368 | 16.09690 | 16.38633 | 16.68214 | 17.29342 | 18.59891 | 20.02359 | 21.57856 | 23.27597 | 27.15211 | 29.36092 | 31.77248 | 37.27971 |
| **16** | 16.61423 | 16.93228 | 17.25786 | 17.59116 | 17.93237 | 18.63929 | 20.15688 | 21.82453 | 23.65749 | 25.67253 | 30.32428 | 33.00340 | 35.94973 | 42.75328 |
| **17** | 17.69730 | 18.05927 | 18.43044 | 18.81105 | 19.20136 | 20.01207 | 21.76159 | 23.69751 | 25.84037 | 28.21288 | 33.75023 | 36.97370 | 40.54470 | 48.88367 |
| **18** | 18.78579 | 19.19472 | 19.61475 | 20.04619 | 20.48938 | 21.41231 | 23.41444 | 25.64541 | 28.13238 | 30.90565 | 37.45024 | 41.30134 | 45.59917 | 55.74971 |
| **19** | 19.87972 | 20.33868 | 20.81090 | 21.29677 | 21.79672 | 22.84056 | 25.11687 | 27.67123 | 30.53900 | 33.75999 | 41.44626 | 46.01846 | 51.15909 | 63.43968 |
| **20** | 20.97912 | 21.49122 | 22.01900 | 22.56298 | 23.12367 | 24.29737 | 26.87037 | 29.77808 | 33.06595 | 36.78559 | 45.76196 | 51.16012 | 57.27500 | 72.05244 |
| **21** | 22.08401 | 22.65240 | 23.23919 | 23.84502 | 24.47052 | 25.78332 | 28.67649 | 31.96920 | 35.71925 | 39.99273 | 50.42292 | 56.76453 | 64.00250 | 81.69874 |
| **22** | 23.19443 | 23.82230 | 24.47159 | 25.14308 | 25.83758 | 27.29898 | 30.53678 | 34.24797 | 38.50521 | 43.39229 | 55.45676 | 62.87334 | 71.40275 | 92.50258 |
| **23** | 24.31040 | 25.00096 | 25.71630 | 26.45737 | 27.22514 | 28.84496 | 32.45288 | 36.61789 | 41.43048 | 46.99583 | 60.89330 | 69.53194 | 79.54302 | 104.60289 |
| **24** | 25.43196 | 26.18847 | 26.97346 | 27.78808 | 28.63352 | 30.42186 | 34.42647 | 39.08260 | 44.50200 | 50.81558 | 66.76476 | 76.78981 | 88.49733 | 118.15524 |
| **25** | 26.55912 | 27.38488 | 28.24320 | 29.13544 | 30.06302 | 32.03030 | 36.45926 | 41.64591 | 47.72710 | 54.86451 | 73.10594 | 84.70090 | 98.34706 | 133.33387 |

**Table 23-1** Future Value Annuity Factors *(continued)*

| Period | 0.50% | 0.75% | 1.00% | 1.25% | 1.50% | 2.00% | 3.00% | 4.00% | 5.00% | 6.00% | 8.00% | 9.00% | 10.00% | 12.00% |
|---|---|---|---|---|---|---|---|---|---|---|---|---|---|---|
| **26** | 27.69191 | 28.59027 | 29.52563 | 30.49963 | 31.51397 | 33.67091 | 38.55304 | 44.31174 | 51.11345 | 59.15638 | 79.95442 | 93.32398 | 109.18177 | 150.33393 |
| **27** | 28.83037 | 29.80470 | 30.82089 | 31.88087 | 32.98668 | 35.34432 | 40.70963 | 47.08421 | 54.66913 | 63.70577 | 87.35077 | 102.72313 | 121.09994 | 169.37401 |
| **28** | 29.97452 | 31.02823 | 32.12910 | 33.27938 | 34.48148 | 37.05121 | 42.93092 | 49.96758 | 58.40258 | 68.52811 | 95.33883 | 112.96822 | 134.20994 | 190.69889 |
| **29** | 31.12439 | 32.26094 | 33.45039 | 34.69538 | 35.99870 | 38.79223 | 45.21885 | 52.96629 | 62.32271 | 73.63980 | 103.96594 | 124.13536 | 148.63093 | 214.58275 |
| **30** | 32.28002 | 33.50290 | 34.78489 | 36.12907 | 37.53868 | 40.56808 | 47.57542 | 56.08494 | 66.43885 | 79.05819 | 113.28321 | 136.30754 | 164.49402 | 241.33268 |
| **31** | 33.44142 | 34.75417 | 36.13274 | 37.58068 | 39.10176 | 42.37944 | 50.00268 | 59.32834 | 70.76079 | 84.80168 | 123.34587 | 149.57522 | 181.94342 | 271.29261 |
| **32** | 34.60862 | 36.01483 | 37.49407 | 39.05044 | 40.68829 | 44.22703 | 52.50276 | 62.70147 | 75.29883 | 90.88978 | 134.21354 | 164.03699 | 201.13777 | 304.84772 |
| **33** | 35.78167 | 37.28494 | 38.86901 | 40.53857 | 42.29861 | 46.11157 | 55.07784 | 66.20953 | 80.06377 | 97.34316 | 145.95062 | 179.80032 | 222.25154 | 342.42945 |
| **34** | 36.96058 | 38.56458 | 40.25770 | 42.04530 | 43.93309 | 48.03380 | 57.73018 | 69.85791 | 85.06696 | 104.18375 | 158.62667 | 196.98234 | 245.47670 | 384.52098 |
| **35** | 38.14538 | 39.85381 | 41.66028 | 43.57087 | 45.59209 | 49.99448 | 60.46208 | 73.65222 | 90.32031 | 111.43478 | 172.31680 | 215.71075 | 271.02437 | 431.66350 |
| **36** | 39.33610 | 41.15272 | 43.07688 | 45.11551 | 47.27597 | 51.99437 | 63.27594 | 77.59831 | 95.83632 | 119.12087 | 187.10215 | 236.12472 | 299.12681 | 484.46312 |
| **37** | 40.53279 | 42.46136 | 44.50765 | 46.67945 | 48.98511 | 54.03425 | 66.17422 | 81.70225 | 101.62814 | 127.26812 | 203.07032 | 258.37595 | 330.03949 | 543.59869 |
| **38** | 41.73545 | 43.77982 | 45.95272 | 48.26294 | 50.71989 | 56.11494 | 69.15945 | 85.97034 | 107.70955 | 135.90421 | 220.31595 | 282.62978 | 364.04343 | 609.83053 |
| **39** | 42.94413 | 45.10817 | 47.41225 | 49.86623 | 52.48068 | 58.23724 | 72.23423 | 90.40915 | 114.09502 | 145.05846 | 238.94122 | 309.06646 | 401.44778 | 684.01020 |
| **40** | 44.15885 | 46.44648 | 48.88637 | 51.48956 | 54.26789 | 60.40198 | 75.40126 | 95.02552 | 120.79977 | 154.76197 | 259.05652 | 337.88245 | 442.59256 | 767.09142 |
| **41** | 45.37964 | 47.79483 | 50.37524 | 53.13318 | 56.08191 | 62.61002 | 78.66330 | 99.82654 | 127.83976 | 165.04768 | 280.78104 | 369.29187 | 487.85181 | 860.14239 |
| **42** | 46.60654 | 49.15329 | 51.87899 | 54.79734 | 57.92314 | 64.86222 | 82.02320 | 104.81960 | 135.23175 | 175.95054 | 304.24352 | 403.52813 | 537.63699 | 964.35948 |
| **43** | 47.83957 | 50.52194 | 53.39778 | 56.48231 | 59.79199 | 67.15947 | 85.48389 | 110.01238 | 142.99334 | 187.50758 | 329.58301 | 440.84566 | 592.40069 | 1081.08262 |
| **44** | 49.07877 | 51.90086 | 54.93176 | 58.18834 | 61.68887 | 69.50266 | 89.04841 | 115.41288 | 151.14301 | 199.75803 | 356.94965 | 481.52177 | 652.64076 | 1211.81253 |
| **45** | 50.32416 | 53.29011 | 56.48107 | 59.91569 | 63.61420 | 71.89271 | 92.71986 | 121.02939 | 159.70016 | 212.74351 | 386.50562 | 525.85873 | 718.90484 | 1358.23003 |
| **46** | 51.57578 | 54.68979 | 58.04589 | 61.66464 | 65.56841 | 74.33056 | 96.50146 | 126.87057 | 168.68516 | 226.50812 | 418.42607 | 574.18602 | 791.79532 | 1522.21764 |
| **47** | 52.83366 | 56.09996 | 59.62634 | 63.43545 | 67.55194 | 76.81718 | 100.39650 | 132.94539 | 178.11942 | 241.09861 | 452.90015 | 626.86276 | 871.97485 | 1705.88375 |
| **48** | 54.09783 | 57.52071 | 61.22261 | 65.22839 | 69.56522 | 79.35352 | 104.40840 | 139.26321 | 188.02539 | 256.56453 | 490.13216 | 684.28041 | 960.17234 | 1911.58980 |
| **49** | 55.36832 | 58.95212 | 62.83483 | 67.04374 | 71.60870 | 81.94059 | 108.54065 | 145.83373 | 198.42666 | 272.95840 | 530.34274 | 746.86565 | 1057.18957 | 2141.98058 |
| **50** | 56.64516 | 60.39426 | 64.46318 | 68.88179 | 73.68283 | 84.57940 | 112.79687 | 152.66708 | 209.34800 | 290.33590 | 573.77016 | 815.08356 | 1163.90853 | 2400.01825 |

**Table 23-2** Present Value Annuity Factors

| Period | 0.50% | 0.75% | 1.00% | 1.25% | 1.50% | 2.00% | 3.00% | 4.00% | 5.00% | 6.00% | 8.00% | 9.00% | 10.00% | 12.00% |
|---|---|---|---|---|---|---|---|---|---|---|---|---|---|---|
| 1 | 0.99502 | 0.99256 | 0.99010 | 0.98765 | 0.98522 | 0.98039 | 0.97087 | 0.96154 | 0.95238 | 0.94340 | 0.92593 | 0.91743 | 0.90909 | 0.89286 |
| 2 | 1.98510 | 1.97772 | 1.97040 | 1.96312 | 1.95588 | 1.94156 | 1.91347 | 1.88609 | 1.85941 | 1.83339 | 1.78326 | 1.75911 | 1.73554 | 1.69005 |
| 3 | 2.97025 | 2.95556 | 2.94099 | 2.92653 | 2.91220 | 2.88388 | 2.82861 | 2.77509 | 2.72325 | 2.67301 | 2.57710 | 2.53129 | 2.48685 | 2.40183 |
| 4 | 3.95050 | 3.92611 | 3.90197 | 3.87806 | 3.85438 | 3.80773 | 3.71710 | 3.62990 | 3.54595 | 3.46511 | 3.31213 | 3.23972 | 3.16987 | 3.03735 |
| 5 | 4.92587 | 4.88944 | 4.85343 | 4.81784 | 4.78264 | 4.71346 | 4.57971 | 4.45182 | 4.32948 | 4.21236 | 3.99271 | 3.88965 | 3.79079 | 3.60478 |
| 6 | 5.89638 | 5.84560 | 5.79548 | 5.74601 | 5.69719 | 5.60143 | 5.41719 | 5.24214 | 5.07569 | 4.91732 | 4.62288 | 4.48592 | 4.35526 | 4.11141 |
| 7 | 6.86207 | 6.79464 | 6.72819 | 6.66273 | 6.59821 | 6.47199 | 6.23028 | 6.00205 | 5.78637 | 5.58238 | 5.20637 | 5.03295 | 4.86842 | 4.56376 |
| 8 | 7.82296 | 7.73661 | 7.65168 | 7.56812 | 7.48593 | 7.32548 | 7.01969 | 6.73274 | 6.46321 | 6.20979 | 5.74664 | 5.53482 | 5.33493 | 4.96764 |
| 9 | 8.77906 | 8.67158 | 8.56602 | 8.46234 | 8.36052 | 8.16224 | 7.78611 | 7.43533 | 7.10782 | 6.80169 | 6.24689 | 5.99525 | 5.75902 | 5.32825 |
| 10 | 9.73041 | 9.59958 | 9.47130 | 9.34553 | 9.22218 | 8.98259 | 8.53020 | 8.11090 | 7.72173 | 7.36009 | 6.71008 | 6.41766 | 6.14457 | 5.65022 |
| 11 | 10.67703 | 10.52067 | 10.36763 | 10.21780 | 10.07112 | 9.78685 | 9.25262 | 8.76048 | 8.30641 | 7.88687 | 7.13896 | 6.80519 | 6.49506 | 5.93770 |
| 12 | 11.61893 | 11.43491 | 11.25508 | 11.07931 | 10.90751 | 10.57534 | 9.95400 | 9.38507 | 8.86325 | 8.38384 | 7.53608 | 7.16073 | 6.81369 | 6.19437 |
| 13 | 12.55615 | 12.34235 | 12.13374 | 11.93018 | 11.73153 | 11.34837 | 10.63496 | 9.98565 | 9.39357 | 8.85268 | 7.90378 | 7.48690 | 7.10336 | 6.42355 |
| 14 | 13.48871 | 13.24302 | 13.00370 | 12.77055 | 12.54338 | 12.10625 | 11.29607 | 10.56312 | 9.89864 | 9.29498 | 8.24424 | 7.78615 | 7.36669 | 6.62817 |
| 15 | 14.41662 | 14.13699 | 13.86505 | 13.60055 | 13.34323 | 12.84926 | 11.93794 | 11.11839 | 10.37966 | 9.71225 | 8.55948 | 8.06069 | 7.60608 | 6.81086 |
| 16 | 15.33993 | 15.02431 | 14.71787 | 14.42029 | 14.13126 | 13.57771 | 12.56110 | 11.65230 | 10.83777 | 10.10590 | 8.85137 | 8.31256 | 7.82371 | 6.97399 |
| 17 | 16.25863 | 15.90502 | 15.56225 | 15.22992 | 14.90765 | 14.29187 | 13.16612 | 12.16567 | 11.27407 | 10.47726 | 9.12164 | 8.54363 | 8.02155 | 7.11963 |
| 18 | 17.17277 | 16.77918 | 16.39827 | 16.02955 | 15.67256 | 14.99203 | 13.75351 | 12.65930 | 11.68959 | 10.82760 | 9.37189 | 8.75563 | 8.20141 | 7.24967 |
| 19 | 18.08236 | 17.64683 | 17.22601 | 16.81931 | 16.42617 | 15.67846 | 14.32380 | 13.13394 | 12.08532 | 11.15812 | 9.60360 | 8.95011 | 8.36492 | 7.36578 |
| 20 | 18.98742 | 18.50802 | 18.04555 | 17.59932 | 17.16864 | 16.35143 | 14.87747 | 13.59033 | 12.46221 | 11.46992 | 9.81815 | 9.12855 | 8.51356 | 7.46944 |
| 21 | 19.88798 | 19.36280 | 18.85698 | 18.36969 | 17.90014 | 17.01121 | 15.41502 | 14.02916 | 12.82115 | 11.76408 | 10.01680 | 9.29224 | 8.64869 | 7.56200 |
| 22 | 20.78406 | 20.21121 | 19.66038 | 19.13056 | 18.62082 | 17.65805 | 15.93692 | 14.45112 | 13.16300 | 12.04158 | 10.20074 | 9.44243 | 8.77154 | 7.64465 |
| 23 | 21.67568 | 21.05331 | 20.45582 | 19.88204 | 19.33086 | 18.29220 | 16.44361 | 14.85684 | 13.48857 | 12.30338 | 10.37106 | 9.58021 | 8.88322 | 7.71843 |
| 24 | 22.56287 | 21.88915 | 21.24339 | 20.62423 | 20.03041 | 18.91393 | 16.93554 | 15.24696 | 13.79864 | 12.55036 | 10.52876 | 9.70661 | 8.98474 | 7.78432 |
| 25 | 23.44564 | 22.71876 | 22.02316 | 21.35727 | 20.71961 | 19.52346 | 17.41315 | 15.62208 | 14.09394 | 12.78336 | 10.67478 | 9.82258 | 9.07704 | 7.84314 |

**Table 23-2** Present Value Annuity Factors *(continued)*

| Period | 0.50% | 0.75% | 1.00% | 1.25% | 1.50% | 2.00% | 3.00% | 4.00% | 5.00% | 6.00% | 8.00% | 9.00% | 10.00% | 12.00% |
|---|---|---|---|---|---|---|---|---|---|---|---|---|---|---|
| **26** | 24.32402 | 23.54219 | 22.79520 | 22.08125 | 21.39863 | 20.12104 | 17.87684 | 15.98277 | 14.37519 | 13.00317 | 10.80998 | 9.92897 | 9.16095 | 7.89566 |
| **27** | 25.19803 | 24.35949 | 23.55961 | 22.79630 | 22.06762 | 20.70690 | 18.32703 | 16.32959 | 14.64303 | 13.21053 | 10.93516 | 10.02658 | 9.23722 | 7.94255 |
| **28** | 26.06769 | 25.17071 | 24.31644 | 23.50252 | 22.72672 | 21.28127 | 18.76411 | 16.66306 | 14.89813 | 13.40616 | 11.05108 | 10.11613 | 9.30657 | 7.98442 |
| **29** | 26.93302 | 25.97589 | 25.06579 | 24.20002 | 23.37608 | 21.84438 | 19.18845 | 16.98371 | 15.14107 | 13.59072 | 11.15841 | 10.19828 | 9.36961 | 8.02181 |
| **30** | 27.79405 | 26.77508 | 25.80771 | 24.88891 | 24.01584 | 22.39646 | 19.60044 | 17.29203 | 15.37245 | 13.76483 | 11.25778 | 10.27365 | 9.42691 | 8.05518 |
| **31** | 28.65080 | 27.56832 | 26.54229 | 25.56929 | 24.64615 | 22.93770 | 20.00043 | 17.58849 | 15.59281 | 13.92909 | 11.34980 | 10.34280 | 9.47901 | 8.08499 |
| **32** | 29.50328 | 28.35565 | 27.26959 | 26.24127 | 25.26714 | 23.46833 | 20.38877 | 17.87355 | 15.80268 | 14.08404 | 11.43500 | 10.40624 | 9.52638 | 8.11159 |
| **33** | 30.35153 | 29.13712 | 27.98969 | 26.90496 | 25.87895 | 23.98856 | 20.76579 | 18.14765 | 16.00255 | 14.23023 | 11.51389 | 10.46444 | 9.56943 | 8.13535 |
| **34** | 31.19555 | 29.91278 | 28.70267 | 27.56046 | 26.48173 | 24.49859 | 21.13184 | 18.41120 | 16.19290 | 14.36814 | 11.58693 | 10.51784 | 9.60857 | 8.15656 |
| **35** | 32.03537 | 30.68266 | 29.40858 | 28.20786 | 27.07559 | 24.99862 | 21.48722 | 18.66461 | 16.37419 | 14.49825 | 11.65457 | 10.56682 | 9.64416 | 8.17550 |
| **36** | 32.87102 | 31.44681 | 30.10751 | 28.84727 | 27.66068 | 25.48884 | 21.83225 | 18.90828 | 16.54685 | 14.62099 | 11.71719 | 10.61176 | 9.67651 | 8.19241 |
| **37** | 33.70250 | 32.20527 | 30.79951 | 29.47878 | 28.23713 | 25.96945 | 22.16724 | 19.14258 | 16.71129 | 14.73678 | 11.77518 | 10.65299 | 9.70592 | 8.20751 |
| **38** | 34.52985 | 32.95808 | 31.48466 | 30.10250 | 28.80505 | 26.44064 | 22.49246 | 19.36786 | 16.86789 | 14.84602 | 11.82887 | 10.69082 | 9.73265 | 8.22099 |
| **39** | 35.35309 | 33.70529 | 32.16303 | 30.71852 | 29.36458 | 26.90259 | 22.80822 | 19.58448 | 17.01704 | 14.94907 | 11.87858 | 10.72552 | 9.75696 | 8.23303 |
| **40** | 36.17223 | 34.44694 | 32.83469 | 31.32693 | 29.91585 | 27.35548 | 23.11477 | 19.79277 | 17.15909 | 15.04630 | 11.92461 | 10.75736 | 9.77905 | 8.24378 |
| **41** | 36.98729 | 35.18307 | 33.49969 | 31.92784 | 30.45896 | 27.79949 | 23.41240 | 19.99305 | 17.29437 | 15.13802 | 11.96723 | 10.78657 | 9.79914 | 8.25337 |
| **42** | 37.79830 | 35.91371 | 34.15811 | 32.52132 | 30.99405 | 28.23479 | 23.70136 | 20.18563 | 17.42321 | 15.22454 | 12.00670 | 10.81337 | 9.81740 | 8.26194 |
| **43** | 38.60527 | 36.63892 | 34.81001 | 33.10748 | 31.52123 | 28.66156 | 23.98190 | 20.37079 | 17.54591 | 15.30617 | 12.04324 | 10.83795 | 9.83400 | 8.26959 |
| **44** | 39.40823 | 37.35873 | 35.45545 | 33.68640 | 32.04062 | 29.07996 | 24.25427 | 20.54884 | 17.66277 | 15.38318 | 12.07707 | 10.86051 | 9.84909 | 8.27642 |
| **45** | 40.20720 | 38.07318 | 36.09451 | 34.25817 | 32.55234 | 29.49016 | 24.51871 | 20.72004 | 17.77407 | 15.45583 | 12.10840 | 10.88120 | 9.86281 | 8.28252 |
| **46** | 41.00219 | 38.78231 | 36.72724 | 34.82288 | 33.05649 | 29.89231 | 24.77545 | 20.88465 | 17.88007 | 15.52437 | 12.13741 | 10.90018 | 9.87528 | 8.28796 |
| **47** | 41.79322 | 39.48617 | 37.35370 | 35.38062 | 33.55319 | 30.28658 | 25.02471 | 21.04294 | 17.98102 | 15.58903 | 12.16427 | 10.91760 | 9.88662 | 8.29282 |
| **48** | 42.58032 | 40.18478 | 37.97396 | 35.93148 | 34.04255 | 30.67312 | 25.26671 | 21.19513 | 18.07716 | 15.65003 | 12.18914 | 10.93358 | 9.89693 | 8.29716 |
| **49** | 43.36350 | 40.87820 | 38.58808 | 36.47554 | 34.52468 | 31.05208 | 25.50166 | 21.34147 | 18.16872 | 15.70757 | 12.21216 | 10.94823 | 9.90630 | 8.30104 |
| **50** | 44.14279 | 41.56645 | 39.19612 | 37.01288 | 34.99969 | 31.42361 | 25.72976 | 21.48218 | 18.25593 | 15.76186 | 12.23348 | 10.96168 | 9.91481 | 8.30450 |

## Notes

24

# Business Statistics

## Learning Objectives

By studying this chapter and completing all assignments, you will be able to:

Learning Objective 1 Compute the mean.

Learning Objective 2 Determine the median.

Learning Objective 3 Determine the mode.

Learning Objective 4 Construct frequency tables.

Learning Objective 5 Construct histograms.

Learning Objective 6 Construct bar graphs.

Learning Objective 7 Construct line graphs.

Learning Objective 8 Construct pie charts.

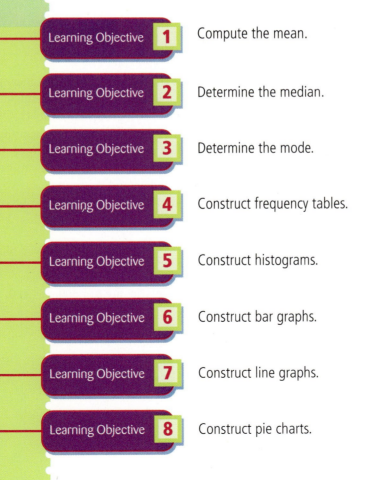

Burger King has sold billions of hamburgers. Housing prices are higher in Boston than in Atlanta. The United States has a trade deficit, which means that the country has been importing more goods than it has been exporting. Families tend to spend more money in retail stores during December than during any other single month of the year. These examples are based on collections of information about businesses. The information is called **business statistics.** The word **statistics** also refers to a field of study that includes the collection, organization, analysis, and presentation of data. Businesses use statistics for two primary purposes: (1) to summarize and report the performance of the business and (2) to analyze their options in making business decisions.

Individuals and groups who want information about the business performance of a company include the company's management, board of directors, investors, and government agencies like the IRS. Once statistics have been reported, individuals and groups use the statistics to make business decisions. For example, depending on the amount of profits, the board of directors decides how much dividend to pay the shareholders. Likewise, after hearing about current profits and projected profits, investors decide whether to purchase or sell shares of the company's stock. After studying sales figures for its products and those of competitors, management makes decisions about which markets to enter, what products to emphasize, and how to advertise.

If a Burger King analyst wants to report data on sales of hamburgers, she could list the number of hamburgers sold at every restaurant. But Burger King has so many restaurants that there would be too many numbers to be meaningful. To make the data meaningful, the analyst can make some summary calculations and/or organize the data in tables. To make her presentations of the data more meaningful and easier to interpret, she may draw charts, diagrams, and/or graphs.

## Statistical Averages: Computing the Mean

**Learning Objective 1**

Compute the mean.

The objective in reporting statistics is to summarize the data in a simple, yet meaningful, manner. One way to simplify data is to compute an **average.** An average is a single number that is supposed to be "typical" or "representative" of a group of numbers. One common way to find an average is to add all the data values and divide by the number of values. In statistics, this particular average is called the *mean*. When the mean isn't typical or representative of an entire group of data, another average might be more representative. We also discuss two other averages: the median and the mode.

The **mean** of a group of values is computed by dividing the sum of the group of values by the number of values in the group.

**EXAMPLE A**

Find the mean salary of five employees whose actual salaries are \$51,500, \$54,400, \$57,600, \$62,000, and \$64,500.

Sum = \$51,500 + \$54,400 + \$57,600 + \$62,000 + \$64,500 = \$290,000
Mean = \$290,000 ÷ 5 = \$58,000

## CONCEPT CHECK 24.1

Find the mean for the following set of numbers: 14, 11, 12, 15, 10, 16, 15, 12, 13, 11, 15, 17, 13, 14, 15, 12, 18

There are 17 numbers. The mean equals their sum divided by 17.

Sum = 233

Mean = 233 ÷ 17 = 13.706, or 13.7 rounded to one decimal place

# Determining the Median

Learning Objective 2

Determine the median.

The **median** of a group of numbers is determined by arranging the numbers in numerical order and finding the middle number. The median is useful when one value in the group is much larger or much smaller than the rest of the numbers.

### EXAMPLE B

Find the median salary of five employees whose salaries are $51,500, $54,400, $57,600, $62,000, and $254,500.

The salaries are already in numerical order; the median is $57,600 because it is the middle number of the five numbers arranged in order.

In example B, the mean is $480,000 ÷ 5 = $96,000, but $96,000 is not representative of the salaries of the five employees. The mean is very large because one employee (perhaps the owner) has a very large salary compared to the rest of the group. The median salary, $57,600, is more typical of the group.

If the number of values is even, the median will be halfway between the two middle values. The median will be the mean of the middle two values.

### EXAMPLE C

Find the median salary of six employees whose salaries are $57,600, $64,500, $51,500, $254,500, $62,000, and $54,400.

Rearranged in numerical order, the salaries are $51,500, $54,400, $57,600, $62,000, $64,500, and $254,500.

The median is halfway between the middle two numbers, $57,600 and $62,000. The median is ($57,600 + $62,000) ÷ 2, or $119,600 ÷ 2 = $59,800.

## CONCEPT CHECK 24.2

Find the median for the following set of numbers: 14, 11, 12, 15, 10, 16, 15, 12, 13, 11, 15, 17, 13, 14, 15, 12, 18

The median is the middle number, after all the numbers have been arranged by order of size: 10, 11, 11, 12, 12, 12, 13, 13, 14, 14, 15, 15, 15, 15, 16, 17, 18

The median is the ninth number, or 14.

# Determining the Mode

Learning Objective 3

Determine the mode.

The **mode** of a group of numbers is the number that occurs most often. None of examples A, B, and C has a mode because each number occurs only once. The mode is useful when the word *average* implies "most typical" or "happening most often." Retail businesses keep track of the items that sell most frequently so that they can avoid shortages of those items.

**EXAMPLE D**

Find the mode shoe size of 12 pairs of cross trainer running shoes, sizes 6, 6, $7\frac{1}{2}$, $7\frac{1}{2}$, 8, $8\frac{1}{2}$, 9, 9, 9, 9, 9, and $9\frac{1}{2}$.

The mode is size 9, because 9 occurs most frequently.

In example D neither the mean nor the median makes any sense. The mean is $98 \div 12 = 8.17$, or $8\frac{1}{6}$. The median is halfway between sizes $8\frac{1}{2}$ and 9, which would be 8.75, or $8\frac{3}{4}$. The store owner could not buy any shoes in either size $8\frac{1}{6}$ or size $8\frac{3}{4}$ because those shoe sizes do not exist. However, the store owner does want to stock several shoes in size 9.

**CONCEPT CHECK 24.3**

Find the mode for the following set of numbers: 14, 11, 12, 15, 10, 16, 15, 12, 13, 11, 15, 17, 13, 14, 15, 12, 18

The mode is the number that occurs most often. It is easier to find if you arrange the numbers by size first:

10, 11, 11, 12, 12, 12, 13, 13, 14, 14, 15, 15, 15, 15, 16, 17, 18

There are four 15s, so the mode is 15.

# Constructing Frequency Tables

Learning Objective 4

Construct frequency tables.

The data in examples A–D are sometimes called **ungrouped data** because the numbers are listed individually. Business applications, such as sales results for all Burger King restaurants, often involve hundreds or thousands of numbers. Interpreting data that are literally pages of raw numbers is impossible. To make sense of such data, we organize the individual values into groups called **classes of data** or *data classes.* Adjacent classes "touch each other," but cannot overlap, not even by one cent. Also, classes are normally the same width. In example E, the width of each class is $5,000. The number of values in each class, called the **frequency** of the class, is summarized in a table called a **frequency table.**

**STEPS to Develop a Frequency Table**

1. Determine the classes of data, and list the classes in one column.
2. Tally the data by making one mark for each data item in the column next to the appropriate class.
3. Count the tally marks for each class and write the number in the column next to the tally marks.

**EXAMPLE E**

Listed below are the salaries of 25 full-time office employees of a large insurance company. Make a frequency table with five classes: $40,000 up to *but not including* $45,000, $45,000 up to *but not including* $50,000, and so on.

| | | | | |
|---|---|---|---|---|
| $42,500 | $41,300 | $53,500 | $62,400 | $47,500 |
| 45,400 | 54,600 | 41,000 | 44,400 | 59,100 |
| 48,000 | 52,000 | 57,500 | 62,500 | 44,000 |
| 53,600 | 46,200 | 53,500 | 51,800 | 56,400 |
| 55,500 | 46,000 | 45,200 | 46,000 | 60,800 |

The frequency table for these salaries appears in Figure 24-1.

**Figure 24-1 Frequency Table**

| Class | Tally | Frequency (F) |
|---|---|---|
| $40,000 up to $45,000 | 𝍸 | 5 |
| $45,000 up to $50,000 | 𝍸 II | 7 |
| $50,000 up to $55,000 | 𝍸 I | 6 |
| $55,000 up to $60,000 | IIII | 4 |
| $60,000 up to $65,000 | III | +3 |
| Total | | 25 |

## COMPUTING THE MEAN OF LARGE DATA SETS

When a data set contains many numbers, as in example E, a computer spreadsheet is usually used to compute the mean. If you use a calculator, be sure to check your work. One way to do so is to add all the numbers twice. One method to add them twice, but in two different orders, is shown in the following steps.

**STEPS to Compute the Mean for a Large Data Set**

1. Add all the numbers in each column.
2. Add all the numbers in each row.
3. Compute the grand total by adding all the column totals.
4. Check the grand total by adding all the row totals.
5. Divide the grand total by the number of values to get the mean.

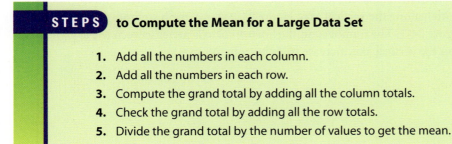

**EXAMPLE F**

Compute the mean of the 25 salaries in example E.

| | | | | | |
|---|---|---|---|---|---|
| $ 42,500 | $ 41,300 | $ 53,500 | $ 62,400 | $ 47,500 | $ 247,200 |
| 45,400 | 54,600 | 41,000 | 44,400 | 59,100 | 244,500 |
| 48,000 | 52,000 | 57,500 | 62,500 | 44,000 | 264,000 |
| 53,600 | 46,200 | 53,500 | 51,800 | 56,400 | 261,500 |
| + 55,500 | + 46,000 | + 45,200 | + 46,000 | + 60,800 | + 253,500 |
| $245,000 | $240,100 | $250,700 | $267,100 | $267,800 | $1,270,700 |

The sum of the row totals and the sum of the column totals are both $1,270,700.

Mean = $1,270,700 ÷ 25 = $50,828

**CONCEPT CHECK 24.4**

Make a frequency table for the following set of data. Use the classes 1,500 up to 2,000, 2,000 up to 2,500, and so on.

| | | | | |
|---|---|---|---|---|
| 2,550 | 3,275 | 3,410 | 2,650 | 3,140 |
| 3,480 | 3,400 | 2,860 | 3,810 | 3,480 |
| 1,660 | 3,280 | 2,940 | 2,480 | 3,325 |
| 1,975 | 4,270 | 3,520 | 2,440 | 2,325 |
| 4,110 | 3,300 | 2,290 | 4,140 | 3,990 |
| 2,570 | 2,150 | 2,840 | 4,325 | 2,720 |

| Class | Tally | Frequency |
|---|---|---|
| 1,500 up to 2,000 | II | 2 |
| 2,000 up to 2,500 | ~~IIII~~ | 5 |
| 2,500 up to 3,000 | ~~IIII~~ II | 7 |
| 3,000 up to 3,500 | ~~IIII~~ IIII | 9 |
| 3,500 up to 4,000 | III | 3 |
| 4,000 up to 4,500 | IIII | +4 |
| Total | | 30 |

COMPLETE ASSIGNMENT 24.1.

# Charts and Graphs: Constructing Histograms

**Learning Objective 5**

Construct histograms.

In business, statistical information is first summarized clearly in tables. For presentation, the results are then often displayed in charts or graphs. Popular graphs include the histogram, the bar graph, the line graph, and the pie chart (circle graph). Histograms, bar graphs, and line graphs all have perpendicular axes. Labels are placed at the left (the vertical axis) and bottom (the horizontal axis).

A **histogram** is a diagram that presents the **grouped data** from a frequency table. The classes are positioned adjacent to each other along the horizontal axis, and the frequencies are written along the vertical axis. Figure 24-2 shows the histogram for the frequency table in Figure 24-1. The numbers on the horizontal axis increase from left to right. The numbers on the vertical axis increase from bottom to top.

**Figure 24-2** **Histogram**

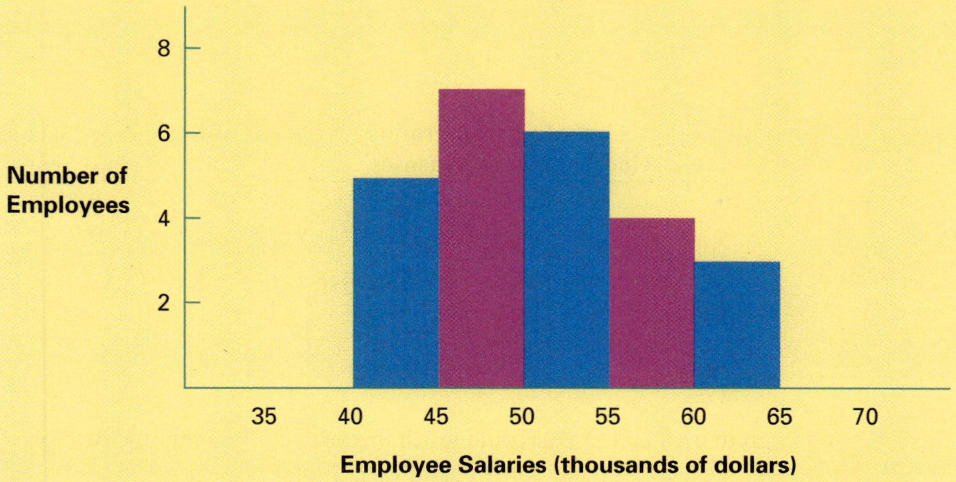


**CONCEPT CHECK 24.5**

Construct a histogram from the following frequency table.

| Class | Frequency |
|---|---|
| 1,500 up to 2,000 | 2 |
| 2,000 up to 2,500 | 5 |
| 2,500 up to 3,000 | 7 |
| 3,000 up to 3,500 | 9 |
| 3,500 up to 4,000 | 3 |
| 4,000 up to 4,500 | +4 |
| Total | 30 |

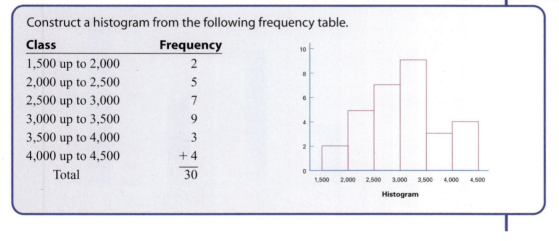

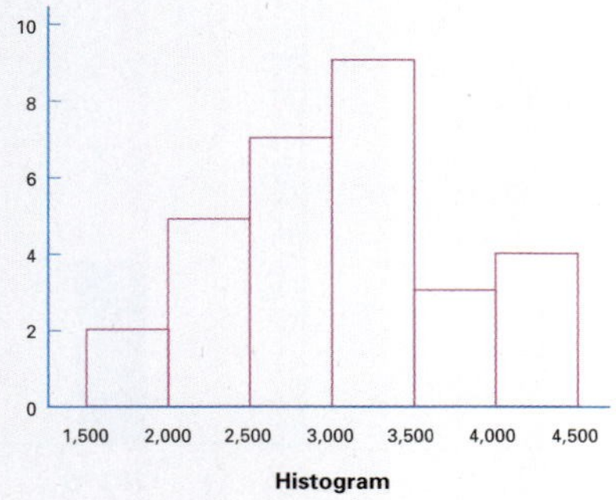


## Constructing Bar Graphs

Learning Objective 6

Construct bar graphs.

A **bar graph,** or bar chart, resembles the histogram except that there may not be a numeric scale on the horizontal axis and the bars normally do not touch each other. Sosa's Markets has grocery stores in four different towns: Davis, Hubbard, Bay View, and Easton, although the Davis store just opened last year in July. The table in Figure 24-3 shows the annual sales revenue, cost of goods sold, operating expenses, and net profits for both the current year and the previous year. The bar graph in Figure 24-4 illustrates the data from the current year. Data from the table in Figure 24-3 are used in various examples throughout the remainder of this chapter.

*Note:* It does not make sense to have the vertical bars "touch each other" as in a histogram. The four stores are distinct objects. If the horizontal axis were "time," like consecutive months of the year, then you could make a bar graph. But it would also make

Figure 24-3 Revenues, Expenses, and Net Profits (in millions of dollars)

**SOSA'S MARKETS SALES DATA FOR THE CURRENT YEAR (IN MILLIONS OF DOLLARS)**

| Location | Sales Revenue | Cost of Goods Sold | Operating Expenses | Net Profit (This Year) | Net Profit (Last Year) |
|---|---|---|---|---|---|
| **Davis** | 1.50 | 0.75 | 0.50 | 0.25 | 0.15 |
| **Hubbard** | 3.25 | 1.75 | 1.00 | 0.50 | 0.75 |
| **Bay View** | 2.00 | 1.00 | 0.75 | 0.25 | 0.50 |
| **Easton** | 4.00 | 2.00 | 1.25 | 0.75 | 0.50 |

sense to use a histogram because last year could touch this year at midnight on December 31. However, as you will see, we can make some useful variations of bar graphs that we really cannot do with histograms.

Figure 24-4 Bar Graph

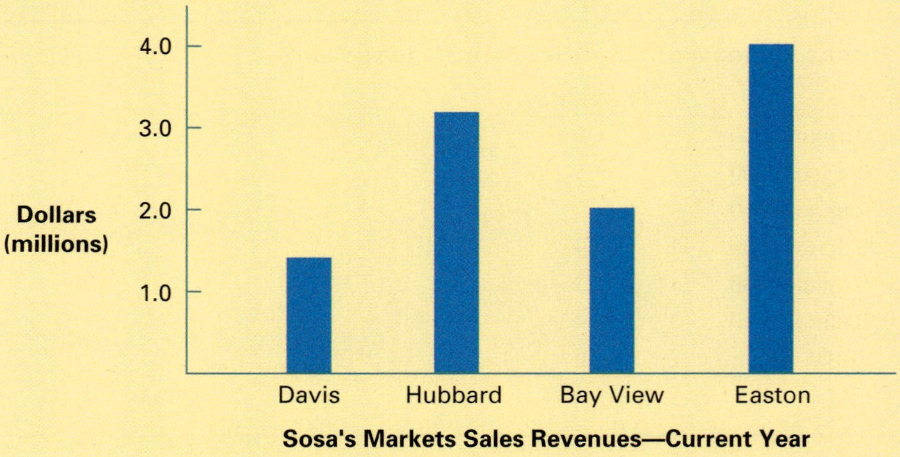


## COMPARATIVE BAR GRAPH

Two bar graphs can be combined on one grid to make a **comparative bar graph.** This permits the statistician to make a graph that will compare two different sets of data. The graph for Sosa's Markets in Figure 24-5 compares each store's net profit this year with its net profit last year. Each store has one pair of bars and the two bars in each pair need to be colored or shaded differently to help the reader distinguish between the two years.

Figure 24-5 Comparative Bar Graph

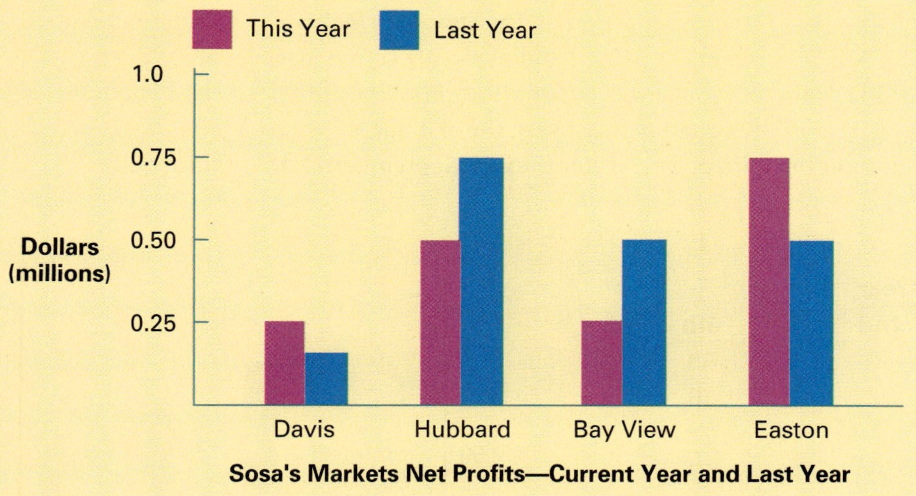


## COMPONENT BAR GRAPH

A bar graph constructed to show how certain data are composed of various segments is a **component bar graph.** Figure 24-6 shows how the current sales revenue is composed of cost of goods sold, operating expenses, and net profit. As in the comparative bar graph, the component parts are colored or shaded differently to permit easier reading.

Figure 24-6 Component Bar Graph

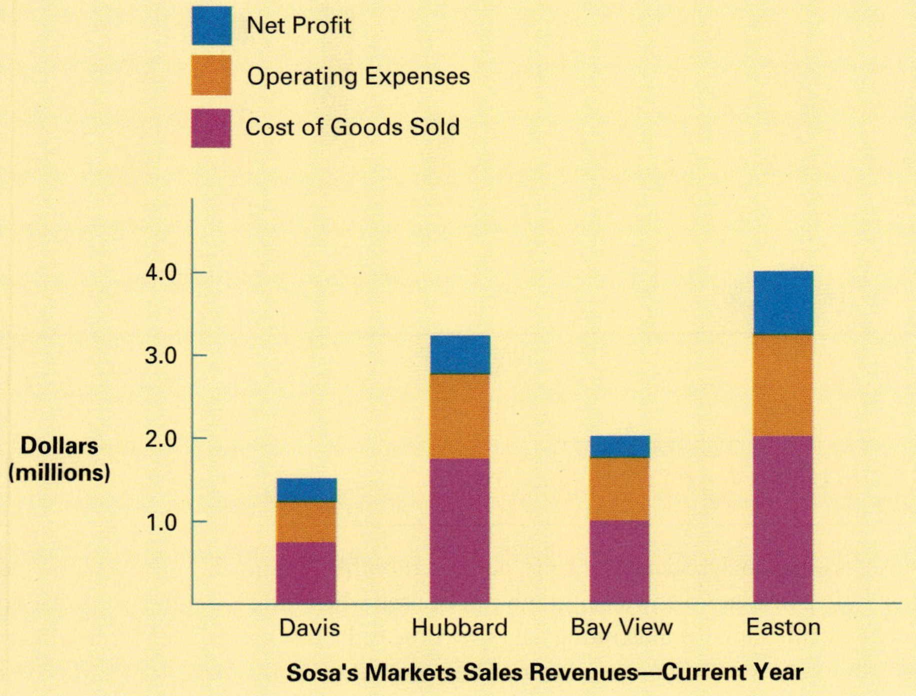

## CONCEPT CHECK 24.6

A real estate agency has three offices, all of which sell some homes. The Shopping Mall Office sells homes almost exclusively; last year it sold 150 homes. The Downtown Office handles mostly commercial property, but it sold 60 homes last year. The Mountain Office primarily manages various resort properties, but it did sell 30 homes. Following are the numbers of homes sold in each quarter of last year. The first quarter is January through March; the second quarter is April through June; the third quarter is July through September; and the fourth quarter is October through December.

**Home Sales Last Year**

| **Quarter** | **1st** | **2nd** | **3rd** | **4th** |
|---|---|---|---|---|
| Shopping Mall Office | 20 | 60 | 40 | 30 |
| Downtown Office | 5 | 20 | 25 | 10 |
| Mountain Office | +10 | +3 | +5 | +12 |
| Total sales last year | 35 | 83 | 70 | 52 |
| Total sales prior year | 30 | 75 | 65 | 55 |

a. Construct a bar graph showing total home sales for each quarter last year. Make the vertical scale from 0 to 100, and mark the four quarters on the horizontal scale.

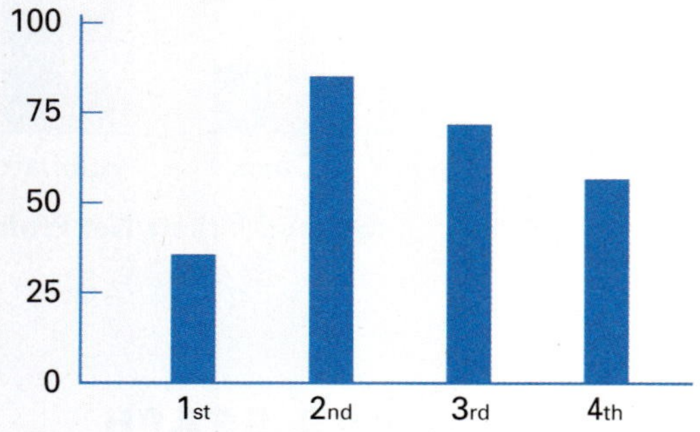


**Home Sales by Quarter—Last Year**

b. Construct a comparative bar graph showing total home sales for each quarter, both last year and the prior year.

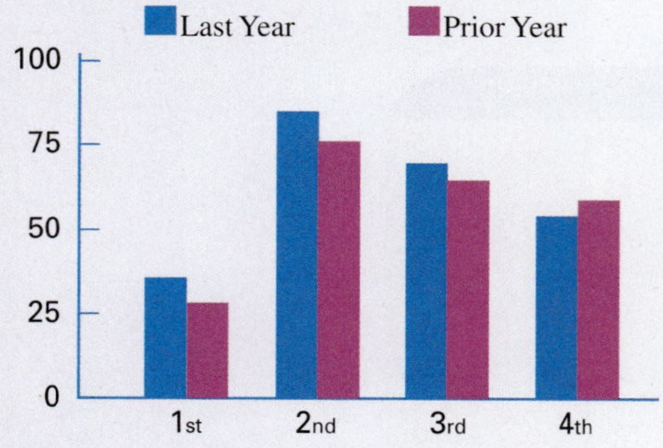


**Home Sales Last Year vs. Prior Year**

c. Construct a component bar graph showing quarterly home sales for each office last year.

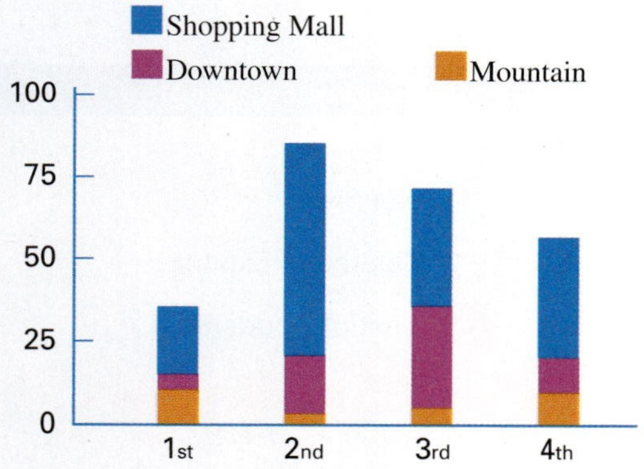


**Home Sales by Office—Last Year**

# Constructing Line Graphs

Learning Objective 7

Construct line graphs.

Businesses often analyze data over time, perhaps monthly or annually. As we mentioned earlier, both a histogram and a bar graph can be used when time is on the horizontal axis. Another useful graph for illustrating data over time is the **line graph.** Plot the heights with single points above each month (or year). Then connect the consecutive points with straight line segments. Notice that it would not make sense to put time on the vertical axis.

Following are five months of expenses for materials for the residential and commercial divisions of Solar Metals, Inc., a custom metal-fabricating business.

| | Jan. | Feb. | Mar. | Apr. | May |
|---|---|---|---|---|---|
| **Residential** | 24,000 | 30,000 | 26,000 | 36,000 | 32,000 |
| **Commercial** | 46,000 | 40,000 | 50,000 | 46,000 | 54,000 |

Figure 24-7 shows a comparative bar graph for this data. Figure 24-8 shows two line graphs with one line for the Residential Division and the other for the Commercial Division.

**Figure 24-7** Comparative Bar Graph

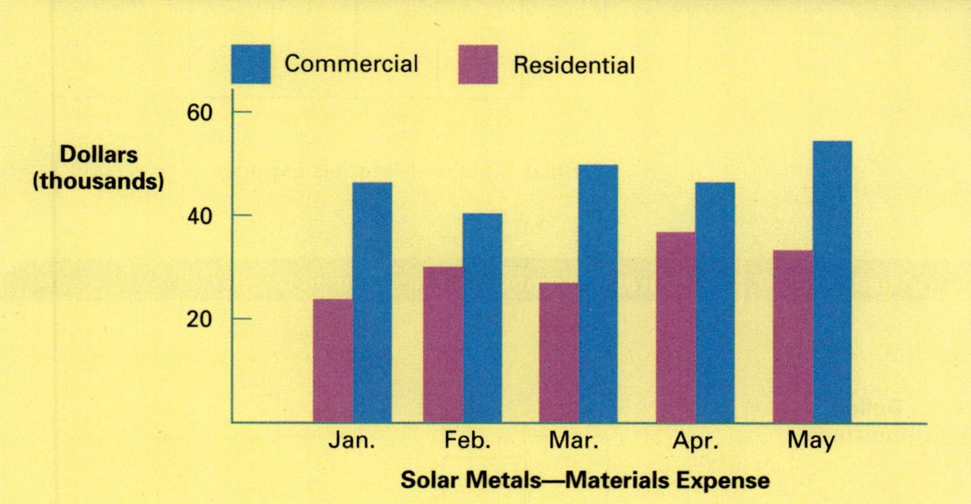


**Figure 24-8** Line Graph

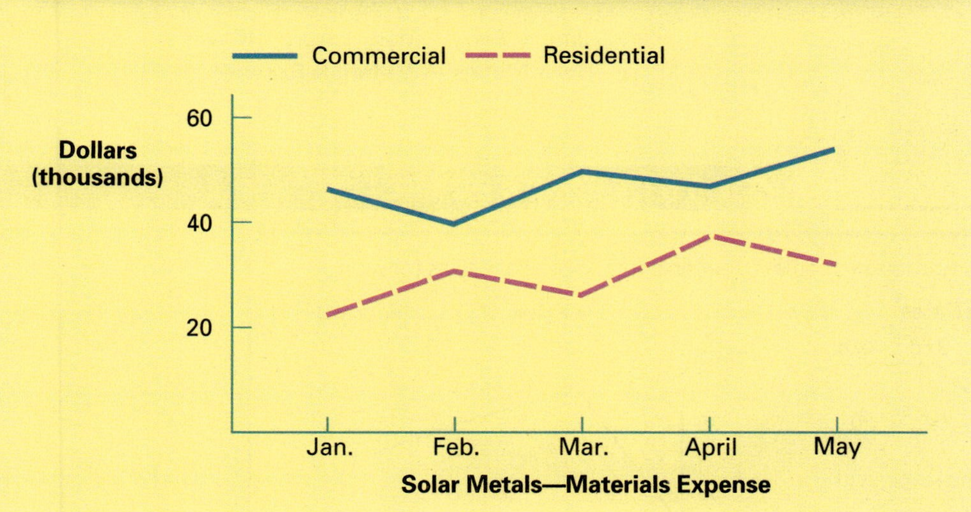


As we mentioned earlier, there is not a convenient, unconfusing method to make one histogram show all of the information. If you simply take the comparative bar graph, but draw the vertical bars all adjacent, the result is NOT a histogram. Histograms are simply not normally used for this kind of data. Histograms for the Residential and Commercial Divisions are shown in Figures 24-9 and 24-10. Their only purpose here is for you to see that the line graph and the comparative bar graph are much better suited to illustrate the differences in the data.

**Figure 24-9** Histogram—Residential Division

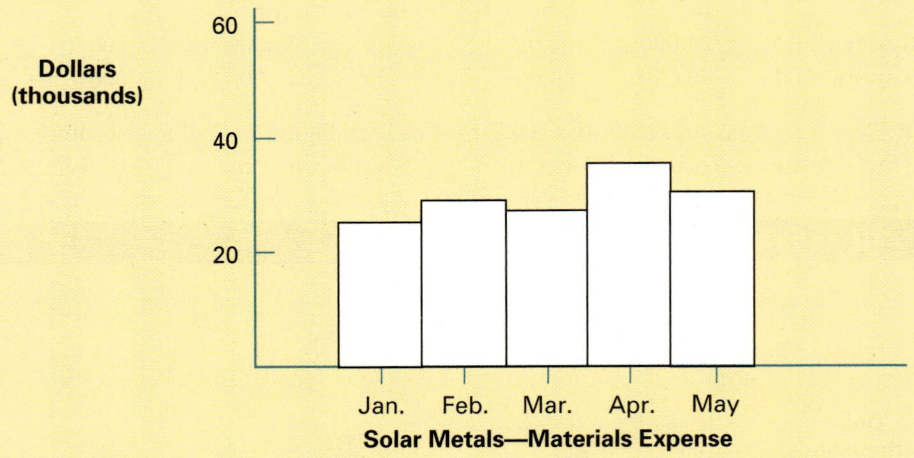


**Figure 24-10** Histogram—Commercial Division

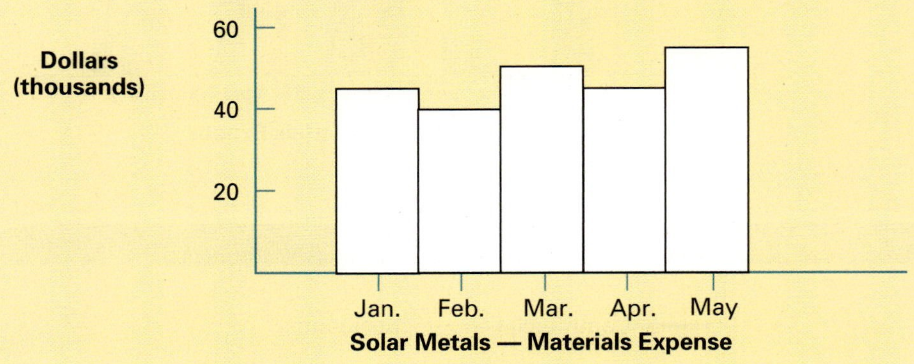


## CONCEPT CHECK 24.7

The real estate firm's quarterly home sales for last year and the prior year are as follows.

**Quarterly Home Sales**

| Quarter | 1st | 2nd | 3rd | 4th |
|---|---|---|---|---|
| Sales last year | 35 | 85 | 75 | 62 |
| Sales prior year | 25 | 73 | 64 | 50 |

Construct two line graphs on the same grid showing quarterly home sales for last year and for the prior year. Make the vertical scale from 0 to 100, and mark the four quarters on the horizontal scale.

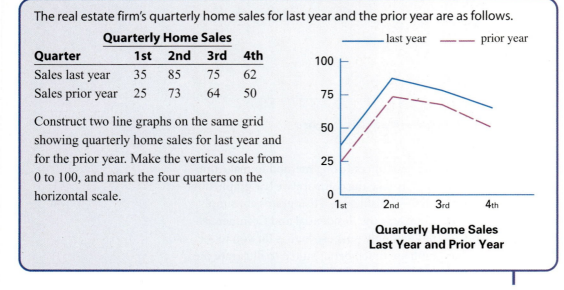

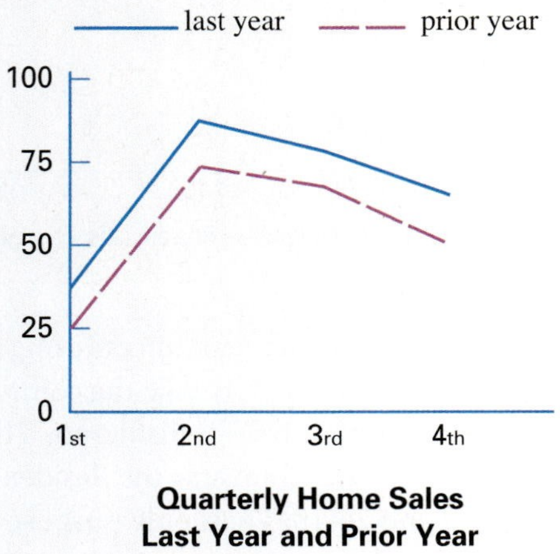

# Constructing Pie Charts

A **pie chart,** sometimes called a circle graph, resembles a component bar graph because it shows how one quantity is composed of different parts. In a pie chart, however, the parts normally are written as percents. Figure 24-11 gives the sales data breakdown for just the Bay View location of Sosa's Markets. (Refer back to Figures 24-3 and 24-6.) The pie chart shown in Figure 24-12 indicates how the Bay View sales revenue for the current year is composed of cost of goods sold, operating expenses, and net profit.

Before the pie chart is drawn, the data are changed into percents, as shown in Figure 24-11. The size of each part of the circle can be reasonably estimated by using the fractional equivalents of the percents. In Figure 24-12, cost of goods sold is 50%, or $\frac{1}{2}$, of the circle. Operating expenses make up 37.5%, or $\frac{3}{8}$, of the circle. The remaining $\frac{1}{8}$ represents net profit.

Learning Objective 8

Construct pie charts.

**Figure 24-11** Sales Revenue for Bay View Market—Current Year

| | Amount | Percent |
|---|---|---|
| Cost of Goods Sold | $1,000,000 | 50.0% |
| Operating Expenses | 750,000 | 37.5% |
| Net Profit Last Year | + 250,000 | + 12.5% |
| Sales Revenue | $2,000,000 | 100.0% |

$1,000,000 ÷ $2,000,000 = 50.0%
$750,000 ÷ $2,000,000 = 37.5%
$250,000 ÷ $2,000,000 = 12.5%

**Figure 24-12** Pie Chart

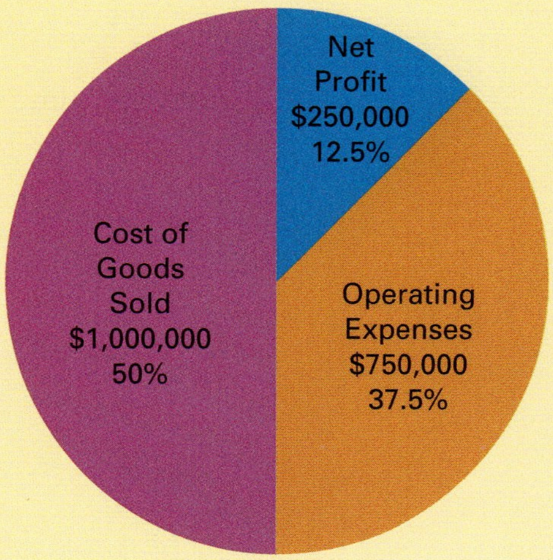


**Bay View Market Sales Revenue—Current Year**

Compare the pie chart in Figure 24-12 with the Bay View part of the component bar graph in Figure 24-6.

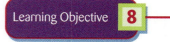

## CONCEPT CHECK 24.8

The home sales by three real estate offices for the past year are shown. Calculate the percent of the total sales for each office, and make a pie chart showing each office's share of the total sales.

| Office | Homes | Percent |
|---|---|---|
| Shopping Mall Office | 150 | 150 ÷ 240 = 62.5% |
| Downtown Office | 60 | 60 ÷ 240 = 25% |
| Mountain Office | + 30 | 30 ÷ 240 = 12.5% |
| Total | 240 | 240 ÷ 240 = 100% |

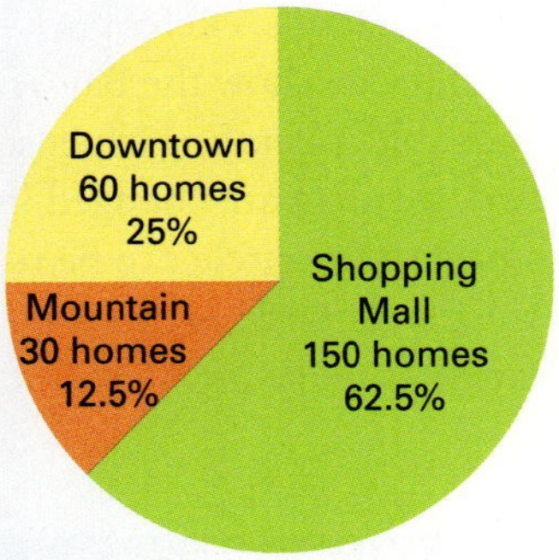

**Home Sales Last Year**

25% is $\frac{1}{4}$ of the circle; 12.5% is half of another quarter, or $\frac{1}{8}$; 62.5% is the remaining eighth plus the remaining half, or $\frac{5}{8}$.

COMPLETE ASSIGNMENT 24.2.

## Chapter Terms for Review

- average
- bar graph
- business statistics
- classes of data
- comparative bar graph
- component bar graph
- frequency
- frequency table
- grouped data
- histogram
- line graph
- mean
- median
- mode
- pie chart
- statistics
- ungrouped data

# THE BOTTOM LINE

*Summary of chapter learning objectives:*

| Learning Objective | Example |
|---|---|
| **24.1**<br>Compute the mean. | 1. Compute the mean (rounded to one decimal place) for these seven values: 34, 26, 18, 9, 21, 24, and 15. |
| **24.2**<br>Determine the median. | 2. Determine the median for these seven values: 15, 26, 18, 9, 21, 24, and 15. |
| **24.3**<br>Determine the mode. | 3. Determine the mode for these seven values: 24, 21, 17, 9, 21, 26, and 15. |
| **24.4**<br>Construct a frequency table. | 4. Use the following set of data to construct a frequency table. Use the classes 0 up to 100, 100 up to 200, and so on. |
| **24.5**<br>Construct histograms. | 5. Construct a histogram from the following frequency table. |

Data for example 4:

| | | | | |
|---|---|---|---|---|
| 150 | 427 | 134 | 254 | 75 |
| 8 | 134 | 228 | 317 | 284 |
| 347 | 289 | 129 | 180 | 125 |
| 197 | 27 | 430 | 246 | 308 |
| 210 | 330 | 297 | 141 | 182 |

Frequency table for example 5:

| Class | Frequency |
|---|---|
| 0 up to 100 | 6 |
| 100 up to 200 | 4 |
| 200 up to 300 | 7 |
| 300 up to 400 | 5 |
| 400 up to 500 | +3 |
| Total | 25 |

Answers: 1. 21 2. 18 3. 21

4.

| Class | Tally | Frequency |
|---|---|---|
| 0 up to 100 | III | 3 |
| 100 up to 200 | 卌 IIII | 9 |
| 200 up to 300 | 卌 II | 7 |
| 300 up to 400 | IIII | 4 |
| 400 up to 500 | II | +2 |
| Total | | 25 |

5.

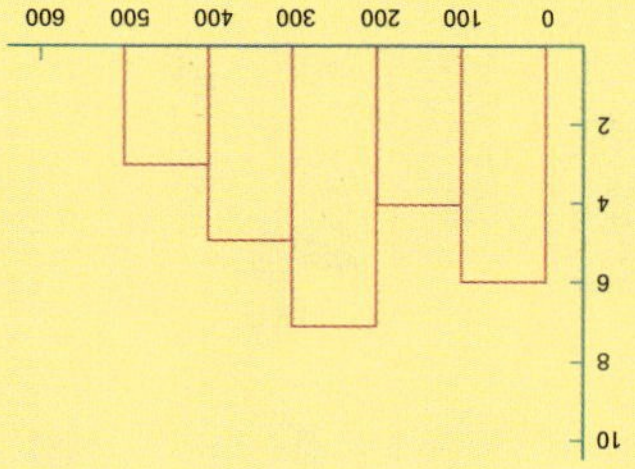

# THE BOTTOM LINE

*Summary of chapter learning objectives:*

| Learning Objective | Example |
|---|---|
| **24.6**<br><br>Construct bar graphs. | 6. Georgia Bailey is an automobile salesperson who sells coupes, sedans, and sport utility vehicles. Her vehicle sales for April, May, June, and July of this year are arranged in the table below. Also given are Georgia's total sales for the same four months last year. |

| Vehicle Type | April | May | June | July |
|---|---|---|---|---|
| Coupe | 9 | 6 | 9 | 8 |
| Sports sedan | 12 | 8 | 6 | 9 |
| Sport utility vehicle | +3 | +12 | +5 | +10 |
| Totals this year | 24 | 26 | 20 | 27 |
| Totals last year | 15 | 20 | 16 | 22 |

Construct a bar graph showing the four monthly totals for this year. Make a vertical scale from 0 to 30, and mark the horizontal scale April, May, June, and July.

7. Construct a comparative bar graph showing the four monthly totals for this year and last year.
8. Construct a component bar graph showing car sales by model for April through July of this year.

Answers: 6.

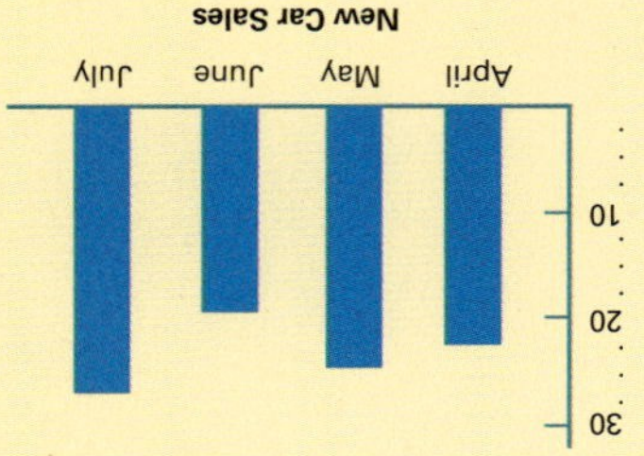


7.

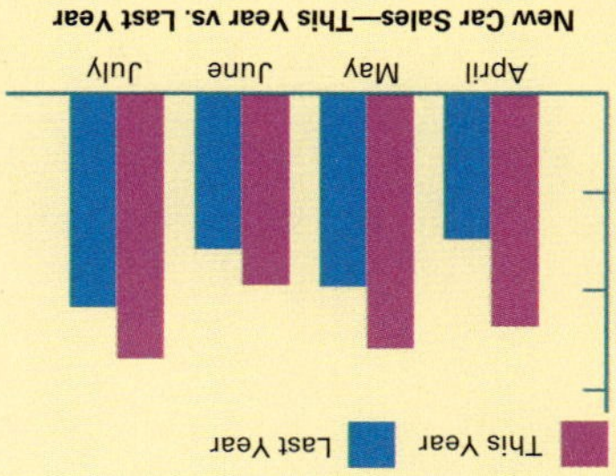


8.

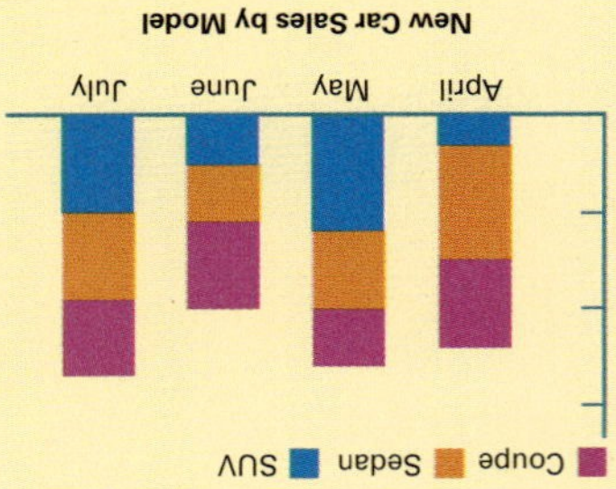

# THE BOTTOM LINE

*Summary of chapter learning objectives:*

| Learning Objective | Example |
|---|---|
| **24.7**<br>Construct line graphs. | 9. The monthly car sales for April, May, June, and July of this year and last year for Georgia Bailey are as follows. |

| Period | April | May | June | July |
|---|---|---|---|---|
| This year | 24 | 26 | 20 | 27 |
| Last year | 15 | 20 | 16 | 22 |

On one grid, construct line graphs showing her sales for these 4 months during this year and last year.

| Learning Objective | Example |
|---|---|
| **24.8**<br>Construct pie charts. | 10. In April of this year, Georgia Bailey sold the following numbers of cars, arranged by type of vehicle. |

| Vehicle Type | Sales | Percent |
|---|---|---|
| Coupe | 9 | |
| Sedan | 12 | |
| Sport utility vehicle | + 3 | |
| Totals | 24 | |

Calculate the percent for each model. Then make a pie chart showing Georgia's sales for each model in April.

Answers: 9.

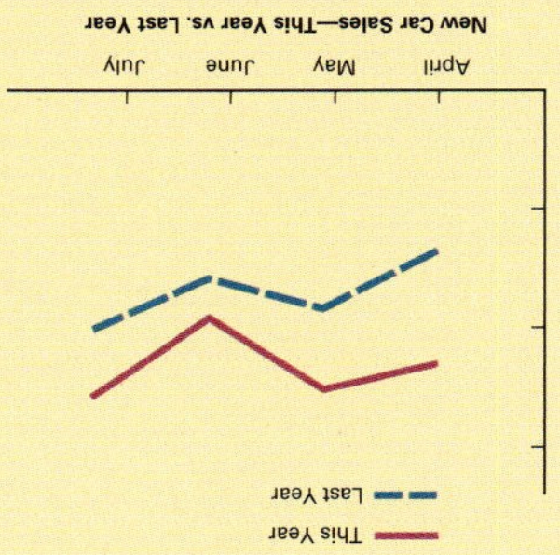


10. 37.5%, 50%, 12.5%

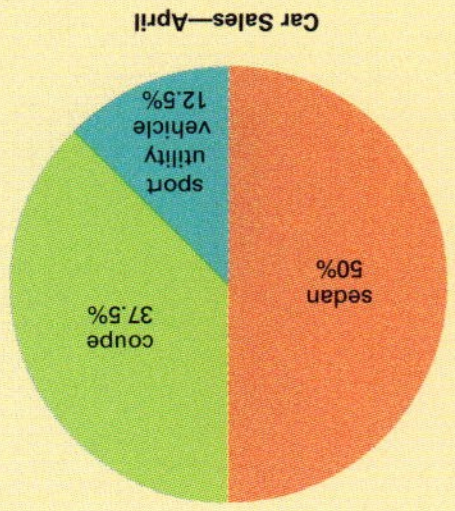

## SELF-CHECK

# Review Problems for Chapter 24

1 For the data 58, 65, 55, 77, 88, 58, 82, 66, 53, 58, 62, 52, 68, 58, 78, 61, 49, find (a) the mean, (b) the median, and (c) the mode.

2 Use the data given to complete the following frequency distribution:

86, 67, 85, 57, 72
61, 77, 53, 85, 67
69, 83, 79, 68, 71
59, 62, 88, 64, 81

| Class | Tally | Frequency |
|---|---|---|
| 50 up to 60 | ________ | a. ________ |
| 60 up to 70 | ________ | b. ________ |
| 70 up to 80 | ________ | c. ________ |
| 80 up to 90 | ________ | d. ________ |

3 Use the frequency distributions from problem 2(a)–(d) to create the appropriate histogram. (Each vertical bar should represent one part of the problem)

4 Kevin and Al Bianchini own two markets, Bianchini's and Foodville. In a typical week, each store sells approximately 2,400 lb of meat, fish, and poultry. Typical amounts are as follows:

| Location | Meat | Fish | Poultry |
|---|---|---|---|
| Bianchini's | 900 | 900 | 600 |
| Foodville | 1,200 | 300 | 900 |

**a.** Draw a comparative bar graph showing the sales of the two markets (two vertical bars for each type of product).

**b.** Draw a component bar graph showing the sales of the two markets. Make one vertical bar for each store, and each bar should show the amount of each product sold in that store.

**c.** Draw a pie chart for the sales for Bianchini's market only.

**Answers to the Self-Check can be found in Appendix B at the back of the text.**

# Assignment 24.1: Statistical Averages

Name ______________________

Date ______________ Score ______________

Learning Objectives 1 2 3 4

**A** **(52 points) Solve the following problems. (points for correct answers as marked)**

**1.** A department store has three local locations: Mason Plaza, Corbin Center, and Balbo Mall. The store gives every applicant for any type of managerial job a test of basic business skills. Listed here are the scores from the tests given to applicants at the three locations last week.

| Mason Plaza | Corbin Center | Balbo Mall |
|---|---|---|
| 59 | 89 | 64 |
| 88 | 60 | 44 |
| 62 | 89 | 53 |
| 47 | 55 | 77 |
| 68 | 46 | 58 |
| 88 | 74 | 43 |
| 78 | 64 | 77 |
| 59 | 89 | 82 |
| 45 | +46 | 66 |
| 88 | | +62 |
| +87 | | |
| ____ | ____ | ____ |

**b.** Combine all the scores into one frequency distribution with the classes as shown. (1 point for each correct answer)

| Class | Tally | Frequency |
|---|---|---|
| 40 up to 50 | ________ | ________ |
| 50 up to 60 | ________ | ________ |
| 60 up to 70 | ________ | ________ |
| 70 up to 80 | ________ | ________ |
| 80 up to 90 | ________ | ________ |

**a.** Find the mean, median, and mode for each location. (3 points for each correct answer)

| | Mason | Corbin | Balbo |
|---|---|---|---|
| Mean | ________ | ________ | ________ |
| Median | ________ | ________ | ________ |
| Mode | ________ | ________ | ________ |

**2.** Cirano Aguilar operates a popular coffee cart from which he also sells sandwiches. He has the opportunity to open another cart in the inner patio of a complex of office buildings, but he won't be allowed to sell sandwiches. Perform a statistical analysis on Cirano's sales receipts for nonsandwich items for the first 15 work days of May and September. (3 points for each correct answer)

| May | | | September | | |
|---|---|---|---|---|---|
| \$430 | \$470 | \$450 | \$200 | \$320 | \$430 |
| 240 | 350 | 240 | 340 | 240 | 295 |
| 280 | 260 | 340 | 280 | 230 | 360 |
| 305 | 360 | 370 | 290 | 370 | 420 |
| 325 | 190 | 250 | 220 | 250 | 180 |

**a.** Find the mean for May. ________

**b.** Find the mean for September. ________

**c.** Find the median for May. ________

**d.** Find the median for September. ________

**e.** Find the combined mean for all 30 days. (*Hint:* Add the two sums and divide by 30.)

________

Score for A (52)

**B (48 points) Solve the following problems. (points for correct answers as marked)**

**3.** La Morra Bank & Trust Co. has several retail branches. Bank management wants to compare the ages of personal banking customers at two specific branches—the Financial District Branch, downtown, and the University Branch, located in a residential area between the local university and a retirement community. The bank's analyst randomly selects 30 personal banking customers from each bank and writes down their ages. The following two tables show the results.

| Financial District Branch | | | | | | University Branch | | | | | |
|---|---|---|---|---|---|---|---|---|---|---|---|
| 43 | 30 | 43 | 51 | 60 | ______ | 74 | 82 | 46 | 19 | 20 | ______ |
| 68 | 32 | 72 | 52 | 27 | ______ | 21 | 36 | 73 | 57 | 18 | ______ |
| 28 | 73 | 43 | 19 | 64 | ______ | 54 | 17 | 18 | 75 | 84 | ______ |
| 70 | 35 | 56 | 55 | 31 | ______ | 76 | 22 | 24 | 19 | 68 | ______ |
| 63 | 24 | 47 | 44 | 34 | ______ | 27 | 21 | 75 | 34 | 18 | ______ |
| 52 | 61 | 66 | 57 | 58 | ______ | 81 | 64 | 22 | 60 | 70 | ______ |
| ______ | ______ | ______ | ______ | ______ | ______ | ______ | ______ | ______ | ______ | ______ | ______ |

**a.** Compute the mean age of the group of customers from the Financial District Branch. (8 points) ______

**b.** Compute the mean age of the group of customers from the University Branch. (8 points) ______

**c.** Make two frequency tables of customer ages, one for the Financial District Branch and one for the University Branch. For each table, use frequency classes 10 up to 20, 20 up to 30, . . . , 80 up to 90. (2 points for each correct row in each table)

**Financial District Branch**

| Class | Tally | Frequency |
|---|---|---|

**University Branch**

| Class | Tally | Frequency |
|---|---|---|

Score for B (48)

# Assignment 24.2: Graphs and Charts

Name

Date Score

Learning Objectives 5 6 7 8

**A (18 points) Complete the following problem as directed. (9 points for each correct graph)**

**1.** After doing the initial research in problem 3 of Assignment 24.1, the analyst from La Morra Bank randomly selected 100 customers from the Financial District Branch and 100 customers from the University Branch. She found the age of each customer and summarized the data in the following two frequency tables.

**Financial District Branch**

| Class | Frequency |
|---|---|
| 10 up to 20 | 5 |
| 20 up to 30 | 10 |
| 30 up to 40 | 15 |
| 40 up to 50 | 21 |
| 50 up to 60 | 18 |
| 60 up to 70 | 16 |
| 70 up to 80 | 12 |
| 80 up to 90 | + 3 |
| Total | 100 |

**University Branch**

| Class | Frequency |
|---|---|
| 10 up to 20 | 20 |
| 20 up to 30 | 21 |
| 30 up to 40 | 10 |
| 40 up to 50 | 9 |
| 50 up to 60 | 5 |
| 60 up to 70 | 7 |
| 70 up to 80 | 15 |
| 80 up to 90 | +13 |
| Total | 100 |

**a.** Draw a histogram for the Financial District Branch. Label each axis, and write a title under the graph.

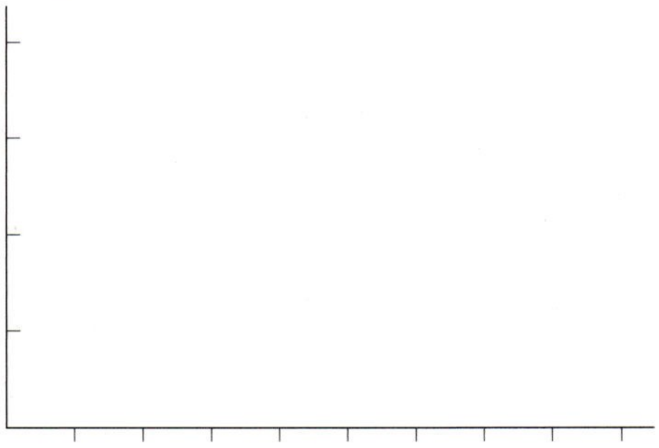

**b.** Draw a histogram for the University Branch. Label each axis, and write a title under the graph.

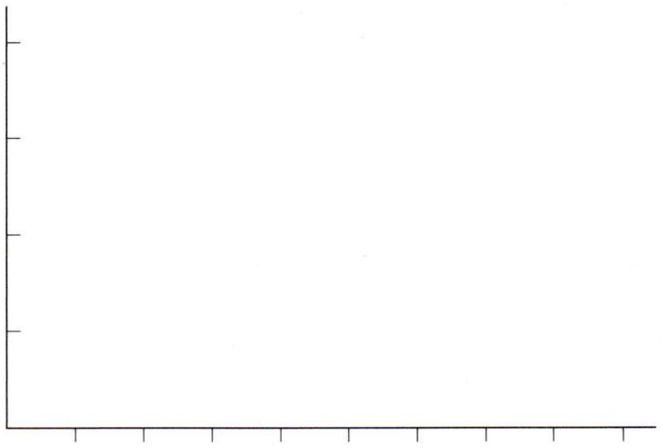

Score for A (18)

**B** **(54 points) Complete the following problems as directed. (18 points for each correct graph)**

**2.** Carla Viberti owns two printing/copying businesses: Viberti Printing and Copies by Carla. Viberti Printing is near City Hall and does most of its work for corporations. Copies by Carla is in a residential district and does primarily printing and copying for individuals and small businesses. The following table shows sales revenues for the two shops for the last 4 months of the year.

| Shop | September | October | November | December |
|---|---|---|---|---|
| Viberti Printing | $300,000 | $225,000 | $275,000 | $200,000 |
| Copies by Carla | 125,000 | 150,000 | 100,000 | 175,000 |

**a.** Make a comparative bar graph showing the monthly sales revenue for each shop. Label each axis, and write a title under the graph. Shade the bars for each shop differently.

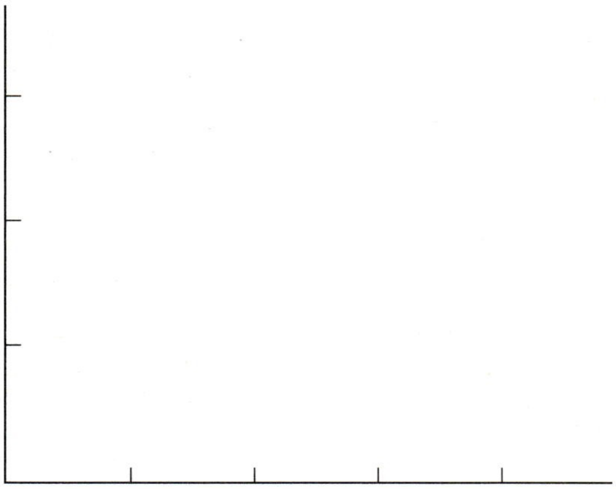

**b.** On the same grid, make line graphs showing the monthly sales revenue for each shop. Label each axis, and write a title under the graph. Use a solid line for Viberti Printing and a dashed line for Copies by Carla.

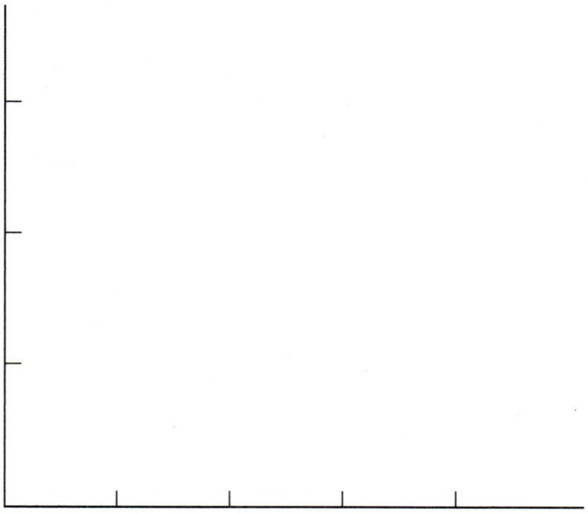

**3.** Atlantic General Insurance Brokers records the totals of residential (as opposed to commercial) insurance policy premiums billed each month. The results for the first 4 months of the year are shown classified by automobile insurance, homeowner's insurance, and life insurance. Construct a component bar graph showing the premiums for each insurance type each month. Label each axis, and write a title under the graph. Shade the three types of insurance differently.

| Insurance Type | January | February | March | April |
|---|---|---|---|---|
| Auto | $200,000 | $200,000 | $160,000 | $240,000 |
| Home | 360,000 | 320,000 | 440,000 | 360,000 |
| Life | +160,000 | +120,000 | +200,000 | +160,000 |
| Total | $720,000 | $640,000 | $800,000 | $760,000 |

Score for B (54)

**C (28 points) Complete the following problem. (points for correct answers as marked)**

**4.** KinatosMedia.com is an Internet web site selling CDs and DVDs, as well as downloadable audio and video recordings. For its own internal sales analysis, KinatosMedia.com classifies every CD music sale as either Rock, Country Western, Classical/Jazz, or Folk. In December, KinatosMedia.com had the CD music sales shown in the table below.

**a.** Compute the percent of the total and the fraction of the total represented by each category of music. (2 points for each correct percent, 1 point for each correct fraction)

| Music Type | Sales | Percent | Fraction |
|---|---|---|---|
| Rock | $276,000 | ______ | ______ |
| Country | 138,000 | ______ | ______ |
| Classical/Jazz | 69,000 | ______ | ______ |
| Folk | + 69,000 | ______ | ______ |
| Total | ______ | 100.0% | $\frac{8}{8}$, or 1 |

**b.** Complete the pie chart to approximate the percent of total December CD music sales for each category of music. Label each section with the category and percent and write a title under the graph. (8 points)

**c.** The percents of CD music sales at KinatosMedia.com for November are shown. Complete the pie chart to approximate the percent of total November sales for each category of music. Label each section with the category and percent, and write a title under the graph. (*Hint:* 37.5% is $\frac{3}{8}$; 12.5% is $\frac{1}{8}$; 30% is somewhere between 25% and 37.5%; 20% is between 12.5% and 25%.) (8 points)

| Music Type | Percent |
|---|---|
| Rock | 37.5% |
| Country | 30.0% |
| Classical/Jazz | 12.5% |
| Folk | +20.0% |
| | 100.0% |

Score for C (28)

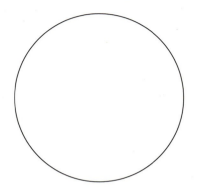

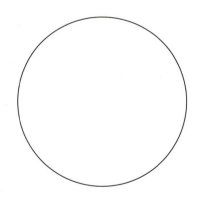

# Appendix A: Answers to Odd-Numbered Problems

## Chapter 1

### Assignment 1.1

1. 310
3. 377
5. 491
7. 639
9. 337
11. 1,215
13. 2,437
15. 1,626
17. 1,589
19. 2,362
21. 1,897.20
23. 1,286.33
25. 929.90
27. 1,904.78
29. 7,269.37
31. 175.93
33. 132.44
35. 265.86
37. 296.36
39. 224.25

### Assignment 1.2

1. 61
3. 47
5. 36
7. 76
9. 16
11. 7
13. 59
15. 29
17. 14
19. 584
21. 103
23. 616
25. $73.98
27. $60.82
29. $38.61
31. ($1,388.96)
33. $8,216.01
35. $3,151.61
37. ($211.31)
39. $48.80
41. $1,790,906.69

### Assignment 1.3

1. 26
3. 728
5. 90
7. 240
9. 72
11. 144
13. 48
15. 80
17. 36
19. 88
21. 28
23. 136
25. 72,576
27. 317,327,062
29. 1,080,000
31. 4,184,998
33. 548,784
35. 2,266,875
37. 184,200
39. 166,050
41. 37,500
43. 27,540
45. 9,800
47. 1,000
49. 585,514
51. 144.00
53. 366.08
55. 1,787.50
57. 2,352
59. 3,234
61. 26,400

### Assignment 1.4

1. 12
3. 3
5. 42
7. 4
9. 18
11. 30
13. 13
15. 99
17. 52
19. 18
21. 5 (153)
23. 976
25. 390
27. 90 (5)
29. 7 (600)
31. 22 (16)
33. 612
35. 178 (28)
37. 184 (137)
39. 1,000 (7)
41. 20 (118)
43. 517 (597)
45. 1,111 (49)
47. $2.20
49. 1 (49)
51. 1,112 (36)
53. 260 (49)
55. 2,000,148 (24)
57. 45
59. 105 (9)

### Assignment 1.5

1. 400,000
3. 2,400,000
5. 5,400,000
7. 30,000
9. 2,000,000
11. 640,000
13. 7,000,000
15. 1,000,000
17. 4,000
19. 4,000
21. 270,000; 259,602
23. 10,000,000; 9,822,780
25. 140,000; 139,867
27. 60; 51
29. 200; 208

## Chapter 2

### Assignment 2.1

1. $2\frac{1}{6}$
3. 3
5. $1\frac{10}{13}$
7. $\frac{37}{10}$
9. $\frac{21}{8}$
11. $\frac{33}{5}$
13. $\frac{2}{5}$
15. $\frac{3}{5}$
17. $\frac{2}{3}$
19. $\frac{7}{10}$

21. $\frac{15}{18}$

23. $\frac{15}{24}$

25. $\frac{15}{35}$

27. $\frac{36}{45}$

29. $\frac{10}{10} = 1$

31. $3\frac{17}{12} = 4\frac{5}{12}$

33. $7\frac{12}{6} = 9$

35. $6\frac{58}{45} = 7\frac{13}{45}$

37. $1\frac{2}{12} = 1\frac{1}{6}$

39. $1\frac{8}{12} = 1\frac{2}{3}$

41. $1\frac{17}{20}$

43. $2\frac{17}{30}$

45. $7\frac{11}{12}$ qt

47. $\frac{7}{8}$ in.

### Assignment 2.2

1. $\frac{1}{6}$
3. $\frac{5}{8}$
5. 7
7. $6\frac{3}{4}$
9. $1\frac{1}{6}$
11. $1\frac{7}{8}$
13. $1\frac{3}{7}$
15. $4\frac{1}{6}$
17. $13\frac{1}{3}$ cu yd
19. $1\frac{1}{2}$ qt
21. $14\frac{2}{3}$ times

## Chapter 3

### Assignment 3.1

1. 0.0613
3. 0.64
5. 860.00098
7. three hundred eight and ninety-seven hundredths
9. four hundred ninety-two and three tenths
11. forty-two and four hundred eighty-one ten-thousandths
13. one thousand seven and four tenths
15. 49.0 mi
17. 374.3 lb
19. 6.4 oz
21. \$0.10
23. \$8.10
25. \$53.00
27. 0.005 gal
29. 8.186 in.
31. 0.200 lb
33. \$0.16
35. \$2.10
37. \$0.66
39. 22.2363
41. 104.4996
43. 29.281
45. 249.202
47. 0.364
49. 17.415
51. 3.682
53. 0.4095
55. 0.176
57. 1.677

### Assignment 3.2

1. \$1,311.58
3. \$338.52
5. 79.3354
7. 79.9969128
9. \$1.85
11. \$45.25
13. 6.12
15. 62.5
17. 470
19. 0.632
21. \$21,723.00
23. \$720.00
25. \$0.43
27. c. 0.04
29. c. 28
31. b. 0.048
33. c. 270
35. d. 120,000
37. a. 0.004
39. b. 1.2
41. a. 70

### Assignment 3.3

1. 8.25 ft
3. 16.85 mi
5. \$302.13
7. \$460
9. \$125
11. \$0.19
13. 67.1 gal

## Chapter 4

### Assignment 4.1

1. \$12,000
3. AUTO
5. \$31.60
7. \$44.85
9. 11
11. \$400
13. \$310
15. \$28
17. \$62.50
19. \$114
21. 22
23. 385
25. 7
27. 3
29. 21
31. **a.** 30, 25
    **b.** 36, 31
    **c.** 66, 60
33. **a.** 25, 5
    **b.** 9, 3
    **c.** 100, 20

### Assignment 4.2

1. \$1.44
3. \$6.12
5. 103 lb
7. \$1.50
9. 900 mi

11. $9.95
13. $79.92
15. $14.85
17. $23.70
19. $760
21. $801
23. $799.60
25. $240
27. $55.79
29. $89.40
31. 6 + 4 + 2 = 17 − 5
33. 9 − 3 − 1 = 2 + 3
35. 20 + 1 + 2 = 16 + 7
37. 12 + 3 − 3 = 7 + 5
39. 64 − 32 − 8 = 8 + 16

## Chapter 5

### Assignment 5.1

1. 0.31
3. 0.0333
5. 300%
7. 15%
9. 175%
11. 2.245
13. 52%
15. 8.25%
17. 400%
19. 0.0001
21. 0.21
23. 11.17
25. 0.34
27. $0.29
29. $1.65
31. 16
33. 75
35. 0.96
37. 20%
39. 200%
41. $1.20
43. 150%
45. $48
47. $8,000
49. 56
51. 480
53. 40%
55. $21.00
57. 160%
59. 25

### Assignment 5.2

1. 210
3. 30
5. $8,320
7. 544
9. $170
11. 16%
13. 25%
15. 20%
17. (25); (4.6%)
19. +230; +12.7%
21. (1,318); (8.9%)
23. (189); (17.4%)
25. +310; +17.2%
27. ($63.53); (9.4%)
29. +55.60; +14.9%
31. +22.74; +15%
33. +193.39; +4.0%
35. (216.61); (4.7%)

### Assignment 5.3

1. 220
3. 6,500
5. 38%
7. 280,000
9. $720
11. $3,250
13. $52,942
15. 10%
17. $62,500
19. 100%

### Assignment 5.4

1. **a.** 1,200; 16%; $2,400
   **b.** 1,800; 24%; 3,600
   **c.** 2,100; 28%; 4,200
   **d.** 2,400; 32%; 4,800
3. $6,400; $3,200; $4,800; $5,600
5. $8,840; $6,760; $4,940; $5,460

## Chapter 6

### Assignment 6.1

1. $3,600; $3,600
3. 2,100; 3,600
5. 3,840; 5,640
7. 3,040
9. 3,720
11. 4,900
13. $1,152; $36,997
15. $504; $7,612
17. $987; $12,841
19. $539; $5,634
21. $388; $5,456

### Assignment 6.2

1. $6,275
3. $3,450
5. $3,680
7. $1,834.20
9. $952
11. $10,800

## Chapter 7

### Assignment 7.1

1. $441; $819
3. $2,120; $6,360
5. 80%; $5,592
7. $720; $420; —; $1,260
9. 60%; 80%; —; $864
11. 70%; 80%; 95%; 46.8%
13. $466

### Assignment 7.2

1. June 1; June 21; $86.25; $2,788.87
3. Sept. 4; Oct. 4; $6.75; $443.25
5. Apr. 8; 98%; $570.85
7. $625.00; $356.94

## Chapter 8

### Assignment 8.1

1. $655.95
3. $455.48
5. $280.99
7. $340; $1,190
9. $1,050; $2,550
11. $480; $1,120
13. $2,250; $4,750
15. 160%; $775
17. 220%; $50
19. 135%; $440
21. 150%; $1,500
23. $1,575; $3,675
25. $1,116; 55%

### Assignment 8.2

1. $149.49
3. $1,819
5. $37.49
7. $66; $54
9. $144; $216
11. $999; $999
13. $494.40; $329.60
15. 60%; $1,425
17. 55%; $260
19. 70%; $3,600

**21.** 65%; $820
**23.** $174; $174
**25.** $72.96; 60%

## Chapter 9

### Assignment 9.1

**1.** 585.00; 4,782.50; 3,262.50; 2,272.50; 2,207.20; 1,917.50; 5,762.75; 5,636.33; 4,671.33; 4,021.33
**3.** 1,190.85; 1,190.85; 1,190.85; 878.05
**5.** 877.76; 3,037.76; 3,037.76; 1,837.49
**7.** $1,669.35
**9.** 2,141.70; 1,993.50; 2,970.30; 2,156.30; $1,871.13
**11.** 3,020.10; 2,754.38; 2,668.68; 3,604.30; $2,374.16

### Assignment 9.2

**1.** 802.50; 752.90; 678.71; 904.21; 791.89; 758.56; 746.56; 678.79; 466.79; 328.79; 422.79
**3.** **a.** $728.47 **b.** $1,630.27 **c.** $951.41 **d.** $737.40 **e.** $962.18

### Assignment 9.3

**1.** Cogswell Cooling, Inc.
Reconciliation of Bank Statement, November 30

| | | |
|---|---|---|
| Checkbook balance | | $ 480.77 |
| Minus unrecorded bank charges: | | |
| Service charge | | 9.50 |
| | | $ 471.27 |
| Plus bank interest credit | | 12.00 |
| Adjusted checkbook balance | | $ 483.27 |
| Bank balance on statement | | $1,050.82 |
| Minus outstanding checks: | | |
| No. 148 | $ 13.90 | |
| No. 156 | 235.10 | |
| No. 161 | 96.35 | |
| No. 165 | $222.20 | 567.55 |
| Adjusted bank balance | | $ 483.27 |

**3.** Linberg Floors
Reconciliation of Bank Statement, May 31

| | | |
|---|---|---|
| Checkbook balance | | $19,512.54 |
| Plus bank interest credited | | 35.20 |
| | | $19,547.74 |
| Minus unrecorded bank charges: | | |
| Service charge | $ 18.00 | |
| Automatic transfer—insurance | 1,765.00 | |
| Returned check | 920.00 | 2,703.00 |
| Adjusted checkbook balance | | $16,844.74 |
| Bank balance on statement | | $18,120.16 |
| Plus deposit not recorded by bank | | 2,004.35 |
| | | $20,124.51 |
| Minus outstanding checks: | | |
| No. 730 | $ 85.17 | |
| No. 749 | 1,216.20 | |
| No. 753 | 462.95 | |
| No. 757 | 512.80 | |
| No. 761 | 19.75 | |
| No. 768 | 982.90 | 3,279.77 |
| Adjusted bank balance | | $16,844.74 |

## Chapter 10

### Assignment 10.1

**1.** $360.00; $108.00; $18.00; $486.00
320.00; —; —; 320.00
400.00; 120.00; 40.00; 560.00
360.00; 67.50; —; 427.50
352.00; —; —; 352.00
280.00; —; —; 280.00
320.00; 84.00; —; 404.00
360.00; 13.50; —; 373.50
352.00; 105.60; 17.60; 475.20
352.00; —; —; 352.00
380.00; 114.00; 38.00; 532.00
400.00; 60.00; —; 460.00
$4,236.00; $672.60; $113.60; $5,022.20
**3.** $2,838.98
**5.** $637.54
**7.** $9.49; $10.00; $0.51
**9.** $41.59; $42.00; $0.41

### Assignment 10.2

**1.** $592.00; $592.00; $36.70; $8.58; $65.00; $125.28; $466.72
600.00; 5; 22.50; 112.50; 712.50; 44.18; 10.33; 50.00; 116.51; 595.99
432.00; 432.00; 26.78; 6.26; 50.00; 95.04; 336.96
600.00; 600.00; 37.20; 8.70; 26.00; 89.90; 510.10
496.00; 8; 18.60; 148.80; 644.80; 39.98; 9.35; 39.00; 106.33; 538.47
592.00; 4; 22.20; 88.80; 680.80; 42.21; 9.87; 27.00; 97.08; 583.72
424.00; 424.00; 26.29; 6.15; 39.00; 83.44; 340.56
571.20; 2; 21.42; 42.84; 614.04; 38.07; 8.90; 13.00; 71.97; 542.07
500.00; 500.00; 31.00; 7.25; 51.00; 104.25; 395.75
$4,807.20; $392.94; $5,200.14; $322.41; $75.39; $360.00; $889.80; $4,310.34
**3.** $27.94; $6.53; $16.58; $55.05; $395.55
25.54; 5.97; 12.72; 48.23; 363.77
25.54; 5.97; 12.72; 48.23; 363.77
29.48; 6.89; 19.07; 59.44; 416.06
25.74; 6.02; 13.04; 48.80; 366.40
30.40; 7.11; 20.55; 62.06; 428.19
26.51; 6.20; 14.27; 50.98; 376.52
27.03; 6.32; 15.11; 52.46; 383.44
31.62; 7.40; 22.52; 65.54; 444.46
31.35; 7.33; 22.08; 64.76; 440.84
31.99; 7.48; 23.12; 66.59; 449.41
30.91; 7.23; 21.37; 63.51; 434.99
33.22; 7.77; 25.10; 70.09; 465.71
$377.27; $88.22; $238.25; $755.74; $5,329.11
**5.** **a.** $22,528.40
**b.** $1,396.75
**c.** $326.67
**d.** $2,500.95
**e.** $4,224.37
**7.** **a.** $19,500.00; $7,000.00
**b.** $56.00
**c.** $378.00
**d.** $434.00

## Chapter 11

### Assignment 11.1

1. $0.59; $8.96; $1.04
   0.16; 2.51; 2.50
   2.44; 37.29; 2.71
   1.37; 20.93; 4.07
   0.36; 5.48; 4.52
   1.16; 17.66; 2.34
   1.30; 19.85; 0.15
   0.07; 1.05; 0.20
   0.70; 10.68; 4.32
   1.24; 19.02; 0.98
3. $106.26
5. **a.** Discount Carpets
   **b.** $312

### Assignment 11.2

1. **a.** $625,000,000
   **b.** $732,997,500
   **c.** $361,760,000
3. $1.30
   $0.98
5. $2,565
7. $539.75
9. **a.** 1.7% (0.017)
   1.5% (0.015)
   1.35% (0.0135)
   2.0% (0.02)
   **b.** 17 mills
   15 mills
   13.5 mills
   20 mills
11. $1,392

### Assignment 11.3

1. **a.** $19,950
   **b.** $31,000
   **c.** $17,200
   **d.** $7,092
   **e.** $11,082
3. **a.** $350
   **b.** $35
5. **a.** $35,550
   **b.** $4,550

## Chapter 12

### Assignment 12.1

1. **a.** $960
   **b.** $220
   **c.** $1,650
   **d.** $1,430
3. **a.** $3,600
   **b.** $2,400
   **c.** $279
   **d.** $3,600
5. **a.** $53,340
   **b.** $50,000
   **c.** $6,000
   **d.** $3,440
   **e.** $56,000

### Assignment 12.2

1. **a.** $3,724
   **b.** $2,793
   **c.** $558.60
3. $200,000
5. **a.** $165,000
   **b.** $55,000
   **c.** $180,000
   **d.** $120,000
7. $360,000

### Assignment 12.3

1. $19.30; $3,860.00
   $8.26; $2,643.20
   $27.04; $540.80
   $4.91; $2,356.80
   $16.83; $3,366.00
   $53.86; $4,578.10
3. $4,800
5. **a.** $9,050
   **b.** $9,500
   **c.** $6,545
7. **a.** $600
   **b.** $1,896

## Chapter 13

### Assignment 13.1

1. $30.00
3. $48.00
5. $187.50
7. $2,240.00
9. $130.00
11. $48.00; $47.34; $0.66
13. $480.00; $473.42; $6.58
15. $375.00; $369.86; $5.14
17. $9.65; $9.25; $0.40
19. $60.32; $60.00; $0.32
21. $4,800
23. 8%
25. 225 days
27. $91.80
29. 7.5%

### Assignment 13.2

1. $12.75
   $862.75
3. $90
   $3,690
5. $2,080
   $62,080
7. $924.66
   $45,924.66
9. $67.81
   $5,067.81

## Chapter 14

### Assignment 14.1

1. **a.** 1.5%
   **b.** 1.25%
   **c.** 1.4%
   **d.** 0.6%
   **e.** 0.55%
   **f.** 1.6%
   **g.** 1.2%
   **h.** 0.7%
   **i.** 0.75%
   **j.** 0.8%
3. $29.34; $1,748.68
5. $45.15; $1,151.95
7. $1,690.26; $23.63; $993.55
9. $1,098.40; $12.23;
   $1,783.02
11. $790.12; $9.15; $1,571.62

### Assignment 14.2

1. $36.00; $1,636.00;
   $3,200.00
   3,200.00; 24.00; 1,624.00;
   1,600.00
   1,600.00; 12.00; 1,612.00
3. $36.00; $1,636.00;
   $3,200.00
   3,200.00; 36.00; 1,636.00;
   1,600.00
   1,600.00; 36.00; 1,636.00
5. **a.** $3,200
   **b.** $115.50
   **c.** 14.4%
7. **a.** $3,200
   **b.** $108
   **c.** 13.5%

### Assignment 14.3

**A.** 1. $204.52242; $3,681.40
3. $6.32649; $1,739.78

**B.** 5. $254.70501
7. 4,516.77; 33.88;
   1,494.35; 3,022.42
9. 1,516.86; 11.38;
   1,528.24; 1,516.86

**C.** 11. 4,845.00; 36.34; 1,163.66; 3,681.34
13. 2,508.95; 18.82; 2,527.77; 2,508.95

**D.** 15. 159,769.12; 798.85; 232.03; 159,537.09

## Chapter 15

### Assignment 15.1

**1.** 188
**3.** 122
**5.** 121
**7.** January 30, 2012
**9.** December 5, 2012
**11.** March 9, 2010
**13.** Jan. 10, 2011; $403.00; $26,403.00
**15.** Oct. 28, 2009; $583.92; $36,333.92
**17.** 125; $730.07; $42,530.07
**19.** Aug. 10, 2009; $2,115.62; $54,115.62

### Assignment 15.2

**1.** $31.25
$2,531.25
May 15
32
$24.75
$2,506.50

**3.** $0
$4,500
Jan. 22
39
$48.75
$4,451.25

**5.** $71.01
$3,671.01
July 19
44
$57.53
$3,613.48

**7.** $0
$4,000
Oct. 15
45
$49.32
$3,950.68

### Assignment 15.3

**1.** $250; $7,250; 10.34%
**3.** $825; $15,675; 12.63%
**5.** $27.18; $952.82; 7.71%
**7.** $100.00; 20; $26.85; $73.15
**9.** $407.19; 33; $254.48; $152.71
**11.** $92.00; 30; $71.87; $20.13
**13.** $650.00; 20; $118.07; $531.93

## Chapter 16

### Assignment 16.1

**1.** $7,622.94; $1,622.94
**3.** $37,690.80; $17,690.80
**5.** $5,719.80; $719.80
**7.** $5,713.00; $1,713.00
**9.** $4,381.50
**11.** $46,140.66
**13.** $2,062.88
**15.** $22,510.44
**17.** $7,590.85
**19.** $7,142.85
**21.** $31,622.58
**23.** $1,750.71
**25.** $308.99

### Assignment 16.2

**1.** $3,266.17; $633.83
**3.** $12,116.17; $10,883.83
**5.** $5,512.60; $4,487.40
**7.** $2,285.35; $214.65
**9.** $1,060.20
**11.** $9,230.00
**13.** $4,407.62
**15.** $2,714.50
**17.** $2,218.98
**19.** $4,273.90
**21.** $18,561.75
**23.** $4,884.72
**25.** $360.49

## Chapter 17

### Assignment 17.1

**1.** $696.00
$546.00
$552.00
$781.20
$1,260.00
$648.00
$4,483.20

**3.** **a.** $21,420
**b.** $22,200
**c.** $21,700

### Assignment 17.2

**1.** $120,000; $96,000
120,000; 72,000; 93,000
86,000
$75,000; 82,000; 87,000; $61,000

**3.** **a.** $61,400
**b.** 5.73

**5.** **a.** $30,123
**b.** $50,205

**7.** $1,555,829

**9.** **a.** $200,000; $4,000
**b.** $182,000; $86,000
**c.** $255,500; $188,500
**d.** $275,591; $168,409
**e.** $24,000; $13,500
**f.** $160,000; $208,000
**g.** $360,000; $60,000
**h.** $313,043; $126,957
**i.** $112,500; $12,500
**j.** $100,000; $30,000

## Chapter 18

### Assignment 18.1

**1.** **a.** $2,700; $21,600; $8,400
**b.** $6,100; $36,600; $11,400
**c.** $10,500; $52,500; $31,500
**d.** $5,600; $5,600; $29,000

**3.** **a.** $14,000
**b.** $18,000

**5.** **a.** $4,000.00; $3,062.50
**b.** $3,715.20; $343.68
**c.** $2,000.00; $1,000.00
**d.** $1,920.00; $1,228.80
**e.** $2,362.50; $1,328.91
**f.** $7,695.00; $6,232.95

**7.** $1,540.39

**9.** $8,000
$5,333
$2,667

**11.** straight-line, $22,286

### Assignment 18.2

**1.** **a.** $2,475
**b.** $8,640

**3.** $97,200

**5.** $15,670

## Chapter 19

### Assignment 19.1

1. 11.81%; 11.37%; $100,000; 13.33%
   18.06%; 15.92%; $250,000; 23.81%
   10.83%; 9.86%; $129,500; 19.91%
   40.69%; 37.14%; $479,500; 19.57%
   14.17%; 14.70%; $50,000; 5.15%
   5.00%; 4.48%; $64,200; 21.70%
   9.17%; 10.22%; $(14,200); 2.11%
   43.19%; 45.47%; $110,000; 3.67%
   6.94%; 7.17%; $27,200; 5.75%
   59.31%; 62.86%; $123,000; 2.97%
   100.00%; 100.00%; $602,500; 9.13%
   0.53%; 0.94%; $(24,000); −38.71%
   1.53%; 1.33%; $22,530; 25.75%
   0.33%; 0.30%; $4,000; 20.41%
   2.38%; 2.56%; $2,530; 1.50%
   24.31%; 23.86%; $176,200; 11.19%
   2.50%; 3.18%; $(30,000); −14.29%
   26.81%; 27.04%; $146,200; 8.19%
   29.19%; 29.61%; $148,730; 7.61%
   62.50%; 61.70%; $429,200; 10.54%
   6.25%; 6.67%; $10,000; 2.27%
   2.06%; 2.02%; $14,570; 10.91%
   70.81%; 70.39%; $453,770; 9.77%
   100.00%; 100.00%; $602,500; 9.13%
3. 43.23%; 41.79%; $928,778; 13.52%
   7.25%; 7.77%; $29,333; 2.29%
   2.37%; 2.13%; $77,888; 22.25%
   52.85%; 51.69%; $1,035,999; 12.19%
   9.63%; 10.22%; $56,403; 3.36%
   −4.35%; −4.20%; −$94,767; −13.73%
   5.28%; 6.02%; $(38,364); −3.87%
   26.44%; 25.35%; $602,365; 14.45%
   15.44%; 16.94%; $44; 0.00%
   47.15%; 48.31%; $564,045; 7.10%
   100.00%; 100.00%; $1,600,044; 9.73%
   20.66%; 24.77%; $(345,473); −8.48%
   15.82%; 13.85%; $575,666; 25.27%
   4.26%; 4.22%; $73,683; 10.61%
   40.74%; 42.85%; $303,876; 4.31%
   20.95%; 22.75%; $39,273; 1.05%
   7.11%; 5.95%; $305,603; 31.24%
   28.06%; 28.70%; $344,876; 7.31%
   68.80%; 71.55%; $648,752; 5.51%
   26.30%; 24.80%; $667,520; 16.37%
   2.78%; 2.81%; $40,372; 8.75%
   2.12%; 0.85%; $243,400; 174.63%
   31.20%; 28.45%; $951,292; 20.33%
   100.00%; 100.00%; $1,600,044; 9.73%

### Assignment 19.2

1. 103.95%; 103.76%; $93,000; 11.25%
   3.95%; 3.76%; $5,000; 16.67%
   100.00%; 100.00%; $88,000; 11.04%
   23.73%; 24.72%; $13,000; 6.60%
   51.98%; 49.56%; $65,000; 16.46%
   75.71%; 74.28%; $78,000; 13.18%
   27.12%; 26.35%; $30,000; 14.29%
   48.59%; 47.93%; $48,000; 12.57%
   51.41%; 52.07%; $40,000; 9.64%
   14.98%; 15.06%; $12,600; 10.50%
   9.49%; 10.04%; $4,000; 5.00%
   2.03%; 2.51%; $(2,000); −10.00%
   0.51%; 0.53%; $300; 7.14%
   0.41%; 0.39%; $500; 16.13%
   0.14%; 0.18%; $(200); −14.29%
   0.79%; 0.65%; $1,800; 34.62%
   0.36%; 0.26%; $1,100; 52.38%
   28.71%; 29.61%; $18,100; 7.67%
   22.70%; 22.46%; $21,900; 12.23%
   3.62%; 3.51%; $4,000; 14.29%
   19.08%; 18.95%; $17,900; 11.85%
3. 102%; 102%; $12,200; 16%
   2%; 2%; $200; 11%
   100%; 100%; $12,000; 16%
   26%; 24%; $4,500; 26%
   45%; 48%; $3,000; 9%
   71%; 72%; $7,500; 14%
   28%; 30%; $2,100; 10%
   42%; 42%; $5,400; 18%
   58%; 58%; $6,600; 16%
   13%; 15%; $300; 3%
   9%; 8%; $1,500; 25%
   2%; 2%; $200; 17%
   1%; 1%; $70; 18%
   1%; 1%; $50; 8%
   0%; 1%; $(70); −17%
   2%; 2%; $200; 12%
   0%; 0%; $(30); −14%
   28%; 29%; $2,220; 10%
   30%; 29%; $4,380; 21%
   3%; 3%; $200; 10%
   27%; 26%; $4,180; 22%

### Assignment 19.3

**1.** $5,400; 5.2%
19,100; 16.5%
40,000; 27.6%
$64,500; 17.6%
$(3,500); −7.2%
13,000; 9.8%
$9,500; 5.3%
$74,000; 13.6%
$4,800; 17.0%
7,100; 6.3%
$11,900; 8.4%
$(20,000); −16.7%
$(8,100); −3.1%
82,100; 28.8%
$74,000; 13.6%
$(55,000); −6.6%
$7,000; 5.1%
(35,000); −5.6%
$(28,000); −3.7%
40,000; 27.6%
$(68,000); −11.1%
$13,000; 5.9%
$3,400; 4.3%
(1,000); −3.3%
$2,400; 2.2%
$10,600; 9.4%

**3.** $9,000; 56.3%
4,000; 50.0%
15,000; 48.4%
$28,000; 50.9%
$(4,000); −9.3%
4,000; 36.4%
$0; 0.0%
$28,000; 25.7%
$(1,000); −18.2%
3,500; 58.3%
$2,500; 21.7%
$(8,000); −21.1%
$(5,500); −11.1%
$33,500; 56.3%
$28,000; 25.7%
$85,000; 70.8%
$3,500; 12.7%
69,500; 82.2%
$73,000; 65.2%
15,000; 48.4%
$58,000; 71.6%
$27,000; 69.2%
$9,500; 44.2%
5,750; 79.3%
$15,250; 53.0%
$11,750; 114.6%

## Chapter 20

### Assignment 20.1

**1.** **a.** $271.05
**b.** $445.53
**c.** $83.80
**d.** $172.04
**e.** $301.84
**f.** $41.76
**g.** $40.23

**3.** **a.** $156,008
**b.** $4,552
**c.** $1,496

**5.** **a.** 28,272
**b.** $18,500

### Assignment 20.2

**1.** **a.** $2,700
**b.** $86.40
**c.** $2,786.40

**3.** $1,296

**5.** **a.** $16,608
**b.** $17,054.40
**c.** $2,592
**d.** $760.32

**7.** **a.** $36,750
**b.** $14,700
**c.** 0; No duty is paid on exports

**9.** $195,000

**11.** **a.** 590.55 in.
**b.** 49.215 ft
**c.** 16.35 yd
**d.** 9.315 mi
**e.** .875 oz
**f.** .055 lb
**g.** 55 lb
**h.** 63.39 pt
**i.** 31.71 qt
**j.** 7.92 gal

## Chapter 21

### Assignment 21.1

**1.** **a.** $85,400
**b.** $10,846

**3.** 7.9%

**5.** 10.52%

**7.** **a.** $2.10; 6.56%
**b.** $6; 7.5%
**c.** $2; 4.49%
**d.** $5.50; 6.11%
**e.** $3.25; 5.6%

### Assignment 21.2

**1.** 5,000 shares; 90,000 shares

**3.** **a.** $67,500
**b.** $8,750
**c.** $1.75
**d.** $270,000
**e.** $305,000
**f.** $4.00

**5.** $9,750; $0.16

**7.** $38,000 ÷ 25,000 = $1.52;
-0-
$42,000 ÷ 25,000 = $1.68;
$14,000 ÷ 50,000 = $0.28
$40,000 ÷ 25,000 = $1.60;
$25,000 ÷ 50,000 = $0.50

**9.** $550

**11.** **a.** 17
**b.** 15

## Chapter 22

### Assignment 22.1

**1.** $9,625

**3.** $5,400,000

**5.** **a.** $4,000.00; $300.00
**b.** 2,940.00; 236.25
**c.** 7,740.00; 911.25
**d.** 6,540.00; 562.50
$21,220.00; 2,010.00

**7.** **a.** 73; $2,096.50
**b.** 100; $2,852.50

**9.** **a.** 8.33%
**b.** 7.89%
**c.** 8.93%
**d.** 7.32%

### Assignment 22.2

**1.** **a.** 8.22%
**b.** 9.11%

**3.** **a.** $3,661.67
**b.** 9.66%

**5.** **a.** $640.00; $−80.00; $8,200.00; 6.83%
**b.** $600.00; +30.00; 9,850.00; 6.40%
**c.** $900.00; +210.00; 11,160.00; 9.95%
**d.** $510.00; −200.00; 5,300.00; 5.85%
**e.** $70.00; +20.00; 950.00; 9.47%
**f.** $1,950.00; −62.50; 20,250.00; 9.32%

## Chapter 23

### Assignment 23.1

**1.** $57,614.63
**3.** $104,223.28
**5.** $22,557.76
**7.** $75,298.83
**9.** $1,829.35
**11.** $34,335.28
**13.** $8,124.48
**15.** $15,609.04
**17.** $869.25
**19.** $55,070.54
**21.** $6,614.16
**23.** $26,754,941.60
**25.** $334.54

### Assignment 23.2

**1.** $18,988.95
**3.** $34,064.26
**5.** $58,670.83
**7.** $23,585.11
**9.** $1,067.02
**11.** $1,543.04
**13.** $57,738.20
**15.** $1,776.98
**17.** $913.89
**19.** $60,195.40
**21.** $395.01
**23.** $6,450.00; $32.25; $1,600.45; $4,849.55
**25.** $3,241.10; $16.21; $1,616.49; $1,624.61

## Chapter 24

### Assignment 24.1

**1.** **a.** Mean: 69.9; 68; 62.6
Median: 68; 64; 63
Mode: 88; 89; 77
**b.** 6; 5; 7; 4; 8
**3.** **a.** 48.6
**b.** 45.8
**c.** Financial District Branch
10 up to 20: 1
20 up to 30: 3
30 up to 40: 5
40 up to 50: 5
50 up to 60: 7
60 up to 70: 6
70 up to 80: 3
80 up to 90: 0
Total: 30

University Branch
10 up to 20: 6
20 up to 30: 7
30 up to 40: 2
40 up to 50: 1
50 up to 60: 2
60 up to 70: 3
70 up to 80: 6
80 up to 90: 3
Total: 30

### Assignment 24.2

**1.** **a.**

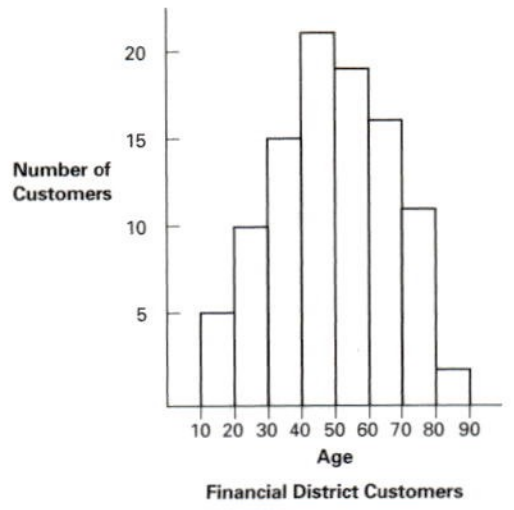


**b.**

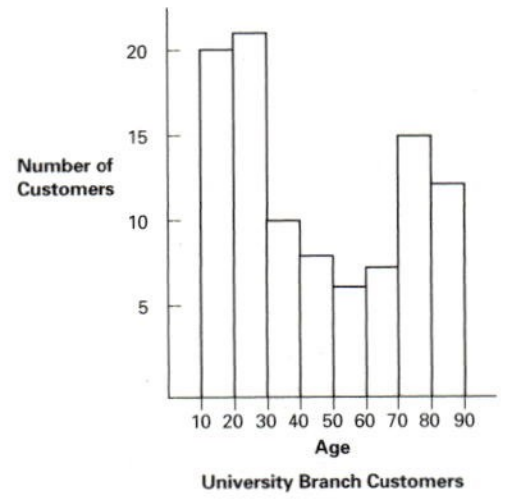


**3.**

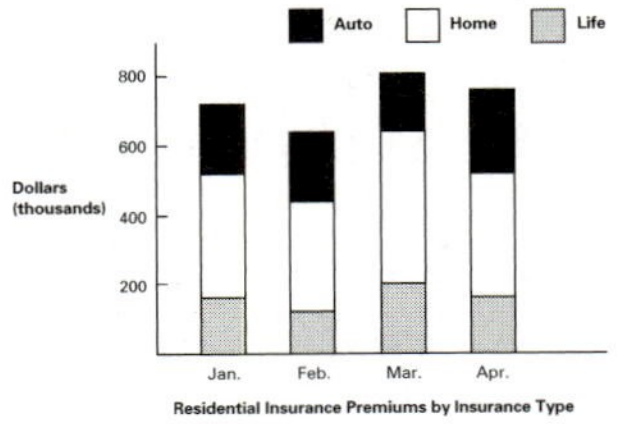

# Appendix B: Answers to Self-Check Review Problems

## Chapter 1

1. 38
2. 127; 67; 240; 204; 638
   140; 229; 121; 148; 638
3. 2,696
4. 51 (3)
5. 1,274
6. 21 (33)
7. 4 (42)
8. 81 (2)
9. 32 R.12
10. 609,824
11. 5
12. 32
13. 10,000
14. 222; 313; 205; 740
    1,774; 1,034; 740
15. 41,216
16. 705,408
17. 28 (4)
18. 640
19. 20,000 (6)
20. 110 (7)
21. $80 \times 30 = 2,400$
22. $100 \times 20 = 2,000$
23. $400 \times 200 = 80,000$
24. $4,000 \times 100 = 400,000$
25. $1,500 \times 600 = 900,000$
26. $400 \div 80 = 5$
27. $900 \div 30 = 30$
28. $10,000 \div 500 = 20$
29. $3,000 \div 60 = 50$
30. $6,000 \div 3,000 = 2$

## Chapter 2

1. $\frac{17}{6}$
2. $7\frac{1}{2}$
3. $\frac{6}{7}$
4. $\frac{40}{56}$
5. $1\frac{17}{30}$
6. $1\frac{19}{24}$
7. $7\frac{11}{20}$
8. $\frac{7}{15}$
9. $1\frac{17}{18}$
10. $1\frac{34}{45}$
11. $\frac{2}{7}$
12. $1\frac{1}{20}$
13. $2\frac{1}{3}$
14. $2\frac{1}{4}$
15. $2\frac{1}{10}$
16. $1\frac{1}{5}$
17. $8\frac{1}{4}$ qt
18. $2\frac{1}{12}$ ft
19. $6\frac{1}{8}$ tbsp
20. 9 pieces; $\frac{7}{8}$ in.

## Chapter 3

1. 116.0014
2. six thousand four hundred thirty-one and seven hundred nineteen thousandths
3. 3.5
4. $12.67
5. 743.64475
6. 20.807
7. 2.717
8. 122.4881
9. 1.797726
10. $443.39
11. 3.23
12. $0.74
13. 8,649.30, or 8,649.3
14. $2.76
15. **d.** 500
16. **c.** $0.80
17. $3,825.75
18. $281,971.57
19. 590.8 cubic feet
20. 21.88 cu yd

## Chapter 4

1. $35.94
2. $7.44
3. $47.76
4. $80.80
5. $31,256
6. $43,244
7. 427 miles
8. $400
9. $225.75
10. $250
11. 23 hours
12. 19 hours
13. 300
14. 8
15. 156
16. 3
17. 3
18. 13
19. 20
20. $2.00; $0.01

## Chapter 5

1. 0.1475
2. 62.5%
3. 1.5
4. $\frac{3}{4}$%
5. 0.0006
6. 40%
7. 11.2
8. 150
9. 180
10. 70
11. 87.5%
12. 160%
13. $120,000
14. $96,000
15. 100%
16. 50%
17. 1,625 rose bushes
18. 225%
19. $3,440
20. 64%

## Chapter 6

1. **a.** $3,480
   **b.** $6,480

2. **a.** $4,300
   **b.** $6,800
3. **a.** $3,114
   **b.** $6,714
4. **a.** $6,926
   **b.** $6,926
5. $6,000
6. $2,550
7. $7,750
8. $3,300
9. $1,400
10. $6,900
11. $3,750
12. $5,500
13. $8,550
14. $33,910
15. $3,210
16. $25,256

## Chapter 7

1. **a.** $190
   **b.** $570
2. **a.** $360
   **b.** $168
   **c.** $672
3. **a.** 60%
   **b.** $525
4. **a.** 70%
   **b.** 85%
   **c.** $1,071
5. **a.** 60%
   **b.** 80%
   **c.** 90%
   **d.** 56.8%
6. **a.** Aug. 4
   **b.** Aug. 24
   **c.** $17.49
   **d.** $857.06
7. **a.** Jan. 2
   **b.** Feb. 11
   **c.** 97%
   **d.** $1,787.15
8. **a.** $10,204.08
   **b.** $6,335.92

## Chapter 8

1. **a.** $43.35
   **b.** $211.83
   **c.** $1,570
   **d.** $572.63
2. **a.** $250
   **b.** $750
3. **a.** $23.40
   **b.** $59.40
4. **a.** 160%
   **b.** $360
5. **a.** 175%
   **b.** $420
6. **a.** 200%
   **b.** $506
7. **a.** 140%
   **b.** $70
8. **a.** $300
   **b.** 125%
9. **a.** $400
   **b.** 25%
10. **a.** $72
    **b.** $168
11. **a.** $36
    **b.** $108
12. **a.** 60%
    **b.** $744
13. **a.** 25%
    **b.** $132
14. **a.** 40%
    **b.** $2,400
15. **a.** 75%
    **b.** $48
16. **a.** $320
    **b.** 40%
17. **a.** $2,250
    **b.** 60%
18. **a.** $10
    **b.** 25%
    **c.** 20%

## Chapter 9

1. **a.** B
   **b.** D
   **c.** A
   **d.** D
   **e.** C
   **f.** C
   **g.** D
   **h.** D
2.

| | |
|---|---|
| Bank Balance | $10,961.65 |
| + Deposit in transit | 1,850.15 |
| Subtotal | 12,811.80 |
| − O/S checks | 342.90 |
| Adj. Bank Balance | $12,468.90 |

| | |
|---|---|
| Book Balance | $12,583.40 |
| + Interest | 52.50 |
| + Error | 3.00 |
| Subtotal | 12,638.90 |
| − Svc Chg | 20.00 |
| − NSF CK | 150.00 |
| Adj. Book Balance | $12,468.90 |

## Chapter 10

1. **a.** Gross pay = $712.50
   **b.** Social Security = $ 44.18
   Medicare = $ 10.33
   **c.** FIT withheld = $ 82.43
   **d.** Net pay = $575.56
2. **a.** Percentage method = $ 40.04
   Wage-bracket method = $ 41.00
   **b.** Percentage method = $ 54.09
   Wage-bracket method = $ 54.00
3. Jan. $1,260.35; Feb. $1,198.35; Mar. $888.35
4. Social Security, $7,688; Medicare, $1,798, Federal income tax, $7,800; Total, $17,286
5. Social Security, 322.40; Medicare, $110.20; Total, $432.60
6. $614.08; $532.00; $464.40

## Chapter 11

1. Choose A because the cost is less than B.
2. **a.** 1.5%
   **b.** $2,100; $1,161
3. **a.** $443.50
   **b.** 295.67
4. $27,300
5. $17,000 (5 exemptions × $3,400)
6. Standard deduction ($12,800 standard for joint return with one person 65 or older)
7. $23,350 ($38,000 − $7,850 − $6,800)
8. $9,098 ($8,772.50 + 25% of excess over $63,700)

## Chapter 12

1. Jim's insurance pays $5,300, Jim's medical expenses. Joshua's insurance pays -0-.
2. $313.20
3. $2,695
4. $29.250
5. $30,000
6. $4,389
7. $3,255
8. $1,440

## Chapter 13

1. **a.** $75.60
   **b.** $74.56
   **c.** $1.04
2. **a.** $140.00
   **b.** $138.08
   **c.** $1.92
3. **a.** $114.94
   **b.** $120.00
   **c.** $5.06
4. **a.** $58.98
   **b.** $60.00
   **c.** $1.02
5. $1,500
6. 5%
7. 270 days
8. $2,512.50
9. $289.97

## Chapter 14

1. **a.** 9.0%
   **b.** 7.5%
   **c.** 14.4%
   **d.** 4.8%
2. **a.** 0.5%
   **b.** 1.25%
   **c.** 1.1%
   **d.** 0.8%
3. **a.** $26.72
   **b.** $2,387.35
4. **a.** $30.00
   **b.** $1,030.00
   **c.** $2,000.00
   **d.** $2,000.00
   **e.** $20.00
   **f.** $1,020.00
   **g.** $1,000.00
   **h.** $1,000.00
   **i.** $10.00
   **j.** $1,010.00
5. 12%
6. $1,721.23
7. **a.** $30.00
   **b.** $990.07
   **c.** $2,009.93
   **d.** $2,009.93
   **e.** $20.10
   **f.** $999.97
   **g.** $1,009.96
   **h.** $1,009.96
   **i.** $10.10
   **j.** $1,020.06
   **k.** $1,009.96

## Chapter 15

1. **a.** Feb. 7, 2011
   **b.** $3,463.75
2. **a.** 151 days
   **b.** $4,532.88
3. **a.** Jan. 6, 2012
   **b.** $15,255.21
4. **a.** 123 days
   **b.** $3,045.27
5. **a.** $77.85
   **b.** $3,037.85
   **c.** September 12
   **d.** 59 days
   **e.** $73.66
   **f.** $2,964.19
6. **a.** $3,100
   **b.** February 8
   **c.** 60 days
   **d.** $61.15
   **e.** $3,038.85
7. **a.** $135.00
   **b.** $4,365
   **c.** 9.28%
8. **a.** $32.00
   **b.** 20 days
   **c.** $8.59
   **d.** $23.41

## Chapter 16

1. **a.** $4,786.72
   **b.** $786.72
   **c.** $20,892.24
   **d.** $8,892.24
   **e.** $137,849.10
   **f.** $107,849.10
   **g.** $21,226.40
   **h.** $13,226.40
2. **a.** $14,797.50
   **b.** $10,202.50
   **c.** $2,340.72
   **d.** $3,659.28
   **e.** $10,479.15
   **f.** $4,520.85
   **g.** $29,698.80
   **h.** $10,301.20
3. $7,927.74
4. $27,450.94
5. $6,691.12
6. $4,104.25

## Chapter 17

1. 80
2. **a.** 86,371; 352,129
   **b.** 87,562.50; 350,937.50
   **c.** 83,125; 355,375
3. $76,000
4. **a.** $38,600
   **b.** $271,800
   **c.** 7.04 times

## Chapter 18

1. **a.** 12.5%
   **b.** 25%
   **c.** 25%
   **d.** 40%
2. $\frac{4}{10}, \frac{3}{10}, \frac{2}{10}, \frac{1}{10}$
3. Declining Balance
4. **a.** $9,000
   **b.** $71,000
   **c.** $3,000
   **d.** $.90/hr
   **e.** $2,124
5. **a.** $9,000
   **b.** $13,500
6. **a.** $9,280
   **b.** $16,620
7. **a.** $1,040.00
   **b.** $1,487.00

## Chapter 19

1. **a.** $285,000
   **b.** $382,000
   **c.** 14.84%; 1.49%; 34.04%
2. $139,650; 30.34%
3. 16.34%
4. **a.** 16.67% increase
   **b.** 25.00% decrease
   **c.** 100% increase
   **d.** 0% no change
   **e.** $33\frac{1}{3}$% decrease
5. **a.** 1.65:1
   **b.** 1.08:1
   **c.** 1.05 times
   **d.** 17.72%
   **e.** 10.79%
   **f.** 56.44%

## Chapter 20

1. 465.75
2. $0.48
3. 4,026.81
4. $72.41
5. $40,230
6. $1,655 less
7. $99,194
8. $79,355
9. $979.20
10. $2,170
11. 3.784 liters
12. 113.70 miles farther

## Chapter 21

1. **a.** 37,700,000 shares
   **b.** $25.71
   **c.** Boeing $80.54 + $0.04 = $80.58
   General Motors $25.71 + $0.76 = $26.47
   **d.** $107.38 − $74.12 = $33.26
   **e.** $80.54 ÷ 15.4 = $5.23
2. **a.** $20,400
   **b.** $5,429.25
   **c.** $3,574
3. **a.** $400.10 gain
   **b.** $400.10 ÷ $8,579.95 = 4.7%
4. **a.** 11.36%
   **b.** 16.0268%
5. 400 × 4 = 1,600 shares
6. 400 × $20 × 8% = $640 preferred dividend
   1,600 × $0.60 = $960 common dividend
   $960 − $640 = $320 more
7. 8,000 × 50 × 7.5% = $30,000 ÷ 8,000 = $3.75/share preferred; $85,000 − $30,000 = $55,000 ÷ 50,000 sh = $1.10/share common
8. $30,000 × 2 = $60,000 ÷ 8,000 = $7.50/share preferred; $90,000 − $60,000 = $30,000 ÷ 50,000 = $0.60/share common

## Chapter 22

1. **a.** $15,600 ($15,000 × 1.04)
   **b.** Semiannually
   **c.** $562.50 $\left(\$15{,}000 \times 7.5\% \times \frac{1}{2}\right)$
   **d.** $206.25 ($15,000 × 7.5% × 66 days ÷ 360)
   **e.** $15,806.25 ($15,600 + $206.25)
   **f.** Premium (104 = 4% above face value)
   **g.** $600 ($15,000 × 4%) or ($15,600 − $15,000)
   **h.** 2018
   **i.** 7.21% ($1,125 annual interest ÷ $15,600)
   **j.** 7.03%; $600 premium ÷ 12 yrs = $50 amortization
   $1,125 − $50 = $1,075 annual interest adjusted for amortization
   ($15,000 + $15,600) ÷ 2 = $15,300 average principal invested
   $1,075 ÷ $15,300 = 7.03% yield to maturity
2. **a.** 180 (30 × 6)
   **b.** $7,560 (180 shares × $42)
   **c.** $1,860 gain; $7,560 − $5,700 ($6,000 × 95%)
   **d**. Yes, because she realizes a gain of $600 (180 shares × $35 = $6,300)
3. $10,500,000
4. MCD because the MCD bond offers the best return

## Chapter 23

1. **a.** $142,286.06
   **b.** $6,286.06
   **c.** $475,127.60
   **d.** $275,127.60
   **e.** $1,066.39
   **f.** $10,804.98
   **g.** $977.87
   **h.** $4,531.12
2. **a.** $6,063.94
   **b** $936.06
   **c.** $78,834.59
   **d.** $21,965.41
   **e.** $2,991.94
   **f.** $26,862.98
   **g.** $2,240.89
   **h.** $7,226.70
3. $40,573.37
4. $407,768.37
5. $2,507.03
6. $16,663.06

## Chapter 24

1. **a.** 64
   **b.** 61
   **c.** 58
2. **a.** 3
   **b.** 7
   **c.** 4
   **d.** 6
3. **a.**

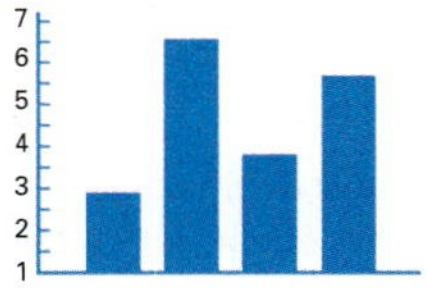


4. **a.**

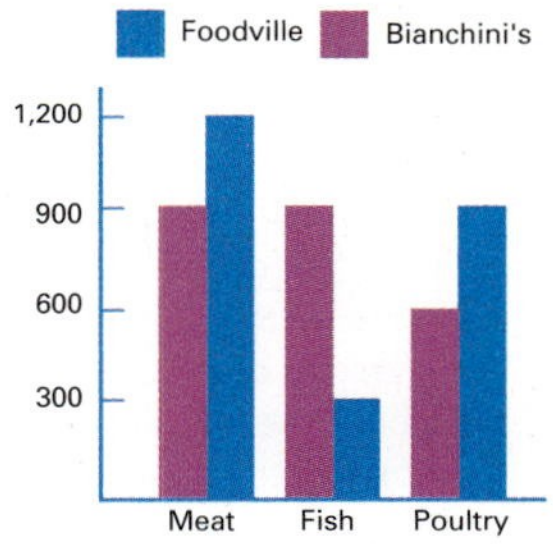


**b.**

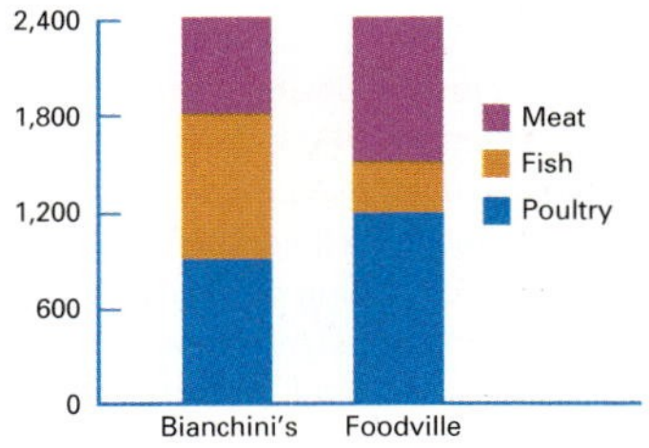


**c.**

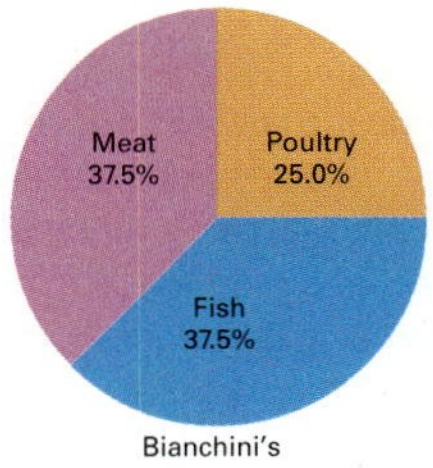

## A

**Account purchase.** A detailed statement from the commission merchant to the principal.

**Account sales.** A detailed statement of the amount of the sales and the various deductions sent by the commission merchant to the consignor.

**Accounts receivable.** Amounts owed to a business for services performed or goods delivered.

**Accrued interest.** Interest earned from the last payment date to the purchase date.

**Accumulated depreciation.** The total of all the depreciation recognized up to a specified time.

**Acid test ratio.** Used to determine the amount of assets that can be quickly turned into cash to pay current liabilities; acid test ratio = total of cash plus receivables ÷ total current liabilities.

**Ad valorem duty.** A tax charged as a percent of the value of the item.

**Addend.** Any of a set of numbers to be added.

**Additional death benefit (ADB).** Benefits, available with some life insurance policies, that allow the insured to purchase, at a low rate per thousand dollars of coverage, additional insurance up to the full face value of the policy. In case of death of the insured by accident, both the full value of the policy and the ADB would be paid to the beneficiaries of the insured. If death occurs other than by accident, the full value of the policy is paid but no ADB is paid. Sometimes referred to as accidental death benefit.

**Adjusted bank balance.** The dollar amount obtained by adding to or subtracting from the bank statement balance checkbook activities not yet known to the bank. This amount should equal the adjusted checkbook balance.

**Adjusted checkbook balance.** The dollar amount obtained by adding to or subtracting from the checkbook balance those activities appearing on the bank statement that do not yet appear in the checkbook. This amount should equal the adjusted bank statement balance.

**Adjusted gross income (AGI).** Gross income minus certain income adjustments.

**Allocate.** Assign representative proportions of a business expense to the different departments of a company.

**Amortization.** The process by which a loan's monthly payments are always equal in dollar amount while the interest amount, which is calculated on the unpaid balance, always varies.

**Amortization payment factor.** A number which, when multiplied by the per $1,000 loan amount, calculates the amount of each loan payment.

**Amortization schedule.** A schedule of payments; the schedule shows the amount of interest and the amount of principal in each payment.

**Amount credited.** The total amount paid plus the amount of cash discount.

**Amount of decrease.** The rate of decrease times the base amount.

**Amount of increase.** The rate of increase times the base amount.

**Annual discount amortization.** Also known as the annual premium amortization, determined by dividing the discount (or premium) by the number of years from purchase to maturity.

**Annual percentage rate (APR).** The annual equivalent interest rate charged.

**Annual premium amortization.** Also known as the annual discount amortization, determined by dividing the premium (or discount) by the number of years from purchase to maturity.

**Annuity.** A sum of money paid out in a series of equal payments.

**Annuity insurance.** Life insurance that pays a certain sum of money to the insured every year after the insured reaches a specified age or until the insured's death.

**Assessed valuation.** A property value determined by a representative of the local or state government.

**Assets.** Things of value owned by a business or a person.

**Auto collision insurance.** Insurance that protects the vehicle of the insured against collision damage.

**Auto comprehensive insurance.** Insurance that protects the vehicle of the insured against fire, water, theft, vandalism, falling objects, and other damage not caused by collision.

**Auto liability and property damage insurance.** Insurance that protects the insured against claims resulting from personal injuries and property damage.

**Automatic teller machine (ATM).** A computerized electronic machine, many of which are located outside of banks and in numerous other locations, that allows customers to perform various banking functions, such as checking balances, making deposits, and withdrawing funds.

**Average.** A single number that is supposed to be "typical" or "representative" of the group, such as the mean, median, or mode.

**Average cost method.** A method of valuing inventory that is based on the assumption that the costs of all items on hand are averaged and shared evenly among all units.

**Average daily balance.** The sum of each day's balance divided by the number of days in the month. Payments are usually included; new purchases may or may not be included.

**Average inventory.** The inventory average calculated by summing each inventory valuation (determined by physical inventory) and dividing by the number of physical inventories over a specified period of time; average annual inventory = (beginning inventory value + ending inventory value) ÷ 2.

**Average principal.** The average unpaid balance of a note or loan.

**Average principal invested.** Determined by adding the maturity value and the cost price and then dividing by 2.

**Average unpaid balance.** The sum of all of the unpaid monthly balances divided by the number of months.

## B

**Balance sheet.** The financial statement of what is owned (assets), what is owed (liabilities), and the difference between the two (net worth) on a specific date.

**Bank charge.** A fee for services performed by the bank.

**Bank discount loan.** Bank loan for which the interest is subtracted from the face value at the time the loan is made.

**Bank statement.** A formal accounting by a bank of the adding and subtracting activities that have occurred in one bank account over a stated period of time (usually a month).

**Bar graph.** Also known as a bar chart, a graphic presentation of statistical information resembling the histogram except that there may not be a numeric scale on the horizontal axis and the bars normally do not touch each other.

**Base (B).** The whole quantity, or 100%, of an amount.

**Basic depreciation rate.** A rate of depreciation determined by dividing 100% by the estimated total years of useful life of the item.

**Bearer.** The lender of a note.

**Beginning inventory (BI).** The cost of inventory on hand at the beginning of a time period.

**Beneficiary.** A person, a company, or an organization that benefits from an insurance policy.

**Board of directors.** A group of people elected by shareholders to oversee the operation of the corporation.

**Bond ratings.** Information on the presumed safety of a bond investment, provided by firms such as Standard & Poor's and based on experience and research.

**Bonds.** Long-term notes that are bought and sold on the open market, much like stocks.

**Book value.** The original cost of an asset minus accumulated depreciation.

**Broker.** A person who performs services of buying and/or selling for a commission.

**Business statistics.** Collections of information about businesses.

## C

**Callable bonds.** Bonds that have a provision that the issuer can repurchase, or call in, the bonds at specified dates if the board of directors authorizes the retirement (payoff) of the bonds before their maturity date.

**Cancel.** "Divide out" common factors that occur in both the numerator and denominator.

**Cancellation.** Process of dividing out common factors.

**Capital stock.** The general term applied to the shares of a corporation.

**Cash discount.** A reduction in an invoice amount available to the buyer for paying all or part of the amount due within a stated period of time.

**Cash surrender value.** The amount of cash that a company will pay the insured on the surrender, or "cashing-in," of an insurance policy.

**Charges.** The commission and any other sales expenses, such as transportation, advertising, storage, and insurance.

**Charter.** A corporation's basic approval document, issued by the state, under which the corporation operates.

**Check.** A written order directing the bank to pay a certain sum to a designated party.

**Checkbook.** Checks and check stubs to record deposits, withdrawals, check numbers, dates of transactions, other additions or subtractions, and the account balance.

**Check register.** A place for recording important information about each transaction.

**Child Tax Credit.** Taxpayers with dependent children under age 17 can receive a credit of $1,000 per qualifying child. The credit phases out at higher income levels.

**Classes of data.** Individual values organized into groups, to more easily make sense of raw numbers.

**Coinsurance clause.** An insurance policy clause specifying that, if a property is not insured up to a certain percentage of its value, the owner is the bearer of part of the insurance and will not be covered for the full amount of damages.

**Commercial paper.** Documentation of a promise to repay a loan or pay for merchandise.

**Commission.** Payment to an employee or to an agent for performing or helping to perform a business transaction or service.

**Commission merchant.** A person who performs services of buying and/or selling for a commission.

**Common denominator.** A denominator that is shared by two or more fractions. The product of the denominators of two or more fractions is always a common denominator.

**Common stock.** The usual type of stock issued by a corporation, often with different rights compared to preferred stock.

**Comparative bar graph.** Two bar graphs combined on one grid, to compare two different sets of comparable data.

**Complement method.** Method of computing the net price directly, using the complement of the trade discount rate.

**Complement rate.** A rate equal to 100% minus the discount rate; used with the complement method in determining trade or cash discounts.

**Component bar graph.** A bar graph constructed to show how certain data are composed of various parts.

**Compound amount.** Also known as the future value, the total value of an investment; equal to the principal plus all the compound interest.

**Compound amount factors.** Also known as future value factors, the numbers in a compound interest or future value table that are used to compute the total amount of compound interest.

**Compound interest.** Interest computed by performing the simple interest formula periodically during the term of the investment.

**Consignee.** The party to whom a consignment shipment is sent.

**Consignment.** Goods from a producer to a commission merchant for sale at the best possible price.

**Consignor.** The party who sends a consignment.

**Convertible bonds.** Corporate bonds that have a provision that they may be converted to a designated number of shares or to a designated value of the corporation's stock.

**Convertible preferred stock.** Preferred stock that gives the owner the option of converting those preferred shares into a stated number of common shares.

**Corporate bonds.** Long-term notes, such as convertible bonds and callable bonds, issued by a corporation.

**Corporation.** A body that is granted a charter by a state legally recognizing it as a separate entity, with its own rights, privileges, and liabilities distinct from those of its owners.

**Cost of goods sold (CGS).** The seller's cost of items (goods) that have been sold during a certain time.

**Credit.** A deposit to a bank account.

**Credit balance.** A negative difference.

**Credit card.** Credit extended by a third party.

**Cross-checking.** Adding columns vertically and then adding those totals horizontally.

**Cumulative preferred stock.** Preferred stock that, if the corporation doesn't pay the specified percentage, has the unpaid amount (the dividend in arrears) carried over to the following year or years.

**Current yield.** The annual interest income of a bond, calculated by dividing the annual interest by the current purchase price.

## D

**Decimal equivalent.** The presentation of a nondecimal number in decimal form.

**Decimal places.** The places for digits to the right of the decimal point, representing tenths, hundredths, thousandths, and so forth.

**Decimal point.** The period between two numerals.

**Declare a dividend.** A board of directors' distribution of earnings to shareholders.

**Declining-balance depreciation rate.** A multiple of the basic depreciation rate, such as two (double-declining-balance) or 1.5 (150%-declining-balance).

**Declining-balance (DB) method.** A method to depreciate assets based on the theory that depreciation is greatest in the first year and less in each succeeding year.

**Deductible clause.** An insurance policy clause that stipulates that the insured will pay the first portion of collision damage and that the insurance company will pay the remainder up to the value of the insured vehicle.

**Denominator.** In a fraction, the number below the line.

**Dependency exemptions.** Reductions to taxable income for each of one or more dependents.

**Deposit slip.** A written form that lists cash and checks being deposited in a bank account and cash received from the amount being deposited.

**Depreciation.** The decrease in the value of an asset through use.

**Difference.** The result of subtracting the subtrahend from the minuend.

**Discount.** A fee charged when someone buys a note before maturity. With regard to bonds, a bond sells at a discount if the market value becomes less than the face value.

**Discount amount.** The decrease in value of a discounted note.

**Discount date.** The last day on which a cash discount may be taken. The day on which a note is discounted (sold).

**Discount method.** Method of computing the net price using the trade discount rate to calculate the amount of trade discount, and, subsequently, the net price.

**Discount period.** A certain number of days after the invoice date, during which a buyer may receive a cash discount. The time between a note's discount date and its maturity date.

**Discount rate.** The percent used for calculating a trade or cash discount. The interest percent charged by the buyer of a discounted note.

**Discounted note.** A loan that the original lender has sold to a new lender, at a price that is less than the loan's original maturity value.

**Dividend.** The number being divided.

**Dividend in arrears.** The unpaid amount carried over to the following year or years due to holders of cumulative preferred stock.

**Divisor.** The number used to divide another number.

**Dollar markup.** The total of operating expenses and net profit. Markup expressed as an amount rather than as a percent.

**Double-declining-balance.** A method that determines a depreciation amount for the first year that is approximately twice the straight-line rate.

**Down payment.** A partial payment made at the time of a purchase with the balance due at a later time.

**Due date.** The final day an invoice is to be paid. After that day the buyer may be charged interest. Also the date by which a loan is to be repaid.

**Duty.** A charge or tax often levied against imported items to protect the domestic market against foreign competition.

## E

**Effective interest rate.** The actual annual rate of interest.

**Electronic fund transfer (EFT).** Money that is transmitted electronically, primarily via computers and automatic teller machines.

**Employee's earnings record.** Summary by quarter of the employee's gross earnings, deductions, and net pay.

**Employer's Quarterly Federal Tax Return.** A tax report, filed on Form 941 every three months by all employers, that provides the IRS with details about the number of employees, total wages paid, income and FICA taxes withheld, and other figures that determine whether a tax balance is due from the company.

**Ending inventory (EI).** The cost of the inventory on hand at the end of a time period.

**Endowment insurance.** Insurance payable upon the insured's death if it occurs within a specified period, and an endowment of the same amount as the policy, payable if the insured is alive at the end of that period.

**Equation.** A sentence consisting of numbers and/or letters that represent numbers, divided into two sections by an equal sign (=).

**Equivalent single discount rate.** A single trade discount rate that can be used in place of two or more trade discount rates to determine the same discount amount.

**Estimated service life.** The amount of usefulness that an owner expects to get from an item before it will need to be replaced owing to obsolescence.

**Exact interest method.** The calculation of interest based on the assumption that a year is 365 (or 366) days long.

**Excise tax.** A tax assessed on each unit, such as is levied on the sale of gasoline, cigarettes, and alcoholic beverages.

**Exponent.** A number written above and to the right of a number used to indicate raising to the power.

**Export.** The shipment of goods made in one country for sale in other countries.

**Export Administration Regulations.** In the U.S., the set of International Trade Administration/Department of Commerce rules and regulations that governs trade between domestic and foreign companies.

**Extension.** When taking an inventory, the dollar amount derived by multiplying the quantity of an item by its unit price or average cost.

## F

**Face value.** The dollar amount written on a note; it is the same as the amount borrowed, or the principal (P). With regard to corporate and government bonds, the amount that will be paid to the holder when a bond is redeemed at maturity.

**Factors.** Term used in multiplication to mean numbers.

**Federal Insurance Contributions Act (FICA).** Provides for a federal system of old-age, survivors, disability, and hospital insurance.

**Federal Unemployment Tax Act (FUTA).** Law that requires employers to pay the IRS an annual tax of 6.2% on the first $7,000 paid to each employee. The federal government uses the money to help fund State Employment Security Agencies, which administer unemployment insurance and job service programs.

**Filing status.** One of five conditions, including single, married, and married filing separate returns, that a taxpayer qualifies for on Form 1040 that will determine such factors as tax rates and allowable deductions.

**Finance charge.** The fee that the seller charges for the privilege of buying on credit.

**Financial statements.** Statements presenting financial information about a company; two of these statements are the balance sheet and the income statement.

**First-in, first-out (FIFO) costing method.** A method of valuing inventory that assumes that costs for units used or sold are charged according to the order in which the units were manufactured or purchased.

**Fixed interest rate.** An interest rate that stays the same for the entire length of the loan.

**Foreign trade zones.** Domestic sites in the United States that are used for import and export activity and are considered to be outside U.S. Customs territory.

**Form 1040.** One of the basic income tax return forms filed by taxpayers.

**Form W-4.** The form used to inform the government of a person's marital status and to claim withholding allowances.

**Fractions.** Number expressions of one or more equal parts of whole units.

**Frequency.** The number of values in a class of data.

**Frequency table.** A table that summarizes the number of values in each class.

**Future value.** Also known as the compound amount, the total value of an investment; equal to the principal plus all the compound interest.

**Future value factor.** Also known as compound amount factors, the numbers in a compound interest or future value table that are used to compute the total amount of compound interest.

**Future value of an annuity.** The total value of a set of equal deposits into a sinking fund.

**Future value of annuity factor (FVAF).** Numbers used in annuity tables to compute total interest earned.

## G

**Government bonds.** Long-term notes such as the treasury bonds issued by the federal government and the municipal bonds issued by states, cities, school districts, and other public entities.

**Graduated commission rates.** A system of rates by which graduated commissions increase as the level of sales increase.

**Gross cost.** The prime cost and all charges paid by the principal.

**Gross proceeds.** The price that a commission merchant gets for a consignment; also, the full sales price before any allowances, returns, or other adjustments are considered.

**Gross profit method.** A method of estimating inventory without a physical count or perpetual inventory system.

**Gross sales.** Total sales before deducting any returns, cancelled orders, or sales expenses.

**Group insurance.** Health insurance coverage extended to a group of people. The cost for each person's coverage is less expensive than it would be under an individual policy.

**Grouped data.** Individual values that have been organized into data classes, as for use in a frequency table.

## H

**Health maintenance organization (HMO).** Group health insurance coverage with limited options as a means of keeping health insurance costs lower than that of regular group policies.

**Higher terms.** A fraction in which both the numerator and denominator have been multiplied by the same number.

**High-risk driver.** A driver with a record of numerous citations or accidents.

**Histogram.** A diagram that presents the grouped data from a frequency table.

## I

**Import.** Acquiring and selling goods made in a foreign country.

**Improper fraction.** One whole unit or more. The numerator is greater than or equal to the denominator.

**Income statement.** The financial statement that shows the revenues, the expenses, and the net income for a certain period of time.

**Installments.** Monthly payments, which for a credit sale typically include the purchase price plus credit charges.

**Insured.** For life insurance, the person whose life is being insured; for other types of insurance, the person who receives the benefit of the insurance.

**Interest.** A fee, usually charged for the use of money.

**Interest-bearing note.** A note that has a maturity value greater than its face value.

**Interest dollars.** The interest stated as an amount of money rather than as a percent.

**Interest period.** The period of time between the loan date and the repayment date.

**Inventory sheet.** A form used for recording information when taking a physical inventory.

**Inventory turnover.** The number of times the average inventory is converted into sales during the year.

**Inventory turnover at cost.** Cost of goods sold divided by average inventory for the same period computed at cost prices.

**Inventory turnover at retail.** Net sales divided by average inventory for the same period computed at retail prices.

**Invoice.** A document from a seller requesting payment from the buyer; the supplier's bill.

**Invoice date.** The date stated on an invoice; the beginning of the discount period.

**Itemized deductions.** Potential reductions to income allowed for certain payments made during the tax year.

## J

**Junk bond.** A high-risk bond with a low rating.

## L

**Last-in, first-out (LIFO) costing method.** A method of valuing inventory based on the assumption that the inventory on hand at the end of a period of time is composed of the units received first.

**Least common denominator.** The lowest shared multiple of two or more denominators.

**Levy.** A government charge or fee.

**Liabilities.** The sum total of all that a business owes at any point in time; debt.

**Limited-payment life insurance.** A certain premium to be paid every year for a certain number of years specified at the time of insuring, or until the death of the insured, should that occur during the specified period. The policy is payable on the death of the insured, although there may be some options available at the end of the payment period.

**Line graph.** A type of graph often used for illustrating data over time.

**List price.** The price amount listed in the catalog.

**Loan value.** The amount that an insured may borrow on a policy from the insurance company.

**Long-term credit.** Loans that are for longer than 1 year.

**Lower of cost or market value (LCM).** An inventory valuation method by which the lower amount of either the market value or the cost value is chosen.

**Lower terms.** A fraction that has been reduced by a common divisor.

**Lowest terms.** A fraction that cannot be reduced by any common divisor.

**Low-risk driver.** A driver with a long-standing, clear driving record.

## M

**Maker.** With regard to a note, the borrower.

**Market value.** The dollar amount required to replace the inventory as of the inventory date.

**Markup.** The difference between price and a seller's cost of an item for sale. In dollars it is the amount added to the cost of the goods in order to have a gross profit high enough to cover operating expenses and to make a net profit.

**Markup based on selling price.** The percent that is calculated by dividing the desired amount of dollar markup by the selling price.

**Markup percent.** A percent that is used to compute the amount of dollar markup by multiplication. It could be a percent that multiplies the cost to find the dollar markup; or, it could be a percent that multiplies the selling price to find that dollar markup.

**Markup percent based on cost.** The percent that is calculated by dividing the desired amount of dollar markup by the cost.

**Markup rate.** Markup percent.

**Maturity date.** The final day of a note on which the borrower (the maker of the note) pays the face value and any interest due to the holder of the note. The due date.

**Maturity value.** For an interest-bearing note, it is the sum of the face value (principal) and the interest dollars: $MV = P + I$.

**Mean.** An average of a group of values, computed by dividing the sum of the group of values by the number of values in the group.

**Median.** An average of a group of values, computed by arranging the numbers in numerical order and finding the middle number.

**Metric system.** The decimal system of weights (grams, kilograms, etc.) and measures (meters, kilometers, etc.) used in most countries of the world, with the major exception of the U.S.

**Mill.** One tenth of one cent, or $0.001; a tax rate may be expressed in mills.

**Minuend.** Number from which subtraction is being made.

**Mixed decimal.** A number containing a decimal point and both a whole-number part and a decimal part.

**Mixed number.** A number that represents more than one whole unit by combining a whole number and a proper fraction.

**Mode.** An average of a group of values, computed by identifying the number that occurs most often.

**Modified Accelerated Cost Recovery System (MACRS).** The accelerated depreciation method required by the IRS.

**Mortgage.** A loan, usually amortized over 15 to 30 years, used to purchase a home.

**Multiplicand.** The factor that is multiplied.

**Multiplier.** The factor that indicates how many times to multiply.

**Municipal bonds.** Long-term notes issued by states, cities, school districts, and other public entities.

## N

**Negotiable promissory note.** A promissory note that may be sold to a third party.

**Net price.** The price that a distributor will charge a customer after any trade discounts have been subtracted from the list price.

**Net proceeds.** The amount sent to the consignor as a result of consignment sales; gross proceeds minus charges.

**Net purchase amount.** The price of the merchandise actually purchased, including allowances for returns but excluding handling and other costs.

**Net revenue.** Total revenue less any returns and allowances; frequently called net sales.

**Net sales.** Total sales for the time period minus sales returned and adjustments made during the same time.

**Net worth.** The difference between what a business owns (its assets) and what it owes (its liabilities). Also known as owners' or stockholders' equity.

**No-fault insurance.** Insurance coverage under which the driver of each vehicle involved in an injury accident submits a claim to his or her own insurance company to cover medical costs for injuries to the driver and passengers in that person's own vehicle. The insurance does not cover damage to either vehicle involved in an accident.

**No-par stock.** Stock issued without par value.

**Non-interest-bearing promissory note.** A note having a maturity value equal to its face value.

**Number of compounding periods.** The number of compounding periods per year times the number of years of the loan.

**Numerator.** In a fraction, the number above the line.

**Numerical sentence.** A mathematical or logical statement, such as an equation, expressed in numbers and symbols.

## O

**Obsolescence.** Becoming out-of-date.

**Odd lot.** Shares of stock for sale, consisting of any number of shares less than 100.

**Odd-lot differential.** A small extra charge, commonly added to the round-lot price, when odd lots are purchased.

**Of.** "Multiply," particularly when "of" is preceded by the Rate and followed by the Base.

**150%-declining-balance.** A method that determines a depreciation amount for the first year that is approximately one and one-half the straight-line rate.

**Ordinary annuity.** An annuity in which the payments occur at the end of each period.

**Ordinary interest method.** The calculation of interest based on the assumption that a year is 360 days long.

**Original cost.** The cost of building or buying an asset and getting it into use.

**Outstanding check.** One that has been written but hasn't yet cleared the bank and been charged to the customer's account.

**Outstanding deposit.** A credit that hasn't yet been recorded by the bank.

**Overhead costs.** General costs not directly related to sales merchandise.

## P

**Par.** A value assigned the shares of capital stock and stated on the stock certificate.

**Payee.** Party to whom a check is written.

**Payroll register.** A summary of wages earned, payroll deductions, and final take-home pay.

**Percent.** Word and symbol used to communicate a fraction or decimal number, verbally or in writing, as a numerator whose denominator is 100.

**Percentage (P).** A portion of the Base.

**Percentage method.** One of two primary methods for calculating the amount of income tax to withhold from employee paychecks. After the total withholding allowance is subtracted from an employee's gross earnings, the amount to be withheld is determined by taking a percentage of the balance. The percentage to be used is specified by the IRS.

**Period (compounding period).** The unit of time of the compounding.

**Periodic interest rate.** The rate of interest charged each period.

**Perpetual inventory.** A running count of all inventory units and unit costs based on a physical tracking of every item as it comes into and goes out of inventory.

**Personal exemptions.** Reductions to taxable income for the primary taxpayer and a spouse.

**Physical inventory.** An actual counting of the inventory.

**Pie chart.** Also known as a circle graph, a graphic presentation of statistics resembling a component bar graph because it shows how one quantity is composed of different parts.

**Power.** The number of times as indicated by an exponent that a number is multiplied by itself.

**Preferred provider organization (PPO).** Group health insurance coverage with benefits based on use of contracted providers as a means of keeping health insurance costs lower than that of regular group policies.

**Preferred stock.** A type of stock issued by corporations, which gives holders a right to share in earnings and liquidation before common shareholders do.

**Premium.** Fee for insurance coverage, usually paid every year by the insured person. The difference between a bond's par value and its market value when the market value is more. When bonds are sold at a premium, the yield rate will be lower than the stated (face) rate.

**Premium (bond).** The amount above the face value that a purchaser pays for a bond.

**Present value.** The amount needed to invest today to reach a stated future goal, given a certain rate of return.

**Present value factors.** The numbers in a present value factors table that are used to compute present value.

**Present value of an annuity.** The current value of a series of future payments.

**Present value of annuity factor (PVAF).** The numbers in a present value annuity factors table that are used to compute present value and total interest earned.

**Price/earnings ratio (P/E).** A measure of a stock's value, based on the per-share earnings as reported by the company for the four most recent quarters.

**Prime cost.** The price that commission merchants pay for the merchandise when they purchase goods for their principals.

**Principal.** The person (client) for whom a service is performed. Amount that is borrowed using credit.

**Proceeds.** The amount that a seller receives from the buyer of a note being discounted; the difference between the maturity value and the discount amount. In a stock transaction, the proceeds received by the seller are equal to the selling price minus the commission.

**Proceeds (from sale of stock).** The amount of money received by the seller of stock, which is the price minus commission.

**Product.** The answer to a multiplication problem.

**Promissory note.** An agreement signed by the borrower that states the conditions of a loan.

**Proper fraction.** Smaller than one whole unit. The numerator is smaller than the denominator.

**Property insurance.** Insurance against loss of or damage to property.

**Property tax.** A tax on real estate or other property owned by the business or an individual.

**Purchases (P).** Those goods for sale that have been acquired during the current time period.

**Pure decimal.** A number with no whole-number part.

## Q

**Quotient.** The answer to a division problem.

## R

**Rate (R).** The stated or calculated percent of interest.

**Rate of decrease.** The negative change in two values stated as a percent.

**Rate of increase.** The positive change in two values stated as a percent.

**Rate of return on investment.** A rate that approximates the interest rate that owners are earning on their investment in a company; rate of return on investment = net income ÷ owner's equity.

**Rate of yield.** From an investment in stock, the ratio of the dividend to the total cost of the stock.

**Rate of yield to maturity.** The rate of interest investors will earn if they hold a bond to its maturity date.

**Ratio.** The relation of one amount to another.

**Ratio of accounts receivable to net sales.** Indicates the percentage of sales that have not yet been paid for by customers; ratio of accounts receivable to net sales = accounts receivable ÷ net sales.

**Reconciliation of the bank balance.** Comparison of the check stubs or check register with the bank statement to determine the adjusted bank balance.

**Recovery amount.** The maximum amount that an insurance company will pay on a claim.

**Relationship of net income to net sales.** This ratio indicates the portion of sales that is income; relationship of net income to net sales = net income ÷ net sales.

**Remainder.** A part of a dividend that is left after even division is complete. The leftover part of division into which the divisor cannot go a whole number of times.

**Remittance.** Amount that a buyer actually pays after deducting a cash discount.

**Round lot.** A unit of stocks for sale, usually 100 shares.

**Rounding off.** Rounding up or down.

## S

**Sales tax.** A government charge on retail sales of certain goods and services.

**Scrap value (SV).** The amount the owner of an asset expects to receive upon disposing of it at the end of its estimated service life.

**Series of discounts.** Two or more trade discount rates available to a buyer for different volume purchases.

**Short rates.** Insurance premium rates charged for less than a full term of insurance.

**Short-term credit.** Loans that are 1 year or less in length.

**Simple interest.** The fundamental interest calculation.

**Sinking fund.** A fund of deposits made by the issuer of a corporate or government bond and managed by a neutral third party in order to ultimately pay off a bond.

**State Unemployment Tax Act (SUTA).** Any of various laws passed by states that require the employer to pay a tax, such as 5.4% on the first $7,000 paid to each employee, used to help fund unemployment programs.

**Statistics.** A field of study that includes the collection, organization, analysis, and presentation of data.

**Stock certificate.** A paper document that establishes ownership of a stock.

**Stock exchanges.** Formal marketplaces, such as the New York Stock Exchange and the National Association of Securities Dealers Automated Quotations, that are set up for the purpose of trading stocks.

**Stock transactions.** The purchase and sale of stocks.

**Stockbroker.** An agent who handles stock transactions for clients.

**Straight (ordinary) life insurance.** Insurance requiring a certain premium to be paid every year until the death of the insured person. The policy then becomes payable to the beneficiary.

**Straight-line (SL) method.** A depreciation method that distributes the depreciable cost of an item in equal amounts to designated units or periods covering its useful life; (original cost − scrap value) ÷ estimated total life in units or periods of time = depreciation amount for one unit or period.

**Subtrahend.** Number being subtracted.

**Sum.** The total of two or more addends.

**Sum-of-the-years-digits (SYD) method.** A depreciation method based on the assumption that greater use (and greater productivity) occurs in the earlier years of an asset's life; the rate of depreciation is greater than the straight-line method but less than the declining-balance method in the earlier years.

## T

**Tax rate.** The percent used to calculate a tax.

**Tax Rate Schedules.** Tables formulated by the IRS to compute, depending upon filing status, the tax owed for various levels of taxable income.

**Taxable income.** The amount of income on which the income tax is determined.

**Term insurance.** Insurance protection issued for a limited time. A certain premium is paid every year during the specified time period, or term. The policy is payable only in the case of death of the insured during the term. Otherwise, neither the insured nor the specified beneficiaries receive any payment, and the protection stops at the end of the term.

**Term of the loan.** The period of time between the loan date and the repayment date.

**Terms of payment.** A statement on the invoice that informs the buyer of any available discount rate and discount date as well as the due date.

**Time.** Stated in terms of all or part of a year, the length of time used for calculating the interest dollars, the rate, or the principal.

**Time line.** A line representing time onto which marks are placed to indicate the occurrence of certain activities.

**Total cost (for purchaser of stock).** The purchase price of the stock plus a brokerage fee.

**Trade discounts.** Discounts given to buyers that generally are based on the quantity purchased.

**Treasury bonds.** Bonds issued by the United States government.

**Truth in Lending Act (TILA).** A federal law to assist consumers in knowing the total cost of credit.

## U

**Ungrouped data.** Numbers listed individually.

**Units-of-production method.** A method for determining depreciation that distributes depreciation based on how much the asset is used.

## V

**Variable-rate loans.** Loans that permit the lender to periodically adjust the interest rate depending on current financial market conditions.

## W

**Wage-bracket method.** One of two primary methods for calculating the amount of income tax to withhold from employee paychecks. This method starts by granting a deduction for each withholding allowance claimed. The amount for each withholding allowance is provided by the IRS. This method involves use of a series of wage-bracket tables published by the IRS.

**Withholding allowance.** An amount claimed on tax Form W-4 that determines how much income tax the employer will withhold from each paycheck. Each allowance claimed (as for a spouse or dependents) reduces the amount of income tax withheld.

**Working capital.** The amount of current assets less current liabilities.

**Working capital ratio.** The amount of current assets that would remain if all a company's current liabilities were paid immediately; total current assets ÷ total current liabilities.

## Y

**Yield.** Income from an investment; generally stated as a percent, or rate.

# INDEX

Note: Page numbers referencing figures are italicized and followed by an *f*. Page numbers referencing tables are italicized and followed by a *t*.